# 60th Annual Meeting of the Association for Computational Linguistics (ACL 2022)



System Demonstrations

Dublin, Ireland
22 – 27 May 2022

ISBN: 978-1-7138-6724-1

**Printed from e-media with permission by:**

Curran Associates, Inc.
57 Morehouse Lane
Red Hook, NY 12571

**Some format issues inherent in the e-media version may also appear in this print version.**



Printed with permission by Curran Associates, Inc. (2023)

For permission requests, please contact the Association for Computational Linguistics at the address below.

Association for Computational Linguistics
209 N. Eighth Street
Stroudsburg, Pennsylvania 18360

Phone: 1-570-476-8006
Fax: 1-570-476-0860

acl@aclweb.org

**Additional copies of this publication are available from:**

Curran Associates, Inc.
57 Morehouse Lane
Red Hook, NY 12571 USA
Phone: 845-758-0400
Fax: 845-758-2633
Email: curran@proceedings.com
Web: www.proceedings.com

ACL 2022

# The 60th Annual Meeting of the Association for Computational Linguistics

## Proceedings of System Demonstrations

May 22-27, 2022

# Introduction

Welcome to the proceedings of the system demonstration track of the Joint Conference of the 60th Annual Meeting of the Association for Computational Linguistics (ACL 2022) on May 22nd – May 27th, 2022. For the ACL 2022 system demonstration track, we received 75 submissions, of which 27 were selected for inclusion in the program (acceptance rate of 36%) after being reviewed by at least three members of the program committee. We would like to thank the members of the program committee for their timely help in reviewing the submissions. Lastly, we thank the many authors that submitted their work to the demonstrations track. This year, the ACL conference is a hybrid event. The demonstration paper will be presented through pre-recorded talks and in presence during the poster sessions.

Valerio Basile, Zornitsa Kozareva, Sanja Štajner
ACL 2022 System Demonstration Chairs

# Program Committee

### System Demonstrations Chairs

Valerio Basile, University of Turin
Zornitsa Kozareva, Facebook AI
Sanja Štajner, Symanto Research

### System Demonstrations Program Committee

Ahmed Abdelali, Qatar Computing Research Institute
Omri Abend, The Hebrew University of Jerusalem
Abdalghani Abujabal, Amazon Alexa AI
Heike Adel, Bosch Center for Artificial Intelligence
Rodrigo Agerri, HiTZ Center - Ixa, University of the Basque Country UPV/EHU
Željko Agić, Unity Technologies
Roee Aharoni, Google
Alan Akbik, Humboldt-Universität zu Berlin
Zeynep Akkalyoncu, University of Waterloo
Khalid Al Khatib, Groningen University
Miguel A. Alonso, Universidade da Coruña
Rafael Anchiêta, Federal Institute of Piauí
Diego Antognini, EPFL
Rahul Aralikatte, University of Copenhagen
Eleftherios Avramidis, German Research Center for Artificial Intelligence (DFKI)
Ioana Baldini, IBM Research
Gianni Barlacchi, Amazon Alexa
Mohaddeseh Bastan, Stony Brook University
Timo Baumann, Ostbayerische Technische Hochschule Regensburg
Gábor Berend, University Of Szeged
Sumit Bhatia, IBM Research
Eduardo Blanco, Arizona State University
Rexhina Blloshmi, Sapienza University of Rome
Aljoscha Burchardt, DFKI
Daniel Campos, University of Illinois Urbana Champaign
Ed Cannon, Expedia Group
Erion Çano, Research Group Data Mining, University of Vienna
Jiarun Cao, University of Manchester
Yixin Cao, Singapore Management University
Daniel Cer, Google Research; University of California at Berkeley
Alberto Cetoli, QBE
Yee Seng Chan, Raytheon BBN Technologies
Wanxiang Che, Harbin Institute of Technology
Long Chen, Columbia University
Guanyi Chen, Utrecht University
Shizhe Chen, INRIA
Jhih-jie Chen, National Tsing Hua University
Lu Chen, Shanghai Jiao Tong University
Chung-chi Chen, Department of Computer Science and Information Engineering National Taiwan University, Taipei, Taiwan

Hongshen Chen, JD.com
Hai Leong Chieu, DSO National Laboratories
Christos Christodoulopoulos, Amazon Research
Yagmur Gizem Cinar, Amazon
Miruna Clinciu, Edinburgh Centre for Robotics
Danilo Croce, University of Roma, Tor Vergata
Shaobo Cui, Alibaba Group
Marina Danilevsky, IBM Research
Pradipto Das, Rakuten USA, Inc.
Alok Debnath, Trinity College, Dublin
Thierry Declerck, DFKI GmbH
Shumin Deng, Zhejiang University
Yuntian Deng, Harvard University
Michael Desmond, IBM Research
Joseph P. Dexter, Harvard University
Chenchen Ding, NICT
Carl Edwards, University of Illinois, Urbana-Champaign
Carsten Eickhoff, Brown University
Patrick Ernst, Amazon
James Fan, Google
Federico Fancellu, Samsung AI Research Canada
Paulo Fernandes, Merrimack College
Dimitris Galanis, Institute for Language and Speech Processing, Athena Research Center
Sudeep Gandhe, Google Inc
Xiang Gao, Microsoft Research
Andrew Gargett, The Open University
Mozhdeh Gheini, University of Southern California
Chi Han, ByteDance AI Lab
Xianpei Han, Institute of Software, Chinese Academy of Sciences
Han He, Emory University
Yun He, Texas A&M University
Leonhard Hennig, German Research Center for Artificial Intelligence
Daniel Hershcovich, University of Copenhagen
Ales Horak, Masaryk University
Xiaodan Hu, University of Illinois at Urbana-Champaign
Hen-hsen Huang, Institute of Information Science, Academia Sinica
Ali Hürriyetoğlu, Koç University
Jeff Jacobs, Columbia University
Youngsoo Jang, KAIST
Feng Ji, Tencent Technology Ltd.
Zhuoxuan Jiang, Tencent
Ridong Jiang, Institute for Infocomm Research
Zhanming Jie, ByteDance AI Lab
Sudipta Kar, Amazon Alexa AI
Eugene Kharitonov, Facebook AI
Joo-kyung Kim, Amazon Alexa AI
Philipp Koehn, Johns Hopkins University
Mamoru Komachi, Tokyo Metropolitan University
Valia Kordoni, Humboldt-Universität zu Berlin
Harshit Kumar, IBM Research
Varun Kumar, Amazon Alexa

Philippe Laban, UC Berkeley
Tuan Lai, University of Illinois at Urbana-Champaign
Mark Last, Ben-Gurion University of the Negev
Dong-ho Lee, University of Southern California
John Lee, City University of Hong Kong
Sha Li, University of Illinois at Urbana-Champaign
Yanran Li, The Hong Kong Polytechnic University
Xintong Li, The Ohio State University
Manling Li, UIUC
Lizi Liao, National University of Singapore
Constantine Lignos, Brandeis University
Marina Litvak, Shamoon College of Engineering
Qian Liu, Beihang University
Xiaodong Liu, Microsoft Research
Nikola Ljubešić, Jožef Stefan Institute
Clare Llewellyn, University of Edinburgh
Nitin Madnani, Educational Testing Service
Wolfgang Maier, Mercedes-Benz AG
Benjamin Marie, None
Alex Marin, Microsoft Corporation
Stella Markantonatou, ILSP/R.C. Athena
Marie-jean Meurs, Université du Québec à Montréal
Margot Mieskes, University of Applied Sciences, Darmstadt
Koji Mineshima, Keio University
Yusuke Miyao, University of Tokyo
Junta Mizuno, NICT
Hamdy Mubarak, Qatar Computing Research Institute
Aldrian Obaja Muis, None
Philippe Muller, IRIT, University of Toulouse
Diane Napolitano, The Associated Press
Denis Newman-griffis, University of Pittsburgh
Tae-gil Noh, OMQ GmbH
Pierre Nugues, Lund University
Benjamin Nye, Northeastern University
Yusuke Oda, LegalForce
Tsuyoshi Okita, Kyushu institute of technology
Xiaoman Pan, Tencent AI Lab
Feifei Pan, Rensselaer Polytechnic Institute
Alexandros Papangelis, Amazon Alexa AI
Xutan Peng, The University of Sheffield
Oren Pereg, AI Lab, Intel Labs
Stelios Piperidis, Athena RC/ILSP
Prokopis Prokopidis, ILSP/Athena RC
Yada Pruksachatkun, Alexa AI
Stephen Pulman, Apple Inc.
Peng Qi, JD AI Research
Pablo Ruiz Fabo, LiLPa, Université de Strasbourg
Irene Russo, ILC CNR
Saurav Sahay, Intel Labs
Gözde Şahin, UKP Lab, Technische Universität Darmstadt
Sashank Santhanam, University of North Carolina at Charlotte

Sebastin Santy, Microsoft Research
Sven Schmeier, Researcher
Djamé Seddah, Inria
Jiaming Shen, University of Illinois at Urbana-Champaign
Liang-hsin Shen, National Taiwan University
Michal Shmueli-scheuer, IBM Research
Lei Shu, Amazon AWS AI
Amy Siu, Berliner Hochschule für Technik
Yuanfeng Song, Hong Kong University of Science and Technology, WeBank Co., Ltd
Jacopo Staiano, reciTAL
Josef Steinberger, University of West Bohemia
Michael Stewart, The University of Western Australia
Carl Strathearn, Edinburgh Napier University
Shang-yu Su, National Taiwan University
Chenkai Sun, University of Illinois at Urbana-Champaign
Jian Sun, Alibaba Group
Natalia Vanetik, Shamoon College of Engineering
Andrea Varga, CUBE
Ivan Vulić, University of Cambridge
Rui Wang, Vipshop (China) Co., Ltd.
Qingyun Wang, University of Illinois at Urbana-Champaign
Jingjing Wang, Soochow University
Zhenhailong Wang, University of Illinois at Urbana-Champaign
Zhongqing Wang, Soochow University
Changhan Wang, Facebook AI Research
Xuan Wang, University of Illinois at Urbana-Champaign
Chien-sheng Wu, Salesforce
Xianchao Wu, NVIDIA
Deyi Xiong, Tianjin University
Zhen Xu, Tencent PCG
Runxin Xu, Institute of Computational Linguistic, Peking University
Ziqing Yang, iFLYTEK Research
Yujiu Yang, tsinghua.edu.cn
Wonsuk Yang, Korea Advanced Institute of Science and Technology
Tae Yano, Expedia Group
Wenlin Yao, Tencent AI Lab
Seid Muhie Yimam, Universität Hamburg
Pengfei Yu, Department of Computer Science, University of Illinois at Urbana-Champaign
Dian Yu, University of California, Davis
Liang-chih Yu, Yuan Ze University
Hamada Zahera, Paderborn University
Qi Zeng, University of Illinois at Urbana-Champaign
Huaping Zhang, Beijing Institute of Technology
Chengzhi Zhang, Nanjing University of Science and Technology
Zixuan Zhang, University of Illinois Urbana-Champaign
Qi Zhang, Fudan University
Tiancheng Zhao, SOCO.AI
Guangyou Zhou, School of Computer Science, Central China Normal University
Cangqi Zhou, Nanjing University of Science and Technology
Deyu Zhou, Southeast University
Imed Zitouni, Google

This page intentionally left blank.

# Table of Contents

# DoTAT: A Domain-oriented Text Annotation Tool

**Yupian Lin[1], Tong Ruan[1,*], Ming Liang[1], Tingting Cai[1], Wen Du[2], Yi Wang[3]**
[1]East China University of Science and Technology, Shanghai 200237, China
[2]DS Information Technology Co., Ltd., Shanghai 200032, China
[3]Fudan University Shanghai Cancer Center,
ruantong@ecust.edu.cn
duwen@dscomm.com.cn, tonywang@shca.org.cn

## Abstract

We propose DoTAT, a domain-oriented text annotation tool. The tool designs and implements functions heavily in need in domain-oriented information extraction. Firstly, the tool supports a multi-person collaborative process with automatically merging and review, which can greatly improve the annotation accuracy. Secondly, the tool provides annotation of events, nested event and nested entity, which are frequently required in domain-related text structuring tasks. Finally, DoTAT provides visual annotation specification definition, automatic batch annotation and iterative annotation to improve annotation efficiency. Experiments on the ACE2005 dataset show that DoTAT can reduce the event annotation time by 19.7% compared with existing annotation tools. The accuracy without review is 84.09%, 1.35% higher than Brat and 2.59% higher than Webanno. The accuracy of DoTAT even reaches 93.76% with review. The demonstration video can be accessed from https://ecust-nlp-docker.oss-cn-shanghai.aliyuncs.com/dotat_demo.mp4. A live demo website is available at https://github.com/FXLP/MarkTool.

## 1 Introduction

A high-quality corpus is a prerequisite in supervised machine learning, especially for most neural Natural Language Processing (NLP) systems. However, annotation is also one of the most time-consuming and costly components of many NLP research work, and the quality of the annotation results greatly affects the effect of the trained model.

Currently more and more domain-oriented information extraction tasks (Pyysalo et al., 2011, 2012; Miwa and Ananiadou, 2013; Huang et al., 2020) are proposed, therefore annotation tools should be redesigned to meet the new requirements:

**1) Multiple specifications support.** There are many document types in each domain, and the specifications of the target structured data are different. Therefore, different annotation specifications need to be defined for each document type.

**2) Nested event.** (Espinosa et al., 2019; Trieu et al., 2020) An event is called nested event when it has other events in its arguments, while an event is called flat event when there are only entities in its arguments. Domain-oriented information extraction tasks often require event and nested event annotation.

**3) Multi-person support with merging and reviewing.** Single-person annotation often leads to missing and wrong annotation due to human errors, the ambiguity of the words, or particular language phenomenon not covered by the specifications. When there are multiple annotation specifications in domain-oriented annotation tasks, more errors may appear since specifications vary and more annotators are required. Therefore, multi-person collaborative annotation is required to improve the annotation quality. Furthermore the divergence between multiple annotators should be detected and the improved result can be achieved by automatic merging and human reviewing.

However, the existing annotation tools only support one or two of the above requirements. Only Brat (Stenetorp et al., 2012), Webanno (Yimam et al., 2013; Eckart de Castilho et al., 2016) and INCEpTION (Klie et al., 2018; Boullosa et al., 2018) support event annotation, but they do not design event annotation as a core function and do not contain enough features for specification management and quality improvement. To address the challenges above, we propose DoTAT, a domain-oriented text annotation tool for complex event annotation tasks. Specifically, it satisfies the above-mentioned new requirements through the following methods which even support iterative annotation and automatic batch annotation:

- **Visual annotation specifications definition** The annotation specifications are defined by



*Proceedings of the 60th Annual Meeting of the Association for Computational Linguistics*
*System Demonstrations*, pages 1 - 8

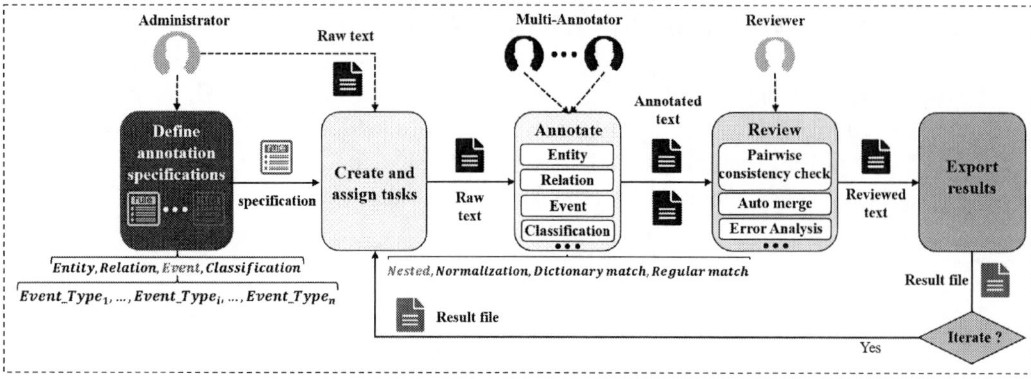


Figure 1: Typical workflow using DoTAT.

a visual interface instead of manual configuration so that administrators can easily define multiple specifications and annotators can dynamically select the specification to match their documents.

- **Nested event and nested entity** The tool not only supports nested event (Figure 2) but also supports nested entity (Figure 4). Nested Entity means that one entity is inside another entity. Besides complex event annotation, DoTAT also supports entity normalization annotation (Figure 5) that is useful when annotating domain-specific corpora, especially in medical domain.

- **Merge and review** It provides pairwise consistency checking and automatic merging of content annotated by pairwise people. The reviewer can also manually edit the merged content.

- **Iterative annotation** Annotators can re-load previous exported result file for further annotation. The function is frequently used in the situation that new version of a domain specification is designed and existing annotation file should be reused and revised. The above three features forms the basis of DoTAT annotation process and help to improve the quality of the annotation.

- **Automatic batch annotation** The tool provides automatic batch annotation by text matching based on regular expressions (Figure 6) and dictionaries (Figure 7).

In the following section, we summarize annotation tools. Section 3 describes the overall workflow of DoTAT and its functions. Section 4 introduces the implementation of DoTAT. Section 5 illustrates the comparative experiment. Section 6 shows the case study in the medical and public security domains. Section 7 concludes this paper and gives further directions.

## 2 Related Work

There are various text annotation tools for different scenarios, but most of them do not support event annotation, including Knowtator (Ogren, 2006), WordFreak (Morton and LaCivita, 2003), Anafora (Chen and Styler, 2013), Atomic (Druskat et al., 2014), GATE Teamware (Bontcheva et al., 2013), Doccano and YEDDA (Yang et al., 2018). Each tool has their own special features, e.g., WordFreak supports constituent parse structure and dependent annotations as well as ACE named-entity and coreference annotation. Doccano and YEDDA support the use of shortcut keys for entity annotation, and YEDDA can perform batch annotation through the command line.

Currently only Brat (Stenetorp et al., 2012), Webanno (Yimam et al., 2013; Eckart de Castilho et al., 2016) and INCEpTION (Klie et al., 2018; Boullosa et al., 2018) support event annotation. However, it is difficult for them to annotate nested event. The method used by them for event annotation is to connect multiple entities through directed arcs. If the number of entities is numerous or the distance between entities is far, abundant arcs and intersections will appear on the whole page, resulting in an inferior visualization effect. Except for WordFreak, Anafora and Atomic, most tools declare to support multi-person collaborative annotation. GATE Teamware provides the adjudication interfaces to

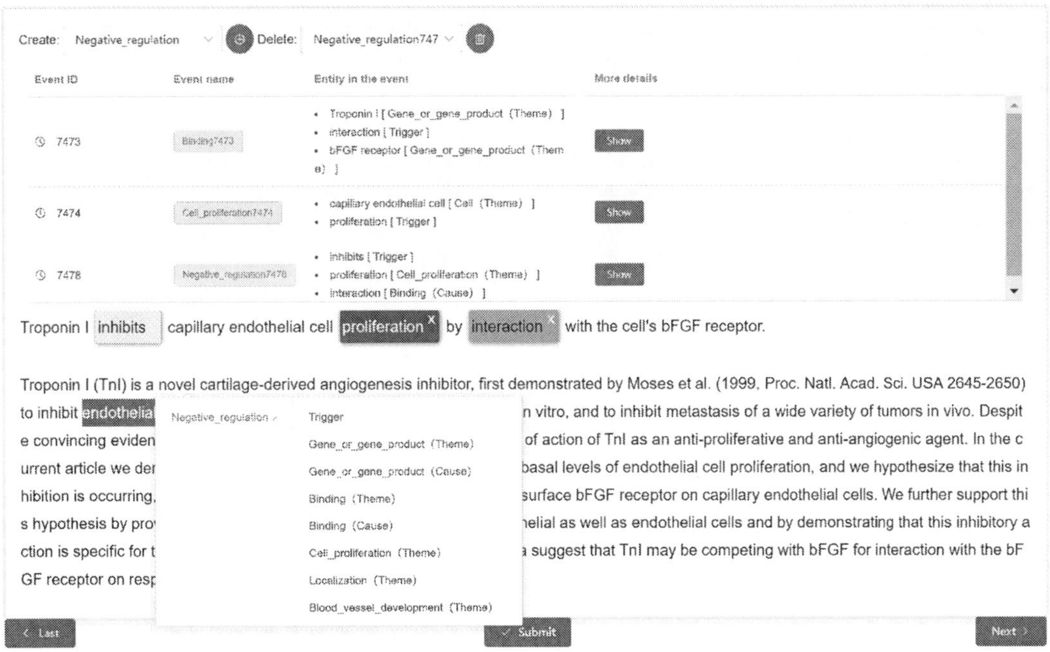

Figure 2: The event annotation of MLEE (Pyysalo et al., 2012). Top: event list panel, bottom: annotation panel.

compare annotations. However, only Webanno and INCEpTION provide the curation with automatic merging function. INCEpTION is partially based on WebAnno (Eckart de Castilho et al., 2016).

Compared to these tools, event annotation in DoTAT is much easier to perform. Furthermore DoTAT designs an iterative process from specification definition to merging and review, which can help the annotation team gradually increase the quality of annotated corpus.

## 3 DoTAT

DoTAT is a web-based multilingual text annotation tool. The raw texts that need to be annotated can be in Chinese or in any other language. There are three types of user roles: administrator, annotator, and reviewer. The fundamental annotation types include entity annotation, relation annotation, event annotation, and text classification. As shown in Figure 1, a typical annotation process using DoTAT may include the following five steps:

- **Define annotation specifications**: The administrator selects the annotation type and visually defines event types, entity types, relation types or text categories in annotation specifications.
- **Create and assign tasks**: Administrator creates and assigns tasks. Each task contains an annotation specification and several raw texts. It is recommended that two annotators and one reviewer are assigned to each task.
- **Annotate**: Before the annotators interactively annotate events or entities, they can use automatic batch annotation to accelerate the speed. The detailed annotation process can be seen in section 3.1.
- **Merge and Review**: The reviewer starts consistency checking and automatic merging of the annotated content by multiple annotators (See section 3.2 for details). The reviewer can visually analyze the errors according to the merged events list. When there are many similar errors, the reviewer can give feedback for administrator to redefine the annotation specification. With iterative annotation function, all existing annotations can be reused.
- **Export results**:After the review process, the annotated content can be exported by administrator to a result file (JSON format).

### 3.1 Annotate

The event annotation interface of DoTAT contains annotation panel and event list panel, as shown in Figure 2. Users can interactively annotate in the former panel, and the results are summarized in the latter one. Users can select an event in the event list panel and view this event in another panel.

When beginning annotation, the user first selects the event type. Then he can use dictionary matching or regular expression matching to automatically annotate text span which reduces manual efforts. On this basis, the user manually annotates the trigger or other parameters in the event. Specifically, he uses the mouse to pick a text span in the annotation panel, and then all arguments of this event type will appear immediately, then the user can select an argument to annotate. As shown in Figure 2, the annotator selects the argument "Cell proliferation (Theme)" to annotate the text span "endothelial cell". The user repeatedly selects each span and corresponding argument to finish the event annotation. For the nested events, where the trigger of one event becomes an argument of another event, as shown in Figure 2, the trigger "interaction" of the Binding event (7473) is nested in the negative regulation event (7478) as an argument.

### 3.2 Merge and Review

The review procedure supports consistency checking, automatic merging, and manual revision. Before the review, the system will check the consistency of the annotated content of the two annotators. The problem is to find matched events between two annotated text, the detail is shown in Algorithm 1.

**1)** We calculate the event similarity between pairwise annotators. The event similarity is calculated as the number of matched entities divided by the number of all entities. The result is recorded as matrix $S_{n,m}$. **2)** Then the problem is defined as the maximum weight matching of weighted bipartite graphs. We apply the Kuhn-Munkres Algorithm to find optimized matching pairs. The consistency checking score is the sum of similarity values of matched pairs divided by the maximum number of events. When consistency checking score reaches the threshold, the system can start the merging process. **3)** The merge criteria depends on the state, and there are four states for each event, "Consistent", "Only A", "Only B" and "Inconsistent". The system automatically merges all the arguments for events in "Inconsistent" state. For the other three states, the system will only keep the larger event.

In the review procedure, the reviewer can view the merged annotations, as shown in Figure 8. If the reviewer doubts on the merged event, he can trace the source to view the original annotated event by clicking role switching bar to change current view. The reviewer can also perform manual modification. He should modify the events in "Inconsistent" state. The whole annotation process finishes after the reviewer submits the refined result.

**Algorithm 1** Automatically merge event annotations by using the Kuhn-Munkres Algorithm.

**Input:** $A_n$: the n events of annotator-A; $B_m$: the m events of annotator-B
**Output:** $C$: the set of merged events; $K$: the consistency checking score

$S_{n,m} = similarity(A_n, B_m)$, where $S_{i,j} = similarity(a_i, b_j)$, $a_i \in A_n$ and $b_j \in B_m$.
$W_n = Kuhn - Munkres(S_{n,m})$ denote the optimal event merging strategy.
**for** $\forall a_i \in A_n$ **do**
    **if** $a_i \in W_n$ **then**
        $C_i = a_i \cup b_k$, where $b_k = W_i(a_i)$
        **if** $a_i = b_k$ **then**
            $state_{C_i} = Consistent$
        **else** $state_{C_i} = Inconsistent$
        **end if**
    **else** $C_i = a_i$ and $state_{C_i} = OnlyA$
    **end if**
**end for**
**for** $\forall b_j \in B_m$ **do**
    **if** $b_j \notin W_n$ **then**
        $C_{i+j} = b_j$ and $state_{C_{i+j}} = OnlyB$
    **end if**
**end for**
$K = \sum S_{i,j}/n$, where $a_i \in W_n \wedge b_j \in W_n$
**return** $C$,$K$;

## 4 Implementation

DoTAT is a web-based text annotation tool with the software license Apache-2.0. We used the Vue.js and Element UI to build the user interface. The core of Vue.js is a responsive data binding framework, which makes it pretty easy to synchronize data with the DOM (Document Object Model). Therefore, Vue.js is particularly suitable for real-time visualization of text annotations. The server side utilizes the Python-based open-source Django framework to build RESTful web services. MySQL database is adopted to organize, store and manage data. The code is available at the GitHub repository `https://github.com/FXLP/MarkTool`, which also contains a live demo website.

| Group | Tool | Annotation Time (seconds) | | | | | |
|---|---|---|---|---|---|---|---|
| | | 20% | 40% | 60% | 80% | 100% | $Time_{avg}$ |
| Group-1 | WebAnno | 1703 | 3493 | 5123 | 6704 | 8359 | 418 |
| | Brat | 1870 | 3113 | 4303 | 5456 | 6374 | 319 |
| | **DoTAT** | **1340** | **2497** | **3937** | **5007** | **5887** | **295** |
| Group-2 | WebAnno | 1518 | 3138 | 4589 | 6055 | 7516 | 386 |
| | Brat | 1767 | 3239 | 4755 | 6077 | 7513 | 375 |
| | **DoTAT** | **1210** | **2385** | **3845** | **4956** | **5645** | **282** |
| Group-3 | WebAnno | 1321 | 2771 | 4119 | 5314 | 6704 | 335 |
| | Brat | 1503 | 3055 | 4218 | 5293 | 7174 | 358 |
| | **DoTAT** | **1156** | **2167** | **3446** | **4592** | **5387** | **269** |

Table 1: Annotation time comparison of annotation tools in ACE2005 Dataset. The average annotation time of annotation tool is arithmetic mean value of $Time_{avg}$ in three group. The average annotation time of Webanno is 380s. The average annotation time of Brat is 351s. The average annotation time of DoTAT is 282s.

## 5 Experiments

We compared DoTAT with the other two text annotation tools (Brat and WebAnno) for annotation time (see section 5.1) and annotation result (see section 5.2) on the event annotation task.

### 5.1 Annotation time

We randomly selected 20 news texts from the ACE2005 dataset (Consortium, 2005), and each text contained at least four sentences. Six students randomly divided into three groups were invited to annotate those texts. For each user, if a tool was used first, more time might be spent since the user was not familiar with the texts. To eliminate the influences, each student was given extra time to view the text before the annotation, and each was assigned a different tool using sequences. We separately recorded the time (in seconds) spent by each group using the three tools when completing 20%, 40%, 60%, 80%, and 100% of the texts. As we could calculate from Table 1, the average annotation time ($Time_{avg}$) of DoTAT was reduced by 19.7% compared with Brat and 25.8% compared with WebAnno. DoTAT spent less time, since it was time consuming for Brat and Webanno to connect arcs between the trigger and multiple arguments. The mouse movements in the process might be forward and backward. However, DoTAT only needed to select the arguments from a pop up menu on a text span, and the mouse typically moved from left to right.

### 5.2 Annotation result

We also evaluated the accuracy by comparing with the gold standard results from ACE20005 data set. The accuracy is computed as:

$$acc = \frac{\sum_{i=1}^{n}(Trig_i^{correct} + \sum_{j=1}^{m_i} Arg_{i,j}^{correct})}{\sum_{i=1}^{n}(1+m_i)} \quad (1)$$

where $n$ is the total number of gold standard events, and $m_i$ is total number of arguments in event $i$. In event $i$, $Trig_i^{correct} = 1$ when trigger is correct, and if argument $j$ is correct then $Arg_{i,j}^{correct} = 1$, otherwise the value is 0. Since annotation quality was too low in real projects with new annotation specifications or new annotators, we often added a particular training process in real application scenarios. Therefore, we designed two rounds of experiments, the first round (Round-1) was for training and the second round (Round-2) was a formal annotation. After Round-1, we have a meeting to discuss with annotators about the error-prone events and entities. In Round-2, we selected five other most error-prone texts from ACE 2005. As we could see from Table 2, the average accuracy of unreviewed annotations was less than 60% in experiment Round-1. The main reason was that annotators often missed a whole event or missed particular arguments. The accuracy of DoTAT was better since it was less possible for DoTAT to miss arguments. When a text span was picked, DoTAT would show all arguments, the pop menu reminded the annotator about the arguments. DoTAT also performed better than Brat and Webanno in Round-2. Besides, the overall accuracy increased in Round-2, which showed that the training process had effects.

In Round-1, the average accuracy of DoTAT's reviewed annotations reached 76.2%, which was an increase of 20.9% compared to the average accuracy of DoTAT's unreviewed annotations. In

| Round | Tool | Accuracy | | | |
|---|---|---|---|---|---|
| | | Group-1 | Group-2 | Group-3 | Average |
| Round-1 | WebAnno | 44.5% | 49.0% | 51.7% | 48.4% |
| | Brat | 34.5% | 44.9% | 47.8% | 42.4% |
| | DoTAT-U | 45.4% | 55.7% | 64.8% | 55.3% |
| | **DoTAT-R** | **67.7%** | **72.6%** | **88.3%** | **76.2%** |
| Round-2 | WebAnno | 75.48% | 82.58% | 86.45% | 81.5% |
| | Brat | 79.19% | 83.87% | 85.16% | 82.74% |
| | DoTAT-U | 78.71% | 86.45% | 87.1% | 84.09% |
| | **DoTAT-R** | **93.54%** | **92.9%** | **94.84%** | **93.76%** |

Table 2: Accuracy comparison of annotation tools in ACE2005 Dataset. DoTAT-U denotes the unreviewed annotation content of DoTAT. DoTAT-R denotes the reviewed annotation content of DoTAT.

| **Domain** | **Task** | **Annotated** |
|---|---|---|
| Public security | 10 types<br>10,000 texts | 6 types<br>6,000 texts<br>20,000 events<br>80,000 entities |
| Medical | 4 types<br>300 long texts | 4 types<br>300 long texts<br>6,000 events<br>18,000 entities |

Table 3: Application of DoTAT.

| | **Fraud file-1** | **Fraud file-2** | **Fraud file-3** | **Fraud file-4** |
|---|---|---|---|---|
| **Victim's name** | 86 | 84.85 | 69.77 | 59.09 |
| **Suspect's phone** | 100 | 88.89 | 66.67 | 94.12 |
| **Fraud method** | 39.39 | 28.77 | 46.25 | 48.76 |

The example annotation of Fraud method:

| Raw Text | Annotator-1 | Annotator-2 |
|---|---|---|
| 自称淘宝客服张三，以理赔为由，骗取李四300元。 | 自称淘宝客服张三，以理赔为由，骗取李四300元。 | 自称淘宝客服张三，以理赔为由，骗取李四300元。 |

Figure 3: The fraud case annotation example.

Round-2, the average accuracy of DoTAT's reviewed annotations had also increased by 9.67%. It indicated that the review procedure could effectively improve the accuracy.

## 6 Case Study

DoTAT has been used in the annotation projects of three different domains. The details in the public security and medical domains are shown in Table 3. For the criminal case type "fraud" which contains 5 event types and altogether 23 arguments in public security domain, the training process before formal annotation involves four original files and eight annotators. Each file contains 20 texts. Consistency checking is performed to inspect the specification understanding of each annotator, and part of the results are shown in Figure 3. We found that the argument "fraud method" scored less than 50% in the four files, because the text span of this argument is not fixed. For the example in Figure 3, some annotator annotated "claim settlement(理赔)" and some annotated "on the ground of claim settlement(以理赔为由)". Besides, we also found that some simple arguments (such as "name" and "phone") did not reach a consistency score of 100%. There are two reasons for this: one is binding an argument to the wrong event, e.g. take the "name" of the victim as suspect; the other is missing annotation, e.g. "name" of victim appears more than once, but only one place is annotated. Therefore, further training is required to solve the disagreement between annotators.

## 7 Conclusions

The demands for annotation corpus in different domains are rapidly increasing with the development of deep learning. We propose a web-based text annotation tool, DoTAT, which is suitable for domain-oriented complex event annotation. We demonstrate the powerfulness of our tool with experiments and real-world scenarios. We find that the pre-annotation and reviewing are critical steps to improve the quality of corpus. In the future, we plan to integrate the active learning algorithm into DoTAT to reduce the manual annotation work.


## Acknowledgments

We would like to appreciate the valuable comments and suggestions from the anonymous reviewers. This work was supported by Zhejiang Lab (No.2019ND0AB01). We also would like to thank Hongli Sun, Chuang Chen, and Yuqiu Song for their assistance with annotation experiments.

## References


Kalina Bontcheva, Hamish Cunningham, Ian Roberts, Angus Roberts, Valentin Tablan, Niraj Aswani, and Genevieve Gorrell. 2013. Gate teamware: a web-based, collaborative text annotation framework. *Language Resources and Evaluation*, 47(4):1007'Ă'Ş1029.

Beto Boullosa, Richard Eckart de Castilho, Naveen Kumar, Jan-Christoph Klie, and Iryna Gurevych. 2018. Integrating knowledge-supported search into the INCEpTION annotation platform. In *Proceedings of the 2018 Conference on Empirical Methods in Natural Language Processing: System Demonstrations*, pages 127–132, Brussels, Belgium. Association for Computational Linguistics.

Wei-Te Chen and Will Styler. 2013. Anafora: A web-based general purpose annotation tool. In *Proceedings of the 2013 NAACL HLT Demonstration Session*, pages 14–19, Atlanta, Georgia. Association for Computational Linguistics.

L. D. Consortium. 2005. Ace ( automatic content extraction ) english annotation guidelines for entities.

Stephan Druskat, Lennart Bierkandt, Volker Gast, Christoph Rzymski, and Florian Zipser. 2014. Atomic: an open-source software platform for multi-level corpus annotation.

Richard Eckart de Castilho, Éva Mújdricza-Maydt, Seid Muhie Yimam, Silvana Hartmann, Iryna Gurevych, Anette Frank, and Chris Biemann. 2016. A web-based tool for the integrated annotation of semantic and syntactic structures. In *Proceedings of the Workshop on Language Technology Resources and Tools for Digital Humanities (LT4DH)*, pages 76–84, Osaka, Japan. The COLING 2016 Organizing Committee.

Kurt Junshean Espinosa, Makoto Miwa, and Sophia Ananiadou. 2019. A search-based neural model for biomedical nested and overlapping event detection. In *Proceedings of the 2019 Conference on Empirical Methods in Natural Language Processing and the 9th International Joint Conference on Natural Language Processing (EMNLP-IJCNLP)*, pages 3679–3686, Hong Kong, China. Association for Computational Linguistics.

Kung-Hsiang Huang, Mu Yang, and Nanyun Peng. 2020. Biomedical event extraction with hierarchical knowledge graphs. In *Findings of the Association for Computational Linguistics: EMNLP 2020*, pages 1277–1285, Online. Association for Computational Linguistics.

Jan-Christoph Klie, Michael Bugert, Beto Boullosa, Richard Eckart de Castilho, and Iryna Gurevych. 2018. The INCEpTION platform: Machine-assisted and knowledge-oriented interactive annotation. In *Proceedings of the 27th International Conference on Computational Linguistics: System Demonstrations*, pages 5–9, Santa Fe, New Mexico. Association for Computational Linguistics.

Makoto Miwa and Sophia Ananiadou. 2013. NaCTeM EventMine for BioNLP 2013 CG and PC tasks. In *Proceedings of the BioNLP Shared Task 2013 Workshop*, pages 94–98, Sofia, Bulgaria. Association for Computational Linguistics.

Thomas Morton and Jeremy LaCivita. 2003. WordFreak: An open tool for linguistic annotation. In *Companion Volume of the Proceedings of HLT-NAACL 2003 - Demonstrations*, pages 17–18.

Philip V. Ogren. 2006. Knowtator: A protégé plug-in for annotated corpus construction. In *Proceedings of the Human Language Technology Conference of the NAACL, Companion Volume: Demonstrations*, pages 273–275, New York City, USA. Association for Computational Linguistics.

Sampo Pyysalo, Tomoko Ohta, Makoto Miwa, Han-Cheol Cho, Jun'ichi Tsujii, and Sophia Ananiadou. 2012. Event extraction across multiple levels of biological organization. *Bioinformatics*, 28(18):i575–i581.

Sampo Pyysalo, Tomoko Ohta, Rafal Rak, Dan Sullivan, Chunhong Mao, Chunxia Wang, Bruno Sobral, Jun'ichi Tsujii, and Sophia Ananiadou. 2011. Overview of the infectious diseases (ID) task of BioNLP shared task 2011. In *Proceedings of BioNLP Shared Task 2011 Workshop*, pages 26–35, Portland, Oregon, USA. Association for Computational Linguistics.

Pontus Stenetorp, Sampo Pyysalo, Goran Topić, Tomoko Ohta, Sophia Ananiadou, and Jun'ichi Tsujii. 2012. brat: a web-based tool for NLP-assisted text annotation. In *Proceedings of the Demonstrations at the 13th Conference of the European Chapter of the Association for Computational Linguistics*, pages 102–107, Avignon, France. Association for Computational Linguistics.

Hai-Long Trieu, Thy Thy Tran, Khoa N A Duong, Anh Nguyen, Makoto Miwa, and Sophia Ananiadou. 2020. DeepEventMine: end-to-end neural nested event extraction from biomedical texts. *Bioinformatics*, 36(19):4910–4917.

Jie Yang, Yue Zhang, Linwei Li, and Xingxuan Li. 2018. YEDDA: A lightweight collaborative text span annotation tool. In *Proceedings of ACL 2018, System Demonstrations*, pages 31–36, Melbourne, Australia. Association for Computational Linguistics.

Seid Muhie Yimam, Iryna Gurevych, Richard Eckart de Castilho, and Chris Biemann. 2013. WebAnno: A flexible, web-based and visually supported system for distributed annotations. In *Proceedings of the 51st Annual Meeting of the Association for Computational Linguistics: System Demonstrations*, pages 1–6, Sofia, Bulgaria. Association for Computational Linguistics.

## A Nested entity annotation

For the nested entity annotation, theoretically, the internal entity overlaps the outer entity. In order to make both entities displayed well, we make the shadow of the internal entity a little smaller and put it in the top layer, the example is shown in Figure 4.

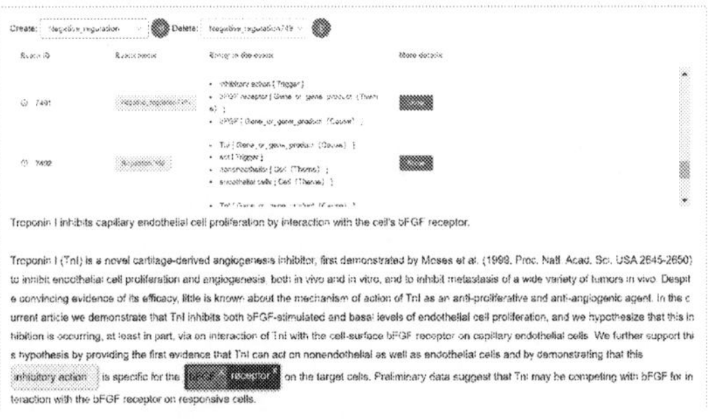

Figure 4: The example of nested entity annotation in DoTAT. The entity "bFGF" is nested in the entity "bFGF receptor".

## B Entity normalization

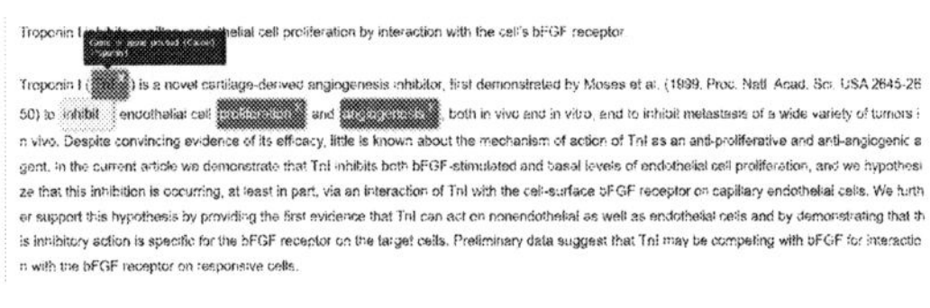

Figure 5: The example of entity normalization in DoTAT. The entity "TnI" has been normalized as "Troponin I".

## C Automatic batch annotation

The example of automatic batch annotation based on regular expressions is shown in Figure 6. Specifically, the user chooses the created regular expression "(angiogenesis|angiogenic){1}" to automatically annotate the trigger of "Blood vessel development" event. And the example of automatic batch annotation based on dictionaries is shown in Figure 7. Specifically, the user chooses the created dictionary to automatically annotate "TnI" as the argument "Gene or gene product(Cause)" of "Negative regulation" event.

## D Review of event annotation

The review interface of event annotation in DoTAT is shown in Figure 8.

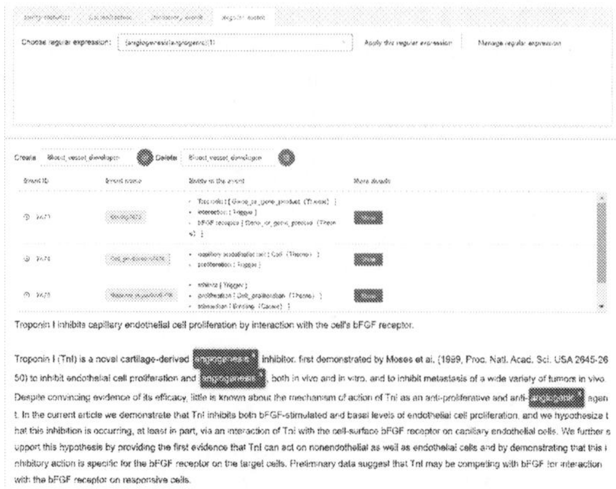

Figure 6: Automatic batch annotation based on regular expressions. Top: regular expression panel, middle: event list panel, bottom: annotation panel.

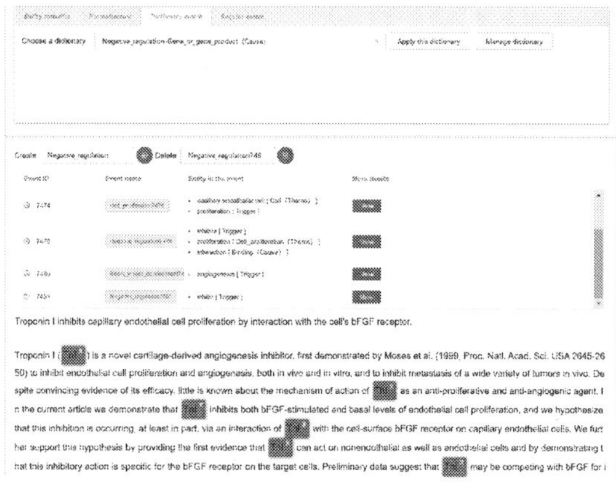

Figure 7: Automatic batch annotation based on dictionaries. Top: dictionary panel, middle: event list panel, bottom: annotation panel.

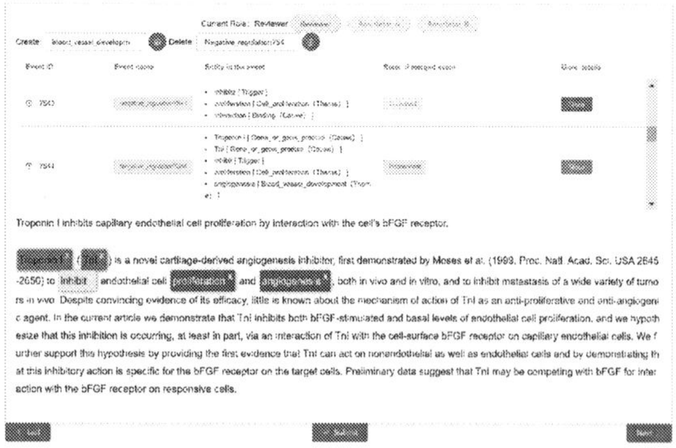

Figure 8: Review of event annotation in DoTAT. Top: role switching bar, middle: event list panel, bottom: annotation panel. Each merged event in the event list has a status and a merged annotation result.

# UKP-SQuARE: An Online Platform for Question Answering Research

**Tim Baumgärtner,[1] Kexin Wang,[1] Rachneet Sachdeva,[1] Max Eichler,[1] Gregor Geigle,[1] Clifton Poth,[1] Hannah Sterz,[1] Haritz Puerto,[1] Leonardo F. R. Ribeiro,[1] Jonas Pfeiffer,[1] Nils Reimers,[2] Gözde Gül Şahin,[3] Iryna Gurevych[1]**

[1]Ubiquitous Knowledge Processing Lab, Department of Computer Science, Technical University of Darmstadt
[2]Hugging Face, [3]Koç University Computer Science and Engineering Department

www.ukp.tu-darmstadt.de

## Abstract

Recent advances in NLP and information retrieval have given rise to a diverse set of question answering tasks that are of different formats (e.g., extractive, abstractive), require different model architectures (e.g., generative, discriminative), and setups (e.g., with or without retrieval). Despite having a large number of powerful, specialized QA pipelines (which we refer to as Skills) that consider a single domain, model or setup, there exists no framework where users can easily explore and compare such pipelines and can extend them according to their needs. To address this issue, we present UKP-SQuARE, an extensible online QA platform for researchers which allows users to query and analyze a large collection of modern Skills via a user-friendly web interface and integrated behavioural tests. In addition, QA researchers can develop, manage, and share their custom Skills using our microservices that support a wide range of models (Transformers, Adapters, ONNX), datastores and retrieval techniques (e.g., sparse and dense). UKP-SQuARE is available on https://square.ukp-lab.de.[1]

## 1 Introduction

Researchers in NLP have devoted significant resources to creating more powerful machine learning models for Question Answering (QA), and collecting high-quality QA datasets. Combined with the recent breakthroughs by large pretrained language models, we have witnessed rapid progress in the field across many different kinds of QA tasks (Rogers et al., 2021).

The great variety in QA tasks has led to specialized, domain-specific models trained on a single QA format such as *multiple choice* (Lai et al., 2017) (i.e., selecting the best answer out of multiple options), *extractive* (Rajpurkar et al., 2016) (i.e., finding the answer span in a context) and *abstractive* (Kocisky et al., 2018) (i.e., generating an answer that is not a contiguous span in the context). The format may influence the model architecture (e.g., discriminative objective for *multiple choice*, generative objective for *abstractive*). Additionally, systems vary with how the context is provided. It can be given by the user, or retrieved from a Datastore which is commonly referred to as *open-domain* or *retriever-reader* setup (Chen et al., 2017). The retrieval mechanism can also be chosen from a set of sparse (e.g., BM25, Robertson et al., 1994) or dense (e.g., DPR, Karpukhin et al., 2020) techniques.

The speed of progress in the field makes it essential for researchers to explore, compare, and combine these different QA components as quickly as possible to identify the strengths and weaknesses

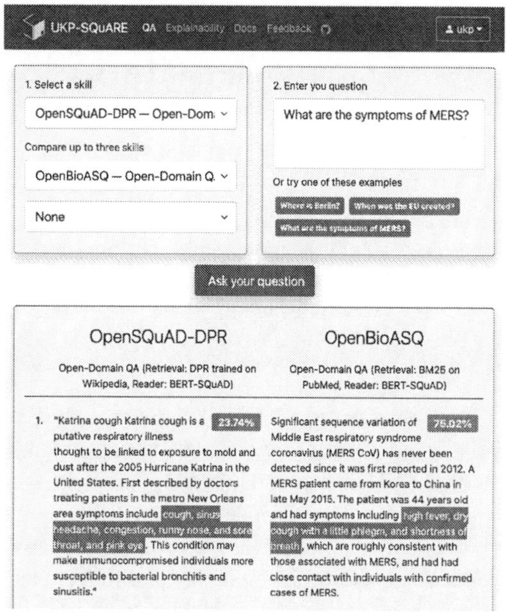


Figure 1: QA page of UKP-SQuARE. The user selects a Skill (in this case, two open-domain Skills are selected), enters a question and then receives an answer.

[1]The code is available on https://github.com/UKP-SQuARE/square-core



*Proceedings of the 60th Annual Meeting of the Association for Computational Linguistics*
*System Demonstrations*, pages 9 - 22

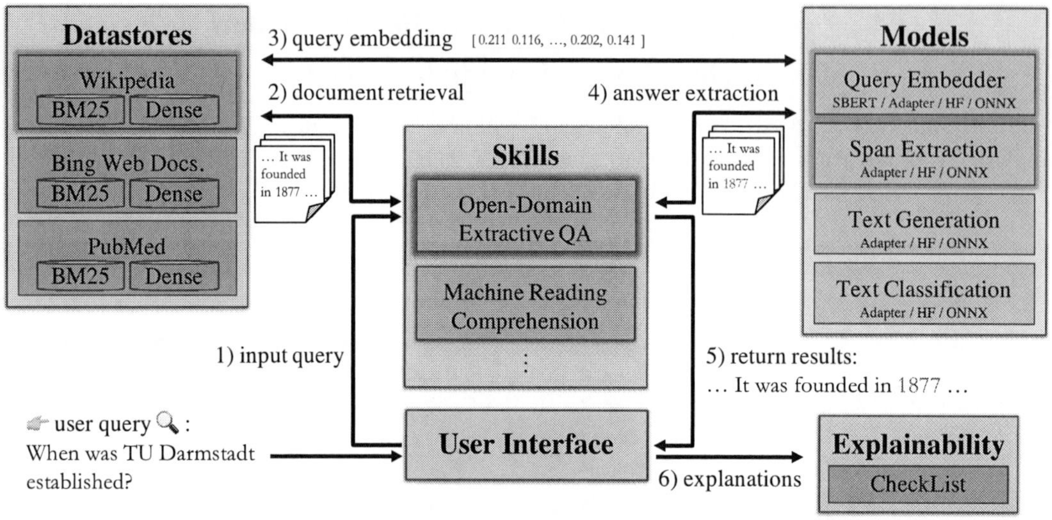


Figure 2: Overall architecture of UKP-SQuARE, illustrating an open-domain, extractive QA Skill. (1) First a user selects a **Skill** and issues a query via the **User Interface**. (2) The selected QA Skill forwards the query to the respective **Datastore** for document retrieval. (3) The **Datastore** gets the query embedding from the **Models**, uses it for semantic document retrieval and returns the top documents to the **Skill**. (4) The **Skill** sends the query and retrieved documents to the reader model for answer extraction. (5) Finally, the answers are shown to the user. (6) Optionally, the user can view the results of the predefined behavioural tests for the **Skill**.

of the current state of the art. Even though there exists a number of powerful QA systems (Dibia, 2020; Khashabi et al., 2020) and frameworks such as Haystack,[2] those approaches focus only on one component (e.g., retrieval, QA format, domain), hence do not allow plug-and-play of different Datastores, domains, model architectures or retrieval techniques. This considerably limits their applicability and reusability across the diverse, rapidly progressing area of QA research, making it infeasible for researchers to quickly integrate novel models and QA pipelines.

To address this gap, we introduce UKP-SQuARE, a flexible and extensible QA platform to enable users to easily implement, manage and share their custom QA pipelines, which we call **Skills**, using our microservices. As shown in Fig. 1, UKP-SQuARE also allows users to query and compare different **Skills** via an easy-to-use user interface and systematically analyze their strengths and weaknesses through integrated behavioural tests.[3]

## 2 UKP-SQuARE

The system is implemented as a modern microservice architecture using Docker containers.[4] The major components are **Skills**, **Datastores**, **Models**, **Explainability** and the **User Interface**. The process flow across the components is illustrated in Fig. 2 on an open-domain, extractive QA Skill. The central component of the system is the **Skill** that specifies how a user query is processed (e.g., which QA type, retrieval mechanism, model or adapter to be used in which order). The **Skill** leverages the other services for query execution. **Datastores** hold multiple collections of documents with sparse indices, e.g., BM25 (Robertson et al., 1994) and dense indices, e.g., DPR (Karpukhin et al., 2020), allowing fast and efficient retrieval of background knowledge in an extensible way. The **Model** service hosts numerous models, combined with Adapters (Houlsby et al., 2019; Pfeiffer et al., 2020), to support a wide range of tasks such as text embedding (for queries in open-domain QA), sequence and token classification (for multiple-choice and extractive QA) and sequence-to-sequence generation (for abstractive QA). The **Explainability** component performs behavioural tests on the deployed Skills for better understanding of the models. Details of each service are provided in the following sections.

Furthermore, while we host UKP-SQuARE on our infrastructure and make it available for the community, we also provide the option to set up the system locally. Additionally, the **Datastores** and

[2] `https://deepset.ai/haystack`

[3] Screenshots for adding Skills, the outputs of different QA formats and behavioural tests are shown in Appendix D.

[4] `https://docker.com`

**Models** services are exposed via an API[5].

### 2.1 Skills

Skills define how the user query should be processed by the Datastores and Models components and how the respective answers are obtained. For question answering, this might involve retrieving background knowledge, extracting spans from context or selecting an answer from multiple choices.

Skills are not necessarily equivalent to a model trained on a dataset. Instead a Skill is more general and can use multiple models to arrive at an output. A Skill might work on a specialized domain (e.g. biomedical, movies, etc.) or a specific format (e.g. extractive, abstractive, etc.), but also combinations are possible. For example, a Skill could combine Wikipedia and a news based extractive reader model to answer factoid and news questions. The degree of specialization or generalization of a Skill is up to its developer. In UKP-SQUARE the Skill only defines the pipeline, i.e., pre-processing, information retrieval or answer extraction/generation/classification. These steps are facilitated and executed by the usage of the other components: Models (§2.2) and Datastores (§2.3).

Importantly, Skills can be added to the system by the community. They can be added privately, thereby only giving a specific user access to it, or made public, allowing everyone to use it (§3.1). This allows great flexibility in the design of question answering pipelines, keeping implementation effort and required compute low, thereby democratizing the usage of question answering models.

### 2.2 Models

The Models component is responsible for hosting NLP models required for document retrieval and answer extraction/generation tasks. Our platform supports a wide variety of models comprising HuggingFace (HF) Transformers (Wolf et al., 2020), Adapters, Sentence-Transformers (Reimers and Gurevych, 2019), and a limited selection of ONNX (Open Neural Network Exchange) (Bai et al., 2019) models. Specifically, the inclusion of memory-efficient adapters in our platform allows having a variety of task-specific models while maintaining storage efficiency. Moreover, for faster inference, the high performance inference engine, ONNX Runtime[6] can be used for the ONNX models provided on our platform.

The Models component comprises of two main services: **inference** and **management**. The inference service is responsible for loading models and getting predictions for the input queries. The management service allows the user to list, deploy, update and remove models (available on HF, Adapterhub and Sentence-Transformers) on the UKP-SQUARE platform. This allows to deploy and query models beyond the ones we already provide, for example multilingual models. To maintain a scalable architecture, we host every deployed model in its separate Docker container and use Traefik[7] to route the user query to the specific model instance for inference. The inference service of the model API can be queried using the Skills (§2.1) as per the end-user's requirements.

### 2.3 Datastores

The Datastores are responsible for storing document collections as knowledge bases of QA Skills, supporting retrieval on these collections. Each Datastore contains a collection of documents and several indices of them for retrieval. The document collections are stored by an Elasticsearch[8] instance. Within one Datastore, the document collection is indexed by sparse or dense retrieval models.

For sparse retrieval, we use BM25 provided by the Elasticsearch instance; for dense retrieval, we use dual-encoder neural networks (Karpukhin et al., 2020; Xiong et al., 2021) with Approximate Nearest Neighbor (ANN) indexing provided by Faiss (Johnson et al., 2021). The Datastores are agnostic to the ANN methods. Among them, we use *IndexIVFScalarQuantizer* (Jégou et al., 2011) from Faiss as the default choice. For scalability, we maintain each dense-retrieval index within one Docker container and use Traefik to route the queries to the specific index. For each query using dense retrieval, the Datastores forward the query to the Models to get the query embedding (e.g., via the Query Embedder in Fig. 2 and Table 2) and then input this embedding to the ANN search for retrieving relevant documents.

As the built-in Datastores, Wikipedia[9] with the DPR encoder (Karpukhin et al., 2020), PubMed[10]

[5]`https://square.ukp-lab.de/docs/`

[6]`https://github.com/microsoft/onnxruntime`

[7]`https://traefik.io`

[8]`https://elastic.co`

[9]The English Wikipedia dump preprocessed by Karpukhin et al. (2020).

[10]From the BioASQ8 edition (Nentidis et al., 2020).

| Minimum Functionality Test (MFT)-*Taxonomy* |
|---|
| **C:** There is a tiny purple box in the room.<br>**Q:** What size is the box?<br>**Test:** Check if the prediction is tiny |
| **INV**ariance-*Robustness* |
| **C:** ...Newcomen designs had a duty of about 7 million, but most were closer to 5 million....<br>**Q:** What was the ideal [duty->udty] of a Newcomen engine?<br>**Test:** Check whether the prediction changes or not. |

Table 1: Examples for two most common test types. **Top:** Minimum Functionality Test (MFT), **Bottom:** Invariance Test (INV). **C:** refers to context and **Q:** is the question.

and Bing web documents[11] with the TAS-B encoder (Hofstätter et al., 2021) are supported. We plan to add more Datastores in the future.

### 2.4 Explainability

Recently, many interpretability techniques to understand black-box neural models such as influence functions and input/token attribution methods (Madsen et al., 2021) have been introduced. Most of these techniques provide only local explanations and require access to the back-propagation function. One exception is *CheckList* (Ribeiro et al., 2020), which is a type of behavioural testing that treats models—in our case Skills—as black-boxes and compares their behaviour against the expected one. This is achieved by *unit tests* designed by the end-users or the system experts. Two most common test types are **M**inimum **F**unctionality **T**est (MFT) and **INV**ariance (INV) as shown in Table 1. MFTs are designed to measure a capability (e.g., *Taxonomy* capacity of matching object properties to categories) via specifying the expected behaviour (e.g., "tiny" in Table 1). INVs tests are similarly refined for capabilities (e.g., robustness under spelling errors in question), however the expected behaviour is already known, i.e., the answer should remain the same. We adapt the machine comprehension tests from Ribeiro et al. (2020) for behavioural testing of our Skills. In our current setup, the tests for all the deployed Skills are curated manually, saved in as JSON file and made available via the UI. The test results are shown on demand via a separate tab (§3.3).

### 2.5 User Interface

We host UKP-SQUARE as a web application built with VueJS[12] to make it easily accessible to re-

[11]From the MS MARCO dataset (Nguyen et al., 2016).

[12]https://vuejs.org

| Training Dataset for Models | Domain |
|---|---|
| **Text Generation (Abstractive QA)** | |
| NarrativeQA (Kocisky et al., 2018) | Stories |
| **Span Extraction (Extractive QA)** | |
| BioASQ (Tsatsaronis et al., 2015) | Biomedical |
| DROP (Dua et al., 2019) | Wikipedia |
| DuoRC (Saha et al., 2018) | Movies |
| Natural Questions (Kwiatkowski et al., 2019) | Wikipedia |
| NewsQA (Trischler et al., 2017) | News |
| Quoref (Dasigi et al., 2019) | Wikipedia |
| SQuAD 1.1 (Rajpurkar et al., 2016) | Wikipedia |
| SQuAD 2.0 (Rajpurkar et al., 2018) | Wikipedia |
| TriviaQA (Joshi et al., 2017) | Wikipedia, Web |
| **Text Classification (Multiple-Choice QA)** | |
| BioASQ (Tsatsaronis et al., 2015) | Biomedical |
| BoolQ (Clark et al., 2019) | Wikipedia |
| CommonsenseQA (Talmor et al., 2019) | - |
| CosmosQA (Huang et al., 2019) | Personal Narratives |
| MultiRC (Khashabi et al., 2018) | Fiction, Textbook, Wikipedia, News, etc. |
| Quail (Rogers et al., 2020) | Fiction, News, Blogs, User Stories |
| Quartz (Tafjord et al., 2019) | Relationships |
| RACE (Lai et al., 2017) | News, Stories, Ads, Biography, Philosophy |
| SocialIQA (Sap et al., 2019) | Social Interactions |
| **Query Embedder (Retrieval)** | |
| Natural Questions (Kwiatkowski et al., 2019) | Wikipedia |
| MS MARCO (Nguyen et al., 2016) | Bing Web Docs. |

Table 2: Available Models fine-tuned on various datasets upon the release of UKP-SQUARE.

searchers. Once a Skill has been created by a user (§3.1) it can be added, edited, and deleted in the Skill management section of the application in the "My Skills" menu. For each Skill, its URL, metadata, requirements for context, and visibility can be adjusted (see Appendix Fig. 3). The functionality of the user interface is split into QA and explainability.

**QA Interface.** The QA section of the user interface provides access to the Skill by allowing the user to enter their question and optionally a context. Public Skills are accessible to everyone while private Skills require the user to be signed in. The UI provides distinct visualizations depending on the selected Skill type. For extractive Skills, e.g., SQuAD (Rajpurkar et al., 2016), a document and multiple spans are returned and ranked by the model's confidence. In this setup, we also provide the option to show the span highlighted in its position in the document (see Fig. 1). Categorical Skills, e.g., BoolQ (Clark et al., 2019), show an interface with boolean output scores (see Appendix Fig. 5). A multiple-choice Skill requires multiple options separated by newlines in the context field. These are then ranked and returned with their respective scores (see Appendix Fig. 6). When multiple Skills are selected, the user can see and compare their outputs side-by-side and better understand their behavioural differences.

**Explainability Interface.** A Skill selector is provided at the top which allows users to visualize and compare the results of the CheckList machine reading tests for the selected Skills. A list of tests with their name, type, capability, and failure rate is shown. The list can be expanded for a detailed description along with a small number of failed examples with their questions, context, and predictions.

## 3 Use Cases

### 3.1 Skill Publishing

A major contribution of our platform is to support developers creating their own Skills. This allows practitioners to easily make their research publicly available, without having to take care of engineering heavy topics such as infrastructure, web development and security. To publish a new Skill, developers need to implement a single function that defines the question answering pipeline. They are provided with utility functions that facilitate interacting with other components such as the Datastores, Models and the UI. A code snippet implementing a Skill is given in Appendix A.

Allowing developers to implement their own Skills enables us to greatly extend the system to have stronger models. For instance, multiple Datastores with potentially different retrieval methods can be combined to find complementary background knowledge, e.g., from Wikipedia and biomedical articles. Similarly, different models could be used to precisely answer a diverse set of questions that might require different capabilities, such as answerability (Rajpurkar et al., 2018), numerical (Dua et al., 2019) or multi-hop (Yang et al., 2018) reasoning. Once a developer creates their Skill, it can be added to UKP-SQUARE via the UI. The Skill developer can further make the Skill publicly available.

Allowing the community to implement Skills comes with a technical challenge such as deploying unreliable code on our servers. We therefore allow three different ways of hosting Skills. (1) First, Skills can be hosted directly on UKP-SQUARE. For this, a pull request for the new Skill should be submitted to our public repository, which can then be added to the system upon a code review. While processing the submitted Skill requires a human in the loop, this option simplifies the hosting process for the Skill developer. (2) Second, in order to provide an option to make Skills instantly and independently available, we also allow Skills to be hosted on third party cloud platforms such as Amazon Web Services, Google Cloud and Microsoft Azure. All these cloud providers allow to easily host a lightweight function that can be used by UKP-SQUARE. (3) Lastly, we allow developers to host Skills on their own hardware. The only requirement is that the Skill needs to be publicly accessible. In the latter two cases, developers will still have access to UKP-SQUARE's components (e.g., Datastores and Models), but the Skill itself will run on the cloud or on other hardware. For quick development of Skills we recommend using options (2) and (3). For long-term availability and usage of a Skill, adding it via the public github repository is recommended. We provide extensive documentation for all possibilities to host Skills.[13]

### 3.2 Skill Querying

Once a developer makes their Skill public in UKP-SQUARE, other users can obtain answers from it. Upon release of the system, we make a wide range of question answering Skills available. These span over different QA formats (extractive, multiple-choice, abstractive), setups (open-domain, machine reading comprehension) and to different domains (wikipedia, web, biomedical, etc.). The list of available models for different formats is given in Table 2. This allows the public to test current state-of-the-art question answering models. Moreover, researchers can use it for qualitative analysis, for example to discover potentials biases, strengths or weaknesses in models by behavioural testing. Furthermore, we support querying multiple Skills at the same time. This is particularly useful to compare capabilities of different models. For example see Fig. 1, where two open domain, extractive Skills can be compared.

### 3.3 Behavioural Testing of Skills

The users can choose the Skill they want to investigate from the drop-down menu. The selected Skill can be analyzed standalone or alongside two different compatible Skills.

The tests are displayed showing the Skill fail-

[13] https://square.ukp-lab.de/docs/

|  | Supported Models | Retrieval | QA Types | Expl. | Ext. |
|---|---|---|---|---|---|
| Haystack | HF Transformers | sparse, dense | EX, AB | × | × |
| Dibia (2020) | HF Transformers | sparse | EX | ✓ | × |
| Karpukhin et al. (2020) | DPR | dense | EX | × | × |
| Khashabi et al. (2020) | T5 | × | EX, AB, MC, YN | × | × |
| UKP-SQuARE | HF Transformers, ONNX, adapters | sparse, dense | EX, AB, MC, YN | ✓ | ✓ |

Table 3: Qualitative comparison of UKP-SQuARE to previous works. HF: HuggingFace, Expl.: Explainability component, Ext.: Extensible by the end-user , EX: Extractive, AB: Abstractive, MC: Multiple-choice, YN: Yes/No

ure rate and the failed examples can be viewed by clicking on the 'Expand' button. An examplary visualization for negation and coreference testing of SQuAD Skills is given in Appendix Fig. 4. For replacement tests, e.g., where names are perturbed, colored markers are used to highlight how the input was modified for the test. This allows the user to quickly identify changes the Skill could not handle. To analyze or process a Skill's test performance in more detail, a full JSON report of all test examples can be downloaded.

## 4 User Study

We evaluate the usability of our system by conducting a pilot attitudinal user study with five participants. We recruited graduate students, our main target user group, and instructed them to compare and analyze several Skills. We provided them with a list of predefined questions to input into the system to help them use it. After the students used the system we asked them several questions to discover whether they understood every element of the interface effortlessly (i.e., the input and the output of the Skills, the list of behavioral cards of the Skills, and their specific contents). All users understood the input and output of the Skills and stated that the interface allows them to compare the Skills effortlessly. They also stated that the behavioral cards of the explainability component are useful to analyze the strong and weak points of the models and could help develop new Skills. However, most of them could not understand them in a glimpse. Hence, we will improve the presentation of these cards in a future update. Appendix C provides the list of questions and responses. To finish the study, we employed the System Usability Scale (SUS) questionnaire (Brooke, 1996) to quantitatively assess the global usability of the system. The average score is 70 out of 100, which refers to a "good usability" (UIUX-Trend, 2021).

## 5 Related Work

A qualitative comparison with similar frameworks is given in Table 3. The closest work to ours is Haystack, which is an open-source and scalable framework for building search systems over large document collections. Although it supports both sparse and dense retrieval techniques, models from the Huggingface (HF), and different QA types (abstractive and extractive) it lacks support for faster ONNX or memory efficient `adapter` models. Furthermore, it has to be set up by the users on their own infrastructure which requires technical expertise and sufficient hardware resources. Dibia (2020) introduce NeuralQA, an interactive tool for QA that leverages the benefits of sparse retrieval along with the HF reader models. However, NeuralQA is limited to extractive QA. Karpukhin et al. (2020) provide a simple user interface that employs efficient dense retrieval but only support models for open-domain QA. Finally, UnifiedQA (Khashabi et al., 2020) provides a demo page[14] that employs a custom T5 based model trained on a wide range of QA datasets, hence supports a variety of QA formats. However, (1) it lacks the retrieval component, (2) is not scalable (to include different model formats), and (3) is not flexible (not possible to use models with different retrieval techniques). Unlike other previous systems, UKP-SQuARE is dynamically extendable allowing users to easily contribute with new Skills. Finally, except from gradient-based explanations in Dibia (2020), none of the systems have an explainability component.

## 6 Conclusion and Future Work

We introduce the UKP-SQuARE platform that enables researchers and developers to study and compare QA pipelines, i.e., Skills, that comprises a selection of Datastores, retrieval mechanisms and reader models. The platform enables querying ex-

[14]`https://unifiedqa.apps.allenai.org/`

isting public Skills, as well as implementing custom ones using UKP-SQuARE's microservices and utility functions that support a large collection of model types and Datastores. Furthermore, users can simultaneously query multiple Skills, and analyze them through integrated behavioural tests.

Our architecture is scalable and flexible to incorporate most of the latest developments in the QA domain. Future versions will include automated deployment of custom models and Datastores, automated Skill selection by incorporating previous works (Puerto et al., 2021; Geigle et al., 2021) and increasing the number of supported Datastores (e.g., wikidata, Vrandečić and Krötzsch, 2014). We also plan to incorporate specialized models (e.g., using graph encoders, Ribeiro et al., 2021), structured reasoning approaches (Yasunaga et al., 2021) and interpretability techniques such as saliency maps (Li et al., 2016).

## Ethics and Broader Impact Statement

**Data** This work does not generate new data. All datasets employed in used to construct Skills as described in §2.2, §2.3, and Table 2. The datasets are well-known to be safe for research purposes and do not contain any personal information or offensive content. We comply with the licenses and intended uses of each dataset. The licenses of each dataset can be seen in Appendix B.

**Intended Use.** The intended use of UKP-SQuARE is i) bringing different QA components together to share them as a skill with the rest of the world and ii) the analysis of these Skills. Our platform allows NLP practitioners to share their Skills with the community removing technical barriers such as configuration and infrastructure so that any person can reuse these models. In addition, users can analyze the available Skills through behavioral tests and compare them thanks to a user-friendly UI. This has a straightforward benefit for the research community (i.e., reproducible research and analysis of prior works), but also to the general public because UKP-SQuARE allows them to run state-of-the-art models without requiring them any special hardware and hiding complex settings such as virtual environments and package management.

**Potential Misuse.** Our platform makes use of Skills uploaded by the community. However, this current version does not incorporate any mechanism to ensure that these models are fair and without bias. Nonetheless, UKP-SQuARE includes a module for explainability that uses CheckLists (Ribeiro et al., 2020) to analyze the strong and weak points of the Skills and to detect their biases and unfair content. Thus, we currently delegate the fairness checks to the authors of the models. We are not held responsible for errors, false, or offensive content generated by the Skills. Users should use them at their discretion.

**Environmental Impact.** Since UKP-SQuARE empowers the community to run publicly available Skills on the cloud, it has the potential to reduce $CO_2$ emissions from retraining previous models to make the comparisons needed when developing new models.

**User Study.** The participants are junior graduate students recruited on a voluntary basis. They are not part of this work, and never saw the user interface before the study. Before starting the study, they were given detailed instructions on the goals and scope of the study, and how the data was going to be used. Only non-personal data was recorded.

## Acknowledgements

We thank Jan-Christoph Klie for his insightful feedback and suggestions on a draft of the paper and the project. We thank Richard Eckart de Castilho for advice on the general infrastructure and Nandan Thakur and Hossain Shaikh Saadi for their preliminary work on the project. We also thank Serkan Bayraktaroğlu for designing our logo.

This work has been funded by: (i) the German Research Foundation (DFG) as part of the UKP-SQuARE project (grant GU 798/29-1), (ii) the DFG as part of the QASciInf project (GU 798/18-3), (iii) the DFG within the project "Open Argument Mining" (GU 798/25-1), associated with the Priority Program "Robust Argumentation Machines (RATIO)" (SPP-1999), (iv) the DFG-funded research training group "Adaptive Preparation of Information form Heterogeneous Sources" (AIPHES, GRK 1994/1), (v) the European Regional Development Fund (ERDF) and the Hessian State Chancellery – Hessian Minister of Digital Strategy and Development under the promotional reference 20005482 (TexPrax), and (vi) the LOEWE initiative (Hesse, Germany) within the emergenCITY center.

## References


Junjie Bai, Fang Lu, Ke Zhang, et al. 2019. ONNX: Open Neural Network Exchange. https://github.com/onnx/onnx.

John Brooke. 1996. SUS-a quick and dirty usability scale. *Usability evaluation in industry*, 189.

Danqi Chen, Adam Fisch, Jason Weston, and Antoine Bordes. 2017. Reading Wikipedia to answer open-domain questions. In *Proceedings of the 55th Annual Meeting of the Association for Computational Linguistics (Volume 1: Long Papers)*, pages 1870–1879, Vancouver, Canada. Association for Computational Linguistics.

Christopher Clark, Kenton Lee, Ming-Wei Chang, Tom Kwiatkowski, Michael Collins, and Kristina Toutanova. 2019. BoolQ: Exploring the surprising difficulty of natural yes/no questions. In *Proceedings of the 2019 Conference of the North American Chapter of the Association for Computational Linguistics: Human Language Technologies, Volume 1 (Long and Short Papers)*, pages 2924–2936, Minneapolis, Minnesota. Association for Computational Linguistics.

Pradeep Dasigi, Nelson F. Liu, Ana Marasović, Noah A. Smith, and Matt Gardner. 2019. Quoref: A reading comprehension dataset with questions requiring coreferential reasoning. In *Proceedings of the 2019 Conference on Empirical Methods in Natural Language Processing and the 9th International Joint Conference on Natural Language Processing (EMNLP-IJCNLP)*, pages 5925–5932, Hong Kong, China. Association for Computational Linguistics.

Victor Dibia. 2020. NeuralQA: A usable library for question answering (contextual query expansion + BERT) on large datasets. In *Proceedings of the 2020 Conference on Empirical Methods in Natural Language Processing: System Demonstrations*, pages 15–22, Online. Association for Computational Linguistics.

Dheeru Dua, Yizhong Wang, Pradeep Dasigi, Gabriel Stanovsky, Sameer Singh, and Matt Gardner. 2019. DROP: A reading comprehension benchmark requiring discrete reasoning over paragraphs. In *Proceedings of the 2019 Conference of the North American Chapter of the Association for Computational Linguistics: Human Language Technologies, Volume 1 (Long and Short Papers)*, pages 2368–2378, Minneapolis, Minnesota. Association for Computational Linguistics.

Gregor Geigle, Nils Reimers, Andreas Rücklé, and Iryna Gurevych. 2021. TWEAC: transformer with extendable QA agent classifiers. *CoRR*, abs/2104.07081.

Sebastian Hofstätter, Sheng-Chieh Lin, Jheng-Hong Yang, Jimmy Lin, and Allan Hanbury. 2021. Efficiently teaching an effective dense retriever with balanced topic aware sampling. In *SIGIR '21: The 44th International ACM SIGIR Conference on Research and Development in Information Retrieval, Virtual Event, Canada, July 11-15, 2021*, pages 113–122. ACM.

Neil Houlsby, Andrei Giurgiu, Stanislaw Jastrzebski, Bruna Morrone, Quentin De Laroussilhe, Andrea Gesmundo, Mona Attariyan, and Sylvain Gelly. 2019. Parameter-efficient transfer learning for NLP. In *Proceedings of the 36th International Conference on Machine Learning*, volume 97 of *Proceedings of Machine Learning Research*, pages 2790–2799. PMLR.

Lifu Huang, Ronan Le Bras, Chandra Bhagavatula, and Yejin Choi. 2019. Cosmos QA: Machine reading comprehension with contextual commonsense reasoning. In *Proceedings of the 2019 Conference on Empirical Methods in Natural Language Processing and the 9th International Joint Conference on Natural Language Processing (EMNLP-IJCNLP)*, pages 2391–2401, Hong Kong, China. Association for Computational Linguistics.

Jeff Johnson, Matthijs Douze, and Hervé Jégou. 2021. Billion-scale similarity search with gpus. *IEEE Transactions on Big Data*, 7(3):535–547.

Mandar Joshi, Eunsol Choi, Daniel Weld, and Luke Zettlemoyer. 2017. TriviaQA: A large scale distantly supervised challenge dataset for reading comprehension. In *Proceedings of the 55th Annual Meeting of the Association for Computational Linguistics (Volume 1: Long Papers)*, pages 1601–1611, Vancouver, Canada. Association for Computational Linguistics.

Herve Jégou, Matthijs Douze, and Cordelia Schmid. 2011. Product quantization for nearest neighbor search. *IEEE Transactions on Pattern Analysis and Machine Intelligence*, 33(1):117–128.

Vladimir Karpukhin, Barlas Oguz, Sewon Min, Patrick Lewis, Ledell Wu, Sergey Edunov, Danqi Chen, and Wen-tau Yih. 2020. Dense passage retrieval for open-domain question answering. In *Proceedings of the 2020 Conference on Empirical Methods in Natural Language Processing (EMNLP)*, pages 6769–6781, Online. Association for Computational Linguistics.

Daniel Khashabi, Snigdha Chaturvedi, Michael Roth, Shyam Upadhyay, and Dan Roth. 2018. Looking beyond the surface: A challenge set for reading comprehension over multiple sentences. In *Proceedings of the 2018 Conference of the North American Chapter of the Association for Computational Linguistics: Human Language Technologies, Volume 1 (Long Papers)*, pages 252–262, New Orleans, Louisiana. Association for Computational Linguistics.

Daniel Khashabi, Sewon Min, Tushar Khot, Ashish Sabharwal, Oyvind Tafjord, Peter Clark, and Hannaneh Hajishirzi. 2020. UNIFIEDQA: Crossing format boundaries with a single QA system. In *Findings of the Association for Computational Linguistics: EMNLP 2020*, pages 1896–1907, Online. Association for Computational Linguistics.

Tomas Kocisky, Jonathan Schwarz, Phil Blunsom, Chris Dyer, Karl Moritz Hermann, Gabor Melis, and Edward Grefenstette. 2018. The narrativeqa reading comprehension challenge. *Transactions of the Association for Computational Linguistics*, 6(0):317–328.

Tom Kwiatkowski, Jennimaria Palomaki, Olivia Redfield, Michael Collins, Ankur Parikh, Chris Alberti, Danielle Epstein, Illia Polosukhin, Jacob Devlin, Kenton Lee, Kristina Toutanova, Llion Jones, Matthew Kelcey, Ming-Wei Chang, Andrew M. Dai, Jakob Uszkoreit, Quoc Le, and Slav Petrov. 2019. Natural questions: A benchmark for question answering research. *Transactions of the Association for Computational Linguistics*, 7:452–466.

Guokun Lai, Qizhe Xie, Hanxiao Liu, Yiming Yang, and Eduard Hovy. 2017. RACE: Large-scale ReAding comprehension dataset from examinations. In *Proceedings of the 2017 Conference on Empirical Methods in Natural Language Processing*, pages 785–794, Copenhagen, Denmark. Association for Computational Linguistics.

Jiwei Li, Xinlei Chen, Eduard H. Hovy, and Dan Jurafsky. 2016. Visualizing and understanding neural models in NLP. In *NAACL HLT 2016, The 2016 Conference of the North American Chapter of the Association for Computational Linguistics: Human Language Technologies, San Diego California, USA, June 12-17, 2016*, pages 681–691.

Andreas Madsen, Siva Reddy, and Sarath Chandar. 2021. Post-hoc interpretability for neural NLP: A survey. *arXiv*, abs/2108.04840.

Anastasios Nentidis, Anastasia Krithara, Konstantinos Bougiatiotis, Martin Krallinger, Carlos Rodríguez Penagos, Marta Villegas, and Georgios Paliouras. 2020. Overview of bioasq 2020: The eighth bioasq challenge on large-scale biomedical semantic indexing and question answering. In *Experimental IR Meets Multilinguality, Multimodality, and Interaction - 11th International Conference of the CLEF Association, CLEF 2020, Thessaloniki, Greece, September 22-25, 2020, Proceedings*, volume 12260 of *Lecture Notes in Computer Science*, pages 194–214. Springer.

Tri Nguyen, Mir Rosenberg, Xia Song, Jianfeng Gao, Saurabh Tiwary, Rangan Majumder, and Li Deng. 2016. MS MARCO: A Human Generated MAchine Reading COmprehension Dataset. In *Proceedings of the Workshop on Cognitive Computation, NIPS*.

Jonas Pfeiffer, Andreas Rücklé, Clifton Poth, Aishwarya Kamath, Ivan Vulić, Sebastian Ruder, Kyunghyun Cho, and Iryna Gurevych. 2020. AdapterHub: A framework for adapting transformers. In *Proceedings of the 2020 Conference on Empirical Methods in Natural Language Processing: System Demonstrations*, pages 46–54, Online. Association for Computational Linguistics.

Haritz Puerto, Gözde Gül Sahin, and Iryna Gurevych. 2021. MetaQA: Combining expert agents for multi-skill question answering. *arXiv*, abs/2112.01922.

Pranav Rajpurkar, Robin Jia, and Percy Liang. 2018. Know what you don't know: Unanswerable questions for SQuAD. In *Proceedings of the 56th Annual Meeting of the Association for Computational Linguistics (Volume 2: Short Papers)*, pages 784–789, Melbourne, Australia. Association for Computational Linguistics.

Pranav Rajpurkar, Jian Zhang, Konstantin Lopyrev, and Percy Liang. 2016. SQuAD: 100,000+ questions for machine comprehension of text. In *Proceedings of the 2016 Conference on Empirical Methods in Natural Language Processing*, pages 2383–2392, Austin, Texas. Association for Computational Linguistics.

Nils Reimers and Iryna Gurevych. 2019. Sentence-BERT: Sentence embeddings using Siamese BERT-networks. In *Proceedings of the 2019 Conference on Empirical Methods in Natural Language Processing and the 9th International Joint Conference on Natural Language Processing (EMNLP-IJCNLP)*, pages 3982–3992, Hong Kong, China. Association for Computational Linguistics.

Leonardo F. R. Ribeiro, Yue Zhang, and Iryna Gurevych. 2021. Structural adapters in pretrained language models for AMR-to-Text generation. In *Proceedings of the 2021 Conference on Empirical Methods in Natural Language Processing*, pages 4269–4282, Online and Punta Cana, Dominican Republic. Association for Computational Linguistics.

Marco Túlio Ribeiro, Tongshuang Wu, Carlos Guestrin, and Sameer Singh. 2020. Beyond accuracy: Behavioral testing of NLP models with checklist. In *Proceedings of the 58th Annual Meeting of the Association for Computational Linguistics, ACL 2020, Online, July 5-10, 2020*, pages 4902–4912.

Stephen E. Robertson, Steve Walker, Susan Jones, Micheline Hancock-Beaulieu, and Mike Gatford. 1994. Okapi at TREC-3. In *Proceedings of The Third Text REtrieval Conference, TREC 1994, Gaithersburg, Maryland, USA, November 2-4, 1994*, volume 500-225 of *NIST Special Publication*, pages 109–126. National Institute of Standards and Technology (NIST).

Anna Rogers, Matt Gardner, and Isabelle Augenstein. 2021. QA dataset explosion: A taxonomy of NLP resources for question answering and reading comprehension. *arXiv*, abs/2107.12708.

Anna Rogers, Olga Kovaleva, Matthew Downey, and Anna Rumshisky. 2020. Getting closer to ai complete question answering: A set of prerequisite real tasks. *Proceedings of the AAAI Conference on Artificial Intelligence*, 34(05):8722–8731.

Amrita Saha, Rahul Aralikatte, Mitesh M. Khapra, and Karthik Sankaranarayanan. 2018. DuoRC: Towards complex language understanding with paraphrased reading comprehension. In *Proceedings of the 56th Annual Meeting of the Association for Computational*

*Linguistics (Volume 1: Long Papers)*, pages 1683–1693, Melbourne, Australia. Association for Computational Linguistics.

Maarten Sap, Hannah Rashkin, Derek Chen, Ronan Le Bras, and Yejin Choi. 2019. Social IQa: Commonsense reasoning about social interactions. In *Proceedings of the 2019 Conference on Empirical Methods in Natural Language Processing and the 9th International Joint Conference on Natural Language Processing (EMNLP-IJCNLP)*, pages 4463–4473, Hong Kong, China. Association for Computational Linguistics.

Oyvind Tafjord, Matt Gardner, Kevin Lin, and Peter Clark. 2019. QuaRTz: An open-domain dataset of qualitative relationship questions. In *Proceedings of the 2019 Conference on Empirical Methods in Natural Language Processing and the 9th International Joint Conference on Natural Language Processing (EMNLP-IJCNLP)*, pages 5941–5946, Hong Kong, China. Association for Computational Linguistics.

Alon Talmor, Jonathan Herzig, Nicholas Lourie, and Jonathan Berant. 2019. CommonsenseQA: A question answering challenge targeting commonsense knowledge. In *Proceedings of the 2019 Conference of the North American Chapter of the Association for Computational Linguistics: Human Language Technologies, Volume 1 (Long and Short Papers)*, pages 4149–4158, Minneapolis, Minnesota. Association for Computational Linguistics.

Adam Trischler, Tong Wang, Xingdi Yuan, Justin Harris, Alessandro Sordoni, Philip Bachman, and Kaheer Suleman. 2017. NewsQA: A machine comprehension dataset. In *Proceedings of the 2nd Workshop on Representation Learning for NLP*, pages 191–200, Vancouver, Canada. Association for Computational Linguistics.

George Tsatsaronis, Georgios Balikas, Prodromos Malakasiotis, Ioannis Partalas, Matthias Zschunke, Michael R. Alvers, Dirk Weissenborn, Anastasia Krithara, Sergios Petridis, Dimitris Polychronopoulos, Yannis Almirantis, John Pavlopoulos, Nicolas Baskiotis, Patrick Gallinari, Thierry Artiéres, Axel-Cyrille Ngonga Ngomo, Norman Heino, Eric Gaussier, Liliana Barrio-Alvers, Michael Schroeder, Ion Androutsopoulos, and Georgios Paliouras. 2015. An overview of the bioasq large-scale biomedical semantic indexing and question answering competition. *BMC Bioinformatics*, 16(1):138.

UIUX-Trend. 2021. Measuring and interpreting system usability scale. `https://uiuxtrend.com/measuring-system-usability-scale-sus`. Accessed: 2022-01-21.

Denny Vrandečić and Markus Krötzsch. 2014. Wikidata: A free collaborative knowledgebase. *Commun. ACM*, 57(10):78–85.

Thomas Wolf, Lysandre Debut, Victor Sanh, Julien Chaumond, Clement Delangue, Anthony Moi, Pierric Cistac, Tim Rault, Rémi Louf, Morgan Funtowicz, Joe Davison, Sam Shleifer, Patrick von Platen, Clara Ma, Yacine Jernite, Julien Plu, Canwen Xu, Teven Le Scao, Sylvain Gugger, Mariama Drame, Quentin Lhoest, and Alexander M. Rush. 2020. Transformers: State-of-the-art natural language processing. In *Proceedings of the 2020 Conference on Empirical Methods in Natural Language Processing: System Demonstrations*, pages 38–45, Online. Association for Computational Linguistics.

Lee Xiong, Chenyan Xiong, Ye Li, Kwok-Fung Tang, Jialin Liu, Paul N. Bennett, Junaid Ahmed, and Arnold Overwijk. 2021. Approximate nearest neighbor negative contrastive learning for dense text retrieval. In *International Conference on Learning Representations*.

Zhilin Yang, Peng Qi, Saizheng Zhang, Yoshua Bengio, William Cohen, Ruslan Salakhutdinov, and Christopher D. Manning. 2018. HotpotQA: A dataset for diverse, explainable multi-hop question answering. In *Proceedings of the 2018 Conference on Empirical Methods in Natural Language Processing*, pages 2369–2380, Brussels, Belgium. Association for Computational Linguistics.

Michihiro Yasunaga, Hongyu Ren, Antoine Bosselut, Percy Liang, and Jure Leskovec. 2021. QA-GNN: Reasoning with language models and knowledge graphs for question answering. In *Proceedings of the 2021 Conference of the North American Chapter of the Association for Computational Linguistics: Human Language Technologies*, pages 535–546, Online. Association for Computational Linguistics.

## A Skill Implementation

The code below implements an open-domain, extractive QA Skill. First, a set of utility classes are loaded and initialized for facilitating interaction with UKP-SQuARE's Models and Datastore components (lines 1-5). Next, in the `predict` function, the Datastores are queried for retrieval. The Datastores component takes the user query, the datastore (Wikipeida snapshot from Natural Questions) and what index to use (dense, based on DPR) as input and returns the top documents. From these results, the document text and respective scores are extracted (lines 11-17). Subsequently, the query and the top documents are passed to an to the Models component for span extraction. In this implementation, a BERT base model with a adapter trained on SQuAD V2.0 is used (lines 21-30). Finally, the top answers are returned (lines 32-36).

```
1  from square_skill_api.models import QueryOutput, QueryRequest
2  from square_skill_helpers import ModelAPI, DataAPI
3
4  model_api = ModelAPI()
5  data_api = DataAPI()
6
7  async def predict(request: QueryRequest) -> QueryOutput:
8
9      # Dense document retrieval using the Datastores
10     # on a Wikipedia snapshot with DPR embeddings
11     data_api_output = await data_api(
12         datastore="nq",
13         index_name="dpr",
14         query=request.query,
15     )
16     context = [d["document"]["text"] for d in data_api_output]
17     context_score = [d["score"] for d in data_api_output]
18
19     # Answer extraction from the top document using the Model API
20     # using bert-base-uncased base model with SQuAD2.0 adapter
21     model_api_request = {
22       "input": [[request.query, c] for c in context],
23       "task_kwargs": {"topk": 1},
24       "adapter_name": "qa/squad2@ukp",
25     }
26     model_api_output = await model_api(
27         model_name="bert-base-uncased",
28         pipeline="question-answering",
29         model_request=model_api_request,
30     )
31
32     return QueryOutput.from_question_answering(
33         model_api_output=model_api_output,
34         context=context,
35         context_score=context_score
36     )
```

Listing 1: Example Implementation of an open-domain, span extraction Skill.

## B Dataset Licences

Table 4 shows the license of each dataset. In the case of RACE, the authors did not provide any license but specified that it can only be used for non-commercial research purposes. In the case of the other datasets without any specified license, the authors did not provide any license, but the datasets are freely available to download and use in a research context. BioASQ is available by Courtesy of the U.S. National Library of Medicine.

| Dataset | License |
|---|---|
| NarrativeQA | Apache 2.0 |
| BioASQ | National Library of Medicine Terms and Conditions |
| DROP | CC BY-SA 4.0 |
| DuoRC | MIT |
| Natural Questions | MIT |
| NewsQA | MIT |
| Quoref | CC BY 4.0 |
| SQuAD 1.1 | CC BY-SA 4.0 |
| SQuAD 2.0 | CC BY-SA 4.0 |
| TriviaQA | Apache 2.0 |
| BoolQ | CC BY-SA 3.0 |
| CommonSenseQA | NA |
| CosmosQA | NA |
| MultiRC | NA |
| Quail | NA |
| Quartz | NA |
| RACE | NA |
| SocialIQA | NA |
| MS MARCO | CC BY 4.0 |

Table 4: License of each dataset.

## C Questions of the User Study

Table 5 contains the answers of the participants of the user study (§4) to each question we asked to evaluate their understanding of the interface.

| Question | Avg. Ans. |
|---|---|
| SQuARE provides a user interface that allows me to tell the difference between both Skills | 4.4 |
| I understand in a glimpse each card. | 2.6 |
| I can get a quick overall view of the weak points of the skill. | 3.8 |
| The examples of each CheckList item are useful. | 4.4 |

Table 5: List of questions to understand the usefulness of the system. 1 represents "strongly disagree" and 5 represents "strongly agree."

## D User Interface

UI screenshots for visualizing categorical and multiple choice Skill results are given in Fig. 5 and 6 respectively. In Fig. 3 the UI for managing a Skill is shown. Navigating through behavioural test results is given in Fig. 4.

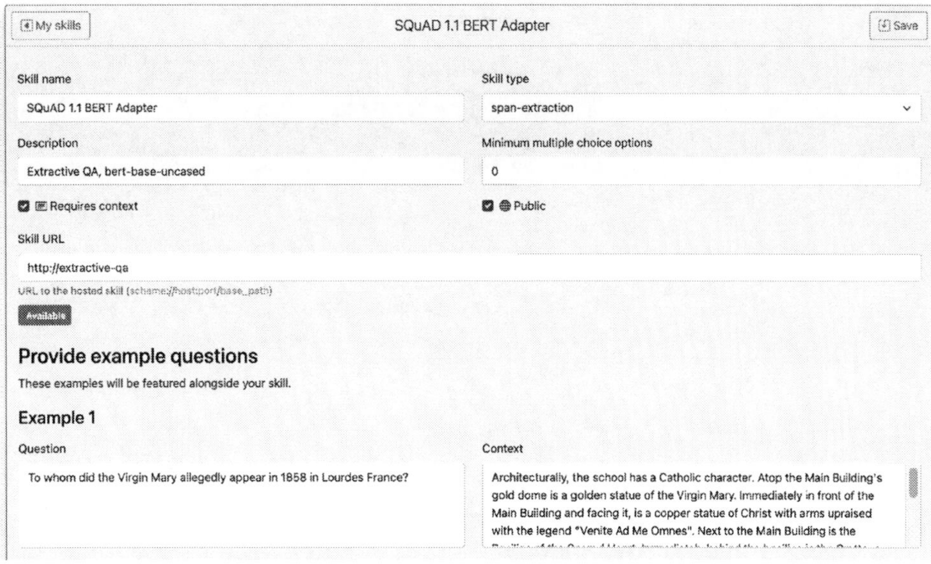


Figure 3: User interface for managing a Skill.

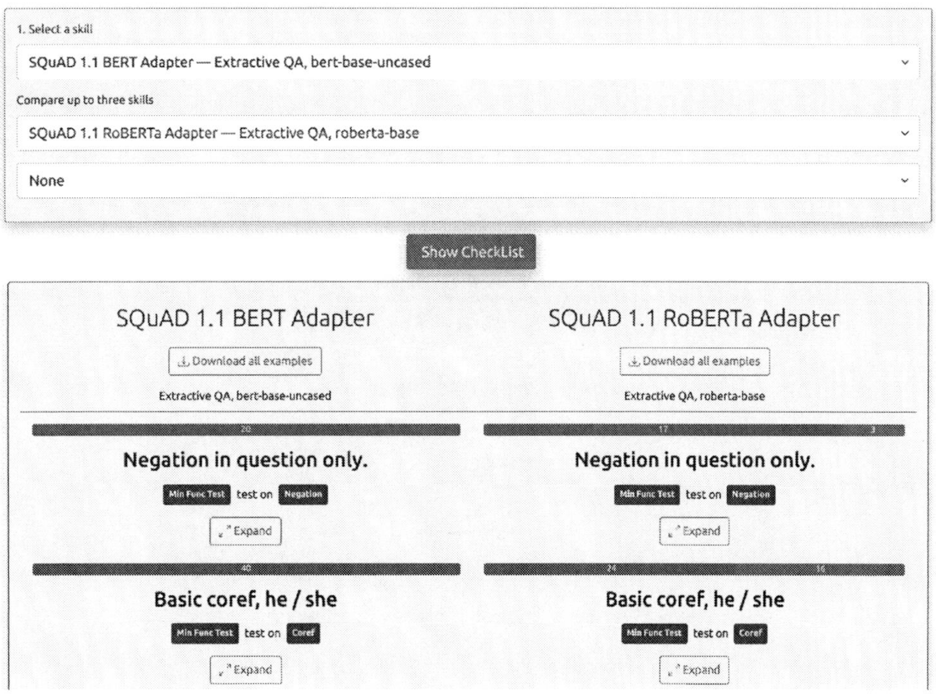


Figure 4: User interface for behavioural tests from CheckList.

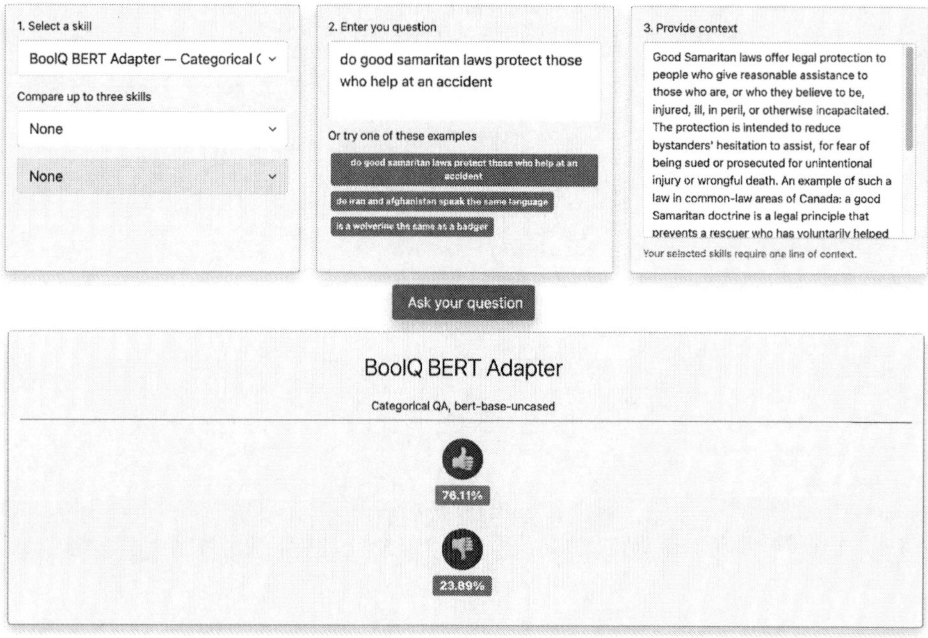


Figure 5: User interface for visualizing categorical Skill results.

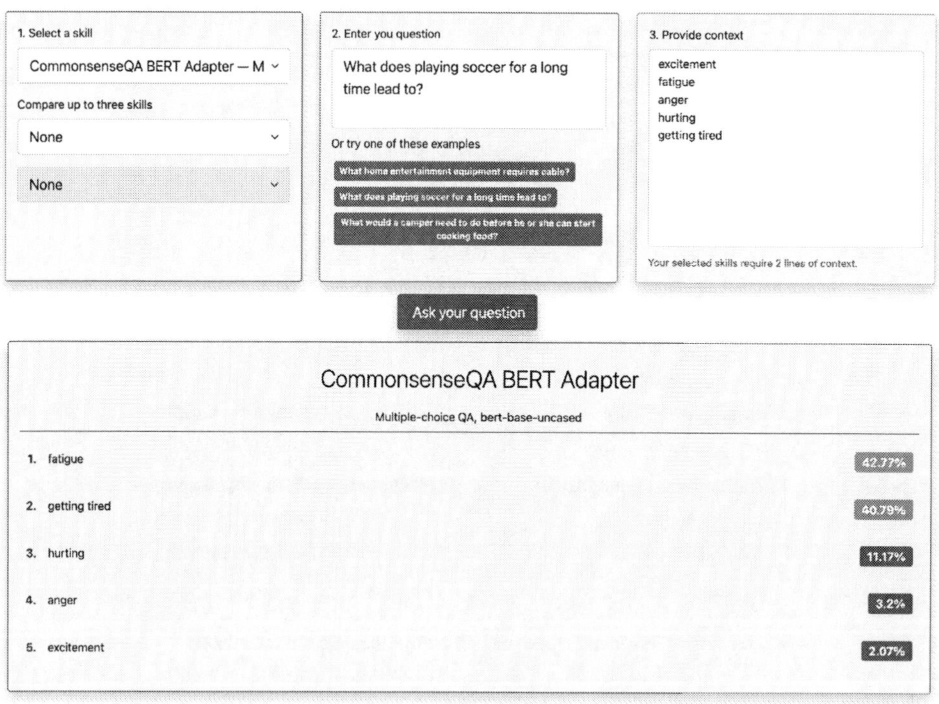


Figure 6: User interface for visualizing multiple choice Skill results.

# ViLMedic: a framework for research at the intersection of vision and language in medical AI

Jean-Benoit Delbrouck, Khaled Saab, Maya Varma, Sabri Eyuboglu,
Jared A. Dunnmon, Pierre Chambon, Juan Manuel Zambrano,
Akshay Chaudhari, Curtis P. Langlotz
Stanford University
{jeanbenoit.delbrouck}@stanford.edu

## Abstract

There is a growing need to model interactions between data modalities (*e.g.*, vision, language) — both to improve AI predictions on existing tasks and to enable new applications. In the recent field of multimodal medical AI, integrating multiple modalities has gained widespread popularity as multimodal models have proven to improve performance, robustness, require less training samples and add complementary information. To improve technical reproducibility and transparency for multimodal medical tasks as well as speed up progress across medical AI, we present ViLMedic, a Vision-and-Language medical library. As of 2022, the library contains a dozen reference implementations replicating the state-of-the-art results for problems that range from medical visual question answering and radiology report generation to multimodal representation learning on widely adopted medical datasets. In addition, ViLMedic hosts a model-zoo with more than twenty pretrained models for the above tasks designed to be extensible by researchers but also simple for practitioners. Ultimately, we hope our reproducible pipelines can enable clinical translation and create real impact. The library is available at `https://github.com/jbdel/vilmedic`.

## 1 Introduction

In the past few years, there has been a surge of interest in multimodal problems, especially involving visio-linguistic data that occurs "in the wild", from image captioning (Chen et al., 2015; Krishna et al., 2017; You et al., 2016) to visual question answering (Antol et al., 2015; Goyal et al., 2017; Yu et al., 2019) and beyond. Multimodal tasks are interesting because many real-world problems are multimodal in nature. This is also the case in medical AI where many repetitive tasks lie at the intersection of vision and language. For example, radiologists must generate and summarize reports from x-ray images, or answer medical questions from patients. As a response, tasks such as radiology report generation (Zhang et al., 2020b; Miura et al., 2021), where assistive systems that take X-ray images of a patient and generate a textual report describing clinical observations or medical visual question answering have been proposed. Recent multimodal training techniques, such as contrastive learning, have also enabled powerful multimodal embeddings that contribute to higher quality in-domain image representations that capture the subtlety of visual features required for medical image understanding tasks and annotation-efficient learning (Zhang et al., 2020a; Huang et al., 2021).

These recent advances have identified new challenges. First, it is not always clear to what extent truly visio-linguistic reasoning and understanding is required for solving tasks where images and text are available. Language can inadvertently impose strong priors that result in seemingly impressive performance without any understanding (or active use) of the visual content. This challenge has been pointed out for tasks involving natural images, such as visual question answering (Jabri et al., 2016; Goyal et al., 2017) or multimodal machine translation (Delbrouck and Dupont, 2017; Caglayan et al., 2019), but also involving medical images, such as slice discovery (Eyuboglu et al., 2022) or multimodal radiology report summarization (Delbrouck et al., 2021). Secondly, multimodal training has been identified as a challenging learning task by nature: multimodal networks are prone to overfitting due to their increased capacity and modalities overfit and generalize at different rates (Wang et al., 2020).

Another challenge in medical AI is transparency. Despite much promising research currently being undertaken, particularly in imaging, the literature as a whole lacks clear reporting to facilitate



*Proceedings of the 60th Annual Meeting of the Association for Computational Linguistics*
*System Demonstrations*, pages 23 - 34
May 22-27, 2022 ©2022 Association for Computational Linguistics

replicability, exploration for potential ethical concerns, and clear demonstrations of effectiveness (Vollmer et al., 2020). Recently, McDermott et al. (2021) evaluated 511 scientific papers across several machine learning subfields and found that machine learning for health compared poorly to other areas regarding reproducibility metrics, such as dataset and code accessibility. As an example, McKinney et al. (2020) demonstrated a system that improves the speed and robustness of breast cancer screening, while highlighting the challenges of making such work reproducible. This absence of sufficiently documented methods and computer code underlying the study has effectively undermined its scientific value (Haibe-Kains et al., 2020).

To address the aforementioned shortcomings related to multimodal training and medical AI, we propose **ViLMedic** (§3), an open-source Vision-and-Language medical library. ViLMedic emphasizes technical reproducibility by packaging common operations (e.g., linguistic or visual encoding) as "**blocks**" (3.1), and by defining "**solutions**" (3.2), the full pipeline of a certain multimodal technique published in the literature, as an assembly of blocks. With the abstraction of blocks and example configurations of these blocks to form solutions, ViLMedic gives the user an easy to use interface to (i) reproduce the results reported in the literature, and (ii) investigate novel multimodal techniques quickly. In addition to blocks and solutions, ViLMedic hosts a **model-zoo** (3.3) containing trained solutions usable in one line of code.

As of 2022, ViLMedic contains dozen of solutions replicating the state-of-the-art results for problems that range from medical visual question answering and radiology report generation to multimodal representation learning on widely adopted medical datasets, and more than twenty pretrained models for the above tasks.

## 2 Related work

Recent progress in natural language processing and computer vision has been driven by advances in both model architecture and model pretraining. Namely, Transformer architectures have facilitated building higher-capacity models and pretraining has made it possible to effectively utilize this capacity for a wide variety of medical tasks. The library HuggingFace Transformers (Wolf et al., 2020) provides thousands of pretrained models to perform tasks on different modalities such as text, vision, and audio. ViLMedic takes advantage of the available medical language representation models hosted on the HuggingFace model hub, such as clinicalBERT (Alsentzer et al., 2019) and BioMed-RoBERTa (Gururangan et al., 2020), to fine-tune their representations on downstream medical multimodal tasks.

Another related work is the MultiModal Framework (MMF, Singh et al. (2018)), a deep learning library for vision and language multimodal research for natural images. MMF has the same philosophy as ViLMedic: the library replicates the architectures and results from the literature and provides baseline implementations for machine learning challenges. However, the MMF framework is oriented towards handling data that occurs "in the wild" (VQA, TextVQA) or on the Internet (Hateful Memes detection). As of today, no medical tasks are addressed. Nevertheless, MMF contains state-of-the-art visio-linguistic architectures, such as VisualBERT (Li et al., 2019) and ViLT (Kim et al., 2021) whose efficiency does not straightforwardly translate in the medical domain but that could be useful for ViLMedic in the future.

In the medical field, TorchXRayVision (Cohen et al., 2020) is an open-source software library for working with chest X-ray datasets and deep learning models. It also provides a common interface and common pre-processing chain for a wide set of publicly available chest X-ray datasets. It differs from ViLMedic in two ways: first, it offers very limited tools and details to re-train the models and second, it primarily focuses on releasing pretrained visual encoder (namely, DenseNet (Huang et al., 2017)). ViLMedic focuses on training and releasing pretrained models that are multimodal across four major medical tasks and also emphasizes technical reproducibility. Nonetheless, we have integrated TorchXRayVision as a component of our library.

## 3 ViLMedic

ViLMedic consists of **blocks**, **solutions** and a **model-zoo**. A **block** (§3.1) is a common operations defined as a snippet of code. Blocks can be a piece of a neural network architecture (e.g., a ResNet (He et al., 2016) encoding the image in a multimodal solution), a loss function, or an evaluation metric. Therefore, a block can be suitable for several solutions. **Solutions** (§3.2) are defined as the full pipeline of a certain multimodal technique published in the literature. That is, a solution contains pre-processed data (or the pre-processing scripts), open-source architecture implementations, proper training parameters, and evaluation scoring. A solution is composed of independent blocks and defined in a configuration file. Finally, most of our solutions are trained and stored in a **model-zoo** (§3.3), saving researchers and practitioners time and effort (Appendix F).

Our blocks, solutions and model-zoo are supported by a documentation available at `https://vilmedic.readthedocs.io/en/latest/`.

## 3.1 Blocks

A block is a snippet of code, usually written in PyTorch, that contains a sub-part of a solution. It can be a piece of a neural network architecture, a loss function, or an evaluation metric. Therefore, a block can be suitable for several solutions. In a configuration file of a solution, a CNN (Convolutional Neural Network) block would look like this:

```
---
my_cnn:
    proto: CNN
    backbone: densenet169
    output_layer: features
    dropout_out: 0.0
    permute: batch_first
    visual_embedding_dim: 1664
    freeze: False
---
```

Code Listing 1: Declaring a CNN block in ViLMedic

This would result in the creation of a CNN block that consists of a Densenet169 network (Huang et al., 2017) whose output is the "features" layer[1]. This block will be referred as the `my_cnn` variable in the solution.

Block instantiation must respect rules, but users can feed the blocks any type of modality. For example, you can feed the Transformer architecture (Vaswani et al., 2017) sequences of words (Vaswani et al., 2017), sequences of image patches (Dosovitskiy et al., 2021), sequences of speech pieces (Pham et al., 2019) or sequences of state, action and reward in reinforcement learning (Parisotto et al., 2020) and still get a strong baseline for your task.

We believe this consolidation in architecture tends to focus and concentrate software and infrastructure, further speeding up progress across AI. This concept of blocks in ViLMedic enables a user to quickly build a solution that acts as a strong baseline for their multimodal task. In the following sections, we provide details on the three primary types of blocks: language (§3.1.1), vision (§3.1.2), and metrics (§3.1.3).

### 3.1.1 Language blocks

In ViLMedic, all language blocks are based on the HuggingFace Transformer library (Wolf et al., 2020). This offers the possibility to load any available pretrained encoder and decoder model[2] in ViLMedic. This also allows the users to benefit from all the implemented HuggingFace functionalities such as beam-search, length penalty, or token exclusion and configurations such as the layer-size, the number of layers, the dropout per layer, etc.

For decoders (i.e., Transformers generating language), ViLMedic creates a block to support model-ensembling. That is, one can train several Natural Language Generation (NLG) models (say, for the Radiology Report Generation task) and ensemble those to further improve generation.

### 3.1.2 Vision blocks

ViLMedic supports all CNN architectures proposed by PyTorch and TorchXRayVision, and offers a block wrapping these models that allows to select sub-parts of a network, add dropout, and change the train-mode (as shown in listing 1).

Some vision blocks, such as the Vision Transformers (Dosovitskiy et al., 2021) or VisualBERT (Li et al., 2019), are implemented in ViLMedic but still unexploited by solutions. We believe they may be important for future research in our field[3].

[1] `https://github.com/pytorch/vision/blob/main/torchvision/models/densenet.py#L215`

[2] `https://huggingface.co/models`

[3] `https://openreview.net/forum?id=3Wybo29gGlx`

#### 3.1.3 Metric blocks

Besides widely used metrics in classification (accuracy, F1-score, etc.) and NLG (BLEU, ROUGE, METEOR), ViLMedic implements metrics specific to radiology report generation that evaluate the factual correctness, completeness, and consistency of the output. To be consistent with the literature, we propose the F1-CheXbert (Smit et al., 2020) metric that consists of scoring the CheXbert classification output of the ground-truth (GT) report and the generated report, a Named Entity Recognition accuracy based on the medical NER model of Stanza (Qi et al., 2020) and the RadGraph (Jain, Saahil et al., 2021) reward that scores the similarities between the generated semantic graphs of two reports.

ViLMedic also supports two metric optimization blocks that use Reinforcement Learning (RL) settings to directly optimize metrics scores as described in previous works (Rennie et al., 2017; Zhang et al., 2020b; Miura et al., 2021). These two methods, Self-critical sequence training (Rennie et al., 2017) and Proximal Policy Optimization (Schulman et al., 2017), require the language decoder to sample words. Because our language blocks are compliant with the HuggingFace Transformer library, we can use their `generate()`[4] method and benefit from all the related features during RL training (such as the arguments top_k, top_p, repetition_penalty, min_length, etc.)

### 3.2 Solutions

We define solutions as implementations of multimodal learning methods published in the literature. That is, a solution contains the corresponding pre-processed data or scripts, the architecture implementations, the proper training parameters, and the evaluation scoring. We present a non-exhaustive list of our solutions and how they compare to previous work in Table 1 in the Appendix.

Technically, a solution is described in a configuration file that lists the pre-processing and the hyper-parameters of the blocks, training, and evaluation. The configuration of a generic multimodal solution would look like this:

```
name: my_experiment
dataset:
  proto: ImSeq
  image:
    file: image.tok
    resize: 256
    crop: 224
    [...]
  seq:
    file: report.tok
    tokenizer: allenai/biomed_roberta_base
    tokenizer_max_len: 128
    processing: r2gen_clean_report
    [...]

model:
  proto: multimodal_encoding
  encoder:
    proto: allenai/biomed_roberta_base
  cnn:
    proto: CNN
    backbone: densenet169
    [...]
 projection:
    in_features: 1664
    out_features: 768

trainer:
    optimizer: Adam
    learning_rate: 5e-5
    [...]

validator:
    metrics: [accuracy, F1-score]
    [...]
```

Code Listing 2: Generic configuration describing a solution in ViLMedic. A solution can be run for training and then evaluation.

In the next sections, we detail the solutions existing in ViLMedic. They consist of results we replicated from the literature but also of new, original results available for future research. We divide our solutions in four medical tasks: Medical Visual Question Answering (§3.2.1), Radiology report generation (§3.2.2) and summarization (§3.2.3), and finally Vision-Language self-supervised learning (§3.2.4).

#### 3.2.1 Medical Visual Question Answering

VQA in the medical domain consists of building systems that answer open-ended questions about medical images ranging from x-rays, MRI to CT scans. Hosted by the ImageCLEF[5] initiative, the goal of the task is twofold: provide help to patients that can access structured and unstructured data related to their health and helping them better understand their conditions and enhance

[4] https://github.com/huggingface/transformers/blob/v4.15.0/src/transformers/generation_utils.py#L742

[5] https://www.imageclef.org/

the clinicians' confidence in interpreting complex medical images by a "second opinion".

ViLMedic replicates and even surpasses in terms of accuracy the winning solution[6] (Gong et al., 2021) on the VQA-Med 2021 dataset (Ben Abacha et al., 2021).

#### 3.2.2 Radiology report generation (RRG)

An important new application of NLG is to build support systems that take x-ray images of a patient and generate a textual report describing clinical observations in the images. This task has evolved quickly over the last year in term of evaluation as most NLG metrics (such as BLEU (Papineni et al., 2002) or METEOR (Banerjee and Lavie, 2005)) were unsuitable to score a generated report. Rather, metrics evaluating factual correctness (Zhang et al., 2020b) or factual completeness and consistency (Miura et al., 2021) were introduced.

ViLMedic replicates the state-of-the-art solutions in terms of these newly introduced metrics. We release these results for the two chest x-rays datasets evaluated in the literature: MIMIC-CXR (Johnson et al., 2019) and Indiana University (IU) - Chest X-Rays (Demner-Fushman et al., 2016). Finally, we provide a third system trained on Spanish radiology reports from the PadChest dataset (Bustos et al., 2020). As far as we know, this is the first attempt at radiology report generation in Spanish.

#### 3.2.3 Radiology report summarization (RRS)

Given the Findings and/or Background sections of a radiology report, the goal is to generate a summary (called an Impression section in radiology reports) that highlights the key observations and conclusions of the radiology study. Automating this summarization task is critical because the Impression section is the most important part of a radiology report, and manual summarization can be time-consuming and error prone.

The evaluation methods are the same as for Radiology Report Generation (the generated impression is treated as the generated report). Nevertheless, major previous works (Zhang et al., 2020b; Ben Abacha et al., 2021) evaluated their contributions on closed test-sets (either for privacy or challenge-related reasons). Our decision was therefore to implement the best and most straightforward solution (Mahajan et al., 2021) of the MEDIQA challenge (Ben Abacha et al., 2021) and to train it on the official splits of the MIMIC-CXR and IU datasets, providing a strong baseline for future research in this direction. Finally, ViLMedic replicates the first attempt in Multimodal Radiology Report Summarization (Delbrouck et al., 2021).

#### 3.2.4 Vision-Language self-supervised learning

Vision-Language self-supervised learning aims to improve visual representations of medical images or text by combining the benefits of both learning from abundant data and unsupervised statistical approaches. Such representations can be learned modality-wise by using autoencoders or improved by maximizing the agreement between true image-text pairs versus random pairs via a bidirectional objective as in contrastive learning. Successful training leads to higher-quality in-domain representations that capture the subtlety of visual and textual features required for multimodal understanding tasks.

The ViLMedic library has replicated the main framework for learning visual representations by exploiting the naturally occurring pairing of images and textual data. In the medical domain, the newly introduced ConVIRT (Zhang et al., 2020a) and GLoRIA (Huang et al., 2021) architectures are available and can be trained to replicate the same validation losses communicated in the author's paper. We also make available the widely adopted CLIP (Radford et al., 2021) network and its components the VAE (Kingma and Welling, 2014) and DALLE (Ramesh et al., 2021) model. These models are available in our model-zoo for one or more of these datasets: CheXpert (Irvin et al., 2019), MIMIC-CXR (Johnson et al., 2019) and IU - Chest X-Rays (Demner-Fushman et al., 2016) and PadChest dataset (Bustos et al., 2020).

### 3.3 Model-zoo

ViLMedic hosts a model-zoo of trained solutions. That is, a trained solution can be downloaded and instantiated in Python using one line of code (§3.3.1). The user can run the model of the solution on custom data as well as access the blocks separately for further investigation (§3.3.2). Our documentation also provides dedicated code ex-

[6] https://www.aicrowd.com/challenges/imageclef-2021-vqa-med-vqa/leaderboards

hibiting the advanced features of our pretrained models, such as personalized language generation or zero shot classification (see example in appendix E).

### 3.3.1 Basic usage

ViLMedic hosts a model-zoo similar to HuggingFace. Each pretrained model is referenced by a model name. The list of available models and their respective name is available in the documentation[7]. For example, say we would like to instantiate a pretrained ConVIRT model on MIMIC-CXR. Here is the corresponding Python code:

```
from vilmedic import AutoModel
model, processor = AutoModel.
from_pretrained("selfsup/convirt-mimic")
```

The `model` variable references the "model" part of the solution, as shown in listing 2. Technically, it is a PyTorch module with all its declared blocks. The `processor` variable is a custom ViLMedic object that contains the pre-processing code used during training and evaluation.

### 3.3.2 Inference

To run the model with a custom example, one can use the `inference` function of processor, that will trigger the required processing on the user input. The object return is a correctly formatted object to be input into the model:

```
batch = processor.inference(
 seq=["acute cardiopulmonary process."],
 image=["my_x_ray.jpg"])

out = model(**batch)

print(out.keys())
>>> dict_keys(['loss', 'loss_l',
 'loss_v', 'linguistic', 'visual'])
```

The images are processed using the `transform` package of PyTorch and the inference text is processed in two steps: preprocessing and tokenization. Preprocessing consists of cleaning the special characters and punctuation while tokenization splits words into word-pieces. The tokenizers supported in ViLMedic are HuggingFace tokenizers (more information is available in Appendix C).

If a user wants more details on the processing performed, they can directly access the said objects:

```
print(processor.seq.processing)
>>> <function r2gen_clean_report at ...>
print(processor.seq.tokenizer)
>>> PreTrainedTokenizerFast(
 name_or_path='allenai/biomed_..',
 vocab_size=50265, model_max_len=512,
 ...)
print(processor.image.transform)
>>> Compose(
    Resize(size=(224, 224),
    interpolation=bilinear),
    ToTensor()
    Normalize(mean=(...),
              std=(...)))
```

In our example, the model returns the global loss, the linguistic and visual loss, and the linguistic and visual embedding. The outputs of each model are detailed in our documentation.

Finally, a user can investigate the block of a solution by directly accessing the model attributes. Our documentation states that a ConVIRT model is composed of a CNN (`visual`) and a Transformer encoder (`linguistic`) and a loss function (`loss_fn`). The user can access the CNN and the loss as such:

```
print(model.visual)
>>> resnet50(output_layer=avgpool,
 dropout_out=0.0, freeze=False,
 pretrained=True)
print(model.loss_fn)
>>> ConVIRTLoss(
        (cos_loss): CosineSimilarity()
        (tau): 0.1
        (lambda_): 0.75
)
```

Because the CNN block is a PyTorch module, a user can simply use `torch.save(model.visual.state_dict(), "cnn_weights.pth")` for their own project.

## 4 Conclusion and Future Work

We presented ViLMedic, a framework for research at the intersection of vision and language in medical AI. We have reproduced and make publicly available state-of-the-art medical AI models, as well as implemented custom solutions that exceed their performance. Our goal is to maintain the library up-to-date with new blocks and solutions that can serve as a standard for benchmarking results across vision and language medical AI tasks. We also hope our library will be used to generate new ideas and publications.

[7] https://vilmedic.readthedocs.io/en/latest/vilmedic/model_zoo/overview.html

## References


Emily Alsentzer, John Murphy, William Boag, Wei-Hung Weng, Di Jin, Tristan Naumann, and Matthew McDermott. 2019. Publicly available clinical BERT embeddings. In *Proceedings of the 2nd Clinical Natural Language Processing Workshop*, pages 72–78, Minneapolis, Minnesota, USA. Association for Computational Linguistics.

Stanislaw Antol, Aishwarya Agrawal, Jiasen Lu, Margaret Mitchell, Dhruv Batra, C Lawrence Zitnick, and Devi Parikh. 2015. Vqa: Visual question answering. In *Proceedings of the IEEE international conference on computer vision*, pages 2425–2433.

Satanjeev Banerjee and Alon Lavie. 2005. METEOR: An automatic metric for MT evaluation with improved correlation with human judgments. In *Proceedings of the ACL Workshop on Intrinsic and Extrinsic Evaluation Measures for Machine Translation and/or Summarization*, pages 65–72, Ann Arbor, Michigan. Association for Computational Linguistics.

Asma Ben Abacha, Yassine Mrabet, Yuhao Zhang, Chaitanya Shivade, Curtis Langlotz, and Dina Demner-Fushman. 2021. Overview of the MEDIQA 2021 shared task on summarization in the medical domain. In *Proceedings of the 20th Workshop on Biomedical Language Processing*, pages 74–85, Online. Association for Computational Linguistics.

Asma Ben Abacha, Mourad Sarrouti, Dina Demner-Fushman, Sadid A. Hasan, and Henning Müller. 2021. Overview of the vqa-med task at imageclef 2021: Visual question answering and generation in the medical domain. In *CLEF 2021 Working Notes*, CEUR Workshop Proceedings, Bucharest, Romania. CEUR-WS.org.

Aurelia Bustos, Antonio Pertusa, Jose-Maria Salinas, and Maria de la Iglesia-Vayá. 2020. Padchest: A large chest x-ray image dataset with multi-label annotated reports. *Medical Image Analysis*, 66:101797.

Ozan Caglayan, Pranava Swaroop Madhyastha, Lucia Specia, and Loïc Barrault. 2019. Probing the need for visual context in multimodal machine translation. In *Proceedings of the 2019 Conference of the North American Chapter of the Association for Computational Linguistics: Human Language Technologies, Volume 1 (Long and Short Papers)*, pages 4159–4170.

Nicholas Carlini, Florian Tramer, Eric Wallace, Matthew Jagielski, Ariel Herbert-Voss, Katherine Lee, Adam Roberts, Tom Brown, Dawn Song, Ulfar Erlingsson, et al. 2021. Extracting training data from large language models. In *30th USENIX Security Symposium (USENIX Security 21)*, pages 2633–2650.

Xinlei Chen, Hao Fang, Tsung-Yi Lin, Ramakrishna Vedantam, Saurabh Gupta, Piotr Dollar, and C. Lawrence Zitnick. 2015. Microsoft coco captions: Data collection and evaluation server.

Zhihong Chen, Yan Song, Tsung-Hui Chang, and Xiang Wan. 2020. Generating radiology reports via memory-driven transformer. In *Proceedings of the 2020 Conference on Empirical Methods in Natural Language Processing (EMNLP)*, pages 1439–1449, Online. Association for Computational Linguistics.

Joseph Paul Cohen, Mohammad Hashir, Rupert Brooks, and Hadrien Bertrand. 2020. On the limits of cross-domain generalization in automated x-ray prediction. In *Medical Imaging with Deep Learning*.

Marcella Cornia, Matteo Stefanini, Lorenzo Baraldi, and Rita Cucchiara. 2020. Meshed-memory transformer for image captioning. In *Proceedings of the IEEE/CVF Conference on Computer Vision and Pattern Recognition*, pages 10578–10587.

Jean-Benoit Delbrouck and Stéphane Dupont. 2017. An empirical study on the effectiveness of images in multimodal neural machine translation. In *Proceedings of the 2017 Conference on Empirical Methods in Natural Language Processing*, pages 910–919.

Jean-Benoit Delbrouck, Cassie Zhang, and Daniel Rubin. 2021. QIAI at MEDIQA 2021: Multimodal radiology report summarization. In *Proceedings of the 20th Workshop on Biomedical Language Processing*, pages 285–290, Online. Association for Computational Linguistics.

Dina Demner-Fushman, Marc D Kohli, Marc B Rosenman, Sonya E Shooshan, Laritza Rodriguez, Sameer Antani, George R Thoma, and Clement J McDonald. 2016. Preparing a collection of radiology examinations for distribution and retrieval. *Journal of the American Medical Informatics Association*, 23(2):304–310.

Alexey Dosovitskiy, Lucas Beyer, Alexander Kolesnikov, Dirk Weissenborn, Xiaohua Zhai, Thomas Unterthiner, Mostafa Dehghani, Matthias Minderer, Georg Heigold, Sylvain Gelly, Jakob Uszkoreit, and Neil Houlsby. 2021. An image is worth 16x16 words: Transformers for image recognition at scale. *ICLR*.

Sabri Eyuboglu, Maya Varma, Khaled Kamal Saab, Jean-Benoit Delbrouck, Christopher Lee-Messer, Jared Dunnmon, James Zou, and Christopher Re. 2022. Domino: Discovering systematic errors with cross-modal embeddings. In *International Conference on Learning Representations*.

Haifan Gong, Ricong Huang, Guanqi Chen, and Guanbin Li. 2021. Sysu-hcp at vqa-med 2021: A data-centric model with efficient training methodology for medical visual question answering. In *CLEF 2021 – Conference and Labs of the Evaluation Forum, September 21–24, 2021, Bucharest, Romania*, CEUR Workshop Proceedings.

Yash Goyal, Tejas Khot, Douglas Summers-Stay, Dhruv Batra, and Devi Parikh. 2017. Making the v in vqa matter: Elevating the role of image understanding in visual question answering. In *Proceedings of the IEEE Conference on Computer Vision and Pattern Recognition*, pages 6904–6913.

Suchin Gururangan, Ana Marasović, Swabha Swayamdipta, Kyle Lo, Iz Beltagy, Doug Downey, and Noah A. Smith. 2020. Don't stop pretraining: Adapt language models to domains and tasks. In *Proceedings of the 58th Annual Meeting of the Association for Computational Linguistics*, pages 8342–8360, Online. Association for Computational Linguistics.

Benjamin Haibe-Kains, George Alexandru Adam, Ahmed Hosny, Farnoosh Khodakarami, Levi Waldron, Bo Wang, Chris McIntosh, Anna Goldenberg, Anshul Kundaje, Casey S Greene, et al. 2020. Transparency and reproducibility in artificial intelligence. *Nature*, 586(7829):E14–E16.

Kaiming He, Xiangyu Zhang, Shaoqing Ren, and Jian Sun. 2016. Deep residual learning for image recognition. In *Proceedings of the IEEE conference on computer vision and pattern recognition*, pages 770–778.

Gao Huang, Zhuang Liu, Laurens Van Der Maaten, and Kilian Q Weinberger. 2017. Densely connected convolutional networks. In *Proceedings of the IEEE conference on computer vision and pattern recognition*, pages 4700–4708.

Shih-Cheng Huang, Liyue Shen, Matthew P Lungren, and Serena Yeung. 2021. Gloria: A multimodal global-local representation learning framework for label-efficient medical image recognition. In *Proceedings of the IEEE/CVF International Conference on Computer Vision*, pages 3942–3951.

Jeremy Irvin, Pranav Rajpurkar, Michael Ko, Yifan Yu, Silviana Ciurea-Ilcus, Chris Chute, Henrik Marklund, Behzad Haghgoo, Robyn Ball, Katie Shpanskaya, Jayne Seekins, David A. Mong, Safwan S. Halabi, Jesse K. Sandberg, Ricky Jones, David B. Larson, Curtis P. Langlotz, Bhavik N. Patel, Matthew P. Lungren, and Andrew Y. Ng. 2019. Chexpert: A large chest radiograph dataset with uncertainty labels and expert comparison. *Proceedings of the AAAI Conference on Artificial Intelligence*, 33(01):590–597.

Allan Jabri, Armand Joulin, and Laurens Van Der Maaten. 2016. Revisiting visual question answering baselines. In *European conference on computer vision*, pages 727–739. Springer.

Jain, Saahil, Agrawal, Ashwin, Saporta, Adriel, Truong, Steven QH, Nguyen Duong, Du, Bui, Tan, Chambon, Pierre, Lungren, Matthew, Ng, Andrew, Langlotz, Curtis, and Rajpurkar, Pranav. 2021. RadGraph: Extracting Clinical Entities and Relations from Radiology Reports. Type: dataset.

Alistair E. W. Johnson, Tom J. Pollard, Nathaniel R. Greenbaum, Matthew P. Lungren, Chih-ying Deng, Yifan Peng, Zhiyong Lu, Roger G. Mark, Seth J. Berkowitz, and Steven Horng. 2019. MIMIC-CXR-JPG, a large publicly available database of labeled chest radiographs. *arXiv e-prints*, page arXiv:1901.07042.

Wonjae Kim, Bokyung Son, and Ildoo Kim. 2021. Vilt: Vision-and-language transformer without convolution or region supervision. In *Proceedings of the 38th International Conference on Machine Learning*, volume 139 of *Proceedings of Machine Learning Research*, pages 5583–5594. PMLR.

Diederik P. Kingma and Max Welling. 2014. Auto-Encoding Variational Bayes. In *2nd International Conference on Learning Representations, ICLR 2014, Banff, AB, Canada, April 14-16, 2014, Conference Track Proceedings*.

Ranjay Krishna, Yuke Zhu, Oliver Groth, Justin Johnson, Kenji Hata, Joshua Kravitz, Stephanie Chen, Yannis Kalantidis, Li-Jia Li, David A Shamma, et al. 2017. Visual genome: Connecting language and vision using crowdsourced dense image annotations. *International journal of computer vision*, 123(1):32–73.

Liunian Harold Li, Mark Yatskar, Da Yin, Cho-Jui Hsieh, and Kai-Wei Chang. 2019. Visualbert: A simple and performant baseline for vision and language. *arXiv preprint arXiv:1908.03557*.

Diwakar Mahajan, Ching-Huei Tsou, and Jennifer J Liang. 2021. IBMResearch at MEDIQA 2021: Toward improving factual correctness of radiology report abstractive summarization. In *Proceedings of the 20th Workshop on Biomedical Language Processing*, pages 302–310, Online. Association for Computational Linguistics.

Matthew B. A. McDermott, Shirly Wang, Nikki Marinsek, Rajesh Ranganath, Luca Foschini, and Marzyeh Ghassemi. 2021. Reproducibility in machine learning for health research: Still a ways to go. *Science Translational Medicine*, 13(586):eabb1655.

Scott Mayer McKinney, Marcin Sieniek, Varun Godbole, Jonathan Godwin, Natasha Antropova, Hutan Ashrafian, Trevor Back, Mary Chesus, Greg S Corrado, Ara Darzi, et al. 2020. International evaluation of an ai system for breast cancer screening. *Nature*, 577(7788):89–94.

Yasuhide Miura, Yuhao Zhang, Emily Tsai, Curtis Langlotz, and Dan Jurafsky. 2021. Improving factual completeness and consistency of image-to-text radiology report generation. In *Proceedings of the 2021 Conference of the North American Chapter of the Association for Computational Linguistics: Human Language Technologies*, pages 5288–5304, Online. Association for Computational Linguistics.

Kishore Papineni, Salim Roukos, Todd Ward, and Wei-Jing Zhu. 2002. Bleu: a method for automatic evaluation of machine translation. In *Proceedings of the 40th Annual Meeting of the Association for Computational Linguistics*, pages 311–318, Philadelphia, Pennsylvania, USA. Association for Computational Linguistics.

Emilio Parisotto, Francis Song, Jack Rae, Razvan Pascanu, Caglar Gulcehre, Siddhant Jayakumar, Max Jaderberg, Raphael Lopez Kaufman, Aidan Clark, Seb Noury, et al. 2020. Stabilizing transformers for reinforcement learning. In *International Conference on Machine Learning*, pages 7487–7498. PMLR.

Ngoc-Quan Pham, Thai-Son Nguyen, Jan Niehues, Markus Müller, Sebastian Stüker, and Alexander Waibel. 2019. Very deep self-attention networks for end-to-end speech recognition. *arXiv preprint arXiv:1904.13377*.

Peng Qi, Yuhao Zhang, Yuhui Zhang, Jason Bolton, and Christopher D. Manning. 2020. Stanza: A python natural language processing toolkit for many human languages. In *Proceedings of the 58th Annual Meeting of the Association for Computational Linguistics: System Demonstrations*, pages 101–108, Online. Association for Computational Linguistics.

Alec Radford, Jong Wook Kim, Chris Hallacy, Aditya Ramesh, Gabriel Goh, Sandhini Agarwal, Girish Sastry, Amanda Askell, Pamela Mishkin, Jack Clark, et al. 2021. Learning transferable visual models from natural language supervision. *arXiv preprint arXiv:2103.00020*.

Aditya Ramesh, Mikhail Pavlov, Gabriel Goh, Scott Gray, Chelsea Voss, Alec Radford, Mark Chen, and Ilya Sutskever. 2021. Zero-shot text-to-image generation. In *Proceedings of the 38th International Conference on Machine Learning*, volume 139 of *Proceedings of Machine Learning Research*, pages 8821–8831. PMLR.

Steven J Rennie, Etienne Marcheret, Youssef Mroueh, Jerret Ross, and Vaibhava Goel. 2017. Self-critical sequence training for image captioning. In *Proceedings of the IEEE conference on computer vision and pattern recognition*, pages 7008–7024.

John Schulman, Filip Wolski, Prafulla Dhariwal, Alec Radford, and Oleg Klimov. 2017. Proximal policy optimization algorithms. *CoRR*, abs/1707.06347.

Amanpreet Singh, Vivek Natarajan, Yu Jiang, Xinlei Chen, Meet Shah, Marcus Rohrbach, Dhruv Batra, and Devi Parikh. 2018. Pythia-a platform for vision & language research. In *SysML Workshop, NeurIPS*, volume 2018.

Akshay Smit, Saahil Jain, Pranav Rajpurkar, Anuj Pareek, Andrew Ng, and Matthew Lungren. 2020. Combining automatic labelers and expert annotations for accurate radiology report labeling using BERT. In *Proceedings of the 2020 Conference on Empirical Methods in Natural Language Processing (EMNLP)*, pages 1500–1519, Online. Association for Computational Linguistics.

Ashish Vaswani, Noam Shazeer, Niki Parmar, Jakob Uszkoreit, Llion Jones, Aidan N Gomez, Ł ukasz Kaiser, and Illia Polosukhin. 2017. Attention is all you need. In *Advances in Neural Information Processing Systems*, volume 30. Curran Associates, Inc.

Sebastian Vollmer, Bilal A Mateen, Gergo Bohner, Franz J Király, Rayid Ghani, Pall Jonsson, Sarah Cumbers, Adrian Jonas, Katherine S L McAllister, Puja Myles, David Grainger, Mark Birse, Richard Branson, Karel G M Moons, Gary S Collins, John P A Ioannidis, Chris Holmes, and Harry Hemingway. 2020. Machine learning and artificial intelligence research for patient benefit: 20 critical questions on transparency, replicability, ethics, and effectiveness. *BMJ*, 368.

Weiyao Wang, Du Tran, and Matt Feiszli. 2020. What makes training multi-modal classification networks hard? In *Proceedings of the IEEE/CVF Conference on Computer Vision and Pattern Recognition*, pages 12695–12705.

Thomas Wolf, Lysandre Debut, Victor Sanh, Julien Chaumond, Clement Delangue, Anthony Moi, Pierric Cistac, Tim Rault, Remi Louf, Morgan Funtowicz, Joe Davison, Sam Shleifer, Patrick von Platen, Clara Ma, Yacine Jernite, Julien Plu, Canwen Xu, Teven Le Scao, Sylvain Gugger, Mariama Drame, Quentin Lhoest, and Alexander Rush. 2020. Transformers: State-of-the-art natural language processing. In *Proceedings of the 2020 Conference on Empirical Methods in Natural Language Processing: System Demonstrations*, pages 38–45, Online. Association for Computational Linguistics.

Qian Xiao, Xiaobing Zhou, Y Xiao, and K Zhao. 2021. Yunnan university at vqa-med 2021: Pretrained biobert for medical domain visual question answering. *Working Notes of CLEF*, 201.

Quanzeng You, Hailin Jin, Zhaowen Wang, Chen Fang, and Jiebo Luo. 2016. Image captioning with semantic attention. In *Proceedings of the IEEE conference on computer vision and pattern recognition*, pages 4651–4659.

Zhou Yu, Jun Yu, Yuhao Cui, Dacheng Tao, and Qi Tian. 2019. Deep modular co-attention networks for visual question answering. In *Proceedings of the IEEE/CVF Conference on Computer Vision and Pattern Recognition*, pages 6281–6290.

Yuhao Zhang, Hang Jiang, Yasuhide Miura, Christopher D Manning, and Curtis P Langlotz. 2020a. Contrastive learning of medical visual representations from paired images and text. *arXiv preprint arXiv:2010.00747*.

Yuhao Zhang, Derek Merck, Emily Tsai, Christopher D. Manning, and Curtis Langlotz. 2020b. Optimizing the factual correctness of a summary: A study of summarizing radiology reports. In *Proceedings of the 58th Annual Meeting of the Association for Computational Linguistics*, pages 5108–5120, Online. Association for Computational Linguistics.

## A Ethical considerations

ViLMedic is a framework to train AI models on medical data. ViLMedic does not offer the possibility to download data requiring the signing of a data use agreement (such as MIMIC-CXR, PadChest and cheXpert). ViLMedic does provide download links for open access and sharable medical data (license CC BY-NC-ND 4.0), such as the Indiana University - Chest X-Rays dataset.

Though extracting training data from large language models have been revealed possible by using adversarial techniques (Carlini et al., 2021), our released pretrained models have been trained on de-identified datataset that are stripped of any personal information.

## B ViLMedic

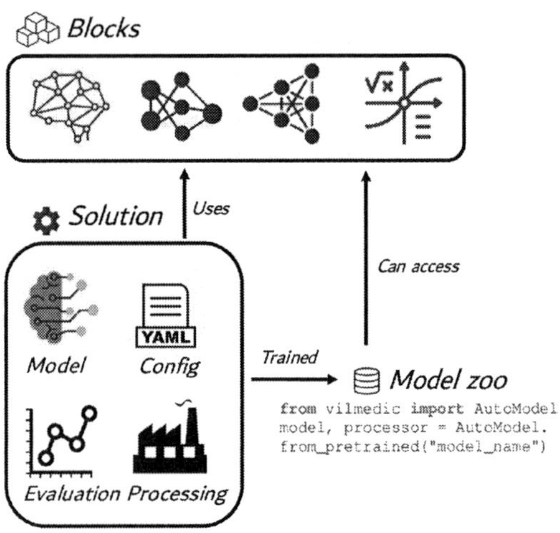


Figure 1: Overview of ViLMedic

## C Formatting, preprocessing and tokenization

In ViLMedic, datasets undergo three stages of processing, namely **formatting**, **preprocessing** and **tokenization**. This pipeline ensures a dataset is correctly process to replicate a solution. **Formatting** concerns the encoding of the dataset content into right file format (ViLMedic uses plain text files for language data and any digital images filetype such as jpg, png or dicom) and the division into the correct training, validation and test splits dictated by the dataset or a paper. The **preprocessing** phase consists of a Python script that takes care of removing stop-words, digits or punctuation from the text. Finally, **tokenization** divides the words into word-pieces. In ViLMedic, tokenization is handled by HuggingFace tokenizers.

## D Results visualization

ViLMedic offer tools to visualize the output of the pretrained models of the model zoo.

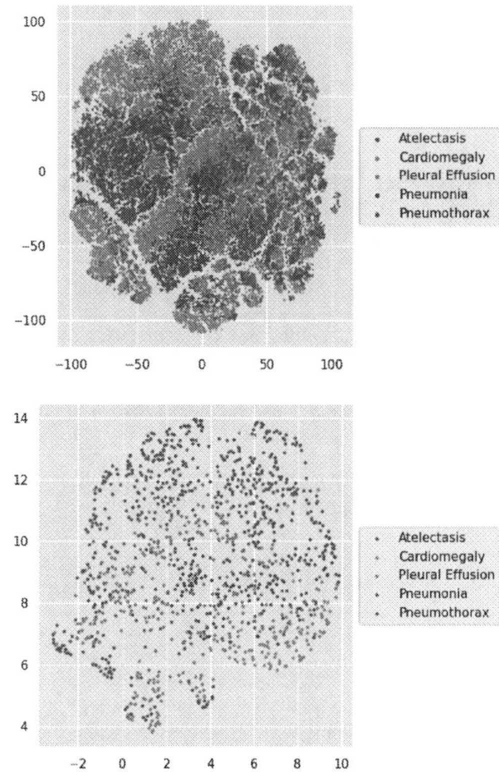


Figure 2: Plot of the linguistic representation learned by ViLMedic ConVIRT (c.f. Table 1). Top: all training data-points. Bottom: sampled data-points from the validation set

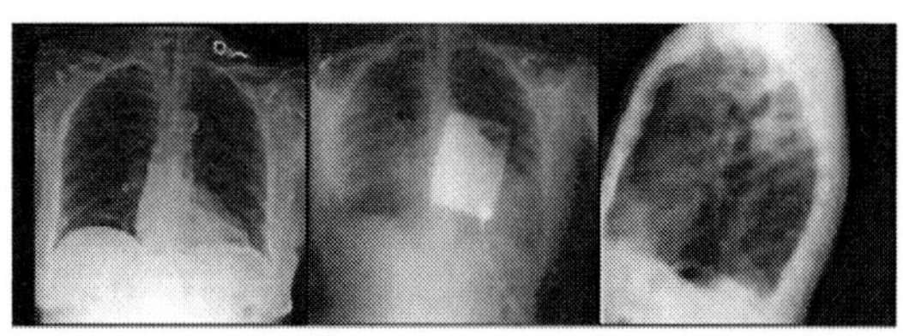

Figure 3: Reconstruction of our VAE for MIMIC-CXR (c.f. ViLMedic VAE Table 1), PadChest and Indiana dataset respectively

| | Loss | BS | Accuracy | BLEU | ROUGE-L | F1-CheXbert | $FC_E$ |
|---|---|---|---|---|---|---|---|
| **RRG** | | | | | | | |
| **MIMIC-CXR test** | | | | | | | |
| R2Gen (Chen et al., 2020) | | | | 8.6 | | 34.60 | |
| M2 Trans (Miura et al., 2021) | | | | 10.5 | | 44.70 | 27.3 |
| ViLMedic biobert | | | | 8.20 | 22.45 | 48.20 | 28.2 |
| **Indiana test** | | | | | | | |
| ViLMedic biobert | | | | 8.78 | 29.19 | 32.20 | |
| **PadChest test** | | | | | | | |
| ViLMedic biobert | | | | 4.02 | 16.32 | | |
| **RRS** | | | | | | | |
| **MIMIC-CXR test** | | | | | | | |
| QIAI (Delbrouck et al., 2021) | | | | | 41.12 | 69.05 | |
| ViLMedic biobert | | | | | 45.98 | 74.64 | |
| **Indiana test** | | | | | | | |
| ViLMedic biobert | | | | | 77.42 | 70.68 | |
| **Medical VQA** | | | | | | | |
| **VQA-Med 2021 out-of-domain** | | | | | | | |
| Yunnan biobert (Xiao et al., 2021) | | | 36.2 | 40.2 | | | |
| SYSU-HCP ensemble (Gong et al., 2021) | | | 38.2 | 41.6 | | | |
| ViLMedic VQA ensemble | | | 37.8 | 41.0 | | | |
| **VQA-Med 2021 in-domain** | | | | | | | |
| SYSU-HCP ensemble (Gong et al., 2021) | | | 69.2 | | | | |
| ViLMedic VQA | | | 69.0 | | | | |
| ViLMedic VQA ensemble | | | 72.0 | | | | |
| **Self-supervised learning** | | | | | | | |
| *ConVIRT* | | | | | | | |
| **MIMIC-CXR validation** | | | | | | | |
| ConVIRT (Zhang et al., 2020a) | 2.20 | 32 | | | | | |
| ViLMedic ConVIRT | 2.09 | 32 | | | | | |
| **Indiana validation** | | | | | | | |
| ViLMedic ConVIRT | 1.97 | 32 | | | | | |
| **PadChest validation** | | | | | | | |
| ViLMedic ConVIRT | 2.91 | 32 | | | | | |
| *GLoRIA* | | | | | | | |
| **CheXpert validation** | | | | | | | |
| GLoRIA (Huang et al., 2021) | 9.67 | 48 | | | | | |
| ViLMedic GLoRIA | 9.67 | 48 | | | | | |
| **MIMIC-CXR validation** | | | | | | | |
| ViLMedic GLoRIA | 9.27 | 48 | | | | | |
| *simCLR* | | | | | | | |
| **MIMIC-CXR validation** | | | | | | | |
| ViLMedic simCLR | 3.06 | 128 | | | | | |
| *DALLE* | | | | | | | |
| **MIMIC-CXR validation** | | | | | | | |
| ViLMedic VAE | 1e-3 | | | | | | |
| ViLMedic DALLE | 2.66 | 32 | | | | | |

Table 1: Non exhaustive list of solutions and pretrained models. Rows highlighted in grey are available in the model-zoo. F1-CheXbert is the micro-avg over atelectasis, cardiomegaly, consolidation, edema, and pleural effusion to stay consistent with the literature. BS means batch-size, which is important to compare contrastive-based loss.

## E Case by case feature

When suitable, we also release code snippets on how to use our solutions to output predictions. For example, a RRG pretrained model can be used to generate reports using HuggingFace Transformers:

```
model, processor = AutoModel.
from_pretrained("rrg/roberta-mimic")
batch = processor.inference(image=[
    "my_x_ray_1.jpg",
    "my_x_ray_2.jpg",
])

# Using huggingface generate method
hyps = model.dec.generate(
    input_ids=torch.ones(...)
    encoder_hidden_states=model.encode(
    **batch),
    num_return_sequences=1,
    max_length=75,
    num_beams=8,
)
hyps = [processor.tokenizer.decode(h...
print(hyps)
>> ['no acute cardiopulmonary process.',
'in comparison with study of ...']
```

Code Listing 3: Sample code available in ViLMedic documentation to generate reports using a pretrained model.

## F Usecase: Replicating a RRG result using ViLMedic

RRG is a difficult task. Not only does it requires complex architecture to generate language (beam-search, sampling, model ensembling) but also the evaluation methodologies differ from natural image captioning. Say a user would like to replicate the latest results (Miura et al., 2021) on the Indiana University - chest xray dataset with the F1-CheXbert score[8], they must:

1. Download the dataset on kaggle
2. Divide the dataset according to the official splits
3. Make sure to process the reports (the three steps of Appendix C) as detailed in the reference paper
4. Bridge the gap between the data and an open-implementation of the Meshed-Memory Transformer (Cornia et al., 2020) as used in Miura et al. (2021)
5. Copy the code of ChexBert[9], download the pretrained weights, and write an interface between the output of the Meshed-Memory Transformer and the input of ChexBert.
6. They must make sure that the Meshed-Memory Transformer supports beam-search, model-ensembling, and SCST training (Rennie et al., 2017) to optimize the F1-ChexBert score using Reinforcement Learning
7. Finally, they must make sure there is no conflict between the Python, HuggingFace Transformers and pyTorch version of the processing scripts (tokenizers), the Meshed-Memory Transformer and ChexBert (exclusively working with HuggingFace transformers 3.0.2)

Using ViLMedic, the said user can download the data using:

```
vilmedic-download RRG,indiana-images-512
```

and train 6 models as such:

```
for i in {1..6}
do
    python bin/train.py \
    config/RRG/biomed-roberta-baseline-
        indiana.yml \
    validator.metrics=[ROUGEL,METEOR,
        chexbert] \
    validator.beam_size=8 \
    name=my_rrg_indiana
done
```

And then ensemble the 3 best trained models:

```
python bin/ensemble.py
config/RRG/biomed-roberta-baseline-
    indiana.yml \
ensemblor.metrics=[chexbert] \
ensemblor.beam_size=8 \
ensemblor.mode=best-3 \
name=my_rrg_indiana
```

Moreover, all language components are base on HuggingFace, so that the user can refer to their documentation for further exploration.

We provide further information for each solution in our documentation[10].

[8]Recall that this metric is the accuracy between the CheXbert classification output of the ground-truth report and the generated report

[9]https://github.com/stanfordmlgroup/CheXbert

[10]https://vilmedic.readthedocs.io/en/latest/vilmedic/solutions/rrg.html

# TextPruner: A Model Pruning Toolkit for Pre-Trained Language Models

**Ziqing Yang**[†], **Yiming Cui**[‡†], **Zhigang Chen**[†]
[†]State Key Laboratory of Cognitive Intelligence, iFLYTEK Research, China
[‡]Research Center for Social Computing and Information Retrieval (SCIR),
Harbin Institute of Technology, Harbin, China
[†]{zqyang5,ymcui,zgchen}@iflytek.com
[‡]ymcui@ir.hit.edu.cn

## Abstract

Pre-trained language models have been prevailed in natural language processing and become the backbones of many NLP tasks, but the demands for computational resources have limited their applications. In this paper, we introduce TextPruner, an open-source model pruning toolkit designed for pre-trained language models, targeting fast and easy model compression. TextPruner offers structured post-training pruning methods, including vocabulary pruning and transformer pruning, and can be applied to various models and tasks. We also propose a self-supervised pruning method that can be applied without the labeled data. Our experiments with several NLP tasks demonstrate the ability of TextPruner to reduce the model size without re-training the model. [1]

## 1 Introduction

Large pre-trained language models (PLMs) (Devlin et al., 2019; Liu et al., 2019) have achieved great success in a variety of NLP tasks. However, it is difficult to deploy them for real-world applications where computation and memory resources are limited. Reducing the pre-trained model size and speeding up the inference have become a critical issue.

Pruning is a common technique for model compression. It identifies and removes redundant or less important neurons from the networks. From the view of the model structure, pruning methods can be categorized into *unstructured pruning* and *structured pruning*. In the unstructured pruning, each model parameter is individually removed if it reaches some criteria based on the magnitude or importance score (Han et al., 2015; Zhu and Gupta, 2018; Sanh et al., 2020). The unstructured pruning results in sparse matrices and allows for significant model compression, but the inference speed can hardly be improved without specialized devices. While in the structured pruning, rows or columns of the parameters are removed from the weight matrices (McCarley, 2019; Michel et al., 2019; Voita et al., 2019; Lagunas et al., 2021; Hou et al., 2020). Thus, the resulting model speeds up on the common CPU and GPU devices.

Pruning methods can also be classified into optimization-free methods (Michel et al., 2019) and the ones that involve optimization (Frankle and Carbin, 2019; Lagunas et al., 2021). The latter usually achieves higher performance, but the former runs faster and is more convenient to use.

Pruning PLMs has been of growing interest. Most of the works focus on reducing transformer size while ignoring the vocabulary (Abdaoui et al., 2020). Pruning vocabulary can greatly reduce the model size for multilingual PLMs.

In this paper, we present TextPruner, a model pruning toolkit for PLMs. It combines both transformer pruning and vocabulary pruning. The purpose of TextPruner is to offer a universal, fast, and easy-to-use tool for model compression. We expect it can be accessible to users with little model training experience. Therefore, we implement the structured optimization-free pruning methods for its convenient use and fast computation. Pruning a base-sized model only requires several minutes with TextPruner. TextPruner can also be a useful analysis tool for inspecting the importance of the neurons in the model.

TextPruner has the following highlights:

- TextPruner is designed to be easy to use. It provides both Python API and Command Line Interface (CLI). Working with either of them requires only a couple of lines of simple code. Besides, TextPruner is non-intrusive and compatible with Transformers (Wolf et al., 2020), which means users do not have to change their models that are built on the Transformers library.

[1]The source code and the documentation are available at http://textpruner.hfl-rc.com



*Proceedings of the 60th Annual Meeting of the Association for Computational Linguistics*
*System Demonstrations*, pages 35 - 43

- TextPruner works with different models and tasks. It has been tested on tasks like text classification, machine reading comprehension (MRC), named entity recognition (NER). TextPruner is also designed to be extensible for other models.
- TextPruner is flexible. Users can control the pruning process and explore pruning strategies via tuning the configurations to find the optimal configurations for the specific tasks.

## 2 Pruning Methodology

We briefly recall the multi-head attention (MHA) and the feed-forward network (FFN) in the transformers (Vaswani et al., 2017). Then we describe how we prune the attention heads and the FFN based on the importance scores.

### 2.1 MHA and FFN

Suppose the input to a transformer is $\boldsymbol{X} \in \mathbb{R}^{n\times d}$ where $n$ is the sequence length and $d$ is the hidden size. the MHA layer with $N_h$ heads is parameterized by $\boldsymbol{W}_i^Q, \boldsymbol{W}_i^K, \boldsymbol{W}_i^V, \boldsymbol{W}_i^O \in \mathbb{R}^{d_h\times d}$

$$\mathrm{MHA}(\boldsymbol{X}) = \sum_i^{N_h} \mathrm{Att}_{\boldsymbol{W}_i^Q,\boldsymbol{W}_i^K,\boldsymbol{W}_i^V,\boldsymbol{W}_i^O}(\boldsymbol{X}) \quad (1)$$

where $d_h = d/N_h$ is the hidden size of each head. $\mathrm{Att}_{\boldsymbol{W}_i^Q,\boldsymbol{W}_i^K,\boldsymbol{W}_i^V,\boldsymbol{W}_i^O}(\boldsymbol{X})$ is the bilinear self-attention

$$\mathrm{Att}_{\boldsymbol{W}_i^Q,\boldsymbol{W}_i^K,\boldsymbol{W}_i^V,\boldsymbol{W}_i^O}(\boldsymbol{X}) = \mathrm{softmax}(\frac{\boldsymbol{X}(\boldsymbol{W}_i^Q)^\top \boldsymbol{W}_i^K \boldsymbol{X}^\top}{\sqrt{d}})\boldsymbol{X}(\boldsymbol{W}_i^V)^\top \boldsymbol{W}_i^O \quad (2)$$

Each transformer contains a fully connected feed-forward network (FFN) following MHA. It consists of two linear transformations with a GeLU activation in between

$$\mathrm{FFN}_{\boldsymbol{W}_1,\boldsymbol{b}_1,\boldsymbol{W}_2,\boldsymbol{b}_2}(\boldsymbol{X}) = \mathrm{GeLU}(\boldsymbol{X}\boldsymbol{W}_1 + \boldsymbol{b}_1)\boldsymbol{W}_2 + \boldsymbol{b}_2 \quad (3)$$

where $\boldsymbol{W}_1 \in \mathbb{R}^{d\times d_{ff}}$, $\boldsymbol{W}_2 \in \mathbb{R}^{d_{ff}\times d}$, $\boldsymbol{b}_1 \in \mathbb{R}^{d_{ff}}$, $\boldsymbol{b}_2 \in \mathbb{R}^d$. $d_{ff}$ is the FFN hidden size. The adding operations are broadcasted along the sequence length dimension $n$.

### 2.2 Pruning with Importance Scores

With the hidden size fixed, The size of a transformer can be reduced by removing the attention heads or removing the intermediate neurons in the FFN layer (decreasing $d_{ff}$, which is mathematically equal to removing columns from $\boldsymbol{W}_1$ and rows from $\boldsymbol{W}_2$). Following Michel et al. (2019), we sort all the attention heads and FFN neurons according to their proxy importance scores and then remove them iteratively.

A commonly used importance score is the sensitivity of the loss with respect to the values of the neurons. We denote a set of neurons or their outputs as $\boldsymbol{\Theta}$. Its importance score is computed by

$$\mathrm{IS}(\boldsymbol{\Theta}) = \mathbb{E}_{x\sim X}\left|\frac{\partial\mathcal{L}(x)}{\partial\boldsymbol{\Theta}}\boldsymbol{\Theta}\right| \quad (4)$$

The expression in the absolute sign is the first-order Taylor approximation of the loss $\mathcal{L}$ around $\Theta = 0$. Taking $\boldsymbol{\Theta}$ to be the output of an attention head $h_i$, $\mathrm{IS}(\boldsymbol{\Theta})$ gives the importance score of the head $i$; Taking $\boldsymbol{\Theta}$ to be the set of the $i$-th column of $\boldsymbol{W}_1$, $i$-the row of $\boldsymbol{W}_2$ and the $i$-th element of $\boldsymbol{b}_1$, $\mathrm{IS}(\boldsymbol{\Theta})$ gives the importance score of the $i$-th intermeidate neuron in the FFN layer.

A lower importance score means the loss is less sensitive to the neurons. Therefore, the neurons are pruned in the order of increasing scores. In practice, we use the development set or a subset of the training set to compute the importance score.

### 2.3 Self-Supervied Pruning

In equation (4), the loss $\mathcal{L}$ usually is the training loss. However, there can be other choices of $\mathcal{L}$. We propose to use the Kullback–Leibler divergence to measure the varitaion of the model outputs:

$$\mathcal{L}_{\mathrm{KL}}(x) = \mathrm{KL}(\mathrm{stopgrad}(q(x))||p(x)) \quad (5)$$

where $q(x)$ is the original model prediction distribution and $p(x)$ is the to-be-pruned model prediction distribution. The `stopgrad` operation is used to stop back-propagating gradients. An increase in $\mathcal{L}_{\mathrm{KL}}$ indicates an increase in the diviation of $p(x)$ from the original prediction $q(x)$. Thus the gradient of $\mathcal{L}_{\mathrm{KL}}$ reflects the sensitivity of the model to the value of the neurons. Evaluation of $\mathcal{L}_{\mathrm{KL}}$ does not require label information. Therefore the pruning process can be performed in a self-supervised way where the unpruned model provides the soft-labels $q(x)$. We call the method *self-supervised pruning*. TextPruner supports both supervised pruning

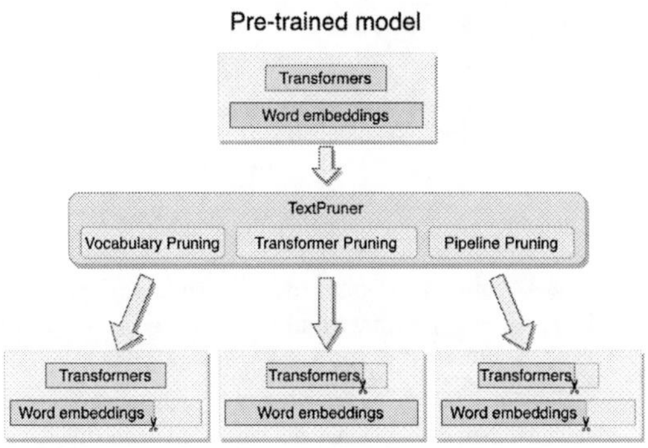


Figure 1: Three pruning modes in TextPruner.

(where $\mathcal{L}$ is the training loss) and self-supervised pruning. We will compare them in the experiments.

## 3 Overview of TextPruner

### 3.1 Pruning Mode

As illustrated in Figure 1, there are three pruning modes In TextPruner.

**Vocabulary Pruning** The pre-trained models have a large vocabulary, but some tokens in the vocabulary rarely appear in the downstream tasks. These tokens can be removed to reduce the model size and accelerate the training speed of the tasks that require predicting probabilities over the whole vocabulary. In this mode, TextPruner reads and tokenizes an input corpus. TextPruner goes through the vocabulary and checks if the token in the vocabulary has appeared in the text file. If not, the token will be removed from both the model's embedding matrix and the tokenizer's vocabulary.

**Transformer Pruning** Previous studies (Michel et al., 2019; Voita et al., 2019) have shown that not all attention heads are equally important in the transformers, and some of the attention heads can be pruned without performance loss (Cui et al., 2022). Thus, Identifying and removing the least important attention heads can reduce the model size and have a small impact on performance.

In this mode, TextPruner reads the examples and computes the importance scores of attention heads and the feed-forward networks' neurons. The heads and the neurons with the lowest scores are removed first. This process is repeated until the model has been reduced to the target size. TextPruner also supports custom pruning from user-provided masks without computing the importance scores.

**Pipeline Pruning** In this mode, TextPruner performs transformer pruning and vocabulary pruning automatically to fully reduce the model size.

### 3.2 Pruners

The pruners are the cores of TextPruner, and they perform the actual pruning process. There are three pruner classes, corresponding to the three aforementioned pruning modes: **VocabularyPruner**, **TransformerPruner** and **PipelinePruner**. Once the pruner is intialized, call the `pruner.prune(...)` to start pruning.

### 3.3 Configurations

The following configuration objects set the pruning strategies and the experiment settings.

**GeneralConfig** It sets the device to use (CPU or CUDA) and the output directory for model saving.

**VocabularyPruningConfig** It sets the token pruning threshold `min_count` and whether pruning the LM head `prune_lm_head`. The token is to be removed from the vocabulary if it appears less than `min_count` times in the corpus; if `prune_lm_head` is true, TextPruner prunes the linear transformation in the LM head too.

**TransformerPruningConfig** The transformer pruning parameters include but not are limited to:

- `pruning_method` can be *mask* or *iterative*. If it is *iterative*, the pruner prunes the model based on the importance scores; if it is *mask*, the pruner prunes the model with the masks given by the users.
- `target_ffn_size` denotes the average FFN hidden size $d_{ff}$ per layer.
- `target_num_of_heads` denotes the average number of attention heads per layer.
- `n_iters` is number of pruning iterations. For example, if the original model has $N_h$ heads per layer, the target model has $N'_h$ heads per layer, the pruner will prune $(N_h - N'_h)/n\_iters$ heads on average per layer per iteration. It also applies to the FFN neurons.
- If `ffn_even_masking` is true, all the FFN layers are pruned to the same size $d_{ff}$; otherwise, the FFN sizes vary from layer to layer and their average size is $d_{ff}$.
- If `head_even_masking` is true, all the MHAs are pruned to the same number of heads; otherwise, the number of attention heads varies from layer to layer.

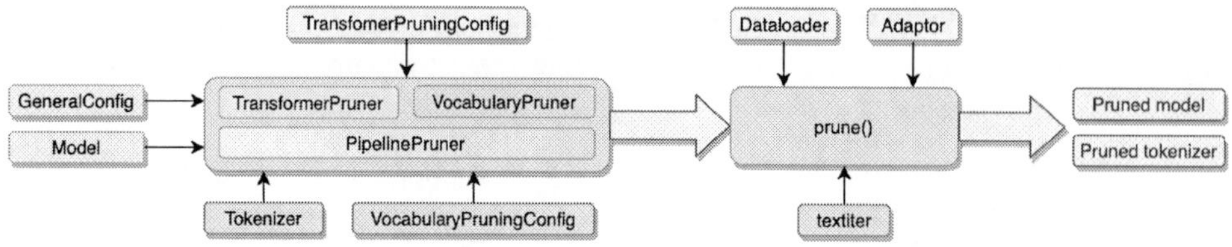


Figure 2: The workflow of TextPruner. The yellow blocks are the general arguments for any pruners. The green blocks should be provided for the TransformerPruner and PipelinePruner. The blue blocks should be provided for the VocabularyPruner and PipelinePruner.

```
from textpruner import VocabularyPruner
from textpruner import TransformerPruner
from textpruner import TransformerPruningConfig

# We omit the initialization of the model, tokenizer,
# dataloader and the texts.
model : torch.nn.Module = ...
tokenizer :PreTrainedTokenizer = ...
dataloader: torch.utils.data.Dataloader = ...
texts : List[str] = ...

# Vocabulary pruning
pruner = VocabularyPruner(model, tokenizer)
pruner.prune(texts)

# Transformer pruning
# Reconstruct the dataset and the dataloader if the
# following is run immediately after vocabulary pruning
transformer_pruning_config = TransformerPruningConfig(
    pruning_method='itereative',
    target_ffn_size=2048,
    target_num_of_heads=8,
    n_iters=4)
pruner = TransformerPruner(
    model, transformer_pruning_config)
pruner.prune(dataloader)
```

Figure 3: A typical TextPruner workflow for transformer pruning and vocabulary pruning.

- If `ffn_even_masking` is false, the FFN hidden size of each layer is restricted to be a multiple of `multiple_of`. It make the model structure friendly to the device that works most efficiently when the matrix shapes are multiple of a specific size.
- If `use_logits` is true, self-supervised pruning is enabled.

All the configurations can be initialized manually in python scripts or from JSON files (for the CLI, the configurations can only be initialized from the JSON files). An example of the configuration in a Python script is shown in Figure 3.

### 3.4 Other utilities

TextPruner contains diagnostic tools such as **summary** which inspects and counts the model parameters, and **inference_time** which measures the model inference speed. Readers may refer to the examples in the repository to see their usages.

### 3.5 Usage and Workflow

TextPruner provides both Python API and CLI. The typical workflow is shown in Figure 2. Before calling or Initializing TextPruner, users should prepare:

1. A trained a model that needs to be pruned.
2. For vocabulary pruning, a text file that defines the new vocabulary.
3. For transformer pruning, a python script file that defines a dataloader and an adaptor.
4. For pipeline pruning, both the text file and the python script file.

**Adaptor** It is a user-defined function that takes the model outputs as the argument and returns the loss or logits. It is responsible for interpreting the model outputs for the pruner. If the adaptor is `None`, the pruner will try to infer the loss from the model outputs.

**Pruning with Python API** First, initialize the configurations and the pruner, then call `pruner.prune` with the required arguments, as shown in Figure 2. Figure 3 shows an example. Note that we have not constructed the GeneralConfig and VocabularyPruningConfig. The pruners will use the default configurations if they are not specified, which simplifies the coding.

**Pruning with CLI** First create the configuration JSON files, then run the `textpruner-cli`. Pipeline pruning example:

```
textpruner-cli  \
  --pruning_mode pipeline \
  --configurations vocab.json trm.json \
  --model_class BertForClassification \
  --tokenizer_class BertTokenizer \
  --model_path models/ \
  --vocabulary texts.txt \
  --dataloader_and_adaptor dataloader.py
```

| Model | Vocabulary size | Model size | Dev (en) | Dev (zh) | Test (en) | Test (zh) |
|---|---|---|---|---|---|---|
| XLM-R | 250002 | 1060 MB (100%) | 84.8 | 75.1 | 85.7 | 75.0 |
| + Vocabulary Pruning on en | 26653 | 406 MB (38.3%) | 84.6 | - | 85.9 | - |
| + Vocabulary Pruning on zh | 23553 | 397 MB (37.5%) | - | 74.7 | - | 74.5 |
| + Vocabulary Pruning on en and zh | 37503 | 438 MB (41.3%) | 84.8 | 74.3 | 85.8 | 74.5 |

Table 1: The accuracy scores ($\times 100\%$) of models with the pruned vocabulary on XNLI dev set and test set.

| Structure | 12 | 10 | 8 | 6 |
|---|---|---|---|---|
| 3072 | 100% (1.00x) | 89% (1.08x) | 78% (1.19x) | 67% (1.30x) |
| 2560 | 94% (1.08x) | 83% (1.18x) | 72% (1.29x) | 61% (1.44x) |
| 2048 | 89% (1.17x) | 78% (1.28x) | 67% (1.43x) | 56% (1.63x) |
| 1536 | 83% (1.29x) | 72% (1.42x) | 61% (1.63x) | 50% (1.90x) |

Table 2: Transformer sizes (listed as percentages) and speedups (listed in the parentheses) of different structures relative to the base model $(12, 3072)$.

### 3.6 Computational Cost

**Vocabulary Pruning** The main computational cost in vocabulary pruning is tokenization. This process will take from a few minutes to tens of minutes, depending on the corpus size. However, the computational cost is negligible if the pre-tokenized text is provided.

**Transformer Pruning** The main computational cost in transformer pruning is the calculation of importance scores. It involves forward and backward propagation of the dataset. This cost is proportional to `n_iters` and dataset size. As will be shown in Section 4.2, in a typical classification task, a dataset with a few thousand examples and setting `n_iters` around 10 can lead to a decent performance. This process usually takes several minutes on a modern GPU (e.g., Nvidia V100).

### 3.7 Extensibility

TextPruner supports different pre-trained models and the tokenizers via the model structure definitions and the tokenizer helper functions registered in the `MODEL_MAP` dictionary. Updating TextPruner for supporting more pre-trained models is easy. Users need to write a model structure definition and register it to the `MODEL_MAP`, so that the pruners can recognize the new model.

## 4 Experiments

In this section, we conduct several experiments to show TextPruner's ability to prune different pre-trained models on different NLP tasks. We mainly focus on the text classification task. We list the results on the MRC task and NER task with different pre-trained models in the Appendix.

### 4.1 Dataset and Model

We use the Cross-lingual Natural Language Inference (XNLI) corpus (Conneau et al., 2018) as the text classification dataset and build the classification model based on XLM-RoBERTa (Conneau et al., 2020). The model is *base*-sized with 12 transformer layers with FFN size 3072, hidden size 768, and 12 attention heads per layer. Since XNLI is a multilingual dataset, we fine-tune the XLM-R model on the English training set and test it on the English and Chinese test sets to evaluate both the in-language and zero-shot performance.

### 4.2 Results on Text Classification

**Effects of Vocabulary Pruning** As XLM-R is a multilingual model, We conduct vocabulary pruning on XLM-R with different languages, as shown in Table 1. We prune XLM-R on the training set of each language, i.e., we only keep the tokens that appear in the training set.

When pruning on the English and Chinese training sets separately, the performance drops slightly . After pruning on both training sets, the model size still can be greatly reduced by about 60% while keeping a decent performance.

Vocabulary pruning is an effective method for reducing multilingual pre-trained model size, and it is especially suitable for tailoring the multilingual model for specific languages.

**Effects of Transformer Pruning** For simplicity, we use the notation $(H, F)$ to denote the model structure, where $H$ is the average number of attention heads per layer, $F$ is the average FFN hidden size per layer. With this notation, the original (unpruned) model is $(12, 3072)$. Before we show the

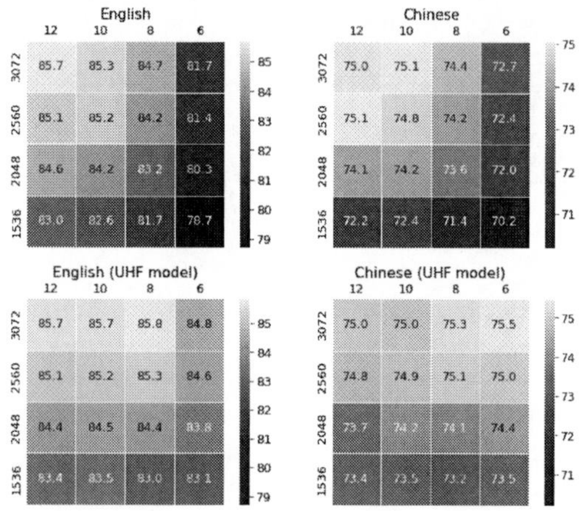


Figure 4: The Performance of the pruned models with different structures on the test sets. The x-axis represents different average numbers of attention heads; the y-axis represents different average FFN sizes. Left column: the accuracy scores on the English test set; Right column: the accuracy scores on the Chinese test set. Models in the first row have homogenous structures, while models in the second row do not. UHF stands for uneven heads and FFN neurons.

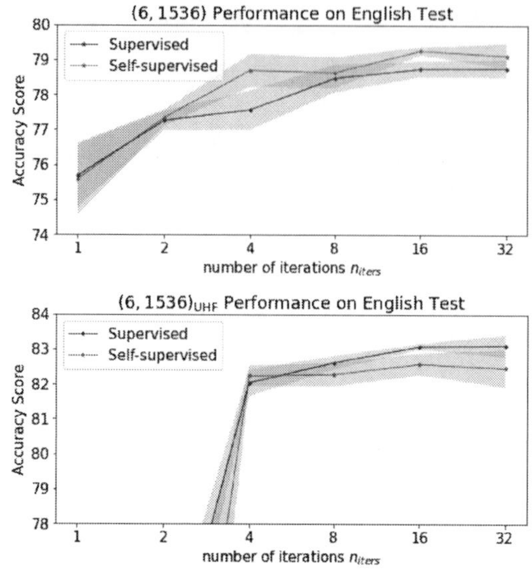


Figure 5: Model Performance on the English test set with different number of iterations.

results on the specific task, we list the transformer sizes and their speedups of different target structures relative to the unpruned model $(12, 3072)$ in the Table 2.

We compute the importance scores on the English development set. The number of iterations $n_{iters}$ is set to 16. We report the mean accuracy of five runs. The performance on English and Chinese test sets are shown in Figure 7. The top-left corner of each heatmap represents the performance of the original model. The bottom right corner represents the model $(6, 1536)$, which contains half attention heads and half FFN neurons.

The models in heatmaps from the first row have homogenous structures: each transformer in the model has the same number of attention heads and same FFN size, while the models in the bottom heatmaps have uneven numbers of attention heads and FFN sizes in transformers. We use the abbreviation *UHF* (**U**neven **H**eads and **FFN** neurons) to distinguish them from homogenous structures. We see that by allowing each transformer to have different sizes, the pruner has more freedom to choose the neurons to prune, thus the UHF models perform better than the homogenous ones.

Note that the model is fine-tuned on the English dataset. The performance on Chinese is zero-shot. After pruning on the English development set, the drops in the performance on Chinese are not larger than the drops in the performance on English. It means the important neurons for the Chinese task remain in the pruned model. In the multilingual model, the neurons that deal with semantic understanding do not specialize in specific languages but provide cross-lingual understanding abilities.

Figure 5 shows how $n_{iters}$ affects the performance. We inspect both the non-UHF model $(6, 1536)$ and the UHF model $(6, 1536)_{\text{UHF}}$. The solid lines denote the average performance over the five runs. The shadowed area denotes the standard deviation. In all cases, the performance grows with the $n_{iters}$. Pruning with only one iteration is a bad choice and leads to very low scores. We suggest setting $n_{iters}$ to at least 8 for good enough performance.

In Figure 5 we also compare the supervised pruning (with $\mathcal{L}$ being the cross-entropy loss with the ground-truth labels) and the proposed self-supervised pruning (with $\mathcal{L}$ being the KL-divergence Eq (5)) . Although no label information is available, the self-supervised method achieves comparable and sometimes even higher results.

How much data are needed for model pruning? To answer this question, we randomly sample 10%, 20%, ..., 90%, 100% examples from the English development set for computing importance scores. We inspect the $(6, 1536)_{\text{UHF}}$ model. Each experiment has been run five times. The results are shown

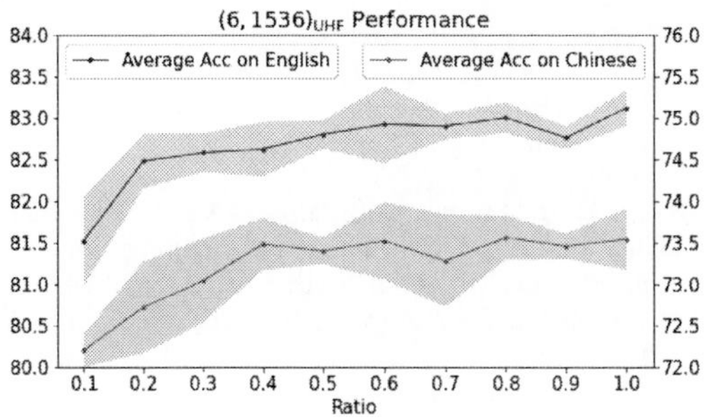


Figure 6: Model Performance on the test set with different number of examples for computing importance scores. Left y-axis: accuracy on Enligh. Right y-axis: accuracy on Chinese.

in Figure 6. With about 70% examples (about 1.7K examples) from the development set, the pruned model achieves a performance that is nearly comparable with the model pruned with the full development set (2490 examples).

## 5 Conclusion and Future Work

This paper presents TextPruner, a model pruning toolkit for pre-trained models. It leverages optimization-free pruning methods, including vocabulary pruning and transformer pruning to reduce the model size. It provides rich configuration options for users to explore and experiment with. TextPruner is suitable for users who want to prune their model quickly and easily, and it can also be used for analyzing pre-trained models by pruning, as we did in the experiments.

For future work, we will update TextPruner to support more pre-trained models, such as the generation model T5 (Raffel et al., 2020). We also plan to combine TextPruner with our previously released knowledge distillation toolkit TextBrewer (Yang et al., 2020) into a single framework to provide more effective model compression methods and a uniform interface for knowledge distillation and model pruning.

## Acknowledgements

This work is supported by the National Key Research and Development Program of China via grant No. 2018YFB1005100.

## References

Amine Abdaoui, Camille Pradel, and Grégoire Sigel. 2020. Load what you need: Smaller versions of mutililingual BERT. In *Proceedings of SustaiNLP: Workshop on Simple and Efficient Natural Language Processing*, pages 119–123, Online. Association for Computational Linguistics.

Alexis Conneau, Kartikay Khandelwal, Naman Goyal, Vishrav Chaudhary, Guillaume Wenzek, Francisco Guzmán, Edouard Grave, Myle Ott, Luke Zettlemoyer, and Veselin Stoyanov. 2020. Unsupervised cross-lingual representation learning at scale. In *Proceedings of the 58th Annual Meeting of the Association for Computational Linguistics*, pages 8440–8451, Online. Association for Computational Linguistics.

Alexis Conneau, Ruty Rinott, Guillaume Lample, Adina Williams, Samuel R. Bowman, Holger Schwenk, and Veselin Stoyanov. 2018. Xnli: Evaluating cross-lingual sentence representations. In *Proceedings of the 2018 Conference on Empirical Methods in Natural Language Processing*. Association for Computational Linguistics.

Yiming Cui, Wei-Nan Zhang, Wanxiang Che, Ting Liu, Zhigang Chen, and Shijin Wang. 2022. Multilingual multi-aspect explainability analyses on machine reading comprehension models. *iScience*, 25(4).

Jacob Devlin, Ming-Wei Chang, Kenton Lee, and Kristina Toutanova. 2019. BERT: Pre-training of deep bidirectional transformers for language understanding. In *Proceedings of the 2019 Conference of the North American Chapter of the Association for Computational Linguistics: Human Language Technologies, Volume 1 (Long and Short Papers)*, pages 4171–4186, Minneapolis, Minnesota. Association for Computational Linguistics.

Jonathan Frankle and Michael Carbin. 2019. The lottery ticket hypothesis: Finding sparse, trainable neural networks. In *International Conference on Learning Representations*.

Song Han, Jeff Pool, John Tran, and William J. Dally. 2015. Learning both weights and connections for efficient neural networks. *CoRR*, abs/1506.02626.

Lu Hou, Zhiqi Huang, Lifeng Shang, Xin Jiang, Xiao Chen, and Qun Liu. 2020. Dynabert: Dynamic BERT with adaptive width and depth. In *Advances in Neural Information Processing Systems 33: Annual Conference on Neural Information Processing Systems 2020, NeurIPS 2020, December 6-12, 2020, virtual*.

François Lagunas, Ella Charlaix, Victor Sanh, and Alexander Rush. 2021. Block pruning for faster transformers. In *Proceedings of the 2021 Conference on Empirical Methods in Natural Language Processing*, pages 10619–10629, Online and Punta Cana, Dominican Republic. Association for Computational Linguistics.

Yinhan Liu, Myle Ott, Naman Goyal, Jingfei Du, Mandar Joshi, Danqi Chen, Omer Levy, Mike Lewis, Luke Zettlemoyer, and Veselin Stoyanov. 2019.

Roberta: A robustly optimized bert pretraining approach.

J. S. McCarley. 2019. Pruning a bert-based question answering model. *CoRR*, abs/1910.06360.

Paul Michel, Omer Levy, and Graham Neubig. 2019. Are sixteen heads really better than one? In *Advances in Neural Information Processing Systems 32: Annual Conference on Neural Information Processing Systems 2019, NeurIPS 2019, December 8-14, 2019, Vancouver, BC, Canada*, pages 14014–14024.

Colin Raffel, Noam Shazeer, Adam Roberts, Katherine Lee, Sharan Narang, Michael Matena, Yanqi Zhou, Wei Li, and Peter J. Liu. 2020. Exploring the limits of transfer learning with a unified text-to-text transformer. *Journal of Machine Learning Research*, 21(140):1–67.

Pranav Rajpurkar, Jian Zhang, Konstantin Lopyrev, and Percy Liang. 2016. SQuAD: 100,000+ questions for machine comprehension of text. In *Proceedings of the 2016 Conference on Empirical Methods in Natural Language Processing*, pages 2383–2392, Austin, Texas. Association for Computational Linguistics.

Victor Sanh, Thomas Wolf, and Alexander M. Rush. 2020. Movement pruning: Adaptive sparsity by fine-tuning. In *Advances in Neural Information Processing Systems 33: Annual Conference on Neural Information Processing Systems 2020, NeurIPS 2020, December 6-12, 2020, virtual.*

Erik F. Tjong Kim Sang and Fien De Meulder. 2003. Introduction to the CoNLL-2003 shared task: Language-independent named entity recognition. In *Proceedings of the Seventh Conference on Natural Language Learning at HLT-NAACL 2003*, pages 142–147.

Ashish Vaswani, Noam Shazeer, Niki Parmar, Jakob Uszkoreit, Llion Jones, Aidan N. Gomez, Lukasz Kaiser, and Illia Polosukhin. 2017. Attention is all you need. In *Advances in Neural Information Processing Systems 30: Annual Conference on Neural Information Processing Systems 2017, December 4-9, 2017, Long Beach, CA, USA*, pages 5998–6008.

Elena Voita, David Talbot, Fedor Moiseev, Rico Sennrich, and Ivan Titov. 2019. Analyzing multi-head self-attention: Specialized heads do the heavy lifting, the rest can be pruned. In *Proceedings of the 57th Annual Meeting of the Association for Computational Linguistics*, pages 5797–5808, Florence, Italy. Association for Computational Linguistics.

Thomas Wolf, Lysandre Debut, Victor Sanh, Julien Chaumond, Clement Delangue, Anthony Moi, Pierric Cistac, Tim Rault, Rémi Louf, Morgan Funtowicz, Joe Davison, Sam Shleifer, Patrick von Platen, Clara Ma, Yacine Jernite, Julien Plu, Canwen Xu, Teven Le Scao, Sylvain Gugger, Mariama Drame, Quentin Lhoest, and Alexander M. Rush. 2020. Transformers: State-of-the-art natural language processing. In *Proceedings of the 2020 Conference on Empirical Methods in Natural Language Processing: System Demonstrations*, pages 38–45, Online. Association for Computational Linguistics.

Ziqing Yang, Yiming Cui, Zhipeng Chen, Wanxiang Che, Ting Liu, Shijin Wang, and Guoping Hu. 2020. TextBrewer: An Open-Source Knowledge Distillation Toolkit for Natural Language Processing. In *Proceedings of the 58th Annual Meeting of the Association for Computational Linguistics: System Demonstrations*, pages 9–16. Association for Computational Linguistics.

Michael Zhu and Suyog Gupta. 2018. To prune, or not to prune: Exploring the efficacy of pruning for model compression. In *6th International Conference on Learning Representations, ICLR 2018, Vancouver, BC, Canada, April 30 - May 3, 2018, Workshop Track Proceedings*. OpenReview.net.

## A Datasets and Models

We experiment with different pre-trained models to test TextPruner's ability to prune different models. For the MRC task, we use SQuAD (Rajpurkar et al., 2016) dataset and RoBERTa (Liu et al., 2019) model; For the NER task, we use CoNLL 2003 (Tjong Kim Sang and De Meulder, 2003) and BERT (Devlin et al., 2019) model. All the models are *base*-sized, i.e., 12 transformer layers with a hidden size of 768, an FFN size of 3072, and 12 attention heads per layer.

## B Transformer Pruning on MRC

We compute the importance scores on a subset of the training set (5120 examples). The F1 score on the SQuAD development set is listed in Table 3. $(12, 3072)$ is the unpruned model. The performance grows with the $n_{iters}$. The number of iterations also plays an important role on model performance in the SQuAD task. We also see that pruning with only one iteration is a bad choice and leads to low scores. Setting $n_{iters}$ to at least 8 achieves good enough performance.

## C Transformer Pruning on NER

We compute the importance scores on the CoNLL 2003 development set. The F1 score on the test is listed in Table 4. We also see large gaps in performance between $n_{iters} = 4$ and $n_{iters} = 8$.

The performance of the pruned models with different structures is shown in Figure 7. We only consider the UHF case for it can achieve the best overall performance. The number of iterations $n_{iters}$ is set to 16.

| Model | 1 | 2 | 4 | 8 | 16 |
|---|---|---|---|---|---|
| $(12, 3072)$ | 91.4 | | | | |
| $(8, 2048)$ | 76.4 | 80.3 | 81.9 | **82.9** | 82.5 |
| $(8, 2048)_{\text{UHF}}$ | 87.5 | 86.4 | 87.6 | 88.3 | **88.4** |
| $(6, 1536)$ | 12.8 | 42.6 | 49.5 | 51.5 | **56.5** |
| $(6, 1536)_{\text{UHF}}$ | 47.2 | 55.6 | 66.1 | 74.1 | **75.2** |

Table 3: The F1 score on SQuAD. Each score is averaged over five runs. Different columns represent results under different number of iterations. We **bold** the best F1 in each row.

| Model | 1 | 2 | 4 | 8 | 16 | 32 |
|---|---|---|---|---|---|---|
| $(12, 3072)$ | 91.3 | | | | | |
| $(8, 2048)$ | 88.5 | 88.4 | 88.7 | 89.2 | 89.2 | 89.4 |
| $(8, 2048)_{\text{UHF}}$ | 81.8 | 90.0 | 90.6 | 90.7 | 90.8 | 90.8 |
| $(6, 1536)$ | 33.6 | 56.2 | 62.4 | 80.5 | 83.4 | 84.1 |
| $(6, 1536)_{\text{UHF}}$ | 9.8 | 67.6 | 80.2 | 86.2 | 87.0 | 87.3 |

Table 4: The F1 score on CoNLL 2003. Each score is averaged over five runs.

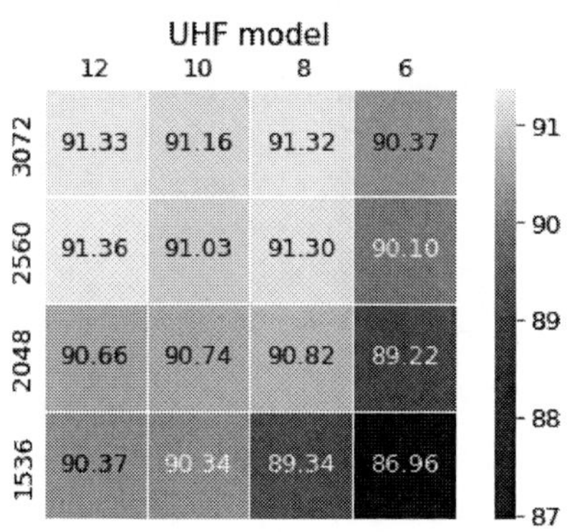


Figure 7: The Performance of the pruned models with different structures on the CoNLL 2003 test set. Each score is averaged over five runs.

# AnnIE: An Annotation Platform for Constructing Complete Open Information Extraction Benchmark

**Niklas Friedrich**[1], **Kiril Gashteovski**[2], **Mingying Yu**[1,2], **Bhushan Kotnis**[2], **Carolin Lawrence**[2], **Mathias Niepert**[2,3], **Goran Glavaš**[1,4]

[1] University of Mannheim, Mannheim, Germany

[2] NEC Laboratories Europe, Heidelberg, Germany

[3] University of Stuttgart, Stuttgart, Germany, [4] LMU Munich, Munich, Germany

{nfriedri,minyu,gglavas}@mail.uni-mannheim.de

{firstname.lastname}@neclab.eu

## Abstract

Open Information Extraction (OIE) is the task of extracting facts from sentences in the form of relations and their corresponding arguments in schema-free manner. Intrinsic performance of OIE systems is difficult to measure due to the *incompleteness* of existing OIE benchmarks: ground truth extractions do not group all acceptable surface realizations of the same fact that can be extracted from a sentence. To measure performance of OIE systems more realistically, it is necessary to manually annotate *complete facts* (i.e., clusters of all acceptable surface realizations of the same fact) from input sentences. We propose AnnIE: an interactive annotation platform that facilitates such challenging annotation tasks and supports creation of *complete fact-oriented OIE evaluation benchmarks*. AnnIE is modular and flexible in order to support different use case scenarios (i.e., benchmarks covering different types of facts) and different languages. We use AnnIE to build two complete OIE benchmarks: one with verb-mediated facts and another with facts encompassing named entities. We evaluate several OIE systems on our complete benchmarks created with AnnIE. We publicly release AnnIE under non-restrictive license.[1]

## 1 Introduction

Open Information Extraction (OIE) is the task of extracting relations and their arguments from natural language text in schema-free manner (Banko et al., 2007). Consider the input sentence *"Edmund Barton, who was born in Australia, was a judge"*. Without the use of a pre-specified schema, an OIE system should extract the triples *("Edmund Barton"; "was born in"; "Australia")* and *("Edmund Barton"; "was"; "judge")*. The output of OIE systems is used in many downstream tasks, including open link prediction (Broscheit et al., 2020), automated knowledge base construction (Gashteovski et al., 2020), question answering (Khot et al., 2017) and text summarization (Xu and Lapata, 2021).

Intrinsic evaluation of OIE systems is done either manually (Mausam et al., 2012; Pal et al., 2016) or with the use of evaluation benchmarks (Stanovsky and Dagan, 2016; Bhardwaj et al., 2019). While manual evaluations are usually of higher quality, they are expensive and time consuming. Automated benchmark evaluations are faster and more economic than manual OIE evaluations (Hohenecker et al., 2020), but are less reliable than human judgments of extraction correctness (Zhan and Zhao, 2020), because they are based on approximate token-level matching of system extractions against ground truth extractions. The main shortcoming of existing OIE benchmarks is their *incompleteness*: they do not exhaustively list all acceptable surface realizations of the same piece of information (i.e., same fact) and, because of this, resort to unreliable scoring functions based on token-level matching between system and gold extractions (Schneider et al., 2017).

Obtaining complete manual OIE annotations is, however, very difficult and time-consuming. Annotating a *complete* OIE benchmark requires human annotators to write *all* possible combinations of extractions expressing the same fact (i.e., exhaustively list all acceptable surface realizations of the same fact; see Section 3). To facilitate and speed up this process, we introduce AnnIE, a dedicated annotation tool for constructing complete fact-oriented OIE benchmark. AnnIE facilitates the annotation process by (1) highlighting the tokens of interest (e.g., for verb-mediated extractions, it highlights the verbs, which are candidates for head words of predicates); (2) providing web-based interface for annotating triples and grouping them into *fact synsets*, i.e., groups of informationally equivalent extractions (Section 3). To the best of our knowledge, AnnIE is the first publicly-available annotation platform for constructing OIE benchmarks.

[1] https://github.com/nfriedri/annie-annotation-platform



*Proceedings of the 60th Annual Meeting of the Association for Computational Linguistics System Demonstrations*, pages 44 - 60

We showcase AnnIE[2] by creating two complete fact-based OIE benchmarks: (1) benchmark of verb-mediated facts on English, German, Chinese, Galician, Arabic and Japanese, making this gold data the first such OIE resource on languages other than English; (2) benchmark for facts associating named entities (for English only). We then benchmark several state-of-the-art OIE systems on these fact-based benchmarks and demonstrate that they are significantly less effective than indicated by existing OIE benchmarks that use token-level scoring. We hope that AnnIE motivates the creation of many more fact-based (as opposed to token-level) OIE evaluation benchmarks.

## 2 Related Work

### 2.1 Evaluation of OIE Systems

OIE systems are evaluated either manually (Mausam et al., 2012; Pal et al., 2016; Gashteovski et al., 2019), w.r.t. a downstream task (Mausam, 2016; Lin et al., 2020), or with the use of evaluation benchmarks (Stanovsky and Dagan, 2016; Bhardwaj et al., 2019). Manual evaluations are usually of higher quality because they are performed by one or more expert annotators (Del Corro and Gemulla, 2013). They are, however, expensive and time consuming, which makes the development of OIE systems very slow. On the other hand, downstream evaluation of OIE systems is faster, but provides insights only about their performance w.r.t. particular tasks and does not provide insights on the intrinsic (i.e., task-agnostic) correctness of the extractions. Finally, using evaluation benchmarks is both task-agnostic and fast, though current benchmarks might contain noise (Zhan and Zhao, 2020). Moreover, current benchmarks suffer from incompleteness; i.e., they are not designed in a manner that aims to contain all possible extractions from an input sentence. Therefore, they rely on lenient token-overlap based evaluation, which could result in misleading results (Lechelle et al., 2019). To address this, we move away from such token-based evaluations and move towards fact-based evaluation (Section 3).

### 2.2 Annotation Tools

To facilitate the annotation process of NLP tasks, many interactive annotation tools have been designed. Such work covers tasks like sequence labelling (Lin et al., 2019; Lee et al., 2020), coreference resolution (Bornstein et al., 2020) and treebank projection across languages (Akbik and Vollgraf, 2017). For annotating OIE extractions, however, there are no publicly available tools. The two commonly used benchmarks—OIE2016 (Stanovsky and Dagan, 2016) and CaRB (Bhardwaj et al., 2019)—only provide annotated data and no dedicated annotation tool. OIE2016 uses a dataset from a similar task (QA-SRL), which is then automatically ported to OIE. This approach does not require an annotation tool, but the quality of the benchmark (i.e., ground truth extractions) decreases due to the automatic label projection (Zhan and Zhao, 2020). CaRB addresses this issue by sampling from the same input sentences used by OIE2016, and then crowdsourcing manual extractions. However, their annotation OIE interface has four major limitations: (1) it cannot be used to create complete fact-based OIE benchmarks (Section 3), i.e., it does not allow for different extractions (e.g., triples) that correspond to the same fact; this leads to incomplete annotations and unreliablly lenient token-overlap-based evaluation measures; (2) it focuses only on one type of OIE (verb-mediated extractions); (3) it is not publicly available; (4) it does not support annotations for languages other than English.

## 3 Fact-Based OIE Evaluation

Due to their incompleteness, previous benchmarks lack clarity about whether an extraction indeed represents a correct fact or not. In particular, given a system extraction, they do not assign a binary score (correct/incorrect), but rather calculate per-slot token overlap scores. Consider, for example, the input sentence from Table 1 and the scores that the recent OIE benchmark CaRB (Bhardwaj et al., 2019) assigns to extractions $t_1$ to $t_3$. Because all tokens for each slot for $t_1 - t_3$ are also present in the gold extraction, CaRB credits these extractions with a perfect precision score, even though the extractions clearly state incorrect facts. In similar vein, the CaRB recall score of the extraction $t_4$ is lower than the recall score of $t_3$, even though $t_4$ captures the correct core fact and $t_3$ does not.

To address these issues, we propose moving away from such lenient token-overlap scoring and going towards fact-level exact matching. To this end, we propose an evaluation framework, dubbed BenchIE (Gashteovski et al., 2022), for OIE evaluation based on facts, not tokens. Here, the annotator is instructed to *exhaustively* list all possible surface

[2]Video demo: `https://youtu.be/2wn75U8Lc5w`

**Input sentence:** *"Sen. Mitchell is confident he has sufficient votes to block such a measure with procedural actions."*
**CaRB gold extraction:** *("Sen. Mitchell"; "is confident he has"; "sufficient votes to block ...procedural actions")*

| | Input OIE extraction | | CaRB (P / R) | | Fact-based |
|---|---|---|---|---|---|
| $t_1$ | *("Sen. Mitchell"; "is confident he has";* | *"sufficient")* | 1.00 | 0.44 | 0 |
| $t_2$ | *("Sen. Mitchell"; "is confident he has";* | *"sufficient actions")* | 1.00 | 0.50 | 0 |
| $t_3$ | *("Sen. Mitchell"; "is confident he has";* | *"sufficient procedural actions")* | 1.00 | 0.56 | 0 |
| $t_4$ | *("Sen. Mitchell"; "is confident he has";* | *"sufficient votes")* | 1.00 | 0.50 | 1 |

Table 1: Difference in scores between CaRB and fact-based evaluation. For the input sentence, CaRB provides only one extraction which covers all the words in the sentence. Then, for each input OIE extraction (from $t_1$ to $t_4$) it calculates token-wise precision and recall scores w.r.t. the golden annotation. Fact-based evaluation (with all acceptable extractions of the fact exhaustively listed) allows for exact matching against OIE extractions.

realizations of the same fact, allowing for a binary judgment (correct/incorrect) of correctness of each extraction (it either exactly matches some of the acceptable gold realizations of some fact or it does not match any). The example in Table 2 illustrates the concept of a *fact synset*: a collection of all acceptable extractions for the same fact (i.e., same piece of knowledge).

Because benchmarks based on fact synsets are supposed to be complete, a system OIE extraction is considered correct if and only if it *exactly* matches any of the gold extractions from any of the fact synsets. The number of *true positives (TPs)* is the number of fact synsets (i.e., different facts) "covered" by at least one system extraction. This way, a system that extracts $N$ different triples of the same fact, will be rewarded only once for the correct extraction of the fact. False negatives (FNs) are then fact synsets not covered by any of the system extractions. Finally, each system extraction that does not exactly match any gold triple (from any synset) is counted as a false positive (FP). We then compute *Precision*, *Recall*, and $F_1$ score from TP, FP, and FN in the standard fashion. For more details on the evaluation framework, see (Gashteovski et al., 2022).

## 4 AnnIE: Platform Description

AnnIE is a web-based platform that facilitates manual annotations of fact-based OIE benchmarks. In this section, we discuss: (1) the functionality of highlighting tokens of interest; (2) how AnnIE facilitates creation of complete fact-based OIE benchmarks; (3) AnnIE's software architecture; and (4) AnnIE's web interface and its multilingual support.

### 4.1 Tokens of Interest

One of the key functionalities of AnnIE is its ability to highlight *tokens of interest* – tokens that commonly constitute parts of extractions of interest. For example, most OIE systems focus on extracting verb-mediated triples (Angeli et al., 2015; Kolluru et al., 2020b). In such case, *verbs* clearly represent tokens of interest and are candidates for head words of fact predicates. Other example of tokens of interest may be named entities, which could be useful for extracting information from domain-specific text. There has been prior work on extracting open information from specific domains, including the biomedical (Wang et al., 2018), legal (Siragusa et al., 2018) and scientific domain (Lauscher et al., 2019). In this work, it is important to extract open relations between named entities. Accordingly, highlighting mentions of named entities then facilitates manual extraction of the type of facts that the benchmark is supposed to cover (i.e., relations between named entities). AnnIE allows the user to define a custom function that yields the tokens of interest from the input sentence and then highlights these tokens for the annotator with a background color (Figure 2).

To further facilitate the manual annotations, future versions of AnnIE could also include recommendations for whole OIE triples (e.g., by recommending high-confidence extractions from already existing OIE systems) or for slots (e.g., given a subject, recommend a potential relation; or given a relation, recommend candidates for the arguments). We leave such improvements for future work.

### 4.2 Annotating Fact Synsets

Given a sentence with highlighted tokens of interest, the annotator can start constructing fact synsets. Fact synsets are clusters of fact-equivalent extractions. AnnIE currently supports only the annotation of triples: for each extraction/triple the user first selects which slot she wants to annotate (subject, predicate, or object) and then selects the tokens

**Input sentence:** *"Sen. Mitchell is confident he has sufficient votes to block such a measure with procedural actions."*

| | Subject | Predicate | Object |
|---|---|---|---|
| $f_1$ | *("Sen. Mitchell" \| "he";* | *"is";* | *"confident [he has sufficient ... actions]")* |
| $f_2$ | *("Sen. Mitchell" \| "he";* | *"is confident he has";* | *"sufficient votes")* |
| | *("Sen. Mitchell" \| "he";* | *"is confident he has";* | *"suff. votes to block [such] [a] measure")* |
| $f_3$ | *("Sen. Mitchell" \| "he";* | *"is conf. he has sufficient votes to block"* | *"[such] [a] measure")* |
| | *("Sen. Mitchell" \| "he";* | *"is confident he has ... to block [such]";* | *"[a] measure")* |
| | *("Sen. Mitchell" \| "he";* | *"is confident he has ... to block [such] [a]";* | *"measure")* |
| $f_4$ | *("Sen. Mitchell" \| "he";* | *"is conf. he has ... [such] [a] measure with";* | *"procedural actions")* |
| | *("Sen. Mitchell" \| "he";* | *"is confident he has ... [such] [a] measure";* | *"with procedural actions")* |

Table 2: Example sentence with four *fact synsets* ($f_1$–$f_4$). We account for entity coreference and accept both *"Sen. Mitchell"* and *"he"* as subjects: the delimiter "|" is a shorthand notation for different extractions. In the same vein, square brackets ([]) are a shorthand notation for multiple extractions: triples both with and without the expression(s) in the brackets are considered correct.

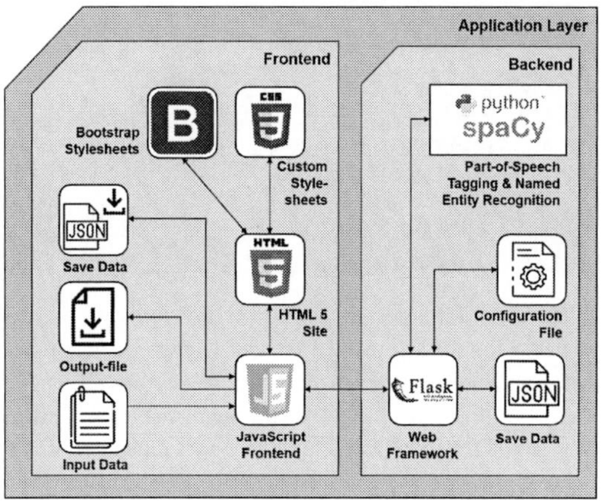


Figure 1: Software architecture of AnnIE.

that constitute that slot. Each token (part of one of the three slots) can additionally be marked as "optional", which means that the tool will create variants of that extraction both with and without those tokens. Once a triple is fully denoted (i.e., tokens for all three slots selected), the annotator chooses whether (1) the triple is a different variant of an already existing fact (i.e., existing fact synset), in which case the triple is added to an existing cluster or (2) a first variant of a new fact, in which case a new cluster (i.e., fact synset) is created and the triple added to it. To facilitate this decision, the annotator can at any time review the already existing fact synsets. Figure 3 shows the interface for creating triples and adding them to fact synsets.

### 4.3 Platform Architecture

AnnIE is a simple local executable web application (Figure 1) that consists of a backend layer and a frontend layer. It starts a local server that provides a user interface accessible from any browser that supports JavaScript.

**Backend.** AnnIE's backend server is based on `Flask`[3], a popular light-weight Python web framework. We implemented HTTP endpoints for receiving requests and sending responses. Additionally, `Flask` hosts the frontend (HTML and CSS) files as a web server. The `Flask` server interacts with (1) the NLP library `SpaCy`[4] (which we employ for POS-tagging and NER, in service of highlighting tokens of interest); (2) a configuration file; (3) data files on the local hard drive and (4) the frontend (i.e., the web interface). AnnIE's backend is highly modularized, so that any component may easily be further customized or replaced with a different module. For example, the `SpaCy`-based NLP module (for POS-tagging and NER) can easily be replaced with any other NLP toolkit, e.g., `Stanza`[5] (Qi et al., 2020). AnnIE is also easily customizable through a configuration file, where the user may specify the types of tokens to be highlighted or select colors for highlighting. The I/O module expects the input (a collection of sentences for OIE annotation) to be in JSON format and saves the annotated fact synsets in JSON as well.

**Frontend.** The application frontend is implemented in JavaScript and based on the `Bootstrap` library and custom CSS stylesheets. We adopt model-view-controller (MVC) architecture for the frontend: it uses a data structure (i.e., *model*) capturing the entire annotation process (i.e., information about the annotation, loaded text file, current triple in annotation, etc.; you can find more details in the Appendix, Section A.2). Based on the current state of the model, the frontend renders the interface (i.e., view) by enabling and disabling particular annotation functionality. The controller connects the two: it renders the view based on the current state of the model. We implemented

[3] `https://github.com/pallets/flask`
[4] `https://spacy.io/`
[5] `https://stanfordnlp.github.io/stanza/`

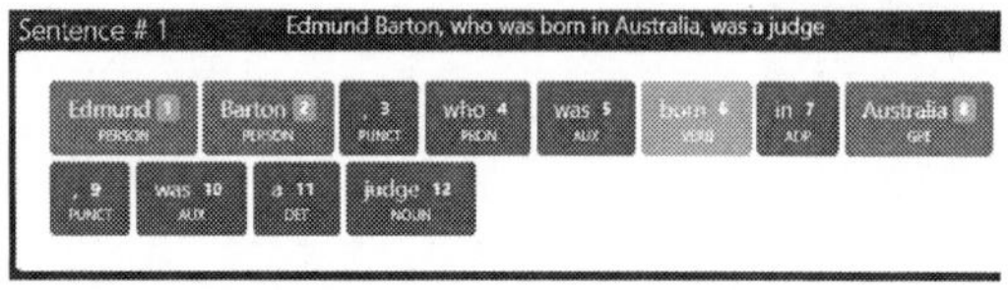


Figure 2: Highlighting tokens of interest. In this example, tokens of interest are verbs and named entities.

additional I/O scripts that complement the core functionality of the main controller. These scripts handle the formatting of the output file as well as the loading of the data from the input files. Saving or loading data is customizable: one merely needs to overwrite the `load()` and `save()` methods of the controller.

**Data Flow.** Upon selection of the input file, the data is sent from the frontend to the backend via an HTTP request. In the backend, the sentence is then tokenized, POS-tagged, and processed for named entities with the NLP module (we rely on `SpaCy`). The tokenized and labeled sentence is then sent as a JSON object to the frontend, where each token is displayed as one button (Figure 2). The default version of the tool allows the user to choose (in the configuration file) between four coloring schemes for highlighting token buttons.

### 4.4 Web Interface and Language Support

The user can start from scratch by uploading a text file that contains unannotated sentences, or load previously saved work (JSON file). For each sentence, the user starts from a full set of sentence tokens with highlighted tokens of interest (Figure 2). The user then constructs triples and places them into fact synsets (Figure 3). At any point during the annotation, the user can generate human-readable output of the annotated extractions and download it as a text file in a tab-separated format (Figure 4). Alternatively, the user can save the annotation progress as a JSON file that can later be loaded in order to continue annotating.

AnnIE supports OIE annotations for sentences in any language supported by its NLP module (i.e., available POS-tagging and NER models). By default, AnnIE relies on `SpaCy` and can therefore support creation of OIE benchmarks for all languages for which `SpaCy` provides POS-tagging and NER models. Section A.3 from the appendix provides details about how this module can be adjusted to the user's preference.

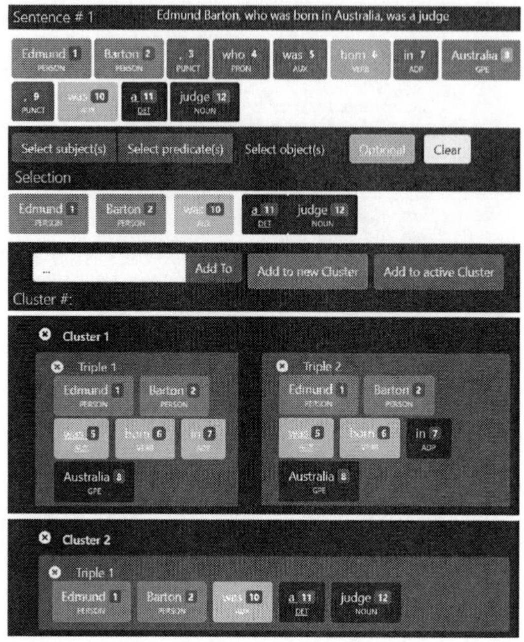


Figure 3: Manual labeling of OIE triples. The user selects tokens from the tokenized input sentence and places them into the correct slot: subject (green), predicate (yellow) or object (blue). Then, the user adds the extracted triple either to an active fact cluster (i.e., fact synset) or to a new one. The user can also select which tokens are optional by clicking the "Optional" button on an active token selection. For larger version of the same figure, see Figure 11 in Appendix A.6.

## 5 Demonstration Study

To showcase our tool's suitability for different OIE scenarios, we generated two complete fact-based OIE benchmarks using AnnIE: (1) a benchmark for verb-mediated facts; (2) a benchmark with facts involving named entities (NEs). We then evaluated several OIE systems and compared their fact-based scores with the token-overlap lenient scores of the existing CaRB benchmark (Bhardwaj et al., 2019).

### 5.1 Experimental Setup

**OIE Systems.** We comparatively evaluated several state-of-the-art OIE systems against the gold fact synsets annotated with AnnIE. For OIE on English, we used ClausIE (Del Corro and Gemulla, 2013), Stanford (Angeli et al., 2015), MinIE (Gashteovski et al., 2017), ROIE (Stanovsky et al., 2018) and OpenIE6 (Kolluru et al., 2020a). For Chinese, German, Galician, Japanese and Arabic, we used the supervised M$^2$OIE (Ro et al., 2020) model, which is based on multilingual BERT (Devlin et al., 2019), trained on large English dataset (Zhan

| | | EN | | | | | ZH | DE | AR | GL | JA |
|---|---|---|---|---|---|---|---|---|---|---|---|
| | | ClausIE | MinIE | Stanford | ROIE | OpenIE6 | M$^2$OIE | M$^2$OIE | M$^2$OIE | M$^2$OIE | M$^2$OIE |
| P | CaRB | **0.58** | 0.45 | 0.17 | 0.44 | 0.48 | / | / | / | / | / |
| | Fact-based | **0.50** | 0.43 | 0.11 | 0.20 | 0.31 | 0.18 | 0.09 | 0.16 | 0.15 | 0.00 |
| | $\Delta$ | +0.08 | +0.02 | +0.06 | **+0.24** | +0.17 | / | / | / | / | / |
| R | CaRB | 0.53 | 0.44 | 0.29 | 0.60 | **0.67** | / | / | / | / | / |
| | Fact-based | 0.26 | **0.28** | 0.16 | 0.09 | 0.21 | 0.10 | 0.03 | 0.03 | 0.06 | 0.00 |
| | $\Delta$ | +0.27 | +0.16 | +0.13 | **+0.51** | +0.46 | / | / | / | / | / |
| $F_1$ | CaRB | **0.56** | 0.44 | 0.22 | 0.51 | **0.56** | / | / | / | / | / |
| | Fact-based | **0.34** | **0.34** | 0.13 | 0.13 | 0.25 | 0.13 | 0.04 | 0.05 | 0.09 | 0.00 |
| | $\Delta$ | +0.22 | +0.10 | +0.09 | **+0.38** | +0.31 | / | / | / | / | / |

Table 3: Comparison of performance of OIE systems on fact-based v.s. CaRB benchmarks for English (EN), Chinese (ZH), German (DE), Arabic (AR), Galician (GL) and Japanese (JA). Metrics used: precision (P), recall (R) and $F_1$ score ($F_1$). $\Delta$ is the difference between the CaRB scores and the fact-based scores. **Bold numbers** indicate highest score for English per row (i.e., highest score for P / R / $F_1$ per benchmark) or highes score difference per row (i.e., highest $\Delta$ for P / R / $F_1$ per benchmark). The fact-based benchmark on English reveals that CaRB overestimates the performance of OIE systems, but with the help of AnnIE it is easily possible to create benchmarks which provide more reliable performance estimates. Creating such fact-based benchmarks for a series of other languages highlights the need for future OIE research to focus on langauges other than English.

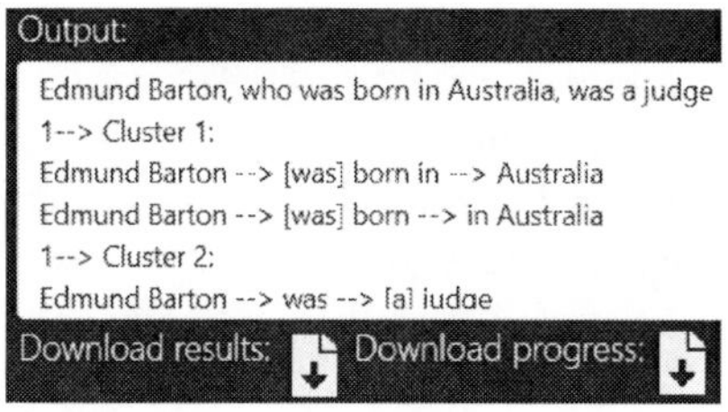


Figure 4: Human-readable representation of the annotated extractions. Annotations can be downloaded as a human-readable file or as a JSON file (loadable for further annotation with AnnIE).

and Zhao, 2020) and transferred to the target language by means of its multilingual encoder. We trained M$^2$OIE using the implementation and recommended hyperparameter setup from the original work (Ro et al., 2020).

**Verb-Mediated Triples.** We first evaluate the OIE systems in the most common setup: for verb-mediated facts. In this scenario, OIE system extractions are triples with verb-phrase predicates. We randomly sampled 300 sentences from the CaRB benchmark, and two experts independently annotated them manually for fact synsets with AnnIE (we provide the annotation guidelines in the Appendix, Section A.4). Then, the annotators merged the annotations by resolving the disagreements through a discussion. The annotation effort was approximately two working weeks per annotator. To show that AnnIE is in principle language agnostic, native speakers of German, Chinese, Japanese and Galician translated these 300 sentences to their respective languages. For Arabic, a native speaker managed to translate the first 100 sentences. only due to limited resources. Then, the native speakers annotated fact synsets in these languages with AnnIE. Due to limited resources, the sentences for these languages were translated and then annotated with OIE extractions by one annotator per language. Finally, we evaluated one OIE system for each language on this benchmark.

**NE-centric Triples.** We used AnnIE to build a benchmark consisting of facts connecting named entities (NEs): triples in which both subjects and objects are named entities. Since NEs are frequently mentioned in news stories, we selected the sentences for annotation from the NYT10k dataset (Gashteovski et al., 2017), a random sample of 10k sentences from the New York Times corpus (Sandhaus, 2008). We split the NE-centric benchmark in two parts: (1) NE-2: 150 sentences from NYT10k with exactly 2 NEs (as detected by `SpaCy`); (2) NE-3$^+$: we sample 150 sentences from NYT10k such that they have 3 or more NE mentions. The annotation guidelines, while similar to those for the verb-mediated triples, differ in two important aspects: (1) the annotator should extract *only* the facts in which both arguments are named entities; (2) besides verb-mediated relations, the annotator was allowed to extract noun-mediated relations too; e.g., *("Sundar Pichai"; "CEO"; "Google")*.

### 5.2 Results and Discussion

**English OIE.** We score the OIE systems against the gold fact synsets produced with AnnIE, using the fact-based evaluation protocol (Section 3). For the verb-mediated extractions, we compare our fact-based evaluation scores against the token-overlap

| | | ClausIE (4 / 10) | MinIE (26 / 48) | Stanford (12 / 22) | ROIE (2 / 7) | OIE6 (8 / 20) |
|---|---|---|---|---|---|---|
| P | NE-2 | **0.75** | 0.58 | 0.45 | 0.05 | 0.38 |
| | NE-3$^+$ | **0.78** | 0.54 | 0.63 | 0.05 | 0.32 |
| R | NE-2 | 0.05 | **0.23** | 0.08 | 0.02 | 0.05 |
| | NE-3$^+$ | 0.04 | **0.13** | 0.06 | 0.02 | 0.03 |
| $F_1$ | NE-2 | 0.09 | **0.33** | 0.13 | 0.03 | 0.08 |
| | NE-3$^+$ | 0.07 | **0.21** | 0.11 | 0.02 | 0.06 |

Table 4: Performance of OIE systems on fact-based evaluation on NE-centric triples. NE-2 / NE-3$^+$: results on sentences that contain 2 / 3 or more NEs (labelled with SpaCy). Numbers in brackets below an OIE system name indicate the number of OIE triples on which the evaluation was done for NE-2 / NE-3$^+$. **Bold numbers** indicate highest score per row.

scores of CaRB (Bhardwaj et al., 2019): the results are shown in Table 3. Comparison of Fact-based and CaRB scores indicates that: (1) CaRB largely overestimates the performance of OIE systems; (2) current OIE systems predominantly fail to extract correct facts, which strongly points to the need for creating complete fact-oriented benchmarks, a task that AnnIE facilitates. For more detailed discussion, multi-faceted evaluation and error analysis, see Gashteovski et al. (2022).

**Multilingual OIE.** Finally, Table 3 shows that the results for OIE systems in languages other than English are significantly worse, which shows that more research is needed in this direction. The results for Chinese OIE seem to be particularly encouraging, as the difference of the $F_1$ score between some OIE systems in English and M$^2$OIE in Chinese is not too large as it is between English and the other languages. For example, M$^2$OIE in Chinese has the same $F_1$ score as Stanford's OIE system and ROIE. We applied the same training strategy for Japanese, but the $F_1$ score of this OIE system is 0. This indicates that more research is needed for Japanese in defining the problem well and proposing methods for solving it. Nevertheless, we release the gold datasets for OIE in all investigated languages: English, German, Galician, Chinese, Japanese and Arabic; which we believe to be an important resource for research for subsequent multilingual OIE. Figure 12 and Figure 13 from the Appendix show an example sentence and its corresponding OIE annotations in different languages. For a more detailed discussion on the results of multilingual OIE evaluation, see Kotnis et al. (2022).

**NE-centric OIE.** Table 4 shows the performance of OIE systems on the NE-centric benchmark. In both subsets of 150 sentences—NE-2 and NE-3$^+$—only a fraction of them contain actual knowledge facts that connect a pair of NEs (59/150 and 97/150 respectively). Because the OIE systems used in the evaluation are not specifically designed to extract NE-centric facts, we make the evaluation fairer by pruning the system extractions before fact-based evaluation: we keep only the triples that contain in both subject and object NEs found among subjects and objects of gold extractions. In other words, we primarily test whether the OIE systems extract acceptable predicates between NEs between which there is a predicate in the gold standard. The results show that the current OIE systems extract very few NE-centric triples (e.g., ClausIE extracts only 4 triples for the NE-2 dataset and 10 for the NE-3$^+$ dataset, see Table 4). Because of this, one should intepret the results in Table 4 with caution. This evaluation, nonetheless shows that the current OIE systems are not ill-suited for a NE-centric OIE task, warranting more research efforts in this direction.

## 6 Conclusions

Exhaustively annotating all acceptable OIE triples is a tedious task, but important for realistic intrinsic evaluation of OIE systems. To support annotators, we introduced AnnIE: annotation tool for constructing comprehensive evaluation benchmarks for OIE. AnnIE allows custom specification of tokens of interests (e.g., verbs) and is designed for creating fact-oriented benchmarks in which the fact-equivalent–yet superficially differing–extractions are grouped into fact synset. AnnIE's lightweight architecture, easy installation and customizable components make it a practical solution for future OIE annotation.

## Acknowledgments

We thank the anonymous reviewers for their invaluable feedback and support.

## References

Alan Akbik and Roland Vollgraf. 2017. The Projector: An Interactive Annotation Projection Visualization Tool. In *Proceedings of the Conference on Empirical Methods in Natural Language Processing (EMNLP): System Demonstrations*, pages 43–48.

Gabor Angeli, Melvin Jose Johnson Premkumar, and Christopher D. Manning. 2015. Leveraging Linguistic Structure For Open Domain Information Extraction. In *Proceedings of the Annual Meeting of the Association for Computational Linguistics (ACL)*, pages 344–354.

Michele Banko, Michael J Cafarella, Stephen Soderland, Matthew Broadhead, and Oren Etzioni. 2007. Open Information Extraction from the Web. In *Proceedings of the International Joint Conferences on Artificial Intelligence (IJCAI)*, pages 2670–2676.

Sangnie Bhardwaj, Samarth Aggarwal, and Mausam Mausam. 2019. CaRB: A Crowdsourced Benchmark for Open IE. In *Proceedings of the Conference on Empirical Methods in Natural Language Processing and the International Joint Conference on Natural Language Processing (EMNLP-IJCNLP)*, pages 6263–6268.

Aaron Bornstein, Arie Cattan, and Ido Dagan. 2020. CoRefi: A Crowd Sourcing Suite for Coreference Annotation. In *Proceedings of the Conference on Empirical Methods in Natural Language Processing (EMNLP): System Demonstrations*.

Samuel Broscheit, Kiril Gashteovski, Yanjie Wang, and Rainer Gemulla. 2020. Can We Predict New Facts with Open Knowledge Graph Embeddings? A Benchmark for Open Link Prediction. In *Proceedings of the Annual Meeting on Association for Computational Linguistics (ACL)*, pages 2296–2308.

Luciano Del Corro and Rainer Gemulla. 2013. ClausIE: Clause-Based Open Information Extraction. In *Proceedings of the International World Wide Web Conferences (WWW)*, pages 355–366.

Jacob Devlin, Ming-Wei Chang, Kenton Lee, and Kristina Toutanova. 2019. BERT: Pre-training of Deep Bidirectional Transformers for Language Understanding. In *Proceedings of the Conference of the North American Chapter of the Association for Computational Linguistics - Human Language Technologies (NAACL-HLT)*, pages 8554–8565.

Kiril Gashteovski, Rainer Gemulla, and Luciano Del Corro. 2017. MinIE: Minimizing Facts in Open Information Extraction. In *Proceedings of the Conference on Empirical Methods in Natural Language Processing (EMNLP)*, pages 2630–2640.

Kiril Gashteovski, Rainer Gemulla, Bhushan Kotnis, Sven Hertling, and Christian Meilicke. 2020. On Aligning Openie Extractions with Knowledge Bases: A Case Study. In *Proceedings of the First Workshop on Evaluation and Comparison of NLP Systems*, pages 143–154.

Kiril Gashteovski, Sebastian Wanner, Sven Hertling, Samuel Broscheit, and Rainer Gemulla. 2019. OPIEC: An Open Information Extraction Corpus. In *In Proceedings of the Conference on Automated Knowledge Base Construction (AKBC)*.

Kiril Gashteovski, Mingying Yu, Bhushan Kotnis, Carolin Lawrence, Mathias Niepert, and Goran Glavaš. 2022. BenchIE: A Framework for Multi-Faceted Fact-Based Open Information Extraction Evaluation. In *Annual Meeting of the Association for Computational Linguistics (ACL)*.

Patrick Hohenecker, Frank Mtumbuka, Vid Kocijan, and Thomas Lukasiewicz. 2020. Systematic Comparison of Neural Architectures and Training Approaches for Open Information Extraction. In *Proceedings of the Conference on Empirical Methods in Natural Language Processing (EMNLP)*, pages 8554–8565.

Tushar Khot, Ashish Sabharwal, and Peter Clark. 2017. Answering Complex Questions Using Open Information Extraction. In *Proceedings of the Annual Meeting on Association for Computational Linguistics (ACL)*, pages 311–316.

Keshav Kolluru, Vaibhav Adlakha, Samarth Aggarwal, Soumen Chakrabarti, et al. 2020a. OpenIE6: Iterative Grid Labeling and Coordination Analysis for Open Information Extraction. In *Proceedings of the Conference on Empirical Methods in Natural Language Processing (EMNLP)*, pages 3748–3761.

Keshav Kolluru, Samarth Aggarwal, Vipul Rathore, Mausam, and Soumen Chakrabarti. 2020b. IMoJIE: Iterative Memory-Based Joint Open Information Extraction. In *Proceedings of the Annual Meeting of the Association for Computational Linguistics (ACL)*, pages 5871–5886.

Bhushan Kotnis, Kiril Gashteovski, Daniel Oñoro Rubio, Ammar Shaker, Vanesa Rodriguez-Tembras, Makoto Takamoto, Mathias Niepert, and Carolin Lawrence. 2022. MILLIE: Modular & Iterative Multilingual Open Information Extraction. In *Proceedings of the Annual Meeting on Association for Computational Linguistics (ACL)*.

Anne Lauscher, Yide Song, and Kiril Gashteovski. 2019. MinScIE: Citation-centered Open Information Extraction. In *2019 ACM/IEEE Joint Conference on Digital Libraries (JCDL)*, pages 386–387. IEEE.

William Lechelle, Fabrizio Gotti, and Phillippe Langlais. 2019. WiRe57: A Fine-Grained Benchmark for Open Information Extraction. In *Proceedings of the Linguistic Annotation Workshop (LAW@ACL)*, pages 6–15.

Dong-Ho Lee, Rahul Khanna, Bill Yuchen Lin, Jamin Chen, Seyeon Lee, Qinyuan Ye, Elizabeth Boschee, Leonardo Neves, and Xiang Ren. 2020. LEAN-LIFE: A Label-Efficient Annotation Framework Towards Learning from Explanation. In *Proceedings of the Annual Meeting on Association for Computational Linguistics (ACL Demo)*, pages 372–379.

Bill Yuchen Lin, Dong-Ho Lee, Frank F Xu, Ouyu Lan, and Xiang Ren. 2019. AlpacaTag: An Active Learning-based Crowd Annotation Framework for Sequence Tagging. In *Proceedings of the Annual*

*Meeting of the Association for Computational Linguistics (ACL): System Demonstrations*, pages 58–63.

Xueling Lin, Haoyang Li, Hao Xin, Zijian Li, and Lei Chen. 2020. KBPearl: A Knowledge Base Population System Supported by Joint Entity and Relation Linking. In *Proceedings of the Very Large Data Base Endowment (PVLDB)*, pages 1035–1049.

Mausam. 2016. Open Information Extraction Systems and Downstream Applications. In *Proceedings of the twenty-fifth international joint conference on artificial intelligence*, pages 4074–4077.

Mausam, Michael Schmitz, Robert Bart, Stephen Soderland, and Oren Etzioni. 2012. Open Language Learning for Information Extraction. In *Proceedings of the Joint Conference on Empirical Methods in Natural Language Processing and Computational Natural Language Learning (EMNLP-CoNLL)*, pages 523–534.

Harinder Pal et al. 2016. Demonyms and Compound Relational Nouns in Nominal Open IE. In *Proceedings of the 5th Workshop on Automated Knowledge Base Construction*, pages 35–39.

Peng Qi, Yuhao Zhang, Yuhui Zhang, Jason Bolton, and Christopher D Manning. 2020. Stanza: A Python Natural Language Processing Toolkit for Many Human Languages. In *Association for Computational Linguistics (ACL)*, page 101–108.

Youngbin Ro, Yukyung Lee, and Pilsung Kang. 2020. Multi^2OIE: Multilingual Open Information Extraction Based on Multi-Head Attention with BERT. In *Findings of the Association for Computational Linguistics: EMNLP 2020*, pages 1107–1117, Online. Association for Computational Linguistics.

Evan Sandhaus. 2008. The new york times annotated corpus. *Linguistic Data Consortium, Philadelphia*, 6(12):e26752.

Rudolf Schneider, Tom Oberhauser, Tobias Klatt, Felix A. Gers, and Alexander Löser. 2017. Analysing errors of open information extraction systems. In *Proceedings of the First Workshop on Building Linguistically Generalizable NLP Systems*, pages 11–18, Copenhagen, Denmark. Association for Computational Linguistics.

Giovanni Siragusa, Rohan Nanda, Valeria De Paiva, and Luigi Di Caro. 2018. Relating Legal Entities via Open Information Extraction. In *Research Conference on Metadata and Semantics Research*, pages 181–187. Springer.

Gabriel Stanovsky and Ido Dagan. 2016. Creating a Large Benchmark for Open Information Extraction. In *Proceedings of the International Conference on Empirical Methods in Natural Language Processing (EMNLP)*, pages 2300–2305.

Gabriel Stanovsky, Julian Michael, Luke Zettlemoyer, and Ido Dagan. 2018. Supervised Open Information Extraction. In *Proceedings of the Conference of the North American Chapter of the Association for Computational Linguistics: Human Language Technologies (NAACL-HLT)*, pages 885–895.

Xuan Wang, Yu Zhang, Qi Li, Yinyin Chen, and Jiawei Han. 2018. Open Information Extraction with Meta-pattern Discovery in Biomedical Literature. In *Proceedings of the 2018 ACM International Conference on Bioinformatics, Computational Biology, and Health Informatics (BCB)*, pages 291–300.

Yumo Xu and Mirella Lapata. 2021. Generating Query Focused Summaries from Query-free Resources. In *Annual Meeting of the Association for Computational Linguistics (ACL)*, page 6096–6109.

Junlang Zhan and Hai Zhao. 2020. Span Model for Open Information Extraction on Accurate Corpus. In *Proceedings of the AAAI Conference on Artificial Intelligence (AAAI)*, pages 9523–9530.

```css
/*Add YOURLABEL class to css file */
.btn-YOURLABEL {
  color: white;
  background-color: #87FF00;
  border-color: #87FF00;
  opacity: 0.5;
}
.btn-YOURLABEL:hover,
.btn-YOURLABEL:focus {
  color: white;
  background-color: #75DE00;
  border-color: #75DE00;
}
```

Figure 5: Add new class to css

# A Appendix

## A.1 Highlighting Functions

The tool is designed to make customizations rather easily. For adjusting the color scheme, the color "hex"-values inside the style.css files need to be set to the desired color codes. This needs to be done to the button itself with the desired color as well as to the "hover" property of the button, where usually a darker version of the same color is used. If complete new labels are introduced to the tool, the css needs to include an approriate class to handle these as shown in Figure 5.

In case any new coloring schemes are required, these can either be entered additionally or exchanged against the standard functions implementing the scheme above. The different colorings are applied using the functions `fullColoring()`, `verbColoring()`, `namedEntitiesColoring()`, and `noneColoring()` inside `GraphicalInterface.js`. These functions can be adjusted by changing the switch statements handling which tokens need to be colorized depending on their label. There, new cases can simply be added or superfluous colored labels can be removed.Another option is to add new coloring functions. These can rely on the provided ones. They simply need to be registered to the tool by being added to the first switch statement inside the function `createTaggedContent()`. An example of such an function is given in Figure 6, while the "register" procedure is shown in Figure 7.

In both cases, additionally, the function `downgrade()` needs to be adjusted accordingly to the above-mentioned changes to ensure that the buttons can be selected and deselected properly. This step is shown in Figure 8.

## A.2 Data model structure used in the frontend

The data model structure used in the frontend is shown on Figure 9.

## A.3 Multilinguality

By extending the definition of the function `read_config_file()` inside the backend file `tokenizer.py`, further languages can be included. Therefore, SpaCy simply needs to be forced to load the appropriate language model. For details, see code snippet showing how to adapt the `tokenizer.py` script to accept further language models in Figure 10.

## A.4 Annotation Guidelines (English)

### A.4.1 General Principle

The annotator should manually extract verb-mediated triples from a natural language sentence. Each triple should represent two entities or concepts, and the verb-mediated relation between them. For example, from the input sentence *"Michael Jordan, who is a former basketball player, was born in Brooklyn."*, there are three entities and concepts—*Michael Jordan, former basketball player* and *Brooklyn*—which are related as follows: *("Michael Jordan"; "is"; "former basketball player")* and *("Michael Jordan"; "was born in"; "Brooklyn").*

Once the triple is manually extracted, it should be placed into the correct fact synset (see Section A.4.2).

### A.4.2 Fact Synsets

Once a triple is manually extracted, the annotator should place the triple into its corresponding fact synset (details about fact synsets in Section 3). In case there is no existing fact synset for the manually extracted triple, the annotator should create one and place the triple in that synset.

**Coreference.** The annotator should place extractions that refer to the same entity or concept under the same fact synset. Consider the following input sentence: *"His son , John Crozie, was an aviation pioneer."*; The following triples should be placed in the same fact synset:

- *("His son"; "was"; "[an][6] aviation pioneer")*
- *("J. Crozie"; "was"; "[an] aviation pioneer")*

[6]words in square brackets indicate optional tokens (see Section A.4.3)

```
function yourLabelColoring(labelText, labelPos, index) {
    let output = '';
    switch (labelPos) {
        //Remove cases not necessary:
        case 'NOUN': output += `<button class="btn btn-noun ml-1 mb-1" id="posLabel-${index}"> `; break;
        case 'VERB': output += `<button class="btn btn-verb ml-1 mb-1" id="posLabel-${index}">`; break;
        case 'ADJ':  output += `<button class="btn btn-adjective ml-1 mb-1" id="posLabel-${index}">`; break;
        case 'ORG':
        case 'GPE':
        case 'LOC':
        case 'PERSON':
            output += `<button class="btn btn-namedEntity ml-1 mb-1" id="posLabel-${index}">`; break;
        // Stop removing
        // Insert following lines and exchange variable YOURLABEL
        case 'YOURLABEL':
            output += `<button class="btn btn-YOURLABEL ml-1 mb-1" id="posLabel-${index}">`;
            break;
        // End Insertion
        default: output += `<button class="btn btn-secondary ml-1 mb-1" id="posLabel-${index}">`; break;
    }
    if (showTag) {
        output += `<text>${labelText}</text> <span class="badge badge-secondary">${index}</span><br/><pos>${labelPos}</pos></button>`;
    } else {
        output += `<text>${labelText}</text> <span class="badge badge-secondary">${index}</span><pos hidden>${labelPos}</pos></button>`;
    }
    return output;
}
```

Figure 6: Example of a new coloring function

```
function createTaggedContent(words) {
    var output = "";
    for (var i = 0; i < words.length; i++) {
        //console.log(i)
        let labelText = words[i].text;
        let labelPos = words[i].posLabel;
        let type = words[i].type;
        let index = words[i].index;
        if (type == '') {
            switch (coloring) {
                case 'full':  output += fullColoring(labelText, labelPos, index); break;
                case 'verbs': output += verbColoring(labelText, labelPos, index); break;
                case 'named-entities': output += namedEntitiesColoring(labelText, labelPos, index); break;
                case 'none':  output += noneColoring(labelText, labelPos, index); break;
                // "Register" new created coloring function, replace "yourLabelColoring" with function name
                case 'YOURLABEL':
                    output += yourLabelColoring(labelText, labelPos, index); break;
                // End
                default:
                    output += verbColoring(labelText, labelPos, index);
                    break;
            }
        }
        // ...
```

Figure 7: "Register" new coloring function

```
function downgrade(targetElement) {
    // ...
    else {
        //Insert if-statement for YOURLABELCOLORING
        if (coloring == 'YOURLABELCOLORING') {
            switch (posLabel) {
                case 'NOUN': targetElement.className = "btn btn-noun ml-1 mb-1"; break;
                case 'VERB': targetElement.className = "btn btn-verb ml-1 mb-1"; break;
                case 'ADJ': targetElement.className = "btn btn-adjective ml-1 mb-1"; break;
                case 'ORG':
                case 'LOC':
                case 'PERSON':
                case 'GPE': targetElement.className = "btn btn-namedEntity ml-1 mb-1"; break;
                // Add case for YOURLABEL
                case 'YOURLABEL':
                    targetElement.className = "btn btn-YOURLABEL ml-1 mb-1";
                    break;
                //END
                default:
                    targetElement.className = "btn btn-secondary ml-1 mb-1";
                    break;
            }
        }
        // ...
```

Figure 8: Necessary adjustments to `downgrade()`

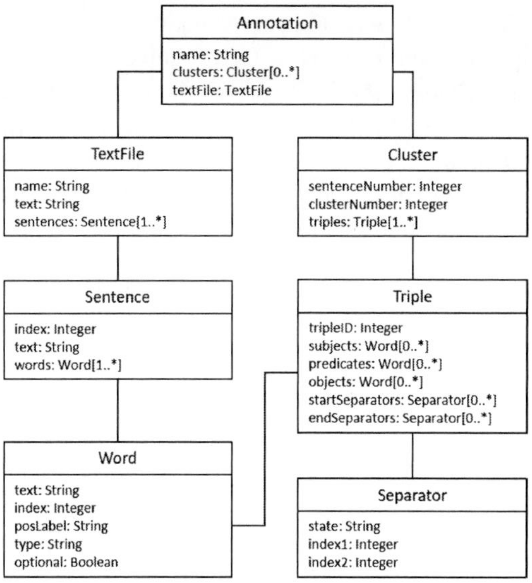


Figure 9: Data model structure used in the frontend

```
def read_config_file(self):
    """..."""
    if configs["Language"] == "English":
        try:
            self.nlp = spacy.load("en_core_web_sm")
        except:
            os.system('python -m spacy download en_core_web_sm')
            self.nlp = spacy.load("en_core_web_sm")
        print("Successfully loaded language: ENGLISH")
    """INSERT """
    if configs["Language"] == "YOURLANGUAGE":
        try:
            self.nlp = spacy.load("SPACY_LANGUAGE_MODULE")
        except:
            os.system('python -m spacy download SPACY_LANGUAGE_MODULE')
            self.nlp = spacy.load("SPACY_LANGUAGE_MODULE")
        print("Successfully loaded language: SPACY_LANGUAGE_MODULE")
    """END"""
```

Figure 10: Code snippet showing how to add further language support

because *"His son"* and *"John Crozie"* refer to the same entity.

**Token placements.** The annotator should consider placing certain tokens in different slots, without damaging the meaning of each the fact. Consider the input sentence *"Michael Jordan was born in Brooklyn."*. There is one fact synset and its corresponding triples:

$f_1$ *("M. J."; "was born in"; "Brooklyn")*
*("M. J."; "was born"; "in Brooklyn")*

In the first triple, the preposition *"in"* is in the relation, while in the second it is in the object. The annotator should allow for such variations, because OIE systems should not be penalized for placing such words in different slots.

### A.4.3 Optional Tokens

If possible, the annotator should label as *optional* all tokens that can be omitted in an extraction without damaging its semantics. Such tokens include determiners (e.g., *a, the, an*), honorifics (e.g., *[Prof.] Michael Jordan*) or certain quantities (e.g., *[some] major projects*. The optional tokens are marked with square brackets [ ].

In what follows, we show examples of considered optional token(s).

**Determiners.** Unless a determiner is a part of a named entity (e.g., *"The Times"*), it is considered as optional. For instance, the following triples are considered to be semantically equivalent:

- *("Michael Jordan"; "took"; "the ball")*
- *("Michael Jordan"; "took"; "ball")*

The annotator, therefore, should annotate *("Michael Jordan"; "took"; "[the] ball")*, where the optional token is in square brackets.

**Titles.** Titles of people are considered optional; e.g., *("[Prof.] Michael Jordan"; "lives in"; "USA")*.

**Adjectives.** The annotator should label adjectives as optional if possible. For example, in the following triple, the adjective *outstanding* can be considered optional: *("Albert Einstein"; "is"; "[an] [outstanding] scientist")*. Note that the annotator should be careful not to label adjectives as optional if they are essential to the meaning of the triple. For instance, the adjective *cold* should not be labeled as optional in the triple *("Berlin Wall"; "is infamous symbol of"; "[the] cold war")*.

**Quantities.** Certain quantities that modify a noun phrase can be considered as optional; e.g.,

*("Mitsubishi"; "has control of"; "[some] major projects").*

**Words indicating some tenses.** The annotator can treat certain verbs that indicate tense as optional. For instance, the word *have* in *("FDA"; "[has] approved"; "Proleukin")* can be considered as optional, since both VPs *"have approved"* and *"approved"* contain the same core meaning.

**Verb phrases.** It is allowed for the annotator to mark verb phrases as optional if possible; e.g. *("John"; "[continues to] reside in"; "Berlin").*

**Passive voice.** When possible, if an extraction is in passive voice, the annotator should place its active voice equivalent into the appropriate fact synset. For instance, suppose we have the sentence *"The ball was kicked by John."*. Then, the fact synset should contain the following triples:

- *("[The] ball"; "was kicked by"; "John")*
- *("John"; "kicked"; "[The] ball")*

Note that the opposite direction is not allowed. If the sentence was *"John kicked the ball."*, then the annotator is not allowed to manually extract the triple *("[The] ball"; "was kicked by"; "John")* because such extraction contains words that are not originally found in the input sentence (*"was"* and *"by"*). These are so-called implicit extractions and we do not consider them (details in Sec. A.4.7)).

**Attribution clauses.** Extractions that indicate attribution of information should be placed in the same fact synset as the original information statement. For example, the core information of the sentence *"Conspiracy theorists say that Barack Obama was born in Kenya."* is that Obama was born in Kenya. As indicated by Mausam et al. (2012), it is important not to penalize OIE systems that would also extract the context about the attribution of such information. Therefore, the annotator should include the following triples into the same fact synset: *("Barack Obama"; "was born in"; "Kenya")* and *("Conspiracy theorists"; "say that"; "Barack Obama was born in Kenya").*

#### A.4.4 Incomplete Clauses

The annotator should not manually extract incomplete clauses, i.e., triples such that they lack crucial piece of information. Suppose there is the input sentence *"He was honored by the river being named after him"*. The following triple should not be manually extracted: *("He"; "was honored by"; "[the] river")*, but the following triples should be: *("He"; "was honored by [the] river being named after"; "him")* and *("[the] river"; "being named after"; "him").*

#### A.4.5 Overly Complex Extractions

The annotators should not manually extract overly specific triples, such that their arguments are complex clauses. For instance, for the input sentence *"Vaccinations against other viral diseases followed, including the successful rabies vaccination by Louis Pasteur in 1886."*, the following triple should not be extracted: *("Vaccinations against other viral diseases"; "followed"; "including the successful rabies vaccination by Louis Pasteur in 1886")* because the object is a complex clause which does not describe a single concept precisely, but rather it is composed of several concepts.

#### A.4.6 Conjunctions

The annotator should not allow for conjunctive phrases to form an argument (i.e., subject or object). Such arguments should be placed into separate extractions (and in separate fact synsets). Consider the sentence *"Michael Jordan and Scottie Pippen played for Chicago Bulls."*. The annotator should manually extract the following triples:

- *("M. Jordan"; "played for"; "Chicago Bulls")*
- *("S. Pippen"; "played for"; "Chicago Bulls")*

The annotator should not, however, manually extract *("Michael Jordan and Scottie Pippen"; "played for"; "Chicago Bulls").*

#### A.4.7 Implicit Extractions

We focus on explicit extractions, which means that every word in the extracted triple must be present in the original input sentence. Therefore, implicit extractions—i.e., extractions that contain inferred information which is not found in the sentence explicitly—are not considered. One example implicit extraction is *("Michael Jordan"; "be"; "Prof.")* from the input sentence *"Prof. Michael Jordan lives in USA."*, where the triple infers that Michael Jordan is professor without being explicitly indicated in the sentence (i.e., the word *"be"* is not present in the input sentence, it is inferred).

### A.5 Annotation Guidelines (Chinese)

The annotator followed the same general principles as with the English annotation guidelines (Sec. A.4. Due to the difference of the languages, we slightly adapted the annotation guidelines for the Chinese language. In what follows, we list those differences.

### A.5.1 Articles

Chinese language does not contain articles (i.e., *"a", "an", "the")*. Therefore, in the manual translation of the sentences, there are no articles in the Chinese counterparts, which also results in labeling such words as optional (for English, see Sec. A.4.3).

### A.5.2 Prepositional Phrases within a Noun Phrase

Certain noun phrases with nested prepositional phrase cannot be translated directly into Chinese the same way as in English. For example, suppose we have the phrase *"Prime Minister of Australia"*. In Chinese, the literal translation of this phrase would be *"Australia's Prime Minister"*. For instance, in the English annotations the sentence *"He was the Prime Minister of Australia"* would have two fact synsets:

$f_1$ *("He"; "was [the] Pr. Min. of"; "Australia")*

$f_2$ *("He"; "was"; "[the] Pr. Min. [of Australia]")*

This is because the the fact synset $f_1$ relates the concepts *"he"* and *"Australia"* with the relation *"was [the] Prime Minister of"*, while the second fact synset relates the concepts *"he"* and *"Prime Minister [of Australia]"* with the relation *"was"*.

In Chinese language, however, the construction of $f_1$ would not be possible, because the phrase *"Prime Mininister of Australia"* cannot be separated into *"Prime Minister"* and *"Australia"*. Therefore, the golden annotation for this particular example in Chinese would be only one fact synset: *("He"; "was"; "[Australia's] Prime Minister")*, which is equivalent with $f_2$.

## A.6 Manual Labeling of OIE Triples

See Figure 11 for a screenshot from AnnIE's GUI, which shows the manual labeling process of OIE triples given an input sentence.

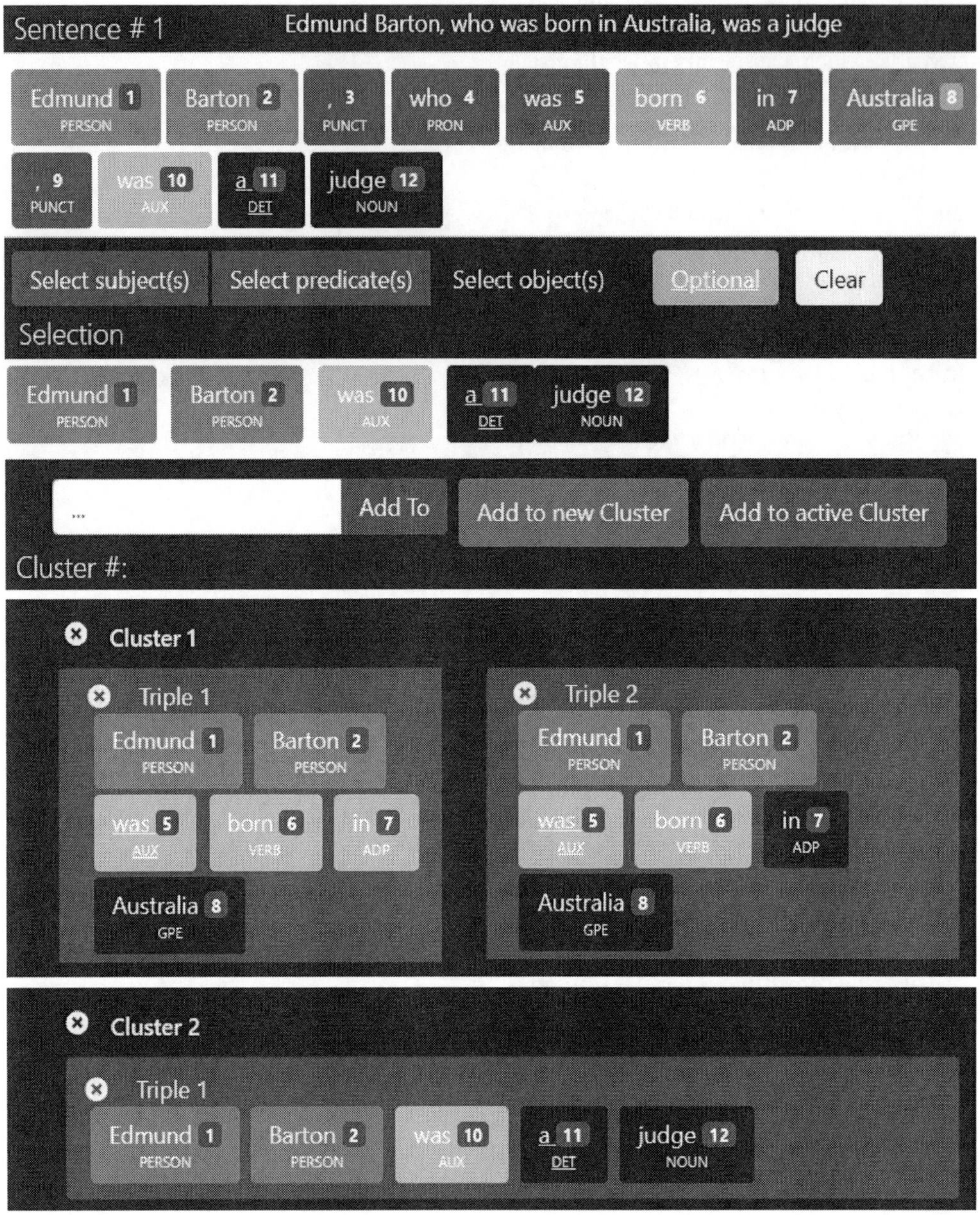


Figure 11: Manual labeling of OIE triples. The user selects tokens from the tokenized input sentence and places them into the correct slot: subject (green), predicate (yellow) or object (blue). Then, the user adds the extracted triple either to an active fact cluster (i.e., fact synset) or to a new one. The user can also select which tokens are optional by clicking the "Optional" button on an active token selection.

| **Input sentence (EN):** *He served as the first Prime Minister of Australia and became a founding justice of the High Court of Australia .* | | | |
|---|---|---|---|
| $f_1$ | *("He";* | *"served as";* | *"[the] [first] Prime Minister [of Australia]")* |
| | *("He";* | *"served";* | *"as [the] [first] Prime Min. [of Australia]")* |
| $f_2$ | *("He";* | *"served as [the] [first] Prime Min. of";* | *"Australia")* |
| | *("He";* | *"served as [the] [first] Prime Min.";* | *"of Australia")* |
| $f_3$ | *("He";* | *"became";* | *"[a] [founding] justice")* |
| | *("He";* | *"became";* | *"[a] [found.] just. of [the] High Court [of Aus.])"* |
| $f_4$ | *("He";* | *"became [a] [founding] justice of";* | *"[the] High Court [of Australia]")* |
| | *("He";* | *"became [a] [founding] justice";* | *"of [the] High Court [of Australia]")* |
| $f_5$ | *("He";* | *"bec. [a] [found.] just. of [the] H. C. of";* | *"Australia")* |
| | *("He";* | *"bec. [a] [found.] just. of [the] H. C.";* | *"of Australia")* |
| **Input sentence (DE):** *Er diente als erster Premierminister von Australien und wurde Gründungsrichter des obersten Gerichts von Australien.* | | | |
| $f_1$ | *("Er";* | *"diente als";* | *"[erster] Premierminister [von Australien]")* |
| | *("Er";* | *"diente";* | *"als [erster] Premierminister [von Australien]")* |
| $f_2$ | *("Er";* | *"diente als [erster] Premiermin. von";* | *"Australien")* |
| | *("Er";* | *"diente als [erster] Premierminister";* | *"von Australien")* |
| $f_3$ | *("Er";* | *"wurde";* | *"Gründungs. [des obersten Gerichts] [von Aus.]")* |
| $f_4$ | *("Er";* | *"wurde Gründungsrichter";* | *"[des] obersten Gerichts [von Australien]")* |
| $f_5$ | *("Er";* | *"wurde Gründungs. [des] oberst. Ger.";* | *"von Australien")* |
| | *("Er";* | *"wurde Gründungs. ... Gerichts von";* | *"Australien")* |
| **Input sentence (GL):** *Serviu como primeiro primeiro ministro de Australia e converteuse nun xuíz fundador do Tribunal Superior de Xustiza de Australia.* | | | |
| $f_1$ | *( /* | *"Serviu";* | *"como [primeiro] primeiro ministro [de Aus.]")* |
| | *( /* | *"Serviu como";* | *"[primeiro] primeiro ministro [de Aus.]")* |
| $f_2$ | *( /* | *"Serviu como prim. primeiro ministro";* | *"de Australia")* |
| | *( /* | *"Serviu como prim. primeiro ministro";* | *"Australia")* |
| $f_3$ | *( /* | *"converteuse";* | *"nun xuíz [fund.] do T. Sup. de Xus. [de Aus.]")* |
| | *( /* | *"converteuse nun";* | *"xuíz [fund.] do Trib. Sup. de Xus. [de Aus.]")* |
| $f_4$ | *( /* | *"converteuse nun xuíz [fundador] do";* | *"Tribunal Superior de Xustiza [de Australia]")* |
| $f_5$ | *( /* | *"con. nun xuíz [fund.] do T. S. de X. de";* | *"Australia")* |
| | *( /* | *"con. nun xuíz [fund.] do T. S. de X.";* | *"de Australia")* |

Figure 12: Example sentence with five *fact synsets* ($f_1$–$f_5$) in several languages: English (EN), German (DE) and Galician (Galician). Square brackets ([]) are a shorthand notation for multiple extractions: triples both with and without the expression(s) in the brackets are considered correct. For continuation of this figure, see Figure 13, whereas the same input sentence and its corresponding OIE annotations are written in Chinese (ZH), Japanese (JA) and Arabic (AR).

| | | | |
|---|---|---|---|
| **Input sentence (ZH):** *他曾担任澳大利亚第一任总理，并成为澳大利亚高等法院的创始法官。* | | | |
| $f_1$ | (“他”; | “[曾] 担任”; | “[澳大利亚] [第一任] 总理”) |
| $f_2$ | (“他”; | “成为”; | “[澳大利亚高等法院的] [创始] 法官”) |
| **Input sentence (JA):** *彼はオーストラリアの初代首相を務め、オーストラリア高等裁判所の創設裁判官になりました。* | | | |
| $f_1$ | (“彼[は]”;<br>(“彼[は]”; | “務め”;<br>“を 務め”; | “[オーストラリア] [の] [初代] 首相 を”)<br>“[オーストラリア] [の] [初代] 首相”) |
| $f_2$ | (“彼[は]”;<br>(“彼[は]”; | “の 初代 首相[を] 務め”;<br>“初代 首相[を] 務め ”; | “オーストラリア”)<br>“オーストラリア の”) |
| $f_3$ | (“彼[は]”;<br>(“彼[は]”; | “なり[まし] [た]”;<br>”なり[まし] [た]”; | “[創設] 裁判 官 に” )<br>”[オーストラリア] 高等 裁判 所 の [創設] 裁判 官 に“) |
| $f_4$ | (“彼[は]”;<br>(“彼[は]”; | “の [創設] [裁判] 官[に] なり まし た“;<br>“[創設] [裁判] 官[に] なり まし た“; | “[オーストラリア] 高等 裁判 所“)<br>“[オーストラリア] 高等 裁判 所 の“) |
| $f_5$ | (“彼 は”; | “高等 裁判 所 の [創設] 裁判 官[に] なり [まし] [た]“ | “オーストラリア“) |
| **Input sentence (AR):** أستراليا في العليا للمحكمة مؤسسًا قاضيًا وأصبح لأستراليا وزراء رئيس أول منصب شغل هو . | | | |
| $f_1$ | (”هو”; | ”غل”; | ”[لأستراليا] وزراء رئيس [أول منصب]”) |
| $f_2$ | (”هو”; | ”وزراء رئيس [أول منصب] غل”; | “أستراليا”) |
| $f_3$ | (”هو”;<br>(”هو”; | ”أصبح”<br>” أصبح” | ”[أستراليا في] العليا للمحكمة [مؤسسًا] اضيًا”)<br>”[مؤسسًا] اضيًا”) |
| $f_4$ | (”هو”; | ”[مؤسسًا] قاضيًا وأصبح” | ”[أستراليا في] العليا لمحكمة”) |
| $f_5$ | (”هو”; | ”للمحكمة [مؤسسًا] قاضيًا أصبح العليا”; | “[في] أستراليا“) |

Figure 13: Example sentence and its corresponding OIE annotations in Chinese (ZH), Japanese (JA) and Arabic (AR). This figure is continuation of Figure 12.

# AdapterHub Playground: Simple and Flexible Few-Shot Learning with Adapters

**Tilman Beck[1], Bela Bohlender[1], Christina Viehmann[2], Vincent Hane[1], Yanik Adamson[1], Jaber Khuri[1], Jonas Brossmann[1], Jonas Pfeiffer[1], Iryna Gurevych[1]**

[1]Ubiquitous Knowledge Processing Lab (UKP Lab)
Department of Computer Science
Technical University of Darmstadt
[2]Institut für Publizistik
Johannes Gutenberg-University Mainz

## Abstract

The open-access dissemination of pretrained language models through online repositories has led to a democratization of state-of-the-art natural language processing (NLP) research. This also allows people outside of NLP to use such models and adapt them to specific use-cases. However, a certain amount of technical proficiency is still required which is an entry barrier for users who want to apply these models to a certain task but lack the necessary knowledge or resources. In this work, we aim to overcome this gap by providing a tool which allows researchers to leverage pretrained models without writing a single line of code. Built upon the parameter-efficient adapter modules for transfer learning, our AdapterHub Playground provides an intuitive interface, allowing the usage of adapters for prediction, training and analysis of textual data for a variety of NLP tasks. We present the tool's architecture and demonstrate its advantages with prototypical use-cases, where we show that predictive performance can easily be increased in a few-shot learning scenario. Finally, we evaluate its usability in a user study. We provide the code and a live interface[1].

## 1 Introduction

The success of transformer-based pretrained language models (Devlin et al., 2019; Liu et al., 2019) was quickly followed by their dissemination, gaining popularity through open-access Python libraries like Huggingface (Wolf et al., 2020), AdapterHub (Pfeiffer et al., 2020a) or SBERT (Reimers and Gurevych, 2019). Researchers and practitioners with a background in computer science are able to download models and fine tune them to their needs. They can then upload their fine-tuned model and contribute to an open-access community of state-of-the-art (SotA) language models for various tasks and in different languages.

This has significantly contributed to the democratization of access to the latest NLP research as the individual implementation process has been simplified through the provision of easy-to-use and actively managed code packages. However, one still needs a certain level of technical proficiency to access these repositories, train models, and predict on new data. This is a limiting factor for researchers in disciplines who could benefit from applying SotA NLP models in their field, but lack the technical ability. Furthermore, there is growing interest for text classification models in interdisciplinary research (van Atteveldt et al., 2021; Boumans and Trilling, 2016), although often the methods are not SotA in NLP.

In this work, we hope to bridge this gap by providing an application which makes the power of pretrained language models available without writing a single line of code. Inspired by the recent progress on parameter-efficient transfer learning (Rebuffi et al., 2017; Houlsby et al., 2019), our application is based on adapters which introduce small and learnable task-specific layers into a pretrained language model. During training, only the newly introduced weights are updated, while the pre-trained parameters are frozen. Adapters have been successfully applied in machine translation Bapna and Firat (2019); Philip et al. (2020), cross-lingual transfer (Pfeiffer et al., 2020b, 2021b; Üstün et al., 2020; Vidoni et al., 2020), community QA (Rücklé et al., 2020), task composition for transfer learning (Stickland and Murray, 2019; Pfeiffer et al., 2021a; Lauscher et al., 2020; Wang et al., 2021) and text generation (Ribeiro et al., 2021). Adapters are additionally computationally more efficient (Rücklé et al., 2021a) and more robust to train (He et al., 2021; Han et al., 2021). In our work, we build our application on top of the AdapterHub (Pfeiffer et al., 2020a) library which stores task-specific adapters with a large variety of architectures and offers upload functionalities

[1]https://adapter-hub.github.io/playground



*Proceedings of the 60th Annual Meeting of the Association for Computational Linguistics System Demonstrations*, pages 61 - 75
May 22-27, 2022 

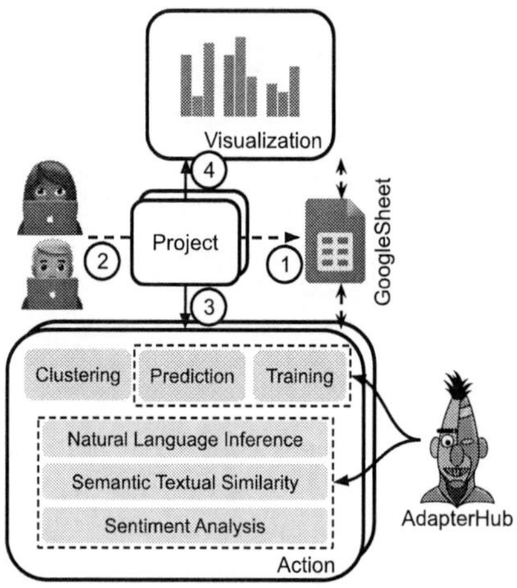


Figure 1: Diagram of the AdapterHub Playground workflow. ① Users upload their text data to GoogleSheets and ② link it to a new project. ③ In each project, users can create multiple actions by selecting a specific action type `Training`, `Prediction`, `Clustering`. For the `Training` and `Prediction` action types, the user needs to define the desired downstream task (e.g. `Sentiment Analysis`). Information about available pretrained adapters for the specified task are dynamically retrieved from AdapterHub. ④ After generating predictions, the user can visualize the results within the project.

for community-developed adapter weights. We leverage this library to allow no-code access to pretrained adapters for a many text classification tasks using dynamic code generation. Finally, our application enables the analysis of multi-dimensional annotations to further investigate model performance.

Our application supports both NLP and interdisciplinary researchers who want to evaluate the transferability of existing pretrained adapters to their specific domains and use cases. We intend this application for both zero-shot as well as few-shot scenarios where a user annotates a small number of data points and monitors model improvements. This is especially interesting for *intermediate* task training (Phang et al., 2018) where models trained on a compatible task are utilized and fine-tuned on the target task.

Some efforts are being made to abstract away engineering requirements to use SotA NLP (Akbik et al., 2019), but their usage still requires certain technical skills. Existing no-code (or AutoML) applications like Akkio[2], Lobe[3], or Teachable Machines[4] allow users to upload data, annotate it using self-defined labels, and train a model for prediction. Most approaches focus on vision tasks and follow commercial goals. To the best of our knowledge, we are the first to provide a non-commercial, no-code application for text classification. Our application is transparent (i.e. details about usable pretrained adapters are traceable), and extendable via the community-supported AdapterHub library. Finally, we enable execution on third party computational servers for users without access to the required GPU hardware for efficient training and prediction (Rücklé et al., 2021b), while also providing the necessary scripts to setup a self-hosted computing instance, mitigating technical dependencies.

Our contributions are: **1)** The AdapterHub Playground application which enables no-code inference and training by utilizing pretrained adapters; **2)** Prototypical showcase scenarios from social sciences using our application for few-shot learning; **3)** An elaborate user study that analyzes the usability of our proposed application.

## 2 AdapterHub Playground

The AdapterHub Playground is a lightweight web application offering no-code usage of pretrained adapters from the AdapterHub library. A user interface accompanied by dynamic code generation allows the utilization of adapters for inference and training of text classification tasks on novel data. Below, we describe the application workflow[5], provide details on the specific functionalities and highlight the technical architecture.

### 2.1 Workflow

The workflow of the AdapterHub Playground is depicted in Figure 1. First, a user creates a GoogleSheet[6] and uploads the input data for the desired classification task. If applicable, additional metadata, for example, annotations or timestamps, can be added. Next, a new project can be created and linked to the data via the GoogleSheet sharing functionality. Within a project, the user can define an *action*, resembling a computational unit (e.g. training an adapter). Upon submission of a new action, the input text data is downloaded and the specified computation is performed. The user is

[2] `https://www.akkio.com/`

[3] `https://lobe.ai/`

[4] `https://tinyurl.com/teachablemachines`

[5] We provide information about user requirements in the Appendix A.

[6] `https://docs.google.com/spreadsheets/`

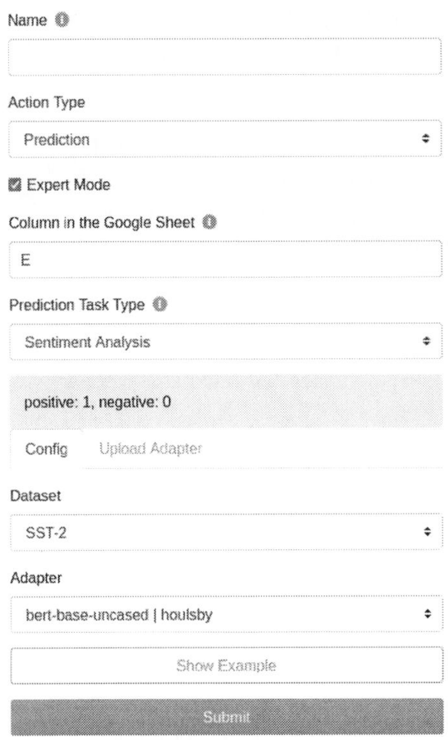


Figure 2: Screenshot of the action creation dialogue. A user has to provide a name for the action, the action type (here `Prediction`), the column in GoogleSheet where results are written to and the downstream task (here `Sentiment Analysis`). In the expert mode, the user has additional options for the pretrained adapter, i.e. the dataset which was used for pretraining and the specific architecture. The available options are dynamically retrieved from AdapterHub. Alternatively a self-provided adapter can be uploaded.

informed visually about the status of the execution in the application. After finishing the computation, the results are written directly into the GoogleSheet by the system and evaluation details are provided in the action interface. By default the system supports accuracy and macro-F1 evaluation metrics. To aid users in estimating model performance we additionally provide the results for random and majority prediction.

A user can create multiple projects, and within each project, multiple actions can be triggered using the same input data.[7] Finally, within a project a user can explore the predictions on the data using different visualization methods.

[7]This allows direct comparison among multiple adapters.

### 2.2 Actions

Our application focuses on three main *actions*, namely `Prediction`, `Training` and `Clustering`. For each action, the respective code is dynamically generated by merging static code snippets with parameters defined by the user (e.g. the specific adapter architecture). In the following we describe the procedure of each action.

**Prediction.** Pretrained task-specific adapters can be utilized for predictions on proprietary data. The user creates a new action in the project detail page and selects as action type `Prediction`, defines the column of the GoogleSheet in which the predictions should be written, and selects the respective downstream task which is dynamically retrieved from the AdapterHub.[8] Execution triggers the backend program to load the specified adapter and data, and produce task-specific labels for the data. A screenshot of the action creation dialogue is provided in Figure 2.

**Training.** To allow for continual training of adapters on labeled data, the user creates a new action of type `Training`. When executed, the backend process loads the specified adapter, downloads both data and target labels, and starts the training procedure. Once training is completed, the user can download the fine-tuned adapters as a zipped file. This makes fine-tuned adapter weights available for another `Prediction` action.

The choice of hyperparameters can have substantial influence on task performance but evaluating these effects is out of scope for this work. Defaults are set based on the literature (Pfeiffer et al., 2021a), however, if necessary, the user can modify training hyperparameters through various dropdown fields. This allows to compare multiple adapters trained with different hyperparameters.

**Clustering.** Discovering recurrent patterns in text data is a common procedure in various research disciplines. To allow for deeper text analysis, we additionally provide the `Clustering` action which enables users to apply clustering algorithms on the data based on their textual similarity. We provide K-Means and hierarchical clustering (Pedregosa et al., 2011) as algorithm choices and support Tf-Idf and SBERT embeddings (Reimers and Gurevych, 2019) as text representations.

[8]We currently focus on (pairwise) text classification tasks.

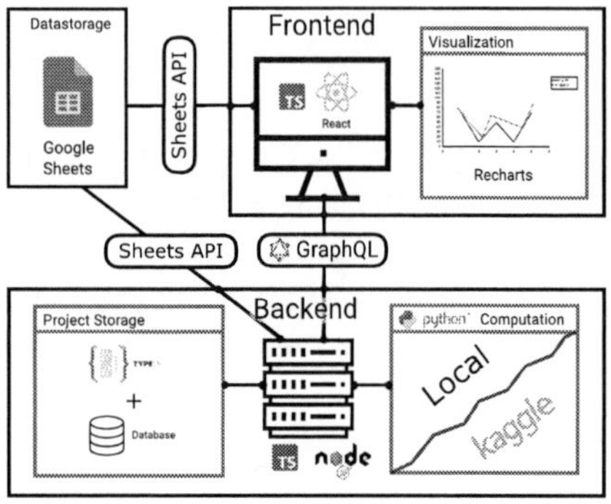


Figure 3: The AdapterHub Playground architecture

### 2.3 Architecture

The architecture of the AdapterHub Playground (Figure 3) is designed to be easy to setup and requires a minimal set of dependencies. The tool is based on three main components; `Frontend`, `Backend` and `Data Storage`. A user interacts with the frontend and triggers various actions as described in §2.2. The backend receives instructions via the frontend and manages the execution on the computational resource. Our application additionally hosts a local database for user and project management.

We chose GoogleSheet as text data storage component due to its similarity to established easy-to-use spreadsheet applications. It supports a variety of import and export mechanisms which simplify the data management process, especially for non-technical users. GoogleSheet also reduces storage requirements on the local computational resource, keeping the application lightweight and manageable. Finally, the Sheets API[9] provides a programmatic interface for communication. Although this requires users to use a Google account, we argue the advantages compensate for this restriction.

Below, we describe the technical details of the implementation for the specific components.

**Frontend.** The frontend provides the visual interface for management (i.e. creation, editing, deletion) of projects and their respective actions. After login with an authentication token[10], a webpage lists all user projects. By selecting a project, a corresponding details page allows actions to be managed (see §2.2) and visualizations to be created using project-specific data storage.

The frontend is implemented using the React[11] framework and is written in TypeScript[12]. The frontend design is based on Bootstrap[13]. Communication with the backend is realized via the GraphQL query language. The data is retrieved using the Sheets API and can be visualized via Recharts[14] which offers seamless integration of the D3[15] visualization library within the React framework.

**Backend.** The backend organizes the storage of application-relevant objects (i.e. users, projects, tasks) and manages both dynamic code generation and execution. User credentials, projects, and tasks are stored in a SQL database. When an action is executed in the frontend, the backend server loads the task-specific code template and dynamically integrates parameter information provided for the individual task. Depending on the choice of the computational node, the generated Python script is scheduled for execution either locally or on a Kaggle compute node via the KaggleAPI[16].

The backend is implemented using Node.js[17] and TypeScript. For application-relevant data, any TypeORM[18]-supported database (e.g. MySQL, PostgreSQL, etc.) can be used. Communication with data storage is realized via Sheets API.

## 3 Few-shot scenario

Several prominent tasks in NLP such as sentiment analysis (Socher et al., 2013; Rosenthal et al., 2017), stance detection (Mohammad et al., 2016; Schiller et al., 2021) or identifying semantically similar texts (Cer et al., 2017; Agirre et al., 2012) are of great interest in social science research (Boumans and Trilling, 2016; Beck et al., 2021; van Atteveldt and Peng, 2021). We therefore replicated two scenarios, namely sentiment analysis and semantic textual similarity.

We envision a situation where a user has collected textual data (e.g. sentence-level) for a given task and wishes to perform analysis using a text classification pipeline. A labeled test set to evaluate the performance of the classifier, and further training data is available.

[9] `https://tinyurl.com/SheetsAPI`

[10] Depending on the chosen backend solution, this can be a JSON file provided by the system administrator of the backend server or the authentication token provided by Kaggle.

[11] `https://reactjs.org/`

[12] `https://www.typescriptlang.org/`

[13] `https://getbootstrap.com/`

[14] `https://recharts.org`

[15] `https://d3js.org/`

[16] `https://www.kaggle.com/docs/api`

[17] `https://nodejs.org`

[18] `https://typeorm.io/`

### 3.1 Experiments

**Data.** For demonstration purposes, we recreated the above-mentioned scenario using existing datasets for both tasks. For sentiment analysis, we use the dataset by Barbieri et al. (2020). In particular, we retrieve text for the Twitter Sentiment Analysis dataset which was originally used for the Semeval2017 Subtask A (Rosenthal et al., 2017). At time of writing, the AdapterHub provides mostly pretrained adapters for binary sentiment classification (*positive*, *negative*). Thus, we discarded all items labeled as *neutral* from the dataset and are left with 24,942 Tweets for training and 6,347 Tweets for testing.

For semantic textual similarity, we use the dataset by Lei et al. (2016) which is a set of pairwise community questions from the AskUbuntu[19] forum annotated for duplicates. Specifically, we use the question titles of the human-annotated development (4k) for training and the test instances (4k) for testing.

**Setup.** For binary sentiment classification, we use the AdapterHub to obtain three different adapters which were previously trained (Pfeiffer et al., 2021a) on English datasets from the movie review domain. The `IMDB` adapter was fine-tuned on the dataset by Maas et al. (2011), the `RT` adapter was trained on the Rotten Tomatoes Movie Reviews dataset by Pang and Lee (2005), and the `SST-2` adapter was trained using a binarized dataset provided by Socher et al. (2013).

For semantic textual similarity, we obtained the `MRPC` adapter trained on the paraphrase dataset by Dolan and Brockett (2005) and the `QQP` adapter trained on the Quora Duplicate Question dataset.[20]

The experiments were conducted using the AdapterHub Playground without writing any code. We experiment with different training dataset sizes, repeated three times with different subsets of the training data randomly selected for each run.[21]. We evaluated statistically significant differences ($p < 0.05$) between zero-shot and few-shot results of each adapter using a paired Bootstrap test (Efron and Tibshirani, 1994).

### 3.2 Results

The results for both tasks are shown in Table 1.

**Sentiment Analysis.** The overall best performance is achieved by the `SST-2` adapter, simultaneously the most robust performance in terms of the standard deviation across different runs and varying amounts of training data. This is most likely due to the substantially larger size of the initial training data (`SST-2`: 67k, `RT`: 8k, `IMDB`: 25k) for the adapter. Although, on average, for all adapters zero-shot performance could be outperformed using a minimum of 10 instances, the differences between individual runs vary largely and statistically significant improvements are only achieved using a larger number of training instances (e.g., at least N≥100 for `SST-2`). We find using a small number of annotated examples (N≤50) leads to worse performance compared to zero-shot performance (N=0) and to less robust results across runs with randomly sampled training data. Providing 1,000 training samples leads to significant improvements for adapters `IMDB` and `SST-2` but only providing the full dataset results in statistically significant improvements for all adapters.

**Semantic Textual Similarity.** The performance gap between both adapters is large, with a difference of 42.10 in the zero-shot setting, favoring `QQP`. The results for the `MRPC` adapter show no clear tendency to improve as the training data size grows, with performance peaking at 50 training instances. Most surprisingly, using 1,000 or all available training samples (4k) leads to a severe performance decrease. For the `QQP` adapter, performance variations are minimal and none of the few-shot experiment settings leads to a significant improvement over zero-shot performance.

**Summary.** Poth et al. (2021) investigated the effects of intermediate task fine-tuning in adapter settings. They showed that domain similarity, task type match and dataset size are good indicators for the identification of beneficial intermediate fine-tuning tasks. Our experiments confirm this finding although we cannot observe consistent improvement with larger training data size. Thus, more research on robust few-shot learning is necessary.

In contrast to relying on off-the-shelf tools for automated content analysis, our application enables direct evaluation of both zero-shot and few-shot performance of existing pretrained adapters. This is especially helpful for assessment of the applicability of such models for interdisciplinary research (Grimmer and Stewart, 2013) but can also be used to test robustness with varying hyperparameter configurations.

[19] `https://askubuntu.com/`

[20] `https://tinyurl.com/quora-qp`

[21] See Appendix B for experimental details.

| Adapter | 0 | 5 | 10 | 20 | 50 | 100 | 1,000 | N |
|---|---|---|---|---|---|---|---|---|
| IMDB | 71.99 | 65.40 ±2.08 | **72.25** ±14.78 | 67.51 ±11.25 | 71.37 ±4.93 | 81.87 ±2.49 | 84.10 ±5.34 | 88.36 |
| RT | 76.24 | 72.33 ±0.97 | **76.76** ±10.08 | 67.38 ±10.09 | 67.44 ±5.57 | 76.88 ±4.22 | 82.64 ±6.01 | 90.50 |
| SST-2 | 84.61 | 84.53 ±0.15 | **86.23** ±2.91 | 84.22 ±0.53 | 82.33 ±2.41 | 83.54 ±0.61 | 88.19 ±2.08 | 92.04 |
| MRPC | 31.18 | **31.64** ±5.37 | 29.22 ±0.08 | 28.46 ±1.30 | 38.57 ±3.66 | 36.66 ±8.54 | 28.31 ±3.18 | 26.23 |
| QQP | 73.28 | 73.10 ±0.16 | 73.19 ±0.06 | 72.79 ±0.44 | 71.08 ±1.17 | 69.60 ±0.48 | 73.01 ±0.30 | **73.68** |

Table 1: Few-shot performance of various pretrained adapters from AdapterHub using increasing size of training data. Underlined scores are significantly ($p < .05$) better than their zero-shot counterpart. Bold scores resemble experiments with minimum training data required for outperforming zero-shot performance of respective adapter. All numbers are accuracy scores. N is for using all available training data.

## 4 Usability Study

AdapterHub Playground is designed to be simple to use, requiring minimal training effort and technical knowledge. While we followed these principles throughout the conception and implementation of the application, we also evaluated the usability with users from our target group. Therefore, we followed the approach by Hultman et al. (2018) and let study participants conduct a series of tasks which were designed to reflect a use-case scenario as described in §3. Afterwards, we used a questionnaire to capture their experiences.

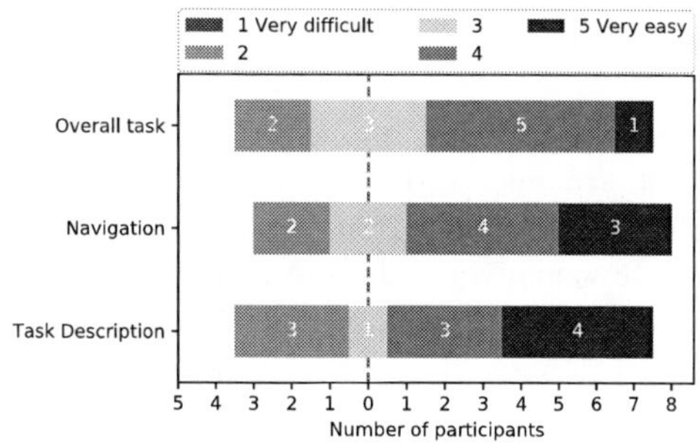


Figure 4: Participants' estimation of difficulty.

**Participants.** We recruited study participants (N=11) from the communication science field, the majority of whom were (post)graduate-level researchers at a university (two Professors, two Post-Docs, six PhDs, one B.Sc.). Our data suggests that the participants have limited or no understanding of the technical computer science concepts but can envision themselves using the AdapterHub Playground (for details see Appendix D). Thus, our participants belong to one of the target groups we aim to aid with this application.

**Procedure.** The participants were provided a textual description of several tasks to be completed.[22] Users were asked to complete a `Training` and `Prediction` action in a sentiment analysis scenario. We provided both labeled test data and unlabeled training data again using the dataset by (Barbieri et al., 2020).[23] After completing the tasks, we asked the participants to complete a questionnaire targeting their experience with the tool.

**Results** The participants were asked to assess the difficulties they faced on a five-point Likert scale, specifically, their experience with the overall task, the navigation of the application, and the difficulty of the task description (see Figure 4). The majority of participants found the task and the navigation of the application to be simple.

Three participants found the task description difficult to understand. We note here that the task description did not explain each individual navigation step in the application. This was designed on purpose - both to reduce the reading volume of the task description and to evaluate the accessibility of each feature of the application.

We further asked the participants about the difficulty of each individual task they had to solve, i.e. prediction, annotation, and training, on a five-point Likert scale ranging *very difficult* (1) to *very easy* (5). Participants had the least trouble with the prediction action (91% voted either category 5 or 4; none voted category 1 or 2). Despite the training action being technically similar to the prediction action, participants perceived it as more difficult with only 64% selecting easier categories (4 and 5) and 27% of the participants being undecided (category 3). This is most likely due to some participants having issues finding the downloadable zip file which required opening the action detail page after training (we received this information as feedback in a free-answer form).

[22] We provide the full task description in the Appendix D.

[23] Our focus is to evaluate the usability of the AdapterHub Playground application. Therefore, we did not require the participants to import the data on their own but rather provided them links to Google Docs containing the imported data.

## 5 Conclusion and Future Work

Open-access dissemination of SotA NLP models has accelerated their use and popularity, yet the required technical proficiency to apply them remains a limiting factor for their democratisation. To mitigate this, we introduced the AdapterHub Playground application which provides an easy-to-use web interface for no-code access to light-weight adapters for text classification tasks. Our system is built on-top of the open-source AdapterHub library and uses a dynamic code generation approach. We demonstrated the features of the application using two exemplary use-case scenarios and evaluated its usability in a user study with researchers from communication sciences. In addition to providing execution on third-party hardware, we also enabled a self-hosted computational instance.

As future work, we plan to extend the application with dynamic user control over all hyperparameter specifications in the expert mode. To support users in efficient sampling of profitable training instances, we plan to investigate the integration of active learning methods (Yuan et al., 2020). A running instance of our tool can be found under `https://adapter-hub.github.io/playground.` and the open-source code[24] under `https://github.com/Adapter-Hub/playground`.

## Broader Impact Statement

**Intended Use** Our proposed application can be used in several ways and by different audiences. First of all, it allows evaluating the performance of already existing fine-tuned adapters for various prominent text classification tasks on hold-out data, possibly from another domain. Further, one can provide annotated data for any of the supported tasks and continue training the corresponding adapter. Training procedures can be repeated using different hyperparameters to investigate the effect of those on the prediction performance. This makes our application interesting for both our target group, i.e. researchers outside of NLP using text classification methods, as well as NLP researchers interested in comparing various adapter models without setting up the required codebase to do so.

**Possible Risks** Primarily, the goal of our application is to lower the technical entry barrier for users interested in using state-of-the-art text classification models. These users usually also lack the expertise to evaluate all aspects of the language understanding capabilities of such a model, as compared to researchers from within the NLP domain. Rightfully, one can argue that publishing such an application increases the opportunities to develop more *bad* black box models, caused by limited evaluation and missing expertise. This can lead to severe misjudgements if conclusions are drawn based on predictions of such a model.

While we cannot eliminate this risk, we would like to raise some points which, in our opinion, put it into perspective with regard to the benefits of having such an application.

From a broader perspective, the AdapterHub Playground contributes to the democratization of access to the latest NLP research by simplifying the process of applying language model adapters for training and prediction. This is especially helpful for interdisciplinary research where the applied text classification tools often rely on outdated methods (Stoll et al., 2020) or off-the-shelf tools (Sen et al., 2020). As a consequence, details about the model architecture, training procedure or out-of-domain performance are mostly omitted. While this does not imply low performance on hold-out data per se, it limits the possibilities for model evaluation and demands a certain level of trust from the end user. In many cases, adapting the model to the target domain is not possible or requires some technical proficiency. In addition, these models are often trained once-and-for-all while our framework allows for an interactive approach to evaluate model performance and offers the rich variety of pretrained adapters being available from the community-driven AdapterHub.

Further, we argue that advancements in NLP research should be made available to the researchers most profiting from them as soon as possible - not only for the sake of accelerating research outside of NLP but also to enable a feedback loop informing NLP researchers about the shortcomings of such models. While the generalization capabilities of state-of-the-art language models are subject to increased scrutiny within NLP (Sanchez et al., 2018; Gururangan et al., 2020; Tu et al., 2020), the datasets and tasks to test them often originate from within the same community, thereby introducing a selection bias (Ramponi and Plank, 2020). By enabling interdisciplinary researchers to eval-

[24] Licensed under Apache License 2.0.

uate NLP models without the technical barriers involved, we are able to gain more insights about the robustness and out-of-domain performance of these models. Our application is a first step into this direction.

## Acknowledgements

This work has been supported by the German Research Foundation (DFG) as part of the Research Training Group KRITIS No. GRK 2222/2 and by the LOEWE initiative (Hesse, Germany) within the emergenCITY center. We want to thank the participants who volunteered to participate in our user study as well as Luke Bates and Ilia Kuznetsov for their valuable feedback.

## References

Eneko Agirre, Daniel Cer, Mona Diab, and Aitor Gonzalez-Agirre. 2012. SemEval-2012 task 6: A pilot on semantic textual similarity. In **SEM 2012: The First Joint Conference on Lexical and Computational Semantics – Volume 1: Proceedings of the main conference and the shared task, and Volume 2: Proceedings of the Sixth International Workshop on Semantic Evaluation (SemEval 2012)*, pages 385–393, Montréal, Canada. Association for Computational Linguistics.

Alan Akbik, Tanja Bergmann, Duncan Blythe, Kashif Rasul, Stefan Schweter, and Roland Vollgraf. 2019. FLAIR: An easy-to-use framework for state-of-the-art NLP. In *Proceedings of the 2019 Conference of the North American Chapter of the Association for Computational Linguistics (Demonstrations)*, pages 54–59, Minneapolis, Minnesota. Association for Computational Linguistics.

Ankur Bapna and Orhan Firat. 2019. Simple, scalable adaptation for neural machine translation. In *Proceedings of the 2019 Conference on Empirical Methods in Natural Language Processing and the 9th International Joint Conference on Natural Language Processing (EMNLP-IJCNLP)*, pages 1538–1548, Hong Kong, China. Association for Computational Linguistics.

Francesco Barbieri, Jose Camacho-Collados, Luis Espinosa Anke, and Leonardo Neves. 2020. TweetEval: Unified benchmark and comparative evaluation for tweet classification. In *Findings of the Association for Computational Linguistics: EMNLP 2020*, pages 1644–1650, Online. Association for Computational Linguistics.

Tilman Beck, Ji-Ung Lee, Christina Viehmann, Marcus Maurer, Oliver Quiring, and Iryna Gurevych. 2021. Investigating label suggestions for opinion mining in German covid-19 social media. In *Proceedings of the 59th Annual Meeting of the Association for Computational Linguistics and the 11th International Joint Conference on Natural Language Processing (Volume 1: Long Papers)*, pages 1–13, Online. Association for Computational Linguistics.

Jelle W Boumans and Damian Trilling. 2016. Taking stock of the toolkit: An overview of relevant automated content analysis approaches and techniques for digital journalism scholars. *Digital journalism*, 4(1):8–23.

Daniel Cer, Mona Diab, Eneko Agirre, Iñigo Lopez-Gazpio, and Lucia Specia. 2017. SemEval-2017 task 1: Semantic textual similarity multilingual and crosslingual focused evaluation. In *Proceedings of the 11th International Workshop on Semantic Evaluation (SemEval-2017)*, pages 1–14, Vancouver, Canada. Association for Computational Linguistics.

Jacob Devlin, Ming-Wei Chang, Kenton Lee, and Kristina Toutanova. 2019. BERT: Pre-training of deep bidirectional transformers for language understanding. In *Proceedings of the 2019 Conference of the North American Chapter of the Association for Computational Linguistics: Human Language Technologies, Volume 1 (Long and Short Papers)*, pages 4171–4186, Minneapolis, Minnesota. Association for Computational Linguistics.

William B. Dolan and Chris Brockett. 2005. Automatically constructing a corpus of sentential paraphrases. In *Proceedings of the Third International Workshop on Paraphrasing (IWP2005)*.

Bradley Efron and Robert J Tibshirani. 1994. *An introduction to the bootstrap*. CRC press.

Justin Grimmer and Brandon M Stewart. 2013. Text as data: The promise and pitfalls of automatic content analysis methods for political texts. *Political analysis*, 21(3):267–297.

Suchin Gururangan, Ana Marasović, Swabha Swayamdipta, Kyle Lo, Iz Beltagy, Doug Downey, and Noah A. Smith. 2020. Don't stop pretraining: Adapt language models to domains and tasks. In *Proceedings of the 58th Annual Meeting of the Association for Computational Linguistics*, pages 8342–8360, Online. Association for Computational Linguistics.

Wenjuan Han, Bo Pang, and Ying Nian Wu. 2021. Robust transfer learning with pretrained language models through adapters. In *Proceedings of the 59th Annual Meeting of the Association for Computational Linguistics and the 11th International Joint Conference on Natural Language Processing (Volume 2: Short Papers)*, pages 854–861, Online. Association for Computational Linguistics.

Ruidan He, Linlin Liu, Hai Ye, Qingyu Tan, Bosheng Ding, Liying Cheng, Jiawei Low, Lidong Bing, and Luo Si. 2021. On the effectiveness of adapter-based tuning for pretrained language model adaptation. In *Proceedings of the 59th Annual Meeting of the Association for Computational Linguistics and the 11th*

International Joint Conference on Natural Language Processing (Volume 1: Long Papers)*, pages 2208–2222, Online. Association for Computational Linguistics.

Neil Houlsby, Andrei Giurgiu, Stanislaw Jastrzebski, Bruna Morrone, Quentin De Laroussilhe, Andrea Gesmundo, Mona Attariyan, and Sylvain Gelly. 2019. Parameter-efficient transfer learning for NLP. In *International Conference on Machine Learning*, pages 2790–2799. PMLR.

Gretchen Hultman, Reed McEwan, Serguei Pakhomov, Elizabeth Lindemann, Steven Skube, and Genevieve B Melton. 2018. Usability Evaluation of an Unstructured Clinical Document Query Tool for Researchers. *AMIA Summits on Translational Science Proceedings*, 2018:84.

Anne Lauscher, Olga Majewska, Leonardo F. R. Ribeiro, Iryna Gurevych, Nikolai Rozanov, and Goran Glavaš. 2020. Common sense or world knowledge? investigating adapter-based knowledge injection into pretrained transformers. In *Proceedings of Deep Learning Inside Out (DeeLIO): The First Workshop on Knowledge Extraction and Integration for Deep Learning Architectures*, pages 43–49, Online. Association for Computational Linguistics.

Tao Lei, Hrishikesh Joshi, Regina Barzilay, Tommi Jaakkola, Kateryna Tymoshenko, Alessandro Moschitti, and Lluís Màrquez. 2016. Semi-supervised question retrieval with gated convolutions. In *Proceedings of the 2016 Conference of the North American Chapter of the Association for Computational Linguistics: Human Language Technologies*, pages 1279–1289, San Diego, California. Association for Computational Linguistics.

Yinhan Liu, Myle Ott, Naman Goyal, Jingfei Du, Mandar Joshi, Danqi Chen, Omer Levy, Mike Lewis, Luke Zettlemoyer, and Veselin Stoyanov. 2019. Roberta: A robustly optimized bert pretraining approach. *arXiv preprint*.

Andrew L. Maas, Raymond E. Daly, Peter T. Pham, Dan Huang, Andrew Y. Ng, and Christopher Potts. 2011. Learning word vectors for sentiment analysis. In *Proceedings of the 49th Annual Meeting of the Association for Computational Linguistics: Human Language Technologies*, pages 142–150, Portland, Oregon, USA. Association for Computational Linguistics.

Saif Mohammad, Svetlana Kiritchenko, Parinaz Sobhani, Xiaodan Zhu, and Colin Cherry. 2016. A dataset for detecting stance in tweets. In *Proceedings of the Tenth International Conference on Language Resources and Evaluation (LREC'16)*, pages 3945–3952, Portorož, Slovenia. European Language Resources Association (ELRA).

Bo Pang and Lillian Lee. 2005. Seeing stars: Exploiting class relationships for sentiment categorization with respect to rating scales. In *Proceedings of the 43rd Annual Meeting of the Association for Computational Linguistics (ACL'05)*, pages 115–124, Ann Arbor, Michigan. Association for Computational Linguistics.

F. Pedregosa, G. Varoquaux, A. Gramfort, V. Michel, B. Thirion, O. Grisel, M. Blondel, P. Prettenhofer, R. Weiss, V. Dubourg, J. Vanderplas, A. Passos, D. Cournapeau, M. Brucher, M. Perrot, and E. Duchesnay. 2011. Scikit-learn: Machine learning in Python. *Journal of Machine Learning Research*, 12:2825–2830.

Jonas Pfeiffer, Aishwarya Kamath, Andreas Rücklé, Kyunghyun Cho, and Iryna Gurevych. 2021a. AdapterFusion: Non-destructive task composition for transfer learning. In *Proceedings of the 16th Conference of the European Chapter of the Association for Computational Linguistics: Main Volume*, pages 487–503, Online. Association for Computational Linguistics.

Jonas Pfeiffer, Andreas Rücklé, Clifton Poth, Aishwarya Kamath, Ivan Vulić, Sebastian Ruder, Kyunghyun Cho, and Iryna Gurevych. 2020a. AdapterHub: A framework for adapting transformers. In *Proceedings of the 2020 Conference on Empirical Methods in Natural Language Processing: System Demonstrations*, pages 46–54, Online. Association for Computational Linguistics.

Jonas Pfeiffer, Ivan Vulić, Iryna Gurevych, and Sebastian Ruder. 2020b. MAD-X: An Adapter-Based Framework for Multi-Task Cross-Lingual Transfer. In *Proceedings of the 2020 Conference on Empirical Methods in Natural Language Processing (EMNLP)*, pages 7654–7673, Online. Association for Computational Linguistics.

Jonas Pfeiffer, Ivan Vulić, Iryna Gurevych, and Sebastian Ruder. 2021b. UNKs everywhere: Adapting multilingual language models to new scripts. In *Proceedings of the 2021 Conference on Empirical Methods in Natural Language Processing*, pages 10186–10203, Online and Punta Cana, Dominican Republic. Association for Computational Linguistics.

Jason Phang, Thibault Févry, and Samuel R Bowman. 2018. Sentence encoders on stilts: Supplementary training on intermediate labeled-data tasks. *arXiv preprint*.

Jerin Philip, Alexandre Berard, Matthias Gallé, and Laurent Besacier. 2020. Monolingual adapters for zero-shot neural machine translation. In *Proceedings of the 2020 Conference on Empirical Methods in Natural Language Processing (EMNLP)*, pages 4465–4470, Online. Association for Computational Linguistics.

Clifton Poth, Jonas Pfeiffer, Andreas Rücklé, and Iryna Gurevych. 2021. What to pre-train on? Efficient intermediate task selection. In *Proceedings of the 2021 Conference on Empirical Methods in Natural Language Processing*, pages 10585–10605, Online and Punta Cana, Dominican Republic. Association for Computational Linguistics.

Yada Pruksachatkun, Jason Phang, Haokun Liu, Phu Mon Htut, Xiaoyi Zhang, Richard Yuanzhe Pang, Clara Vania, Katharina Kann, and Samuel R. Bowman. 2020. Intermediate-task transfer learning with pretrained language models: When and why does it work? In *Proceedings of the 58th Annual Meeting of the Association for Computational Linguistics*, pages 5231–5247, Online. Association for Computational Linguistics.

Alan Ramponi and Barbara Plank. 2020. Neural unsupervised domain adaptation in NLP—A survey. In *Proceedings of the 28th International Conference on Computational Linguistics*, pages 6838–6855, Barcelona, Spain (Online). International Committee on Computational Linguistics.

Sylvestre-Alvise Rebuffi, Hakan Bilen, and Andrea Vedaldi. 2017. Learning multiple visual domains with residual adapters. In *Advances in Neural Information Processing Systems*, volume 30. Curran Associates, Inc.

Nils Reimers and Iryna Gurevych. 2019. Sentence-BERT: Sentence embeddings using Siamese BERT-networks. In *Proceedings of the 2019 Conference on Empirical Methods in Natural Language Processing and the 9th International Joint Conference on Natural Language Processing (EMNLP-IJCNLP)*, pages 3982–3992, Hong Kong, China. Association for Computational Linguistics.

Leonardo F. R. Ribeiro, Yue Zhang, and Iryna Gurevych. 2021. Structural adapters in pretrained language models for AMR-to-Text generation. In *Proceedings of the 2021 Conference on Empirical Methods in Natural Language Processing*, pages 4269–4282, Online and Punta Cana, Dominican Republic. Association for Computational Linguistics.

Sara Rosenthal, Noura Farra, and Preslav Nakov. 2017. SemEval-2017 task 4: Sentiment analysis in Twitter. In *Proceedings of the 11th International Workshop on Semantic Evaluation (SemEval-2017)*, pages 502–518, Vancouver, Canada. Association for Computational Linguistics.

Andreas Rücklé, Gregor Geigle, Max Glockner, Tilman Beck, Jonas Pfeiffer, Nils Reimers, and Iryna Gurevych. 2021a. AdapterDrop: On the efficiency of adapters in transformers. In *Proceedings of the 2021 Conference on Empirical Methods in Natural Language Processing*, pages 7930–7946, Online and Punta Cana, Dominican Republic. Association for Computational Linguistics.

Andreas Rücklé, Gregor Geigle, Max Glockner, Tilman Beck, Jonas Pfeiffer, Nils Reimers, and Iryna Gurevych. 2021b. AdapterDrop: On the efficiency of adapters in transformers. In *Proceedings of the 2021 Conference on Empirical Methods in Natural Language Processing*, pages 7930–7946, Online and Punta Cana, Dominican Republic. Association for Computational Linguistics.

Andreas Rücklé, Jonas Pfeiffer, and Iryna Gurevych. 2020. MultiCQA: Zero-shot transfer of self-supervised text matching models on a massive scale. In *Proceedings of the 2020 Conference on Empirical Methods in Natural Language Processing (EMNLP)*, pages 2471–2486, Online. Association for Computational Linguistics.

Ivan Sanchez, Jeff Mitchell, and Sebastian Riedel. 2018. Behavior analysis of NLI models: Uncovering the influence of three factors on robustness. In *Proceedings of the 2018 Conference of the North American Chapter of the Association for Computational Linguistics: Human Language Technologies, Volume 1 (Long Papers)*, pages 1975–1985, New Orleans, Louisiana. Association for Computational Linguistics.

Benjamin Schiller, Johannes Daxenberger, and Iryna Gurevych. 2021. Stance detection benchmark: How robust is your stance detection? *KI-Künstliche Intelligenz*, pages 1–13.

Indira Sen, Fabian Flöck, and Claudia Wagner. 2020. On the reliability and validity of detecting approval of political actors in tweets. In *Proceedings of the 2020 Conference on Empirical Methods in Natural Language Processing (EMNLP)*, pages 1413–1426, Online. Association for Computational Linguistics.

Richard Socher, Alex Perelygin, Jean Wu, Jason Chuang, Christopher D. Manning, Andrew Ng, and Christopher Potts. 2013. Recursive deep models for semantic compositionality over a sentiment treebank. In *Proceedings of the 2013 Conference on Empirical Methods in Natural Language Processing*, pages 1631–1642, Seattle, Washington, USA. Association for Computational Linguistics.

Asa Cooper Stickland and Iain Murray. 2019. BERT and PALs: Projected Attention Layers for Efficient Adaptation in Multi-Task Learning. In *Proceedings of the 36th International Conference on Machine Learning*, volume 97 of *Proceedings of Machine Learning Research*, pages 5986–5995. PMLR.

Anke Stoll, Marc Ziegele, and Oliver Quiring. 2020. Detecting impoliteness and incivility in online discussions: Classification approaches for german user comments. *Computational Communication Research*, 2(1):109–134.

Lifu Tu, Garima Lalwani, Spandana Gella, and He He. 2020. An empirical study on robustness to spurious correlations using pre-trained language models. *Transactions of the Association for Computational Linguistics*, 8:621–633.

Ahmet Üstün, Arianna Bisazza, Gosse Bouma, and Gertjan van Noord. 2020. UDapter: Language adaptation for truly Universal Dependency parsing. In *Proceedings of the 2020 Conference on Empirical Methods in Natural Language Processing (EMNLP)*, pages

2302–2315, Online. Association for Computational Linguistics.

Wouter van Atteveldt and Tai-Quan Peng. 2021. *Computational Methods for Communication Science*. Routledge.

Wouter van Atteveldt, Mariken ACG van der Velden, and Mark Boukes. 2021. The Validity of Sentiment Analysis: Comparing Manual Annotation, Crowd-Coding, Dictionary Approaches, and Machine Learning Algorithms. *Communication Methods and Measures*, pages 1–20.

Marko Vidoni, Ivan Vulić, and Goran Glavaš. 2020. Orthogonal language and task adapters in zero-shot cross-lingual transfer. *arXiv preprint arXiv:2012.06460*.

Ruize Wang, Duyu Tang, Nan Duan, Zhongyu Wei, Xuanjing Huang, Jianshu Ji, Guihong Cao, Daxin Jiang, and Ming Zhou. 2021. K-Adapter: Infusing Knowledge into Pre-Trained Models with Adapters. In *Findings of the Association for Computational Linguistics: ACL-IJCNLP 2021*, pages 1405–1418, Online. Association for Computational Linguistics.

Thomas Wolf, Lysandre Debut, Victor Sanh, Julien Chaumond, Clement Delangue, Anthony Moi, Pierric Cistac, Tim Rault, Remi Louf, Morgan Funtowicz, Joe Davison, Sam Shleifer, Patrick von Platen, Clara Ma, Yacine Jernite, Julien Plu, Canwen Xu, Teven Le Scao, Sylvain Gugger, Mariama Drame, Quentin Lhoest, and Alexander Rush. 2020. Transformers: State-of-the-art natural language processing. In *Proceedings of the 2020 Conference on Empirical Methods in Natural Language Processing: System Demonstrations*, pages 38–45, Online. Association for Computational Linguistics.

Michelle Yuan, Hsuan-Tien Lin, and Jordan Boyd-Graber. 2020. Cold-start active learning through self-supervised language modeling. In *Proceedings of the 2020 Conference on Empirical Methods in Natural Language Processing (EMNLP)*, pages 7935–7948, Online. Association for Computational Linguistics.

## A Frequently Asked Questions

**What are the requirements to use the AdapterHub Playground?** The most basic usage requirement is an up-to-date modern web browser[25]. To use the application without setting up your own computing instance, one needs to create a Kaggle account and download the API Token for login. We provide information on setting up a local compute instance at `https://github.com/Adapter-Hub/playground`. As we use GoogleSheet as data hosting platform, the user needs an active Google account.

If used for prediction, textual target data must be uploaded to a GoogleSheet and linked with a project within the application. For training, each text must be additionally labelled according to the target task's label matching schema. While we also provide information about each supported task on a separate page in the application, we expect the user to have a basic understanding of the procedure of the targeted task (e.g. *Sentiment Analysis* is about predicting the sentiment tone of a given text).

**How is a user able to identify label mismatch?** For each supported task, we provide the necessary label matching information within the dialogue to create a new Action (e.g. in Figure 2). If the user-provided labels in the Google data sheet do not match the selected task or adapter architecture, an error message will be provided giving information about the indices of the mismatched data points.

**How could a new user determine the task for their data?** In general, this application is intended for users who know what type of predictions (i.e. the task) they want to apply on their data. We provide support for a subset of (pairwise) text classification tasks from AdapterHub.ml with the goal to cover the most prominent ones used in interdisciplinary research. However, we also provide basic information about each supported task on a separate page in the application.

**What if my task is not supported in the AdapterHub Playground?** In general, we can only provide support for the classification tasks which are covered on Adapterhub. We have selected a subset of tasks which we deem to be of interest in interdisciplinary research (e.g. computational social science). Integration of new tasks is possible by extending the application which requires some technical background in coding and web development. If you are a researcher and lack the technical proficiency to do so, we encourage you to get into contact with us to find out if and how we can integrate your task.

[25]We tested the application using Desktop Firefox and Desktop Chrome.

**Which pretrained adapter should be used?** This is still an open research question and we refer to the literature for more details (Phang et al., 2018; Pruksachatkun et al., 2020; Poth et al., 2021). However, there are some heuristics which can be followed. Regarding adapters, it has been shown that domain similarity (e.g. training and test data are both from Twitter) and training dataset size (the more the better) can be indicators for good transfer performance (Poth et al., 2021).

**How should hyperparameters be set?** Hyperparameter optimization for machine learning is a research field of its own and there is no one-size-fits-all solution to this. Especially for users without experience in tuning ML models identifying reasonable hyperparameter values might seem rather arbitrary.

Currently, we support tuning the learning rate and the number of epochs. In general, if the learning rate is high the training may not converge or even diverge. The changes in the weights might become too big such that the optimizer will not find optimal values. A low learning rate is good, but the model will take more iterations to converge because steps towards the minimum of the loss function are tiny. In practice it is good strategy to test different (high and low) learning rates to identify their effect on the model performance.

One epoch describes a full cycle through the entire training dataset. A single epoch can sometimes be enough to improve performance significantly and training text classification adapters longer than for 10 epochs rarely provides substantial improvements. We recommend testing different numbers of epochs (between 2 and 5) to evaluate if longer training is beneficial for the task at hand.

## B Training Details

We did not perform any hyperparameter optimization for our experiments and used the default settings in the AdapterHub Playground application. We adopted a learning rate of 1e-4 from related work (Pfeiffer et al., 2020a) and trained each adapter for three epochs. In Table 2 we provide the

| Adapter | Task | Pretrained Language Model Identifier | Architecture |
|---|---|---|---|
| IMDB | Sentiment Analysis | distilbert-base-uncased | Pfeiffer |
| RT | Sentiment Analysis | distilbert-base-uncased | Pfeiffer |
| SST-2 | Sentiment Analysis | bert-base-uncased | Houlsby |
| MRPC | Semantic Textual Similarity | bert-base-uncased | Houlsby |
| QQP | Semantic Textual Similarity | bert-base-uncased | Houlsby |

Table 2: Adapter architecture details for each specific task.

respective adapter architectures which were used for each specific adapter.

## C Extensibility

Extending the AdapterHub Playground with a new text classification task requires adaptations to both the frontend and backend.

The repository supports a deployment workflow which will update a configuration file with all relevant information from the AdapterHub. This enables that all tasks and their corresponding pretrained adapters (with a classification head) are potentially available within the AdapterHub Playground. The tasks for these adapters are filtered based on a predefined set of tasks which should be available to users of the application. Within the application, the filter list needs to be adapted such that the new task is not filtered during startup of the application. Additionally, the task name and its description need to be added to the frontend code as well as the label mapping information. In the backend we need to add the label mapping and the list of supported tasks such that the evaluation computation is correct.

We provide the technical details within the code repository at `https://github.com/Adapter-Hub/playground`.

## D Usability Study

### D.1 Participants

As can be seen in Figure 5, most participants have only a basic understanding of the technical concepts related to machine learning or natural language processing. However, it is likely they have experience with annotating data. We further asked them if they can envision using the AdapterHub Playground application in their research. Slightly more than half gave a positive answer (54%) and the rest were undecided; no participant claimed they would never use our application.

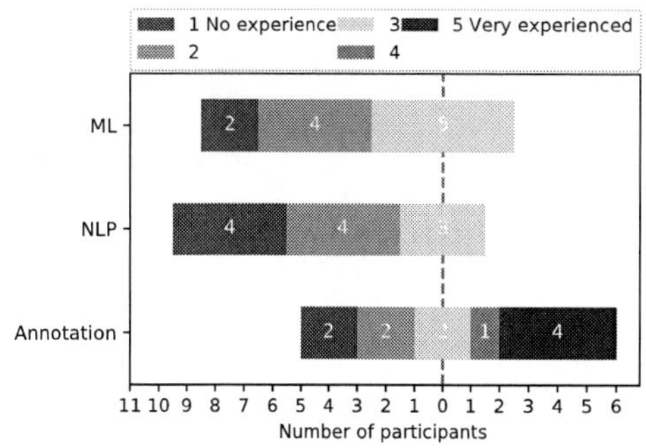


Figure 5: Participants' experience with underlying technical concepts.

Thus, we conclude that our participants belong to our target group.

### D.2 Instructions

We provide the instructions for the usability study in Figure 6.

# User study for the AdapterHub:Playground application

## Study Details

This study is conducted for research purposes by the Ubiquitous Knowledge Processing (UKP) Lab of the Technical University of Darmstadt. Your participation is completely voluntary and you are allowed to cancel at any time. The goal of this study is to evaluate the usability of the Adapterhub:Playground application. The whole study will take approximately 25 minutes. During the study you will be asked to complete certain tasks in the application and fill out a questionnaire afterwards.

Contact Person:
Tilman Beck, M.Sc.
S2|02 B104
Hochschulstraße 10
64289 Darmstadt
beck@ukp.informatik.tu-darmstadt.de
+49 6151 16-25294

## Preliminary

To take part in this study, you need to register on Kaggle.com. After registering, click on your profile picture in the top right corner and choose `Account` in the menu. Then, scroll down to the `Phone verification` field and provide your mobile number for verification (**Important**: without verification we can't use Kaggle as computational resource). Next, scroll to the `API` field, click `Create new API token` and download the `kaggle.json` file to your computer. You are now ready to take part in the study.

## Data:

User ID: <user-ID>
D1: <url-to-data-D1>
D2: <url-to-data-D2>

## Task Description

### Prediction

You are provided a set of Social Media posts and are asked to analyze the sentiment in these texts. The AdapterHub:Playground offers you a tool which allows you to make use of machine learning models to analyze these Social Media posts. They are specialized on a variety of natural language processing tasks such as sentiment analysis.
Please evaluate the performance of those models on the first set of Social Media posts we provided (see D1 above). This Googledocs file does not only contain the Social Media posts, but also their respective sentiment label (`positive` or `negative`). Log into the AdapterHub:Playground tool, create a new project and insert the above mentioned link to the Googlesheet. Enter your new project by clicking on your chosen name in the list, then start a new task with type `Prediction` for `Sentiment Analysis`. In the expert mode you can specify additional details about the model selection like the dataset the model was trained on (e.g. `SST-2`) or the model architecture (e.g. `bert-base-uncased | pfeiffer`). Upon starting the task, the tool will write its predictions directly into the provided Googledocs in the column you provided. This may take some minutes. Once the task is finished, you can investigate the performance of the task using the measures `Accuracy` and `F1`.

### Training

To further improve the performance of the models, the AdapterHub:Playground tool allows you to train existing models with annotated data. Therefore, you are provided a second set of Social Media posts without labels (see D2 above).
Please, visit this Googledocs and start with providing labels (type `positive` or `negative`) in the column `annotation` for the corresponding texts in the first column (`input1`). We recommend annotating at least 10-15 texts, but you are free to annotate more texts.
After you finish your annotation, return to the AdaterHub:Playground tool and create a new project. To do so, please insert the link to the Googledocs (D2 above) where you have made annotations on your own (please be aware, the link is different to the first Googledocs).
Now, create a new `Training task` for `Sentiment Analysis`. Choose the same model selection details as for the previous prediction task and start the training task by submitting. Once the training is finished, download the trained model (`trained_adapter.zip`) to your computer. Congratulations, you have just trained your own sentiment analysis model! Now, please evaluate if your own model achieves better performance than the off-the-shelf model from AdapterHub:Playground. Please, use it to create predictions on your initial set of Social Media posts. Therefore, repeat the process of the first part of this study (Prediction), i.e. create a new project, start a new task with type `Prediction` for `Sentiment Analysis`. However, this time make use of the `Upload Adapter` function in the expert mode and upload the previously downloaded file (`trained_adapter.zip`). After completion of the task, investigate the performance measures again.

Now, please answer the questions in this questionnaire:
<url-to-questionnaire>

Thank you very much for your participation!

Figure 6: Instructions for the participants of the user study.

# QiuNiu: A Chinese Lyrics Generation System with Passage-Level Input

**Le Zhang, Rongsheng Zhang*, Xiaoxi Mao, Yongzhu Chang**
Fuxi AI Lab, NetEase Inc., Hangzhou, China
{zhangle1, zhangrongsheng}@corp.netease.com

## Abstract

Lyrics generation has been a very popular application of natural language generation. Previous works mainly focused on generating lyrics based on a couple of attributes or keywords, rendering very limited control over the content of the lyrics. In this paper, we demonstrate the *QiuNiu*, a Chinese lyrics generation system which is conditioned on passage-level text rather than a few attributes or keywords. By using the passage-level text as input, the content of generated lyrics is expected to reflect the nuances of users' needs. The *QiuNiu* system supports various forms of passage-level input, such as short stories, essays, poetry. The training of it is conducted under the framework of unsupervised machine translation, due to the lack of aligned passage-level text-to-lyrics corpus. We initialize the parameters of *QiuNiu* with a custom pretrained Chinese GPT-2 model and adopt a two-step process to fine-tune the model for better alignment between passage-level text and lyrics. Additionally, a postprocess module is used to filter and rerank the generated lyrics to select the ones of highest quality. The demo video of the system is available at https://youtu.be/OCQNzahqWgM.

Figure 1: This figure depicts a typical creation pattern: the author firstly conceives a rough draft (in the left box) and then polishes it to the final work (in the right box).

## 1 Introduction

AI creation is an important application domain of Natural Language Generation (NLG), including story generation (Zhu et al., 2020; Alabdulkarim et al., 2021), poetry writing (Zhipeng et al., 2019; Liu et al., 2020; Yang et al., 2019), lyrics generation (Potash et al., 2015; Lee et al., 2019; Shen et al., 2019), etc,. Particularly, lyrics generation has always been a popular task of NLG since its intrusiveness and easy data availability. Previous works of lyrics generation (Castro and Attarian, 2018; Watanabe et al., 2018; Manjavacas et al., 2019; Fan et al., 2019; Li et al., 2020; Zhang et al., 2020) mainly focused on generating lyrics conditioned on specified keywords (e.g., *Flower*) or certain attributes such as the lyrics' text style (e.g., *Hip-hop*) and expected theme described by the lyrics (e.g., *Love*). However, these input only provide very limited control over the content of generated lyrics. Sometimes the generated lyrics may deviate far from the user's needs. To improve the usability of AI as a creation tool, we need to improve the controllability of the generated content.

We argue that adopting free form text as the input is an approach to having precise control over the content of generated lyrics. As seen in Figure 1, an author usually conceives a passage (shown in the left text box) in his/her mind that expresses his/her inner feelings and thoughts, and then uses a wealth of writing skills and rhetorical techniques to create the final work (shown in the right text box).

In this paper, we demonstrate *QiuNiu* (the eldest son of the dragon in ancient Chinese mythology, who loves music), a Chinese lyrics generation system conditioned on free form passage-level text. The *QiuNiu* system can receive various forms of passage-level user input, which may be in different

* Corresponding Author



*Proceedings of the 60th Annual Meeting of the Association for Computational Linguistics*
*System Demonstrations*, pages 76 - 82
May 22-27, 2022 ©2022 Association for Computational Linguistics

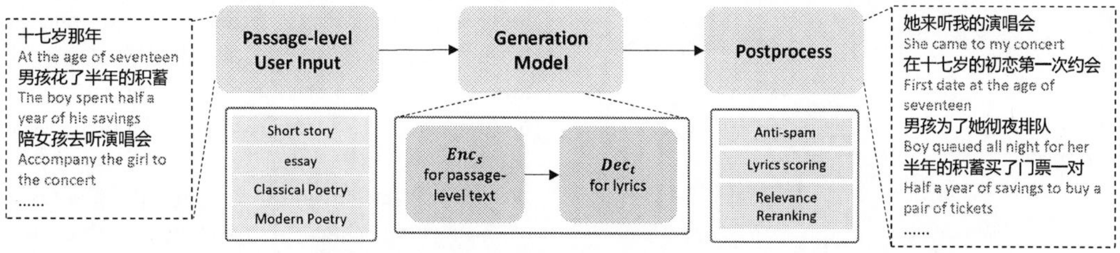


Figure 2: The architecture of *QiuNiu* system. The module of user input can receive various forms of passage-level text. And the generation model generates lyrics conditioned on the passage-level user input. Finally, a postprocess module is used to select the high-quality lyrics.

genres (e.g., short stories, essays, poetry), and eras (e.g., classical poetry, modern poetry). It is basically a text style transfer problem, which greatly suffers from the lack of aligned corpus. To construct the training data, we collected a passage-level corpus $\mathcal{D}_s$ from multiple sources and 300K different styles of lyrics corpus $\mathcal{D}_t$. Note that it is intractable to train a sequence-to-sequence (seq2seq) model from passage-level text to lyrics directly because the $\mathcal{D}_s$ and $\mathcal{D}_t$ are not aligned.

To address the issue, the *QiuNiu* system adopts the framework of unsupervised machine translation (UMT) (Lample et al., 2018; Yang et al., 2019). Specifically, The framework consists of an encoder $Enc_s$ and a decoder $Dec_s$ for the input side, an encoder $Enc_t$ and a decoder $Dec_t$ for lyrics side. The encoder $Enc_s$ (or $Enc_t$) encodes the passage-level input text (or lyrics) into a hidden representation and the decoder $Dec_s$ (or $Dec_t$) decodes it into lyrics (or passage-level text). The objective of the model training is to align the passage-level text and lyrics in the latent representation space.

To train the model, we first initialize the parameters with a custom Chinese GPT-2 (Radford et al., 2019) model, which is pretrained on around 30G Chinese books corpus collected online. Then we adopt a two-step process to finetune the model by jointly optimizing self-reconstruction loss, cross-reconstruction loss and alignment loss. After the training is finished, $Enc_s$ encodes the passage-level input and $Dec_t$ generates the candidate lyrics. Finally, a postprocess module is used to filter and rerank the generated lyrics to select the ones of highest quality. Human evaluation indicates the effectiveness of the framework.

The contributions of the *QiuNiu* system are summarized as follows:

1. The paper demonstrates the *QiuNiu* system, which can generate Chinese lyrics from various forms of passage-level text input for the first time.

2. To better align the passage-level text and lyrics, we propose a two-step process to finetune the UMT model of *QiuNiu*, which is initialized with the pretrained Chinese GPT-2 parameters. And a postprocess module is applied to select the high-quality lyrics by filtering and reranking the generated candidates.

3. The *QiuNiu* system and demo video are available at https://qiuniu.apps.danlu.netease.com/ and https://youtu.be/OCQNzahqWgM.

## 2 Architecture

The architecture of *QiuNiu* system is shown in Figure 2. It mainly consists of three modules: **Passage-level User Input**, **Generation Model** and **Postprocess**. Each module is described in detail below.

### 2.1 Passage-level User Input

The module receives passage-level inputs from the user, performs appropriate pre-processings and passes the results to the trained model to generate lyrics. A passage-level input here refers to a piece of text that can briefly depict the main idea that the lyrics is expected to convey. For the example in Figure 1, the author writes lyrics of lost love, which is based on the experiences of falling in love (e.g., "The boy spent half a year of his savings, accompany the girl to the concert.") and his own understanding of love (e.g., " Love comes and goes quickly, always leaves people in tears."). A passage-level text piece is much stronger than the keywords or attributes at depicting complex stories or nuanced feelings.

The *QiuNiu* system can support various forms of passage-level text inputs, such as short stories, essays, classical poetry, modern poetry. Though

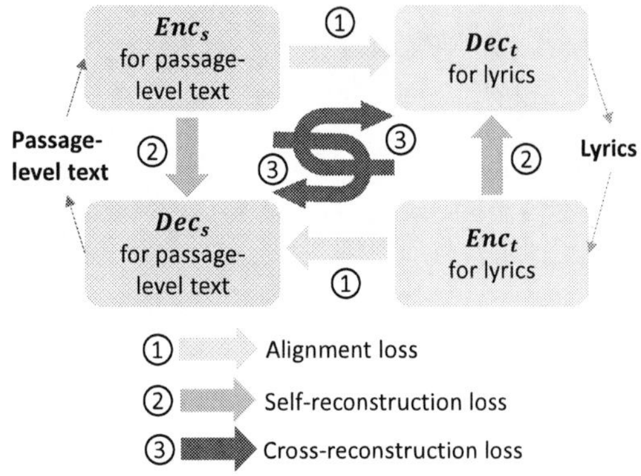


Figure 3: The framework of training the *QiuNiu* model. The framework is composed of two pairs of Encoder-Decoders, one pair for passage-level text and the other for lyrics. And the model is jointly optimized with the self-reconstruction loss, cross-reconstruction loss and alignment loss.

all these passage-level inputs have the same powerful semantic description capabilities, they may be different from each other in genres (e.g., story, poetry), and eras (e.g., classical text, modern text). In order to convert the input text into a form that can be processed by the generation model, preprocessings consists of conversion from traditional Chinese characters to simplified characters, spam filtering, error detection and correction, and conversion to token ids.

## 2.2 Generation Model

The generation model follows the Transformer-based sequence to sequence (seq2seq) framework (Vaswani et al., 2017), which consists of an Encoder for source text $Enc_s$ and a Decoder for target text $Dec_t$. In the inference phrase, it takes in passage-level user inputs and generates several candidate lyrics. As shown in Figure 2, $Enc_s$ encodes the passage-level text into latent representation and $Dec_t$ decodes the latent representation into lyrics. We will describe the details of training below.

### 2.2.1 Corpus

**Lyircs:** We collected 300K different styles of Chinese lyrics from Internet, including Pop, Hip-hop, Chinese Neo-traditional, etc. For the lyrics corpus, we filtered the abnormal characters, removed lyrics less than 100 in length, and de-duplicated. We denote the processed lyrics corpus as $\mathcal{D}_s$.

**Passage-level Text:** To support various forms of passage-level text input, we collected the passage-level corpus covering different genres and eras from many sources. Specifically, the corpus contains short stories or essays collected from social medias, such as Weibo Tree Hole[1], Douban Essay[2], Micro Novel[3]. We filtered out the noisy text and processed them into uniform format. Besides, we also collected refined literature from both classical and modern eras which are naturally the passage-level text, mainly including Chinese classical poetry (e.g., Han Fu, Tang poetry, Song Ci, Yuan Qu, etc.), Chinese modern poetry with different styles (e.g., Philosophy, Love, Child, etc.). Finally, we obtain a passage-level corpus of 600K that denoted as $\mathcal{D}_t$.

**Pseudo-aligned Dataset:** Note that the passage-level text $\mathcal{D}_t$ and the lyrics $\mathcal{D}_s$ are not aligned. To help model for alignment, we further constructed a pseudo-aligned dataset $\mathcal{D}_a$, respectively for classical and modern text. For classical text, we first counted the $n$-gram ($n = 1, 2$) tokens in classical Chinese poetry of $\mathcal{D}_s$. Then for lyrics of each Chinese Neo-traditional song which is most similar to Chinese classical text, we selected these $n$-gram tokens appeared in lyrics and combined them based on the format of classical Chinese poetry (e.g., Five-character Quatrain, a four-line poetry with five characters each line). These pseudo poetry were finally paired with corresponding Chinese Neo-traditional lyrics. For modern text, We constructed pseudo-aligned pairs with back translation. Specifically, for lyrics of each song, we used the API[4] to first translate it into English text and then the English text was translated into Chinese plain text. Finally, we selected several segments of the translated plain text and reordered them, which is regarded as the aligned text with original lyrics.

### 2.2.2 Framework of Model

Due to the lack of aligned corpus from passage-level text to lyrics, we could not train the encoder and decoder of seq2seq model directly. Therefore, our training model adopts the framework of unsupervised machine translation (UMT) (Lample et al., 2018; Yang et al., 2019). As illustrated in Figure 3, the framework is composed of two pairs of Encoder-Decoders, one pair $Enc_s$-$Dec_s$ for passage-level text and the other $Enc_t$-$Dec_t$ for lyrics. $Enc_s$ (or $Enc_t$) encodes passage-level text

[1] https://weibo.com/
[2] https://www.douban.com/
[3] https://www.567876.com/duanwen/weixiaoshuo/
[4] https://fanyi.youdao.com/

| Method | Fluency | Coherence | Relevance | Overall Quality |
|---|---|---|---|---|
| **Two-step Training** | **3.05** | **2.86** | 2.85 | **2.98** |
| **- step 1 (Reconstruction Loss only)** | 2.74 | 2.16 | 2.22 | 2.23 |
| **- step 2 (Alignment Loss only)** | 2.81 | 2.66 | **3.06** | 2.79 |

Table 1: Human evaluation results of Ablation.

(or lyrics) into latent representation, and $Dec_s$ (or $Dec_t$) decodes the latent representation into passage-level text (or lyrics). The training object is to align the passage-level text and lyrics in the latent representation space.

Now we introduce three kinds of losses in the training process as shown in Figure 3.

1) **Alignment Loss:** The loss tries to capture the distribution of lyrics in $Dec_t$ (or passage-level text in $Dec_s$) given the passage-level text in $Enc_s$ (or lyrics in $Enc_t$). It optimizes the model parameters by calculating the negative log likelihood (NLL) on pseudo-aligned dataset $\mathcal{D}_a$:

$$\begin{aligned}\mathcal{L}_a = &-\sum_{\mathcal{D}_a} \log P\left(y_i | Dec_t\left(Enc_s\left(x_i\right)\right)\right) \\ &-\sum_{\mathcal{D}_a} \log P\left(x_i | Dec_s\left(Enc_t\left(y_i\right)\right)\right)\end{aligned} \quad (1)$$

where $(x_i, y_i) \in \mathcal{D}_a$ represent the pseudo-aligned passage-level text and lyrics respectively.

2) **Self-reconstruction Loss:** The loss is to calculate the reconstructed distribution for passage-level text or lyrics itself. Specifically, the passage-level text (or lyrics) is encoded into latent representation by $Enc_s$ (or $Enc_t$) and then decoded by $Dec_s$ (or $Dec_t$). The NLL loss is computed as

$$\begin{aligned}\mathcal{L}_{sr} = &-\sum_{x_{si} \in \mathcal{D}_s} \log P\left(x_{si} | Dec_s\left(Enc_s\left(x_{si}\right)\right)\right) \\ &-\sum_{x_{ti} \in \mathcal{D}_t} \log P\left(x_{ti} | Dec_t\left(Enc_t\left(x_{ti}\right)\right)\right)\end{aligned} \quad (2)$$

3) **Cross-reconstruction loss:** Given a passage-level text (or lyrics), we first generate lyrics (or passage-level text) by $Enc_s$-$Dec_t$ (or $Enc_t$-$Dec_s$). Then the generated text is used to reconstruct the original input by $Enc_t$-$Dec_s$ (or $Enc_s$-$Dec_t$). It is formulated as

$$\begin{aligned}\mathcal{L}_{cr} = &-\sum_{x_{si} \in \mathcal{D}_s} \log P\left(x_{si} | Dec_s\left(Enc_t\left(y^g_{ti}\right)\right)\right) \\ &-\sum_{x_{ti} \in \mathcal{D}_t} \log P\left(x_{ti} | Dec_t\left(Enc_s\left(y^g_{si}\right)\right)\right)\end{aligned} \quad (3)$$

where $y^g_{ti}$ and $y^g_{si}$ are the intermediate generated lyrics or passage-level text.

### 2.2.3 Training

**Model Initialization:** To make the model easier to learn and generate more fluent text, we first initialize the parameters of both the two encoder-decoder pairs with a pretrained GPT-2 model (Radford et al., 2019). Note that the encoders in our system use the unidirectional self-attention to be consistent with the structure of GPT-2. The pretrained GPT-2 with total 210 million parameters has 16 layers, 1,024 hidden dimensions and 16 self-attention heads. The GPT-2 is pretrained on about 30G Chinese novels collected online, whose vocabulary size is 11,400 and context size is 512.

**Two-step Training:** Next we use a two-step training method to finetune the model. In the first step, we train the $Enc_s$-$Dec_t$ and $Enc_t$-$Dec_s$ on constructed pseudo-aligned corpus $\mathcal{D}_a$ with alignment loss $\mathcal{L}_a$ for several epochs. Through this step, we improve the ability of the alignment between encoder and decoder, which is a warm-up for training on unaligned corpus. In the second step, the model is trained on all the corpus ($\mathcal{D}_a$, $\mathcal{D}_s$ and $\mathcal{D}_t$) with jointly optimizing the weighted alignment loss $\mathcal{L}_a$, self-reconstruction loss $\mathcal{L}_{sr}$ and cross-reconstruction loss $\mathcal{L}_{cr}$. In this step, The corpus $\mathcal{D}_s$ of passage-level text and $\mathcal{D}_t$ of lyrics is aligned in the latent representation space (Lample et al., 2018). In general, the training loss can be formulated as

$$\mathcal{L} = \alpha_1 \mathcal{L}_a + \alpha_2 \mathcal{L}_{sr} + \alpha_3 \mathcal{L}_{cr} \quad (4)$$

where $\alpha_1 = 1, \alpha_2 = 0, \alpha_3 = 0$ for the first step and $\alpha_1 = 1, \alpha_2 = 1, \alpha_3 = 1$ for the second step.

## 2.3 Postprocess

After the model training is finished, we use $Enc_s$ and $Dec_t$ to generate lyrics with the passage-level inputs in the inference phrase. Then we postprocess the candidates as followed.

**Lyrics Scoring:** To select the lyrics with high quality, we trained a classifier to judge whether the

Figure 4: The interface of the user input. Users can write multiple forms of passage-level text as input. Several examples of input are provided for each type.

candidate lyrics are good and use its confidence as the lyrics score $Score_l$. We used the lyrics of popular and classic songs as positive examples and the lyrics of less played songs as negative samples. The model is based on pretrained Chinese Bert (Devlin et al., 2019) implemented by Transformers[5]. Experimental results show that our model prefers to give high scores to graceful and ornate lyrics, such as metaphorical sentences, rather than the verbose and plain ones.

**Relevance Reranking:** The metric denoted as $Score_r$ is to measure the relevance between the passage-level inputs and the generated lyrics. The $Score_r$ is computed based on the $n$-gram ($n = 1, 2, 3, 4$) overlapping between the passage-level input $\mathcal{S}$ and the generated lyrics $\mathcal{T}$, which is denoted as $\mathcal{O}_n$. We formulate the $Score_r$ as follows:

$$Score_r = \frac{\sum_{n=1}^{N} \mathcal{O}_n}{N\,|\mathcal{S}|}\ (N = 4) \tag{5}$$

where $|\mathcal{S}|$ is the length of passage-level input.

Finally, we rerank the lyrics filtered by an anti-spam process with the final score $Score_f$.

$$Score_f = Score_l + Score_r \tag{6}$$

## 3 Evaluation

### 3.1 Demonstration

In this section, we demonstrate how the *QiuNiu* system works. And mores details are described in the demo video.

The user input interface is shown in Figure 4. Users can choose one type of the passage-level text input, write passage-level text corresponding to the chosen type or try the provided examples as input. After that, click the button "*Generate!*".

Then we show some generated lyrics of different passage-level inputs, mainly including Chinese modern text and classical text.

**1) Modern Text:** The generated lyrics of two genres (short story, essay), as examples, are shown in the left and middle of Figure 5. For each genre, the *QiuNiu* system can perform well with content expansion and produce fluent and high-quality lyrics relevant to the inputs.

**2) Classical Text:** The *QiuNiu* system also supports Chinese classical poetry input. An example of Song Ci (a type of Chinese classical poetry) is shown in the right of Figure 5. Note that we can also receive other types of Chinese classical poetry, such as Tang poetry, Han Fu and so on. We will not show their generated results due to space limitation, but they are available at the url of *QiuNiu* https://qiuniu.apps.danlu.netease.com/.

### 3.2 Ablation

We conduct ablation study to evaluate our two-step training framework.

**Metrics:** We evaluate the generated lyrics from four perspectives: 1) *Fluency*: Is the lyric grammatically well formed, 2) *Coherence*: Is the lyric itself logical and consistent, 3) *Relevance*: Is the lyric relevant with the input, 4) *Overall quality*: Is the lyric a good lyric overall subjectively. Note *Overall quality* is not the average score of the others. All the metrics are scale from 1 to 5 while 5 is the best.

[5] https://github.com/huggingface/transformers

Figure 5: The examples of generated lyrics for different text inputs, including *short story*, *essay*, *classical poetry*.

**Test set:** We sampled 30 passage-level inputs for each of four genres (short story, essay, modern poetry and classical poetry), totally 120 samples.

**Baselines:** We compare our 1) *Two-step Training* method with 2) *Two-step Training - step 1* (use reconstruction loss only. Here we set $\alpha_1 = 0$ to remove the alignment loss) and 3) *Two-step Training - step 2* (use alignment loss only and can be considered as a seq2seq model with a small corpus).

We invited 3 evaluators to evaluate all the 120 generated lyrics generated independently. The results are shown in Table 1. All the scores are the means of 3*120 human evaluation results. *Two-step training* method gets around 0.2 promotion in perspectives of *Fluency*, *Coherence* and *Overall Quality*, which indicates the effectiveness. Reconstruction loss does make model acquire knowledge from more corpus and improve the fluency and coherence of the generated lyrics. The method *Two-step Training - step 2* achieve the best in *Relevance*. The supervised learning guarantees the correlation between the input and the generated lyrics while the unsupervised step slightly reduces the relevance. The method *Two-step Training - step 1* performs worst except in *Fluency*. This shows that the warm-up step is necessary for model to learn the connection between the input and lyrics.

## 4 Conclusion

In this paper, we demonstrate *QiuNiu*, a Chinese lyrics generation system conditioned on passage-level input. We support various forms of passage-level input, covering different genres and eras. The *QiuNiu* system adopts the framework of unsupervised machine translation due to the lack of aligned corpus from passage-level text to lyrics. Besides, the model of *QiuNiu* is initialized with the pre-trained Chinese GPT-2 parameters and finetuned in a two-step process to improve the alignment between the passage-level text and lyrics. Finally, a postprocess module is used to filter and rerank the generated lyrics to select the high-quality ones.

## Acknowledgements

This work is supported by the Key Research and Development Program of Zhejiang Province (No. 2022C01011).


## References


Amal Alabdulkarim, Siyan Li, and Xiangyu Peng. 2021. Automatic story generation: Challenges and attempts. *NAACL HLT 2021*, page 72.

Pablo Samuel Castro and Maria Attarian. 2018. Combining learned lyrical structures and vocabulary for improved lyric generation. *arXiv preprint arXiv:1811.04651*.

Jacob Devlin, Ming-Wei Chang, Kenton Lee, and Kristina Toutanova. 2019. Bert: Pre-training of deep bidirectional transformers for language understanding. In *NAACL-HLT (1)*.

Haoshen Fan, Jie Wang, Bojin Zhuang, Shaojun Wang, and Jing Xiao. 2019. A hierarchical attention based seq2seq model for chinese lyrics generation. In *Pacific Rim International Conference on Artificial Intelligence*, pages 279–288. Springer.

Guillaume Lample, Myle Ott, Alexis Conneau, Ludovic Denoyer, and Marc'Aurelio Ranzato. 2018. Phrase-based & neural unsupervised machine translation. In *Proceedings of the 2018 Conference on Empirical Methods in Natural Language Processing*, pages 5039–5049.

Hsin-Pei Lee, Jhih-Sheng Fang, and Wei-Yun Ma. 2019. iComposer: An automatic songwriting system for Chinese popular music. In *Proceedings of the 2019 Conference of the North American Chapter of the Association for Computational Linguistics (Demonstrations)*, pages 84–88, Minneapolis, Minnesota. Association for Computational Linguistics.

Piji Li, Haisong Zhang, Xiaojiang Liu, and Shuming Shi. 2020. Rigid formats controlled text generation. *arXiv preprint arXiv:2004.08022*.

Yusen Liu, Dayiheng Liu, and Jiancheng Lv. 2020. Deep poetry: A chinese classical poetry generation system. In *Proceedings of the AAAI Conference on Artificial Intelligence*, volume 34, pages 13626–13627.

Enrique Manjavacas, Mike Kestemont, and Folgert Karsdorp. 2019. Generation of hip-hop lyrics with hierarchical modeling and conditional templates. In *Proceedings of the 12th International Conference on Natural Language Generation*, pages 301–310.

Peter Potash, Alexey Romanov, and Anna Rumshisky. 2015. GhostWriter: Using an LSTM for automatic rap lyric generation. In *Proceedings of the 2015 Conference on Empirical Methods in Natural Language Processing*, pages 1919–1924, Lisbon, Portugal. Association for Computational Linguistics.

Alec Radford, Jeffrey Wu, Rewon Child, David Luan, Dario Amodei, and Ilya Sutskever. 2019. Language models are unsupervised multitask learners. *OpenAI Blog*, 1(8).

Liang-Hsin Shen, Pei-Lun Tai, Chao-Chung Wu, and Shou-De Lin. 2019. Controlling sequence-to-sequence models - a demonstration on neural-based acrostic generator. In *Proceedings of the 2019 Conference on Empirical Methods in Natural Language Processing and the 9th International Joint Conference on Natural Language Processing (EMNLP-IJCNLP): System Demonstrations*, pages 43–48, Hong Kong, China. Association for Computational Linguistics.

Ashish Vaswani, Noam Shazeer, Niki Parmar, Jakob Uszkoreit, Llion Jones, Aidan N Gomez, Łukasz Kaiser, and Illia Polosukhin. 2017. Attention is all you need. In *Advances in neural information processing systems*, pages 5998–6008.

Kento Watanabe, Yuichiroh Matsubayashi, Satoru Fukayama, Masataka Goto, Kentaro Inui, and Tomoyasu Nakano. 2018. A melody-conditioned lyrics language model. In *Proceedings of the 2018 Conference of the North American Chapter of the Association for Computational Linguistics: Human Language Technologies, Volume 1 (Long Papers)*, pages 163–172, New Orleans, Louisiana. Association for Computational Linguistics.

Zhichao Yang, Pengshan Cai, Yansong Feng, Fei Li, Weijiang Feng, Elena Suet-Ying Chiu, et al. 2019. Generating classical chinese poems from vernacular chinese. In *Proceedings of the 2019 Conference on Empirical Methods in Natural Language Processing and the 9th International Joint Conference on Natural Language Processing (EMNLP-IJCNLP)*, pages 6156–6165.

Rongsheng Zhang, Xiaoxi Mao, Le Li, Lin Jiang, Lin Chen, Zhiwei Hu, Yadong Xi, Changjie Fan, and Minlie Huang. 2020. Youling: an ai-assisted lyrics creation system. In *Proceedings of the 2020 Conference on Empirical Methods in Natural Language Processing: System Demonstrations*, pages 85–91.

Guo Zhipeng, Xiaoyuan Yi, Maosong Sun, Wenhao Li, Cheng Yang, Jiannan Liang, Huimin Chen, Yuhui Zhang, and Ruoyu Li. 2019. Jiuge: A human-machine collaborative chinese classical poetry generation system. In *Proceedings of the 57th Annual Meeting of the Association for Computational Linguistics: System Demonstrations*, pages 25–30.

Yutao Zhu, Ruihua Song, Zhicheng Dou, NIE Jian-Yun, and Jin Zhou. 2020. Scriptwriter: Narrative-guided script generation. In *Proceedings of the 58th Annual Meeting of the Association for Computational Linguistics*, pages 8647–8657.

# Automatic Gloss Dictionary for Sign Language Learners

**Chenchen Xu**[1,2], **Dongxu Li**[1,2], **Hongdong Li**[1], **Hanna Suominen**[1,3], **Ben Swift**[1]
[1] The Australian National University (ANU) / Canberra, ACT, Australia
[2] Data61, Commonwealth Scientific and Industrial Research Organization (CSIRO) / Canberra, ACT, Australia
[3] University of Turku / Turku, Finland
`Firstname.Lastname@anu.edu.au`

## Abstract

A multi-language dictionary is a fundamental tool for language learning, allowing the learner to look up unfamiliar words. Searching an unrecognized word in the dictionary does not usually require deep knowledge of the target language. However, this is not true for sign language, where gestural elements preclude this type of easy lookup. This paper introduces GlossFinder, an online tool supporting 2,000 signs to assist language learners in determining the meaning of given signs. Unlike alternative systems of complex inputs, our system requires only that learners imitate the sign in front of a standard webcam. A user study conducted among sign language speakers of varying ability compared our system against existing alternatives and the interviews indicated a clear preference for our new system. This implies that GlossFinder can lower the barrier in sign language learning by addressing the common problem of sign finding and make it accessible to the wider community.

## 1 Introduction

Unlike most language systems, which are composed of their written and spoken forms, sign languages (e.g., American Sign Language (ASL) and the Australian Auslan language) used by the Deaf or Hard-of-Hearing (DHH) community are represented by the rich inputs including facial and gesture movements. As of the year 2020, 430 million people worldwide have developed hearing loss—that is, one in every ten people—and it is estimated that this number may increase to 700 million by 2050 (WHO, 2021). Sign languages are also used by people suffering the loss of ability to speak (e.g., aphasia) or brain stroke. They are spoken by individuals with various relational connections to sign language speakers, e.g., family members or co-workers. Additionally, a substantial and growing number of people are learning a sign language as a second language, e.g., among U.S. university students (Goldberg et al., 2015). Despite the efforts made in building tools to support their learning (Lee et al., 2005; Schioppo et al., 2019; Hou et al., 2019; Scassellati et al., 2018; Li et al., 2021), many sign language learners have limited means of seeking assistance, and are restricted to class offerings or relying on other experienced sign language speakers. It is therefore increasingly important to support the sign language learner community to facilitate better education and communication.

As a fundamental tool in language study, a dictionary is more than a tool to assist sign language learners in searching unfamiliar words. The rich content present in current online dictionaries (e.g., example pronunciation recordings and visual materials) also provide positive feedback to foster the learner's understanding and proficiency in the target language (Corbeil and Archambault, 2006; Laska, 1993). Most existing sign language dictionaries (e.g., AslSearch (ASLSearch, 2009), Handspeak (Lapiak, 1995), and Signing Savvy (Signing Savvy, 2021)) are text-based and centered on one spoken language, with signs presented in an alphabetical order of their corresponding gloss, i.e., the spoken language counterpart. This does not serve the important scenario when someone encounters an unfamiliar sign and does not know its spoken language translation. Another issue with the text-based dictionary is the fact a one-to-one correlation between sign and spoken language words does not always exist, and no standard convention exists for handling these discrepancies. The absence of these types of dictionary for sign language learner is due to the difficulty of processing visual input and the lack of intuitive alphabetics assumed in most language dictionaries. An early effort made towards a sign-centric dictionary is Tennant et al. (1998) where researchers use pre-defined handshapes (finger poses) to formalise the signs so that they can be arranged similar to a conventional dictionary. Follow-up work (Lapiak, 1995; Neidle



*Proceedings of the 60th Annual Meeting of the Association for Computational Linguistics System Demonstrations*, pages 83 - 92

et al., 2012; Alonzo et al., 2019) parameterised the signs by key properties (e.g., handshape, position of hands, and whether the sign involves repetitive movement) to make a filtering-based search system. In addition, Elliott et al. (2011) used the Microsoft Kinect to collect human body movements from the sign language speaker and match the performed signs against the database.

Modern advancements in deep learning algorithms enable processing of unstructured video inputs, and these algorithms have been applied to sign language. Progress has been made in identifying isolated (Li et al. (2020a,c); Albanie et al. (2020); Sincan and Keles (2020); Momeni et al. (2020)) or continuous signs (Li et al. (2020b); Zhou et al. (2021); Bull et al. (2021); Duarte et al. (2021); Chen et al. (2022)) from a video. This presents opportunity to develop a dictionary system, which accepts direct video inputs from a user performing a sign, and attempts to return the meaning of that sign. One of the early attempts on such video-based system is Alonzo et al. (2019) where the author discussed some characteristics in the design and evaluation metrics regarding the user satisfaction. Notably, the work did not build an actual automatic recognition technique and the users are only presented with a predetermined set of results during the study.

In this paper, we present the platform of *GlossFinder*, our new video-based sign dictionary, where users directly provide videos of the target sign by performing it to their webcam or via uploaded clips, and the system will retrieve matched signs without any extra input. To the best of our knowledge, it is the first attempt of user study with a functioning system built. The study identifies some key considerations in designing for this specific sign language context. It also verifies sign language learners' frustration when using previous sign dictionaries, either due to the steep learning curve or the poor quality of results.

## 2 System Design

### 2.1 System Design Criteria

After initial consult with sign language instructors and learners, we determined the following three design criteria items for GlossFinder:

**C1. Result with Feedback:** Unlike with conventional dictionaries, locating the exact target word (i.e., the sign the user is searching for) is laborious with a sign language dictionary. For example, even basic signs such as those for "father" or "mother" can lead to confusion for beginners. Therefore, the system should provide additional materials to support the user in matching the results and guide refining the search, if appropriate.

**C2. Robust to Noise:** Example videos in online sign language learning platforms and related research are sourced in a controlled environment. In contrast, we aspire to our system to be applicable to amateur scenarios so that the system is robust even in less formal noisy situations where such clean inputs are unavailable. Namely, we focus on the following two types of noise commonly presented in the videos from informal sources: First, the user captured videos often include blank segments before and after the informative part, in contrast to the videos from professionals which are trimmed and standardized. Second, the lightning conditions may vary among users. We require the system to be robust to these noises.

**C3. Minimal Learning:** The large sign language learner community includes people of diverse sign language levels and backgrounds. We argue the proposed system should be straightforward to use in order to be perceived as both usable and useful by a broader cohort of sign language learners. With that in mind, a favored dictionary design should be similar to how sign language learners consult peers in practice by performing again the sign to their best ability.

### 2.2 System Architecture

An overview of the GlossFinder system is demonstrated in Figure 2. Gloss Recognizer accepts an incoming video feed of signers performing the target gloss and determines the ranking of predicted gloss categories. Top gloss candidates from the ranking result are relayed to the *Gloss Retriever* component to collect enriched information for each gloss, e.g., the sample gloss video. Users' access to the system through the web-based platform as illustrated in Figure 1 where they can provide the gloss video feed either by using their camera to record or uploading a pre-recorded video file.

### 2.3 Gloss Recognizer

The Gloss Recognizer is based on models from supervised training on a sign recognition dataset. Recent works in this field can be categorized into two streams depending on the input feature, namely, human pose or gesture based approaches inspired by the long-term development in sign language rep-

Figure 1: A screenshot of GlossFinder. The top panel is for the input, with the left part being the real-time capture from a webcam or the user's pre-recorded video. The captured video is played to the right as a preview. After the system has made a prediction, the candidate glosses are displayed in the result panel at the bottom along (including example videos). (Faces have been blurred in this paper for privacy reasons.)

resentation (Wang et al., 2010), and recent works relying on deep learning and raw video frames (Li et al., 2020a; Momeni et al., 2020). We observe that the recent video-based approaches report a higher top-$k$ accuracy, but in comparison the overall results from pose-based approaches are more consistent in retrieving visually similar examples which may be attributed to the sparsity of their pose input. To align with the aforementioned criteria of **C1. Result with Feedback** which promotes returning more similar signs for the user to examine, we construct a model of each kind and ensemble the results to retain the benefits of both.

**Training Material:** To facilitate building the recognition model for the model training, we adopt the public available WLASL dataset (Li et al., 2020a) with $2,000$ sign glosses performed by over 100 signers. This dataset ensures an average of 10.5 examples per sign to support sufficient supervision signals for the model training and vocabulary diversity for our user study.

**Image-Based Model:** We adopt the I3D networks pre-trained on the Kinetics dataset, considering their effectiveness on sign langauge recognition (Li et al., 2020c) and translation (Li et al., 2020b). The pre-trained backbone enjoys the robustness to varying video conditions, remedying the second noise covered in the criterion **C2. Robust to Noise**. We attach a projector on the representation features extracted from the I3D backbone network. The model is finetuned on the WLASL dataset, and achieves an accuracy of 60.21% at top-5, slightly better than those baselines reported in Li et al. (2020a).

**Pose-Based Model:** The pose-based model inherits the setting from (Li et al., 2020a) by first extracting the body and 2D keypoints for each frame applying OpenPose (Cao et al., 2019). Considering that face and lip movements are less reliable in the training corpus WLASL, we only use keypoints of the main upper-body with the both hands. The concatenation of all 2D key point coordinates at each frames forms the input feature, before feeding to the Temporal Graph Convolution Networks (TGCN) (Li et al., 2020a). A complete graph is constructed by connecting all key points present in the input features and the TGCN model is trained by learning to aggregate information over this graph of key points.

**Sliding Window Inference:** Following the cri-

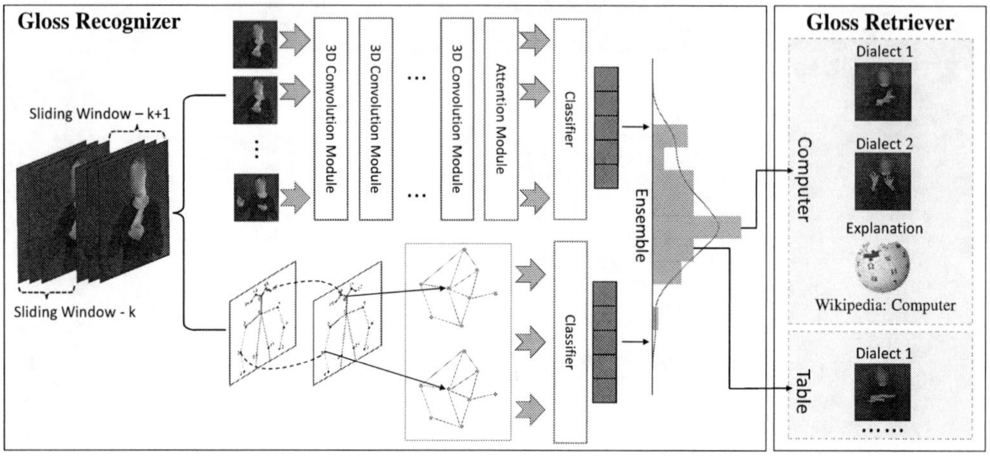


Figure 2: An overview of the main components in GlossFinder. The Gloss Recognizer and Gloss Retriever components jointly generate the enriched view of gloss matches from the input sample video. (Faces have been blurred in this paper for privacy reasons.)

terion of **C2. Robust to Noise**, we incorporate a mechanism to cope with the commonly present short blank segments before and after the representative frames (e.g., users raising or putting down their hands). As demonstrated in Figure 2, We apply the recognition model over several continuous segments of a fixed length of time (sliding windows). As the model slides through the whole input, the result ranking of glosses is obtained from their maximum prediction in all segments. Intuitively, a gloss is predicted as present as long as it appears in any of the segment.

### 2.4 Gloss Retriever

The *Gloss retriever* component collects enriched information for the predicted glosses from *Gloss Recognizer*, including example videos and explanations. We first shortlist a few public ASL sources and construct a database of glosses with their examples in possible dialects. To avoid duplicate in the result, we only include video examples from the source with most examples present for each individual gloss, with the assumption that these ASL sources mostly include one example video for each dialect. The retriever component includes two result modes. The gloss-centric mode lists individual glosses in the predicted order, with one example video for each. The example-centric mode expands the result gloss with their varieties in the database, that is, a gloss with 3 variety videos will take 3 spots in the result list. The gloss-centric mode provides a clearer view of the gloss guesses from the model, while more freedom is given to the user in example-centric mode to inspect examples and match them with their target in the memory.

### 2.5 GlossFinder

Based on the criterion of **C3. Minimal Learning**, GlossFinder avoids any pre-defined parameters and the user is only prompted to give a video input of the target gloss, as illusrated in Figure 1. To start, the system guides the user to focus on their camera to capture a video of the target sign. The "capture" button toggles between the start and stop status during the recording. Whenever the stop status is reached, the recorded video is played in the preview window next to it for any adjustment. The preview window is also initialized with an example video to demonstrate the recommended camera position and hand placement. Once the user is satisfied with the recording, they will click the "Predict" button to issue the request to the back-end *Gloss Recognizer* and *Gloss Retriever* component for results. The "capture" button is disabled during the prediction with the progress bar below indicating the current status. Top predicted gloss candidates are then displayed in the result panel sitting in the bottom panel. Each candidate gloss is featured with some example videos from a professional signer so that the users can quickly compare with the one they are looking for.

## 3 User Evaluation

### 3.1 Benchmark Systems

We include in our comparison the existing public available sign language dictionaries that can serve

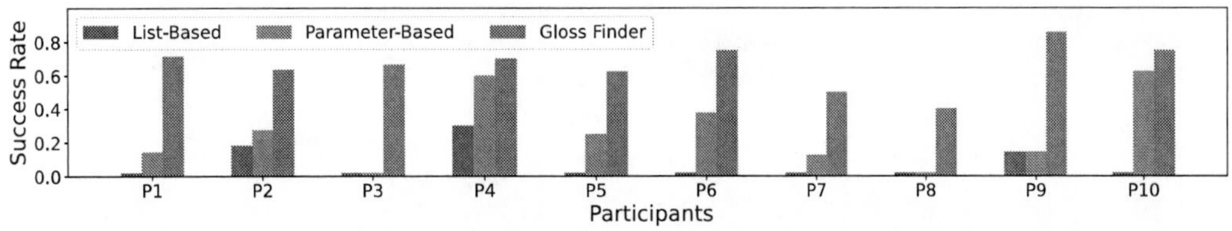


Figure 3: The success rate for each participant P1-P10 in reaching the correct sign during the trials.

the purpose of search for glosses. They are mainly of two categories:

- **List-based Dictionary:** All supported glosses were listed in their alphabetic order or grouped by category. We adopted widely used Signing Savvy (Signing Savvy, 2021) as the default one for participants, with the option of HandSpeak (Lapiak, 1995).
- **Parameter-based Dictionary:** The user was required to tick several parameters such as hand-shape to filter in the glosses. HandSpeak reverse dictionary (Lapiak, 1995) was adopted in our study.

### 3.2 Research Ethics and Recruitment

Ethical approval (Protocol 2021/375) was obtained from the Human Research Ethics Committee of The Australian National University. Each participant provided written informed consent.

Acknowledging that the primary users of this study was sign language leaners, the selection criteria were set to adults of any level of sign language experience. Particularly, experienced sign language users were favored if they were not using ASL. As such, we were able to collect direct feedback from experienced sign language users without forcefully asking them to pretend knowing the target signs. All participation was voluntary to encourage both positive and negative feedback.

### 3.3 Interview Process

The evaluation of the system is conducted in a form of interview with the participants to collect both quantitative and qualitative results. Each participant is guided to try each of the 3 target systems to search for specific signs. They started by experimenting with up to 6 signs from a determined set we constructed based on the consideration of the gesture diversity. The participant also chose a few signs from the vocabulary at will. Within the trial, they are encouraged to play around the systems for a few rounds to simulate the use of a dictionary. After some trials, they are asked to rate their satisfaction with the overall experience of interacting with the system, by taking into account both the quality of retrieved results and the support of the system to refine the search.

### 3.4 Participants

In total, 10 people participated in the study: 3 females and 7 males, and all in the age range of 20–40 years. The participants varied in their level of sign language experience. There were 3 intermediate sign language users with over 10 years of experience, of which 2 were attending professional jobs related to sign language interpretation. Additionally, there was 1 person having going through less than 1 year of systematic study, and 6 junior learners (a.k.a. beginners). All participants self-identified themselves as hearing, and were learning sign language for work, family members, or of their personal interest.

### 3.5 Evaluation Results

In this section, we summarize the ratings of the target systems from the three aspects as described below:

**Ratings of learning to use the system** The list-based dictionary and GlossFinder received higher ratings for easy to learn. A post-hoc analysis was conducted by Wilcoxon Signed-Rank Test to examine the significance of difference in pairwise comparison. Particularly, the corrected p-value were 0.0065 for LB-PB, 0.0103 for GF-PB, and 0.1025 for LB-GF [1]. We considered the difference is significant for the parameter-based method to the other two.

Noticably, the ratings for both the parameter-based system and GlossFinder rose after the trials. For the parameter-based system, the participants

[1] When it is not ambiguous, we will use the abbreviation of List-based (LB), Parameter-based (PB), and GlossFinder (GF) in reporting numeric results.

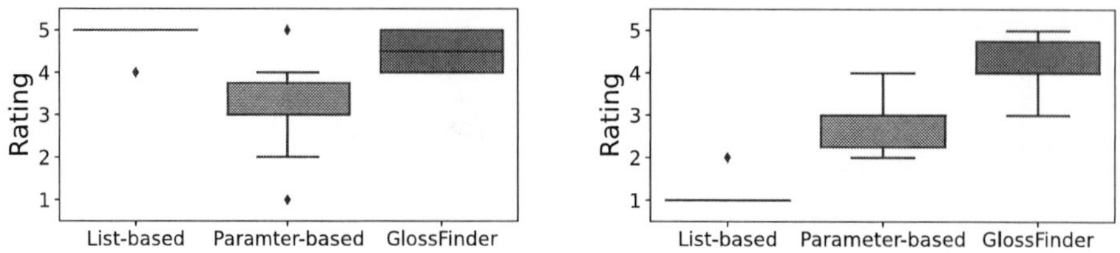


(a) Rating for learning the system

(b) Rating for using the system

Figure 4: Ratings our participants gave to the benchmark systems during the trials. The rating for learning the system was collected both before and after the trial to cope with the bias from the system introduction and long-term effects of the user getting familiar with the system.

had a tendency to be less frustrated when realizing they did not have to always specify all the parameters at once. For example, participant (P5) struggled on several signs about their location parameter especially for signs involving large or circular movements such as "family". He decided to ignore the location in the following trials. In the meantime, the participants also showed more confidence in using GlossFidner as they got comfortable with using their camera. They also attributed the positive change to the capability of system to accommodate imprecise gestures and hand placement.

**Ratings of using the system** It was not surprising to see most participants quickly gave up using the List-based dictionary. Although some disagreement arose here, participants are giving a higher rating to GF in comparision to LB and PB. Similarly, Wilcoxon Signed-Rank Test was conducted to compare the pairwise significance of difference. The corrected p-values were 0.0069 for LB-PB, 0.0276 for GF-PB, and 0.0019 for GF-LB.

The Parameter-based system received controversial feedback among different groups. One of the intermediate signer had particularly used the system before and was reluctant to test it based on his previous experience. Junior learners showed a more optimistic view towards exploring the parameters. However, they reported strong depression over the minimal feedback the system was giving to them, which often confused them about if they were getting close to the target.

The participants expressed their favor to GlossFinder justified by the quality of results with the minimal effort. As pointed out by the participant P6, when he was searching for a sign (e.g., "travel", performed by circulating a hand with two fingers bent forwards) in practice, he might not have been certain if the two fingers should have been pointing towards the front or up. This type of a local change led to less confidence in selecting the parameters. GlossFinder was less demanding on such preciseness. Some other testimonies focused on the interaction. As stressed for the parameter-based system, the users were not receiving feedback regarding their input. In contrast, they were able to compare against the gloss examples present in GlossFinder for possible matches. The participants said that the examples provided more than simply evidence for the correct match, but also guidance on how to proceed next if the target sign was not seen.

**Success rate of search** For quantitatively analyzing the system performance, we kept a record of the exact success rate for each trial of search during the interview, as the target sign was known to us. Detailed results can be found in Figure 3. For the list-based system, a success was defined as whenever the user clicks in the correct sign, no matter if they realized it is correct. It was extended for the parameter-based system to when the correct sign was in the first page of returned results (noticeably it was slightly favoring the system as the user might not be patient enough to examine all candidates even though they are certain with the correctness of parameters). For GlossFinder, we considered a success if the correct sign appears in the top-$k$ results with $k = 12$ for that was the maximum number of videos to display in a common monitor resolution without scrolling. As shown in Figure 3, the success rate correlated positively with the user rating on usability and was clearly favoring the GlossFinder system. The average success rate for LB, PB and GF are 6%, 25% and 66% respectively. Most participants succeeded in locating the correct sign with 1 or 2 rounds of trials possibly by capturing a new video. Only the experienced signers were able to use the list-based system by relating the ASL sign here to the sign language they mastered and thus making a reasonable guess. In comparison, the results from the parameter-based system were relatively diverse, which unexpectedly was regardless of sign language experience. The testimony from participants of higher success rate suggested the method of only combining 2 parameters they were certain and brute force searching the candidates.

## 4 Conclusion

We construct, to the best of our knowledge, the first automatic sign dictionary digesting direct video capture as its inputs. Our user study validates the improved usability from the new system. The participants describe it as less demanding to learn in comparison to the existing parameter-based systems. Retrieved results are said to be more accurate and able to accommodate the varying video capture quality. Enriched results include example videos and explanations are agreed to largely help the user in correctly locating and refining the search. Overall, the reported success rate in reaching the searched sign is on average 66% from GlossFinder, significantly surpassing the benchmarks. We also conduct analysis to compare different views for presenting the results. It is favored by the participants for the system to include more examples of varieties even at the cost that less glosses can be shown in a single page. Our study strengthens the belief that the sign language dictionary design should be visual-based to imitate the practical form of actual sign language teaching and learning. We hope it can also motivate the related research to make sign language learning increasingly accessible to a broader community.

As one of the early attempts in building such system, we notice some limitations in the current study:

- The benchmark systems are comparatively weak, for which it is to blame the fact that sign language learners community is receiving insufficient support and no such stronger peers are public available. Existing systems are in majority made with voluntary contribution and limited in resource. While the incorporated benchmark systems are still receiving some positive feedback, stronger benchmarks are subject to encourage the participants to discover more places to improve in the current designs.
- The target audience of this study is set to general sign language learners, which is in concept a larger community covering DHH. We recruit people of both intermediate and junior level of sign knowledge to collect plausible data. Yet future research may be framed to be more customized for the DHH community. Space may still remain to improve based on their need.

## References


Samuel Albanie, Gül Varol, Liliane Momeni, Triantafyllos Afouras, Joon Son Chung, Neil Fox, and Andrew Zisserman. 2020. BSL-1K: Scaling up co-articulated sign language recognition using mouthing cues. In *ECCV*.

Oliver Alonzo, Abraham Glasser, and Matt Huenerfauth. 2019. Effect of automatic sign recognition performance on the usability of video-based search interfaces for sign language dictionaries. In *The 21st International ACM SIGACCESS Conference on Computers and Accessibility*, pages 56–67.

LLC ASLSearch. 2009. Aslsearch.com.

Hannah Bull, Triantafyllos Afouras, Gül Varol, Samuel Albanie, Liliane Momeni, and Andrew Zisserman. 2021. Aligning subtitles in sign language videos. In *Proceedings of the IEEE/CVF International Conference on Computer Vision*, pages 11552–11561.

Zhe Cao, Gines Hidalgo, Tomas Simon, Shih-En Wei, and Yaser Sheikh. 2019. Openpose: realtime multi-person 2d pose estimation using part affinity fields. *IEEE Transactions on Pattern Analysis and Machine Intelligence*, 43(1):172–186.

Yutong Chen, Fangyun Wei, Xiao Sun, Zhirong Wu, and Stephen Lin. 2022. A simple multi-modality transfer learning baseline for sign language translation. *arXiv preprint arXiv:2203.04287*.

Jean Claude Corbeil and Ariane Archambault. 2006. *Merriam-Webster's Visual Dictionary*. Merriam Webster.

Amanda Duarte, Shruti Palaskar, Lucas Ventura, Deepti Ghadiyaram, Kenneth DeHaan, Florian Metze, Jordi Torres, and Xavier Giro-i Nieto. 2021. How2sign: a large-scale multimodal dataset for continuous american sign language. In *Proceedings of the IEEE/CVF Conference on Computer Vision and Pattern Recognition*, pages 2735–2744.

Ralph Elliott, Helen Cooper, Eng-Jon Ong, John Glauert, Richard Bowden, and François Lefebvre-Albaret. 2011. Search-by-example in multilingual sign language databases. In *2nd Intl. Workshop on Sign Language Translation and Avatar Technology (SLTAT)*.

David Goldberg, Dennis Looney, and Natalia Lusin. 2015. Enrollments in languages other than english in united states institutions of higher education, fall 2013. In *Modern Language Association*. ERIC.

Jiahui Hou, Xiang-Yang Li, Peide Zhu, Zefan Wang, Yu Wang, Jianwei Qian, and Panlong Yang. 2019. Signspeaker: A real-time, high-precision smartwatch-based sign language translator. In *The 25th Annual International Conference on Mobile Computing and Networking*, pages 1–15.

Jolanta Lapiak. 1995. Sign language • asl dictionary | handspeak. `https://www.handspeak.com/`.

Vera Laska. 1993. The macmillan visual dictionary (book review). *International Journal on World Peace*, 10(4):107.

Seungyon Lee, Valerie Henderson, Harley Hamilton, Thad Starner, Helene Brashear, and Steven Hamilton. 2005. A gesture-based american sign language game for deaf children. In *CHI'05 Extended Abstracts on Human Factors in Computing Systems*, pages 1589–1592.

Dongxu Li, Cristian Rodriguez, Xin Yu, and Hongdong Li. 2020a. Word-level deep sign language recognition from video: A new large-scale dataset and methods comparison. In *Proceedings of the IEEE/CVF Winter Conference on Applications of Computer Vision*, pages 1459–1469.

Dongxu Li, Chenchen Xu, Liu Liu, Yiran Zhong, Rong Wang, Lars Petersson, and Hongdong Li. 2021. Transcribing natural languages for the deaf via neural editing programs. *arXiv preprint arXiv:2112.09600*.

Dongxu Li, Chenchen Xu, Xin Yu, Kaihao Zhang, Benjamin Swift, Hanna Suominen, and Hongdong Li. 2020b. Tspnet: Hierarchical feature learning via temporal semantic pyramid for sign language translation. *Advances in Neural Information Processing Systems*, 33:12034–12045.

Dongxu Li, Xin Yu, Chenchen Xu, Lars Petersson, and Hongdong Li. 2020c. Transferring cross-domain knowledge for video sign language recognition. In *Proceedings of the IEEE/CVF Conference on Computer Vision and Pattern Recognition*, pages 6205–6214.

Liliane Momeni, Gul Varol, Samuel Albanie, Triantafyllos Afouras, and Andrew Zisserman. 2020. Watch, read and lookup: learning to spot signs from multiple supervisors. In *Proceedings of the Asian Conference on Computer Vision*.

Carol Neidle, Ashwin Thangali, and Stan Sclaroff. 2012. Challenges in development of the american sign language lexicon video dataset (asllvd) corpus. In *5th Workshop on the Representation and Processing of Sign Languages: Interactions between Corpus and Lexicon, LREC*. Citeseer.

Brian Scassellati, Jake Brawer, Katherine Tsui, Setareh Nasihati Gilani, Melissa Malzkuhn, Barbara Manini, Adam Stone, Geo Kartheiser, Arcangelo Merla, Ari Shapiro, et al. 2018. Teaching language to deaf infants with a robot and a virtual human. In *Proceedings of the 2018 CHI Conference on Human Factors in Computing Systems*, pages 1–13.

Jacob Schioppo, Zachary Meyer, Diego Fabiano, and Shaun Canavan. 2019. Sign language recognition: Learning american sign language in a virtual environment. In *Extended Abstracts of the 2019 CHI Conference on Human Factors in Computing Systems*, pages 1–6.

LLC Signing Savvy. 2021. Signing savvy | asl sign language video dictionary.

Ozge Mercanoglu Sincan and Hacer Yalim Keles. 2020. Autsl: A large scale multi-modal turkish sign language dataset and baseline methods. *IEEE Access*, 8:181340–181355.

Richard A Tennant, Marianne Gluszak, and Marianne Gluszak Brown. 1998. *The American sign language handshape dictionary*. Gallaudet University Press.

Haijing Wang, Alexandra Stefan, Sajjad Moradi, Vassilis Athitsos, Carol Neidle, and Farhad Kamangar. 2010. A system for large vocabulary sign search. In *European Conference on Computer Vision*, pages 342–353. Springer.

WHO. 2021. Deafness and hearing loss.

Hao Zhou, Wengang Zhou, Weizhen Qi, Junfu Pu, and Houqiang Li. 2021. Improving sign language translation with monolingual data by sign back-translation. In *Proceedings of the IEEE/CVF Conference on Computer Vision and Pattern Recognition*, pages 1316–1325.

## A Testimony and Discussion

We extend the semi-structured open discussion with the participants on the general thoughts about sign language dictionary.

**What should be the input format for a sign language dictionary?**
Strong preference is given by the participants towards a rather simple input format to use the dictionary. One surprising finding is that despite experienced users are able to understand better the specification required in the parameter-based system (e.g. to choose the correct handshape and hand location), they also show stronger concerns over the capability as less-structured and more-composite signs are taken into scope (e.g. signs involving different movements from both hands). Junior sign learners show neutral altitude to learning the parameter-based system but it is also stressed by them the challenge they faced in understanding the parameters without further instruction.

> It is hard to know the clear definition of these parameters. Like now I feel I have to try each of these as they all look legitimate. (P5)

> Imaging a sign I don't know, maybe I won't really remember the gestures exactly but just a rough idea. (P6)

The participants express their favor towards the video capture used by GlossFinder for its nature correspondence to how people learn from peers. One improvement suggested is on the fact that both the interface and input require hand movements, i.e., they have to click the button and place the hand back to perform the sign. The future design may incorporate other UI elements to help the user focus on performing the sign. Examples include gesture-based UI input and foot controller.

> It would be cool if I can get all things done just by gestures. (P10)

One thing raised by the experienced signer P2 is:

> What are the things the system is looking at? ... Is it reading my lip as well? (P2)

As discussed in Section 2, the lip input is purposely dropped because of the inconsistency of quality and we want to prevent the model from accidentally learning to overfit to the lip-reading instead of the gesture. However, P2 pointed out that lip movement can be crucial in determining some of the signs, potentially a factor to consider in future development.

**What should the dictionary show as the result?**
Consensus is made by the participants on the advantage of displaying example videos:

> I can guess the meaning of some of these signs as I know them in another (sign language). I have no idea what other people would do if they only see the glosses in English (text). (P2)

> It becomes immediate now I know I find it. (P9)

In the meantime, future work is suggested on improving the order among variety examples for each individual gloss in the example-centric view. The matched glosses are ranked by confidence but the examples within each gloss are not. The result can be more reasonable if it can ensure the matched varieties to appear higher.

In addition, GlossFinder retrieves a fixed number of examples each time. It is argued that the number should adapt to cases for a clearer view.

> Some signs have many similar examples and it is good you show all of them. Just I feel like there may not always be so many similar glosses to show, and you see the later examples in the result become less meaningful. (P10)

**As a language learning tool, what else should a dictionary have?**
Since the primary audience of dictionary is language learners. We encourage the participants to think what can be improved from this perspective. A major point raised is that the dictionary may provide guidance on improving their sign. Even in case the dictionary retrieved the correct gloss, it is said:

> If you can put a confidence score for my recording, it sort of tells if I now remember it correctly. (P4)

A more sophisticated design may incorporate more instructions than the a score.

Maybe the dictionary can indicate the problems as I perform it. I see some difference in my form compared to that professional. (P4)

# PromptSource: An Integrated Development Environment and Repository for Natural Language Prompts

**Stephen H. Bach**[*1,2] **Victor Sanh**[*3] **Zheng-Xin Yong**[1] **Albert Webson**[1] **Colin Raffel**[3]

**Nihal V. Nayak**[1] **Abheesht Sharma**[4] **Taewoon Kim**[5] **M Saiful Bari**[6] **Thibault Fevry**[7]

**Zaid Alyafeai**[8] **Manan Dey**[9] **Andrea Santilli**[10] **Zhiqing Sun**[11] **Srulik Ben-David**[12]

**Canwen Xu**[13] **Gunjan Chhablani**[7] **Han Wang**[14] **Jason Alan Fries**[15,2]

**Maged S. Al-shaibani**[8] **Shanya Sharma**[16] **Urmish Thakker**[17] **Khalid Almubarak**[18]

**Xiangru Tang**[19] **Dragomir Radev**[19] **Mike Tian-Jian Jiang**[20] **Alexander M. Rush**[3]

[1] Brown University [2] Snorkel AI [3] Hugging Face [4] BITS Pilani [5] VU Amsterdam
[6] NTU [7] BigScience [8] KFUPM [9] SAP [10] University of Rome [11] CMU [12] Technion
[13] UCSD [14] NYU [15] Stanford University [16] Walmart Labs [17] SambaNova Systems
[18] PSAU [19] Yale University [20] ZEALS * Equal Contribution

## Abstract

*PromptSource* is a system for creating, sharing, and using natural language prompts. Prompts are functions that map an example from a dataset to a natural language input and target output. Using prompts to train and query language models is an emerging area in NLP that requires new tools that let users develop and refine these prompts collaboratively. *PromptSource* addresses the emergent challenges in this new setting with (1) a templating language for defining data-linked prompts, (2) an interface that lets users quickly iterate on prompt development by observing outputs of their prompts on many examples, and (3) a community-driven set of guidelines for contributing new prompts to a common pool. Over 2,000 prompts for roughly 170 datasets are already available in *PromptSource*. *PromptSource* is available at `https://github.com/bigscience-workshop/promptsource`.

## 1 Introduction

Prompt engineering is emerging as a new focus in NLP, particularly in zero- and few-shot learning settings. *Prompting* is the practice of representing a task as a natural language utterance in order to query a language model for a response (Liu et al., 2021). For example, if a language model is conditioned on the text *"She hit a home run. The previous sentence is about ..."*, then the model's subsequent generation would be interpreted as a prediction of the topic of the preceding sentence, e.g. by mapping a response such as *"sports"* to a class label. In specific contexts, prompting has been shown to have advantages over traditional classification, for example facilitating adaptation of language models to ad-hoc tasks and improving sample efficiency in low-data settings (Brown et al., 2020; Schick and Schütze, 2021b; Le Scao and Rush, 2021; Gao et al., 2021). These advantages motivate a practical challenge: *How can we enable users to create, refine, and share prompts?*

The process of prompt engineering is critical for successful deployment as choices in prompting can affect downstream predictions significantly, particularly in the zero-shot setting (Perez et al., 2021; Zhao et al., 2021; Webson and Pavlick, 2021). Furthermore, training directly on collections of prompts can enable large models to generalize to new prompts more robustly (Sanh et al., 2021; Wei et al., 2021; Min et al., 2021; Mishra et al., 2021). There is therefore a growing need for tools that support the creation of corpora of prompts.

*PromptSource* is an integrated development environment and repository for natural language prompts to use in the context of zero-shot (or gradient-based few-shot) learning. It provides a Web-based GUI that enables developers to write prompts in a templating language and immediately view their outputs on different examples. The system is integrated with the HuggingFace Datasets library (Lhoest et al., 2021), so that users can load any dataset automatically, browse existing prompts, and create new ones. Through the course of writing thousands of prompts, we converged on three key



*Proceedings of the 60th Annual Meeting of the Association for Computational Linguistics*
*System Demonstrations*, pages 93 - 104
May 22-27, 2022 

aspects to the design of *PromptSource*:

- **Flexible Templating Language.** We adapt a templating language to represent prompts. Prompt authors can define prompts in terms of dataset fields, hard-coded text, and simple control logic. This choice provides the flexibility of a programming environment without the mental overhead of having to write and read arbitrary code. Prompt templates can easily be distributed and used in other systems.
- **Tools for Prompt Management.** *PromptSource* has multiple view to address the needs of prompt authors at different stages of the prompt engineering cycle. A global view lets authors browse datasets and existing prompt templates. A local view facilitates iteration on prompt wording and metadata, as well as testing on individual examples.
- **Community-Driven Quality Standards.** *PromptSource* includes a set of guidelines for prompting based on a large-scale prompt writing pilot. *PromptSource*'s collection is meant to be useful for a wide range of research, based on iterative refinement of a set of quality standards. Prompts in *PromptSource* are also annotated with various pieces of metadata to make finding and using prompts easier.

The *PromptSource* system includes over 2,000 open-source prompts for roughly 170 datasets, which have all been reviewed to meet the quality standards. This collection, which we call the Public Pool of Prompts (P3), allows users to materialize prompted forms of datasets for hundreds of different tasks. The T0 series of models (Sanh et al., 2021) for zero-shot inference were fine-tuned on a subset of P3. Since then, *PromptSource* and P3 have been extended for research on multi-lingual prompting (Lin et al., 2021) and priming, i.e., in-context few-shot learning (Min et al., 2021). The *PromptSource* system and associated content is a first step in the study of systems for prompt engineering, an area that is likely to continue to grow.

## 2 Background and Related Work

*PromptSource* builds on recent work in prompting and prompt engineering. It is also related to work on systems for other types of annotations.

**Prompting** Recently, prompting has emerged as a new focus within NLP as it can dramatically improve language models' few-shot and zero-shot performance in a wide range of downstream tasks (Brown et al., 2020; Schick and Schütze, 2021a; Sanh et al., 2021; Wei et al., 2021). Prompts and prompt engineering come in several varieties (Liu et al., 2021). *PromptSource* is focused on facilitating research with human-written prompts, in which natural language is the medium for describing tasks. This approach has the advantage that prompts can be understood, modified, and applied without being tied to a specific model. In contrast, past work has also aimed to automatically construct prompts by framing the search for a good prompt as a learning problem. These prompts can either be expressed in natural language (Gao et al., 2021; Shin et al., 2020) or as arbitrary vectors (a.k.a. "continuous" or "soft" prompts) not corresponding to words in the model's original vocabulary (Lester et al., 2021; Qin and Eisner, 2021)

When using human-written prompts, there are several possible approaches to learning. One is a zero-shot setting, where the goal is to generalize to prompts for which no training examples are given. Prompts can also be used in a few-shot setting, in which a model is either (1) trained on prompted examples of the target task via gradient updates, or (2) priming (i.e. in-context learning), in which labeled examples are included in an input sequence in order to prime models to make predictions without gradient updates (Brown et al., 2020).

*PromptSource* was originally designed for zero-shot learning, so it emphasizes explicit task instructions and no priming examples. If needed, users can extend *PromptSource* for few-shot learning (e.g., as done in Lin et al., 2021 and Min et al., 2021, described in §7).

**Systems for Annotating Data** Most work on collecting annotations has focused on labels and other annotations at the level of individual examples (Neves and Ševa, 2021). GATE (Cunningham et al., 2002) was an early system for annotating text, and includes support for many data types such as labels and entity tags. Since then, many Web-based systems for annotating text have been developed (Stenetorp et al., 2012; Salgado et al., 2012; Wei et al., 2013; Yimam et al., 2013; Chen and Styler, 2013; Eckart de Castilho et al., 2016; Putra et al., 2020). Other systems support collaboration among multiple annotators (Yang et al., 2018; Stewart et al., 2019). More recently, many annotation systems have begun to incorporate learned models to improve workflow, using techniques such as active learning (Lin et al., 2019; Li et al., 2021) and

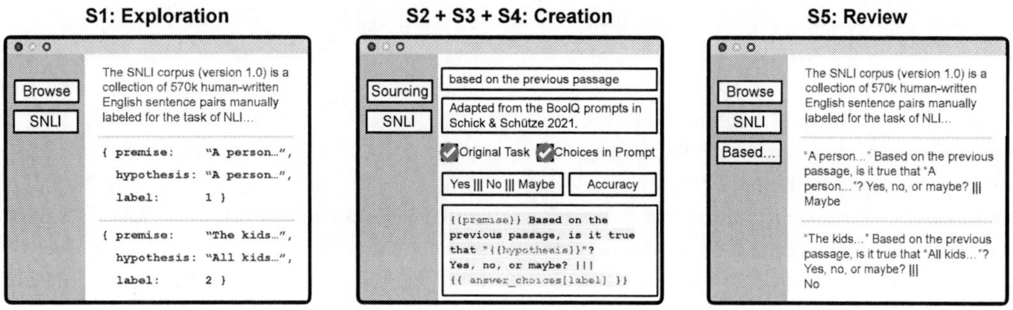


Figure 1: The five stages of creating prompts in *PromptSource*. The Browse view for Dataset Exploration (S1). The Sourcing view for Prompt Writing (S2), Prompt Documentation (S3), and Iteration and Variation (S4). The Browse view for performing a Global Review (S5).

example recommendation (Lee et al., 2020; Kiela et al., 2021). These systems are possible because the annotations to be collected are labels, for which metrics like inter-annotator agreement and model confidence are available.

There has also been some work on collecting annotations other than labels. AlvisAE (Papazian et al., 2012) and TreeAnnotator (Helfrich et al., 2018) support creating ontologies and other structured annotations. Prompts differ from these annotations in that they are semi-structured functions, requiring new tools for developers.

## 3 System Design and Workflow

Creating prompts differs from other types of data collection and annotation. We focus on three challenging aspects on which prompting differs from traditional NLP annotation:

- **Functions, not Labels.** A single prompt is a function that maps dataset examples (dictionaries of arbitrary fields) to natural language input/target pairs. Creating a prompt is therefore more like programming than typical data annotation. How should a prompt format trade off between expressivity and simplicity?
- **Dataset-Level Choices.** Prompts are associated with datasets, unlike label annotations that are local to single examples. Prompt engineering requires developers to evaluate their choices across all examples. What interfaces do authors need to inspect and debug their prompts?
- **Variation in Prompt Construction.** Unlike with labels, it is often desirable to have variation within prompt construction, as different prompt choices may lead to different results. However, variation complicates quality judgment, and makes it impossible to apply simple metrics like inter-annotator agreement. How can multiple authors collaborate to build a high-quality corpus of prompts and associated metadata?

To illustrate these distinct aspects, we start with a concrete overview of the prompt creation process of *PromptSource*. For this example, we imagine that a user of *PromptSource* is creating prompts for a natural language inference dataset, specifically SNLI (Bowman et al., 2015). The goal is to design a prompt query such that the answer can be mapped onto the SNLI classes. A prompt author can accomplish this goal with *PromptSource* via the following five steps (Figure 1):

**S1: Dataset Exploration** The prompt author starts in the *Browse* view to read the dataset description, including linked READMEs and papers, and to browse through examples. In this case, they would see that SNLI is a dataset for natural language inference: assume a given premise sentence is true, the goal is to determine whether a hypothesis sentence is true (entailment), false (contradiction), or undetermined (neutral).

**S2: Prompt Writing** The prompt author uses the *Sourcing* view to try out a prompt wording, and then adjusts it by observing prompted examples (Figure 1 middle, full example in Figures 3 and 4).

**S3: Prompt Documentation** To facilitate using the prompt, the author fills in various metadata including possible metrics to evaluate the prompt, valid outputs if applicable, whether the prompt expresses the original intended task of the dataset, and whether the template explicitly states the valid outputs.

**S4: Iteration and Variation** The prompt author then iterates through S2 and S3 to create multiple prompts for the dataset. Authors are encouraged to vary multiple factors such as the formulation of the prompt and the targeted task (see Section 6).

**S5: Global Review** The author saves the draft prompts in a structured file which are then verified by other contributors through code reviews. New prompts need to meet the quality standard with a series of automatic tests and by validation through prompted instances. Upon passing review, the new prompts can be merged into a global prompts collection.

Upon submission, prompts can be viewed through *PromptSource* by other users. The full collection is stored globally and can be used outside of the tool, for instance to be applied on an example from a dataset of the *Datasets* library (Lhoest et al., 2021).

```
from promptsource.templates import DatasetTemplates
from datasets import load_dataset

prompts = DatasetTemplates("snli")
prompt_key = "based on the previous passage"
p = prompts[prompt_key]

dataset = load_dataset("snli", split="train")
example = dataset[0]

result = p.apply(example)
print("INPUT: ", result[0])
print("TARGET: ", result[1])
```

With this workflow in mind, we next describe the key aspects of the *PromptSource* system in greater detail.

## 4 Prompting Language

A key design decision is the format for prompts. Previous works on prompting tended to use code for specifying each prompt. We experimented with this format and found a trade-off between expressivity and explicit structure. On one side, a maximally expressive format such as pure Python code would let users write complex programs to manipulate the semi-structured examples into prompted examples. However, interpreting and analyzing these programs becomes difficult. This difficulty limits downstream manipulation and analysis of the prompts, for example for possible future work on automatic prompt augmentation. On the other side, a maximally structured format, such as rule-based generation, limits the kinds of prompts that users can create. We found it infeasible to enumerate types of rules sufficient for the wide range of tasks and data formats for which we wanted prompts.

We therefore settled on a middle ground between the two: a templating language. Specifically, we use the Jinja2 templating engine,[1] originally designed for producing web markup. Users write templates as prompts with placeholders, such as `If {{premise}} is true, is it also true that {{hypothesis}}? ||| {{entailed}}`. The separator `|||` denotes the break between the conditioning text and the desired completion. Placeholders refer to fields in the underlying example (represented as a Python `dict` by *Datasets* (Lhoest et al., 2021)). Users also have access to Jinja's built-in functions, such as manipulating strings and structured data. For each prompt, prompted examples are created by applying the prompt to all examples in the corresponding dataset. While Jinja is a complete programming language, our review guidelines encourage simple functions with minimal additional logic (see Figure 3 and 4 for example).

During the development of *PromptSource*, we found that a few idioms were particularly useful. First, not all templates are applicable to all examples in a dataset. Users can wrap templates in Jinja's built-in conditional statements, and any example that results in an empty prompted example is simply skipped. Second, many examples can be used to make multiple training instances, such as a question that has multiple valid answers. We therefore added a `choice` function that selects an element from a list in a way that can be controlled during dataset generation, such as picking a random element using a seeded random number generator or generating different prompts for each combination of elements in the template. Third, many tasks such as classification and binary question answering have a small set of possible valid completions, and it is common to make predictions for these tasks by scoring only the valid completions and returning the highest one (Brown et al., 2020; Sanh et al., 2021; Wei et al., 2021). Users therefore can list the valid completions in a separate field and access them as a list in their prompts (displayed as `Answer choices` in Figure 3). These completions are then explicitly available when evaluating predictions for these prompted examples.

## 5 The *PromptSource* UI

The *PromptSource* system is designed to enable prompt creators to view data (S1), write prompts in a standard format (S2, S3, and S4), and ver-

[1]`https://jinja.palletsprojects.com`

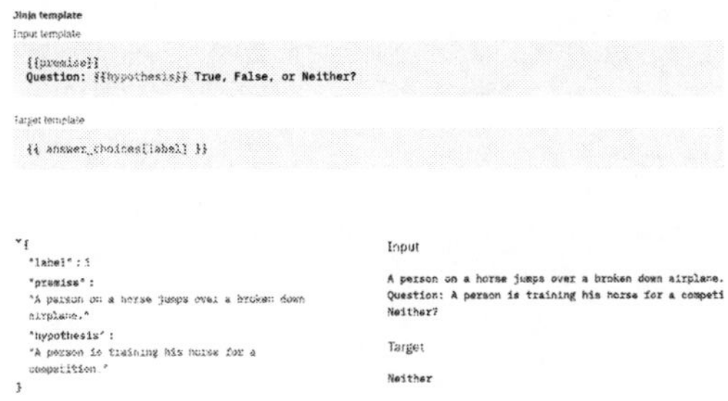


Figure 2: Prompt creators can browse through the dataset examples (left-column) and their prompted form (right column) using the *Browse* view.

ify that their templates work correctly (S5). We implemented a lightweight interface for the tool in Streamlit[2] so that users could download, run locally in a web browser, and then upload their results to a central repository. Testing iterations of the interface on pilot template-writing tasks, we converged on three views for the interface.

**V1: Browse** This view (Figure 2) lets users inspect datasets before creating prompts (S1). Once prompts are created, they can select prompts and browse the prompted examples generated by them (S5). The original example is viewed side-by-side with the resulting prompted example, with the substituted text highlighted to distinguish from text hard-coded in the template. Users can quickly scroll through many examples, verify the behavior of their prompt, and return to the sourcing view if changes are needed.

**V2: Sourcing** This view (Figures 3 and 4) allows users to select a dataset to prompt, browse examples from that dataset in the form of tables, and enter a prompt for that dataset. As the user writes their template (S2, S3, and S4), every time they save it, the output of the template applied to the current example is displayed next to the editor. We also collect metadata like a name for the template, and a reference for any bibliographic information or rationale for the template.

**V3: Helicopter** This view (Figure 5) allows users to see what datasets are available for writing templates and how many are written for each, to prioritize user attention. This view is particularly useful for moving between datasets and for the prompt reviewers (S5).

[2]https://streamlit.io/

## 6 Community Guidelines and Process

Due to the variety of existing NLP datasets, we found it challenging to exhaustively describe the characteristics of a good prompt: there are no simple metrics like inter-annotator agreement on example-level labels. Instead, over a few iterations, we converged on community guidelines[3] with three objectives in mind: (a) provide a standardized vocabulary for discussing prompts between prompt authors, reviewers and users, and minimum requirements for a valid prompt, (b) highlight common errors and best practices, (c) collect the necessary information about the prompts to support current and future research on prompt engineering. The guidelines were enforced in the use of *PromptSource* by a code review process in which each prompt was reviewed before being committed to the central repository.

Guidelines apply to the combination of a template (a function that maps an example into an input/target pair in natural language) and a set of metadata about the template. The most important constraint we imposed for a template to be valid is that it is formulated in natural language (both for the input and the target). We forbid the use of non-natural language prompts such as pure code. Each prompt should clearly state what task should be solved, in a way a non-specialist adult can understand. We found this guideline strikes a good balance between freedom and expressivity in the wording of the prompts on one side and short generic prompts on the other side.

In early experiments, we found that user-written prompts that did not explicitly state the possible valid completions tended to perform worse in experiments than their counterparts in which the possible valid completions were listed. We encouraged prompt authors to explicitly state the valid outputs in some of their prompts. In addition, when working with training prompts that include target text, we found it useful to remove variations on the target format that led to spurious ambiguity. For instance, the target template should only contain the answer to the task. It should not contain any extra text such as "The answer is ...", which can be equivalently moved to the input template.

One of the research question we hope to enable with *PromptSource* is whether the diversity of the

[3]Complete guidelines can be found at https://github.com/bigscience-workshop/promptsource/blob/main/CONTRIBUTING.md.

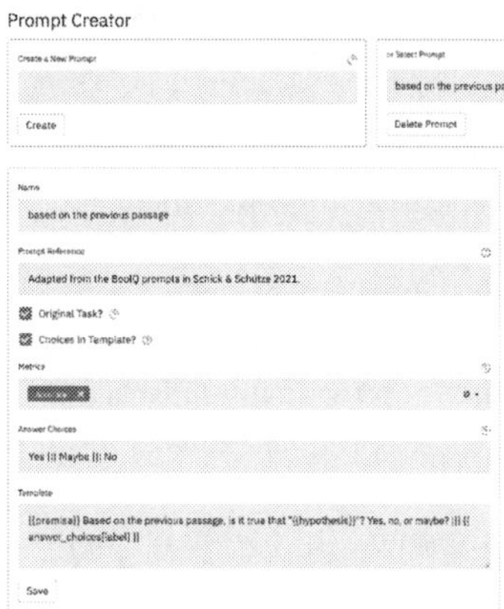


Figure 3: With the *Sourcing* view, prompt authors can write new prompts, fill in the associated metadata, observe the result on examples, and iterate.

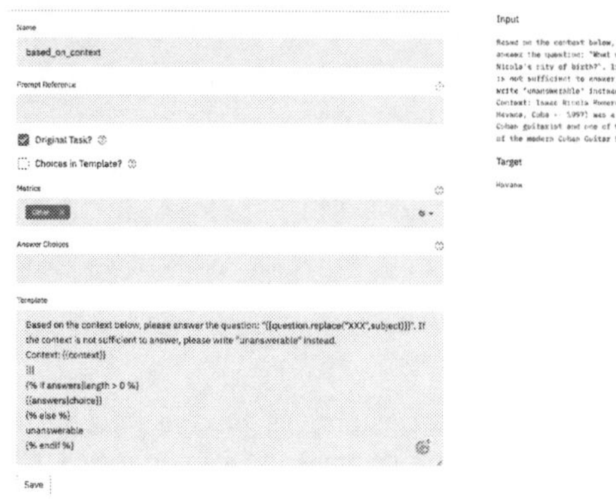


Figure 4: Another example of the the *Sourcing* view, focusing on the editor. The templating language strikes a balance between expressivity and explicit structure. This prompt for QA-ZRE (Levy et al., 2017), a dataset for zero-shot relation extraction, shows how to manipulate strings and do conditional statements with Jinja.

prompt formulation during training leads to models that are more robust to the prompt formulation at test time. Therefore, we encouraged prompt authors to create between 5 and 10 (or more) prompts per dataset while varying the prompt formulation. For a given dataset, authors produce multiple prompts per example, sometimes for task formulations that differed from the original dataset. For instance, for question answering dataset, one prompt can ask to extract the answer to a given question from a given passage, while a second prompt can ask to generate a potential question given an answer and a passage.

As part of the community process and to facilitate future research, *PromptSource* asks prompt authors to include additional metadata for each prompt. Metadata fields include a name for the prompt, a reference to the paper it was extracted from (or any relevant explanation), whether the prompt expresses the task originally intended by the dataset, the valid outputs (if relevant), whether the input template states the valid outputs, and possible metrics to evaluate the prompted examples. These can be used in future systems to evaluate how the style and structure of prompts leads to different downstream results.

## 7 Case Studies

A system for creating, maintaining, and using prompts is a key tool for supporting the emerging research area of prompting in a standardized and reproducible manner. We highlight three recent research projects for which *PromptSource* was a key resource.

**Massively multitask prompted training** Sanh et al. (2021) study the question of zero-shot behaviors in large language models and ask whether zero-shot generalization can be induced by training a language model on a massively multitask mixture of prompts. To test this question, they use *PromptSource* to create diverse prompts for a large collection of NLP datasets. Their training and evaluation prompts are a subset of P3. This work demonstrates that *PromptSource* allows training a language model on a massively multitask mixture of prompted datasets and evaluating the ability of models trained with such a procedure to perform unseen tasks.

**Multilingual prompting** Lin et al. (2021) study the zero- and few-shot learning abilities of an multilingual autoregressive language model trained on 30 languages. In particular, they are interested in the cross-lingual generalization of such models and benchmark a variety of tasks in multiple languages. *PromptSource* allows using a massive set of high-quality English prompts. Moreover, the English prompts serve as support to create prompts in other languages (through either machine or human translation).

**Priming (in-context learning)** Min et al. (2021) study improving models' few-shot priming performance by first fully training a model (with gradient updates) on a multitask mixture formatted with priming examples. They find that incorporating templates from P3 significantly further improves performance compared to training on priming ex-

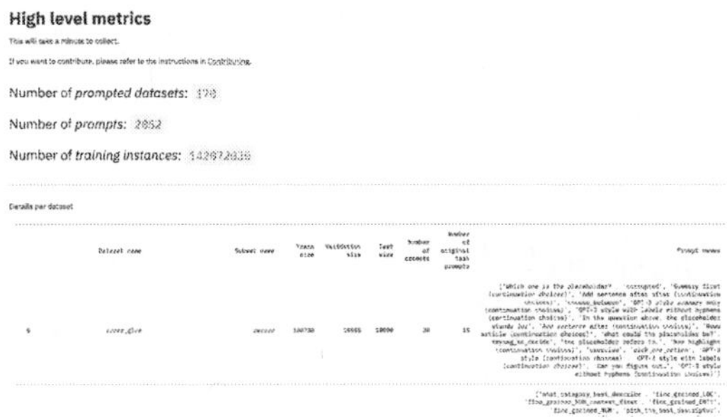


Figure 5: The *Helicopter* view indicates what datasets have prompts and how many prompts are available for each dataset.

amples alone. Although *PromptSource* was not originally designed for this specific form of prompting, users were able to easily use P3's template collection and the templating language for their own priming methods.

## 8 Conclusion

*PromptSource* is an open-source system for creating, sharing, and using natural language prompts and addresses the need for new collaborative and centralized tools to support the emerging research around prompting. The tool is designed to answer three key needs: a flexible template language, a suite of tools for prompt management, and community-driven quality standards. As of January 2022, *PromptSource* includes a growing collection of 2,000 public prompts for roughly 170 datasets, and has already been an instrumental resource for multiple recent research projects.

## Acknowledgements

This research was conducted under the BigScience project for open research,[4] a year-long initiative targeting the study of large models and datasets. The goal of the project is to research language models in a public environment outside large technology companies. The project has over 950 researchers from over 65 countries and more than 250 institutions. The BigScience project was initiated by Thomas Wolf at Hugging Face, and this collaboration would not have been possible without his effort. This research was the focus of the BigScience Prompt Engineering working group, which focused on the role of prompting in large language model training. Disclosure: Stephen Bach contributed to this work as an advisor to Snorkel AI.

[4] `https://bigscience.huggingface.co/`

## References

Samuel R. Bowman, Gabor Angeli, Christopher Potts, and Christopher D. Manning. 2015. A large annotated corpus for learning natural language inference. In *Proceedings of the 2015 Conference on Empirical Methods in Natural Language Processing*, pages 632–642, Lisbon, Portugal. Association for Computational Linguistics.

Tom B. Brown, Benjamin Mann, Nick Ryder, Melanie Subbiah, Jared Kaplan, Prafulla Dhariwal, Arvind Neelakantan, Pranav Shyam, Girish Sastry, Amanda Askell, Sandhini Agarwal, Ariel Herbert-Voss, Gretchen Krueger, Tom Henighan, Rewon Child, Aditya Ramesh, Daniel M. Ziegler, Jeffrey Wu, Clemens Winter, Christopher Hesse, Mark Chen, Eric Sigler, Mateusz Litwin, Scott Gray, Benjamin Chess, Jack Clark, Christopher Berner, Sam McCandlish, Alec Radford, Ilya Sutskever, and Dario Amodei. 2020. Language models are few-shot learners. In *Advances in Neural Information Processing Systems 33: Annual Conference on Neural Information Processing Systems 2020, NeurIPS 2020, December 6-12, 2020, virtual.*

Wei-Te Chen and Will Styler. 2013. Anafora: A web-based general purpose annotation tool. In *Proceedings of the 2013 NAACL HLT Demonstration Session*, pages 14–19, Atlanta, Georgia. Association for Computational Linguistics.

Hamish Cunningham, Diana Maynard, Kalina Bontcheva, and Valentin Tablan. 2002. GATE: an architecture for development of robust HLT applications. In *Proceedings of the 40th Annual Meeting of the Association for Computational Linguistics*, pages 168–175, Philadelphia, Pennsylvania, USA. Association for Computational Linguistics.

Richard Eckart de Castilho, Éva Mújdricza-Maydt, Seid Muhie Yimam, Silvana Hartmann, Iryna Gurevych, Anette Frank, and Chris Biemann. 2016. A web-based tool for the integrated annotation of semantic and syntactic structures. In *Proceedings of the Workshop on Language Technology Resources and Tools for Digital Humanities (LT4DH)*, pages 76–84, Osaka, Japan. The COLING 2016 Organizing Committee.

Tianyu Gao, Adam Fisch, and Danqi Chen. 2021. Making pre-trained language models better few-shot learners. In *Proceedings of the 59th Annual Meeting of the Association for Computational Linguistics and the 11th International Joint Conference on Natural Language Processing (Volume 1: Long Papers)*, pages 3816–3830, Online. Association for Computational Linguistics.

Philipp Helfrich, Elias Rieb, Giuseppe Abrami, Andy Lücking, and Alexander Mehler. 2018. TreeAnnotator: Versatile visual annotation of hierarchical text relations. In *Proceedings of the Eleventh International Conference on Language Resources and Evaluation (LREC 2018)*, Miyazaki, Japan. European Language Resources Association (ELRA).

Douwe Kiela, Max Bartolo, Yixin Nie, Divyansh Kaushik, Atticus Geiger, Zhengxuan Wu, Bertie Vidgen, Grusha Prasad, Amanpreet Singh, Pratik Ringshia, Zhiyi Ma, Tristan Thrush, Sebastian Riedel, Zeerak Waseem, Pontus Stenetorp, Robin Jia, Mohit Bansal, Christopher Potts, and Adina Williams. 2021. Dynabench: Rethinking benchmarking in NLP. In *Proceedings of the 2021 Conference of the North American Chapter of the Association for Computational Linguistics: Human Language Technologies*, pages 4110–4124, Online. Association for Computational Linguistics.

Teven Le Scao and Alexander Rush. 2021. How many data points is a prompt worth? In *Proceedings of the 2021 Conference of the North American Chapter of the Association for Computational Linguistics: Human Language Technologies*, pages 2627–2636, Online. Association for Computational Linguistics.

Dong-Ho Lee, Rahul Khanna, Bill Yuchen Lin, Seyeon Lee, Qinyuan Ye, Elizabeth Boschee, Leonardo Neves, and Xiang Ren. 2020. LEAN-LIFE: A label-efficient annotation framework towards learning from explanation. In *Proceedings of the 58th Annual Meeting of the Association for Computational Linguistics: System Demonstrations*, pages 372–379, Online. Association for Computational Linguistics.

Brian Lester, Rami Al-Rfou, and Noah Constant. 2021. The power of scale for parameter-efficient prompt tuning. In *Proceedings of the 2021 Conference on Empirical Methods in Natural Language Processing*, pages 3045–3059, Online and Punta Cana, Dominican Republic. Association for Computational Linguistics.

Omer Levy, Minjoon Seo, Eunsol Choi, and Luke Zettlemoyer. 2017. Zero-shot relation extraction via reading comprehension. In *Proceedings of the 21st Conference on Computational Natural Language Learning (CoNLL 2017)*, pages 333–342, Vancouver, Canada. Association for Computational Linguistics.

Quentin Lhoest, Albert Villanova del Moral, Yacine Jernite, Abhishek Thakur, Patrick von Platen, Suraj Patil, Julien Chaumond, Mariama Drame, Julien Plu, Lewis Tunstall, Joe Davison, Mario Šaško, Gunjan Chhablani, Bhavitvya Malik, Simon Brandeis, Teven Le Scao, Victor Sanh, Canwen Xu, Nicolas Patry, Angelina McMillan-Major, Philipp Schmid, Sylvain Gugger, Clément Delangue, Théo Matussière, Lysandre Debut, Stas Bekman, Pierric Cistac, Thibault Goehringer, Victor Mustar, François Lagunas, Alexander Rush, and Thomas Wolf. 2021. Datasets: A community library for natural language processing. In *Proceedings of the 2021 Conference on Empirical Methods in Natural Language Processing: System Demonstrations*, pages 175–184, Online and Punta Cana, Dominican Republic. Association for Computational Linguistics.

Yanzeng Li, Bowen Yu, Li Quangang, and Tingwen Liu. 2021. FITAnnotator: A flexible and intelligent text annotation system. In *Proceedings of the 2021 Conference of the North American Chapter of the Association for Computational Linguistics: Human Language Technologies: Demonstrations*, pages 35–41, Online. Association for Computational Linguistics.

Bill Yuchen Lin, Dong-Ho Lee, Frank F. Xu, Ouyu Lan, and Xiang Ren. 2019. AlpacaTag: An active learning-based crowd annotation framework for sequence tagging. In *Proceedings of the 57th Annual Meeting of the Association for Computational Linguistics: System Demonstrations*, pages 58–63, Florence, Italy. Association for Computational Linguistics.

Xi Victoria Lin, Todor Mihaylov, Mikel Artetxe, Tianlu Wang, Shuohui Chen, Daniel Simig, Myle Ott, Naman Goyal, Shruti Bhosale, Jingfei Du, Ramakanth Pasunuru, Sam Shleifer, Punit Singh Koura, Vishrav Chaudhary, Brian O'Horo, Jeff Wang, Luke Zettlemoyer, Zornitsa Kozareva, Mona T. Diab, Veselin Stoyanov, and Xian Li. 2021. Few-shot learning with multilingual language models. *CoRR*, abs/2112.10668.

Pengfei Liu, Weizhe Yuan, Jinlan Fu, Zhengbao Jiang, Hiroaki Hayashi, and Graham Neubig. 2021. Pre-train, prompt, and predict: A systematic survey of prompting methods in natural language processing. *CoRR*, abs/2107.13586.

Sewon Min, Mike Lewis, Luke Zettlemoyer, and Hannaneh Hajishirzi. 2021. Metaicl: Learning to learn in context. *CoRR*, abs/2110.15943.

Swaroop Mishra, Daniel Khashabi, Chitta Baral, and Hannaneh Hajishirzi. 2021. Cross-task generalization via natural language crowdsourcing instructions. *arXiv preprint arXiv:2104.08773*.

Mariana Neves and Jurica Ševa. 2021. An extensive review of tools for manual annotation of documents. *Briefings in bioinformatics*, 22(1):146–163.

Frédéric Papazian, Robert Bossy, and Claire Nédellec. 2012. AlvisAE: a collaborative web text annotation editor for knowledge acquisition. In *Proceedings of the Sixth Linguistic Annotation Workshop*, pages 149–152, Jeju, Republic of Korea. Association for Computational Linguistics.

Ethan Perez, Douwe Kiela, and Kyunghyun Cho. 2021. True few-shot learning with language models. *NeurIPS*.

Jan Wira Gotama Putra, Simone Teufel, Kana Matsumura, and Takenobu Tokunaga. 2020. TIARA: A tool for annotating discourse relations and sentence reordering. In *Proceedings of the 12th Language Resources and Evaluation Conference*, pages 6912–6920, Marseille, France. European Language Resources Association.

Guanghui Qin and Jason Eisner. 2021. Learning how to ask: Querying LMs with mixtures of soft prompts. In *Proceedings of the 2021 Conference of the North*

*American Chapter of the Association for Computational Linguistics: Human Language Technologies*, pages 5203–5212, Online. Association for Computational Linguistics.

David Salgado, Martin Krallinger, Marc Depaule, Elodie Drula, Ashish V. Tendulkar, Florian Leitner, Alfonso Valencia, and Christophe Marcelle. 2012. MyMiner: a web application for computer-assisted biocuration and text annotation. *Bioinformatics*, 28(17):2285–2287.

Victor Sanh, Albert Webson, Colin Raffel, Stephen H. Bach, Lintang Sutawika, Zaid Alyafeai, Antoine Chaffin, Arnaud Stiegler, Teven Le Scao, Arun Raja, Manan Dey, M Saiful Bari, Canwen Xu, Urmish Thakker, Shanya Sharma Sharma, Eliza Szczechla, Taewoon Kim, Gunjan Chhablani, Nihal Nayak, Debajyoti Datta, Jonathan Chang, Mike Tian-Jian Jiang, Han Wang, Matteo Manica, Sheng Shen, Zheng Xin Yong, Harshit Pandey, Rachel Bawden, Thomas Wang, Trishala Neeraj, Jos Rozen, Abheesht Sharma, Andrea Santilli, Thibault Fevry, Jason Alan Fries, Ryan Teehan, Stella Biderman, Leo Gao, Tali Bers, Thomas Wolf, and Alexander M. Rush. 2021. Multitask prompted training enables zero-shot task generalization.

Timo Schick and Hinrich Schütze. 2021a. Exploiting cloze-questions for few-shot text classification and natural language inference. In *Proceedings of the 16th Conference of the European Chapter of the Association for Computational Linguistics: Main Volume*, pages 255–269, Online. Association for Computational Linguistics.

Timo Schick and Hinrich Schütze. 2021b. It's not just size that matters: Small language models are also few-shot learners. In *Proceedings of the 2021 Conference of the North American Chapter of the Association for Computational Linguistics: Human Language Technologies*, pages 2339–2352, Online. Association for Computational Linguistics.

Taylor Shin, Yasaman Razeghi, Robert L. Logan IV, Eric Wallace, and Sameer Singh. 2020. AutoPrompt: Eliciting Knowledge from Language Models with Automatically Generated Prompts. In *Proceedings of the 2020 Conference on Empirical Methods in Natural Language Processing (EMNLP)*, pages 4222–4235, Online. Association for Computational Linguistics.

Pontus Stenetorp, Sampo Pyysalo, Goran Topić, Tomoko Ohta, Sophia Ananiadou, and Jun'ichi Tsujii. 2012. brat: a web-based tool for NLP-assisted text annotation. In *Proceedings of the Demonstrations at the 13th Conference of the European Chapter of the Association for Computational Linguistics*, pages 102–107, Avignon, France. Association for Computational Linguistics.

Michael Stewart, Wei Liu, and Rachel Cardell-Oliver. 2019. Redcoat: A collaborative annotation tool for hierarchical entity typing. In *Proceedings of the 2019 Conference on Empirical Methods in Natural Language Processing and the 9th International Joint Conference on Natural Language Processing (EMNLP-IJCNLP): System Demonstrations*, pages 193–198, Hong Kong, China. Association for Computational Linguistics.

Albert Webson and Ellie Pavlick. 2021. Do prompt-based models really understand the meaning of their prompts? *ArXiv*, abs/2109.01247.

Chih-Hsuan Wei, Hung-Yu Kao, and Zhiyong Lu. 2013. PubTator: a web-based text mining tool for assisting biocuration. *Nucleic Acids Research*, 41(W1):W518–W522.

Jason Wei, Maarten Bosma, Vincent Y. Zhao, Kelvin Guu, Adams Wei Yu, Brian Lester, Nan Du, Andrew M. Dai, and Quoc V. Le. 2021. Finetuned language models are zero-shot learners. *CoRR*, abs/2109.01652.

Jie Yang, Yue Zhang, Linwei Li, and Xingxuan Li. 2018. YEDDA: A lightweight collaborative text span annotation tool. In *Proceedings of ACL 2018, System Demonstrations*, pages 31–36, Melbourne, Australia. Association for Computational Linguistics.

Seid Muhie Yimam, Iryna Gurevych, Richard Eckart de Castilho, and Chris Biemann. 2013. WebAnno: A flexible, web-based and visually supported system for distributed annotations. In *Proceedings of the 51st Annual Meeting of the Association for Computational Linguistics: System Demonstrations*, pages 1–6, Sofia, Bulgaria. Association for Computational Linguistics.

Tony Z. Zhao, Eric Wallace, Shi Feng, Dan Klein, and Sameer Singh. 2021. Calibrate before use: Improving few-shot performance of language models. *CoRR*, abs/2102.09690.

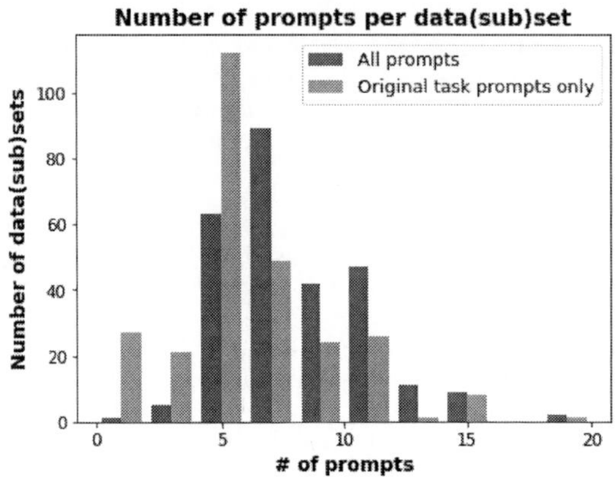


Figure 6: Most of the datasets have between 5 and 10 prompts.

## A Data and Statistics

P3 is the largest public collection of English prompts and is actively growing. As of January 2022, it contains 2'052 English prompts for 170 English datasets (or 269 subsets, one dataset can contain multiple subsets with different prompts). There is an average of 7.6 prompts per data subset and an average 5.6 original-task prompts per data subset (see Figure 6).

P3 was developed as part of the BigScience project for open research[5]. There was a open hackathon to collect prompts for as many English NLP dataset (or English subsets of datasets) as possible. Almost 50 unique contributors affiliated with more than 25 institutions in 10 countries participated.

## B Complete Views

We show higher resolution examples of the full interfaces for the *Browse* (Figure 7), *Sourcing* (Figure 8), and *Helicopter* (Figure 9) views.

[5]https://bigscience.huggingface.co

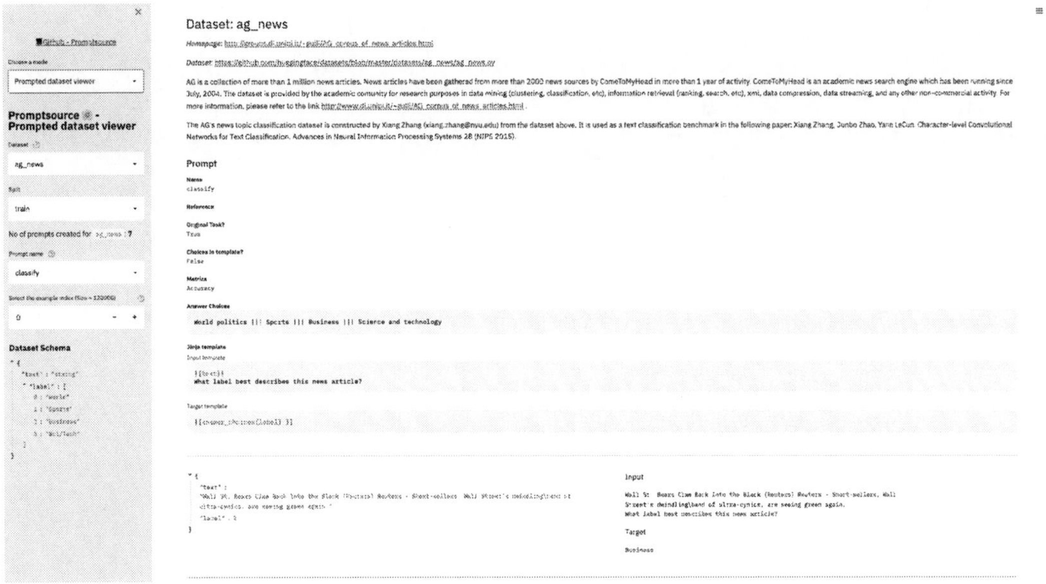


Figure 7: Complete example of the *Browse* view.

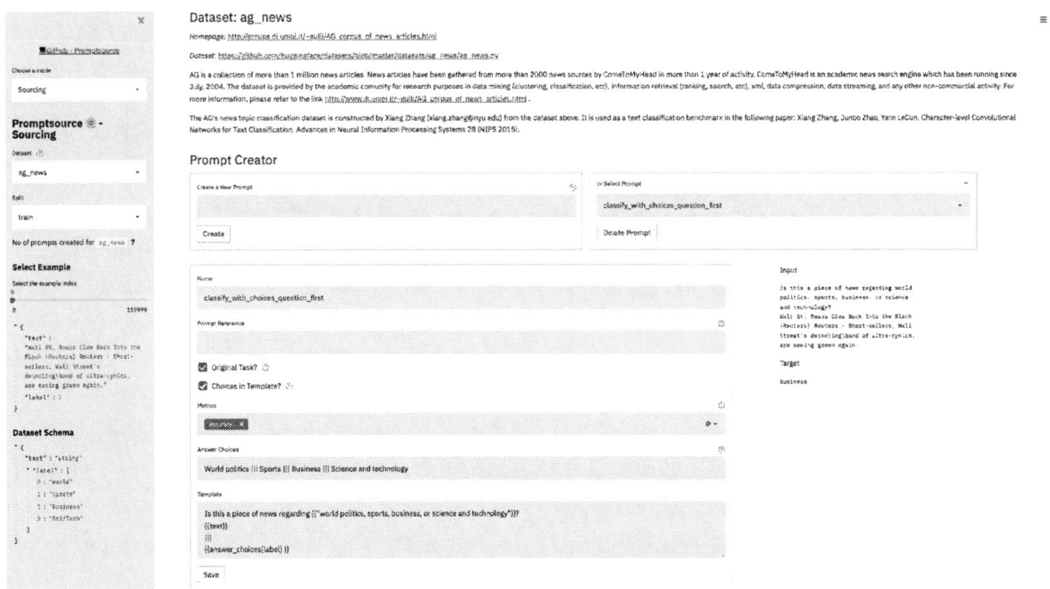


Figure 8: Complete example of the *Sourcing* view.

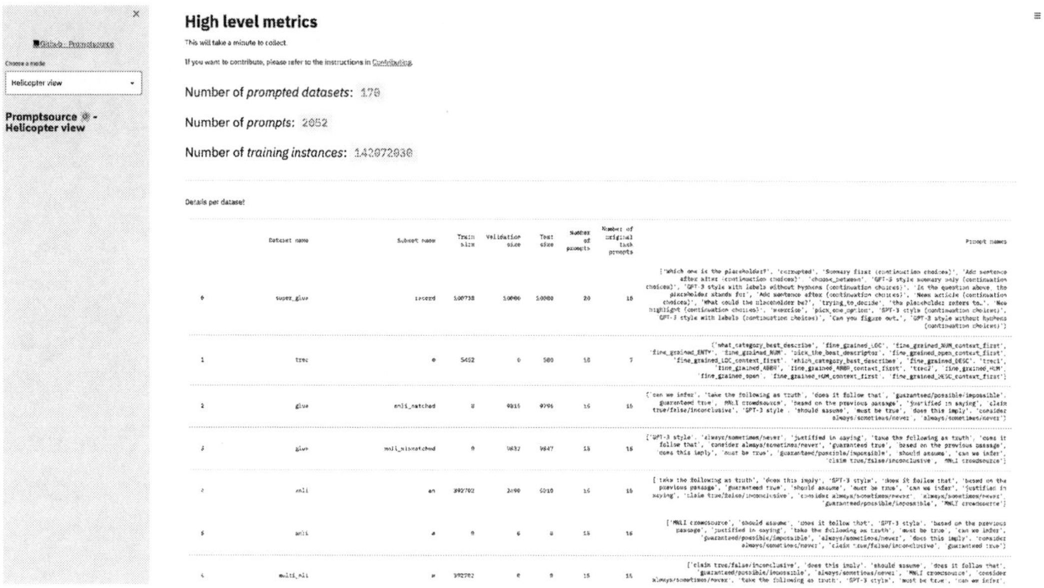


Figure 9: Complete example of the *Helicopter* view.

# OpenPrompt: An Open-source Framework for Prompt-learning

**Ning Ding**[1*], **Shengding Hu**[1*], **Weilin Zhao**[1*], **Yulin Chen**[5],
**Zhiyuan Liu**[1,2,3,4†], **Hai-Tao Zheng**[5†], **Maosong Sun**[1,2,3]
[1]Dept. of Comp. Sci. & Tech., Institute for AI, Tsinghua University, Beijing, China
Beijing National Research Center for Information Science and Technology
[2]Institute Guo Qiang, Tsinghua University, Beijing, China
[3]International Innovation Center of Tsinghua University, Shanghai, China,[4] BAAI, China
[5] Shenzhen International Graduate School, Tsinghua University, China, Peng Cheng Laboratory
{dingn18, hsd20, zwl19, yl-chen21}@mails.tsinghua.edu.cn

## Abstract

Prompt-learning has become a new paradigm in modern natural language processing, which directly adapts pre-trained language models (PLMs) to *cloze*-style prediction, autoregressive modeling, or sequence to sequence generation, resulting in promising performances on various tasks. However, no standard implementation framework of prompt-learning is proposed yet, and most existing prompt-learning codebases, often unregulated, only provide limited implementations for specific scenarios. Since there are many details such as templating strategy, initializing strategy, and verbalizing strategy, etc., need to be considered in prompt-learning, practitioners face impediments to quickly adapting the desired prompt learning methods to their applications. In this paper, we present OpenPrompt, a unified easy-to-use toolkit to conduct prompt-learning over PLMs. OpenPrompt is a research-friendly framework that is equipped with efficiency, modularity, and extendibility, and its combinability allows the freedom to combine different PLMs, task formats, and prompting modules in a unified paradigm. Users could expediently deploy prompt-learning frameworks and evaluate the generalization of them on different NLP tasks without constraints.[1]

## 1 Introduction

Pre-trained language models (PLMs) (Han et al., 2021a; Qiu et al., 2020) have been widely proven to be effective in natural language understanding and generation, ushering in a new era of modern natural language processing (NLP). In the early stage of this revolution, a standard approach to adapt PLMs to various specific NLP tasks is the *pretraining-finetuning* paradigm, where additional parameters and task-specific objectives are introduced in the tuning procedure. However recently, the paradigm of the adaptation of PLMs is shifting. Originated in T5 (Raffel et al., 2019) and GPT-3 (Brown et al., 2020), researchers find that PLMs can be effectively stimulated by textual prompts or demonstrations, especially in low-data scenarios.

Take a simple prompt-based sentiment classification for example, the pipeline consists of a template and a verbalizer, where a template is used to process the original text with some extra tokens, and a verbalizer projects original labels to words in the vocabulary for final prediction. Assume the template is "<text> *It is* <mask>", where the token <text> stands for the original text, and the verbalizer is {*"positive":"great", "negative":"terrible"*}. The sentence "*Albert Einstein was one of the greatest intellects of his time.*" will first be wrapped by the pre-defined template as "*Albert Einstein was one of the greatest intellects of his time. It is* <mask>". The wrapped sentence is then tokenized and fed into a PLM to predict the distribution over vocabulary on the <mask> token position. It is expected that the word *great* should have a larger probability than *terrible*.

As illustrated above, prompt-learning projects the downstream tasks to pre-training objectives for PLMs with the help of textual or soft-encoding prompts. A series of studies of prompt-learning (Liu et al., 2021a) have been proposed to investigate the strategies of constructing templates (Schick and Schütze, 2021; Gao et al., 2021; Liu et al., 2021b), verbalizers (Hu et al., 2021), optimization (Lester et al., 2021), and application (Li and Liang, 2021; Han et al., 2021b; Ding et al., 2021a) for this paradigm.

A prompt-learning problem could be regarded as a synthesis of PLMs, human prior knowledge, and specific NLP tasks that need to be handled.

* equal contribution
† corresponding authors
[1]OpenPrompt is released at https://github.com/thunlp/OpenPrompt.



*Proceedings of the 60th Annual Meeting of the Association for Computational Linguistics*
*System Demonstrations*, pages 105 - 113
May 22-27, 2022 ©2022 Association for Computational Linguistics

| Example | PLM | Template | Verbalizer | Task | Reference |
|---|---|---|---|---|---|
| Naive TC | MLM & Seq2Seq | M. text | M. One-Many | Text Classification | - |
| Naive KP | LM & Seq2Seq | M. text | - | Knowledge Probing | - |
| Naive FET | MLM | M. text (meta info) | M. One-Many | Entity Typing | (Ding et al., 2021a) |
| PTR | MLM | M. text (complex) | M. One-One | Relation Extratcion | (Han et al., 2021b) |
| P-tuning | LM | Soft tokens | M. One-One | Text Classification | (Liu et al., 2021b) |
| Prefix-tuning | LM, Seq2Seq | Soft tokens | - | Text Generation | (Li and Liang, 2021) |
| LM-BFF | MLM | A. text | M. One-Many | Text Classification | (Gao et al., 2021) |

Table 1: Some examples implemented by OpenPrompt, where M. is the abbreviation of manually defined and A. is the abbreviation of automatically generated. Note that different approaches focus on different parts in prompt-learning. Additional to the whole pipeline, our specific implementations of these methods are integrated into the specific classes of OpenPrompt.

Hence, it is hard to support the particular implementations of prompt-learning elegantly with the current deep learning or NLP libraries while there is also a lack of a standard paradigm. Previous works pursue the most efficient way to implement prompt-learning with the least modification to the existing framework for traditional fine-tuning, resulting in poor readability and even unstable reproducibility. Moreover, the performance of a prompt-learning pipeline varies greatly with the choice of templates and verbalizers (Zhao et al., 2021), creating more barriers for implementations. Lastly, there is no comprehensive open-source framework particularly designed for prompt-learning at present, which makes it difficult to try out new methods and make rigorous comparisons for previous approaches.

We present OpenPrompt, an open-source, easy-to-use, and extensible toolkit for prompt-learning. OpenPrompt modularizes the whole framework of prompt-learning and considers the interactions between each module. We highlight the feature of combinability of OpenPrompt, which supports flexible combinations of diverse task formats, PLMs, and prompting modules. For example, we can easily adapt prefix-tuning (Li and Liang, 2021) to a text classification task in OpenPrompt. This feature enables users to assess the generalization of their prompt-learning models on various tasks, but not only the performance on specific tasks.

Specifically, a `Template` class is used to define or generate textual or soft-encoding templates to wrap the original input. To flexibly support various templates under a unified paradigm, we design a new template language that could easily conduct token-level customization for the corresponding attributes. A `Verbalizer` projects the classification labels to words in the vocabulary, and a `PromptModel` is responsible for the training and inference process. Each module in OpenPrompt is clearly defined while retaining its independence and coupling so that researchers can easily deploy a model and make targeted improvements. We also implement baselines with OpenPrompt and evaluate them on a broad scope of NLP tasks, demonstrating the effectiveness of OpenPrompt.

The area of prompt-learning is in the exploratory stage with rapid development. Hopefully, OpenPrompt could help beginners quickly understand prompt-learning, enable researchers to efficiently deploy prompt-learning research pipeline, and empower engineers to readily apply prompt-learning to practical NLP systems to solve real-world problems. OpenPrompt will not only keep all the code open source, but will also continue to update the documentation to provide detailed tutorials.

## 2 Design and Implementation

As stated in § 1, prompt-learning is a comprehensive process that combines PLMs, human knowledge, and specific NLP tasks. Keeping that in mind, the design philosophy is to simultaneously consider the independence and mutual coupling of each module. As illustrated in Figure 1, OpenPrompt provides the full life-cycle of prompt-learning based on PyTorch (Paszke et al., 2019). In this section, we first introduce the combinability of OpenPrompt, and then the detailed design and implementation of each component in OpenPrompt.

### 2.1 Combinability

In the NLP world, we usually adopt different PLMs with corresponding objective functions to different underlying tasks (roughly, classification and generation). But in prompt learning, given that the core idea of the framework is to mimic pre-training tasks in the downstream task, which are essentially "predicting words based on context", we can further unify the execution of downstream tasks. Open-

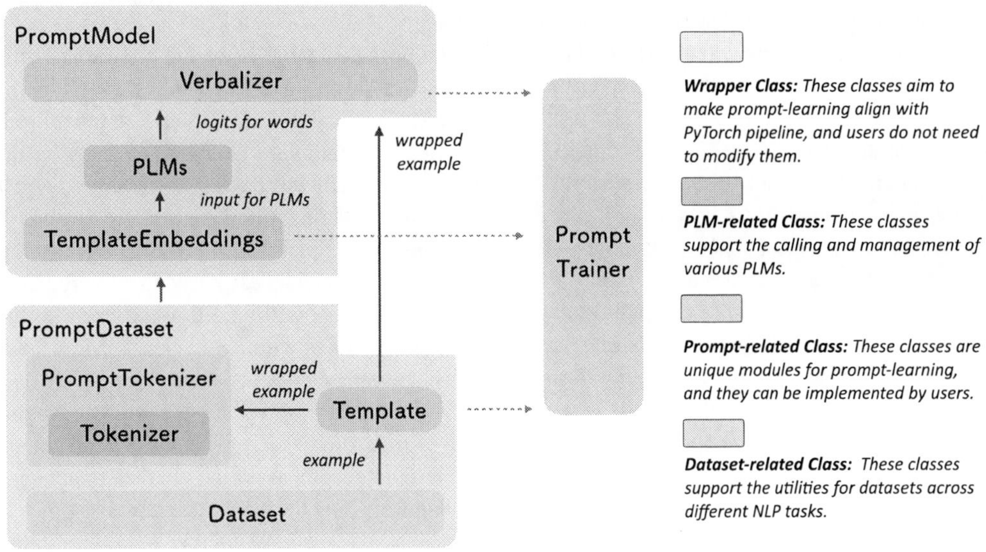


Figure 1: The overall architecture of OpenPrompt. Note that according to the prompt-learning strategies, not all the modules are necessarily used. For example, in generation tasks, there are no verbalizers in the learning procedure. The `PromptTrainer` is a controller that controls the data flow and the training process with some unique attributes, users can also implement the training process in a conventional fashion.

Prompt supports a combination of tasks, PLMs, and prompt modules in a flexible way. For example, from a model perspective, T5 (Raffel et al., 2019) is not only used for span prediction and GPT (Brown et al., 2020) is not only used for generative tasks. From the perspective of prompting, prefix-tuning can also be used for classification, and soft prompt can be used for generation. All these combinations can easily be implemented and validated on NLP tasks in our framework so that we can better understand the mechanisms involved.

## 2.2 Pre-trained Language Models

One core idea of prompt-learning is to use additional context with masked tokens to imitate the pre-training objectives of PLMs and better stimulate these models. Hence, the choice of PLMs is crucial to the whole pipeline of prompt-learning. PLMs could be roughly divided into three groups according to their pre-training objectives.

The first group of PLMs use masked language modeling (MLM) to reconstruct a sequence corrupted by random masked tokens, where only the losses of the masked tokens are computed. Typical PLMs with MLM objective include BERT (Devlin et al., 2019), RoBERTa (Liu et al., 2019), etc, and such an objective is regarded suitable for natural language understanding (NLU). The second group exploits the autoregressive-style language modeling (LM) to predict the current token according to its leading tokens. GPT-3 (Brown et al., 2020) is one of the representative works adopting this objective. The third part is the sequence-to-sequence (Seq2Seq) models, which aim to generate a sequence with a decoder conditioned on a separate encoder for an input sequence. Typical seq2seq PLMs include T5 (Raffel et al., 2020), MASS (Song et al., 2019) and BART (Lewis et al., 2020), etc.

Different PLMs have different attributes, resulting in various adaptation capabilities for different NLP tasks in prompt-learning. Practically in OpenPrompt, we support directly loading PLMs from huggingface transformers (Wolf et al., 2020), and PLMs implemented by other libraries will be supported in the future. Once the PLM is determined, researchers could deploy a known valid prompt-learning pipeline (e.g., RoBERTa for few-shot sentiment classification) or explore other uses of PLM that could exploit its potential. Users of OpenPrompt do not need to implement objective heads for different PLMs to calculate the corresponding loss, a unified interface can perform these operations automatically (§ 2.6).

## 2.3 Tokenization

Tokenization is a crucial step in processing data for NLP, and it faces new challenges in prompt-learning. After designing the template, the specific implementation of the tokenization for original input and the designed template could be time-consuming and error-prone. First, in prompt-learning, some specific information such as the indices of entities and masked tokens should be carefully tackled in tokenization. Some small errors, such as the mismatch of masked token indices, may lead to serious consequences. Moreover, concatenation and truncation issues after tokenization (templates are not supposed to be truncated) should also be handled. Since different PLMs may have different tokenization strategies, we should also consider the inconsistency in the details of additional context processing. We specifically design the tokenization module for prompt-learning and significantly simplify the process. By using our encapsulated data processing APIs, users could use the human-readable style to design templates and conveniently operate on the input and the template at the same time. Our component integrates complex information from input and template and then conducts tokenization. Based on the choice of PLMs, OpenPrompt automatically chooses the appropriate tokenizer in prompt-learning, which could save considerable time for users to process prompt-related data.

### 2.4 Templates

As one of the central parts of prompt-learning, a template module wraps the original text with the textual or soft-encoding template. A template normally contains contextual tokens (textual or soft) and masked tokens. In OpenPrompt, all the templates are inherited from a common base class with universal attributes and abstract methods.

Previous works design a wide variety of templates, including manually written template (Schick and Schütze, 2021) and pure soft template (Lester et al., 2021). Gu et al. (2021) report a mix of manual template tokens and soft (trainable) tokens sometimes yields better results than separate manual template and soft template. In Liu et al. (2021b), a promising performance is achieved by fixing the majority of manual tokens while tuning a small number of the others. In Han et al. (2021b), the template is contextualized, which needs to be filled with the head entity and the tail entity to form a complete one, moreover, the output of multiple positions is used in the loss calculation in their template. Logan IV et al. (2021) design null template with simple concatenation of the inputs and an appended `<mask>` token.

It's not reasonable to design a template format for each prompt since it will require high learning cost for practical use. To this end, in OpenPrompt, we design a template language to ease the problem, with which we can construct various types of templates under a unified paradigm. Our template language takes insight from the dict grammer of Python. And such a design ensures flexibility and clarity at the same time, allowing users to build different prompts with relative ease. More specifically, a template node is a text (or empty text) with an attributes' description. In our template language, one is free to edit the attributes of each token in the template, such as which characters are shared embedding, how the characters are post-processed (e.g. by MLP), etc. We show some template examples in Figure 2, and the detailed tutorial for writing templates is in the documentation [2].

### 2.5 Verbalizers

When it comes to prompt-based classification, a verbalizer class should be constructed to map original labels to label words in the vocabulary. When a PLM predicts a probability distribution over the vocabulary for one masked position, a verbalizer will extract the logits of label words and integrate the logits of label words to the corresponding class, thereby responsible for the loss calculation. Figure 3 shows a simple way to define a binary sentiment classification verbalizer.

Similar to templates, all the verbalizer classes are also inherited from a common base class with necessary attributes and abstract methods. Additional to manually-defined verbalizers, we implement automatic verbalizers like AutomaticVerbalizer and KnowledgeableVerbalizer (Hu et al., 2021). Moreover, important operations like calibrations (Zhao et al., 2021) are also realized in OpenPrompt.

Prompt-learning could also facilitate the unification of NLP tasks. In such kind of paradigm, a span of text (i.e., the target text) is expected to be generated in the masked position. Then the final prediction will be based on a mapping from the target texts to the labels (Ye et al., 2021; Du et al., 2021). To fully support such a paradigm, we implement a novel `GenerationVerbalizer`, which supports designating any kind of text, including a piece of text from the input, as the target text. To compose a target text for a

[2] https://thunlp.github.io/OpenPrompt

```
# Example A. Hard prompt for topic classification
a {"mask"} news: {"meta": "title"} {"meta": "description"}

# Example B. Hard prompt for entity typing
{"meta": "sentence"}. In this sentence, {"meta": "entity"} is a {"mask"},

# Example C. Soft prompt (initialized by textual tokens)
{"meta": "premise"} {"meta": "hypothesis"} {"soft": "Does the first sentence
    entails the second ?"} {"mask"} {"soft"}.

# Example D. Pure soft template in Lester et al., 2021.
{"soft": None, "duplicate": 100} {"meta": "text"} {"mask"}

# Example E. Post processing script support
# e.g. write an lambda expression to strip the final punctuation in data
{"meta": "context", "post_processing": lambda s: s.rstrip(string.punctuation)}. {"
    soft": "It was"} {"mask"}

# Example F. Mixed prompt with two shared soft tokens
{"meta": "premise"} {"meta": "hypothesis"} {"soft": "Does"} {"soft": "the", "
    soft_id": 1} first sentence entails {"soft_id": 1} second?

# Example G. Specify the title should not be truncated
a {"mask"} news: {"meta": "title", "shortenable": False} {"meta": "description"}
```

Figure 2: Some examples of our template language. In our template language, we can use the key "meta" to refer the original input text (Example B), parts of the original input (Example A, C, G), or other key information. We can also freely specify which tokens are hard and which are soft (and their initialization strategy). We could assign an id for a soft token to specify which tokens are sharing embeddings (Example F). OpenPrompt also supports the post processing (Example E) for each token, e.g., lambda expression or MLP.

```
from openprompt import
    ManualVerbalizer

promptVerbalizer = ManualVerbalizer(
    classes = classes,
    label_words = {
        "negative": ["bad"],
        "positive": ["good", "
    wonderful", "great"],
    },
    tokenizer = bertTokenizer,
)
```

Figure 3: An example to define a Verbalizer, the number of the label words for each class is flexible.

```
from openprompt import
    GenerationVerbalizer

promptVerbalizer =
    GenerationVerbalizer(
    classes = classes,
    label_words = {
        0: ["other words."],
        1: ["word {'meta': 'word0'}"],
    },
    is_rule = True,
    tokenizer = T5Tokenizer,
)
```

Figure 4: An example to use GenerationVerbalizer to conduct a co-reference resolution task. This task requires the model to distinguish whether a pronoun refers to the 'word0' in the sentence.

`GenerationVerbalizer`, the syntax is the same as the template language (See Figure 4). Different evaluation metrics are then used for different types of task, For example, exact match for classification tasks and BLEU score (Papineni et al., 2002) for generation tasks.

## 2.6 PromptModel

In OpenPrompt, we use a `PromptModel` object to be responsible for training and inference, which contains a PLM, a `Template` object, and a `Verbalizer` object (optional). Users could flexibly combine these modules and define advanced interactions among them. A model-agnostic forward method is implemented in the base class to predict words for the masked positions. One goal of this module is that users do not need to specifically implement heads for different PLMs, but use a unified API to "predict words for positions that need to be predicted" regardless of the pre-training objective. An example to define a `PromptModel` is shown in Figure 6.

## 2.7 Training

From the perspective of trainable parameters, the training of prompt-learning could be divided into two types of strategies. The first strategy simulta-

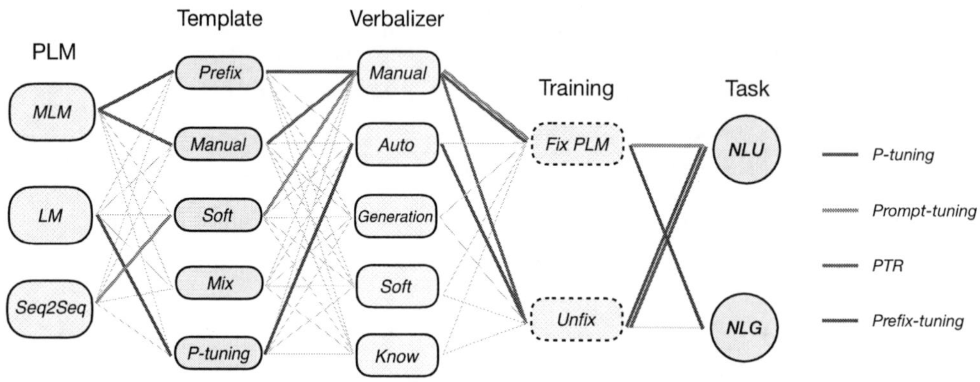


Figure 5: The illustration of the validation space of OpenPrompt. By driving different modules of the framework, we could implement and evaluate different methods on a broad set of NLP tasks. We show four examples in this illustration, the colored lines denote the implementation flow of the corresponding method.

```
from openprompt import
    PromptForClassification

promptModel = PromptForClassification(
    template = promptTemplate,
    model = bertModel,
    verbalizer = promptVerbalizer,
)

promptModel.eval()
with torch.no_grad():
    for batch in data_loader:
        logits = promptModel(batch)
        preds = torch.argmax(logits,
    dim = -1)
        print(classes[preds])
```

Figure 6: An example to define a `PromptModel` and conduct evaluation.

neously tunes the prompts and the PLM, which is verified to be effective in a low-data regime (OpenPrompt also provides a `FewshotSampler` to support the few-shot learning scenario). The second strategy is to only train the parameters of prompts and keep the PLM frozen, this is regarded as a parameter-efficient tuning method and is considered as a promising way to stimulate super-large PLMs. Both of these strategies can be called with one click in the trainer (or runner) module of OpenPrompt. Trainer modules in OpenPrompt implement training process accompanied with prompt-oriented training tricks, e.g. the ensemble of templates. Meanwhile, OpenPrompt supports experimentation through configuration to easily drive large-scale empirical study. We provide several complete tutorials[3] to use the basic and advanced attributes of OpenPrompt.

## 3 Evaluation

OpenPrompt aims to support a broad set of NLP tasks under the paradigm of prompt-learning. In terms of evaluation, we use OpenPrompt to implement various baselines and assess them on the corresponding NLP tasks. We show the validation space in Figure 5. And the evaluation tasks include WebNLG (Gardent et al., 2017) for conditional generation, GLUE (Wang et al., 2018) and SuperGLUE (Wang et al., 2019) for natural language understanding; SemEval (Hendrickx et al., 2010), Few-NERD (Ding et al., 2021b) for information extraction; MNLI (Williams et al., 2017), AG's News (Zhang et al., 2015), DBPedia (Lehmann et al., 2015) and IMDB (Maas et al., 2011) for text classification; LAMA (Petroni et al., 2019) for knowledge probing. The processors of these datasets have already been implemented in OpenPrompt, and they are all inherited from a common base `DataProcessor` class. To keep the results up to date, we are constantly updating and reporting the latest results on our GitHub repository[4].

## 4 Discussion

Although PLMs have achieved tremendous success on almost all the subtasks in NLP, one problem still hangs in the air, *have we really fully exploited the potential of PLMs, especially the big ones?* Conventional fine-tuning uses extra task-specific heads and objectives for adaptation, but this strategy may face two issues. On the one hand, such an approach creates a natural gap between model tuning and pre-training. On the other hand, as the

[3] `https://github.com/thunlp/OpenPrompt/tree/main/tutorial`

[4] `https://github.com/thunlp/OpenPrompt/tree/main/results/`

number of model parameters increases, this fine-tuning approach becomes increasingly difficult to operate due to the massive computational volume (e.g., GPT-3 (Brown et al., 2020)).

By mimicking the process of pre-training, prompt-learning intuitively bridges the gap between pre-training and model tuning. Practically, this paradigm is surprisingly effective in low-data regime (Le Scao and Rush, 2021; Gao et al., 2021). For example, with appropriate template, zero-shot prompt-learning could even outperform 32-shot fine-tuning (Ding et al., 2021a). Another promising empirical attribute of prompt-learning is the potential to stimulate large-scale PLMs. When it comes to a 10B model, solely optimizing prompts (the parameters of the model are fixed) could achieve comparable performance to full parameter fine-tuning (Lester et al., 2021). These practical studies imply that we may use prompts to more effectively and efficiently dig the knowledge kept in PLMs, leading to a deeper understanding of the underlying principles of their mechanisms (Wei et al., 2021; Qin et al., 2021; Vu et al., 2021). In addition to prompt-based methods, there are also other techniques exploring the parameter-efficient stimulation of large-scale PLMs (Houlsby et al., 2019; Hu et al., 2022; He et al., 2022; Ding et al., 2022). Although it is possible to achieve non-trivial results on the large-scale PLMs by just adjusting the prompt. However, in small and medium-sized models, prompt still faces optimization problems that need to be addressed.

From a practical implementation point of view, prompt-learning is actually complex and requires a lot of detailed consideration. With general-purpose NLP under the prompt-learning paradigm as our target, we present OpenPrompt, a unified toolkit to effectively and efficiently implement prompt-learning approaches. OpenPrompt demonstrates a comprehensive view of the programming details of prompt-learning, and enables practitioners to quickly understand the mechanisms and practical attributes of this technique. And one can quickly deploy existing representative prompt-learning algorithms that are already implemented in the package under a unified programming framework. Moreover, OpenPrompt allows researchers or developers to quickly try out new ideas of prompt-learning, which not only includes newly designed templates or verbalizers, but also the exploration of the attributes of prompt-learning, e.g., prompt-based adversarial attacking.

## 5 Conclusion and Future Work

We propose OpenPrompt, a unified, easy-to-use, and extensible toolkit for prompt-learning. OpenPrompt establishes a unified framework with clearly defined blocks and flexible interactions to support solid research on prompt-learning. At the application level, OpenPrompt could facilitate researchers and developers to effectively and efficiently deploy prompt-learning pipelines. In the future, we will continue to integrate new techniques and features to OpenPrompt to facilitate the research progress of prompt-learning. Focusing on organizing input and output and training processes, Openprompt will be easily combined with tools that focus on specific optimization execution processes in the future.

## Acknowledgements

This research is supported by National Key R&D Program of China (No. 2020AAA0106502), National Natural Science Foundation of China (Grant No. 6201101015), Beijing Academy of Artificial Intelligence (BAAI), Natural Science Foundation of Guangdong Province (Grant No. 2021A1515012640), the Basic Research Fund of Shenzhen City (Grant No. JCYJ20210324120012033 and JCYJ20190813165003837), and Overseas Cooperation Research Fund of Tsinghua Shenzhen International Graduate School (Grant No. HW2021008), Institute Guo Qiang at Tsinghua University, International Innovation Center of Tsinghua University, Shanghai, China. Ning Ding is supported by Baidu Scholarship. The authors would like to thank Guoyang Zeng, Jie Zhou, Jun Zhang and Huadong Wang for their valuable suggestions of the project.

## Contributions

Zhiyuan Liu, Ning Ding and Hai-Tao Zheng initiated and led the project. Ning Ding and Shengding Hu designed the original working flow and APIs. Shengding Hu, Weilin Zhao, Yulin Chen, Ning Ding developed basic classes and advanced attributes of OpenPrompt, as well as the tutorials. Ning Ding and Shengding Hu drafted the documentation and the paper. Zhiyuan Liu, Hai-Tao Zheng and Maosong Sun gave suggestions and feedback about the organization of the project.

## References


Tom B Brown, Benjamin Mann, Nick Ryder, Melanie Subbiah, Jared Kaplan, Prafulla Dhariwal, Arvind Neelakantan, Pranav Shyam, Girish Sastry, Amanda Askell, et al. 2020. Language models are few-shot learners. *arXiv preprint arXiv:2005.14165*.

Jacob Devlin, Ming-Wei Chang, Kenton Lee, and Kristina Toutanova. 2019. BERT: Pre-training of deep bidirectional transformers for language understanding. In *Proceedings of ACL*, pages 4171–4186, Minneapolis, Minnesota.

Ning Ding, Yulin Chen, Xu Han, Guangwei Xu, Pengjun Xie, Hai-Tao Zheng, Zhiyuan Liu, Juanzi Li, and Hong-Gee Kim. 2021a. Prompt-learning for fine-grained entity typing. *Arxiv preprint*, 2108.10604.

Ning Ding, Yujia Qin, Guang Yang, Fuchao Wei, Zonghan Yang, Yusheng Su, Shengding Hu, Yulin Chen, Chi-Min Chan, Weize Chen, et al. 2022. Delta tuning: A comprehensive study of parameter efficient methods for pre-trained language models. *arXiv preprint arXiv:2203.06904*.

Ning Ding, Guangwei Xu, Yulin Chen, Xiaobin Wang, Xu Han, Pengjun Xie, Hai-Tao Zheng, and Zhiyuan Liu. 2021b. Few-nerd: A few-shot named entity recognition dataset. In *Proceedings of ACL*.

Zhengxiao Du, Yujie Qian, Xiao Liu, Ming Ding, Jiezhong Qiu, Zhilin Yang, and Jie Tang. 2021. All nlp tasks are generation tasks: A general pretraining framework. *arXiv preprint arXiv:2103.10360*.

Tianyu Gao, Adam Fisch, and Danqi Chen. 2021. Making pre-trained language models better few-shot learners. In *Proceedings of ACL*, pages 3816–3830, Online.

Claire Gardent, Anastasia Shimorina, Shashi Narayan, and Laura Perez-Beltrachini. 2017. The webnlg challenge: Generating text from rdf data. In *Proceedings of INLG*, pages 124–133.

Yuxian Gu, Xu Han, Zhiyuan Liu, and Minlie Huang. 2021. Ppt: Pre-trained prompt tuning for few-shot learning. *arXiv preprint arXiv:2109.04332*.

Xu Han, Zhengyan Zhang, Ning Ding, Yuxian Gu, Xiao Liu, Yuqi Huo, Jiezhong Qiu, Liang Zhang, Wentao Han, Minlie Huang, Qin Jin, Yanyan Lan, Yang Liu, Zhiyuan Liu, Zhiwu Lu, Xipeng Qiu, Ruihua Song, Jie Tang, Ji-Rong Wen, Jinhui Yuan, Wayne Xin Zhao, and Jun Zhu. 2021a. Pre-trained models: Past, present and future. *ArXiv preprint*, abs/2106.07139.

Xu Han, Weilin Zhao, Ning Ding, Zhiyuan Liu, and Maosong Sun. 2021b. Ptr: Prompt tuning with rules for text classification. *ArXiv preprint*, 2105.11259.

Junxian He, Chunting Zhou, Xuezhe Ma, Taylor Berg-Kirkpatrick, and Graham Neubig. 2022. Towards a unified view of parameter-efficient transfer learning. In *Proceedings of ICLR*.

Iris Hendrickx, Su Nam Kim, Zornitsa Kozareva, Preslav Nakov, Diarmuid Ó Séaghdha, Sebastian Padó, Marco Pennacchiotti, Lorenza Romano, and Stan Szpakowicz. 2010. SemEval-2010 task 8: Multi-way classification of semantic relations between pairs of nominals. In *Proceedings of SemEval*, pages 33–38.

Neil Houlsby, Andrei Giurgiu, Stanislaw Jastrzebski, Bruna Morrone, Quentin De Laroussilhe, Andrea Gesmundo, Mona Attariyan, and Sylvain Gelly. 2019. Parameter-efficient transfer learning for NLP. In *Proceedings of ICML*, pages 2790–2799. PMLR.

Edward J Hu, Yelong Shen, Phillip Wallis, Zeyuan Allen-Zhu, Yuanzhi Li, Shean Wang, Lu Wang, and Weizhu Chen. 2022. Lora: Low-rank adaptation of large language models. In *Proceedings of ICLR*.

Shengding Hu, Ning Ding, Huadong Wang, Zhiyuan Liu, Juanzi Li, and Maosong Sun. 2021. Knowledgeable prompt-tuning: Incorporating knowledge into prompt verbalizer for text classification. *ArXiv preprint*, 2108.02035.

Teven Le Scao and Alexander M Rush. 2021. How many data points is a prompt worth? In *Proceedings of NAACL*, pages 2627–2636.

Jens Lehmann, Robert Isele, Max Jakob, Anja Jentzsch, Dimitris Kontokostas, Pablo N Mendes, Sebastian Hellmann, Mohamed Morsey, Patrick Van Kleef, Sören Auer, et al. 2015. Dbpedia–a large-scale, multilingual knowledge base extracted from wikipedia. *Semantic web*, 6(2):167–195.

Brian Lester, Rami Al-Rfou, and Noah Constant. 2021. The power of scale for parameter-efficient prompt tuning. *ArXiv preprint*, abs/2104.08691.

Mike Lewis, Yinhan Liu, Naman Goyal, Marjan Ghazvininejad, Abdelrahman Mohamed, Omer Levy, Veselin Stoyanov, and Luke Zettlemoyer. 2020. BART: Denoising sequence-to-sequence pre-training for natural language generation, translation, and comprehension. In *Proceedings of ACL*, pages 7871–7880, Online.

Xiang Lisa Li and Percy Liang. 2021. Prefix-tuning: Optimizing continuous prompts for generation. In *Proceedings ACL*, pages 4582–4597, Online. Association for Computational Linguistics.

Pengfei Liu, Weizhe Yuan, Jinlan Fu, Zhengbao Jiang, Hiroaki Hayashi, and Graham Neubig. 2021a. Pre-train, prompt, and predict: A systematic survey of prompting methods in natural language processing. *ArXiv preprint*, abs/2107.13586.

Xiao Liu, Yanan Zheng, Zhengxiao Du, Ming Ding, Yujie Qian, Zhilin Yang, and Jie Tang. 2021b. Gpt understands, too. *arXiv preprint arXiv:2103.10385*.

Yinhan Liu, Myle Ott, Naman Goyal, Jingfei Du, Mandar Joshi, Danqi Chen, Omer Levy, Mike Lewis, Luke Zettlemoyer, and Veselin Stoyanov. 2019. RoBERTa: A robustly optimized BERT pretraining approach. *ArXiv preprint*, abs/1907.11692.

Robert L Logan IV, Ivana Balažević, Eric Wallace, Fabio Petroni, Sameer Singh, and Sebastian Riedel. 2021. Cutting down on prompts and parameters: Simple few-shot learning with language models. *arXiv preprint arXiv:2106.13353*.

Andrew Maas, Raymond E Daly, Peter T Pham, Dan Huang, Andrew Y Ng, and Christopher Potts. 2011. Learning word vectors for sentiment analysis. In *Proceedings of ACL*.

Kishore Papineni, Salim Roukos, Todd Ward, and Wei-Jing Zhu. 2002. Bleu: a method for automatic evaluation of machine translation. In *Proceedings of ACL*, pages 311–318.

Adam Paszke, Sam Gross, Francisco Massa, Adam Lerer, James Bradbury, Gregory Chanan, Trevor Killeen, Zeming Lin, Natalia Gimelshein, Luca Antiga, et al. 2019. Pytorch: An imperative style, high-performance deep learning library. *Proceedings of NeurIPS*, 32:8026–8037.

Fabio Petroni, Tim Rocktäschel, Patrick Lewis, Anton Bakhtin, Yuxiang Wu, Alexander H Miller, and Sebastian Riedel. 2019. Language models as knowledge bases? *arXiv preprint arXiv:1909.01066*.

Yujia Qin, Xiaozhi Wang, Yusheng Su, Yankai Lin, Ning Ding, Zhiyuan Liu, Juanzi Li, Lei Hou, Peng Li, Maosong Sun, et al. 2021. Exploring low-dimensional intrinsic task subspace via prompt tuning. *arXiv preprint arXiv:2110.07867*.

Xipeng Qiu, Tianxiang Sun, Yige Xu, Yunfan Shao, Ning Dai, and Xuanjing Huang. 2020. Pre-trained models for natural language processing: A survey. *Science China Technological Sciences*, pages 1–26.

Colin Raffel, Noam Shazeer, Adam Roberts, Katherine Lee, Sharan Narang, Michael Matena, Yanqi Zhou, Wei Li, and Peter J Liu. 2019. Exploring the limits of transfer learning with a unified text-to-text transformer. *ArXiv preprint*, abs/1910.10683.

Colin Raffel, Noam Shazeer, Adam Roberts, Katherine Lee, Sharan Narang, Michael Matena, Yanqi Zhou, Wei Li, and Peter J. Liu. 2020. Exploring the limits of transfer learning with a unified text-to-text transformer. *Journal of Machine Learning Research*, 21(140):1–67.

Timo Schick and Hinrich Schütze. 2021. Exploiting cloze-questions for few-shot text classification and natural language inference. In *Proceedings of EACL*, pages 255–269, Online. Association for Computational Linguistics.

Kaitao Song, Xu Tan, Tao Qin, Jianfeng Lu, and Tie-Yan Liu. 2019. Mass: Masked sequence to sequence pre-training for language generation. *arXiv preprint arXiv:1905.02450*.

Tu Vu, Brian Lester, Noah Constant, Rami Al-Rfou, and Daniel Cer. 2021. Spot: Better frozen model adaptation through soft prompt transfer. *arXiv preprint arXiv:2110.07904*.

Alex Wang, Yada Pruksachatkun, Nikita Nangia, Amanpreet Singh, Julian Michael, Felix Hill, Omer Levy, and Samuel R Bowman. 2019. Superglue: A stickier benchmark for general-purpose language understanding systems. *arXiv preprint arXiv:1905.00537*.

Alex Wang, Amanpreet Singh, Julian Michael, Felix Hill, Omer Levy, and Samuel R Bowman. 2018. Glue: A multi-task benchmark and analysis platform for natural language understanding. *arXiv preprint arXiv:1804.07461*.

Colin Wei, Sang Michael Xie, and Tengyu Ma. 2021. Why do pretrained language models help in downstream tasks? an analysis of head and prompt tuning. In *Proceedings of NeurIPS*.

Adina Williams, Nikita Nangia, and Samuel R Bowman. 2017. A broad-coverage challenge corpus for sentence understanding through inference. *arXiv preprint arXiv:1704.05426*.

Thomas Wolf, Lysandre Debut, Victor Sanh, Julien Chaumond, Clement Delangue, Anthony Moi, Pierric Cistac, Tim Rault, Rémi Louf, Morgan Funtowicz, Joe Davison, Sam Shleifer, Patrick von Platen, Clara Ma, Yacine Jernite, Julien Plu, Canwen Xu, Teven Le Scao, Sylvain Gugger, Mariama Drame, Quentin Lhoest, and Alexander M. Rush. 2020. Transformers: State-of-the-art natural language processing. In *Proceedings of EMNLP*, pages 38–45, Online.

Qinyuan Ye, Bill Yuchen Lin, and Xiang Ren. 2021. CrossFit: A few-shot learning challenge for cross-task generalization in NLP. In *Proceedings of EMNLP*, pages 7163–7189. Association for Computational Linguistics.

Xiang Zhang, Junbo Zhao, and Yann LeCun. 2015. Character-level convolutional networks for text classification. In *Proceedings of NIPS*.

Tony Z Zhao, Eric Wallace, Shi Feng, Dan Klein, and Sameer Singh. 2021. Calibrate before use: Improving few-shot performance of language models. *arXiv preprint arXiv:2102.09690*.

# Guided $K$-best Selection for Semantic Parsing Annotation

**Anton Belyy**[*1], **Chieh-Yang Huang**[*2], **Jacob Andreas**[3],
**Emmanouil Antonios Platanios**[3], **Sam Thomson**[3], **Richard Shin**[3],
**Subhro Roy**[3], **Aleksandr Nisnevich**[3], **Charles Chen**[3], **Benjamin Van Durme**[3]
[1]Johns Hopkins University, [2]Pennsylvania State University, [3]Microsoft Semantic Machines
`abel@jhu.edu`, `chiehyang@psu.edu`, `sminfo@microsoft.com`

## Abstract

Collecting data for conversational semantic parsing is a time-consuming and demanding process. In this paper we consider, given an incomplete dataset with only a small amount of data, how to build an AI-powered human-in-the-loop process to enable efficient data collection. A **guided $K$-best selection** process is proposed, which (*i*) generates a set of possible valid candidates; (*ii*) allows users to quickly traverse the set and filter incorrect parses; and (*iii*) asks users to select the correct parse, with minimal modification when necessary. We investigate how to best support users in efficiently traversing the candidate set and locating the correct parse, in terms of speed and accuracy. In our user study, consisting of five annotators labeling 300 instances each, we find that combining *keyword searching*, where keywords can be used to query relevant candidates, and *keyword suggestion*, where representative keywords are automatically generated, enables fast and accurate annotation.[1]

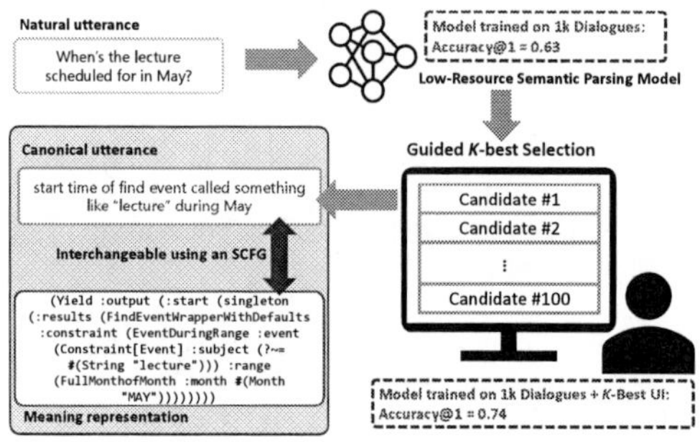


Figure 1: Guided $K$-best selection approaches achieve accuracy up to 74% when applied to VACSP-1k (Platanios et al., 2021), a conversational semantic parsing model trained on only 1k dialogues. The canonical utterance, used as the annotation target, is interchangeable with the meaning representation using an SCFG.

## 1 Introduction

Conversational Semantic Parsing (CSP), which aims to turn an utterance into a meaning representation such as an executable program or logical form, plays an important role in task-oriented dialogue systems (Zettlemoyer and Collins, 2009; Cheng et al., 2020; Platanios et al., 2021). In practice, building a complete task-oriented dialogue system requires back-and-forth revision of the meaning representation design. Such a mutable nature makes the data collection process difficult and costly. Depending on the complexity of the meaning representation, annotators might even need further training to equip them with basic domain knowledge about the task. Inspired by Computer Assisted Translation (CAT) (Green et al., 2013, 2014), we would like to know if we can accelerate the annotation process with AI-powered human-in-the-loop interfaces. The main difference between our task and the traditional CAT task lies in the facts that (*i*) only a prototype model trained on a small amount of initial data is available (low-resource setting), leading to limited prediction performance; and (*ii*) annotators have relatively little or no knowledge about the meaning representation.

Because neither the model nor the annotators are 100% accurate in our scenario, we propose the **$K$-best selection approach** as shown in Figure 1, where we (*i*) generate a set of candidates using a low-resource model; and (*ii*) ask annotators to traverse the set to select the correct parse and only modify it if necessary. This formulation allows annotators to focus on **reading and verification** and thus minimizes the need for annotators to write the complicated meaning representation. While the notion of $K$-best selection is established (Duan et al., 2016; He et al., 2016), to our knowledge there has been no investigation into optimizing this approach beyond a simple enumeration of candidates ranked by model score. In addition, a standard $K$-best

*Equal contribution. Work performed during an internship at Microsoft Semantic Machines.

[1]Demo video: `https://youtu.be/AtbCCYxjKIY`



*Proceedings of the 60th Annual Meeting of the Association for Computational Linguistics*
*System Demonstrations*, pages 114 - 126
May 22-27, 2022 

| Natural Utterance | Canonical Utterance |
|---|---|
| Okay, I'll get in touch with them. Can you tell me if Sqirl in Los Angeles has waiter service? | Does "Sqirl in Los Angeles" have waiter service |
| What do I have on my calendar after 12 pm tomorrow? | find event tomorrow after 12 PM |
| Can you add a workout with Kim between the sales meeting and dinner? | create event called "workout" starting between find event called something like "sales meeting" to find event called something like "dinner" with recipient "Kim" |
| The first one. Also make a Stand-up meeting for early next Monday | Yes, create the first one and then create event called "Stand-up meeting" starting next Monday early morning |
| Yes please do so. | Looks good! |
| Is it cloudy in Florida? | weather at "Florida" now is cloudy |

Table 1: Examples of natural and canonical utterances extracted from the SMCalFlow training set (Semantic Machines et al., 2020). The canonical utterances are generated by the SCFG defined by Shin et al. (2021a)[2].

selection approach may face challenges such as:

- Annotation *speed*: as $K$ grows larger, an annotator needs to spend more time reading the candidate list. Can we organize the candidates list in a way that allows for fast filtering?
- Annotation *accuracy*: early plausible candidates in a ranked list may bias interpretation; an annotator may commit early to a less-than-perfect result without exploring further. Can we encourage exploration without adversely affecting speed?

In this work we demonstrate the validity of these concerns and propose a solution called **guided $K$-best selection**, consisting of: (*i*) a *search interface* that allows annotators to type keywords and narrow down the $K$ choices, (*ii*) a *keyword suggestion* method that guides the exploration of $K$-best lists for less experienced users. We show that it is the combination of efficient search and guidance that strikes the optimal balance between accuracy and speed while achieving high annotator satisfaction.

## 2 Conversational Semantic Parsing

For our study we focus on a version of Conversational Semantic Parsing (Figure 1), where we are given a user's natural utterance, and the goal of the task is to annotate it into a *canonical utterance*. The use of canonical utterances formulates semantic parsing as a paraphrasing task that paraphrases a natural utterance into a "canonical" utterance in a constrained language (Berant and Liang, 2014; Marzoev et al., 2020; Shin et al., 2021a; Wu et al., 2021). A synchronous context-free grammar (*SCFG*) defines a mapping between task-specific meaning representations and their corresponding constrained languages. That is to say, using such an SCFG, a complicated meaning representation can be presented as a human-readable canonical utterance (more similar to natural language) so models can focus on learning how to paraphrase a natural utterance to a canonical utterance. We choose to annotate canonical utterances also because it substantially reduces the task complexity, since annotators no longer need to learn the syntax of the meaning representation itself. We use canonical utterances induced by an SCFG defined in (Shin et al., 2021a). The corresponding meaning representation is defined in the SMCalFlow dataset (Semantic Machines et al., 2020), which contains 41.5K task-oriented dialogues about calendar events, weather, places, and people. Examples of natural and canonical utterances are shown in Table 1.

## 3 Guided $K$-best Selection Interfaces

In this section, we describe three proposed and two baseline annotation interfaces. Figure 2 shows their basic components. The user utterance and its context are given in (A) and the $K$-best candidate list is provided in (C). (C) and its variants provide different functions to help users efficiently get to the correct parse. Note that (A), (B), (D), and (E) are shared across all UIs.

**`no-kbest`** This interface, shown on Figure 2 (C-1), is an "annotate from scratch" baseline. Users need to type the canonical utterance without seeing the $K$-best list. They can use (D) to validate whether the current utterance is grammatical.

[2]SCFG implementation is available on the Github repository (Shin et al., 2021b).

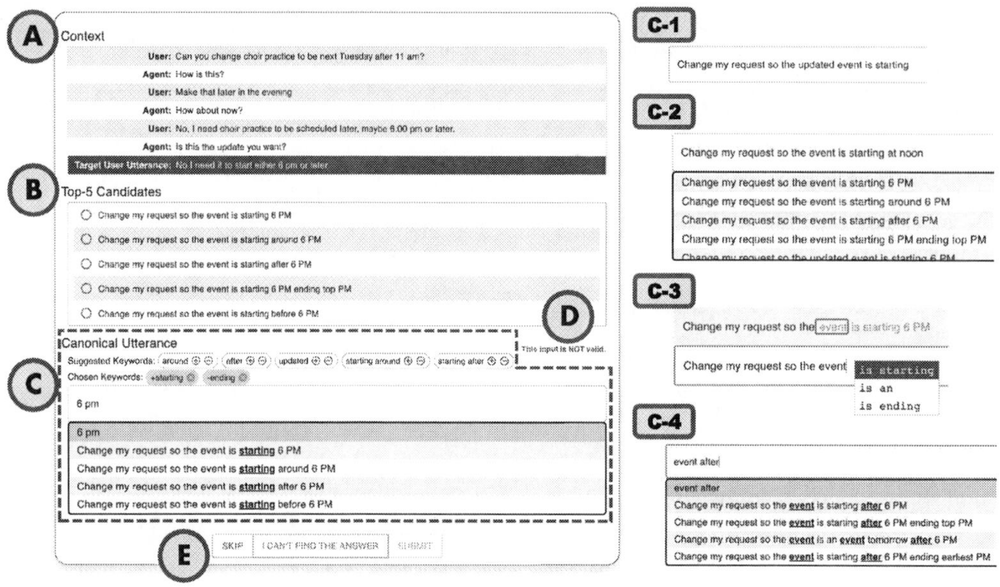


Figure 2: The main components of `search-keywords` and other interfaces. (A), (B), (D) and (E) are shared across all interfaces. (A) shows the dialog context and the target user utterance to annotate; (B) shows the top 5 candidates to serve as the options and hints; (D) indicates whether the current input is grammatical, i.e. can be parsed with an SCFG (the latency of the grammar verification function is around 70 ms, which is quick enough for real-time querying); (E) presents buttons for submitting the current task, "skipping" it to work on later, or "escalating" it for manual annotation (via the "I can't find the answer" button, which declares that the correct parse is not in the top $K$). `Search-keywords` (C) suggests a set of keywords for users to query relevant candidates on. `No-kbest` (C-1) only provides an input box for manually entering the annotation. `Scroll` (C-2) simply presents all the candidates for users to select. `Autocomplete` (C-3) shows both a full sentence completion and possible next chunks of the tokens. `Search` (C-4) allows users to enter keywords to query relevant candidates.

**`scroll`** Figure 2 (C-2) shows the `scroll` interface. `scroll` serves as another baseline in our experiments. We simply present all the candidates ordered by their model scores. Users are able to use their mouse or keyboard to traverse the list.

**`autocomplete`** As shown in Figure 2 (C-3), `autocomplete` shows a full sentence completion above the input area and possible next chunks of tokens next to the cursor. To generate the suggestions, we insert all candidates into a trie (Browning, 2021). The full sentence completion is the one that satisfies the prefix constraint and has the highest model score; and the next chunks of tokens are generated by traversing the trie until different tokens appear. The red box serves as a cursor around the current token in the full sentence completion. When using `autocomplete`, users essentially explore the $K$ candidates by traversing the trie.

**`search`** Figure 2 (C-4) shows the `search` interface. It aims to break the *left-to-right* nature of `autocomplete`, where users need to traverse the trie in a certain order. `search` allows users to enter keywords in arbitrary order to remove irrelevant candidates. After entering the keywords, valid candidates ordered by the model scores will be shown below the input area. The matched keywords are highlighted in bold and underlined for quick reference. We use flexsearch (Wilkerling, 2021) to index the candidate list in the frontend UI to further reduce the latency.

**`search-keywords`** As shown in Figure 2 (C), `search-keywords` extends the `search` interface by showing a list of top 5 discriminative keywords. These keywords are used to narrow down the current candidates. They also give users a rough overview of the candidate list and the annotation grammar. Users can choose to include (+) or exclude (−) the keyword in the correct parse.

To provide suggestions, we develop a Keyword Suggestion (KS) method inspired by post-decoding clustering (PDC) from (Ippolito et al., 2019). We similarly perform $k$-means clustering over the $K$-

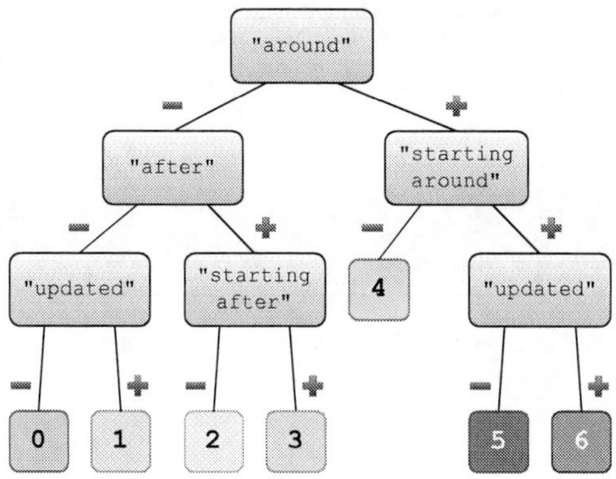


Figure 3: KS example. We generate an explanation tree over a $k$-means clustering ($k$=7) and use $k' = 5$ unique intermediate nodes' $n$-grams as suggested keywords.

| | Top-5 | Top-20 | Top-100 | Escalate |
|---|---|---|---|---|
| Stratified | 25% | 25% | 25% | 25% |
| True | 76% | 6% | 4% | 14% |

Table 2: We apply stratified sampling to control the distribution of gold answers. **Escalate** is the case where the gold parse is not in top 100. The **True** distribution gives each stratum's real distribution in the dev set.

best list and choose the candidate with the highest model score to represent each cluster. This distills the original $K$ candidates into fewer but more diverse candidates, where $k \ll K$. In addition, we employ a cluster explanation technique recently proposed by Dasgupta et al. (2020) to further distill the $k$ diverse candidates into $k'$ *keywords*. This is done by approximating the $k$ clusters' decision boundaries (which are arbitrarily shaped) with $k$ axis-aligned rectangles. As a result, this approximated $k$-means clustering can be summarized with a binary tree, consisting of $k$ leaf nodes and at most $k - 1$ intermediate split nodes. Split nodes correspond to $n$-grams ($n = 1, 2, 3$) formed from the canonical representations of candidate parses. We use the set of all unique split nodes' $n$-grams to form a set of suggested keywords. Thus, the $k$ diverse candidates are distilled even further into $k'$ keywords, $k' < k \ll K$. An example of this process is given on Figure 3. Finally, the $k'$ keywords are re-ranked based on their *discriminativeness*, or how evenly they split the current candidates, and the 5 most discriminative keywords are shown in the interface. This allows combining keyword suggestion with the `search` interface. In Section 4.3, we compare keyword suggestion with other mechanisms to guide annotators.

## 4 Experiments

### 4.1 Protocol

**Data** 300 utterances were sampled from the SMCalFlow development set (Semantic Machines et al., 2020). For each utterance, we used the state-of-the-art conversational semantic parser VACSP (Platanios et al., 2021) to generate $K = 100$ candidate parses.[3] To simulate a low-resource setting, we used the variant of VACSP trained on 1k dialogues (VACSP-1k). We sampled utterances according to the stratified distribution from Table 2 in order to represent multiple rank settings equally. For **Escalate** samples, where the gold answer was not presented in the candidate list, we expected the participants to either choose the "I can't find the answer" option,[4] or edit one of the candidates to obtain the correct parse.

**Participants** A total of 5 participants joined the experiment. All participants were not previously exposed to the canonical language and the proposed interfaces. To help annotators get familiar with the canonical grammar, they were asked to read 300 (user utterance, canonical utterance) pairs.[5] Participants were then randomly assigned to a particular interface and data split. Each interface was used along with a different data split to reduce potential bias. After finishing, participants filled out a questionnaire, evaluating (*i*) interface preference on a 5-point Likert scale, (*ii*) cognitive load using the NASA Task Load Index (Hart, 2006) on a 7-point Likert scale, and (*iii*) free-text suggestions.

### 4.2 Interface Comparison

We compare interfaces from (*i*) the requester's perspective by evaluating annotation accuracy and time and (*ii*) the annotator's perspective by evaluating their UI preference across multiple criteria.

**Accuracy and time** Table 3 shows the exact match accuracy and the time usage per utterance.

To verify how accuracy and time differ depending on the difficulty of each instance, we measure the rank of the gold parse in the $K$-best list, and aggregate the results over three non-overlapping set-

[3]We used Accuracy@$K$ as a proxy to decide the best $K$. We chose $K = 100$ since larger values of $K$ did not substantially improve Accuracy@$K$ with our prototype model: e.g. Accuracy@200 was only 0.8% higher than Accuracy@100.

[4]Practically, **Escalate** means sending this hard instance to experienced and knowledgeable annotators to handle.

[5]The 300 pairs were selected to represent a diverse set of functions in the canonical and meaning representations.

| | Exact Match Accuracy ↑ | | | | | | | Median Time (sec) ↓ | | | | |
|---|---|---|---|---|---|---|---|---|---|---|---|---|
| | **Top-5** | **Top-20** | **Top-100** | **Escalate** | **Escalate$_m$** | **All** | **True** | **Top-5** | **Top-20** | **Top-100** | **Escalate** | **All** |
| No-KBest | .411 | .189 | .123 | .400 | .067 | .197 | .339 | 56.13 | 73.17 | 97.48 | 74.29 | 69.43 |
| Scroll | .880 | .320 | .213 | .453 | .067 | .370 | .706 | 13.00 | 25.84 | 26.47 | 30.23 | 24.73 |
| Autocomplete | **.919** | .370 | **.333** | .427 | .067 | **.422** | **.743** | 13.71 | 26.01 | 30.02 | 31.47 | 25.53 |
| Search | .878 | .320 | .213 | .400 | .080 | .373 | .707 | **8.48** | **19.09** | **17.16** | **19.55** | **16.02** |
| Search-Keywords | .880 | **.419** | .213 | **.480** | **.093** | .401 | .716 | 12.78 | 24.51 | 36.26 | 31.15 | 23.91 |

Table 3: Accuracy and time usage of the baseline and proposed interfaces. In the last stratum, Escalate, in which answer is not provided, we present two values: **Escalate$_m$**, where only matching the gold answer is correct, and **Escalate**, where in addition to that selecting "I Can't Find The Answer" is also treated as correct. **All** is the mean accuracy over all the strata. **True** stands for the true accuracy weighted by the true distribution in the dev set (Table 2). Note **All** and **True** are computed using **Escalate$_m$**. **Bolded** is the best result; underlined is the second-best result. `Autocomplete` achieves the highest accuracy and `Search` help reduce time usage up to 35% compared to `Scroll`. `Search-keywords` strikes the balance between accuracy and time usage.

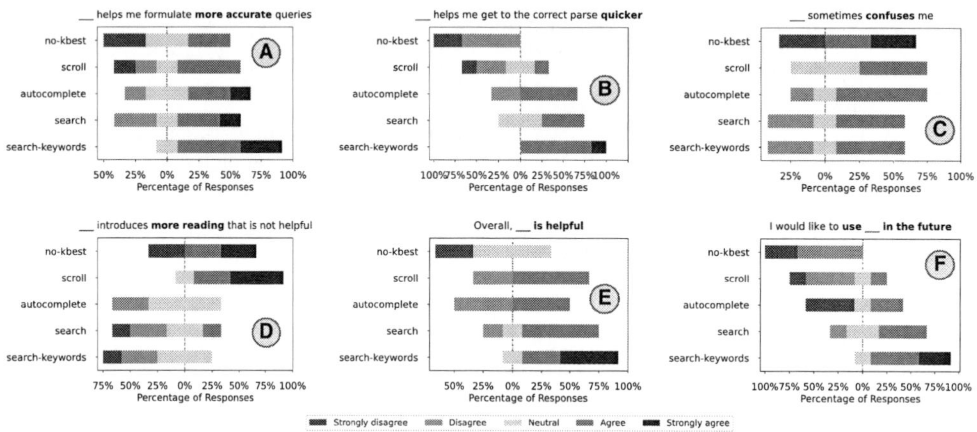


Figure 4: Summary of the user feedback on the interface preference. Across six evaluation criteria, the users preferred the proposed UIs over baselines, with `search-keywords` being their top choice across all criteria.

tings: "Top-5", "Top-20", and "Top-100",[6] which correspond to varying difficulties of instances.

We further compute the *true accuracy* by estimating the real distribution of the strata in our dataset to compare with Platanios et al. (2021)'s VACSP-1k results. As shown in the **True** accuracy column in Table 3, by introducing humans into the semantic parsing process, no matter which $K$-best interface they use, the performance always improves (the **True** accuracy of the VACSP-1k model is 0.630). When comparing each interface, `autocomplete` achieves the highest accuracy overall but it also takes a longer time. We hypothesize that the accuracy gain comes from the fact that annotators are required to review tokens individually. Compared to `scroll`, `search` does not substantially improve the accuracy, but it does reduce the overall time usage by up to 35%. `No-KBest` shows that, with only the grammar verification, annotators are much slower (69s vs 25s) and less accurate (.339 vs .706) even compared to `scroll` (see Appendix B for more analysis on annotation time distribution). Overall, `search-keywords` strikes a balance between the trade-offs, being generally either best or close to best in both accuracy and time usage.

**User feedback** Figure 4 summarizes user answers to UI preference questions from the questionnaire.[7] Annotators generally preferred the proposed interfaces to the `no-kbest` and `scroll` baselines: they found that the proposed UIs enable them to be more accurate (A) and faster (B), as well as requiring less unnecessary reading (D). The level of confusion was roughly the same across UIs (C), perhaps due to non-UI related factors (such as an-

[6] "Top-5" corresponds to the rank in [1, 5] "Top-20" corresponds to [6, 20], and "Top-100" corresponds to [21, 100].

[7] More feedback, incl. excerpts of free-form suggestions and NASA task load index results, is provided in Appendix C.

| | Oracle simulation results ($k=5$) Average number of turns ↓ | | | | Human annotation results ($k=5$) Median time (sec) ↓ | | | |
|---|---|---|---|---|---|---|---|---|
| | **Top-5** | **Top-20** | **Top-100** | **All** | **Top-5** | **Top-20** | **Top-100** | **All** |
| KS (ours) | <u>1.10</u> | **2.39** | **2.80** | **1.24** | **15.30** | <u>46.99</u> | **48.20** | **36.71** |
| PDC ($k$-means, canonical) | 1.11 | <u>2.40</u> | <u>2.84</u> | **1.24** | 25.09 | 73.23 | <u>55.42</u> | 52.94 |
| PDC (agglomerative, canonical) | 1.16 | 2.73 | 3.10 | 1.31 | — | — | — | — |
| PDC (agglomerative, meaning) | 1.15 | 2.68 | 2.91 | <u>1.29</u> | — | — | — | — |
| Scroll | **1.00** | 2.63 | 7.75 | 1.33 | <u>24.18</u> | **42.30** | 56.37 | <u>37.21</u> |

Table 4: Comparison of $K$-best guidance strategies: by suggesting keywords (top row), diverse candidates (middle rows), or all $K$ candidates (bottom row). In both oracle and human settings, $k=5$ candidates are displayed per each interaction turn. **Bolded** is the best result, <u>underlined</u> is the second-best result. While KS and PDC perform similarly in the oracle setting, the former leads to faster annotation when tested with real human annotators.

notation grammar or stratified distribution of examples). The annotators also preferred the proposed UIs for future use (F), with `search-keywords` being the most preferred one by a large margin.

### 4.3 Guidance Comparison

We compare our keyword suggestion (KS) method, based on explainable $k$-means clustering, with the PDC algorithm from (Ippolito et al., 2019) and the `scroll` baseline from Section 3. We compare multiple variants of PDC, exploring whether agglomerative clustering (based on string edit distance) or $k$-means is better, and whether canonical or meaning representation is better. All algorithms are used interactively: e.g., during one turn of PDC, a user would pick one out of $k$ clusters (represented by the top scoring parse each) that looks most correct to them, and on the next turn, they would only see candidates from the cluster chosen previously. In KS, one turn corresponds to choosing whether a single suggested keyword (e.g. "create event") should or should not be included in the correct parse while seeing the currently best scoring $k$ candidates. Finally, in `scroll` the user simply scrolls over $K$ candidates using a size-$k$ window. To achieve a fair comparison and manageable workload, all methods display $k=5$ candidates per interaction turn.

We evaluate guidance methods in two ways: with a simulated (oracle) user, and with a pool of human annotators described in Section 4.1. The simulated user will always make the best choice at each interaction turn: that is, pick the keyword or the candidate parse that will be included in, or will be closest to, the best parse. Human annotators, however, might make mistakes. Thus, in all interfaces, they are allowed to go several turns back and fix mistakes before submitting. We report the number of turns for the simulated user and the wall annotation time for human annotators in Table 4.

**Oracle simulation results** Table 4 (left) shows several trends: first, adding explanations and "coarsening" clusters' decision boundary in KS does not hurt annotation speed, compared to the otherwise similar "PDC ($k$-means, canonical)". Second, both KS and PDC substantially decrease the gap between the easiest Top-5 and the hardest Top-100 settings observed for `scroll`, contributing to a more predictable annotator experience. Finally, comparing the results across PDC variants, we can conclude that $k$-means over canonical representation is a reasonable default setting, and we lock on to it for human annotation experiments.

**Human annotation results** Table 4 (right) agrees with the simulation finding that KS and PDC help decrease the gap between Top-5 and Top-100 settings, albeit to a lesser extent than in the simulation experiment. Most notable is the difference in speed between KS and PDC: while in simulation it was only marginal, here the lack of explanations substantially slows the human annotators down. In addition, in the post-experiment survey, the annotators were confused by "non-intuitive similarity relations" and "too much extra reading" of the clustering-based PDC while praising the keyword-based KS for being "intuitive" and "engaging".

## 5 Related Work

### 5.1 Interactive Semantic Parsing

$K$-best selection is aligned with *interactive semantic parsing*. These approaches assume access to an existing parsing model, and to a user that provides corrections in binary (Clarke et al., 2010; Artzi and Zettlemoyer, 2013; Iyer et al., 2017), multiple-choice (Iyer et al., 2017; Gur et al., 2018; Yao et al., 2019), or natural language form (Elgohary et al., 2021). Many of these methods also rely on separate trainable modules or parsing model's parameters to identify inference steps the parser is most uncertain about. In contrast, $K$-best selection is parameter-free (making it well-suited for low-resource settings).

### 5.2 Computer-Assisted Translation

Our search and autocomplete UIs are motivated by *computer-assisted translation.* There are three main directions in CAT. **Post-Editing (PE)** asks users to revise and verify a machine translated text (Green et al., 2013; Aranberri et al., 2014; Toral et al., 2018; Herbig et al., 2020; Lee et al., 2021). **Interactive Translation Prediction (ITP)** suggests translations dynamically based on users' input (Langlais et al., 2000; Foster et al., 2002; Bender et al., 2005; Barrachina et al., 2009; Koehn, 2009; Alabau et al., 2014; Green et al., 2014; Cheng et al., 2016). Both PE and ITP assume users' translations are nearly perfect which is not always the case in CSP. **Iterative translation (IT)** asks two groups of monolingual speakers to iterate over the translation back and forth to improve translation quality (Morita and Ishida, 2009; Hu et al., 2010, 2011). Although IT ensures quality, its low throughput (2.5 to 6 times slower compared to professional translators (Hu et al., 2011)) prevents us from using it.

### 5.3 Diverse Generation

Our keyword suggestion mechanism is motivated by *diverse text generation.* Typical strategies for improving the collective diversity (Hu et al., 2019) of the output candidates include: modifications to beam search (Vijayakumar et al., 2018; Tam, 2020), modifications to the sampling method (Fan et al., 2018; Holtzman et al., 2020), stratified sampling based on semantic codes (Weir et al., 2020), and post-decoding clustering (Kriz et al., 2019; Ippolito et al., 2019). The latter approach involves over-generating candidates by using a large beam size, clustering the final candidates, and selecting one or a few representative candidates per cluster.

## 6 Conclusion

In this paper, we tackled the challenge of efficient data collection for conversational semantic parsing. In the presence of little available training data, we propose human-in-the-loop interfaces for **guided $K$-best selection**, using a prototype model trained on limited data. Guided $K$-best selection interfaces generate a set of possible candidates with functions for fast traversal and ask annotators to select the correct parse. User studies show that combining keyword search functionality with a keyword suggestion system strikes an optimal balance between annotation accuracy and speed.

## References


Vicent Alabau, Christian Buck, Michael Carl, Francisco Casacuberta, Mercedes García-Martínez, Ulrich Germann, Jesús González-Rubio, Robin Hill, Philipp Koehn, Luis A Leiva, et al. 2014. Casmacat: A computer-assisted translation workbench. In *Proceedings of the Demonstrations at the 14th Conference of the European Chapter of the Association for Computational Linguistics*, pages 25–28.

Nora Aranberri, Gorka Labaka, Arantza Diaz de Ilarraza, and Kepa Sarasola. 2014. Comparison of post-editing productivity between professional translators and lay users. In *Proceedings of the 11th Conference of the Association for Machine Translation in the Americas*, pages 20–33.

Yoav Artzi and Luke Zettlemoyer. 2013. Weakly supervised learning of semantic parsers for mapping instructions to actions. *Transactions of the Association for Computational Linguistics*, 1:49–62.

Sergio Barrachina, Oliver Bender, Francisco Casacuberta, Jorge Civera, Elsa Cubel, Shahram Khadivi, Antonio Lagarda, Hermann Ney, Jesús Tomás, Enrique Vidal, and Juan-Miguel Vilar. 2009. Statistical approaches to computer-assisted translation. *Computational Linguistics*, 35(1):3–28.

Oliver Bender, Saša Hasan, David Vilar, Richard Zens, and Hermann Ney. 2005. Comparison of generation strategies for interactive machine translation. In *Proceedings of the 10th EAMT Conference: Practical applications of machine translation*, Budapest, Hungary. European Association for Machine Translation.

Jonathan Berant and Percy Liang. 2014. Semantic parsing via paraphrasing. In *Proceedings of the 52nd Annual Meeting of the Association for Computational Linguistics (Volume 1: Long Papers)*, pages 1415–1425.

Lyndsey Browning. 2021. Github repository: trie-prefix-tree.

Mia Xu Chen, Benjamin N. Lee, Gagan Bansal, Yuan Cao, Shuyuan Zhang, Justin Lu, Jackie Tsay, Yinan Wang, Andrew M. Dai, Zhifeng Chen, Timothy Sohn, and Yonghui Wu. 2019. Gmail smart compose: Real-time assisted writing. In *Proceedings* of the 25th ACM SIGKDD International Conference on Knowledge Discovery & Data Mining, KDD '19, page 2287–2295, New York, NY, USA. Association for Computing Machinery.

Jianpeng Cheng, Devang Agrawal, Héctor Martínez Alonso, Shruti Bhargava, Joris Driesen, Federico Flego, Dain Kaplan, Dimitri Kartsaklis, Lin Li, Dhivya Piraviperumal, Jason D. Williams, Hong Yu, Diarmuid Ó Séaghdha, and Anders Johannsen. 2020. Conversational semantic parsing for dialog state tracking. In *Proceedings of the 2020 Conference on Empirical Methods in Natural Language Processing (EMNLP)*, pages 8107–8117, Online. Association for Computational Linguistics.

Shanbo Cheng, Shujian Huang, Huadong Chen, Xinyu Dai, and Jiajun Chen. 2016. Primt: A pick-revise framework for interactive machine translation. In *Proceedings of the 2016 Conference of the North American Chapter of the Association for Computational Linguistics: Human Language Technologies*, pages 1240–1249.

James Clarke, Dan Goldwasser, Ming-Wei Chang, and Dan Roth. 2010. Driving semantic parsing from the world's response. In *Proceedings of the fourteenth conference on computational natural language learning*, pages 18–27.

Sanjoy Dasgupta, Nave Frost, Michal Moshkovitz, and Cyrus Rashtchian. 2020. Explainable k-means and k-medians clustering. In *Proceedings of the 37th International Conference on Machine Learning, Vienna, Austria*, pages 12–18.

Manjuan Duan, Ethan Hill, and Michael White. 2016. Generating disambiguating paraphrases for structurally ambiguous sentences. In *Proceedings of the 10th Linguistic Annotation Workshop held in conjunction with ACL 2016 (LAW-X 2016)*, pages 160–170.

Ahmed Elgohary, Christopher Meek, Matthew Richardson, Adam Fourney, Gonzalo Ramos, and Ahmed Hassan Awadallah. 2021. NL-EDIT: Correcting semantic parse errors through natural language interaction. In *Proceedings of the 2021 Conference of the North American Chapter of the Association for Computational Linguistics: Human Language Technologies*, pages 5599–5610, Online. Association for Computational Linguistics.

Angela Fan, Mike Lewis, and Yann Dauphin. 2018. Hierarchical neural story generation. In *Proceedings of the 56th Annual Meeting of the Association for Computational Linguistics (Volume 1: Long Papers)*, pages 889–898, Melbourne, Australia. Association for Computational Linguistics.

George Foster, Philippe Langlais, and Guy Lapalme. 2002. User-friendly text prediction for translators. In *Proceedings of the 2002 Conference on Empirical Methods in Natural Language Processing (EMNLP 2002)*, pages 148–155. Association for Computational Linguistics.

Spence Green, Jason Chuang, Jeffrey Heer, and Christopher D Manning. 2014. Predictive translation memory: A mixed-initiative system for human language translation. In *Proceedings of the 27th annual ACM symposium on User interface software and technology*, pages 177–187.

Spence Green, Jeffrey Heer, and Christopher D Manning. 2013. The efficacy of human post-editing for language translation. In *Proceedings of the SIGCHI conference on human factors in computing systems*, pages 439–448.

Izzeddin Gur, Semih Yavuz, Yu Su, and Xifeng Yan. 2018. Dialsql: Dialogue based structured query generation. In *Proceedings of the 56th Annual Meeting of the Association for Computational Linguistics (Volume 1: Long Papers)*, pages 1339–1349.

Sandra G. Hart. 2006. Nasa-task load index (nasa-tlx); 20 years later. *Proceedings of the Human Factors and Ergonomics Society Annual Meeting*, 50(9):904–908.

Luheng He, Julian Michael, Mike Lewis, and Luke Zettlemoyer. 2016. Human-in-the-loop parsing. In *Proceedings of the 2016 Conference on Empirical Methods in Natural Language Processing*, pages 2337–2342.

Nico Herbig, Tim Düwel, Santanu Pal, Kalliopi Meladaki, Mahsa Monshizadeh, Antonio Krüger, and Josef van Genabith. 2020. Mmpe: A multimodal interface for post-editing machine translation. In *Proceedings of the 58th Annual Meeting of the Association for Computational Linguistics*, pages 1691–1702.

Ari Holtzman, Jan Buys, Li Du, Maxwell Forbes, and Yejin Choi. 2020. The curious case of neural text degeneration. In *International Conference on Learning Representations*.

Chang Hu, Benjamin B Bederson, and Philip Resnik. 2010. Translation by iterative collaboration between monolingual users. In *Proceedings of the ACM SIGKDD Workshop on Human Computation*, pages 54–55.

Chang Hu, Benjamin B Bederson, Philip Resnik, and Yakov Kronrod. 2011. Monotrans2: A new human computation system to support monolingual translation. In *Proceedings of the SIGCHI Conference on Human Factors in Computing Systems*, pages 1133–1136.

J Edward Hu, Abhinav Singh, Nils Holzenberger, Matt Post, and Benjamin Van Durme. 2019. Large-scale, diverse, paraphrastic bitexts via sampling and clustering. In *Proceedings of the 23rd Conference on Computational Natural Language Learning (CoNLL)*, pages 44–54.

Daphne Ippolito, Reno Kriz, João Sedoc, Maria Kustikova, and Chris Callison-Burch. 2019. Comparison of diverse decoding methods from conditional language models. In *Proceedings of the 57th*

*Annual Meeting of the Association for Computational Linguistics*, pages 3752–3762, Florence, Italy. Association for Computational Linguistics.

Srinivasan Iyer, Ioannis Konstas, Alvin Cheung, Jayant Krishnamurthy, and Luke Zettlemoyer. 2017. Learning a neural semantic parser from user feedback. In *Proceedings of the 55th Annual Meeting of the Association for Computational Linguistics (Volume 1: Long Papers)*, pages 963–973, Vancouver, Canada. Association for Computational Linguistics.

Rebecca Knowles, Marina Sanchez-Torron, and Philipp Koehn. 2019. A user study of neural interactive translation prediction. *Machine Translation*, 33(1):135–154.

Philipp Koehn. 2009. A process study of computer-aided translation. *Machine Translation*, 23(4):241–263.

Reno Kriz, João Sedoc, Marianna Apidianaki, Carolina Zheng, Gaurav Kumar, Eleni Miltsakaki, and Chris Callison-Burch. 2019. Complexity-weighted loss and diverse reranking for sentence simplification. In *Proceedings of the 2019 Conference of the North American Chapter of the Association for Computational Linguistics: Human Language Technologies, Volume 1 (Long and Short Papers)*, pages 3137–3147, Minneapolis, Minnesota. Association for Computational Linguistics.

Philippe Langlais, George Foster, and Guy Lapalme. 2000. TransType: a computer-aided translation typing system. In *ANLP-NAACL 2000 Workshop: Embedded Machine Translation Systems*.

Dongjun Lee, Junhyeong Ahn, Heesoo Park, and Jaemin Jo. 2021. IntelliCAT: Intelligent machine translation post-editing with quality estimation and translation suggestion. In *Proceedings of the 59th Annual Meeting of the Association for Computational Linguistics and the 11th International Joint Conference on Natural Language Processing: System Demonstrations*, pages 11–19, Online. Association for Computational Linguistics.

Alana Marzoev, Samuel Madden, M Frans Kaashoek, Michael Cafarella, and Jacob Andreas. 2020. Unnatural language processing: Bridging the gap between synthetic and natural language data. *arXiv preprint arXiv:2004.13645*.

Daisuke Morita and Toru Ishida. 2009. Designing protocols for collaborative translation. In *Proceedings of the 12th International Conference on Principles of Practice in Multi-Agent Systems*, PRIMA '09, page 17–32, Berlin, Heidelberg. Springer-Verlag.

Emmanouil Antonios Platanios, Adam Pauls, Subhro Roy, Yuchen Zhang, Alexander Kyte, Alan Guo, Sam Thomson, Jayant Krishnamurthy, Jason Wolfe, Jacob Andreas, and Dan Klein. 2021. Value-agnostic conversational semantic parsing. In *ACL-IJCNLP 2021*.

Semantic Machines, Jacob Andreas, John Bufe, David Burkett, Charles Chen, Josh Clausman, Jean Crawford, Kate Crim, Jordan DeLoach, Leah Dorner, Jason Eisner, Hao Fang, Alan Guo, David Hall, Kristin Hayes, Kellie Hill, Diana Ho, Wendy Iwaszuk, Smriti Jha, Dan Klein, Jayant Krishnamurthy, Theo Lanman, Percy Liang, Christopher H. Lin, Ilya Lintsbakh, Andy McGovern, Aleksandr Nisnevich, Adam Pauls, Dmitrij Petters, Brent Read, Dan Roth, Subhro Roy, Jesse Rusak, Beth Short, Div Slomin, Ben Snyder, Stephon Striplin, Yu Su, Zachary Tellman, Sam Thomson, Andrei Vorobev, Izabela Witoszko, Jason Wolfe, Abby Wray, Yuchen Zhang, and Alexander Zotov. 2020. Task-oriented dialogue as dataflow synthesis. *Transactions of the Association for Computational Linguistics*, 8:556–571.

Richard Shin, Christopher H. Lin, Sam Thomson, Charles Chen, Subhro Roy, Emmanouil Antonios Platanios, Adam Pauls, Dan Klein, Jason Eisner, and Benjamin Van Durme. 2021a. Constrained language models yield few-shot semantic parsers. In *Proceedings of the 2021 Conference on Empirical Methods in Natural Language Processing*, Punta Cana.

Richard Shin, Christopher H. Lin, Sam Thomson, Charles Chen, Subhro Roy, Emmanouil Antonios Platanios, Adam Pauls, Dan Klein, Jason Eisner, and Benjamin Van Durme. 2021b. Github repository: Constrained language models yield few-shot semantic parsers.

Yik-Cheung Tam. 2020. Cluster-based beam search for pointer-generator chatbot grounded by knowledge. *Computer Speech & Language*, 64:101094.

Antonio Toral, Martijn Wieling, and Andy Way. 2018. Post-editing effort of a novel with statistical and neural machine translation. *Frontiers in Digital Humanities*, 5:9.

Ashwin K Vijayakumar, Michael Cogswell, Ramprasath R Selvaraju, Qing Sun, Stefan Lee, David Crandall, and Dhruv Batra. 2018. Diverse beam search: Decoding diverse solutions from neural sequence models. In *Proceedings of the AAAI Conference on Artificial Intelligence*, pages 7371–7379. AAAI.

Nathaniel Weir, João Sedoc, and Benjamin Van Durme. 2020. COD3S: Diverse generation with discrete semantic signatures. In *Proceedings of the 2020 Conference on Empirical Methods in Natural Language Processing (EMNLP)*, pages 5199–5211, Online. Association for Computational Linguistics.

Thomas Wilkerling. 2021. Github repository: flexsearch.

Shan Wu, Bo Chen, Chunlei Xin, Xianpei Han, Le Sun, Weipeng Zhang, Jiansong Chen, Fan Yang, and Xunliang Cai. 2021. From paraphrasing to semantic parsing: Unsupervised semantic parsing via synchronous semantic decoding. In *Proceedings of the 59th Annual Meeting of the Association for Computational Linguistics and the 11th International Joint*

*Conference on Natural Language Processing (Volume 1: Long Papers)*, pages 5110–5121, Online. Association for Computational Linguistics.

Ziyu Yao, Yu Su, Huan Sun, and Wen-tau Yih. 2019. Model-based interactive semantic parsing: A unified framework and a text-to-SQL case study. In *Proceedings of the 2019 Conference on Empirical Methods in Natural Language Processing and the 9th International Joint Conference on Natural Language Processing (EMNLP-IJCNLP)*, pages 5447–5458, Hong Kong, China. Association for Computational Linguistics.

Luke Zettlemoyer and Michael Collins. 2009. Learning context-dependent mappings from sentences to logical form. In *Proceedings of the Joint Conference of the 47th Annual Meeting of the ACL and the 4th International Joint Conference on Natural Language Processing of the AFNLP*, pages 976–984, Suntec, Singapore. Association for Computational Linguistics.

## A Discussion

In this section, we share additional lessons we learned while interacting with expert annotators in the preliminary experiments and adapting our final proposed interfaces according to their feedback.

**Latency is a critical issue when generating completions dynamically.** We initially experimented with the autocomplete interface suggesting completions fully **dynamically**, similar to recent works on CAT (Green et al., 2014; Knowles et al., 2019). To achieve this, we periodically sent users' inputs to the backend BART model (Shin et al., 2021a) that would perform completions using beam search decoding. We found the latency of the BART model to be around 300-600 ms even with the beam size of one and constrained decoding turned off (turning the constrained decoding on ensures the generated completions are grammatical but doubles the latency). In a small preliminary study, participants generally noted the dynamic interface to be "laggy". Similar issues also happened in prior studies, e.g. Green et al. (2014) noticed that users deemed the interface as "sluggish" unless the latency was reduced to less than 300 ms by using the phrase-based decoding algorithm to reduce the search space; Chen et al. (2019) examined the latency of LSTM as well as Transformer and concluded that Transformer's high latency was not suitable for production despite the performance gain. We thus concluded that generating completions dynamically is infeasible and directed our study towards $K$-best selection.

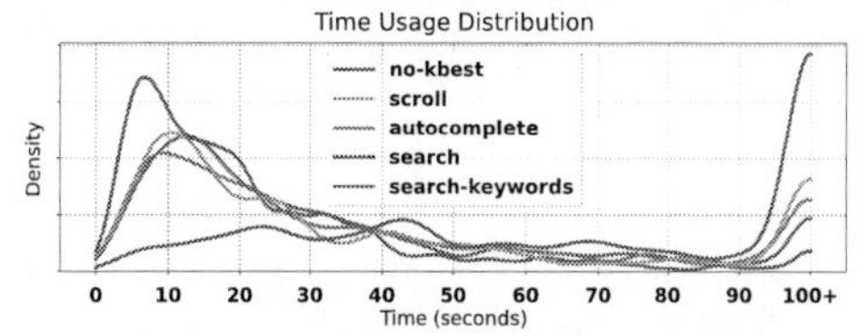


Figure 5: KDE plot of the time usage for the baseline and proposed interfaces. `Search` has a higher distribution between 5-20 seconds; The long tail is merged and forms another peak in 100+ where we can clearly see that `no-kbest` $\gg$ `scroll` $>$ `autocomplete` $>$ `search-keywords` $>$ `search`.

**Users are not able to produce a full canonical utterance from scratch.** Compared to CAT tasks (Section 5.2), one of the difficulties of annotating semantic representations is that the canonical language is hard and subject to change. In CAT, people assume that the produced translation is always valid which is not always true for semantic representation annotation tasks. Annotators found it substantially harder to author a complete annotation from scratch using the `no-kbest` interface (Figure 4), as compared to selecting from a list of $K$ options with all other UIs. We thus believe that a $K$-best framework should be a preferred approach as it relies on people's ability to **read and verify** the candidates rather than producing an answer from scratch.

## B Additional Experiments

**Oracle simulation results** In addition to $k = 5$ (Section 4.3), we experiment with displaying less ($k = 2$) and more ($k = 10$) items per turn. The results are shown on Table 5. When displaying $k = 2$ (left) items per turn, the difference between Top-100 "tail" performance of the scroll baseline vs proposed methods is very high, thus making proposed methods more predictable on the tail. For $k = 10$ (right) items per turn, this difference is more leveled and the overall performance is essentially the same across all methods, at the expense of increased reading per turn. In the human experiments, we chose $k = 5$ to strike balance between workload per turn and reasonable number of turns.

**Overall time usage distribution** In addition to the user study results presented in Section 4.2, we show the kernel density estimation (KDE) plot of the time usage distribution in Figure 5. The KDE

|  | Oracle simulation results ($k = 2$) Average number of turns ↓ |  |  |  | Oracle simulation results ($k = 10$) Average number of turns ↓ |  |  |  |
|---|---|---|---|---|---|---|---|---|
|  | **Top-5** | **Top-20** | **Top-100** | **All** | **Top-5** | **Top-20** | **Top-100** | **All** |
| KS (ours) | 1.19 | 4.22 | 5.90 | 1.53 | 1.06 | 1.79 | 2.09 | **1.14** |
| PDC ($k$-means, canonical) | 1.19 | **4.19** | **5.85** | **1.52** | 1.06 | 1.81 | 2.11 | **1.14** |
| PDC (agglomerative, canonical) | 1.24 | 5.38 | 7.14 | 1.68 | 1.10 | 1.92 | 2.10 | 1.18 |
| PDC (agglomerative, meaning) | 1.23 | 5.00 | 6.55 | 1.63 | 1.10 | 1.94 | **2.03** | 1.18 |
| Scroll | **1.09** | 5.65 | 18.58 | 1.96 | **1.00** | **1.45** | 4.15 | **1.14** |

Table 5: Additional oracle simulation results with $k = 2$ (left) and $k = 10$ (right) candidates displayed per turn. **Bolded** is the best result, underlined is the second-best result.

plots are produced using seaborn[8] with bandwidth adjustment `bw_adjust` = 3 and `clip` = (0, 100). Note that we clip the time to the range $[0, 100]$ to better display the distribution tail. We find that a huge portion of `search` locates within 5–20 seconds showing that users indeed can finish the task much faster. In another peak (100+ seconds), the distribution clearly shows `no-kbest` $\gg$ `scroll` $>$ `autocomplete` $>$ `search-keywords` $>$ `search` meaning that `no-kbest` takes much longer time in general; and a higher portion from `scroll` and `autocomplete` takes much longer time to finish; whereas `search-keywords` and `search` have fewer such cases. This peak is contributed almost evenly by the four different strata, perhaps because users tend to read through all candidates to make sure they get the right answer.

**Time usage distribution per interface** We plot the time usage distribution using KDE for the proposed interfaces to illustrate the time usage for each stratum. Again, the KDE plots are produced using seaborn with bandwidth adjustment `bw_adjust` = 3 and `clip` = (0, 100). The plots shown on Figure 6 tell us that, for $K$-best interfaces, only Top-5 shows a different behavior where tasks can be mostly finished within 10 seconds; while Top-20, Top-100, and Escalate have very similar distributions. We hypothesize this is because we explicitly show the top 5 candidates in the interface (Figure 2 (B)). When the gold parse is not in the top 5 candidate list, annotators go through a similar process to find the answer, resulting in a similar time usage distribution for Top-20, Top-100, and Escalate. The `no-kbest` shows that without any supports, a huge portion of the tasks took more than 100 seconds to finish.

[8]https://seaborn.pydata.org

## C Additional User Feedback

**NASA Task Load Index** Figure 7 summarizes user responses to a NASA Task Load Index questionnaire (Hart, 2006) that evaluates participants' subjective workload across six dimensions. The original 7-point Likert scale was mapped to a 5-point scale for conciseness: "very low", "very high", and "medium" labels were preserved, and the four intermediate labels were mapped into two. This feedback was not collected for `search-keywords`; for `autocomplete` and `search` we observe that, compared to baselines, users report lower temporal demand and higher performance, which correspond to higher perceived speed and accuracy, respectively. This agrees with the interface preference feedback (Figure 4) and quantitative results of our user study (Table 3).

**Free-form suggestions** We collected participants' free-form suggestions by asking four questions: (*i*) "I like the provided function because ...", (*ii*) "I do not like the provided function because ...", (*iii*) "I think provided function can be improved by ...", and (*iv*) "I would like to have some other functions such as ...". Tables 6 to 9 summarize the responses. In general, participants expressed positive impression towards `autocomplete`, `search`, and `search-keywords`. Users especially like `search-keywords` as it helps quickly narrow down the options; gives insights into grammar; and even when the suggestions fail, it can be figured out very quickly and do not cause a huge negative impact (Table 6). Participants suggested to add more keywords and allow pulling keywords from natural utterances to further improve `search-keywords` (Table 8). We also found that participants believe a grammar guide would improve their annotation process (Table 9) which might be infeasible in a rapid prototyping setup.

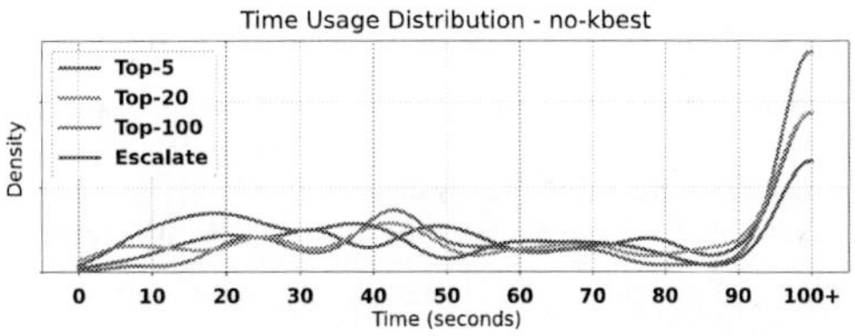


(a) Time usage for `no-kbest`.

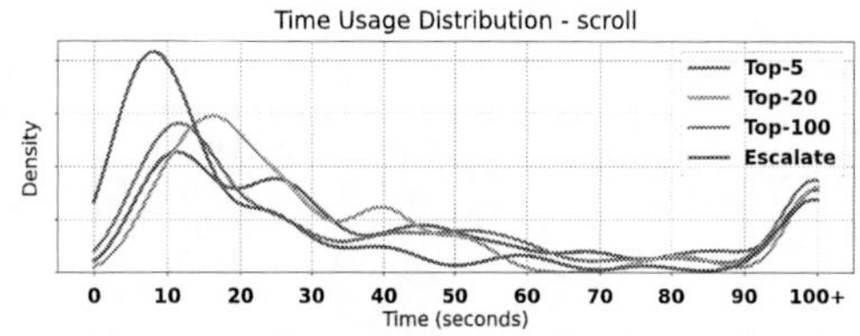


(b) Time usage for `scroll`.

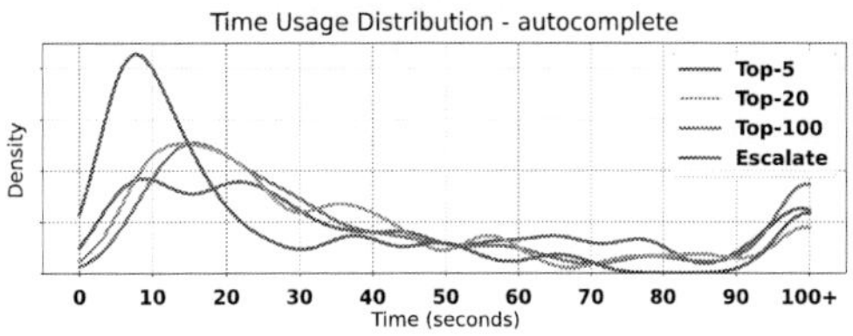


(c) Time usage for `autocomplete`.

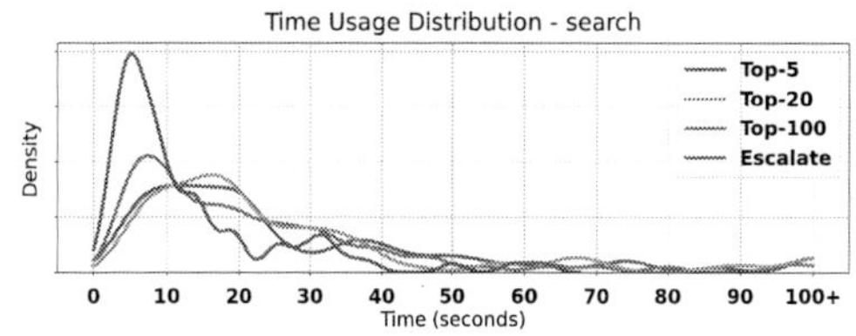


(d) Time usage for `search`.

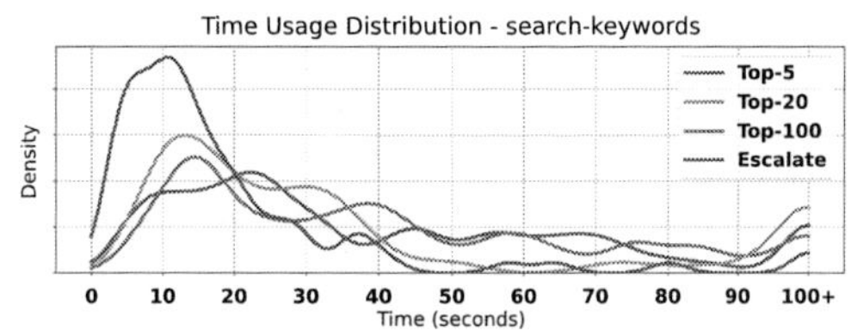


(e) Time usage for `search-keywords`.

Figure 6: For interfaces with $K$-best supports ((a), (b), (c), (d)), only Top-5 has a different shape of distribution where there is a much higher peak around 10 seconds; Top-20, Top-100, and Escalate have very similar time distribution which suggests that annotators might need to go through the same searching process no matter which stratum it is. The distribution of `no-kbest` is relatively **flat** with a huge peak in 100+, meaning that it takes much more time to finish in general.

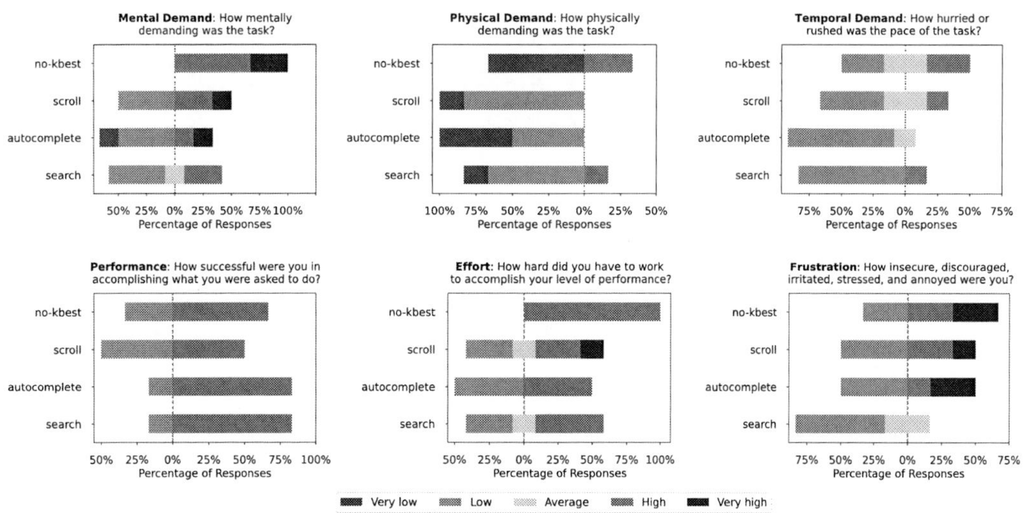


Figure 7: Summary of the user feedback on NASA Task Load Index (Hart, 2006) across six different criteria.

| I **like** the provided function because ... | |
|---|---|
| `scroll` | "You can **easily comb** through the many **variations of grammar**." |
| `autocomplete` | "... the ability to create the correct grammar with assistance was very helpful and **lowered the frustration** overall"<br>"... it has enough context/information to **quickly determine the right path forward**."<br>"It seemed to be focused and direct ... It seemed to give the **right amount of predictive assistance**." |
| `search` | "Being able to **narrow down the options** based on a **keyword** is nice, especially in cases **where the bot mostly gets it wrong right at the start**"<br>"... nicely and succinctly. It seems more **intuitive** to use ..." |
| `search-keywords` | "... the suggested keywords can **very quickly narrow down the list of displayed options** (without having to type in a single search parameter myself) so that **the correct one is easy to locate**."<br>"It was useful for **narrowing things down quicker** and helped **minimize typos** in the search."<br>"It **gave insight into the grammar**, but **was also very efficient**. It allowed myself **more control over the options** I was seeing, meaning it was much more streamlined and was very fast."<br>"Even in those cases where the suggested keywords don't end up helping much, **it only takes a few second to figure that out**. It has minimal impact on the interface, too, so its presence doesn't hurt even when it doesn't help." |

Table 6: Free-form suggestions for question "I like the provided function because ...".

| I **do not like** the provided function because ... | |
|---|---|
| `scroll` | "the scrollable list is just **annoying to look at**."<br>"It is **hard to navigate**. And makes little sense." |
| `autocomplete` | "... sometimes it presenting two options that **both look like they could be valid side-by-side** ..." |
| `search` | "... it sometimes **highlights in odd ways that decreases readability**." |
| `search-keywords` | "They weren't usually presented **in an order that I would immediately search by**." |

Table 7: Free-form suggestions for question "I do not like the provided function because ...".

| I think the provided function can be **improved** by ... | |
|---|---|
| `scroll` | "It would be nice if the **options displayed in the list respected what you had in the answer line**. For example, I type "update" and all the ones which aren't that disappear."<br>"Have **the top 5 candidates be attached to the scrollable list** function, but frozen as the top 5 results (in the same way you can **freeze rows or columns in excel**)." |
| `autocomplete` | "Maybe the ability to **hide the top 5 suggestions or hide specific options** would be nice for some users." |
| `search` | "It would be nice **if the list were a little more readable**, especially when it constantly **changes the boldness/underlines**." |
| `search-keywords` | "If we could add **more suggest words** to help us find the answer even faster."<br>"the ability to **pull "must include" elements of the utterance into** the initial set of **suggested keywords** would be helpful."<br>"the main thing that would make it work better is just **the model being improved** so predictions are better in general."<br>"**the way matched terms** are both bolded and underlined changes the list of predictions in a way that **sometimes confuses the eyes as you're matching things**." |

Table 8: Free-form suggestions for question "I think provided function can be improved by ...".

| I would like to have some **other functions** such as ... | |
|---|---|
| `scroll` | "... **change suggestions** based on the text in the annotation box."<br>"**the displayed list respecting the contents** of the type-box would be nice." |
| `autocomplete` | "A **searchable dictionary** or **index listing common translation**." |
| `search` | "An accompanying **lexicon or index of common translations**." |
| `search-keywords` | "A method of **manually filtering out words** ..." |

Table 9: Free-form suggestions for question "I would like to have some other functions such as ...".

# Hard and Soft Evaluation of NLP models with BOOtSTrap SAmpling - BooStSa

**Tommaso Fornaciari**
Università Bocconi
fornaciari@unibocconi.it

**Alexandra Uma**
Queen Mary University
a.n.uma@qmul.ac.uk

**Massimo Poesio**
Queen Mary University
m.poesio@qmul.ac.uk

**Dirk Hovy**
Università Bocconi
dirk.hovy@unibocconi.it

## Abstract

Natural Language Processing (NLP)'s applied nature makes it necessary to select the most effective and robust models. However, just producing slightly higher performance is insufficient; we want to know whether this advantage will carry over to other data sets. Bootstrapped significance tests can indicate that ability. Computing the significance of performance differences has many levels of complexity, though. It can be tedious, especially when the experimental design has many conditions to compare and several runs of experiments. We present BooStSa, a tool that makes it easy to compute significance levels with the BOOtSTrap SAmpling procedure. BooStSa can evaluate models that predict not only standard hard labels but soft labels (i.e., probability distributions over different classes) as well.

## 1 Introduction

Text classification is one of the main applications of NLP, with hundreds of papers published every year at NLP conferences. While these publications cover various domains, they essentially follow the same steps: *Pick a classification problem. Identify baseline models, standard models from previous literature, and State-Of-The-Art (SOTA) models. Propose a novel approach to the problem. Show that it outperforms the previous ones on benchmark data sets.*

Developing better methods for a task is a common feature of the computational linguistics literature, and selecting the best model from a range of options is crucial for the whole experimental procedure. However, showing absolute improvements on several data sets (let alone one) is not sufficient. Variations in model initialization, batch sampling and other factors might result in an improvement that does not generalize. We can use significance tests to assess whether the observed improvements are likely to hold on future data sets.

However, identifying the best method(s) depends on two different but correlated aspects of the evaluation process. The *metrics* adopted for the performance measurement and the *significance test* carried out for the models' comparison.

To compute the significance of the models' improvements over comparison sets, BooStSa relies on bootstrap sampling (Efron and Tibshirani, 1994; Berg-Kirkpatrick et al., 2012). As Søgaard et al. (2014) discussed, the effect size, that is, the performance gap between different methods, can be modelled as a random variable. When this random variable follows a normal distribution, it is possible to use Student's $t$-test to estimate the significance in the performance difference. However, the assumption of normal distribution does not hold in most NLP applications. Therefore, randomized, sample-based, non-parametric tests such as bootstrap sampling are better suited for NLP.

However, the correct implementation of this method can be non-trivial (especially on top of other experiments). To allow for a safe, flexible application, we release BooStSa to the community. Since the results of bootstrap methods are "very sensitive to sample size, [...] as well as to the existence of multiple metrics" (Søgaard et al., 2014, p. 1), BooStSa incorporates some constraints in the hyper-parameter choice (Section 2.3) to prevent the accidental misuse of the methods.

Concerning the *metrics*, the scenario differs when the prediction uses hard labels or soft labels. Hard labels are standard one-hot encoded labels, where one class is correct and is assigned the value of 1, and the others are wrong and have a value of 0. In the case of soft labels, the actual label value is ultimately uncertain. This uncertainty is expressed as a probability distribution over classes, each receiving a value from 0 to 1, all summing up to 1. In the first case, the use and the interpretation of metrics such as accuracy (*Acc*), precision (*Prec*), recall (*Rec*), and F-measure (*F1*) are well-understood



*Proceedings of the 60th Annual Meeting of the Association for Computational Linguistics System Demonstrations*, pages 127 - 134
May 22-27, 2022 ©2022 Association for Computational Linguistics

in the literature (Forman et al., 2003; Uma et al., 2021). BooStSa computes these metrics for hard labels. In the second case, no metric is generally accepted to evaluate the divergence between probability distributions. BooStSa follows the approach of Uma et al. (2021) and provides cross entropy (*CE*), Jensen-Shannon divergence (*JSD*), entropy similarity (*E-Sim*) and entropy correlation (*E-Corr*) for soft labels.

**Contributions.** We release BooStSa, an open-source application that computes:

- Standard metrics for hard labels, macro-averaged or over selected target classes;
- Metrics for soft labels, following best practices form previous literature;
- The bootstrap sampling significance test, with safety-constraints for hyper-parameter choices.

The tests can be run efficiently, even for complex experimental designs comparing many different models trained in several runs of experiments. The package can be installed with `pip` and is released on github/fornaciari/boostsa (documentation at boostsa.readthedocs.io).

## 2 Methods

### 2.1 Metrics for hard labels

We adopt the standard metrics for classification tasks – F-measure (*F1*), precision (*Prec*), recall (*Rec*), and accuracy (*Acc*). They have been widely studied in literature and their interpretation is generally shared and accepted (Goutte and Gaussier, 2005; Forman et al., 2003).

### 2.2 Metrics for soft labels

For the soft label evaluation, we consider the four metrics proposed by Uma et al. (2021): 1) cross entropy (*CE*), 2) Jensen-Shannon divergence (*JSD*), 3) entropy similarity (*E-Sim*) and 4) entropy correlation (*E-Corr*). The first two measure the divergence between target and predicted probability distribution (*CE* and *JSD*), the second two evaluate how well the predicted distributions capture the uncertainty embodied in the target distribution, usually generated by humans (*E-Sim* and *E-Corr*).

**Cross-entropy.** Cross-entropy is a widely used loss-function to measure the divergence between probability distribution. Peterson et al. (2019) also suggest using it to measure the confidence of trained models with respect to target distributions, typically resulting from human predictions.

**Jensen-Shannon divergence.** Based on the Kullback-Leibler divergence (Kullback and Leibler, 1951) and proposed by Lin (1991), the *JSD* is another common measure of divergence from probability distributions. Compared to the Kullback-Leibler divergence, it is symmetric, making *JSD* more easily interpretable.

**Entropy similarity.** Proposed by Uma et al. (2021), the *E-Sim* is given by the cosine similarity between two vectors, containing the normalized entropy of the probability distribution of each data point, target or prediction.

**Entropy correlation.** It relies on Pearson's correlation (Pearson, 1896), applied to the same vectors used for the *E-Sim* (Uma et al., 2021). Based on the probability distributions' entropy, *E-Sim* and *E-Corr* measure how well the predicted distributions detect the uncertainty of the target distributions.

### 2.3 Bootstrap sampling

We follow the algorithm as described by Berg-Kirkpatrick et al. (2012). The bootstrap sampling procedure relies on the iterative simulation of "new" data sets. Random test sets are repeatedly sub-sampled (with replacement) from the whole test data. At each iteration, we compare the performance difference between baseline and experimental model, $\delta_{sample}$, computed on the original test set, to the difference computed on the sampled subset, $\delta_{sub-sample}$. By counting how many times the sub-sample differences are at least twice as large as the overall difference value, $\delta_{sub-sample} > 2\delta_{sample}$, we can derive the $p$-value by dividing this count by the number of iterations.

Bootstrap sampling is agnostic to the chosen performance metric, making the tool very versatile. It allows, for example, to use all the metrics described in the previous sections, as long as they follow the Central Limit Theorem (CLT) (Pólya, 1920; Rosenblatt, 1956): i.e., it is required that the distribution of sample means approximates a normal distribution as the sample size becomes wider, regardless of the population's distribution.

However, bootstrap sampling is still sensitive to some experimental parameters, that is, the *overall test set size*, the *sub-sampled test set size* and the *number of iterations*. This point is critical, as the notion of significance is not grey-scaled: a $p$-value

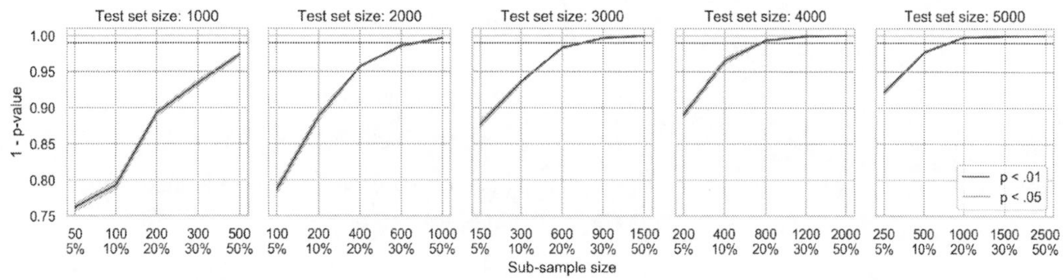


Figure 1: Significance test simulation for classification, showing the effect of interaction between test set size and sub-sample sizes. The test set is perfectly balanced (50% instances for each class). The baseline and model predictions are also balanced (*F1* = *Prec* = *Rec* = *Acc*), and the difference is one percentage point, $\delta = .01$. Each data point comes from 10 simulations. Every significance test simulation was carried out with 1 000 iterations. The narrow confidence interval (light blue) across the 10 simulations, indicates that 1 000 iterations are sufficient to obtain stable results.

is either significant or not with respect to a chosen threshold, but its value is also affected by the bootstrap hyper-parameters. Their effect can be summarized as follows.

**Test set size.** The wider the sample, the more robust the results, and the easier to reach significance levels.

If several experiments are run for each experimental condition, BooStSa concatenates the test data, the baseline and experimental predictions as if each of them was a single experiment.

**Sub-sample size.** The previous hyper-parameter is usually determined by the availability of the data sets, limiting the possibilities of control for the researcher. However, the size of the sub-samples can freely be chosen by the experimenter. Determining its correct value is not trivial, though.

Søgaard et al. (2014, p. 3) observe that "for the bootstrap test to work, the original sample has to capture most of the variation in the population. If the sample is very small, though, this is likely not the case. Consequently, with small sample sizes, there is a risk that the calculated $p$-value will be artificially low–simply because the bootstrap samples are too similar".

The opposite risk exists as well: if the sub-sample is too similar to the size of the whole test set, the bootstrap samples will be too similar to the test set, producing $p$-values that are artificially high. In other words, too broad a sample implies that the test set sample actually represents the whole population, which is quite a strong assumption indeed.

Figure 1 shows a simulation of the relationship between test size and sub-sample size. The curves come from an artificially created test set and perfectly balanced predictions, where the experimental model beats the baseline by one point per cent on every standard classification metric (*F1*, *Prec*, *Rec* and *Acc*). The trends are similar to those shown by Berg-Kirkpatrick et al. (2012) on real data.

To the best of our knowledge, there are no clear guidelines in the literature for selecting the "correct" sample size. In BooStSa, we prevent the selection of extreme sub-sample sizes (too small or too big) by only allowing a range between 5% and 50% of the test set size. Beyond this, we suggest choosing smaller sub-sample sizes, if the test set size allows, as this should keep the sub-sample size far from the dangerous extreme values. We also encourage practitioners to use bootstrap sampling responsibly and transparently by always specifying the chosen test parameters.

**Number of iterations.** On the other hand, tuning the number of iterations is straightforward: the more, the better. The confidence intervals shown in figure 1 suggest that $1,000$ iterations are already sufficient to obtain quite stable results; therefore, the often suggested $10,000$ iterations are a perfectly safe amount.

## 3 Experiment

Figure 2 shows the BooStSa's output for a real use case. We use the barely significant results of the Part-Of-Speech (POS) tagging classification task carried out by Fornaciari et al. (2021, p.2593, table 1, POS tag, separate test set, STL vs. MTL + Cross-Entropy). In that task, a Single-Task Learning (STL) model (*h0*) is compared with a Multi-Task Learning (MTL) model (*h1*). A hold-out validation procedure is followed, with a test set containing

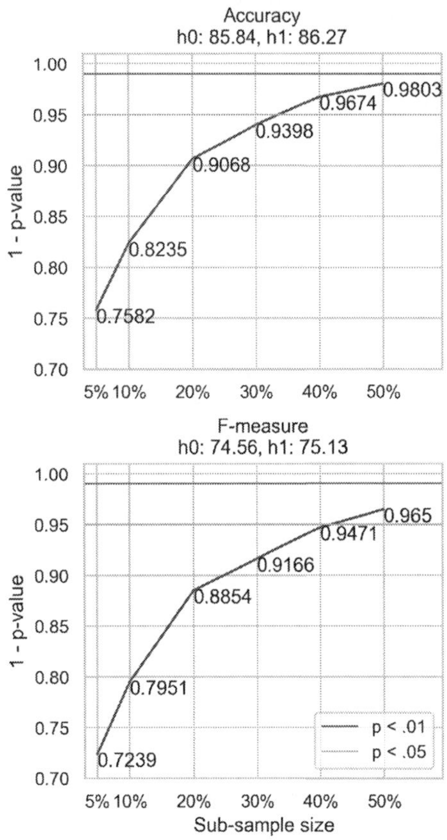


Figure 2: P-levels from significance test simulations with different sub-sample rates and 10 000 iterations. The results concern a POS-tagging classification task from the study of Fornaciari et al. (2021), where a Single-Task Learning (STL) model (*h0*) is compared with a Multi-Task Learning (MTL) model (*h1*).

3064 instances.

We consider two metrics, accuracy and F-measure, and six different sub-sample sizes, from 5% to 50% of test set rate. The *h0*'s accuracy and F-measure were 85.84 and 74.56, the *h1*'s accuracy and F-measure were 86.27 and 75.13, with a delta of 0.43 and 0.57, respectively. Similar to the results shown by Fornaciari et al. (2021), significant $p$-values appear only for sample sizes greater than 30% of the whole test set.

## 4 Usage

### 4.1 Installation

BooStSa can be installed in the shell simply via: `pip install -U boostsa`.

### 4.2 Getting started

To use BooStSa in a Python script, the first step is to import the library:

```
from boostsa import Bootstrap
```

Second, we need to create a bootstrap instance:

```
boot = Bootstrap()
```

This instance will store the experiments' outcomes and compute performances and the significance test between the experiments that need to be compared.

#### 4.2.1 Inputs

The basic assumption for using BooStSa is that at least two classification models have been trained.

One model is considered the baseline, *control*, or null hypothesis (*h0*). The other is the experimental model, *treatment*, or hypothesis 1 (*h1*). In most settings, we expect this model to beat the baseline.

Their respective performance is tested against the same test set. It does not matter if this is a dedicated test set or resulting from a $k$-fold cross-validation procedure. In any case, the test set (*targets*) must be the same for both models.

The *h0* predictions, *h1* predictions and *targets* are the inputs for the Bootstrap instance.

#### 4.2.2 Outputs

BooStSa's outputs are directly printed to standard out, and returned as a pandas `DataFrame`, that can be directly used, for example, to export them to a LaTex table.

However, when the `Boostsa()` object is instantiated, it is possible to define which output to save on disk. BooStSa can produce two kinds of outputs:

**`results.tsv`** It contains the experiments' performance and the (possible) significance levels of the experimental against the *control* conditions;

**`outcomes.json`** It contains targets and predictions for all the experimental conditions.

Target and predictions are the same that BooStSa takes as inputs. However, as described in Section 4.4, it can be useful to save them in JSON format if the test needs to be rerun, for example, when adding new experimental conditions to those that had already been considered. In these cases, feeding BooStSa with `outcomes.json` allows us to recreate the previous inputs' configuration without needing to instantiate BooStSa again from scratch.

These outputs can be created using the following parameters:

**save_results** Type: `bool`; default: `True`. Boolean variable to determine whether to save the performances and the tests' results.

**save_outcomes** Type: `bool`; default: `True`. Boolean variable to determine whether to save as json the input predictions and targets.

**dir_out** Type: `str`; default: `''`. String variable that indicates the directory where to save `results.tsv` and `outcomes.json`.

The box below shows an example:

```
boot = Bootstrap(save_outcomes=False, dir_out='my/favourite/directory/')
```

### 4.3 Simple use-case

In the simplest use case, it is necessary to carry out the significance test between the predictions of two experiments. This can be done with the `test` function, which accepts the following parameters:

**targs** Type: `list`, `numpy.array` or `str`. They are the *targets*, or test set, that is the benchmark to measure the *h0* and *h1* predictions' performance. BooStSa automatically infers from the input shape if hard or soft labels are provided, according to these cases:

- A simple `list` will be assumed to be a list of integers, each corresponding to hard classes' indexes.
- A `list` of `list`s will be assumed to contain in each sub-list, as a row in a 2D matrix, float numbers summing up to one, which will be treated as soft labels.
- A 1D or 1-column `numpy.array` will be considered as containing integers for hard labels.
- A 2D `numpy.array` will be treated as containing float numbers constituting a soft label in each row.
- The `str` input will be processed as a full path to a file, which will have to comply with the following rules:
  - A file with extension '.txt' has to contain an integer in each row, representing hard classes' indexes.
  - A file with extension '.csv' has to contain comma-separated values for soft labels.
  - A file with extension '.tsv' has to contain tab-separated values for soft labels.
  - A file with extension '.npy' has to contain a NumPy binary file.

**h0_preds** Type: `list`, `numpy.array` or `str`. The *h0* predictions, in the same formats of `targs`.

**h1_preds** Type: `list`, `numpy.array` or `str`. The *h1* predictions, in the same formats as above.

**h0_name** Type: `str`, default: `h0`. Expression to describe the *h0* condition.

**h1_name** Type: `str`, default: `h1`. Expression to describe the *h1* condition.

**n_loops** Type: `int`, default: `1000`. Number of iterations for computing the bootstrap sampling.

**sample_size** Type: `float`, default: `.1`. Percentage of data points sampled from their whole set. The admitted values range between 0.05 (5%) and 0.5 (50%).

**targetclass** Type: `int`, default: `None`. If provided, it is interpreted as a label index, and for hard labels BooStSa will provide performance and significance levels with respect to that class. The parameter has no effect with soft labels.

**verbose** Type: `bool`, default: `False`. If true, the experiments' performance is printed on the shell.

An example of `test` function use is shown in figure 3. The significance levels are indicated by $** : p \leq .01$ and $* : p \leq .05$. Figure 4 shows an example with soft labels as inputs. Note that, for *CE* and *JSD*, the difference between the baseline and experimental model is negative. In fact, they are distance measures; therefore, lower is better in their case.

```
boot.test(targs='test_boot/hard/h0.0/targs.txt', h0_preds='test_boot/hard/h0.0/preds
    .txt', h1_preds='test_boot/hard/h1.0/preds.txt', h0_name='baseline', h1_name='
    experiment', n_loops=1000, sample_size=.2, verbose=True)
```

```
data shape:  (1000, 1)
sample size: 200
h0: h0 - h1: h1
targs count:      ['class 0 freq 465 perc 46.50%', 'class 1 freq 535 perc 53.50%']
h0 preds count: ['class 0 freq 339 perc 33.90%', 'class 1 freq 661 perc 66.10%']
h1 preds count: ['class 0 freq 500 perc 50.00%', 'class 1 freq 500 perc 50.00%']
F-measure...... - h0: 0.6776  - h1: 0.7407  - diff: 0.0631
accuracy....... - h0: 0.6900  - h1: 0.7410  - diff: 0.0510
precision...... - h0: 0.6994  - h1: 0.7410  - diff: 0.0416
recall......... - h0: 0.6796  - h1: 0.7422  - diff: 0.0626
bootstrap: 100%|==========================| 1000/1000 [00:09<00:00, 100.40it/s]
count sample diff f1   is twice tot diff f1....... 15   / 1000     p < 0.015  *
count sample diff prec is twice tot diff prec..... 65   / 1000     p < 0.065
count sample diff rec  is twice tot diff rec ..... 9    / 1000     p < 0.009  **
count sample diff acc  is twice tot diff acc...... 38   / 1000     p < 0.038  *
```

Figure 3: Input and output of the `test` function.

```
data shape:  (1000, 3)
sample size: 200
h0: h0 - h1: h1
targs distribution:          [0.33241763 0.33790091 0.32968146]
h0_preds distribution:       [0.33571912 0.33230295 0.33391209]
h1_preds distribution:       [0.33337905 0.3336012  0.33301975]
Jensen-Shannon divergence: - h0: 0.2143  - h1: 0.1817  - diff: -0.0326
cross-entropy:             - h0: 1.3515  - h1: 1.0886  - diff: -0.2629
entropy similarity:        - h0: 0.9816  - h1: 0.9857  - diff: 0.0041
entropy correlation:       - h0: 0.0064  - h1: 0.0529  - diff: 0.0465
bootstrap: 100%|==========================| 1000/1000 [00:05<00:00, 181.20it/s]
count sample diff jsd is twice tot diff jsd....... 0    / 1000     p < 0.0    **
count sample diff ce  is twice tot diff ce........ 0    / 1000     p < 0.0    **
count sample diff sim is twice tot diff sim....... 7    / 1000     p < 0.007  **
count sample diff cor is twice tot diff cor....... 315  / 1000     p < 0.315
```

Figure 4: Output of the `test` function with soft labels.

```
boot = Bootstrap(dir_out='my/favourite/dir/')
boot.feed(h0='h0', exp_idx='h0.0', preds=h0_exp1_preds, targs=targs)
boot.feed(h0='h0', h1='h1', exp_idx='h1.0', preds=h1_exp1_preds, targs=targs)
```

```
next_boot = Bootstrap() # if not already instantiated
next_boot.loadjson('my/favourite/dir/outcomes.json')
next_boot.feed(h0='h0', exp_idx='h0.1', preds=h0_exp2_preds, targs=targs)
next_boot.feed(h0='h0', h1='h1', exp_idx='h1.1', preds=h1_exp2_preds, targs=targs)
next_boot.run(n_loops=1000, sample_size=.2)
```

Figure 5: `feed`, `loadjson` and `run` functions.

### 4.4 BooStSa in a pipeline

In most cases, the experimental conditions are complex and imply the comparison between several baselines and several different experimental models, and for all of them, several runs of experiments can be planned. In those cases, BooStSa can be included in the whole pipeline, collecting the experiments' outcomes while they are produced, storing them and computing performance and significance levels at the end of the whole procedure.

This is done with two functions, `feed` and `run`. The first one collects BooStSa's inputs while they are produced by the experiments; the second one computes performance and bootstrap sampling. The `feed` functions feeds the `outcomes.json` file and takes the following inputs:

**`h0`** Type: `str`. This is a string that identifies a *control* condition. It must be provided both in the case of *control* experiments (*h0*) and *treatment* experiments (*h1*s) because BooStSa needs to know with which baseline the *treatment* results have to be compared.

**`h1`** Type: `str`; default: `None`. This is a string

that identifies a *treatment* condition. It must be provided only in case of *treatment* experiments (*h1*s).

**exp_idx** Type: `str` ; default: `None` . This string (ideally, an index) identifies each unique experiment within its experimental condition, defined by `h0` or `h1` . This is useful in case of multiple experiments for the same experimental condition.

**targs , preds** Type: `list` , `numpy.array` or `str` ; default: `None` . Equivalent to the `targs` , `h0_preds` , and `h1_preds` parameters in `test` .

**idxs** Type: `list` , `numpy.array` or `str` ; default: `None` . Treated like `targs` and `preds` , `idxs` stores the indexes of the data points, that might have been shuffled during the experiments. The data point order does not affect the bootstrap sampling, but storing the shuffled indexes allows us to link the predictions to the original data points later on.

**epochs** Type: `int` . Lastly, `epoch` can store the number of training epochs run by the experiment.

The flexibility of `feed` allows storing together several *control* conditions and the relatives *treatments* for comparison. Also, the process can be stopped and resumed: the function `loadjson` allows to load a previously saved `outcomes.json` file and to keep on feeding it. Once all the inputs are provided, the `run` function computes performance and bootstrap sampling. The `run` parameters are:

**n_loops** Type: `int` ; default: `1000` . The iterations' number of bootstrap sampling.

**sample_size** Type: `float` ; default: `.1` . The sub-sample size, expressed as percent part of the test set. The value is constrained between .05 and .5 (inclusive).

**targetclass** Type: `int` , default: `None` . Equal to the same parameter in `test` .

**verbose** Type: `bool` , default: `False` . If true, the experiments' performance is printed on the shell.

Figure 5 shows the whole process.

## 5 Limitations

Besides the constraints discussed in Section 2.3, aimed to prevent the significance test misuse, BooStSa assumes that *h0* predictions, *h1* predictions, and *targets* are available. When comparing with results from previous literature, this assumption might not hold: in these cases, to apply BooStSa it is necessary to find or reproduce the *h0* outcomes.

## 6 Conclusion

We present BooStSa, a Python package to allow NLP practitioners to efficiently compute significance values for hard and soft labels using a safe set of hyper-parameters.

We discuss how the test hyper-parameters can affect the outcome, introducing safety constraints for the test use and suggesting, as a good practice, to report the hyper-parameters with the experiments' results.

While the metrics for hard labels consolidated in literature, those for soft labels that measure the divergence between probability distributions are not yet widely used, and the consensus about their interpretation is still on the way to be reached. We follow the extensive survey of Uma et al. (2021), which takes into consideration the most recent trends in NLP.

We also agree with Basile et al. (2021), who point out that incorporating into the models the information about the intrinsic entities' ambiguity, expressed as inter-coders disagreement and represented as a probability distribution over different classes, is a necessary step to create models that carry out NLP task with human-like performance.

## Acknowledgments

This research has been partially funded from the European Research Council (ERC) under the European Union's Horizon 2020 research and innovation program No. 949944, INTEGRATOR and No. 695662, DALI. TF and DH are members of the Data and Marketing Insights Unit at the Bocconi Institute for Data Science and Analysis.

## 7 Ethical Considerations

Psychology has seen a growing scandal around $p$-hacking, i.e., the generation of enough experimental variations to produce a significant outcome in one of them. This risk is low in NLP, as significance alone is not sufficient for publication: typically, proof of predictive performance on ideally several test sets is necessary instead. Reporting significance in NLP is therefore an additional robustness measure, indicating the model's generalizability. While users might abuse the capabilities of BooStSa to make significant results more likely, this would require deliberate tampering (and even then would not guarantee significance). If used as intended, however, BooStSa should reduce unintended variance via researcher degrees of freedom and make results more comparable and reproducible.

## References


Valerio Basile, Michael Fell, Tommaso Fornaciari, Dirk Hovy, Silviu Paun, Barbara Plank, Massimo Poesio, and Alexandra Uma. 2021. We need to consider disagreement in evaluation. In *Proceedings of the 1st Workshop on Benchmarking: Past, Present and Future*, pages 15–21, Online. Association for Computational Linguistics.

Taylor Berg-Kirkpatrick, David Burkett, and Dan Klein. 2012. An empirical investigation of statistical significance in NLP. In *Proceedings of the 2012 Joint Conference on Empirical Methods in Natural Language Processing and Computational Natural Language Learning*, pages 995–1005, Jeju Island, Korea. Association for Computational Linguistics.

Bradley Efron and Robert J Tibshirani. 1994. *An introduction to the bootstrap*. CRC press.

George Forman et al. 2003. An extensive empirical study of feature selection metrics for text classification. *J. Mach. Learn. Res.*, 3(Mar):1289–1305.

Tommaso Fornaciari, Alexandra Uma, Silviu Paun, Barbara Plank, Dirk Hovy, and Massimo Poesio. 2021. Beyond black & white: Leveraging annotator disagreement via soft-label multi-task learning. In *Proceedings of the 2021 Conference of the North American Chapter of the Association for Computational Linguistics: Human Language Technologies*, pages 2591–2597, Online. Association for Computational Linguistics.

Cyril Goutte and Eric Gaussier. 2005. A probabilistic interpretation of precision, recall and f-score, with implication for evaluation. In *European conference on information retrieval*, pages 345–359. Springer.

Solomon Kullback and Richard A Leibler. 1951. On information and sufficiency. *The annals of mathematical statistics*, 22(1):79–86.

Jianhua Lin. 1991. Divergence measures based on the shannon entropy. *IEEE Transactions on Information theory*, 37(1):145–151.

Karl Pearson. 1896. Vii. mathematical contributions to the theory of evolution.—iii. regression, heredity, and panmixia. *Philosophical Transactions of the Royal Society of London. Series A, containing papers of a mathematical or physical character*, sblindo(187):253–318.

Joshua C Peterson, Ruairidh M Battleday, Thomas L Griffiths, and Olga Russakovsky. 2019. Human uncertainty makes classification more robust. In *Proceedings of the IEEE/CVF International Conference on Computer Vision*, pages 9617–9626.

Georg Pólya. 1920. Üon the central limit theorem of probability theory and the problem of moments. *Mathematical Journal*, 8(3):171–181.

Murray Rosenblatt. 1956. A central limit theorem and a strong mixing condition. *Proceedings of the National Academy of Sciences of the United States of America*, 42(1):43.

Anders Søgaard, Anders Johannsen, Barbara Plank, Dirk Hovy, and Hector Martínez Alonso. 2014. What's in a p-value in NLP? In *Proceedings of the Eighteenth Conference on Computational Natural Language Learning*, pages 1–10, Ann Arbor, Michigan. Association for Computational Linguistics.

Alexandra N Uma, Tommaso Fornaciari, Dirk Hovy, Silviu Paun, Barbara Plank, and Massimo Poesio. 2021. Learning from disagreement: A survey. *Journal of Artificial Intelligence Research*, 72:1385–1470.

# COVID-19 Claim Radar: A Structured Claim Extraction and Tracking System

**Manling Li, Revanth Gangi Reddy, Ziqi Wang, Yi-Shyuan Chiang, Tuan M. Lai, Pengfei Yu, Zixuan Zhang, Heng Ji**
Computer Science Department
University of Illinois Urbana-Champaign
{manling2, revanth3, ziqiw9, hengji}@illinois.edu

## Abstract

The COVID-19 pandemic has received extensive media coverage, with a vast variety of claims made about different aspects of the virus. In order to track these claims, we present *COVID-19 Claim Radar*[1], a system that automatically extracts claims relating to COVID-19 in news articles. We provide a comprehensive structured view of such claims, with rich attributes (such as claimers and their affiliations) and associated knowledge elements (such as events, relations and entities). Further, we use this knowledge to identify inter-claim connections such as equivalent, supporting, or refuting relations, with shared structural evidence like claimers, similar centroid events and arguments. In order to consolidate claim structures at the corpus-level, we leverage Wikidata[2] as the hub to merge coreferential knowledge elements, and apply machine translation to aggregate claims from news articles in multiple languages. The system provides users with a comprehensive exposure to COVID-19 related claims, their associated knowledge elements, and related connections to other claims. The system is publicly available on GitHub[3] and DockerHub[4], with complete documentation[5].

## 1 Introduction

Claims present in daily news are unfiltered and potentially of great value, but can also have negative effects when misinformation is widespread. The COVID-19 pandemic is a crucial example of when false claims can be particularly harmful, with the torrent of misinformation impacting public perception. For example, a claim such as "*Vaccines are DNA changers*" is likely to discourage vaccinations. Further, a study by KFF[6] COVID-19 Vaccine Monitor project found that 78% of U.S. adults agree with one of eight false claims regarding the pandemic.

In order to distinguish misleading information, a fundamental step is to first identify claims and discover their supporting or refuting relations. Automatic claim detection (Palau and Moens, 2009; Eger et al., 2017; Stab et al., 2018; Li et al., 2019) aims to mine arguments regarding a topic of consideration and has been applied to the COVID-19 scenario (Saakyan et al., 2021; Liu et al., 2020; Reddy et al., 2021). However, existing approaches ignore rich claim structures, or fail to associate claims with structured knowledge elements, thereby being incapable of supporting a more structured analysis. Further, they do not support real-time claim discovery, a feature required to process the rapidly updating COVID-19 pandemic information.

In this paper, we release a claim detection system that aims to automatically mine rich claim structures from news. Different from traditional claim detection systems that discover claims in isolation, we introduce a structured view for claims that consists of:

**(1) Structured Claim Attributes** including claim TOPIC, SUBTOPIC, TEMPLATE, CLAIMOBJECT, CLAIMER, AFFILIATION, LOCATION, and TIME. Our extraction is performed at the corpus-level with entity linking and coreference resolution, which allows for the construction of such comprehensive structures. For example, Table 1 shows a claim related to the topic *Wearing Masks*, where the claimer's AFFILIATION can not be directly extracted from the local sentence, but it can be derived from the "General Affliation" of the CLAIMER that is extracted from the corpus.

**(2) Associated Knowledge Elements** namely the entities, relations and events associated with the

[1] Live Demo: http://18.221.187.153/
[2] https://www.wikidata.org/
[3] GitHub: https://github.com/uiucnlp/covid-claim-radar
[4] DockerHub: https://hub.docker.com/repository/docker/blendernlp/covid-claim-radar
[5] Video: http://blender.cs.illinois.edu/aida/covid_claim_radar.mp4
[6] Kaiser Family Foundation, an American non-profit organization.



*Proceedings of the 60th Annual Meeting of the Association for Computational Linguistics System Demonstrations*, pages 135 - 144
May 22-27, 2022 ©2022 Association for Computational Linguistics

| | |
|---|---|
| ClaimText | Cloth face coverings are most likely to reduce the spread of COVID-19 when they are widely used by people in public settings |
| Topic | Wearing Masks |
| Template | Wearing masks is necessary in location [X] |
| ClaimObject | public settings<br>[Identity Qnode] Q294440 (public space)<br>[Type Qnode] Q7551384 (social space) |
| Claimer | Reed<br>[Identity Qnode] Q30105757 (Carrie Reed)<br>[Type Qnode] Q1650915 (researcher) |
| Affiliation | Centers for Disease Control and Prevention<br>[Identity Qnode] Q583725 (CDC)<br>[Type Qnode] Q20857065 (United States federal agency) |
| Location | None |
| Time | EarliestStart: 2020-01-01<br>LatestStart: 2020-07-27<br>EarliestEnd: 2020-07-27<br>LatestEnd: None |
| Stance | affirm |
| Associated Knowledge | Cloth face coverings [COM.Equipment] are most likely to reduce [CONTROL.IMPEDEINTERFERE] the spread [DISASTER.DISEASEOUTBREAK] of COVID-19 [MHI] when they are widely used [SOCIALBEHAVIOR.WEAR] by people in public settings [LOC] |
| Supporting Claims | 33,000 deaths could be avoided by October 1 if 95 percent of people wore masks in public |
| | masks can prevent transmission in high-risk scenarios |
| Refuting Claims | face masks can be harmful, because they force the wearer to breathe in too much carbon dioxide |
| | with an N95 mask, some people have an elevated blood carbon dioxide level, and some also reduced oxygen level |
| | Masks can cause carbon dioxide poisoning |

Table 1: An example of claim structure.

claims as claim evidence. For example, *reduce* is identified as a CONTROL.IMPEDEINTERFERE event with *COVID-19* as TARGET and *cloth face coverings* as INSTRUMENT. This representation provides a structured perspective of thr claim semantics and enables discovery of semantic relatedness across multiple claims via knowledge elements.

**(3) Inter-Claim Connections** for identifying supporting, refuting and equivalent claims, with complex structured connections via claim attributes and knowledge elements. For example, Table 1 shows the supporting claims that share the *mask* entity and CONTROL.IMPEDEINTERFERE event, as well as refuting claims about masks having negative effects of elevating blood carbon dioxide level.

**(4) Wikidata Linking** for linking claim attributes (including CLAIMER, CLAIMOBJECT, AFFILIATION and LOCATION) and knowledge elements (entities, events and relations) to Wikidata, as shown in Table 1. It enables corpus-level knowledge consolidation and provides external references for users. Note that we use the terms "Qnode" and "Wikidata item" interchangeably.

**(5) Structured Search Queries** to support multi-dimensional search and analysis. Figure 1a shows our multi-dimensional search interface for searching multiple claim attributes jointly, as well as their associated knowledge elements. Each search dimension also provides some frequent candidates as references, such as *Centers for Disease Control and Prevention* for CLAIMER.

*COVID-19 Claim Radar* automatically provides users with a comprehensive and structured overview about COVID-19 related claims, allowing an accurate understanding of rapidly emerging claims, their importance, and their interconnections. The structured view enables seamless search with complex queries and discovery of alternative claims over the rich claim structures. The system is particularly useful for tracking current claims, providing alerts, and predicting possible changes, as well as topics related to the ongoing incidents.

## 2 Overview

The architecture of our structured claim extraction system is illustrated in Figure 2. The system pipeline consists of different components with two main modules, namely, Claim Extraction (CE) (Section 3) and Knoweldge Extraction (KE) (Section 4). Each module creates a separate knowledge base, using the document corpus as input. The corpus-level knowledge base is then associated to claims according to the justifications, as well as coreferential entities and events. Inter-claim relations such as equivalent, supporting or refuting are then identified based on their structural connections (Section 5).

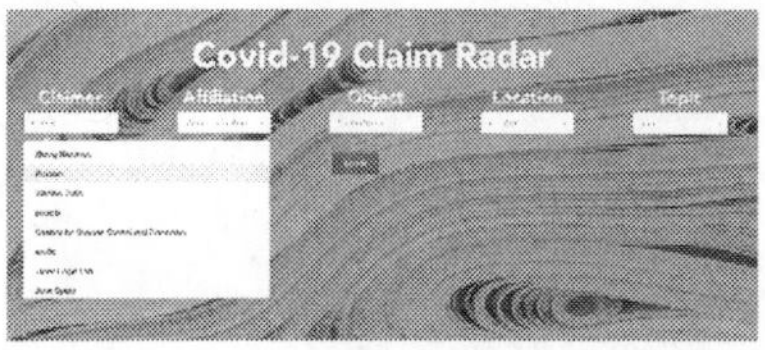


(a) Home page with a multi-dimensional search interface.

(b) List of claims returned corresponding to a search for claimer *"Center for Disease Control and Prevention."*

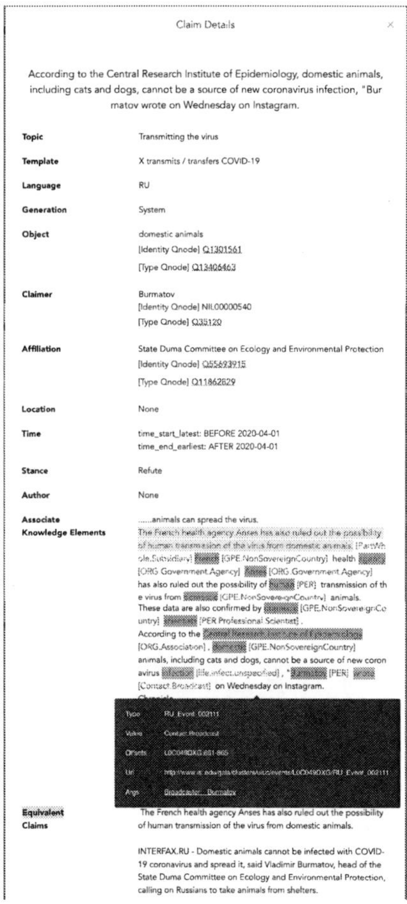


(c) Structured claim view with associated knowledge elements and equivalent claims shown. Hovering over a knowledge element shows its corresponding arguments.

Figure 1: Screenshots of the demo corresponding to (a) main page, (b) list of claims returned from search, and (c) the structure claim view.

# 3 Claim Extraction

## 3.1 Core Claim Extraction

We employ a zero-shot claim detection framework that identifies claims relating to COVID-19 in addition to background attributes such as the CLAIMER and CLAIMOBJECT. Specifically, the system consists of a claim-spotting model to identify sentences that contain claims, with additional modules for filtering topics, and detecting the claimer and claim objects.

For the claim-spotting model, we use ClaimBuster[7] (Hassan et al., 2017) to identify sentences which contain claims. Next, we leverage an extractive Question Answering (QA) system (Alberti et al., 2019) in a zero-shot setting for topic filtering, claimer detection and claim object detection. We use a QA model that is trained on SQuAD 2.0 (Rajpurkar et al., 2018) and Natural Questions (Kwiatkowski et al., 2019).

For each topic, we have two topic filtering approaches: (1) hand-crafting questions corresponding to the topic, and (2) retrieving topic-related questions from Google Search API to handle unseen topics [8]. Then, we use the claim sentence as context and pass these questions as input to the QA model. The answer score for each question is used as the corresponding topic score and a threshold is set on the highest topic score in order to select the claim. Table 2 shows the examples of individual questions used to select claims relating to specific topics about COVID-19.

For claim object detection, we use the answer span for the question corresponding to the claim topic as the CLAIMOBJECT. For identifying the claim span, we use the claim boundary detection service released as part of the Project Debater (Bar-Haim et al., 2021). Next, we leverage the same QA model for claimer detection, by using the answer corresponding the question "*Who said that <claim span>?*", with the entire news article as context.

## 3.2 Knowledge-Enhanced Claim Extraction

To identify the knowledge elements associated to the extracted claims, we leverage entities, relations and events that are extracted from the Knowledge Extraction module (detailed in Section 4). We extract knowledge elements within each claim span

[7]https://idir.uta.edu/claimbuster/api/

[8]We employ the topic as the query, the API we used is https://serpapi.com, and we select top two questions for each topic.

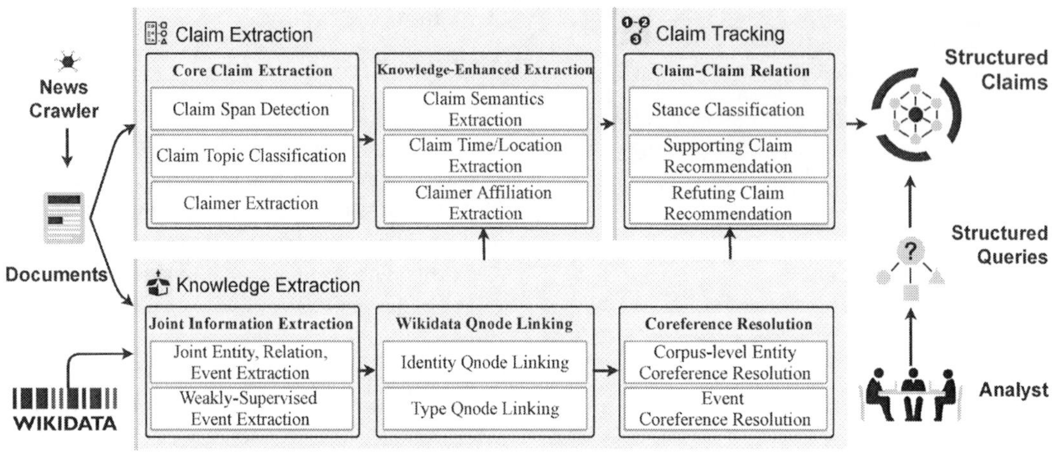


Figure 2: Architecture of the structured claim and knowledge extraction system.

| Topic | Question |
|---|---|
| Tranmission of COVID-19 | What transmits the virus? |
| Contraction of COVID-19 | Who can contract the virus? |
| Protection from COVID-19 | What can protect from the virus? |
| Origin of COVID-19 | What animal is associated with the origin of the virus? |
| Origin of COVID-19 | Where did the first case of the virus occurr? |
| Wearing Masks | What are the harmful effects of wearing masks? |
| Wearing Masks | Where is it necessary to wear masks to prevent the virus? |
| Cure for COVID-19 | What can cure the virus? |

Table 2: Examples of questions corresponding to individual topics about COVID-19.

and within the sentences before and after the claim span. To provide a comprehensive understanding of claim attributes such as the AFFILIATION of the claimer, we extract entity-entity relations of types "General Affiliation" and "Organization Affiliation" from the entire corpus and perform corpus-level entity conference resolution. We also fill in each claim's LOCATION and TIME according to the spatial and temporal attributes of the events mentioned in the claim span.

## 4 Knowledge Extraction

### 4.1 Joint Information Extraction

We first perform joint extraction of events of 144 types, entities of 7 types and relations of 38 types using the state-of-the-art supervised Information Extraction system (Lin et al., 2020) [9]. To extract event types and entity types newly emerging in the COVID-19 pandemic scenario, we employ a keyword-based event detection system. Specifically, we manually collected a list of keywords for each new event type, and compute keyword representations by averaging the contextualized representations from BERT (Devlin et al., 2019) of keyword occurrences in an unlabeled pandemic-related corpus. We provide 4.9 keywords for each type in average. Then we aggregate keyword representations for the same event type to get the event type representation. For event trigger detection, we first compute BERT representations of all the tokens in a sentence, and consider a token as an event trigger if its cosine similarity with an event type representation is larger than a threshold.

### 4.2 WikiData Qnode Linking

Wikidata is the most extensive crowdsourced knowledge graph. As such, it allows us to tie claimers, claim objects, and knowledge elements (e.g., entities) together to consolidate claim structures at the corpus level.

The massive number of entities in Wikidata (i.e., QNodes) makes entity linking challenging. To effectively narrow down the search space, we propose a candidate retrieval paradigm based on entity profiling. Wikidata entities and their textual fields are first indexed into a Elasticsearch. During inference, given a mention and its context, we follow EPGEL (Lai et al., 2022) using a trained sequence-to-sequence (seq2seq) model to generate the profile of the target entity, which consists of a generated title and a generated description. We use the profile to query the indexed search engine to retrieve

[9] We use the extended version (Li et al., 2020) that supports the most comprehensive DARPA AIDA ontology. The ontology is attached to the Appendix.

candidate entities. We use Wikipedia anchor texts and their corresponding Wikidata entities as the supervision signals for training the framework. In addition to instance-level linking, we also perform Qnode linking on the fine-grained entity types in our ontology.

### 4.3 Coreference Resolution

We conduct entity coreference resolution within each document (Lai et al., 2021b) by employing SpanBERT (large) (Joshi et al., 2020) as the base Transformer encoder and train the entire neural model on ACE 2005 (Walker et al., 2006), NIST TAC-KBP EDL 2016[10] (Ji et al., 2015), EDL 2017[11] (Ji et al., 2017), and OntoNotes (English) (Pradhan et al., 2012). After that, we utilize the Wikidata entity linking results to refine the predictions of the neural model. We prevent two entity mentions from being directly merged if they are linked to different entities (i.e., Qnodes) with high confidence. To construct a corpus-level knowledge graph, all entities that are linked to the same Qnode will be merged into the same cluster (even if the entities are from different documents).

Our event coreference resolution is performed within each document and adopts a similar method as entity coreference resolution, while incorporating additional symbolic features such as the event type information (Lai et al., 2021a). We use the multilingual XLM-RoBERTa (XLM-R) (Conneau et al., 2020) as the base Transformer encoder. We train the model on ACE 2005 (Walker et al., 2006) and ERE (Song et al., 2015a).

## 5 Claim-Claim Relation Extraction

We consolidate the claims from the entire corpus according to the Wikidata Qnode linking results and claim attributes.

### 5.1 Stance Classification

We identify the stance from the perspective of each claimer, namely whether the claimer *affirms* or *refutes* a claim. This is different from prior stance detection tasks (Hardalov et al., 2021), which define stance with respect to target-context pairs, such as claim-evidence or headline-article.

In this setting, we follow Reddy et al. (2021) to use pre-trained Natural Language Inference (NLI) models for stance detection. Specifically, we formulate hypotheses for both of the *affirm* and *refute* labels, using the claim's corresponding topic. Then, the claim sentence is used as the premise as input to the NLI model, with the hypothesis corresponding to higher entailment score considered as the stance. We use a Bart-large (Lewis et al., 2020) model trained on MultiNLI (Williams et al., 2018) as our pre-trained NLI model.

### 5.2 Equivalent Claims

We use the structured claim information to identify claims that are equivalent. Specifically, we consider claims that share the same SUBTOPIC, CLAIMOBJECT and STANCE as equivalent. For CLAIMOBJECT, we use the corresponding Wikipedia QNode to account for diversity in the object mentions.

### 5.3 Supporting and Refuting Claims

We also identify claims that are supporting or refuting each other. We formulate this as an NLI task where the claims are corresponding premise-hypthosis pairs. We use high entailment or contradiction scores as an indication of whether two claims are supporting or refuting each other respectively. We leverage the same pre-trained NLI model as used in Section 5.1.

## 6 Experiment

### 6.1 Dataset

The system can take any set of news articles to extract claims and perform visualization. The live demo [12] supports two functions: (1) **Real-time Extraction**: Users are able to copy a piece of news content and extract claims; (2) **Periodical Update**: To track claims in this rapidly evolving pandemic, we periodically collect newly emerging COVID-19 related news articles from Google News [13], and perform claim extraction and knowledge extraction to update the *COVID-19 Claim Radar*.

### 6.2 System Performance

The performance of each component is shown in Table 4. We evaluate the end-to-end performance of our system on 1,139 COVID-19 news articles released by the Linguistic Data Consortium (LDC2021E11). We translated the Spanish and Russian news into English and perform end-to-end

[10]LDC2017E03

[11]LDC2017E52

[12]`http://18.221.187.153/`

[13]`https://news.google.com/rss/search?q=xx`

| | #doc | #claim | #claimer | #affiliation | #location | $\#start_{earliest}$ | $\#start_{latest}$ | $\#end_{earliest}$ | $\#end_{latest}$ | #entity | #event |
|---|---|---|---|---|---|---|---|---|---|---|---|
| **English** | 484 | 905 | 581 | 133 | 166 | 714 | 693 | 661 | 336 | 11,302 | 1,718 |
| **Spanish** | 385 | 427 | 285 | 94 | 76 | 324 | 318 | 309 | 114 | 5,812 | 722 |
| **Russian** | 234 | 566 | 362 | 73 | 135 | 466 | 457 | 442 | 237 | 6,751 | 1,179 |

Table 3: Results of structured claim extraction.

extraction on the entire corpus. More analysis on the extraction results are detailed in the Appendix.

| Component | | | Benchmark | Metric | Score |
|---|---|---|---|---|---|
| Claim Extraction | Claim | | NewsClaims | $F_1$ | 36.0% |
| | Claim Object | | NewsClaims | $F_1$ | 57.0% |
| | Claimer | | NewsClaims | $F_1$ | 50.1% |
| | Stance | | NewsClaims | Acc. | 87.5% |
| Knowledge Extraction | Entity | | ACE | $F_1$ | 89.6% |
| | Relation | | ACE | $F_1$ | 58.6% |
| | Event | Trigger | ACE | $F_1$ | 72.8% |
| | | Argument | ACE | $F_1$ | 54.8% |
| Wikidata Qnode Linking | | | TACKBP-2010 | Acc. | 90.9% |
| Coreference | Entity | | OntoNotes | CoNLL | 92.4% |
| | Event | | ACE | CoNLL | 84.8% |

Table 4: Performance of each component. The benchmark references are: NewsClaims (Reddy et al., 2021), ACE (Walker et al., 2006), ERE (Song et al., 2015b), TACKBP-2010 (Ji et al., 2010), OntoNotes (Pradhan et al., 2012).

### 6.3 Case Study

In the context of comprehensive claim structures, our system can perform explainable and reliable predictions in terms of supporting and refuting claims, by exploiting the shared or related attributes and stances. For example, for the claim "*masks should be carefully taken off after getting inside a car or room*", we are able to discover its refuting claim as "*wear them in your car, your bed, the shower, wear three of them if you want just leave it to the rest of us to decide when it is necessary*", since they share the entities *mask* and *car*, but their STANCE is conflicting, i.e., *refute* and *affirm* respectively.

In addition, we compare the claims extracted from multiple languages, which can be refuting. For example, regarding the TOPIC about "*transmitting the virus*", the claim extracted from a Spanish document "*...small mammals might have transmitted coronavirus to a worker...*" (STANCE = affirm) is refuting with the claim extracted from Russian document " *domestic animals cannot be infected with COVID-19 coronavirus and spread it*" (STANCE = refute).

### 6.4 Discussions

**Generality.** Our claim extraction system can be easily adapted to newly emerging topics by retrieving topic-related questions from the Google Search API, as illustrated in 3.1. It is capable of extracting claims and knowledge elements of other scenarios, by providing in-domain questions in Section 3.1 and several keywords for unseen types in Section 4.1.

**Downstream Applications.** Our system provides a way to transform the massive unstructured news to structured claims with knowledge elements. The structured claim attributes enable users to consolidate claims from multiple sources and to explore the connections between claims, such as shared claimers, related claimer affiliations, etc. It is then can support to exploit the constructed claim base for various downstream tasks, such as question answering, misinformation detection, report generation, etc.

## 7 Related Work

Claim detection is a central task in argumentation mining (Palau and Moens, 2009; Goudas et al., 2014; Sardianos et al., 2015; Eger et al., 2017; Stab et al., 2018). It aims to identify argument components and their relations, including context-denpendent methods (Levy et al., 2014) with topics as input, and context-independent methods (Lippi and Torroni, 2015) without predefined topics. Levy et al. (2017) proposes corpus-wide claim detection to extend the traditional document-level setting. Related work also involves claimer dectection (Pareti, 2016; Elson and McKeown, 2010) and stance detection (Hanselowski et al., 2019; Allaway and McKeown, 2020).

COVID-19 related claim detection and argument mining are generally still limited. The majority of other argument mining approaches for the biomedical domain focus on research literature (Li et al.,

2019; Saakyan et al., 2021; Liu et al., 2020). The work by Reddy et al. (2021) is one of the few exceptions that tackle this challenge and propose a pipeline to extract health-related claims with claim attributes from news articles. However, it does not attempt associating claims and their attributes with structured knowledge elements. To the best of our knowledge, detecting structured COVID-19 claims associated with structured knowledge elements has not been approached yet. Our system leverages the state-of-the-art information extraction and Wikidata entity linking techniques to dynamically construct a COVID-19 claim knowledge base.

## 8 Conclusions and Future Work

We present our *COVID-19 Claim Radar* system, to automatically extract claims in real time from rapidly updating information on the COVID-19 pandemic. We provide users with an in-depth structured view of claims, along with associated knowledge elements. Our system enables exploring various inter-claim connections, including supporting and refuting relations, shared claimers and claim objects, along with related events and entities. In future work, we plan to validate claims from multiple modalities, languages, and sources, as well as support information surgery to correct false claims automatically. In addition, we aim to track claims so as to predict changes in perspectives of claimers and facilitate generating alerts for such changes.

## Ethical Considerations

### Usage Requirements

COVID-19 Claim Radar provides investigative leads rather than final results, so it should not be used as direct conclusions or be applied to any human subjects directly. Research involving human subjects should first be approved by the stakeholder's IRB (Institutional Review Board) who will ensure the safety of the studies.

**Required workflow** Our system is designed to facilitate the understanding of rapidly updating and expanding news articles regarding COVID-19 pandemic, which is difficult for human to keep track of newly emerging claims and to discern false claims from the true ones. Our claim extraction tool (and all claim discovery tools for biomedical applications) is not intended to be used for direct applications involving decisions or human subjects. Instead, our tool aims to highlight structures of claims from a large amount of news text data, which would be too time-consuming for humans to digest. As a result, the tool would be useful to identify claims and analyze the inter-connections between claims. It allows users to narrow down concerned claims from the claimers or affiliations, and then followed by a careful evidence checking to validate claims before making further decisions. Our system does not perform claim verification, which we leave as future work. Failure to follow this workflow, and use of the system without the required human validation, could lead to undesired experimental design wasting time and resources.

**Evidence checking** We provide evidence in the form of structured output in the surrounding contexts with confidence values, as well as the original news article and raw text content as justification. In addition, we provide Wikidata as external knowledge for the user's reference. In order to minimize potential harm caused by extraction errors, consumers of the extracted claims and knowledge elements should double-check the source information and verify the accuracy of the discovered leads prior to undertaking expensive or time-consuming experimental studies.

### Limitations of System Performance

COVID-19 Claim Radar is capable of converting a large number of news articles into structured claims. However, none of our extraction components is perfect, as reported in the experiments. However, as we described in the workflow, the output of our system is intended to be interpreted by humans. Without human validation, incorporating the system output into a decision-making application could result in undesirable results.

### Limitations of Data Collection

The system output might cause harm if it is used in a manner that magnifies the errors or bias in its training data or source input data.

**Bias in training and development data** The performance of our system components as reported is based on the specific benchmark datasets, which could be affected by such data biases. Thus questions concerning generalizability and fairness should be carefully considered. In our paper, most components rely on weak distant supervision such as external knowledge base Wikidata or manually selected keywords. In order to ensure proper application, we recommend: ethical considerations are expected to be included in every step of the system design, the system ensures high transparency and interpretability of data, algorithms, models, and functionalities.

**Bias in source data** Proper use of the technology requires that input documents are legally and ethically obtained. Our goal is to automatically process unstructured text from diverse sources to obtain structured claims, and highlight the complex connections across claims to better identify refuting and supporting claims. The input should not disclose personally identifiable health information, and is expected to have countermeasures for protecting vulnerable groups.

## Acknowledgement

We thank the anonymous reviewers helpful suggestions. This research is based upon work supported by U.S. DARPA AIDA Program No. FA8750-18-2-0014, U.S. DARPA KAIROS Program No. FA8750-19-2-1004, DARPA SemaFor Program No. HR001120C0123, and DARPA INCAS Program No. HR001121C0165. The views and conclusions contained herein are those of the authors and should not be interpreted as necessarily representing the official policies, either expressed or implied, of DARPA, or the U.S. Government. The U.S. Government is authorized to reproduce and distribute reprints for governmental purposes notwithstanding any copyright annotation therein.

## References

Chris Alberti, Kenton Lee, and Michael Collins. 2019. A bert baseline for the natural questions. *arXiv preprint arXiv:1901.08634*.

Emily Allaway and Kathleen McKeown. 2020. Zero-shot stance detection: A dataset and model using generalized topic representations. *arXiv preprint arXiv:2010.03640*.

Roy Bar-Haim, Yoav Kantor, Elad Venezian, Yoav Katz, and Noam Slonim. 2021. Project Debater APIs: Decomposing the AI grand challenge. In *Proceedings of the 2021 Conference on Empirical Methods in Natural Language Processing: System Demonstrations*, pages 267–274, Online and Punta Cana, Dominican Republic. Association for Computational Linguistics.

Alexis Conneau, Kartikay Khandelwal, Naman Goyal, Vishrav Chaudhary, Guillaume Wenzek, Francisco Guzmán, Edouard Grave, Myle Ott, Luke Zettlemoyer, and Veselin Stoyanov. 2020. Unsupervised cross-lingual representation learning at scale. In *Proceedings of the 58th Annual Meeting of the Association for Computational Linguistics*, pages 8440–8451, Online. Association for Computational Linguistics.

Jacob Devlin, Ming-Wei Chang, Kenton Lee, and Kristina Toutanova. 2019. BERT: Pre-training of deep bidirectional transformers for language understanding. In *Proceedings of the 2019 Conference of the North American Chapter of the Association for Computational Linguistics: Human Language Technologies, Volume 1 (Long and Short Papers)*, pages 4171–4186, Minneapolis, Minnesota. Association for Computational Linguistics.

Steffen Eger, Johannes Daxenberger, and Iryna Gurevych. 2017. Neural end-to-end learning for computational argumentation mining. *arXiv preprint arXiv:1704.06104*.

David K Elson and Kathleen R McKeown. 2010. Automatic attribution of quoted speech in literary narrative. In *Twenty-Fourth AAAI Conference on Artificial Intelligence*.

Theodosis Goudas, Christos Louizos, Georgios Petasis, and Vangelis Karkaletsis. 2014. Argument extraction from news, blogs, and social media. In *Hellenic Conference on Artificial Intelligence*, pages 287–299. Springer.

Andreas Hanselowski, Christian Stab, Claudia Schulz, Zile Li, and Iryna Gurevych. 2019. A richly annotated corpus for different tasks in automated fact-checking. *arXiv preprint arXiv:1911.01214*.

Momchil Hardalov, Arnav Arora, Preslav Nakov, and Isabelle Augenstein. 2021. A survey on stance detection for mis-and disinformation identification. *arXiv preprint arXiv:2103.00242*.

Naeemul Hassan, Gensheng Zhang, Fatma Arslan, Josue Caraballo, Damian Jimenez, Siddhant Gawsane, Shohedul Hasan, Minumol Joseph, Aaditya Kulkarni, Anil Kumar Nayak, et al. 2017. Claimbuster: The first-ever end-to-end fact-checking system. *Proceedings of the VLDB Endowment*, 10(12):1945–1948.

Heng Ji, Heng Ji, Ralph Grishman, Hoa Trang Dang, Kira Griffitt, and Joe Ellis. 2010. Overview of the tac 2010 knowledge base population track.

Heng Ji, Joel Nothman, Ben Hachey, and Radu Florian. 2015. Overview of TAC-KBP2015 tri-lingual entity discovery and linking. In *Proc. Text Analysis Conference (TAC2015)*.

Heng Ji, Xiaoman Pan, Boliang Zhang, Joel Nothman, James Mayfield, Paul McNamee, and Cash Costello. 2017. Overview of TAC-KBP2017 13 languages entity discovery and linking. In *Proc. Text Analysis Conference (TAC2017)*.

Mandar Joshi, Danqi Chen, Yinhan Liu, Daniel S. Weld, Luke Zettlemoyer, and Omer Levy. 2020. Spanbert: Improving pre-training by representing and predicting spans. *Transactions of the Association for Computational Linguistics*, 8:64–77.

Tom Kwiatkowski, Jennimaria Palomaki, Olivia Redfield, Michael Collins, Ankur Parikh, Chris Alberti, Danielle Epstein, Illia Polosukhin, Jacob Devlin, Kenton Lee, et al. 2019. Natural questions: A benchmark for question answering research. *Transactions of the Association for Computational Linguistics*, 7.

Tuan Lai, Heng Ji, Trung Bui, Quan Hung Tran, Franck Dernoncourt, and Walter Chang. 2021a. A context-dependent gated module for incorporating symbolic semantics into event coreference resolution. In *Proceedings of the 2021 Conference of the North American Chapter of the Association for Computational Linguistics: Human Language Technologies*, pages 3491–3499, Online. Association for Computational Linguistics.

Tuan Manh Lai, Trung Bui, and Doo Soon Kim. 2021b. End-to-end neural coreference resolution revisited: A simple yet effective baseline. *arXiv preprint arXiv:2107.01700*.

Tuan Manh Lai, Heng Ji, and ChengXiang Zhai. 2022. Improving candidate retrieval with entity profile generation for wikidata entity linking. *ACL 2022 Findings*.

Ran Levy, Yonatan Bilu, Daniel Hershcovich, Ehud Aharoni, and Noam Slonim. 2014. Context dependent claim detection. In *Proceedings of COLING 2014, the 25th International Conference on Computational Linguistics: Technical Papers*, pages 1489–1500.

Ran Levy, Shai Gretz, Benjamin Sznajder, Shay Hummel, Ranit Aharonov, and Noam Slonim. 2017. Unsupervised corpus–wide claim detection. In *Proceedings of the 4th Workshop on Argument Mining*, pages 79–84.

Mike Lewis, Yinhan Liu, Naman Goyal, Marjan Ghazvininejad, Abdelrahman Mohamed, Omer Levy, Veselin Stoyanov, and Luke Zettlemoyer. 2020. Bart: Denoising sequence-to-sequence pre-training for natural language generation, translation, and comprehension. In *Proceedings of the 58th Annual Meeting of the Association for Computational Linguistics*, pages 7871–7880.

Manling Li, Alireza Zareian, Ying Lin, Xiaoman Pan, Spencer Whitehead, Brian Chen, Bo Wu, Heng Ji, Shih-Fu Chang, Clare Voss, et al. 2020. Gaia: A fine-grained multimedia knowledge extraction system. In *Proceedings of the 58th Annual Meeting of the Association for Computational Linguistics: System Demonstrations*, pages 77–86.

Xiangci Li, Gully Burns, and Nanyun Peng. 2019. Scientific discourse tagging for evidence extraction. *arXiv preprint arXiv:1909.04758*.

Ying Lin, Heng Ji, Fei Huang, and Lingfei Wu. 2020. A joint neural model for information extraction with global features. In *Proceedings of the 58th Annual Meeting of the Association for Computational Linguistics*, pages 7999–8009.

Marco Lippi and Paolo Torroni. 2015. Context-independent claim detection for argument mining. In *Twenty-Fourth International Joint Conference on Artificial Intelligence*.

Zhenghao Liu, Chenyan Xiong, Zhuyun Dai, Si Sun, Maosong Sun, and Zhiyuan Liu. 2020. Generalizing open domain fact extraction and verification to covid-fact thorough in-domain language modeling. In *Proceedings of the 2020 Conference on Empirical Methods in Natural Language Processing: Findings*, pages 2395–2400.

Raquel Mochales Palau and Marie-Francine Moens. 2009. Argumentation mining: the detection, classification and structure of arguments in text. In *Proceedings of the 12th international conference on artificial intelligence and law*, pages 98–107.

Silvia Pareti. 2016. Parc 3.0: A corpus of attribution relations. In *Proceedings of the Tenth International Conference on Language Resources and Evaluation (LREC'16)*, pages 3914–3920.

Sameer Pradhan, Alessandro Moschitti, Nianwen Xue, Olga Uryupina, and Yuchen Zhang. 2012. Conll-2012 shared task: Modeling multilingual unrestricted coreference in ontonotes. In *Joint Conference on Empirical Methods in Natural Language Processing and Computational Natural Language Learning - Proceedings of the Shared Task: Modeling Multilingual Unrestricted Coreference in OntoNotes, EMNLP-CoNLL 2012, July 13, 2012, Jeju Island, Korea*, pages 1–40. ACL.

Pranav Rajpurkar, Robin Jia, and Percy Liang. 2018. Know what you don't know: Unanswerable questions for squad. In *Proceedings of the 56th Annual Meeting of the Association for Computational Linguistics (Volume 2: Short Papers)*, pages 784–789.

Revanth Gangi Reddy, Sai Chinthakindi, Zhenhailong Wang, Yi R Fung, Kathryn S Conger, Ahmed S Elsayed, Martha Palmer, and Heng Ji. 2021. Newsclaims: A new benchmark for claim detection from news with background knowledge. *arXiv preprint arXiv:2112.08544*.

Arkadiy Saakyan, Tuhin Chakrabarty, and Smaranda Muresan. 2021. Covid-fact: Fact extraction and verification of real-world claims on covid-19 pandemic. *arXiv preprint arXiv:2106.03794*.

Christos Sardianos, Ioannis Manousos Katakis, Georgios Petasis, and Vangelis Karkaletsis. 2015. Argument extraction from news. In *Proceedings of the 2nd Workshop on Argumentation Mining*, pages 56–66.

Zhiyi Song, Ann Bies, Stephanie Strassel, Tom Riese, Justin Mott, Joe Ellis, Jonathan Wright, S. Kulick, Neville Ryant, and Xiaoyi Ma. 2015a. From light to rich ere: Annotation of entities, relations, and events. In *EVENTS@HLP-NAACL*.

Zhiyi Song, Ann Bies, Stephanie Strassel, Tom Riese, Justin Mott, Joe Ellis, Jonathan Wright, Seth Kulick, Neville Ryant, and Xiaoyi Ma. 2015b. From light to rich ere: annotation of entities, relations, and events. In *Proceedings of the the 3rd Workshop on EVENTS: Definition, Detection, Coreference, and Representation*, pages 89–98.

Christian Stab, Tristan Miller, and Iryna Gurevych. 2018. Cross-topic argument mining from heterogeneous sources using attention-based neural networks. *arXiv preprint arXiv:1802.05758*.

Christopher Walker, Stephanie Strassel, Julie Medero, and Kazuaki Maeda. 2006. Ace 2005 multilingual training corpus. *Linguistic Data Consortium, Philadelphia*, 57.

Adina Williams, Nikita Nangia, and Samuel Bowman. 2018. A broad-coverage challenge corpus for sentence understanding through inference. In *Proceedings of the 2018 Conference of the North American Chapter of the Association for Computational Linguistics: Human Language Technologies, Volume 1 (Long Papers)*, pages 1112–1122.

# TS-ANNO: An Annotation Tool to Build, Annotate and Evaluate Text Simplification Corpora

**Regina Stodden** and **Laura Kallmeyer**
Heinrich Heine University
Düsseldorf, Germany
{stodden,kallmeyer}@phil.hhu.de

## Abstract

We introduce TS-ANNO, an open-source web application for manual creation and for evaluation of parallel corpora for text simplification. TS-ANNO can be used for i) sentence–wise alignment, ii) rating alignment pairs (e.g., w.r.t. grammaticality, meaning preservation, ...), iii) annotating alignment pairs w.r.t. simplification transformations (e.g., lexical substitution, sentence splitting, ...), and iv) manual simplification of complex documents. For evaluation, TS-ANNO calculates inter-annotator agreement of alignments i) and annotations ii).

## 1 Introduction

A large number of texts are difficult to understand for many people, e.g., people with low literacy skills, non-native speakers, or people with cognitive disabilities (Alva-Manchego et al., 2020b). Text simplification (TS) aims to make complex texts more accessible by editing their wording and syntax, while preserving the original meaning (Alva-Manchego et al., 2020b).

In automatic TS, parallel corpora that align sentences from the original text with corresponding professionally simplified sentences are precious resources for training and evaluating TS systems. Currently, however, high-quality corpora of this type are rare and often of comparably small size (e.g., Zero Hora (Caseli et al., 2009) or Terence & Teacher (Brunato et al., 2015)). Therefore, often resources that were not designed for TS in the first place are used to train TS systems (e.g., Simple Wikipedia texts (Coster and Kauchak, 2011; Hwang et al., 2015)) (Štajner, 2021). As text simplification is often performed on sentence-level, two further problems of TS corpora arise: missing sentence-level alignment (e.g., see Newsela (Xu et al., 2015)) or error-prone automatic sentence alignment (e.g., see PWKP (Zhu et al., 2010)) (Štajner, 2021).

Furthermore, TS corpora are provided, if at all, with the alignment, e.g., WikiLarge (Zhang and Lapata, 2017) or Wiki-Auto (Jiang et al., 2020). Only a few corpora contain information about the actual types of simplification (simplification transformations, respective grammaticality, lexical complexity etc. of the aligned sentences, etc.) (e.g., see PorSimple Corpus Caseli et al. (2009), SimpleSEW corpus Amancio and Specia (2014) or Terence & Teacher corpus Brunato et al. (2015)). Collecting such data is difficult but could be useful to analyze the advantages and limitations of TS systems (Alva-Manchego et al., 2020b).

To facilitate the creation of manually annotated high-quality TS corpora with $n$:$m$ alignments of full documents, we developed TS-ANNO, an open-source, language-independent, all-in-one web application. The web application supports:

- web scraping of parallel websites and local files upload,
- $n$:$m$ sentence-wise manual alignment,
- sentence-wise rating of grammaticality, simplicity, coherence and ambiguity,
- pair-wise rating of meaning preservation, information gain, overall simplicity, structural simplicity and lexical simplicity,
- pair-wise annotation of (fine-grained) simplification transformations on word-level, phrase-level, sentence-level and paragraph-level, and
- evaluation of the data collected.

The main functionalities of the annotation tool are illustrated in Figure 1. A demonstration of the tool and a demo video can be found here `https://ts-anno.phil.hhu.de/`.[1] The source code is also available to create an own copy of the annotation tool.[2]

[1] Register yourself to annotate on a test basis or log in as *test*-User (password: *TS_anno22*) to test evaluations and downloads.

[2] https://github.com/rstodden/TS_annotation_tool



*Proceedings of the 60th Annual Meeting of the Association for Computational Linguistics System Demonstrations*, pages 145 - 155

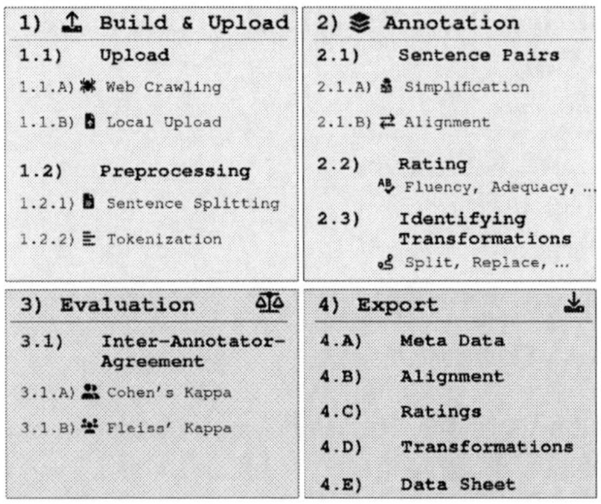


Figure 1: Visualization of TS-ANNO's main functionalities: i) build & upload, ii) annotation, iii) evaluation, and iv) export. The numbered lists describe consecutive steps, whereas the lettered lists describe alternatives.

In the remainder of the paper, we elaborate technical details and functionalities of TS-ANNO and exemplify its usage.

## 2 TS-ANNO: Preparing the data

This section introduces implementation details, user administration, data uploading and preprocessing options of TS-ANNO.

### 2.1 System Architecture

TS-ANNO is an open-source web-based application implemented in Python (Version 3.8)[3] using the Django web framework (Version 4)[4] and PostgreSQL[5] for the underlying database structure. NGINX[6] is used to configure the server of TS-ANNO. The responsive interface of the application is designed with Bootstrap (Version 4.5)[7]. Currently, all interface instructions are in English, but they can also be translated to other languages if required. For each annotation step, the time is measured to identify more or less difficult corpora or domains. To further develop the tool, contributions by the community are welcome by participation on GitHub or by using the changelog function of the annotation tool itself.

[3] https://www.python.org/downloads/

[4] https://www.djangoproject.com/

[5] https://www.postgresql.org/

[6] https://www.nginx.com/

[7] https://getbootstrap.com/

### 2.2 Administration + User Management

Django comes by default with an administrator interface. In our case, it is helpful for the control of corpora, users and annotations. In addition to the basic user information of Django, upon registration, users are asked for some optional demographic characteristics, such as native language and language level of the language to annotate. This information can help to better understand the users' ratings, especially regarding simplicity, which has been shown to be subjective (Štajner, 2018).

### 2.3 Uploading and Metadata

TS-ANNO supports different approaches for data insertion. Either local data can be uploaded or online data can be automatically crawled and read to the database.

**Local Upload.** TS-ANNO permits the upload of parallel documents either as plain texts, paragraph segmented texts, or pre-aligned texts.[8] If no simple version of a document exists, the "to_simplify" option can be ticked to add the data for the manual simplification part of the tool. Furthermore, before uploading, additional metadata regarding copyright, domain and language levels of the documents are requested to incorporate practices for responsible data (re-)use (Rogers et al., 2021) from the start.

The functionality of uploading pre-aligned data is illustrated in the online demo with the manual simplifications of the ASSET corpus (Alva-Manchego et al., 2020a). This corpus is selected because a further analysis regarding the rewriting transformations applied in combination with fine-grained manual ratings of the simplification seems to be a relevant supplement to ASSET.

**Web Crawling.** More and more manually and professionally simplified texts are available on websites. Among others, it might be due to the recommendation of the European standard for digital accessibility (European Telecommunications Standards Institute, 2021) to provide easy-to-read texts on (at least public authority) websites. Mostly these texts are aligned with parallel versions in standard language.

[8] TS-ANNO does not support automatic sentence alignment, but it can handle already aligned sentences. Before uploading, the texts can be aligned manually or with any automatic alignment algorithm (e.g., MASSalign (Paetzold et al., 2017), CATS (Štajner et al., 2018), or a neural CRF model (Jiang et al., 2020)).

Battisti et al. (2020) have shown that TS can benefit from these websites by developing a web crawler to download their texts, images and typography. In order to also access the texts of the parallel web pages, TS-ANNO integrates a web crawler (build with the Python library Beautiful Soup[9]) that enables the extraction and alignment of these valuable documents. The web crawler automatically aligns complex documents with parallel, simple documents and recognizes paragraph endings.[10]

Currently, the system contains example web crawlers for the websites of "Inclusion Europe"[11] and "Alumniportal Deutschland"[12]. On the website of Alumniportal Deutschland, openly licensed, parallel German documents (original: CEFR level B1-B2, simple A1-A2) are published, which exemplify the annotation of everyday documents in TS-ANNO. The website of Inclusion Europe includes parallel complex-simple documents in four languages (German, English, Spanish and French), which make possible to create a multi-lingual simplification corpus with TS-ANNO.

### 2.4 Pre-processing

During upload, no matter whether local or online, the data will be pre-processed with a language-specific NLP pipeline of SpaCy (Version 3) (Honnibal et al., 2020).[13]

Possible pre-processing problems, e.g., segmentation errors or HTML left-over of crawling, can be reported per sentence in the interface.

## 3 TS-ANNO: Annotation

The main functionality of TS-ANNO is the annotation, which comprises alignment, transformation annotation, rating and manual simplification. Overall, the annotation is structured by the corpora to annotate. Each corpus contains at least one document pair, which in turn consists of a complex document and a parallel simplified document (except for manual simplification). For detailed instructions on how to annotate and how to use the annotation tool, we refer to the annotation guidelines.[14]

The online demo contains pre-aligned senentece pairs of ASSET (Alva-Manchego et al., 2020a) and a few annotated document pairs of Alumniportal to illustrate the functionalities of TS-ANNO.

### 3.1 Aligning Sentences

Alignment is the process of finding and grouping text elements, such as documents, paragraphs or sentences, of at least two parallel or comparable texts with a quite similar meaning. In TS-ANNO, in any case, complex and simple documents are aligned when uploading the data (see subsection 2.3). Depending on the input data, sentence pairs can also be already aligned during the upload. The annotation tool further supports the manual alignment (or alignment correction) of paragraphs and sentences. Each complex and simple sentence co-occurs with a button that highlights the most similar sentence(s) in the corresponding text (based on SpaCy's word embeddings) to facilitate sentence alignment.

In TS, sentence alignment pairs mostly contain only one sentence *of each* document (1:1, e.g., copying or rephrasing the text). However they can also contain only one sentence *of one* document (1:0 or 0:1, e.g., sentence omitting for removing unimportant text or sentence insertion for explanations), several sentences in *one* document (1:$n$ or $n$:1, e.g., splitting a sentence or merging sentences) or several sentences in *both* documents ($n$:$m$, e.g., sentence fusion) (Alva-Manchego et al., 2020b). As illustrated in Figure 2, any number of sentences of both documents can be selected, therefore, TS-ANNO supports all of the named ($n$:$m$) alignments.

All sentences which are identical in the complex and simplified document are automatically aligned and disabled in the front-end to speed-up manual alignment. Furthermore, after the manual alignment of a document, all not aligned simple and complex sentences are automatically aligned as insertion or omitting.

Currently, for most existing corpora, the alignments are automatically generated. However, TS-ANNO does not include alignment algorithms due to their questionable quality. The automatic alignment models can often only identify pairs of (nearly) identical sentences but cannot correctly extract "strong paraphrases" where the structure and semantic were highly changed (Štajner, 2021). Therefore, at least for test sets, manually alignment or alignment post-editing are highly recommended.

[9] https://www.crummy.com/software/BeautifulSoup/

[10] If the web crawler is used, please pay attention to the copyright of the texts of the websites.

[11] https://www.inclusion-europe.eu/

[12] https://www.alumniportal-deutschland.org/

[13] SpaCy currently supports 18 languages, 44 are planned and a multi-language model exists for other languages.

[14] https://github.com/rstodden/TS_annotation_tool/tree/master/annotation_schema

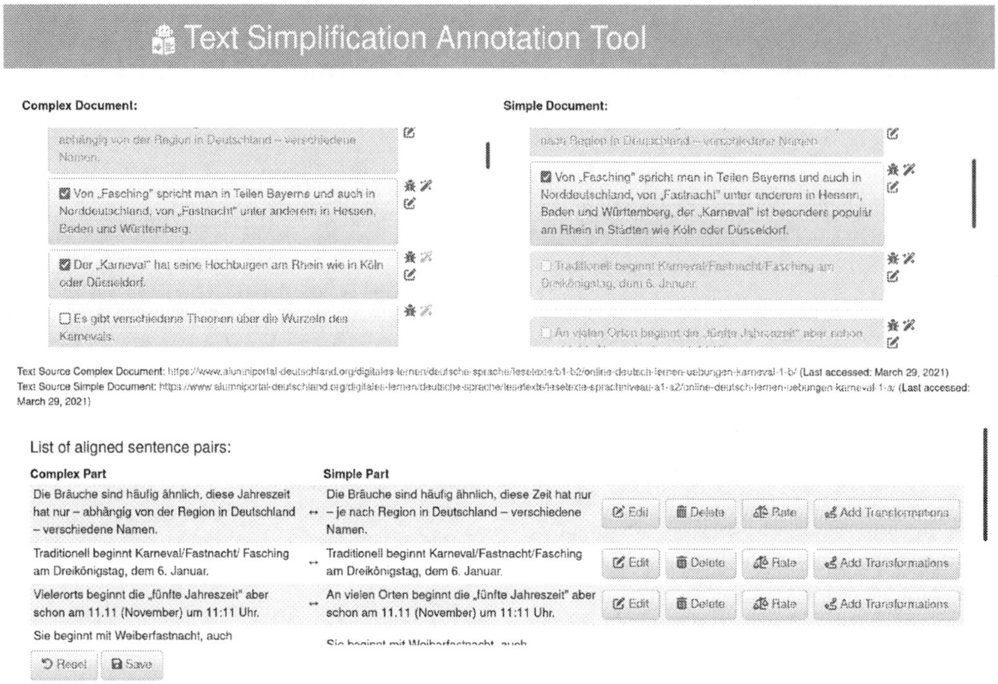


Figure 2: Screenshot of TS-ANNO during the sentence alignment of two complex and one simple sentences of a German document pair of Alumniportal Deutschland. The upper part contains the complex document on the left and the simple document on the right. Per each document, all sentences are listed, including paragraph markers and three buttons: i) a bug button to report content issues, ii) a button to focus most similar sentences in the counterpart, and iii) an edit button to change the alignment of the sentence. In the lower part, all already aligned sentences are shown accompanied with buttons i) to edit or ii) to delete the alignment, iii) to rate the aligned sentence pair or iv) to add the rewriting transformations of the pair.

### 3.2 Transformation Annotation of Alignment Pairs

In the simplification process, various different rewriting strategies can be applied to the complex texts and, hence, it can result in several different simplified sentences. For the creation of some TS corpora, annotators were asked to simplify the text following a given list of rewriting transformations, e.g., Barancikova and Bojar (2020); Alva-Manchego et al. (2020a) or were asked to add the transformations during (or after) alignment, e.g., Caseli et al. (2009); Bott and Saggion (2011b); Amancio and Specia (2014); Brunato et al. (2015).

Enriching aligned corpora with transformation annotations could help to improve TS systems by adding a preceding sequence labeling step for transformation identification (e.g., Dong et al. (2019); Kumar et al. (2020); Omelianchuk et al. (2021)). TS systems with other approaches could benefit from the transformation annotations by splitting and mixing the data splits based on the annotations or gaining more insights into the generated simplifications (Alva-Manchego et al., 2020b). Furthermore, the number of different transformations can be used to quantify the "simplicity gain" (Xu et al., 2016).

TS-ANNO permits the annotator to choose affected tokens in the alignment pair and to assign transformation labels to it; multiple labels are possible. The tokens can optionally be color-coded, e.g., red for delete, orange for replaced, and blue for added, to emphasize the changes in the sentences. The label can correspond to the general transformation level (paragraph, sentence, phrase or word), or a transformation class name can be specified per level. In addition, the labels can be chosen even more fine-grained as for some transformation classes sub-transformation labels are provided.

The transformation levels, classes and sub-transformations can be dynamically changed to consider language-wise differences and preferred annotation schemes. As default, TS-ANNO contains transformations that were used (with similar terms) in existing TS annotation schemes (Bott and Saggion, 2014; Brunato et al., 2015; Gonzalez-Dios et al., 2018; Koptient et al., 2019): 1. *delete*, 2. *insert*, 3. *merge*, 4. *reorder*, 5. *split*, 6. *lexical simplification*. In addition, we add *verbal changes* as transformation because, in German text simplification, the verb's voice or mood are often changed. A list of the default labels of TS-ANNO is provided in Appendix A.2.

### 3.3 Rating of Alignment Pairs

Following Alva-Manchego et al. (2020b), human assessment of system predictions is for now the most reliable evaluation method of text simplification systems. Furthermore, rating of the simplification pairs helps to reveal the unclear initial state of a (web-) corpus, e.g., i) are the original and simplified sentences grammatically correct, ii) is the (simplified) sentence really simple, iii) to which extent are the simplified sentences simpler than the original sentences or iv) to which extent are the pairs lexically or syntactically simplified. An imbalance in the data could for instance lead to training a TS system to only correct grammar issues, to only produce syntactic simplifications or only weak simplifications.

Therefore, TS-ANNO supports relative rating of the aligned sentence pairs, i.e., change between original and simplified sentence (see example iii) and iv)), and absolute ratings of the original and simplified sentence (see example i) and ii)) on a Likert-scale. As many different rating schemes for TS exist (for a summary see Alva-Manchego et al. (2020b); Štajner (2021)), the rating aspects and the rating scale size can be dynamically changed in TS-ANNO.

All aspects are accompanied by a statement for which the annotators are asked to agree or disagree, following Alva-Manchego et al. (2020a); Maddela et al. (2021). An overview of all default aspects, including all statements, is provided in Appendix A.1. The chosen default scale is a 5-point Likert-scale, normally ranging from 1 to 5. However, rating of simplicity is a subjective task (Štajner, 2018), hence, different ratings are expected. To ensure that the ratings are due to subjective perspectives on simplicity and not due to different understandings of the scale,[15] the scale endpoints of some aspects can be changed to $-2$ to $+2$ to emphasize the meaning of the lowest ($-2$, reverse change) and the middle point (0, no change). Furthermore, annotation guidelines with the annotation scheme chosen should be handed out to all annotators.

### 3.4 Manual Simplification

As an additional feature, TS-ANNO supports sentence-wise manual simplification. Most of the available simplification corpora focus on Wikipedia data or news texts (Štajner, 2021). However, in 2014, Pellow and Eskenazi already justified the need to simplify everyday documents. Therefore, we encourages the simplification of texts of other domains, such as illustrated with how-to-articles of wikiHow[16] (Koupaee and Wang, 2018) in the online demo. Furthermore, the manual simplification option can be used to generate alternative simplifications of existing simplification pairs for a better evaluation (Alva-Manchego et al., 2020a).

After the complex data upload, an annotator can select at least one sentence of a complex document on the left and add a simpler version in the text box on the right. To ease the simplification, the guideline of Inclusion Europe is linked as simplification instructions for easy-to-read language (CEFR level A1);[17] as soon as the ISO standard of plain language is published these instructions will also be linked for plain language (CEFR level A2 to B1).[18]

Furthermore, TS-ANNO exemplary integrates the multi-lingual TS system MUSS (Martin et al., 2020) to provide suggestions on how to simplify the marked complex sentence(s); it can be easily exchanged with other TS systems.

## 4 TS-ANNO: Evaluation and Export

### 4.1 Evaluation / Inter-Annotator Agreement

The annotation tool also provides some evaluation approaches.The inter-annotator agreement (IAA) of the alignment and the rating is calculated per all corpora, each corpus, each domain and each document.[19]

However, a low level of IAA does not always indicate a bad quality of the annotations. On the

[15] Stodden (2021) shows that annotators of TS corpora have different understandings of the lowest scale point in simplicity rating, i.e., either same and higher complexity or only higher complexity.

[16] https://www.wikihow.com/Main-Page

[17] Guidelines in many languages: https://www.inclusion-europe.eu/easy-to-read-standards-guidelines/

[18] The ISO/WD 24495-1 is currently under development see: https://www.iso.org/standard/78907.html.

[19] Depending on the number of annotators, either Cohen's Kappa (2 annotators) or Fleiss' Kappa (> 2 annotators) is calculated.

one hand, it can be due to annotation errors, but on the other hand, it can also be due to different subjective perspectives on the task (see Reidsma and op den Akker (2008)). Rating of simplicity is such a subjective task. Hence, we plan to implement a disagreement metric, similar to the polarization index of (Akhtar et al., 2019), that relates annotation choices to the demographic characteristics of the annotators.

### 4.2 Data Export

**Alignment Export.** TS-ANNO supports three formats of alignment export: i) parallel files with a simplification instance per line as most common practice is TS research (Xu et al., 2016; Alva–Manchego et al., 2020a), ii) crossed sentence pairs of full documents with a label specifying whether aligned or not (e.g., see Jiang et al. (2020)), or iii) parallel files with a continuous document text per line (e.g., see Sun et al. (2021)). The first format encourages sentence-level simplification, the second training of a automatic sentence alignment model and the third document-level simplification.

**Annotation and Rating Export.** Furthermore, the data can also be exported in a CSV file containing all annotated information per aligned sentence pair per user, e.g., one column per evaluation aspect and one column per transformation. The output can be filtered per corpus and per annotator.

Following the recommendations of Prabhakaran et al. (2021) on transparency and increased utility of datasets for downstream use cases, in the export of the annotation tool, all annotations of all raters are included without any aggregation to keep all possibly subjective annotations and to facilitate evaluation with disagreements.

**Metadata Export.** TS-ANNO provides automatic support for completing data sheets based on Huggingface Data Cards[20] as demanded for producing responsible NLP (Rogers et al., 2021). The system makes proposals for the data sheets questions based on the given metadata, e.g., demographics of the annotators or domains of the corpora.

## 5 Use Case

TS-ANNO was already tested by aligning German parallel web texts, e.g., the openly licensed, parallel documents of the website "Alumniportal Deutschland". The documents have been uploaded with the internal web crawler and were automatically pre-processed. Two annotators have manually aligned the sentence pairs and annotated them with rewriting transformations and rating aspects.[21] The demonstration version of TS-ANNO contains a few annotated documents of this corpus, including different alignment types, ratings and rewriting transformations to exemplify the evaluation and download options.

Overall, the test usage of TS-ANNO led to some minor improvements, which are already included in this system description.

## 6 Related Work

Several aligned TS corpora exist, some with annotated rewriting transformations and some test sets with rated evaluation aspects (see (Alva-Manchego et al., 2020b) as an overview). However, most authors have not provided a reusing option for their annotation interfaces or have only focused on one of the TS annotation tasks, e.g., aligning, simplification, rating, or transformation annotation. Therefore, we present the related work per TS task.

**Alignment.** The most comparable manual alignment annotation frameworks to TS-ANNO are Tiedemann (2006); Bott and Saggion (2011a); Paetzold et al. (2017), and Jiang et al. (2020), which show also both documents (the original and simplified), in parallel and highlight paragraph blocks. However, in contrast to TS-ANNO, ISA (Tiedemann, 2006) supports only 1:1 alignment, and, in the annotation interface of Jiang et al. (2020), sentence borders can be changed as they are highlighted and not tagged as in our tool.

**Simplification.** For writing simplifications, several commercial and non-commercial tools, or computer-aided translation software exist to facilitate writing easy to understand texts. Some of them offer more writing support than the others: e.g., LanguageTool for German,[22] FriendlyReader for

[20] https://github.com/huggingface/datasets/blob/master/templates/README_guide.md

[21] Both annotators are German native speakers, trained in linguistics as well as simple languages, have at least a graduation diploma, and were paid for their work with at least the minimum wage of their country of residence. The annotators were provided with the following annotation guidelines and instructions on how to use the annotation tool: https://github.com/rstodden/TS_annotation_tool/blob/master/annotation_schema/Annotationsrichtlinien_TS_anno-DE.pdf.

[22] https://languagetool.org/de/leichte-sprache/

Swedish,[23] or Hero-App for English and Dansk,[24] offer most of it by highlighting complex passages and showing rewriting suggestions. The simplification annotation editor of Caseli et al. (2009) also offers rewriting suggestions, which the annotator can accept or decline.

TS-ANNO does not support rewriting suggestions yet and is more similar to the simplification procedure described in Alva-Manchego et al. (2020a), in which crowd workers were provided only with annotation guidelines and should rewrite the sentences without any assistance. However, they added their simplifications within a crowdsourcing platform and not in an annotation tool.

**Rating.** Even if manual rating of TS output is performed on many TS system outputs, no shared annotation tool for rating exists. Often crowdsourcing platforms, e.g., Amazon Mechanical Turk or Figure Eight, are used to ask the rating questions, such as for the ASSET Corpus (Alva-Manchego et al., 2020a) and the Simplicity-DA Data Set (Alva-Manchego et al., 2021).

**Transformations.** The annotation of rewriting transformations is a general sequence labeling problem, therefore, popular sequence labeling tools such as BRAT (Stenetorp et al., 2012) could be used. Gonzalez-Dios et al. (2018) adapt BRAT for TS rewriting annotation by pointing an affected sequence in the original sentence and labeling it with the transformation. In contrast, Koptient et al. (2019) annotated the transformations on the word-level at the parallel text using a modification of YAWAT (Germann, 2008). TS-ANNO is more similar to YAWAT as it facilitates the annotation within a parallel setting, but extends it via the annotation of also phrase-, sentence-, and paragraph-level transformations.

To the best of the authors' knowledge, no annotation tool exists yet, combining all needs of building text simplification corpora, i.e., manual simplification, pair rating, transformation annotation and sentence alignment.

## 7 Limitations

So far, TS-ANNO has been tested only for English, Spanish, French, Farsi, and German. SpaCy, which is used for pre-processing, should support many languages, though maybe not always be with the same quality. For languages that SpaCy does not support, corpora have to be sentence split and tokenized before uploading them. However, it is also possible to exchange SpaCy with another NLP framework.

The annotation tool does not support active learning yet; its current focus is on high-quality manual alignment, rating and annotation of parallel data.

Štajner (2021); Alva-Manchego et al. (2020b) state that rating is not enough to evaluate TS texts, comprehension tests, measuring reading time and eye fixations are also relevant. Unfortunately, TS-ANNO only supports rating as it is yet the most dominant approach.

## 8 Conclusion & Further Work

We presented TS-ANNO, an open-source, web-based application for the purpose of facilitating the time-consuming process of building high-quality corpora for text simplification or of evaluating quality of existing corpora. The annotation tool combines relevant functionalities for building TS corpora, e.g., crawling parallel web documents, sentence-wise alignment of parallel documents, human assessment of alignment pairs, annotation of transformations applied to get the simplified sentence of the pair and evaluating the data, e.g., via inter-annotator agreement. The human assessment of simplification pairs could help to identify and filter out pairs of sentences with an increase of complexity (rather than a decrease) from the complex to the simple document. Furthermore, transformation labels allow characterizing the performed changes. Both information could be used to evaluate TS systems and give insights in their "black boxes".

In future work, we plan to extend the simplification option by highlighting complex phrases. In addition, it would be interesting to integrate active learning or a neural alignment system, which could suggest possible sentence alignments. It is also planned to add more websites to the crawler option of TS-ANNO to facilitate creating corpora with texts of other languages or other domains.

## Acknowledgements

This research is part of the PhD-program "Online Participation", supported by the North Rhine-Westphalian (German) funding scheme "Forschungskolleg". We thank Font Awesome Free for providing the icons used in this paper and in the annotation tool.

[23]http://www.friendlyreader.se/

[24]https://heroapp.ai/en/

## 9 Ethics/Impact Statement

**Intended Use.** In general, simplifying texts makes sense in order to give more people access to information. In addition to analog information dissemination via newspapers or books, digital information dissemination via websites is becoming increasingly relevant. In addition to technical barriers, such as the readability and user guidance of a website, the complexity or language level of texts on websites also plays an important role. The simpler the text, the more people can understand it. The more people understand the text, the more people have the chance to get involved, e.g., in the form of discussions or dissemination of information.

The here proposed annotation tool is designed to create parallel datasets with aligned sentence pairs, one complex and one simplified for TS. Additionally, the sentence pairs can be rated regarding their complexity, grammaticality, meaning preservation and added with transformations applied during the simplification process. The output, a dataset for TS, could be used to train an automatic TS system which helps people with reading problems to understand more texts.

**Failure modes & Misuse Potential.** The usage of the annotation tool highly depends on what the administrator and user do with it. Undesired texts could be inserted or annotators could write harmful comments or simplifications. The resulting corpus could be misused to train a system to make texts even more difficult to read than, as intended, more simpler. Also, the annotations (ratings, alignments or transformation annotations) could be intentionally manipulated or unintentionally wrongly preprocessed by the underlying systems, e.g., sentence splitting or tokenization.

However, the dataset's quality is essential for the use case of TS, as people will rely on it. Hence, TS-ANNO tries to support quality checks of the produced data, e.g., by calculating the inter-annotator agreement, reporting errors in the texts due to preprocessing, and by rating the sentence pairs before publishing the dataset. Users identified as not reliable or even harmful could be banned from the annotation platform by the administrator. Additionally, some unexpected behavior of the annotation tool cannot be precluded entirely. However, users can report issues either on GitHub to the developers or via the changelog feature to the administrator.

**Biases.** ML systems can get biased based on the data they are trained on, therefore we show texts from different domains in our example. Administrators of TS-ANNO should be aware of this bias and carefully select the texts to annotate. Furthermore, the ratings regarding simplicity are highly subjective, hence, the selection of annotators, e.g., only people with high literacy and language level, can bias the rating. The ratings might be completely different if the target group of the simplified texts would rate the sentence pairs. Administrators should keep it in mind and always describe the annotator group. Therefore, the metadata export of TS-ANNO includes metadata of the texts and the annotators to support the administrators.

**Annotators.** During registration, annotators are asked to voluntarily add some relevant demographic characteristics, such as native language and language level of the language to annotate. Also, the username is freely selectable, hence, if not desired, no personal information must be shared. All information is optional but highly preferable as they are helpful to understand the users' annotations.

Furthermore, the annotators of the example dataset were paid for their annotations following with at least the minimum wage of Germany, the country of residence.

**Computing Time.** The annotation tool is a web application, hence, a server is required to run the annotation tool. Administrators can run it either locally or on an external server. No additional computing power or hardware is required. However, to ensure access to the annotation tool, the server needs to be permanently run or the access time should be restricted.

## References


Sohail Akhtar, Valerio Basile, and Viviana Patti. 2019. A new Measure of Polarization in the Annotation of Hate Speech. In *Proceedings of the XVIIIth International Conference of the Italian Association for Artificial Intelligence (AI*IA 2019)*, pages 588–603. Springer International Publishing.

Fernando Alva-Manchego, Louis Martin, Antoine Bordes, Carolina Scarton, Benoît Sagot, and Lucia Specia. 2020a. ASSET: A Dataset for Tuning and Evaluation of Sentence Simplification Models with Multiple Rewriting Transformations. In *Proceedings of the 58th Annual Meeting of the Association for Computational Linguistics*, pages 4668–4679, Online. Association for Computational Linguistics.

Fernando Alva-Manchego, Carolina Scarton, and Lucia Specia. 2020b. Data-Driven Sentence Simplification: Survey and Benchmark. *Computational Linguistics*, 46(1):135–187.

Fernando Alva-Manchego, Carolina Scarton, and Lucia Specia. 2021. The (Un)Suitability of Automatic Evaluation Metrics for Text Simplification. *Computational Linguistics*, pages 1–29.

Marcelo Amancio and Lucia Specia. 2014. An Analysis of Crowdsourced Text Simplifications. In *Proceedings of the 3rd Workshop on Predicting and Improving Text Readability for Target Reader Populations (PITR)*, pages 123–130, Gothenburg, Sweden. Association for Computational Linguistics.

Petra Barancikova and Ondřej Bojar. 2020. COSTRA 1.0: A Dataset of Complex Sentence Transformations. In *Proceedings of the 12th Language Resources and Evaluation Conference*, pages 3535–3541, Marseille, France. European Language Resources Association.

Alessia Battisti, Dominik Pfütze, Andreas Säuberli, Marek Kostrzewa, and Sarah Ebling. 2020. A Corpus for Automatic Readability Assessment and Text Simplification of German. In *Proceedings of the 12th Language Resources and Evaluation Conference*, pages 3302–3311, Marseille, France. European Language Resources Association.

Stefan Bott and Horacio Saggion. 2011a. An Unsupervised Alignment Algorithm for Text Simplification Corpus Construction. In *Proceedings of the Workshop on Monolingual Text-To-Text Generation*, pages 20–26, Portland, Oregon. Association for Computational Linguistics.

Stefan Bott and Horacio Saggion. 2011b. Spanish Text Simplification: An Exploratory Study. *PROCESAMIENTO DEL LENGUAJE NATURAL*, 47(0):87–95.

Stefan Bott and Horacio Saggion. 2014. Text Simplification Resources for Spanish. *Language Resources and Evaluation*, 48(1):93–120.

Dominique Brunato, Felice Dell'Orletta, Giulia Venturi, and Simonetta Montemagni. 2015. Design and Annotation of the First Italian Corpus for Text Simplification. In *Proceedings of The 9th Linguistic Annotation Workshop*, pages 31–41, Denver, Colorado, USA. Association for Computational Linguistics.

Helena Caseli, Tiago F. Pereira, Lucia Specia, Thiago Alexandre Salgueiro Pardo, Caroline Gasperin, and Sandra Maria Aluísio. 2009. Building a Brazilian Portuguese Parallel Corpus of Original and Simplified Texts. In *In: 10th Conference on Intelligent Text Processing and Computational Linguistics, Mexico City*, pages 59–70.

William Coster and David Kauchak. 2011. Simple English Wikipedia: A New Text Simplification Task. In *Proceedings of the 49th Annual Meeting of the Association for Computational Linguistics: Human Language Technologies*, pages 665–669, Portland, Oregon, USA. Association for Computational Linguistics.

Yue Dong, Zichao Li, Mehdi Rezagholizadeh, and Jackie Chi Kit Cheung. 2019. EditNTS: An Neural Programmer-Interpreter Model for Sentence Simplification through Explicit Editing. In *Proceedings of the 57th Annual Meeting of the Association for Computational Linguistics*, pages 3393–3402, Florence, Italy. Association for Computational Linguistics.

European Telecommunications Standards Institute. 2021. Accessibility requirements for ICT products and services - EN 301 549 (V3.2.1). https://www.etsi.org/deliver/etsi_en/301500_301599/301549/03.02.01_60/en_301549v030201p.pdf.

Ulrich Germann. 2008. Yawat: Yet Another Word Alignment Tool. In *Proceedings of the ACL-08: HLT Demo Session*, pages 20–23, Columbus, Ohio. Association for Computational Linguistics.

Itziar Gonzalez-Dios, María Jesús Aranzabe, and Arantza Díaz de Ilarraza. 2018. The Corpus of Basque Simplified Texts (CBST). *Language Resources and Evaluation*, 52(1):217–247.

Matthew Honnibal, Ines Montani, Sofie Van Landeghem, and Adriane Boyd. 2020. spaCy: Industrial-strength Natural Language Processing in Python.

William Hwang, Hannaneh Hajishirzi, Mari Ostendorf, and Wei Wu. 2015. Aligning Sentences from Standard Wikipedia to Simple Wikipedia. In *Proceedings of the 2015 Conference of the North American Chapter of the Association for Computational Linguistics: Human Language Technologies*, pages 211–217, Denver, Colorado. Association for Computational Linguistics.

Chao Jiang, Mounica Maddela, Wuwei Lan, Yang Zhong, and Wei Xu. 2020. Neural CRF Model for Sentence Alignment in Text Simplification. In *Proceedings of the 58th Annual Meeting of the Association for Computational Linguistics*, pages 7943–7960, Online. Association for Computational Linguistics.

Anaïs Koptient, Rémi Cardon, and Natalia Grabar. 2019. Simplification-induced Transformations: Typology and some Characteristics. In *Proceedings of the 18th BioNLP Workshop and Shared Task*, pages 309–318, Florence, Italy. Association for Computational Linguistics.

Mahnaz Koupaee and William Yang Wang. 2018. WikiHow: A Large Scale Text Summarization Dataset. *CoRR*, abs/1810.09305.

Dhruv Kumar, Lili Mou, Lukasz Golab, and Olga Vechtomova. 2020. Iterative Edit-Based Unsupervised Sentence Simplification. In *Proceedings of the 58th Annual Meeting of the Association for Computational Linguistics*, pages 7918–7928, Online. Association for Computational Linguistics.

Mounica Maddela, Fernando Alva-Manchego, and Wei Xu. 2021. Controllable Text Simplification with Explicit Paraphrasing. In *Proceedings of the 2021 Conference of the North American Chapter of the Association for Computational Linguistics: Human Language Technologies*, pages 3536–3553, Online. Association for Computational Linguistics.

Louis Martin, Angela Fan, Éric de la Clergerie, Antoine Bordes, and Benoît Sagot. 2020. Multilingual Unsupervised Sentence Simplification. *CoRR*, abs/2005.00352.

Kostiantyn Omelianchuk, Vipul Raheja, and Oleksandr Skurzhanskyi. 2021. Text Simplification by Tagging. In *Proceedings of the 16th Workshop on Innovative Use of NLP for Building Educational Applications*, pages 11–25, Online. Association for Computational Linguistics.

Gustavo Paetzold, Fernando Alva-Manchego, and Lucia Specia. 2017. MASSAlign: Alignment and annotation of comparable documents. In *Proceedings of the IJCNLP 2017, System Demonstrations*, pages 1–4, Tapei, Taiwan. Association for Computational Linguistics.

David Pellow and Maxine Eskenazi. 2014. An Open Corpus of Everyday Documents for Simplification Tasks. In *Proceedings of the 3rd Workshop on Predicting and Improving Text Readability for Target Reader Populations (PITR)*, pages 84–93, Gothenburg, Sweden. Association for Computational Linguistics.

Vinodkumar Prabhakaran, Aida Mostafazadeh Davani, and Mark Diaz. 2021. On Releasing Annotator-Level Labels and Information in Datasets. In *Proceedings of The Joint 15th Linguistic Annotation Workshop (LAW) and 3rd Designing Meaning Representations (DMR) Workshop*, pages 133–138, Punta Cana, Dominican Republic. Association for Computational Linguistics.

Dennis Reidsma and Rieks op den Akker. 2008. Exploiting 'Subjective' Annotations. In *Coling 2008: Proceedings of the workshop on Human Judgements in Computational Linguistics*, pages 8–16, Manchester, UK. Coling 2008 Organizing Committee.

Anna Rogers, Timothy Baldwin, and Kobi Leins. 2021. 'Just What do You Think You're Doing, Dave?' A Checklist for Responsible Data Use in NLP. In *Findings of the Association for Computational Linguistics: EMNLP 2021*, pages 4821–4833, Punta Cana, Dominican Republic. Association for Computational Linguistics.

Sanja Štajner. 2018. How to Make Troubleshooting Simpler? Assessing Differences in Perceived Sentence Simplicity by Native and Non-native Speakers. In *Proceedings of the Eleventh International Conference on Language Resources and Evaluation (LREC 2018)*, Paris, France. European Language Resources Association (ELRA).

Sanja Štajner. 2021. Automatic Text Simplification for Social Good: Progress and Challenges. In *Findings of the Association for Computational Linguistics: ACL-IJCNLP 2021*, pages 2637–2652, Online. Association for Computational Linguistics.

Sanja Štajner, Marc Franco-Salvador, Paolo Rosso, and Simone Paolo Ponzetto. 2018. CATS: A Tool for Customized Alignment of Text Simplification Corpora. In *Proceedings of the Eleventh International Conference on Language Resources and Evaluation (LREC 2018)*, Miyazaki, Japan. European Language Resources Association (ELRA).

Pontus Stenetorp, Sampo Pyysalo, Goran Topić, Tomoko Ohta, Sophia Ananiadou, and Jun'ichi Tsujii. 2012. BRAT: a Web-based Tool for NLP-Assisted Text Annotation. In *Proceedings of the Demonstrations at the 13th Conference of the European Chapter of the Association for Computational Linguistics*, pages 102–107, Avignon, France. Association for Computational Linguistics.

Regina Stodden. 2021. When the Scale is Unclear – Analysis of the Interpretation of Rating Scales in Human Evaluation of Text Simplification. In *Proceedings of the First Workshop on Current Trends in Text Simplification (CTTS 2021)*, pages 84–95. CEUR-WS.

Renliang Sun, Hanqi Jin, and Xiaojun Wan. 2021. Document-Level Text Simplification: Dataset, Criteria and Baseline. In *Proceedings of the 2021 Conference on Empirical Methods in Natural Language Processing*, pages 7997–8013, Online and Punta Cana, Dominican Republic. Association for Computational Linguistics.

Jörg Tiedemann. 2006. ISA & ICA - Two Web Interfaces for Interactive Alignment of Bitexts alignment of parallel texts. In *Proceedings of the Fifth International Conference on Language Resources and Evaluation (LREC'06)*, Genoa, Italy. European Language Resources Association (ELRA).

Wei Xu, Chris Callison-Burch, and Courtney Napoles. 2015. Problems in Current Text Simplification Research: New Data Can Help. *Transactions of the Association for Computational Linguistics*, 3:283–297.

Wei Xu, Courtney Napoles, Ellie Pavlick, Quanze Chen, and Chris Callison-Burch. 2016. Optimizing Statistical Machine Translation for Text Simplification. *Transactions of the Association for Computational Linguistics*, 4:401–415.

Xingxing Zhang and Mirella Lapata. 2017. Sentence Simplification with Deep Reinforcement Learning. In *Proceedings of the 2017 Conference on Empirical Methods in Natural Language Processing*, pages 584–594, Copenhagen, Denmark. Association for Computational Linguistics.

Zhemin Zhu, Delphine Bernhard, and Iryna Gurevych. 2010. A Monolingual Tree-based Translation Model for Sentence Simplification. In *Proceedings of the 23rd International Conference on Computational Linguistics (Coling 2010)*, pages 1353–1361, Beijing, China. Coling 2010 Organizing Committee.

# A Appendix

## A.1 Rating Aspects

| Aspect | Statement |
|---|---|
| **Grammaticality** | The simplified sentence is fluent, there are no grammatical errors. |
| **Grammaticality (original)** | The original sentence is fluent, there are no grammatical errors. |
| **Meaning Preservation** | The simplified sentence adequately expresses the meaning of the original sentence, perhaps omitting the least important information. |
| **Information Gain** | In the simplified sentence, information is added or gets more explicit than in the original sentence. |
| **Overall Simplicity** | The simplified sentence is easier to understand than the original sentence. |
| **Structural Simplicity** | The structure of the simplified sentence is easier to understand than the structure of the original sentence. |
| **Lexical Simplicity** | The words of the simplified sentence are easier to understand than the words of the original sentence. |
| **Simplicity (simple)** | The simplified sentence is easy to understand. |
| **Simplicity (original)** | The original sentence is easy to understand. |
| **Coherence (simple)** | The simplified sentence is understandable without reading the whole paragraph. |
| **Coherence (original)** | The original sentence is understandable without reading the whole paragraph. |
| **Ambiguity (simple)** | The simplified sentence is ambiguous. It can be read in different ways. |
| **Ambiguity (original)** | The original sentence is ambiguous. It can be read in different ways. |

Table 1: Default rating aspects of TS-ANNO.

## A.2 Rewriting Transformation Label Scheme

| Level | Class Name | Sub Transformation |
|---|---|---|
| **Word** | Deletion | Discourse Marker<br>Abbreviation<br>Filler Words<br>Other |
| | Lexical Substitution | Compound Segmentation<br>More Frequent Word<br>Abbreviation<br>Anaphora<br>Shorter Word<br>Synonym<br>Hyponym<br>Hypernym<br>Nominalization<br>Methaphor<br>Number<br>Date<br>Other |
| | Inflection | |
| | Insert | Ellipsis Filled<br>Other |
| **Phrase** | Reorder | Discontinuity Resolution<br>Other |
| | Deletion | Phrase<br>Clause<br>Replace<br>Less Adjunct Phrase<br>Other |
| | Rephrase | |
| **Sentence** | Split | Coordinate Clause<br>Subordinate Clause<br>Appositive Phrase<br>Adverbial Phrase<br>Relative Clause<br>Other |
| | Verbal Changes | Voice of Verb<br>Verb Tense<br>Verb Mood |
| | Lexical Substitution | Verbalization<br>Other |
| | Reorder | Subject-Verb Reorder<br>Genetive to Dative<br>Negative to Positive<br>Other |
| | Rephrase | |
| | No Operation | |
| **Paragraph** | Reorder | Sentence-Order Changed<br>Other |
| | Merge | |
| | Deletion | |
| | Insert | Explanation<br>Exemplification<br>Other |

Table 2: Default rewriting transformation labels of TS-ANNO.

# Language Diversity: Visible to Humans, Exploitable by Machines

**Gábor Bella**
University of Trento
via Sommarive, 5, 38123 Trento, Italy
gabor.bella@unitn.it

**Erdenebileg Byambadorj**
University of Trento
via Sommarive, 5, 38123 Trento, Italy
e.byambadorj@unitn.it

**Yamini Chandrashekar**
University of Trento
via Sommarive, 5, 38123 Trento, Italy
yamini.chandrashekar@unitn.it

**Khuyagbaatar Batsuren**
National University of Mongolia
NUM 1, 14200, Ulaanbaatar, Mongolia
khuyagbaatar@num.edu.mn

**Danish Asghar Cheema**
University of Trento
via Sommarive, 5, 38123 Trento, Italy
danish.cheema@unitn.it

**Fausto Giunchiglia**
University of Trento
via Sommarive, 5, 38123 Trento, Italy
fausto.giunchiglia@unitn.it

## Abstract

The *Universal Knowledge Core* (UKC) is a large multilingual lexical database with a focus on language diversity and covering over two thousand languages. The aim of the database, as well as its tools and data catalogue, is to make the abstract notion of linguistic diversity visually understandable for humans and formally exploitable by machines. The UKC website lets users explore millions of individual words and their meanings, but also phenomena of cross-lingual convergence and divergence, such as shared interlingual meanings, lexicon similarities, cognate clusters, or lexical gaps. The *UKC LiveLanguage Catalogue*, in turn, provides access to the underlying lexical data in a computer-processable form, ready to be reused in cross-lingual applications.

## 1 Introduction

A recent challenge in computational linguistics has been the development of efficient multilingual and cross-lingual techniques for language understanding and processing. In terms of solutions, a mainstream, yet often implicit assumption has been that shared meaning unites languages beyond superficial differences in lexicon and grammar: after all, humankind on the whole has been successful in getting ideas across linguistic borders. Hence the recent trend of massively multilingual resources—lexical databases, cross-lingual transfer matrices, pre-trained multilingual language models—exploiting a common meaning-based mapping across linguistic units.

*Linguistic diversity* remains, nevertheless, a key concept insomuch as it refers to deep-running, irreducible, meaning-level differences across languages and underlying cultural concepts. To take real examples from state-of-the-art machine translation, syntactically correct but semantically absurd outputs such as *'my older brother is younger than me'* or *'this raw rice is tasty'* are not rare exceptions but recurrent consequences of diversity: the diverging ways languages express culturally significant concepts such as *brother* or *rice*. While phenomena such as lexical gaps (Lehrer, 1970), culturally diverse terminology, or the varying relevance of the notion of *word* itself across languages are not unfamiliar to us computational linguists, this intuitive and high-level understanding is hard to translate into actual 'diversity-aware' computational applications, not the least because of the lack of formal datasets that would provide such information.

Lexical typology has described and catalogued many of such phenomena (Koptjevskaja-Tamm et al., 2015). A few online databases also provide contrastive data and visualisations, sometimes over thousands of languages (Dryer and Haspelmath, 2013; Rzymski et al., 2020; Holman et al., 2011; Arora et al., 2021). The These databases are rarely used in the NLP community, probably because they are often targeted towards historical linguistics and use phonetic representations of words or are limited to a few hundred core concepts. Yet, our position is that typological data can and should be reused for computational purposes, provided that they are meaningfully integrated with existing resources on



*Proceedings of the 60th Annual Meeting of the Association for Computational Linguistics*
*System Demonstrations*, pages 156 - 165

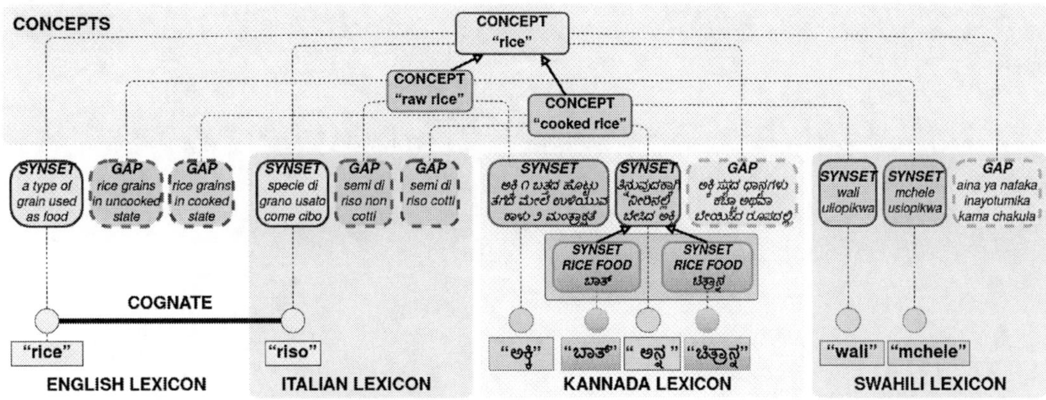


Figure 1: Structural elements in the UKC lexical database for representing cross-lingual unity and diversity.

contemporary language.

Computationally-oriented resources that address language diversity or linguistic typology have so far been concentrating on multilingual morphosyntax (Ponti et al., 2019; Batsuren et al., 2021b; Nivre et al., 2016). On diversity in lexical semantics, only a few studies (Giunchiglia et al., 2017) and sporadic data have been available for specific languages, such as a few hundred lexical gaps in Hebrew (Ordan and Wintner, 2007) or in Italian (Pianta et al., 2002). Large-scale multilingual lexical databases (MLDB), such as BabelNet (Navigli and Ponzetto, 2012) or the Open Multilingual Wordnet (Bond and Foster, 2013), have so far ignored phenomena related to language diversity and have concentrated on shared meaning.

The *Universal Knowledge Core* (UKC) database and system presented in this paper provides computer-readable cross-lingual lexical data, covering both the common and the diverse among more than a thousand lexicons. The data is being made available for download from the *UKC LiveLanguage* catalogue[1], while the *UKC website*[2] provides a set of interactive tools that allow both high-level visualisations and an in-depth exploration of diversity data. The rest of the paper provides an overview of the UKC database structure and contents, the online tools, and the data catalogue.[3]

## 2 A Multilingual Lexical Database on Language Diversity

Among existing large-scale MLDBs, those with a published formal, computer-exploitable data model—such as the Open Multilingual WordNet, BabelNet, or EuroWordNet (Vossen, 1997)—concentrate solely on *language unity*, i.e. shared supra-lingual meaning, through linking together words with the same meaning across languages. The UKC offers a richer, two-layered representation of language unity, as well as introducing *language diversity* as formal data, both in terms of lexical model and actual content.

The UKC data model, the theoretical underpinnings of which have been exposed in (Giunchiglia et al., 2018), is illustrated in Figure 1. On the top of the figure, a supra-lingual *concept layer* contains hierarchies of concepts that represent lexical meaning shared across languages. Concepts thus act as bridges across languages. The only criterion for a concept to be present in the concept layer is that it is lexicalised by at least one language.

The bottom *lexicon layer* consists of language-specific lexicons. As in other lexical databases, these provide lexicalisations for concepts, such as the English *'rice'* and the Italian *'riso'* for the concept of *rice* in Figure 1. Beyond lexicalisations, however, the UKC lexicons also provide rich cross-lingual information on language unity and diversity through the additional constructs detailed below.

**Lexical gaps.** As evoked in the introduction, when unrecognised, lexical untranslatability can decrease the performance of cross-lingual applications. Syntactically correct yet meaningless Google translations, such as the Hungarian sentence

*'A bátyám három évvel fiatalabb nálam,'*

meaning 'my older brother is three years younger than me,' are systematically produced due to non-existent equivalent translations, in this case for the

[1] `http://www.livelanguage.eu`

[2] `http://ukc.datascientia.eu`

[3] See `http://youtu.be/b90SdCJjtCw` for a video.

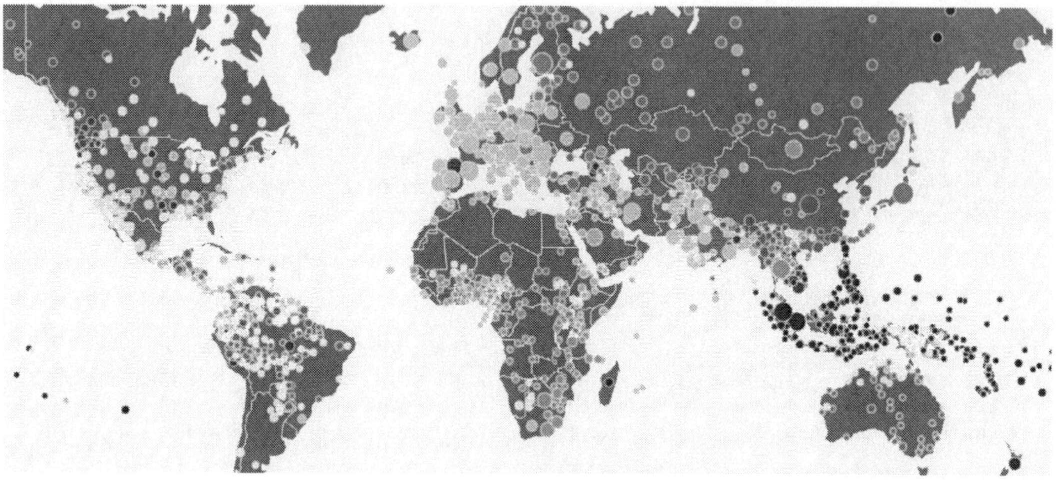

Figure 2: Lexicons in the UKC: circle sizes indicate lexicon size and their colour the language family (phylum).

word *brother* in Hungarian.[4] Likewise, as shown in Figure 1, English has no single word for *raw, uncooked rice* while Swahili—and many other languages, cf. (Joo, 2021)—has no equivalent for the general term *rice*. The UKC provides evidence of untranslatability by representing lexical gaps inside lexicons. Such information can be used, among others, to indicate the absence of equivalent terms to downstream cross-lingual applications.

**Cross-lingual sense relations.** Beyond providing shared word meanings as other MLDBs do, the UKC represents a richer set of interlingual connections between word senses. For example, in Figure 1, the English *'rice'* and the Italian *'riso'* are connected through a *cognate* relationship. Cognates are words in different languages that sound the same and have the same (or similar) meaning due to a common etymological origin. Cognates are key indicators of language unity on the lexical level, i.e. of the cross-lingual similarity of lexicons. Such information can thus be exploited e.g. as seeds in cross-lingual tasks such as bilingual lexicon induction (Batsuren et al., 2021a).

**Metadata on language diversity.** Beyond standard typological metadata such as language phylogeny or the geographical locations of speakers, the UKC also integrates cross-linguistic metadata computed from its own lexico-semantic content. Based on cross-lingual cognate relationships, we computed large-scale *lexicon similarity* data across 27 thousand language pairs over 331 languages. Lexicon similarity (Bella et al., 2021) formally characterises the extent to which the vocabularies of two languages 'resemble each other', taking differing writing systems and orthographies into account. This metric has, in our view, a better potential in predicting the success of cross-lingual tasks (such as transfer learning or joint supervised training) than language phylogeny, as it is based on the overlaps of contemporary lexicons as opposed to historical relatedness.

**Language-specific word meanings.** Diversity also means acknowledging our partial understanding of how specific languages conceptualise lexical meaning and the ultimate impossibility of an exhaustive interlingual model. The UKC is the only lexical database to allow the co-existence of shared and language-specific word meaning hierarchies, inside the concept layer and the lexicons, respectively. Figure 1 shows culture-specific words and meanings (of rice-based foods) represented inside the Kannada lexicon, not yet integrated into the shared concept layer.

**Language-specific lexical relations.** Lexical relations within individual languages are sometimes part of lexical databases, such as antonymy or derivation in the Princeton WordNet (Miller, 1998). The UKC integrates derivational relationships for 20 languages, introduces relation types not typically part of lexical databases—such as *metonym-of* or *homograph-of*—and provides corresponding relation instances.

Table 1 shows the current contents of the UKC (as of January 2022) in terms of the data types

[4] Apart from the laborious and thus rarely used *fiútestvér*.

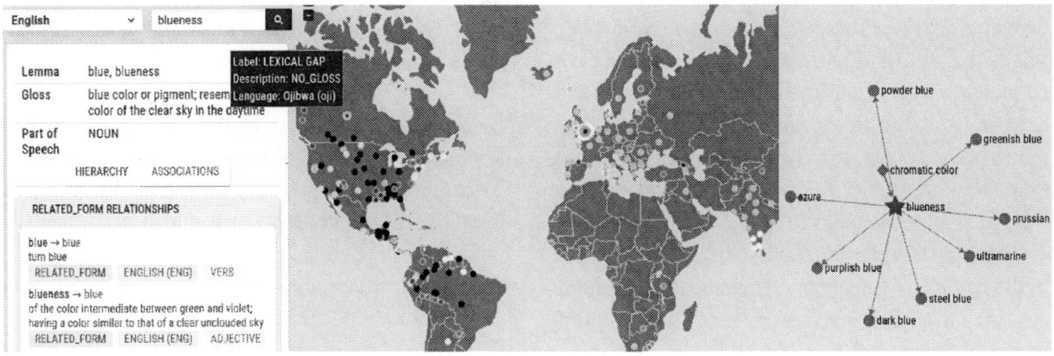


Figure 3: Exploring the concept of *blueness* as lexicalised in the English language (left), in the world (middle), and as part of the supra-lingual concept hierarchy (right).

enumerated above. Concepts and concept relations were initially derived from the Princeton WordNet, as in all other MLDBS, but then extended with 400 new concepts and 490 new relations. We obtained lexicalisations from Wiktionary, NorthEuraLex (Dellert et al., 2020), the *Native Languages of the Americas*[5], as well as from 28 monolingual wordnets cited at the end of our paper. Lexical gaps were mostly obtained from original research (about 33k from diversity-rich domains such as kinship and colours, but also 600 gaps from (Bella et al., 2020)), and over a thousand gaps from the few third-party resources providing such information (Pianta et al., 2002; Ordan and Wintner, 2007). We computed cross-lingual sense relations from UKC data, reusing our method published in (Batsuren et al., 2019a, 2021a). Language-specific sense relations were obtained in a minor part from wordnets providing such data (48k relations), and in a major part from our own research on multilingual morphology (Batsuren et al., 2021b) (770k derivations in 16 languages) and metonymy (25k metonyms in 191 languages). Finally, lexicon-level metadata on language diversity combines online sources (Dryer and Haspelmath, 2013) with results of our own research on the similarity of lexicons (Bella et al., 2021).

## 3 Exploring Diversity Data

The website of the UKC database provides browseable online access to the full database contents, data visualisation tools, extensive information on related projects, publications, source materials, as well as example downstream services, such as word translation between any two languages or multilingual word sense disambiguation (to be released soon).

| Content type | Data size |
|---|---|
| Languages | 2,176 |
| Concepts | 106k |
| Concept relations | 109k |
| Lexicalisations (word senses) | 2.8M |
| Lexical gaps | 35k |
| Cross-lingual sense relations | 8M |
| Language-specific relations | 840k |
| Lexicon-level diversity metadata | 30k |

Table 1: UKC contents and data sizes.

A major feature of the website is the interactive exploration of lexicons and diversity data. The user can browse: (1) linguistic metadata of the 2k lexicons, selecting the language from an interactive map (Figure 2) or by name; (2) within a language, all meanings of a word typed in by the user; and (3) lexicalisations and gaps of a concept in the current language and in all languages of the world.

A screenshot of the last—and richest—concept exploration functionality, taking the example concept of *blueness*, is provided in Figure 3. On the left-hand side of the screen, details are provided on the lexicalisation of the concept in the current language, such as synonyms, definition, part of speech, as well as lexical relationships to other word senses (e.g. derivations, metonyms, cognates in other languages). The middle part of the screen shows an interactive clickable map of all languages that either lexicalise the concept in the database or, on the contrary, *are known not to lexicalise it*. The colour-coded dots (indicating the language family while 'black holes' stand for gaps) thus provide an

[5] `http://www.native-languages.org`

instant global typological overview for the concept selected, e.g. from Figure 3 one can see that a lot of languages in the Americas do not lexicalise blue as a separate colour. Some language do not appear on the map due to lexicon incompleteness: for those languages the UKC has no information whether they lexicalise *blueness* or not.

The right-hand side, finally, shows the concept in the context of the lexico-semantic concept hierarchy, displayed as a graph. A detail of the full graph is shown, including the currently observed concept *blueness*, the parent (broader), and the child (narrower) concepts. Other lexico-semantic relationships (e.g. meronymy and metonymically related concepts) are also shown when they exist. While for usability reasons the graph only displays a part of the full hierarchy, it is interactive, allowing the entire concept graph to be explored in the currently selected language. Changing the language is as simple as clicking on the map or selecting it from the drop-down in the upper left corner of the screen. Colours in the graph are indicative of language diversity: they show whether a concept is lexicalised in the current language (dark-coloured nodes), are missing from its lexicon (light-coloured nodes), or are lexical gaps (black nodes).

## 4 Visualising Language Diversity

Beyond the fine-grained word and concept exploration presented in the previous section, the UKC website also offers visualisation tools that allow humans to grasp diversity both in its globality and from different angles. Currently the following tools are provided, three of which we present below: (1) cognate diversity clusters; (2) colexifications; (3) a gap explorer for a fixed set of domains that are lexically diverse; (4) lexical similarity graphs; and (5) visual statistics.

**Cognate diversity clusters.** This tool shows *cognate clusters* on the map for a given concept selected by the user, computed from cognate data inside the UKC. In Figure 4, the concept of *fish* is selected: each dot represents a lexicon that contains a word for *fish*. Two dots are of the same colour if the two words are cognates of each other. For example, the English *'fish'* and the Italian *'pesce'* are within one cognate cluster (in light green in the figure) while the Hungarian *'hal'* and the Finnish *'kala'* are in another cluster (in turquoise). The number and distribution of clusters for a given concept provide information about its universality or diversity: *coffee* is a so-called *universal concept* while *woman* is an extremely diverse one.

**Lexical gap explorer.** Certain domains—such as kinship, food, colours, or body parts—are known by linguists to be lexically diverse, for reasons related to culture, geography, but also grammar and other factors (Lehrer, 1970). The *gap explorer tool* displays a full concept hierarchy for a domain or subdomain selected by the user. Figure 5 shows the UKC concept structure of the subdomain of *siblings* from the *kinship* domain. For the language selected (Danish in the figure), the tool displays existing lexicalisations, indicates incompleteness (missing word), and provides known lexical gaps. This allows for quick comparisons of how different languages lexicalise (or not) a given domain. For example, for the *cousins* subdomain that consists of 67 concepts, English only lexicalises the root concept *cousin* with all other concepts as gaps, while South Indian languages provide no less than 16 distinct words depending on the age, sex, and lineage (patrilineal/matrilineal) of the cousin.

**Lexical similarity graphs.** Relying on the extensive lexical data inside the UKC, we compute pairwise similarities between languages based on the amount of shared cognates, using the method described in our recent paper (Bella et al., 2021). In order to interpret the resulting similarity data for humans, i.e. provide a global overview of lexical similarity, we compute a dynamic graph visualisation where nodes are languages and edge lengths are proportional to lexical similarities. The graph computation relies on a physical model of attraction and repulsion among nodes, using the *ForceAtlas2* library (Jacomy et al., 2014). We provide two distinct colourings for the same graph: one based on language families (shown in Figure 6) and the other based on geographical distance. These graphs visualise how the similarity of contemporary lexicons correlates with (historic) phylogeny and with the geographical closeness of speakers. As a way to make language evolution visual, we also provide the equivalent graph computed over data from historical linguistics, obtained from the ASJP database (Holman et al., 2011). Insights gained from these graphs may also help computational linguists predict the performance of automated tasks that involve some form of lexicon mapping (e.g. bilingual lexicon induction or machine translation) over specific language pairs.

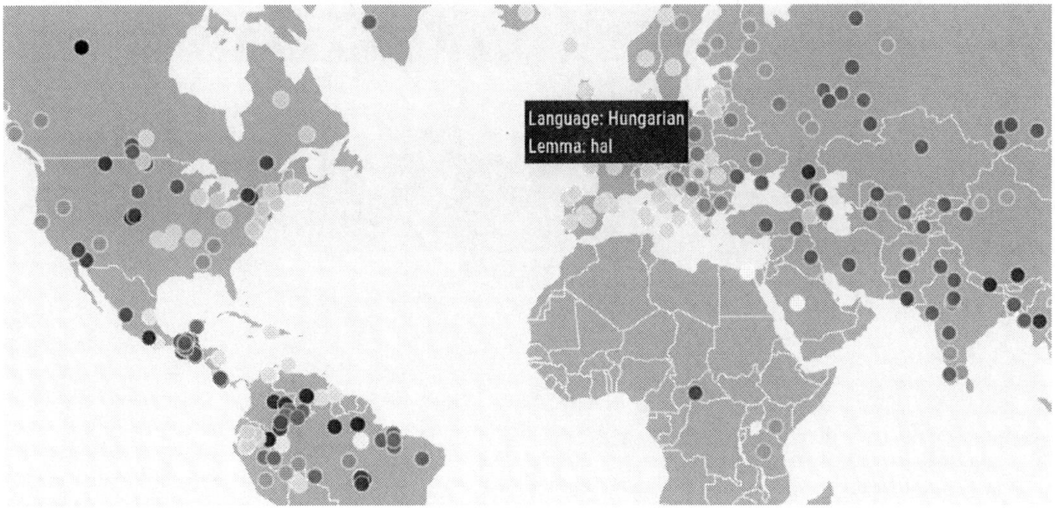


Figure 4: Cognate clusters for the concept of *fish*.

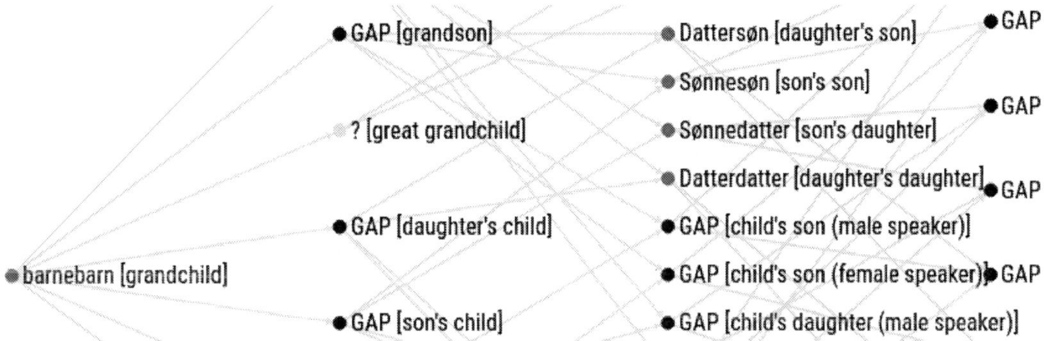


Figure 5: Detail of the *grandchild* subdomain as lexicalised by the Danish language.

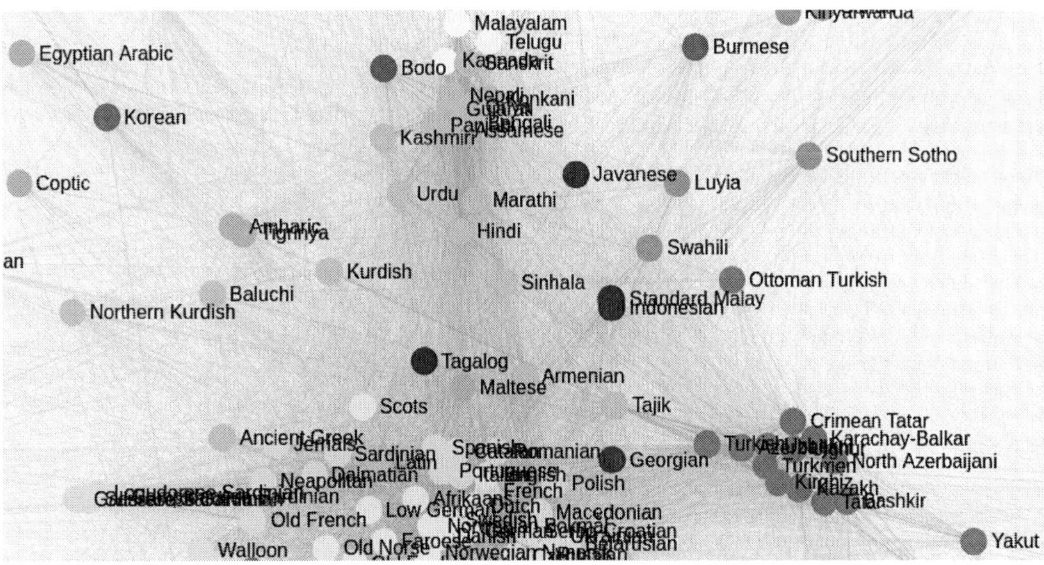


Figure 6: Detail from the lexical similarity graph coloured according to language families.

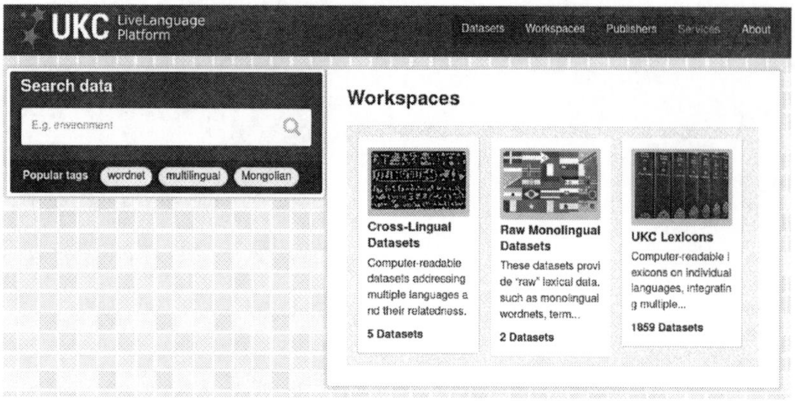


Figure 7: The UKC LiveLanguage Data Catalogue.

## 5 The LiveLanguage Data Catalogue

As a complement to online exploration, we are also making available the contents of the UKC for computational applications. While an open, fine-grained, API-based access to the data is planned as future work, we are already in the process of publishing data for download through the *UKC LiveLanguage* data catalogue. The catalogue, accessible from the website through any of the numerous download links, provides access to the UKC data through multiple modalities. Accordingly, the structure of the catalogue, shown in Figure 7, consists of (1) cross-lingual datasets; (2) individual lexicons that aggregate all types of data about a single language; and (3) lexicon sets that also provide cross-lingual information. All datasets are published in full respect of the licensing constraints of their constituting resources; data that disallow redistribution are excluded from the catalogue.

**Raw data on cross-lingual diversity.** These datasets originate from projects on diversity and cover domain-specific lexical gaps, multilingual morphology, lexical similarity, and cognate relationships. Datasets are distributed in their original formats, with concepts linked to Princeton WordNet 3.0 identifiers for interoperability with third-party data.

**Individual lexicons.** These datasets are produced as language-specific 'cross-sections' of the full UKC data. Their added value lies in the integration of multiple sources—words from wordnets and Wiktionary, language-specific morphological and lexico-semantic relationships, gaps—into a single formal representation. These datasets will be provided in multiple formats (under development), including the ISO standard Lexical Markup Framework (LMF) format as well as OntoLex.

**Lexicon sets.** The notion of language diversity gains full significance *across* languages. Consequently, the development of an online service is underway to allow the simultaneous download of multiple concept-aligned lexicons as a single multilingual resource. The service will export multilingual data from the UKC database in real time. Such datasets will be directly exploitable in cross-lingual training and evaluation tasks.

## 6 Conclusions and Future Work

We see a huge research potential both in the creation and in the reuse of diversity-aware language resources. Exploiting diversity to improve state-of-the-art cross-lingual applications is a direction that we expect to gain importance and popularity in the community. The UKC database, website, and data catalogue aims to contribute to such efforts. All components of the system are going through a rapid evolution: the database contents in terms of language support, lexicon correctness and completeness, the data exploration and visualisation tools, new demonstrators, and APIs are continually being created and extended. We are also deploying regional instances of the UKC—e.g. for the Middle-East or the Indian subcontinent—where diversity among local languages and dialects is studied in fine detail by local communities of linguists.

**Acknowledgement** This paper and the underlying research were supported by the European Union's H2020 Research and Innovation programme under grant agreement no. 826106, project *InteropEHRate*.

## References


Aryaman Arora, Adam Farris, Gopalakrishnan R, and Samopriya Basu. 2021. Bhāṣācitra: Visualising the dialect geography of South Asia. In *Proceedings of the 2nd International Workshop on Computational Approaches to Historical Language Change 2021*, pages 51–57, Online. Association for Computational Linguistics.

Khuyagbaatar Batsuren, Gábor Bella, and Fausto Giunchiglia. 2019a. Cognet: A large-scale cognate database. In *Proceedings of the 57th annual meeting of the association for computational linguistics*, pages 3136–3145.

Khuyagbaatar Batsuren, Gábor Bella, and Fausto Giunchiglia. 2021a. A large and evolving cognate database. *Language Resources and Evaluation*, pages 1–25.

Khuyagbaatar Batsuren, Gábor Bella, and Fausto Giunchiglia. 2021b. Morphynet: a large multilingual database of derivational and inflectional morphology. In *Proceedings of the 18th SIGMORPHON Workshop on Computational Research in Phonetics, Phonology, and Morphology*, pages 39–48.

Khuyagbaatar Batsuren, Amarsanaa Ganbold, Altangerel Chagnaa, and Fausto Giunchiglia. 2019b. Building the mongolian wordnet. In *Proceedings of the 10th global WordNet conference*, pages 238–244.

Gábor Bella, Khuyagbaatar Batsuren, and Fausto Giunchiglia. 2021. A database and visualization of the similarity of contemporary lexicons. In *International Conference on Text, Speech, and Dialogue*, pages 95–104. Springer.

Gábor Bella, Fiona McNeill, Rody Gorman, Caoimhín Ó Donnaíle, Kirsty MacDonald, Yamini Chandrashekar, Abed Alhakim Freihat, and Fausto Giunchiglia. 2020. A major wordnet for a minority language: Scottish gaelic. In *Proceedings of the 12th Language Resources and Evaluation Conference*, pages 2812–2818.

Luisa Bentivogli, Pamela Forner, Bernardo Magnini, and Emanuele Pianta. 2004. Revising the wordnet domains hierarchy: semantics, coverage and balancing. In *Proceedings of the workshop on multilingual linguistic resources*, pages 94–101.

Pushpak Bhattacharyya. 2010. Indowordnet. In *In Proc. of LREC-10*. Citeseer.

Francis Bond and Ryan Foster. 2013. Linking and extending an open multilingual wordnet. In *Proceedings of the 51st Annual Meeting of the Association for Computational Linguistics (Volume 1: Long Papers)*, pages 1352–1362.

Lars Borin, Markus Forsberg, and Lennart Lönngren. 2008. The hunting of the blark–saldo, a freely available lexical database for swedish language technology. *Resourceful language technology. Festschrift in honor of Anna Sågvall Hein*, (7):21–32.

Johannes Dellert, Thora Daneyko, Alla Münch, Alina Ladygina, Armin Buch, Natalie Clarius, Ilja Grigorjew, Mohamed Balabel, Hizniye Isabella Boga, Zalina Baysarova, et al. 2020. Northeuralex: a wide-coverage lexical database of northern eurasia. *Language resources and evaluation*, 54(1):273–301.

Matthew S. Dryer and Martin Haspelmath, editors. 2013. *WALS Online*. Max Planck Institute for Evolutionary Anthropology, Leipzig.

Darja Fišer, Jernej Novak, and Tomaž Erjavec. 2012. slownet 3.0: development, extension and cleaning. In *Proceedings of 6th International Global Wordnet Conference (GWC 2012)*, pages 113–117.

Ruth Vatvedt Fjeld and Lars Nygaard. 2009. Nornet-a monolingual wordnet of modern norwegian. In *NODALIDA 2009 workshop: WordNets and other Lexical Semantic Resources-between Lexical Semantics, Lexicography, Terminology and Formal Ontologies*, volume 7, pages 13–16.

Amarsanaa Ganbold, Altangerel Chagnaa, and Gábor Bella. 2018. Using crowd agreement for wordnet localization. In *Proceedings of the Eleventh International Conference on Language Resources and Evaluation (LREC-2018)*.

Radovan Garabík. 2010. Slovak national corpus tools and resources. In *5th Workshop on Intelligent and Knowledge oriented Technologies*, page 2. Citeseer.

Radovan Garabík and Indrė Pileckytė. 2013. From multilingual dictionary to lithuanian wordnet. *Natural Language Processing, Corpus Linguistics, E-Learning*, pages 74–80.

Fausto Giunchiglia, Khuyagbaatar Batsuren, and Gabor Bella. 2017. Understanding and exploiting language diversity. In *IJCAI*, pages 4009–4017.

Fausto Giunchiglia, Khuyagbaatar Batsuren, and Abed Alhakim Freihat. 2018. One world–seven thousand languages. In *Proceedings 19th International Conference on Computational Linguistics and Intelligent Text Processing, CiCling2018, 18-24 March 2018*.

Aitor Gonzalez-Agirre, Egoitz Laparra, and German Rigau. 2012. Multilingual central repository version 3.0. In *LREC*, pages 2525–2529.

Marissa Griesel and Sonja Bosch. 2014. Taking stock of the african wordnet project: 5 years of development. In *Proceedings of the Seventh Global Wordnet Conference*, pages 148–153.

Maria Grigoriadou, Harry Kornilakis, Eleni Galiotou, Sofia Stamou, and Evangelos Papakitsos. 2004. The software infrastructure for the development and validation of the greek wordnet. *Romanian Journal of Information Science and Technology*, 7(1-2):89–105.

Eric W Holman, Cecil H Brown, Søren Wichmann, André Müller, Viveka Velupillai, Harald Hammarström, Sebastian Sauppe, Hagen Jung, Dik Bakker, Pamela Brown, et al. 2011. Automated dating of the world's language families based on lexical similarity. *Current Anthropology*, 52(6):841–875.

Chu-Ren Huang, Shu-Kai Hsieh, Jia-Fei Hong, Yun-Zhu Chen, I-Li Su, Yong-Xiang Chen, and Sheng-Wei Huang. 2010. Chinese wordnet: Design, implementation, and application of an infrastructure for cross-lingual knowledge processing. *Journal of Chinese Information Processing*, 24(2):14–23.

Hitoshi Isahara, Francis Bond, Kiyotaka Uchimoto, Masao Utiyama, and Kyoko Kanzaki. 2008. Development of the japanese wordnet. In *LREC*.

Mathieu Jacomy, Tommaso Venturini, Sebastien Heymann, and Mathieu Bastian. 2014. Forceatlas2, a continuous graph layout algorithm for handy network visualization designed for the gephi software. *PloS one*, 9(6):e98679.

Ian Joo. 2021. The etymology of korean ssal 'uncooked grain' and pap 'cooked grain'. *Cahiers de Linguistique Asie Orientale*, 50(1):94 – 110.

Farhad Keyvan, Habib Borjian, Manuchehr Kasheff, and Christiane Fellbaum. 2007. Developing persianet: The persian wordnet. In *3rd Global wordnet conference. Citeseer*, pages 315–318. Citeseer.

Maria Koptjevskaja-Tamm, Ekaterina Rakhilina, and Martine Vanhove. 2015. The semantics of lexical typology. In *The Routledge handbook of semantics*, pages 450–470. Routledge.

Adrienne Lehrer. 1970. Notes on lexical gaps. *Journal of linguistics*, 6(2):257–261.

Krister Lindén and Lauri Carlson. 2010. Finnwordnet–finnish wordnet by translation. *LexicoNordica–Nordic Journal of Lexicography*, 17:119–140.

Marek Maziarz, Maciej Piasecki, and Stan Szpakowicz. 2012. Approaching plwordnet 2.0. In *Proceedings of 6th International Global Wordnet Conference, The Global WordNet Association*, pages 189–196.

George A Miller. 1998. *WordNet: An electronic lexical database*. MIT press.

Roberto Navigli and Simone Paolo Ponzetto. 2012. Babelnet: The automatic construction, evaluation and application of a wide-coverage multilingual semantic network. *Artificial Intelligence*, 193:217–250.

Joakim Nivre, Marie-Catherine De Marneffe, Filip Ginter, Yoav Goldberg, Jan Hajic, Christopher D Manning, Ryan McDonald, Slav Petrov, Sampo Pyysalo, Natalia Silveira, et al. 2016. Universal dependencies v1: A multilingual treebank collection. In *Proceedings of the Tenth International Conference on Language Resources and Evaluation (LREC'16)*, pages 1659–1666.

Nurril Hirfana Bte Mohamed Noor, Suerya Sapuan, and Francis Bond. 2011. Creating the open wordnet bahasa. In *Proceedings of the 25th Pacific Asia Conference on Language, Information and Computation*, pages 255–264.

Noam Ordan and Shuly Wintner. 2007. Hebrew wordnet: a test case of aligning lexical databases across languages. *International Journal of Translation*, 19(1):39–58.

Petya Osenova and Kiril Simov. 2018. The data-driven bulgarian wordnet: Btbwn. *Cognitive Studies| Études cognitives*, (18).

Emanuele Pianta, Luisa Bentivogli, and Christian Girardi. 2002. Multiwordnet: developing an aligned multilingual database. In *First international conference on global WordNet*, pages 293–302.

Edoardo Maria Ponti, Helen O'horan, Yevgeni Berzak, Ivan Vulić, Roi Reichart, Thierry Poibeau, Ekaterina Shutova, and Anna Korhonen. 2019. Modeling language variation and universals: A survey on typological linguistics for natural language processing. *Computational Linguistics*, 45(3):559–601.

Marten Postma, Emiel van Miltenburg, Roxane Segers, Anneleen Schoen, and Piek Vossen. 2016. Open dutch wordnet. In *Proceedings of the 8th Global WordNet Conference (GWC)*, pages 302–310.

Alexandre Rademaker, Valeria de Paiva, Fabricio Chalub, Livy Real, and Claudia Freitas. 2016. Introducing openwordnet-pt: a open portuguese wordnet for reasoning.

Ida Raffaelli, Marko Tadic, Božo Bekavac, and Željko Agic. 2008. Building croatian wordnet. In *Proceedings of GWC*, pages 349–360.

Yasser Regragui, Lahsen Abouenour, Fettoum Krieche, Karim Bouzoubaa, and Paolo Rosso. 2016. Arabic wordnet: New content and new applications. In *Proceedings of the 8th Global WordNet Conference (GWC)*, pages 333–341.

Christoph Rzymski, Tiago Tresoldi, Simon J Greenhill, Mei-Shin Wu, Nathanael E Schweikhard, Maria Koptjevskaja-Tamm, Volker Gast, Timotheus A Bodt, Abbie Hantgan, Gereon A Kaiping, et al. 2020. The database of cross-linguistic colexifications, reproducible analysis of cross-linguistic polysemies. *Scientific data*, 7(1):1–12.

Benoît Sagot and Darja Fišer. 2008. Construction d'un wordnet libre du français à partir de ressources multilingues. In *Actes de la 15ème conférence sur le Traitement Automatique des Langues Naturelles. Articles longs*, pages 171–180.

Sareewan Thoongsup, Thatsanee Charoenporn, Kergrit Robkop, Tan Sinthurahat, Chumpol Mokarat, Virach Sornlertlamvanich, and Hitoshi Isahara. 2009. Thai wordnet construction. In *Proceedings of the 7th Workshop on Asian Language Resources (ALR7)*, pages 139–144.

Dan Tufiş, Radu Ion, Luigi Bozianu, Alexandru Ceauşu, and Dan Ştefănescu. 2007. Romanian wordnet: Current state, new applications and prospects. In *Proceedings of the Fourth Global WordNet Conference (GWC 2008)*, pages 441–452.

PJTM Vossen. 1997. Eurowordnet: a multilingual database for information retrieval.

Shan Wang and Francis Bond. 2013. Building the chinese open wordnet (cow): Starting from core synsets. In *Proceedings of the 11th Workshop on Asian Language Resources*, pages 10–18.

Xinyi Wu, Zhenyao Wu, Hao Guo, Lili Ju, and Song Wang. 2021. Dannet: A one-stage domain adaptation network for unsupervised nighttime semantic segmentation. In *Proceedings of the IEEE/CVF Conference on Computer Vision and Pattern Recognition*, pages 15769–15778.

# CogKGE: A Knowledge Graph Embedding Toolkit and Benchmark for Representing Multi-source and Heterogeneous Knowledge

**Zhuoran Jin*[1,2], Tianyi Men*[1,2], Hongbang Yuan*[1,2], Zhitao He[1,2], Dianbo Sui[1,2], Chenhao Wang[1,2], Zhipeng Xue[1], Yubo Chen[1,2], Jun Zhao[1,2]**

[1] National Laboratory of Pattern Recognition, Institute of Automation, CAS, Beijing, China
[2] School of Artificial Intelligence, University of Chinese Academy of Sciences, Beijing, China
{zhuoran.jin, dianbo.sui, yubo.chen, jzhao}@nlpr.ia.ac.cn
{mentianyi2022, yuanhongbang2022, hezhitao2021}@ia.ac.cn

## Abstract

In this paper, we propose CogKGE, a knowledge graph embedding (KGE) toolkit, which aims to represent the **multi-source** and **heterogeneous** knowledge. For multi-source knowledge, unlike existing methods that mainly focus on entity-centric world knowledge, CogKGE also supports the representations of event-centric world knowledge, commonsense knowledge and linguistic knowledge. For heterogeneous knowledge, besides structured triple facts, CogKGE leverages additional unstructured information, such as text descriptions, node types and temporal information, to enhance the meaning of embeddings. Moreover, CogKGE aims to provide a unified programming framework for KGE tasks and a series of knowledge representations for downstream tasks. As a research framework, CogKGE consists of five parts, including core, data, model, knowledge and adapter module. As a knowledge discovery toolkit, CogKGE provides pre-trained embedders to discover new facts, cluster entities and check facts. Furthermore, we construct two new benchmark datasets for further research on multi-source heterogeneous KGE tasks: EventKG240K and CogNet360K. We also release an online system [1] to discover knowledge visually. Source code, datasets and pre-trained embeddings are publicly available at GitHub [2], with a short instruction video [3].

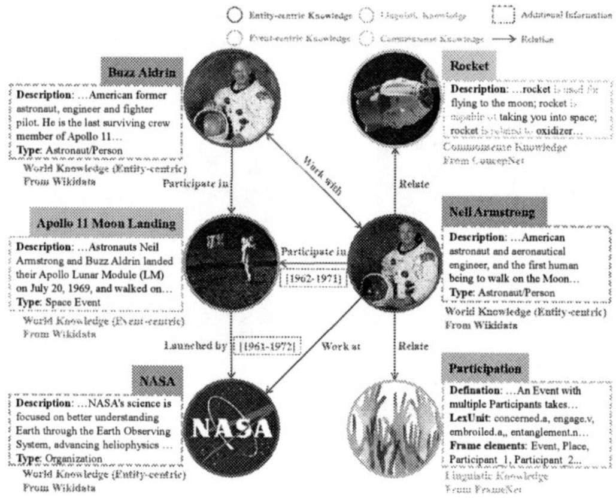


Figure 1: An example of a multi-source heterogeneous KG. Grey, blue, green and purple denote entity-centric world knowledge, event-centric world knowledge, commonsense knowledge and linguistic knowledge, respectively. The dotted boxes show additional information.

## 1 Introduction

In recent years, knowledge graphs (KGs) have experienced rapid development. A large number of KGs, such as FrameNet (Baker et al., 1998), Wikidata (Vrandečić and Krötzsch, 2014), DBpedia (Lehmann et al., 2015) and ConceptNet (Speer et al., 2017), have been built and successfully applied to many real-world applications. Most KGs are originally organized in the form of triples $(h, r, t)$, where $h$ and $t$ indicate head and tail entities, and $r$ indicates the relation between $h$ and $t$. However, a KG is a symbolic system that cannot be directly applied to large-scale deep learning frameworks. To this end, a series of knowledge graph embedding (KGE) models have been proposed to represent the entities and relations into continuous spaces (Bordes et al., 2013; Wang et al., 2014; Lin et al., 2015; Sun et al., 2018; Abboud et al., 2020).

To facilitate the development of KGE models, some remarkable KGE toolkits, such as OpenKE (Han et al., 2018), Graphvite (Zhu et al., 2019), LibKGE (Broscheit et al., 2020), PyKEEN (Ali et al., 2021) and Pykg2vec (Yu et al., 2021) have been released, providing easy-to-use frameworks for a series of KGE models. However, most of them perform the embedding task solely based on entity-related triple facts, so they are still limited to two critical challenges in practical applications: **multi-source** challenge and **heterogeneous** challenge.

As to the multi-source challenge, real-world

*These authors contribute equally to this work.
[1] http://cognlp.com/cogkge/
[2] https://github.com/jinzhuoran/CogKGE/
[3] https://youtu.be/BiA2Rm9JYKs/



*Proceedings of the 60th Annual Meeting of the Association for Computational Linguistics System Demonstrations*, pages 166 - 173
May 22-27, 2022 ©2022 Association for Computational Linguistics

KGs involve not only world knowledge (including entity-centric knowledge and event-centric knowledge), but also linguistic knowledge and commonsense knowledge. In various practical applications, we need to use multi-source knowledge simultaneously. For example, as shown in Figure 1, to understand an article about *"Neil Armstrong"*, we need (1) entity-centric world knowledge, e.g., *"Neil Armstrong worked at NASA"* from Wikidata; (2) event-centric world knowledge, e.g., *"Neil Armstrong is a participator of the Apollo 11 Moon Landing"* from Wikidata; (3) linguistic knowledge, e.g., the linguistic frame of *"Participation"* from FrameNet; (4) commonsense knowledge, e.g., *"rocket is used for flying to the moon"* from ConceptNet. However, most existing toolkits only focus on representing world knowledge, especially entity-centric knowledge, while ignoring other knowledge, like commonsense knowledge and linguistic knowledge. Therefore, developing a toolkit that can represent multi-source knowledge is essential.

As to the heterogeneous challenge, real-world KGs involve not only triple facts, but also additional information, such as text descriptions, node types and temporal information. In many practical applications, we should use these heterogeneous knowledge together. Likewise, as shown in Figure 1, to understand an article about *"Neil Armstrong"*, besides structured triple facts, we also need (1) text descriptions, e.g., *"Neil Armstrong was the first human being to walk on the Moon"*; (2) node types, e.g., *"Neil Armstrong is an astronaut"*; (3) temporal information, e.g., *"Nell Armstrong participated in Apollo 11 Moon Landing from 1962 to 1971"*. All these heterogeneous knowledge can be used for obtaining the embeddings, but conventional KGE models cannot take full advantage of the additional information mentioned above. Therefore, it is highly desirable to have a toolkit that can bridge these heterogeneous knowledge by plug-and-play knowledge adapters.

To solve the above two problems, we propose CogKGE, a knowledge graph embedding toolkit that aims to represent multi-source and heterogeneous knowledge. The toolkit consists of five parts, including core module, data module, model module, adapter module and knowledge module. CogKGE currently supports 17 models, 11 datasets, five evaluation metrics, four knowledge adapters, four loss functions, three samplers and three built-in data containers. Besides, we also construct two large-scale benchmark datasets to promote the research on KGE. In summary, the main features and contributions are as follows:

- **Multi-source and heterogeneous knowledge representation.** CogKGE explores the unified representation of knowledge from diverse sources. Moreover, our toolkit not only contains the triple fact-based embedding models, but also supports the fusion representation of additional information, including text descriptions, node types and temporal information.
- **Comprehensive models and benchmark datasets.** CogKGE has implemented 17 classic KGE models of four categories, including translation distance models, semantic matching models, graph neural network-based models and transformer-based models. Besides nine built-in public datasets, we also release two new large benchmark datasets for further evaluating KGE methods, called EventKG240K and CogNet360K.
- **Extensible and modularized framework.** CogKGE provides a programming framework for KGE tasks. Based on the extensible architecture, CogKGE can meet the requirements of module extension and secondary development, and pre-trained knowledge embeddings can be directly applied to downstream tasks.
- **Open source and online demo.** Besides the toolkit, we also release an online CogKGE demo to discover knowledge visually. Source code, datasets and pre-trained embeddings are publicly available at GitHub.

## 2 System Architecture

The overall system architecture of CogKGE is presented in Figure 2. The top part is composed of the core module and data module. The former is the basis of the toolkit, while the latter provides fundamental data containers, loaders and processors. The bottom part is built upon the top part, the model module contains lots of built-in models, the knowledge module integrates multi-source and heterogeneous knowledge, and the adapter module acts as a bridge between the two. In the following, we will cover these five modules in detail.

### 2.1 Core Module

In the core module, we develop an extensible framework and various ready-to-use components.

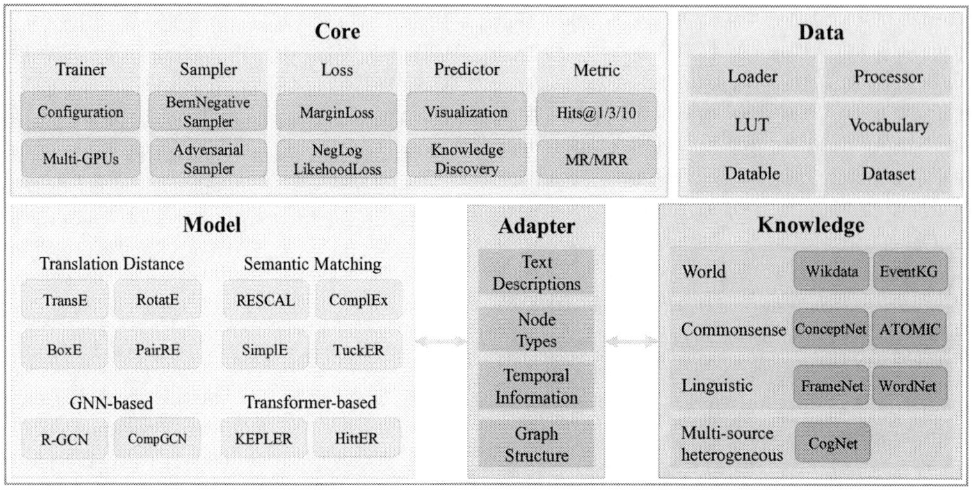


Figure 2: The main architecture of CogKGE.

**Trainer, Evaluator and Predictor.** Since training, evaluation, and prediction are the core processes in the deep learning pipeline, we design `Trainer` class, `Evaluator` class and `Predictor` class to implement them, respectively. To improve the efficiency of our toolkit, we also involve some functions to support multi-GPUs training, breakpoints resume, logs record and result visualization as shown in Appendix A.

**Loss and Sampler.** All models in CogKGE are trained by minimizing `MarginLoss` function or `NegLogLikehoodLoss` function. Both of these loss functions need to construct false triples as negative samples. We encapsulate the efficient process of constructing negative samples in `Sampler` class, including `UniSampler` class, `BernSampler` class and `AdversarialSampler` class.

**Metric.** KGE models are usually evaluated on link prediction, which aims to predict the missing entities in triples $(?, r, t)$ or $(h, r, ?)$. In CogKGE, the `Metric` class computes the ratio of answers ranked top-k (Hits@1/3/10), the mean rank of the answers (MR) and the mean reciprocal rank of the answers (MRR), both raw and filtered results are available.

## 2.2 Data Module

A primary design principle of CogKGE is to support unified KGE tasks. For this purpose, the data module is based on easy-to-use data containers, such as `LUT` class for looking up items in table form, `Vocabulary` class for converting labels to indexes. To improve reusability, CogKGE includes built-in `Loader` and `Processor` class for many benchmarking datasets and is compatible with multi-source heterogeneous KGs with additional information.

## 2.3 Model Module

`BaseModel` class is the base class of all models in CogKGE. `BaseModel` class organizes code into three basic sections: (1) `forward` function for training, (2) `embedding` function for getting the embedding of entities and relations and (3) `scoring` function for computing the score of triples. The model module consists of four parts, which are: translation distance models, semantic matching models, graph neural network-based models and transformer-based models.

**Translation Distance Models.** The translation distance models use distance-based measures to compute the similarity score for a pair of entities and their relationships. In CogKGE, the similarity score function of translation distance models is generally defined as:

$$f_r(h, t) = \|g_h(\mathbf{h}) + \mathbf{r} - g_t(\mathbf{t})\|_{\ell_1/\ell_2}^{1/2}, \quad (1)$$

where $\mathbf{h}$, $\mathbf{r}$, $\mathbf{t}$ are the embedding representations of $h$, $r$, $t$, $g_h(\cdot)$ and $g_t(\cdot)$ are the transformation functions. The translation-based models aim to find a vector representation of entities with relation to the translation of the entities. In CogKGE, we implement several translational distance models, including TransE (Bordes et al., 2013), TransH (Wang et al., 2014), TransR (Lin et al., 2015), TransD (Ji et al., 2015), TransA (Xiao et al., 2015), RotatE (Sun et al., 2018), BoxE (Abboud et al., 2020) and PairRE (Chao et al., 2020).

**Semantic Matching Models.** Compared with the distance-based score function of translation distance models, semantic matching models use the similarity-based score function. They measure the plausibility of facts by matching latent semantics of entities and relations embodied in their vector space representations. RESCAL (Nickel et al., 2011), DistMult (Yang et al., 2015), ComplEx (Trouillon et al., 2016), SimplE (Kazemi and Poole, 2018) and TuckER (Balažević et al., 2019) have been built into CogKGE.

**Graph Neural Network-based Models.** Graph neural network (GNN) has recently been shown to be quite successful in modelling graph-structured data. Considering that KG itself happens to be a kind of graph-structured data, GNN can integrate the topological structure and node feature, then provides a more refined vector representation. We implement R-GCN (Schlichtkrull et al., 2018) and CompGCN (Vashishth et al., 2019) to represent the multi-relational data.

**Transformer-based Models.** Transformer has been widely used in pre-trained language models, and its deep network architecture can learn contextual representations of entities and relations in a KG jointly by aggregating information from graph neighbourhoods. Besides, transformer-based models can also utilize the text descriptions in KGs, encoding the texts and facts into a unified semantic space. We have implemented KEPLER (Wang et al., 2021b) and HittER (Chen et al., 2021).

### 2.4 Knowledge Module

The knowledge module mainly integrates three kinds of knowledge representation, namely world, commonsense and linguistic knowledge.

**World Knowledge.** Encyclopedia KGs such as Freebase, DBpedia and Wikidata mainly focus on explicit world knowledge, containing facts about specific instances, e.g., *(Neil Armstrong, Work at, NASA)*. Besides entity-centric knowledge, event-centric knowledge is also an essential kind of knowledge, which conveys dynamic and procedural knowledge, e.g., *(Neil Armstrong, Participate in, Apollo 11 Moon Landing)*. In CogKGE, we implement entity-centric knowledge representation based on Wikidata and event-centric knowledge representation based on EventKG (Gottschalk and Demidova, 2018). World knowledge representations have been widely used in knowledge-enhanced pre-trained language models, entity disambiguation and event extraction.

**Commonsense Knowledge.** Commonsense knowledge tries to capture implicit general facts and regular patterns in our daily life. Nodes in commonsense KG are semantically rich natural language phrases rather than entities. CogKGE supports the commonsense knowledge representation of ConceptNet, which can be helpful for commonsense completion and reasoning.

**Linguistic Knowledge.** Linguistic knowledge includes considerable information about lexical, conceptual and predicate argument semantics. For example, *"participation"* has hyponymy relation to *"engagement"* in WordNet, while *"take part"* can evoke the *"Participation"* frame in FrameNet. In CogKGE, the knowledge representation of FrameNet can be applied for downstream tasks, such as word sense disambiguation and machine reading comprehension.

### 2.5 Adapter Module

Almost all of the models in Section 2.3 embed KGs to a specific feature space only based on the triple facts $(h, r, t)$. In practice, as shown in Section 2.4, multi-source and heterogeneous knowledge representation is more realistic and valuable. There is a lot of additional information in KGs that can further enhance and refine the knowledge representation. Inspired by the adapter pattern in the design patterns, we leverage plug-and-play knowledge adapters to build a bridge between KGE models and multi-source heterogeneous data.

**Text Descriptions Adapter.** As shown in Figure 1, there are text descriptions of entities in KGs, containing abundant semantic information about them. The challenge of KGE with text description is to embed both structured fact knowledge and unstructured textual information in the same space. According to KEPLER (Wang et al., 2021b), we adopt RoBERTa (Liu et al., 2019) as the encoder to generate the entity embeddings based on text descriptions. For a triple $(h, r, t)$, we have:

$$\mathbf{h} = \text{Encoder}(h_d) \\ \mathbf{t} = \text{Encoder}(t_d), \tag{2}$$

where $h_d$ and $t_d$ are the text descriptions for $h$ and $t$. Users can replace the traditional embedding matrixes with the text descriptions adapter without modifying `scoring` function of models. Models with the text description adapters can generate embeddings from their descriptions for those entities invisible during the training stage.

**Node Types Adapter.** In most KGs, nodes are represented with hierarchical types or categories. For example, *"Neil Armstrong"* belongs to *"Astronaut"* and *"Person"* category. To implement the node types adapter, we use type-specific entity projections based on TKRL (Xie et al., 2016), which is defined as:

$$g_h(\mathbf{h}) = \mathbf{M}_{ch}\mathbf{h}$$
$$g_t(\mathbf{t}) = \mathbf{M}_{ct}\mathbf{t}, \quad (3)$$

where $\mathbf{M}_{ch}$ and $\mathbf{M}_{ct}$ are the projection matrixes of $h$ and $t$ belonging to category $c$.

**Temporal Information Adapter.** KG facts are usually time-sensitive, different events and actions cause entities and relations to change over time. For example, Figure 1 illustrates *"Nell Armstrong"* paticipated in *"Apollo 11 Moon Landing"* from *1962* to *1971*. A fact with temporal information in KGs is represented as a quadruple $(h, r, t, [\tau_b, \tau_e])$, where $\tau_b$ and $\tau_e$ respectively denote the start and end time of the fact. We implement diachronic embedding (DE) (Goel et al., 2020) as the temporal information adapter in CogKGE.

## 3 System Usage

Our goal of designing CogKGE is to provide a unified research framework for KGE tasks and pre-trained knowledge representations for downstream tasks. In this section, we show a detailed guideline on how to use our toolkit.

### 3.1 Pre-trained Embedder for Knowledge Discovery

CogKGE provides a series of pre-trained knowledge representations, such as EventKG, CogNet (Wang et al., 2021a) and other KGs. `Predictor` class serves as the pre-trained embedder, whose model and dataset can be selected by users. As shown in Figure 3, `Predictor` class implements the following functions: similar nodes query, head query according to tail and relation, relation query according to head and tail, etc. Pre-trained embedders can be applicable for knowledge discovery.

```
import cogkge
predictor = cogkge.Predictior(model='BoxE', data='EventKG')
# Fuzzy query nodes by keywords
fuzzy_nodes = predictor.fuzzy_query_node('Copa Colombia')
# Fuzzy query relations by keywords
fuzzy_relations = predictor.fuzzy_query_relation('sport')
# Query similar nodes
similar_nodes = predictor.predict_similar_node(node_id=1)
# Given head node and relation, query the tail node
tails = predictor.predcit_tail(head_id=1, relation_id=2)
# Given head node and tail node, query the relation
relations = predictor.predict_relation(head_id=1, tail_id=2)
```

Figure 3: An example of pre-trained embedder.

```
# Load and process data
loader = EVENTKG2MLoader()
train_data, valid_data, test_data = loader.load_all_data()
node_lut, relation_lut = loader.load_all_lut()
processor = EVENTKG2MProcessor()
train_dataset = processor.process(train_data)
valid_dataset = processor.process(valid_data)
test_dataset = processor.process(test_data)
# Initialize components
model = TransE(embedding_dim=200)
loss = MarginLoss()
optimizer = torch.optim.Adam(model.parameters())
negative_sampler = UniNegativeSampler()
metric = Link_Prediction()
lr_scheduler = torch.optim.lr_scheduler.ReduceLROnPlateau()
# Train and evaluate model
trainer = Trainer(train_dataset, valid_dataset, model, loss,
↪  optimizer, negative_sampler, metric, lr_scheduler)
trainer.train()
evaluator = Evaluator(test_dataset, model, metric)
evaluator.evaluate()
```

Figure 4: An example of programming framework.

### 3.2 Programming Framework for Training Models

As a unified programming framework, CogKGE supports researchers to use various off-the-shelf components to implement new models quickly. Figure 4 shows the sample code of training models. To do this, users need to use `Loader` class to load the lookup tables and process datasets by `Processor` class. Then, `Model`, `Loss`, `Metric`, `Optimizer`, `Sampler` class should be initialized before added to `Trainer` class. And finally, `Trainer` and `Evaluator` class can automatically train and validate the model.

### 3.3 Online System for Visualization

In addition to this toolkit, we also release an online system as shown in Figure 5. We implement high-performance KGE models for large-scale KGs and deploy pre-trained knowledge embedders for online access. The online system can be directly used for querying nodes and relations in various forms, and in the meantime, dimensionality reduction and visualization of nodes are supported.

## 4 Evaluation Benchmark

To evaluate the KGE models on large-scale multi-source heterogeneous KGs, we construct two new benchmark datasets: EventKG240K and

| Model | EventKG240K | | | | | CogNet360K | | | | |
|---|---|---|---|---|---|---|---|---|---|---|
| | Hits@1 | Hits@3 | Hits@10 | MR | MRR | Hits@1 | Hits@3 | Hits@10 | MR | MRR |
| RESCAL | 6.3 | 14.3 | 29.4 | 1644.8 | 13.7 | 1.0 | 2.6 | 7.7 | 1734.9 | 4.0 |
| TransE | 6.2 | 16.1 | 34.7 | 1019.1 | 15.1 | 0.7 | 2.8 | 8.6 | 1167.0 | 4.1 |
| TransH | 6.7 | 15.9 | 32.5 | 1109.4 | 15.0 | 0.6 | 2.6 | 8.3 | 2077.9 | 4.0 |
| DistMult | 7.1 | 15.1 | 31.2 | 1113.6 | 14.8 | 1.4 | 3.7 | 10.4 | 923.9 | 5.1 |
| ComplEx | 8.4 | 19.7 | 41.1 | 1513.5 | 18.4 | 0.7 | 2.2 | 7.4 | 1167.2 | 3.8 |
| RotatE | 8.3 | **22.3** | **45.6** | **717.3** | **19.8** | **1.9** | **4.7** | **12.2** | **230.0** | **6.0** |
| SimplE | **9.2** | 20.6 | 42.8 | 2354.5 | 19.2 | 1.3 | 3.3 | 9.0 | 2973.3 | 4.7 |
| BoxE | 8.3 | 17.5 | 34.5 | 1871.8 | 16.5 | 1.4 | 3.8 | 10.1 | 355.5 | 5.1 |
| PairRE | 7.7 | 20.3 | 39.5 | 1051.0 | 17.7 | 1.3 | 4.1 | 11.3 | 810.6 | 5.4 |

Table 1: Link prediction results on EventKG240K and CogNet360K (% except MR). Under the raw evaluation setting, we do not remove the corrupted triples before ranking. The embedding dimension is 50.

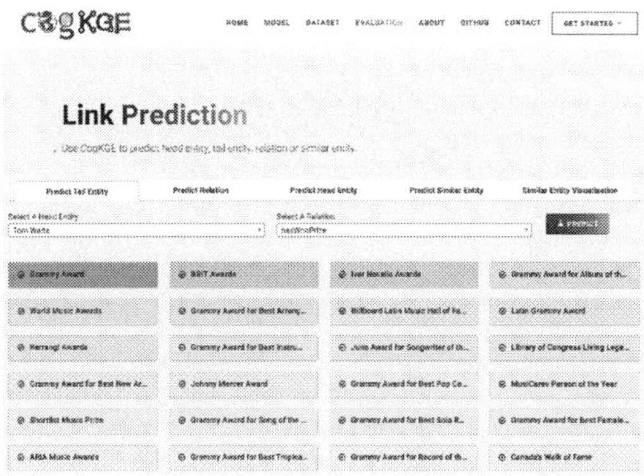


Figure 5: An example of online system.

CogNet360K. In this section, we introduce our datasets and conduct evaluations for classic models included in CogKGE.

### 4.1 EventKG240K

EventKG is an event-centric temporal knowledge graph. To our best knowledge, EventKG240K is the first event-centric KGE dataset. We use EventKG V3.0 data to construct the dataset. First, we filter entities and events based on their degrees. Then, we select the triple facts when both nodes' degrees are greater than 10. At last, we add text descriptions and node types for nodes and translate triples to quadruples by temporal information. The whole dataset contains 238,911 nodes, 822 relations and 2,333,986 triples.

### 4.2 CogNet360K

CogNet is a multi-source heterogeneous KG dedicated to integrating linguistic, world and commonsense knowledge. To build a subset, we count the number of occurrences for each node. Then, we sort frame instances by the minimum occurrences of their connected nodes. After the sorted frame instances, we filter the triple facts according to the preset frame categories. The final dataset contains 360,637 nodes, 45 relations and 1,470,488 triples.

### 4.3 Performance

To assess the challenges of EventKG240K and CogNet360K, we benchmark several popular KGE models on our dataset and select Hits@1/3/10, MR and MRR as the metrics. Table 1 shows the performance of KGE models on EventKG240K and CogNet360K, and the evaluation result shows that both datasets are more challenging due to their multi-source and heterogeneous features. For EventKG240K, traditional KGE models can not distinguish events and entities well. For CogNet360K, it is difficult for vanilla KGE methods to represent multiple kinds of knowledge uniformly. The results advocate for more efforts towards large-scale multi-source heterogeneous KGE tasks.

## 5 Conclusion

In this paper, we propose CogKGE, a knowledge graph embedding toolkit and benchmark for representing multi-source and heterogeneous knowledge. For multi-source knowledge, CogKGE explores the unified representation of world, commonsense and linguistic knowledge. For heterogeneous knowledge, CogKGE incorporates the structured and unstructured knowledge to enhance the meaning of embeddings. So far, we have implemented 17 classic KGE models. Besides nine public datasets, we also release two new benchmark datasets for further evaluating KGE models. Moreover, owing to the extensible and modularized architecture,

CogKGE is not only a KGE research framework, but also a knowledge discovery library. Besides the toolkit, we also release an online system to discover knowledge visually. In the future, more models, benchmark datasets, and knowledge adapters will be incorporated into CogKGE.

## Acknowledgements

We thank the anonymous reviewers for their constructive comments. This work is supported by the National Key Research and Development Program of China (No.2020AAA0106400), the National Natural Science Foundation of China (No.61976211 and No.62176257).

## References

Ralph Abboud, Ismail Ceylan, Thomas Lukasiewicz, and Tommaso Salvatori. 2020. Boxe: A box embedding model for knowledge base completion. *Proc. of NIPS*.

Mehdi Ali, Max Berrendorf, Charles Tapley Hoyt, Laurent Vermue, Sahand Sharifzadeh, Volker Tresp, and Jens Lehmann. 2021. Pykeen 1.0: A python library for training and evaluating knowledge graph embeddings. *Journal of Machine Learning Research*.

Collin F Baker, Charles J Fillmore, and John B Lowe. 1998. The berkeley framenet project. In *Proc. of ACL*.

Ivana Balažević, Carl Allen, and Timothy Hospedales. 2019. Tucker: Tensor factorization for knowledge graph completion. In *Proc. of EMNLP*.

Antoine Bordes, Nicolas Usunier, Alberto Garcia-Duran, Jason Weston, and Oksana Yakhnenko. 2013. Translating embeddings for modeling multi-relational data. In *Proc. of NIPS*.

Samuel Broscheit, Daniel Ruffinelli, Adrian Kochsiek, Patrick Betz, and Rainer Gemulla. 2020. Libkge: A knowledge graph embedding library for reproducible research. In *Proc. of EMNLP: System Demonstrations*.

Linlin Chao, Jianshan He, Taifeng Wang, and Wei Chu. 2020. Pairre: Knowledge graph embeddings via paired relation vectors. *ArXiv:2011.03798*.

Sanxing Chen, Xiaodong Liu, Jianfeng Gao, Jian Jiao, Ruofei Zhang, and Yangfeng Ji. 2021. HittER: Hierarchical transformers for knowledge graph embeddings. In *Proc. of EMNLP*.

Rishab Goel, Seyed Mehran Kazemi, Marcus Brubaker, and Pascal Poupart. 2020. Diachronic embedding for temporal knowledge graph completion. In *Proc. of AAAI*.

Simon Gottschalk and Elena Demidova. 2018. Eventkg: A multilingual event-centric temporal knowledge graph. In *Proc. of ESWC*.

Xu Han, Shulin Cao, Xin Lv, Yankai Lin, Zhiyuan Liu, Maosong Sun, and Juanzi Li. 2018. Openke: An open toolkit for knowledge embedding. In *Proc. of EMNLP: System Demonstrations*.

Guoliang Ji, Shizhu He, Liheng Xu, Kang Liu, and Jun Zhao. 2015. Knowledge graph embedding via dynamic mapping matrix. In *Proc. of ACL*.

Seyed Mehran Kazemi and David Poole. 2018. Simple embedding for link prediction in knowledge graphs. In *Proc. of NIPS*.

Jens Lehmann, Robert Isele, Max Jakob, Anja Jentzsch, Dimitris Kontokostas, Pablo N Mendes, Sebastian Hellmann, Mohamed Morsey, Patrick Van Kleef, Sören Auer, et al. 2015. Dbpedia–a large-scale, multilingual knowledge base extracted from wikipedia. *Semantic web*.

Yankai Lin, Zhiyuan Liu, Maosong Sun, Yang Liu, and Xuan Zhu. 2015. Learning entity and relation embeddings for knowledge graph completion. In *Proc. of AAAI*.

Yinhan Liu, Myle Ott, Naman Goyal, Jingfei Du, Mandar Joshi, Danqi Chen, Omer Levy, Mike Lewis, Luke Zettlemoyer, and Veselin Stoyanov. 2019. Roberta: A robustly optimized bert pretraining approach. *ArXiv:1907.11692*.

Maximilian Nickel, Volker Tresp, and Hans-Peter Kriegel. 2011. A three-way model for collective learning on multi-relational data. In *Proc. of ICML*.

Michael Sejr Schlichtkrull, Thomas N Kipf, Peter Bloem, Rianne van den Berg, Ivan Titov, and Max Welling. 2018. Modeling relational data with graph convolutional networks. In *Proc. of ESWC*.

Robyn Speer, Joshua Chin, and Catherine Havasi. 2017. Conceptnet 5.5: An open multilingual graph of general knowledge. In *Proc. of AAAI*.

Zhiqing Sun, Zhi-Hong Deng, Jian-Yun Nie, and Jian Tang. 2018. Rotate: Knowledge graph embedding by relational rotation in complex space. In *Proc. of ICLR*.

Théo Trouillon, Johannes Welbl, Sebastian Riedel, Éric Gaussier, and Guillaume Bouchard. 2016. Complex embeddings for simple link prediction. In *Proc. of ICML*.

Shikhar Vashishth, Soumya Sanyal, Vikram Nitin, and Partha Talukdar. 2019. Composition-based multi-relational graph convolutional networks. In *Proc. of ICLR*.

Denny Vrandečić and Markus Krötzsch. 2014. Wikidata: a free collaborative knowledgebase. *Communications of the ACM*.

Chenhao Wang, Yubo Chen, Zhipeng Xue, Yang Zhou, and Jun Zhao. 2021a. Cognet: Bridging linguistic knowledge, world knowledge and commonsense knowledge. In *Proc. of AAAI*.

Xiaozhi Wang, Tianyu Gao, Zhaocheng Zhu, Zhengyan Zhang, Zhiyuan Liu, Juanzi Li, and Jian Tang. 2021b. Kepler: A unified model for knowledge embedding and pre-trained language representation. *Transactions of the Association for Computational Linguistics*.

Zhen Wang, Jianwen Zhang, Jianlin Feng, and Zheng Chen. 2014. Knowledge graph embedding by translating on hyperplanes. In *Proc. of AAAI*.

Han Xiao, Minlie Huang, Yu Hao, and Xiaoyan Zhu. 2015. Transa: An adaptive approach for knowledge graph embedding. *ArXiv:1509.05490*.

Ruobing Xie, Zhiyuan Liu, and Maosong Sun. 2016. Representation learning of knowledge graphs with hierarchical types. In *Proc. of IJCAI*.

Bishan Yang, Wen-tau Yih, Xiaodong He, Jianfeng Gao, and Li Deng. 2015. Embedding entities and relations for learning and inference in knowledge bases. In *Proc. of ICLR*.

Shih-Yuan Yu, Sujit Rokka Chhetri, Arquimedes Canedo, Palash Goyal, and Mohammad Abdullah Al Faruque. 2021. Pykg2vec: A python library for knowledge graph embedding. *Journal of Machine Learning Research*.

Zhaocheng Zhu, Shizhen Xu, Jian Tang, and Meng Qu. 2019. Graphvite: A high-performance cpu-gpu hybrid system for node embedding. In *Proc. of WWW*.

## A Visualization in CogKGE

As shown in Figure 6, CogKGE plots training loss and commonly metrics by Tensorboard. To visualize the high-dimensional embeddings, we use t-SNE dimensionality reduction.

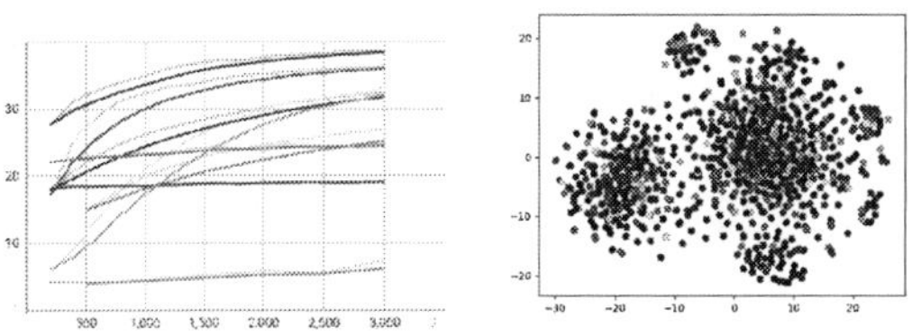

(a) Training Plot. (b) Embedding Plot.

Figure 6: Examples of visualization in CogKGE.

## B EventKG240K Statistics

| Type | Train | Validation | Test |
|---|---|---|---|
| Nodes | 238,911 | 28,844 | 28,848 |
| Relations | 822 | 289 | 301 |
| Event-Event | 219,128 | 1,389 | 1,427 |
| Event-Entity | 1,121,106 | 9,715 | 9,731 |
| Entity-Entity | 953,774 | 8,874 | 8,842 |
| All Triples | 2,294,008 | 19,978 | 20,000 |

Table 2: The statistics of EventKG240K.

In this section, we provide more details of our EventKG240K. As shown in Table 2, EventKG240K contains various event-centirc knowledge, especially event-event triples and event-entity triples.

## C CogNet360K Statistics

In this section, we provide more details of our CogNet360K. As shown in Table 3, CogNet360K contains rich multi-source and heterogeneous knowledge.

| Type | Train | Validation | Test |
|---|---|---|---|
| Nodes | 360,637 | 12,989 | 13,044 |
| Frames | 1,273 | 253 | 258 |
| Mini_frames | 7,673 | 0 | 0 |
| Micro_frames | 12,188 | 1,556 | 1,558 |
| Synset_frames | 5,271 | 1,189 | 1,179 |
| Frame_elements | 5,642 | 256 | 246 |
| Fers | 1,419 | 424 | 420 |
| Fis | 254,384 | 5,611 | 5,655 |
| Entitys | 72,787 | 3,700 | 3,728 |
| Frame-Frame | 5,762 | 250 | 247 |
| Fe-Frame | 5,294 | 0 | 0 |
| Fe-Fe | 14,819 | 230 | 225 |
| Fer-Fer | 6,440 | 368 | 386 |
| Fer-Micro_frame | 5,375 | 462 | 444 |
| Micro_frame-Micro_frame | 63,202 | 9,108 | 9,088 |
| Micro_frame-Frame | 24,075 | 0 | 0 |
| Mini_frame-Frame | 15,346 | 0 | 0 |
| Mini_frame-Micro_frame | 47,548 | 0 | 0 |
| Mini_frame-Synset_frame | 21,084 | 0 | 0 |
| Synset_frame-Frame | 23,133 | 78 | 77 |
| Synset_frame-Synset_frame | 62,215 | 8,267 | 8,316 |
| Synset_frame-Micro_frame | 129,773 | 16,283 | 16,224 |
| Fi-Fer | 220,157 | 16 | 13 |
| Fi-Entity | 488,789 | 6,047 | 6,086 |
| Fi-Micro_frame | 255,035 | 112 | 114 |
| All Triples | 1,388,047 | 41,221 | 41,220 |

Table 3: The statistics of CogNet360K.

# Dynatask: A Framework for Creating Dynamic AI Benchmark Tasks

**Tristan Thrush**[‡,*] **Kushal Tirumala**[†], **Anmol Gupta**[§], **Max Bartolo**[¶], **Pedro Rodriguez**[†],

**Tariq Kane**[††], **William Gaviria Rojas**[††], **Peter Mattson**[⋆], **Adina Williams**[†], **Douwe Kiela**[‡]

[‡] Hugging Face; [†] Facebook AI Research; [§] The University of Hong Kong;
[¶] University College London; [⋆] Google; [††] Coactive AI;
dynabench@fb.com

## Abstract

We introduce Dynatask: an open source system for setting up custom NLP tasks that aims to greatly lower the technical knowledge and effort required for hosting and evaluating state-of-the-art NLP models, as well as for conducting model in the loop data collection with crowdworkers. Dynatask is integrated with Dynabench, a research platform for rethinking benchmarking in AI that facilitates human and model in the loop data collection and evaluation. To create a task, users only need to write a short task configuration file from which the relevant web interfaces and model hosting infrastructure are automatically generated. The system is available at https://dynabench.org/ and the full library can be found at https://github.com/facebookresearch/dynabench.

## 1 Introduction

Data is the backbone of NLP research. One of the most fruitful approaches for making progress on NLP tasks has historically been *benchmarking*. Benchmarking is where the community adopts a high quality dataset for a particular task and tests various models against it to determine which is best. The process of benchmarking requires the effort of a large number of researchers, who collect and clean data, train and evaluate models, and work to understand model weaknesses. This process is iterative: once models perform very highly on the currently accepted community benchmark, another is created to push progress further. Taken as a whole, the benchmarking process is both notoriously difficult and expensive. This is due to a variety of facts: the community is a loose conglomeration of researchers with different areas of expertise, there is ever increasing need for larger datasets (Halevy et al., 2009), and the AI community has historically under-valued (Wagstaff, 2012) and under-invested in data collection and best practices (Kiela et al., 2021; Sambasivan et al., 2021; Mattson et al., 2022).

To make matters worse, in recent years, benchmarks have been saturating with increasing speed. Taking the trends from the greater AI community into account, it took MNIST (LeCun et al., 1998), Switchboard (Godfrey et al., 1992), and ImageNet (Deng et al., 2009) several years to saturate, and newer benchmarks such as SQuAD (Rajpurkar et al., 2016), GLUE (Wang et al., 2018), and SuperGLUE (Wang et al., 2019) about a year. Because of this, data-centric approaches are gaining more attention (Ng et al., 2021; Mattson et al., 2022; Lhoest et al., 2021; Paullada et al., 2021; Luccioni et al., 2021). This trend is clear evidence of the urgency of finding a sustainable and data-centric way to support the full benchmarking ecosystem, from end-to-end, in a way that causes the least amount of friction for anyone who wants to use it.

In this paper, we introduce our answer to these issues: an easy-to-use, open source system that integrates the creation of benchmark datasets for any task, the selection of appropriate metrics, and the evaluation of models while natively supporting revisions to the benchmark as models saturate the original version. We share a unified library that enables these functionalities for the Dynabench platform (Kiela et al., 2021).

## 2 Background

Dynabench was proposed as an open-source and community-driven platform to host dynamic benchmarks. The existing Dynabench tasks avoid saturation by leveraging crowdworkers who continually interact with state-of-the-art models. Crowdworkers either write examples that fool existing models (Nie et al., 2020), or collaborate with generative models to increase example diversity (Bartolo et al., 2021b). Each task is administered by one or more *task owners* from the research community who col-

* TT and DK conducted most of the work for this paper when they were at Facebook AI Research.



*Proceedings of the 60th Annual Meeting of the Association for Computational Linguistics System Demonstrations*, pages 174 - 181
May 22-27, 2022 ©2022 Association for Computational Linguistics

```
context:
- name: context
  type: string
  placeholder: Enter
   ↪ context...
input:
- name: hypothesis
  type: string
  placeholder: Enter
   ↪ hypothesis...
- name: label
  type: multiclass
  labels:
  - entailed
  - neutral
  - contradictory
  as_goal_message: true
output:
- name: label
- name: probs
  type: probs
  reference_name: label
```

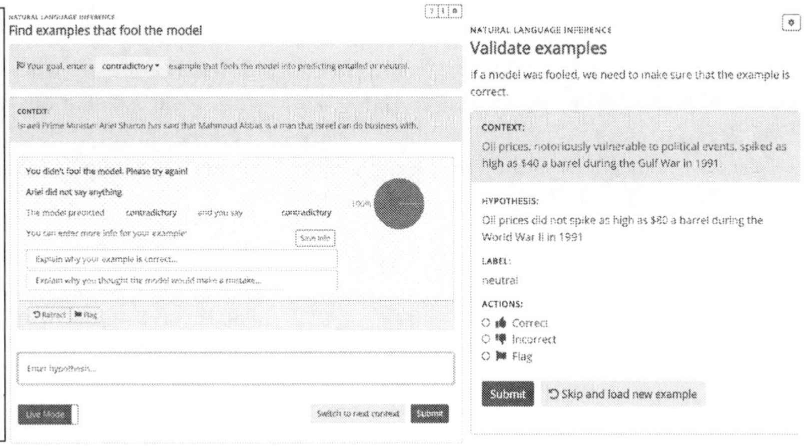


```
input:
- name: image
  type: image
  display_name: image
- name: labels
  type: multilabel
  labels:
  - Bird
  - Canoe
  - Croissant
  - Muffin
  - Pizza
output:
- name: labels
```

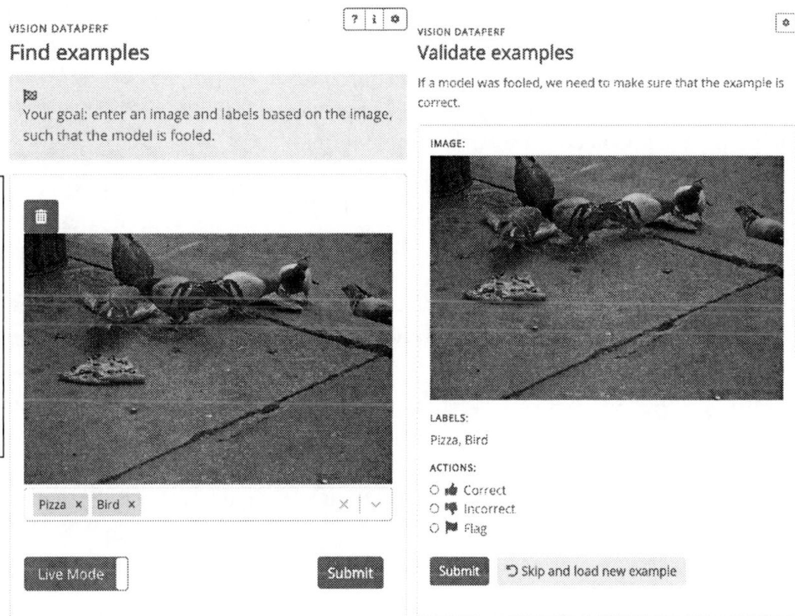


Figure 1: Two example config files and the data collection and validation interfaces they generate. Only config fields that impact the data collection interfaces are shown (e.g. metrics for model ranking are not shown). The Context and Input fields define the type of data that humans can enter. The Output field defines what models will output, given the Context and the Input. Crowdworkers are typically expected to provide the gold truth annotations for a task. In this case, Output will contain some of the object names from Input and Context. These gold truth annotations are removed from the Context and the Input before they are sent to models to get a model-in-the-loop output.

(**Top**) The config implements a natural language inference task. The first image is the collection interface, after a crowdworker submits their example and gets a model-in-the-loop response. The second image is the validation interface. For brevity, the metadata field in the config is omitted. This field is used to define the UI components for additional information, such as the "Explain why your example is correct..." input field.

(**Bottom**) The config implements an image labelling task. The first image is the collection interface, before a crowdworker submits their example. The second image is the validation interface with the same example.

lect data, make the competition's design decisions, select metrics, and configure the task's leaderboard.

Kiela et al. (2021) introduced Dynabench with four English language NLP tasks: Natural Language Inference (Nie et al., 2020), Extractive QA (Bartolo et al., 2020), Sentiment Analysis (Potts et al., 2020) and Hate Speech Detection (Vidgen et al., 2021). In follow-up work, Ma et al. (2021) updated Dynabench with additional leaderboard functionalities that allow task owners to upload task-specific models which are evaluated on each of the task's datasets, and can subsequently be included in model-ensembles that crowdworkers interact with. As the platform kept expanding, it became clear that Dynabench needed a scalable and configurable system for adding new tasks.

A *task* is an essential concept in understanding our work. On Dynabench, a distinct task is a particular relationship between inputs and outputs.[1] Inputs and outputs are framed within some prespecified format. For example, Natural Language Inference is a task on Dynabench. The input format is two strings and the output format is a classification label. The relationship between the inputs and outputs is defined by what humans would do when loosely instructed to treat the input strings as a context (sometimes called the "premise") and a hypothesis, and return a label for whether they think the hypothesis is entailed by the context. MNLI (Williams et al., 2017), SNLI (Bowman et al., 2015), and ANLI (Nie et al., 2020) can be viewed as different datasets that instantiate the same task. Schlangen (2021) takes a similar view.

## 3 Dynatask

Before the introduction of Dynatask, adding a new task required close collaboration between task owners and the Dynabench team, and extensive software contributions to the Dynabench codebase. This paper presents a system that enables Dynabench to scale up to more tasks, including into multimodal and multilingual domains, without such requirements. Now, a task owner can create their own task page on Dynabench with a short task config file. The config file is used to automatically generate crowdworker data collection interfaces, as well as the model and dataset hosting/evaluating infrastructure. The data collection interfaces and hosting overlay existing services such as Amazon Mechanical Turk,[2] which provide a workforce and payment mechanisms, but do not provide crowdworker interfaces for dynamic model-in-the-loop data collection or their corresponding backends. In fact, local installations of Dynabench can be run on Mechanical Turk. Overall, a Dynabench task owner can set up and host:

**Crowdworker data collection:** Task owners can configure interfaces for data collection. Models-in-the-loop can be optionally added, so crowdworkers can receive real-time model responses from their data (Figure 1).

**Crowdworker data validation:** Task owners can configure interfaces for crowdworkers to label collected examples as correct or incorrect. (Figure 1).

**Dynamic dataset metrics:** Metrics on the crowdworker data are computed, such as verified model error rate (vMER) (Nie et al., 2020). Crowdworker example leaderboards are displayed.

**A train file leaderboard:** Task owners can enable users to upload training data files for the automatic creation, training, and evaluation of models in our evaluation cloud.

**A dynamic and interactive model leaderboard (Ma et al., 2021):** Task owners can configure a leaderboard, selecting from a variety of metrics to determine model performance. Owners can also upload new datasets, which triggers automatic evaluation for all of the user-uploaded models. Every leaderboard model can be interacted with in real-time. See Figure 2 for an example.

**A model upload pipeline:** Once a new task goes live on Dynabench, our command line tool[3] allows anyone to create a handler script and upload models by following a few command line instructions. After models are uploaded, they are dockerized and deployed automatically. Models can be viewed on the leaderboard and put in-the-loop with crowdworkers for data collection.

### 3.1 Task Configuration

To become task owners, Dynabench users submit a short written proposal for their task which requires approval by an administrator. We are still developing procedures for how Dynabench accepts tasks;

[1] Although, any user can set up a new task that is a duplicate of an existing one, with a duplicate config file.

[2] `https://www.mturk.com`

[3] `https://github.com/facebookresearch/dynalab`

```
aggregation_metric:
  type: dynascore
perf_metric:
  type: squad_f1
  reference_name:
   ↪ answer
delta_metrics:
- type: fairness
- type: robustness
```

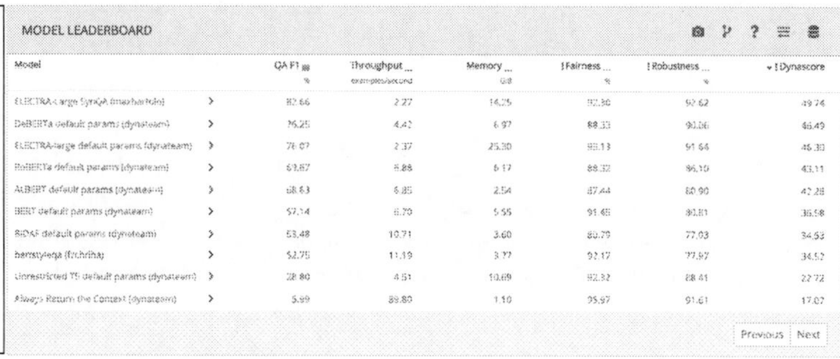


Figure 2: An example of a task config next to the generated model leaderboard. Only config fields that impact the leaderboard are shown. Throughput and memory do not need to be in the config; they are computed by default.

so far, we have reached out to have a discussion with the proposer before accepting their proposal and all non-spam proposals have been slated for acceptance. After approval, the task owner submits a task config file, which can be written in minutes. Once complete, the task is actively hosted on Dynabench; data collection, data validation, model hosting, and model evaluation starts immediately. A complete config file is the combination of a snippet in Figure 1 with that in Figure 2.

The task config is a YAML file which allows someone to encode the specifications for their task—it can be viewed as a lightweight declarative programming language. Task owners can specify:

*The datatypes of the task's inputs and outputs.* There are a variety to choose from, including String, String Selection, Multiclass, Multilabel, Probabilities, and Image. The datatype definition enables Dynatask to automatically construct the UIs for data collection, the dataset uploading and downloading infrastructure, and the model uploading and hosting infrastructure.

*A variety of metrics* to understand the task's datasets and models. Several metrics can currently be computed for the leaderboard: Macro F1, F1 for Visual Question Answering, F1 for Question Answering, Accuracy, BLEU, robustness and fairness (Ma et al., 2021), memory usage, and example throughput. Task owners select or propose an aggregation metric, which combines results across multiple datasets and metrics to arrive at a ranking for the leaderboard. Currently, the only supported aggregation metric is the Dynascore (Ma et al., 2021), which combines metrics across datasets based on microeconomic utility (Ethayarajh and Jurafsky, 2020) of user provided weights. Metrics can also be specified for model-in-the-loop data collection to judge whether a model's output matches that of a crowdworker (i.e., whether the model is "correct"). Dynatask supports a variety of such metrics, including a string F1 threshold (for outputs that are strings), exact match, and simply asking the crowdworker whether the model was correct.

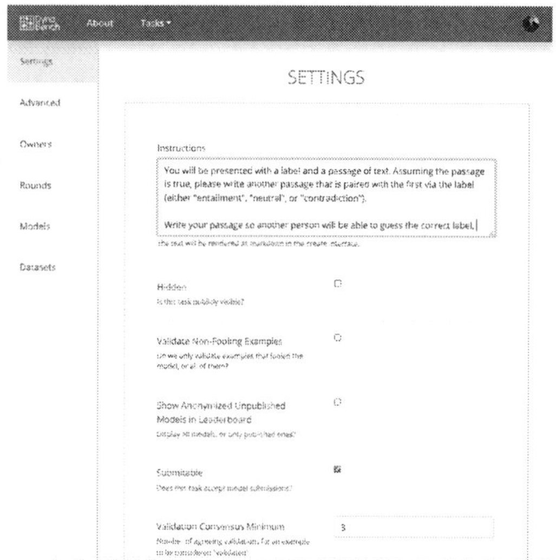


Figure 3: The task owner interface for ANLI.

*Other optional items*, such as messages and instructions that appear in crowdworker interfaces, and options for train-file leaderboards.

### 3.2 Options After Task Configuration

**Crowdworker Interfaces, Data Generation, and Data Evaluation:** Data collection interfaces are automatically hosted at `dynabench.org`. In order for Dynabench to scale, task owners source and pay crowdworkers themselves. If crowdworker management, compensation, and sourcing features are needed, an owner can clone Dynabench and run it on Mechanical Turk by hosting the data col-

Figure 4: A cross-section from a model card. The task owner has enabled downloading of model evaluation logs for each dataset via the buttons on the right.

lection frontend using Mephisto.[4] Task owners can upload context data for crowdworkers to use and download data collected from crowdworkers directly from the Dynabench web interface. Task owners can also initiate new rounds of data collection where they are free to upload entirely new contexts and models. As part of the data collection process, vMER, number of total collected examples, and number of validated examples are computed. Finally, task owners can alter instructions to crowdworkers at any time. They can also specify whether crowdworkers should validate non-model fooling examples, and provide a validation consensus threshold above which examples are considered fully validated. Figure 3 shows an example of the interface that task owners use to adjust settings.

**Model Submission, Interaction, and Evaluation:** Task owners can decide whether their task accepts model submissions, they can upload datasets for model evaluation, and they can download model evaluation logs for any dataset and model. Task owners can optionally allow users to download these logs to debug their models; see the example in Figure 4.

## 4 Decentralized Evaluation-As-A-Service

Most task owners currently use the centralized Dynabench evaluation and model deployment server. With Dynatask, however, we offer a decentralized evaluation feature that will increase the platform's flexibility even further. With this feature, task owners can set up a Dynabench model deployment and evaluation server or select an existing one. To set up a new server, an owner only needs to follow our documentation, creating an AWS account and installing some Dynabench code along the way. Distributed hosting of model building and evaluation enables Dynatask to scale: no one organization needs to fund hosting for all of the models on Dynabench, and every owner of a model deployment and evaluation server can flexibly upload or take down models to suit their budget. It is also designed with re-usability in mind: several tasks can share the same evaluation servers. Task owners do not need to do any setup if they have permission to use an existing evaluation server.

[4] https://github.com/facebookresearch/Mephisto

| Statistic | Count |
|---|---|
| Datasets Hosted | 191 |
| Unique Crowdworkers | 5,595 |
| Model Uploads | 589 |
| Data Collection Rounds | 38 |
| Tasks (incl. private) | 24 |
| Examples Collected | 559,229 |
| Example Validations | 436,922 |

Table 1: Current Dynabench statistics.

## 5 Case Studies of Tasks Enabled so Far

Tables 1 and 2 provide an overview of Dynabench so far. In this section, we report on some use cases. Most of the following projects (besides Image Labelling and Open Domain QA) were added to Dynabench before the introduction of Dynatask, which took months of coding in every case. With Dynatask, they can all be implemented in minutes.

*Hate Speech Detection:* There are a number of hate speech detection projects on Dynabench, where a model must label strings as hateful or not. Groups from Oxford, The Alan Turing Institute, The University of Sheffield, and Facebook AI own task pages that focus on collecting adversarial data (Vidgen et al., 2021), collecting emoji-based hate (Kirk et al., 2021), and evaluating models on a large number of hate speech data perturbations.

*Visual Question Answering:* To combat saturating datasets for the VQA task, which is about answering a question based on an image, Facebook AI and Tecnológico de Monterrey introduced AdVQA (Sheng et al., 2021) using Dynabench. The task's model leaderboard has an additional adversarial VQA dataset from Microsoft and Tsinghua (Li et al., 2021).

*Extractive Question Answering:* Groups from UCL and Facebook AI run SQuAD-style (Rajpurkar et al., 2016) extractive QA projects on Dynabench. The Adversarial QA (Bartolo et al., 2020) project resulted in a popular dataset on the Hugging Face hub (Lhoest et al., 2021). Follow-up

| Selected Dynabench Tasks | Context and Input Types | Output Types |
|---|---|---|
| Hate Speech Detection `https://dynabench.org/tasks/hs` | String, String, Multiclass | Multiclass, Probs |
| Visual QA `https://dynabench.org/tasks/vqa` | Image, String | String |
| Extractive QA `https://dynabench.org/tasks/qa` | String, String, String Select | String Select, Probs |
| Open Domain QA `https://dynabench.org/tasks/qb` | String, String, String | String, Probs |
| Natural Language Inference `https://dynabench.org/tasks/nli` | String, String, Multiclass | Multiclass, Probs |
| Sentiment Analysis `https://dynabench.org/tasks/sentiment` | String, String, Multiclass | Multiclass, Probs |
| Machine Translation `https://dynabench.org/tasks/flores` | String, String, String, String | String |
| Image Labelling `https://dynabench.org/tasks/vision-dataperf` | Image, Multilabel | Multilabel |

Table 2: IO types from the task config, for some tasks on Dynabench. Tasks share the same building blocks.

projects explored the generation of synthetic adversarial QA data (Bartolo et al., 2021a), generative assistants in the loop to help annotators create examples (Bartolo et al., 2021b), and a study of how adversarial model-in-the-loop training data affects generalization out of domain (Kaushik et al., 2021).

*Open-Domain Question Answering:* A team at Facebook AI and The University of Maryland has started a model-in-the-loop data collection effort for the Quizbowl task (Rodriguez et al., 2019; Wallace et al., 2019), as well as a model leaderboard. The task is open domain question answering, where both the question and answer are strings.

*Natural Language Inference:* The NLI dataset ANLI (Nie et al., 2020) is currently a popular dataset on Hugging Face datasets (Lhoest et al., 2021) and an ongoing Dynabench project. Groups from Facebook AI, UC Berkeley, and UNC have set up additional NLI projects on distinct Dynabench task pages. These projects have ranged from an analysis of the contents of adversarially collected development sets (Williams et al., 2022), to an explication of the benefits of dynamic adversarial data collection over multiple rounds (Wallace et al., 2021), to model and leaderboard hosting for a large number of robustness-perturbed NLI datasets.

*Sentiment Analysis:* In later rounds of their work, a team at Stanford used Dynabench to create a new adversarial sentiment analysis dataset, called Dynasent (Potts et al., 2020). They added prompts to their data collection interfaces to encourage crowdworkers to generate naturalistic and diverse data.

*Large-Scale Machine Translation:* The Workshop on Machine Translation (Wenzek et al., 2021) organizers created a Dynabench task page and hosted the FLORES benchmark competition (Goyal et al., 2021) of over 10,000 language pairs. It featured competitors from Microsoft, Huawei, Tencent, and Facebook, and individual competitors. The result of the competition was a BLEU increase of over 10 points on the full task. The owners used Dynabench for its leaderboard, model upload, and evaluation-as-a-service feature, without collecting data on the platform yet.

*Image Labelling:* DataPerf (Mattson et al., 2022) is a working group of the non-profit ML Commons, which focuses on dataset benchmarking for general AI. For their image labelling task hosted on Dynabench, they configured their task via the task config to accept training data file uploads. Users upload train files and models are automatically trained against them and evaluated in the evaluation cloud.

## 6 Conclusion

We introduced Dynatask, a collection of open source features in the Dynabench platform that empowers anyone to create and own a task on Dynabench with only a short config file. Dynabench started as an NLP project with only four English-only tasks. Since then, Dynatask has helped researchers produce several datasets and host competitions, expanding scalably into multimodal and multilingual domains with owners from various corners of the AI community. Dynatask offers the functionalities of Dynabench to the broader research community by allowing them to easily create and host new AI tasks on the platform: it provides a one-stop shop for constructing datasets with or without models in the loop, hosting challenges and competitions, investigating the effects of models in the loop, characterizing distributional shift and continual learning, exploring annotator efficiency and expertise, and improving model robustness through collaboration with humans.

Finally, Dynabench is an open source, community-driven effort. Anyone who wants to add a new input/output type, a new metric, or any other new feature, need only submit a pull request. We hope that our our work can help enable new exciting scientific progress in data-centric AI research in general and dynamic (adversarial) data collection in particular.

## References


Max Bartolo, Alastair Roberts, Johannes Welbl, Sebastian Riedel, and Pontus Stenetorp. 2020. Beat the AI: Investigating adversarial human annotation for reading comprehension. *TACL*.

Max Bartolo, Tristan Thrush, Robin Jia, Sebastian Riedel, Pontus Stenetorp, and Douwe Kiela. 2021a. Improving question answering model robustness with synthetic adversarial data generation. In *EMNLP*.

Max Bartolo, Tristan Thrush, Sebastian Riedel, Pontus Stenetorp, Robin Jia, and Douwe Kiela. 2021b. Models in the loop: Aiding crowdworkers with generative annotation assistants. In *arXiv preprint arXiv:2112.09062*.

Samuel R. Bowman, Gabor Angeli, Christopher Potts, and Christopher D. Manning. 2015. A large annotated corpus for learning natural language inference. In *EMNLP*.

Jia Deng, Wei Dong, Richard Socher, Li-Jia Li, Kai Li, and Li Fei-Fei. 2009. Imagenet: A large-scale hierarchical image database. In *CVPR*.

Kawin Ethayarajh and Dan Jurafsky. 2020. Utility is in the eye of the user: A critique of NLP leaderboards. In *EMNLP*.

John Godfrey, Edward Holliman, and Jane McDaniel. 1992. Switchboard: telephone speech corpus for research and development. In *ICASSP*.

Naman Goyal, Cynthia Gao, Vishrav Chaudhary, Peng-Jen Chen, Guillaume Wenzek, Da Ju, Sanjana Krishnan, Marc'Aurelio Ranzato, Francisco Guzman, and Angela Fan. 2021. The flores-101 evaluation benchmark for low-resource and multilingual machine translation. In *arXiv preprint arXiv:2106.03193*.

Alon Halevy, Peter Norvig, and Fernando Pereira. 2009. The unreasonable effectiveness of data. *IEEE Intelligent Systems*.

Divyansh Kaushik, Douwe Kiela, Zachary C Lipton, and Wen tau Yih. 2021. On the efficacy of adversarial data collection for question answering: Results from a large-scale randomized study. In *ACL-IJCNLP*.

Douwe Kiela, Max Bartolo, Yixin Nie, Divyansh Kaushik, Atticus Geiger, Zhengxuan Wu, Bertie Vidgen, Grusha Prasad, Amanpreet Singh, Pratik Ringshia, Zhiyi Ma, Tristan Thrush, Sebastian Riedel, Zeerak Waseem, Pontus Stenetorp, Robin Jia, Mohit Bansal, Christopher Potts, and Adina Williams. 2021. Dynabench: Rethinking Benchmarking in NLP. In *NAACL*.

Hannah Rose Kirk, Bertram Vidgen, Paul Röttger, Tristan Thrush, and Scott A Hale. 2021. Hatemoji: A test suite and adversarially-generated dataset for benchmarking and detecting emoji-based hate. In *arXiv preprint arXiv:2108.05921*.

Yann LeCun, Corinna Cortes, and Christopher Burges. 1998. The mnist database of handwritten digits.

Quentin Lhoest, Albert Villanova del Moral, Yacine Jernite, Abhishek Thakur, Patrick von Platen, Suraj Patil, Julien Chaumond, Mariama Drame, Julien Plu, Lewis Tunstall, Joe Davison, Mario Šaško, Gunjan Chhablani, Bhavitvya Malik, Simon Brandeis, Teven Le Scao, Victor Sanh, Canwen Xu, Nicolas Patry, Angelina McMillan-Major, Philipp Schmid, Sylvain Gugger, Clément Delangue, Théo Matussière, Lysandre Debut, Stas Bekman, Pierric Cistac, Thibault Goehringer, Victor Mustar, François Lagunas, Alexander Rush, and Thomas Wolf. 2021. Datasets: A community library for natural language processing. In *EMNLP: System Demonstrations*.

Linjie Li, Jie Lei, Zhe Gan, and Jingjing Liu. 2021. Adversarial VQA: A new benchmark for evaluating the robustness of VQA models. In *ICCV*.

Sasha Luccioni, Yacine Jernite, and Meg Mitchell. 2021. Hugging face data measurements tool.

Zhiyi Ma, Kawin Ethayarajh, Tristan Thrush, Somya Jain, Ledell Wu, Robin Jia, Christopher Potts, Adina Williams, and Douwe Kiela. 2021. Dynaboard: An evaluation-as-a-service platform for holistic next-generation benchmarking. In *NeurIPS*.

Peter Mattson, Cody Coleman, Ce Zhang, Praveen Paritosh, Vijay Janapa Reddi, Douwe Kiela, Greg Diamos, Carole-Jean Wu, Sabri Eyuboglu, Joaquin Vanschoren, William Gaviria Rojas, Tariq Kane, Bojan Karlas, Lynn He, Lora Aroyo, Colby Banbury, Mark Mazumder, Bilge Acun, Newsha Ardalani, Tristan Thrush, Adina Williams, Amirata Ghorbani, Emmett Goodman, and Serena Yeung. 2022. Dataperf: Benchmarking data for better ml. In *Forthcoming*.

Andrew Ng, Lora Aroyo, Greg Diamos, Cody Coleman, Vijay Janapa Reddi, Joaquin Vanschoren, Carole-Jean Wu, Sharon Zhou, and Lynn He. 2021. [link].

Yixin Nie, Adina Williams, Emily Dinan, Mohit Bansal, Jason Weston, and Douwe Kiela. 2020. Adversarial NLI: A new benchmark for natural language understanding. In *ACL*.

Amandalynne Paullada, Inioluwa Deborah Raji, Emily M Bender, Emily Denton, and Alex Hanna. 2021. Data and its (dis) contents: A survey of dataset development and use in machine learning research. *Patterns*.

Christopher Potts, Zhengxuan Wu, Atticus Geiger, and Douwe Kiela. 2020. DynaSent: A dynamic benchmark for sentiment analysis. *arXiv preprint arXiv:2012.15349*.

Pranav Rajpurkar, Jian Zhang, Konstantin Lopyrev, and Percy Liang. 2016. SQuAD: 100,000+ questions for machine comprehension of text. In *EMNLP*.

Pedro Rodriguez, Shi Feng, Mohit Iyyer, He He, and Jordan Boyd-Graber. 2019. Quizbowl: The case for incremental question answering. In *arXiv preprint arXiv:1904.04792*.

Nithya Sambasivan, Shivani Kapania, Hannah Highfill, Diana Akrong, Praveen Paritosh, and Lora M. Aroyo. 2021. "everyone wants to do the model work, not the data work": Data cascades in high-stakes AI. In *CHI Conference on Human Factors in Computing Systems*.

David Schlangen. 2021. Targeting the benchmark: On methodology in current natural language processing research. In *ACL-IJCNLP: Short Papers*.

Sasha Sheng, Amanpreet Singh, Vedanuj Goswami, Jose Alberto Lopez Magana, Tristan Thrush, Wojciech Galuba, Devi Parikh, and Douwe Kiela. 2021. Human-adversarial visual question answering. In *NeurIPS*.

Bertie Vidgen, Tristan Thrush, Zeerak Waseem, and Douwe Kiela. 2021. Learning from the worst: Dynamically generated datasets to improve online hate detection. In *ACL*.

Kiri Wagstaff. 2012. Machine learning that matters. In *ICML*.

Eric Wallace, Pedro Rodriguez, Shi Feng, Ikuya Yamada, and Jordan Boyd-Graber. 2019. Trick me if you can: Human-in-the-loop generation of adversarial examples for question answering. In *TACL*.

Eric Wallace, Adina Williams, Robin Jia, and Douwe Kiela. 2021. Analyzing dynamic adversarial training data in the limit. In *arXiv preprint arXiv:2110.08514*.

Alex Wang, Yada Pruksachatkun, Nikita Nangia, Amanpreet Singh, Julian Michael, Felix Hill, Omer Levy, and Samuel R. Bowman. 2019. Superglue: A stickier benchmark for general-purpose language understanding systems. In *NeurIPS*.

Alex Wang, Amanpreet Singh, Julian Michael, Felix Hill, Omer Levy, and Samuel Bowman. 2018. Glue: A multi-task benchmark and analysis platform for natural language understanding. In *BlackboxNLP at EMNLP*.

Guillaume Wenzek, Vishrav Chaudhary, Angela Fan, Sahir Gomez, Naman Goyal, Somya Jain, Douwe Kiela, Tristan Thrush, and Francisco Guzmán. 2021. Findings of the wmt 2021 shared task on large-scale multilingual machine translation. In *WMT*.

Adina Williams, Nikita Nangia, and Samuel R Bowman. 2017. A broad-coverage challenge corpus for sentence understanding through inference. In *arXiv preprint arXiv:1704.05426*.

Adina Williams, Tristan Thrush, and Douwe Kiela. 2022. ANLIzing the adversarial natural language inference dataset. In *SCiL*.

# DataLab: A Platform for Data Analysis and Intervention

**Yang Xiao♣*, Jinlan Fu★, Weizhe Yuan♠, Vijay Viswanathan♠, Zhoumianze Liu♣, Yixin Liu▲, Graham Neubig♠†, Pengfei Liu♠†**

♠Carnegie Mellon University, ♣Fudan University, ★National University of Singapore,
▲Yale University, †Inspired Cognition

## Abstract

Despite data's crucial role in machine learning, most existing tools and research tend to focus on systems on top of existing data rather than how to interpret and manipulate data. In this paper, we propose DataLab, a unified data-oriented platform that not only allows users to interactively analyze the characteristics of data, but also provides a standardized interface for different data processing operations. Additionally, in view of the ongoing proliferation of datasets, DataLab has features for dataset recommendation and global vision analysis that help researchers form a better view of the data ecosystem. So far, DataLab covers 1,715 datasets and 3,583 of its transformed version (e.g., hyponyms replacement ) , where 728 datasets support various analyses (e.g., with respect to gender bias) with the help of 140M samples annotated by 318 feature functions.[1] DataLab is under active development and has been recently upgraded based on reviewers' constructive suggestions.[2] **We have released a wealth of resources** to meet the diverse needs of researchers: *web platform*,[3] open-sourced code of web platform,[4] web API, open-sourced SDK,[5] *PyPI* published package,[6] and online documentation.[7]

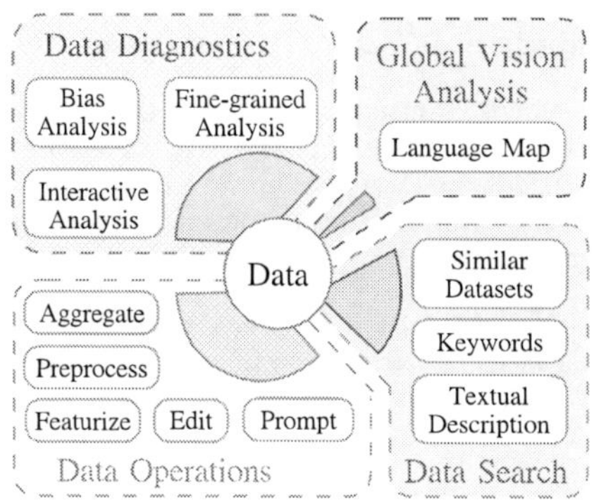


Figure 1: Overview of DataLab functionality

## 1 Introduction

Datasets power modern natural language processing (NLP) systems, playing an essential role in model training, evaluation, and deployment (Paullada et al., 2021). Furthermore, methods to process data and understand have been subject to much research, including on topics such as data augmentation (Fadaee et al., 2017; Feng et al., 2021), adversarial evaluation (Jia and Liang, 2017; Ribeiro et al., 2021), bias analysis (Zhao et al., 2018a; Blodgett et al., 2020), and prompt-based learning (Liu et al., 2021b). Despite the critical role of data in NLP, the majority of open-source tooling regarding NLP has focused on methods to *build models given data*, rather than to *analyze and intervene upon the data itself*. In this paper, we present DataLab, a unified platform that allows NLP researchers to perform a number of data-related tasks in an efficient and easy-to-use manner:

(1) **Data Diagnostics**: While a significant amount of research has focused on interpreting the outputs of machine learning systems (Lipton, 2018; Belinkov and Glass, 2019), data deserves deeper understanding as a first-class citizen of the machine learning ecosystem. DataLab allows for analysis and understanding of data to uncover undesirable traits such as hate speech, gender bias, or label imbalance (as shown in Fig.1 and § 3.1).

(2) **Operation Standardization**: There are a num-

*Work done during a remote research collaboration with CMU

†Corresponding author

[1]Users can also customize their favored feature functions using DataLab SDK.

[2]Recent update: https://datalab.nlpedia.ai/update

[3]http://datalab.nlpedia.ai/

[4]https://github.com/ExpressAI/DataLab_web

[5]https://github.com/ExpressAI/DataLab

[6]https://pypi.org/project/datalabs/

[7]https://expressai.github.io/DataLab/



*Proceedings of the 60th Annual Meeting of the Association for Computational Linguistics*
*System Demonstrations*, pages 182 - 195

| Aspects | Numbers |
|---|---|
| Tasks/Languages | 142/331 |
| Features/Prompts | 318/1007 |
| Plain/Diagnostic Datasets | 1,715/3,583 |
| Annotated Datasets | 728 |
| Annotated Samples | 139,570,057 |

Table 1: Key statistics of DATALAB. "Diagnostic Dataset" refers to a dataset obtained by applying transformations to the original version.[9] "Annotated" indicates datasets or samples where we compute features to obtain additional information that is not originally present in the dataset.

ber of well-designed packages for data-oriented operations such as preprocessing (Loper and Bird, 2002; Manning et al., 2014; Kudo, 2020) or editing (Ribeiro et al., 2021; Dhole et al., 2021). In practice, however, the diversity of requirements makes it necessary for users to install a variety of packages that use different data processing interfaces. This (a) reduces the efficiency of development, (b) can confuse users (e.g., not knowing what preprocessing methods are appropriate for a given dataset?), and (c) is detrimental for reproducibility (Marie et al., 2021). DATALAB provides and standardizes a large number of data processing operations, assigning each operation a unique identifier, to mitigate these issues (§ 3.2).

(3) **Data Search** An important question in practice is which datasets to use in a given scenario, given the huge proliferation of datasets in recent years.[8] DATALAB provides a semantic dataset search tool to help identify appropriate datasets (§ 3.3).

(4) **Global Analysis** Beyond individual datasets, analyzing the entire ecosystem of existing datasets as a whole can yield insights. From a birds-eye view, we can get a clearer picture: *where we are* and *where efforts should be focused* to avoid systemic inequalities (Blodgett et al., 2020; Blasi et al., 2021). DATALAB provides tools to perform similar global analyses over a variety of datasets (§ 3.4).

With the above use cases in mind, DATALAB focuses on the following design principles:

- **Broad-coverage**: DATALAB is designed to cover the majority of NLP tasks, and imports data from a very large number of plain datasets and diagnostic ones as shown in Table 1.[10]
- **Interpretable**: DATALAB has annotated statistical information for many datasets (728 datasets, 139,570,057 samples) that is not originally included in the dataset. These features can help researchers and developers better understand datasets before use, and help data creators improve data quality (e.g., removing artifacts, bias)
- **Unified**: One of the main goals of DATALAB is to unify different data analysis and processing operations into one platform and SDK. To achieve this goal, we design a generalized typology for data and operations (Figure 2).
- **Interactive**: DATALAB makes data exploration, assessment, and processing more accessible and efficient (real-time search, comparison, filtering, **generation of dataset diagnostic reports**). DATALAB can also be used as an off-the-shelf *annotation platform* where some missing yet important crowdsourcable information can be contributed by users.
- **Inspirational**: DATALAB's global view of datasets makes it possible to inspire new research directions, e.g. by (i) finding more appropriate datasets as shown in §3.3 (ii) tracking the global status of dataset development and identifying future directions as illustrated in §3.4.

## 2 Related Work

**Toolkits for NLP Pipelines** There are a wealth of toolkits that support the processing of various NLP tasks, making it easier to build a composable NLP workflow. Typical examples are NLTK (Loper and Bird, 2002), NLPCurate (Clarke et al., 2012), Stanford CoreNLP (Manning et al., 2014), AllenNLP (Gardner et al., 2018), SpaCy (Honnibal and Montani, 2017), GluonNLP (Guo et al., 2020), Forte (Liu et al., 2021c), HuggingFace (Lhoest et al., 2021).

In contrast to these toolkits, DATALAB focuses on data analysis, bias diagnostics, and standardization of data-related operations. Moreover, besides providing the SDK, DATALAB also provides a web-based interactive platform, featuring hundreds of datasets and millions of additional annotations w.r.t. diverse features. KYD (Google, 2021) also provides a web platform for data analysis but it mainly focuses on image data. ExplainaBoard (Liu et al., 2021a) presents an analysis platform while it focuses on system diagnostics.

[8] According to Papers With Code, the number of AI-related academic datasets has doubled in the past two years.

[9] We collect diagnostic datasets by performing an extensive literature review and searching for existing works that released diagnostic samples from different tasks.

[10] Details can be found in Appendix.

**Standardization by Community Wisdom** In ML in general and NLP in particular, researchers have been paying increasing attention to analyzing and improving systems from the perspective of data. In NLP, one major challenge in data processing is the diversity of data formats (e.g., *CONLL*, *BRAT*), task types (e.g., classification, generation) and design considerations (e.g., which types of preprocessing or augmentation) hinders the establishment of a unified platform. Recently, however, researchers in the field are actively trying to alleviate this problem by allowing community members to collectively contribute data-related operations on the same set of code frameworks, and eventually build a data processing platform around those operations. For example, HuggingFace (Lhoest et al., 2021) and Tensorflow (TFData, 2021) Datasets, where researchers in the community contribute data loaders for different tasks and datasets. In XL-Augmentor (Dhole et al., 2021) and Prompt Sourcing (Sanh et al., 2021) different data transformations or prompts are crowdsourced respectively.

After seeing this implicit pattern, we ask, can we have a more general platform above to unify all of these different operations? DATALAB makes a step towards this goal by not only focusing on how to unify data loader interfaces like Huggingface and Tensorflow have done, but also unifying data operations and analysis.

## 3 DATALAB

In this section we detail four major varieties of functionality provided by DATALAB.

### 3.1 Data Diagnostics

Data diagnostics aim to provide users with a comprehensive picture of data through various statistical analyses, enabling better model designs.

#### 3.1.1 Fine-grained Analysis

Fine-grained analysis aims to answer the question: *what are the characteristics of a dataset?* Existing works have shown its advantages in better system designs (Zhong et al., 2019; Fu et al., 2020b; Tejaswin et al., 2021) . Conceptually, this analysis over various dimensions can be performed over each data point (i.e. sample-level) or whole datasets (i.e. dataset-level). These are either generic (*text length* at sample-level or *the average text length* at corpus-level) or task-specific (for summarization: *summary compression* (Chen et al., 2020) or *the average of summary compression*). We detail the features utilized for fine-grained analysis in Appendix.

One key contribution of DATALAB is that we not only design rich sample-level and dataset-level features, but also compute and store those features in a database for easy browsing. As shown in Table 1, so far, we have designed more than 300 features and computed features for 140M samples.

#### 3.1.2 Bias Analysis

The research question to be answered by bias analysis is: *Does the dataset contain potential bias (e.g., artifacts, gender bias)?* Bias problems have been discussed extensively in NLP (Zhao et al., 2018a; Blodgett et al., 2020), and we argue that establishing a unified platform for data bias analysis can more efficiently identify or prevent (for data creators) data bias problems. For example, through the artifact analysis, users can know the shortcut provided by the dataset for model training and be inspired to design more robust systems. So far, DATALAB supports three types of bias analysis.

**Artifact Identification** As observed in many previous works (Gururangan et al., 2018; McCoy et al., 2019), artifacts commonly exist in datasets, which provide shortcuts for model learning and therefore reduce its robustness. DATALAB allows researchers to easily identify potential artifacts in a dataset using the features we have pre-computed for each sample. Specifically, we use PMI (Pointwise mutual information) (Bouma, 2009) to detect whether there is an association between two features (e.g. sentence length vs. label). We detail this method using an example in Appendix.[11]

**Gender Bias Analysis** Gender bias is a prevalent social phenomenon. In this work, we introduce a multidimensional gender biased dictionary[12] used by Dinan et al. (2020) to measure the degree of gender bias in a dataset. Given a dictionary $D_1$ of female names and a dictionary $D_2$ of male names. Suppose a dataset A with $N$ samples has $n_1$ name appearing in $D_1$ and $n_2$ in $D_2$. Following Zhao et al. (2018b), we can calculate the female bias for dataset A as $n_1/N$; the male bias as $n_2/N$.

**Hate Speech Analysis** Hate speech (Badjatiya et al., 2017) can lead to a "dehumanizing effect"

[11] https://expressai.github.io/DataLab/docs/WebUI/bias_analysis_for_artifacts

[12] huggingface.gender_bias

| Aspect | Functionality | Input | Example Output | |
|---|---|---|---|---|
| Diagnostics | Fine-grained Analysis | One dataset | 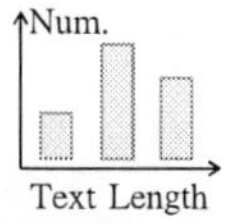  | **Characteristic histogram**: The bar chart on the left shows the distribution of the number of samples of different lengths in a dataset. |
| | Bias Analysis | One dataset |   | **Bias pie chart**: The pie chart on the left shows the hate speech bias of a dataset. The orange portion on the right is the percentage of the data samples containing hate speech, while the green portion on the left is the rest. |
| | Interactive Analysis | Multiple datasets | 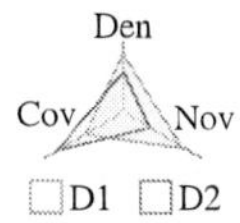  | **Comparison spider chart**: The spider diagram on the left shows the differences between two datasets (D1 and D2) in three dimensions: `Den`: density, `Nov`: novelty, `Cov`: coverage. |
| Operations | Aggregate, Edit, Featurize, Prompt, Preprocess | One dataset | 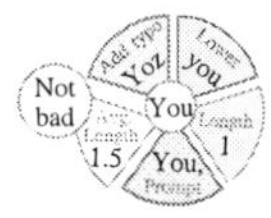  | **Statistics or transformed datasets**: The figure here shows five example operations (one for each category) computed on either one sample (`You`) or the whole dataset (`You` and `Not bad`). |
| Data Search | Search | Keywords, textual descriptions, similar dataset |   | **Related datasets**: The example on the left uses the keyword `Summarization` to search for recommended datasets. . |
| Global Vision | Language Map | Multiple datasets |  | **Heatmap**: We use a heatmap to show how many datasets are available for each country in terms of the languages people speak in that country. |

Table 2: A graphical breakdown of the functionality of DATALAB.

that harms people's mental health by undermining empathy (Tsesis, 2002). We make a first step by following Davidson et al. (2017), classifying the samples into *hate speech*, *offensive language* and *neither* categorizing by the "hatesonar" tool.[13] Users are also allowed to customized other hate speech models using DATALAB SDK. We also averaged the offensiveness of all samples in a dataset to analyze the hate speech bias of the dataset.[14]

### 3.1.3 Interactive Analysis

Interactive analysis aims to meet users' customized data analysis requirements in real time. Although interactivity is present in many aspects of DATALAB, we highlight here its use in three scenarios that make data analysis more accessible. (1) Users can choose two datasets they are interested in and align them for comparative analysis over different dimensions, as shown in Table 2. (2) Users can upload their own datasets and DATALAB will generate diagnostic reports for comprehensive analysis and evaluation of the datasets. (3) Users can contribute some missing metadata information by directly editing in the web interface.

## 3.2 Data Operations

Another key feature of DATALAB is the standardization of different data operations into a unified format to satisfy different data processing requirements in one place. To this end, we devised a general typology for the concepts of data and operation as shown in Figure 2 and curated schemas for these objects. For the operation schema, we introduced (i) "operation id": so that researchers can report them papers for easy re-implementation for follow-up research. (ii) "contributor" to credit those who contributed to the operation. Notably, user-defined operations are also supported (we give an example in Appendix).

[13] pypi.org.hatesonar

[14] Note that deciding whether a sentence contains toxic language is a complex task, which may involve the confounding effects of dialect and the social identity of a speaker Sap et al. (2019), and future iterations of DataLab may use meta-data of datasets to further perform this analysis intersectionally. We have also stored the results of hate speech detector for all samples to make the analysis process more transparent and well-grounded and users could browse them and report error cases.

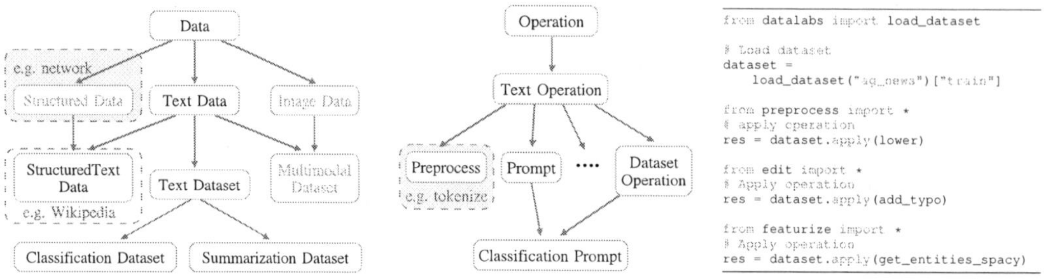


(a) Data (b) Operation (c) SDK

Figure 2: Typology of Data and Operations. Gray-white text (e.g., *Image Data*) indicates that the data type has been defined but we have not yet added data of that type.

**Preprocessing** Data preprocessing (e.g., tokenization) is an indispensable step in training deep learning and machine learning models, and the quality of the dataset directly affects the learning of models. Currently, DATALAB supports both general preprocessing functions and task-specific ones, which are built based on different sources, such as SpaCy (Honnibal and Montani, 2017), NLTK (Loper and Bird, 2002), Huggingface tokenizer.[15]

**Editing** Editing aims to apply certain transformations to a given text, which spans multiple important applications in NLP, for example (i) adversarial evaluation (Ribeiro et al., 2021; Wang et al., 2021), which usually requires diverse perturbations on test samples to test the robustness of a system. (ii) Data augmentation (Wei and Zou, 2019; Dhole et al., 2021; Feng et al., 2021). Essentially, many of the methods for constructing augmented or diagnostic datasets involve some editing operation on the original dataset (e.g., named entity replacement in diagnostic dataset construction (Ribeiro et al., 2021), token deletion in data augmentation (Wei and Zou, 2019)). DATALAB provides a unified interface for data editing and users can easily apply to edit the data they are interested in.

**Featurizing** This operation aims to compute sample-level features of a given text. In DATALAB, in addition to designing some general feature functions (e.g. *get_length* operation calculates the length of the text.), we also customize some feature functions for specific tasks (e.g. *get_oracle* operation for the summarization task that calculates the oracle summary of the source text.).

[15]huggingface.tokenizers

**Aggregating** Aggregation operations are used to compute corpus-level statistics such as TF-IDF (Salton and Buckley, 1988), label distribution. Currently, DATALAB supports both generic aggregation operations applicable to any task and some customized ones for four NLP tasks (classification, summarization, extractive question answering and natural language inference).

**Prompting** Prompt-based learning (Liu et al., 2021b) has received considerable attention, as better utilization of pretrained language models benefits many NLP tasks. In practice, what makes a good prompt is a challenging question. We define the prompt schema as shown in fig. 3. The elements we included in a prompt cover diverse aspects including its features (e.g. length, shape, etc.), metadata (e.g. unique identifier, language, etc.), attributes (e.g. template, answers, etc.) as well as its performance w.r.t. different pre-trained language models and settings. The design can not only help researcher design prompts but also analyze what makes a good prompt.

So far, DATALAB covers 1007 prompts which can be applied to five types of tasks (topic classification, sentiment classification, sentence entailment, summarization, natural language inference), covering 309 datasets in total.

### 3.3 Data Search

Data search aims to answer the research question: which datasets should one use given a description of a research idea? As more datasets are proposed, there is an open question of how to choose the right dataset for a given application. DATALAB takes a step towards solving this problem by including semantic dataset search.

DATALAB data search takes a natural language

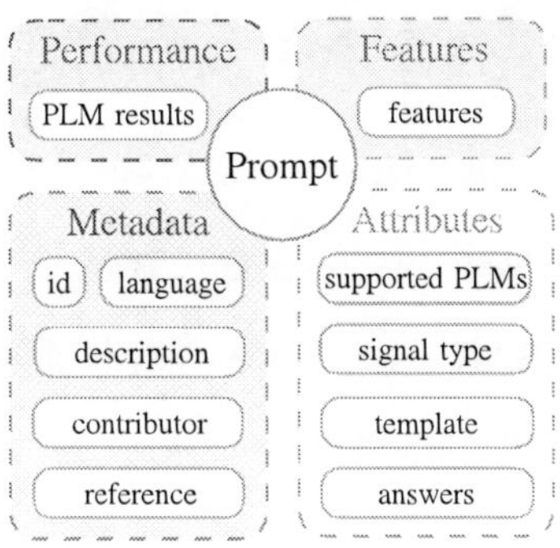


Figure 3: Prompt schema in DATALAB.

description of a research idea,[16] compares it with descriptions of thousands of datasets, and displays the datasets best matching the input (a detailed example is given in Figure 4). This retrieval system goes beyond keyword search by using semantic matching. The algorithm is described in a pending paper; we provide technical details in Appendix.

### 3.4 Global Vision Analysis

**Language Map: Which languages' datasets get less attention?** A language map is used to analyze which languages are more studied and which are less studied from a geographical view (Faisal et al., 2021), identifying potential systemic inequalities. Specifically, we first count how many datasets are available for each language. Then for each country we calculate a distribution over languages,[17] where the ratio of each language represents the proportion of people who speak that language. Finally, for each country, we can get the weighted average number of datasets available for it in terms of its spoken languages (see Appendix for details).

## 4 Case Study

We perform three case studies to show the utility of DATALAB and put more in the appendix.

**Artifacts** One famous example of a dataset artifact reported by Gururangan et al. (2018) (Figure 1) is that in NLI datasets, the length of the hypothesis sentence is closely associated with the assigned label of the premise-hypothesis pair. In fact, DATALAB is able to easily re-discover this artifact, and more. Fig. 4-(a) shows an analysis on the SNLI dataset (Bowman et al., 2015) between two features $\text{length}_{\text{hypothesis}}$ and label (entailment, neutral or contradiction). We can observe that, when $\text{length}_{\text{hypothesis}}$ is larger than 8.4, $\text{PMI}(\text{label}_{\text{neutral}}, \text{length}_{\text{hypothesis}}) > 0.28$, suggesting that "long hypotheses" tend to co-occur with the "neutral" label, even without consideration of the premise. Additionally, when $\text{length}_{\text{hypothesis}} \in [1, 4.7]$, $\text{PMI}(\text{label}_{\text{entailment}}, \text{length}_{\text{hypothesis}}) = 0.359$, implying that "short hypotheses" tend to co-occur with the label "entailment". However, this is not all; **we further observed more than ten potential artifacts on `SNLI` and another popular dataset `SST2`** (Socher et al., 2013) (see Appendix), which demonstrates the ability of DATALAB to efficiently identify these artifacts.

**Systemic Inequalities** Fig. 4-(b) is a statistic of the degree to which languages are studied from a global (w.r.t each country in the world) perspective, with a darker red indicating more datasets studied/-constructed for the languages spoken in a given country, and darker blue indicating the opposite. Unsurprisingly, we observe that *English* is the most studied (large English-speaking countries like the US, Canada, and UK are in dark red), which also benefits those English-speaking African countries (e.g. Madagascar, Uganda, and Libya are in red.). We also observe that the languages spoken in `bm` (Mali), `ee` (Ghana), and `kr` (Niger) are rarely studied, as can be seen from our language map that these three languages have a value of 0.

**Gender Bias** We also showcase the gender bias analysis on `SNLI` as illustrate in Fig. 5. We can find that the samples in the `SNLI` dataset contain more male-oriented words than females ($\text{male}(0.62) > \text{female}(0.38)$).

**Dataset Recommendation** Fig. 4-(c) presents a case study of using our DATALAB to get recommended datasets. When a user enters a research idea "*I want to train a model that can recognize the positive and negative sentiments contained in a beer review.*", DATALAB returns the beer review dataset `BeerAdvocate` (McAuley and Leskovec, 2013) first in the interface, which is a precise result since the dataset consists of beer reviews from beeradvocate.[18]

[16] DATALAB also supports keyword queries as input. However we find the added context provided by natural language descriptions improves search quality.

[17] We refer to some official statistics from this link.

[18] https://www.beeradvocate.com/

| label / hypothesis_length (all count:50000) | 1~4.7 (count:7104) | 4.7~8.4 (count:28726) | 8.4~12.1 (count:10893) | 12.1~15.8 (count:2216) | 15.8~19.5 (count:822) | 19.5~23.2 (count:178) | 23.2~26.9 (count:35) | 26.9~30.6 (count:15) | 30.6~34.3 (count:7) | 34.3~38.1 (count:4) |
|---|---|---|---|---|---|---|---|---|---|---|
| entailment (count:16705) | 0.359 | 0.057 | -0.380 | -0.548 | -0.451 | -0.502 | -0.156 | -0.513 | -0.156 | -0.290 |
| neutral (count:16512) | -0.388 | -0.122 | 0.280 | 0.483 | 0.469 | 0.627 | 0.443 | 0.702 | 0.548 | 0.415 |
| contradiction (count:16783) | -0.120 | 0.053 | -0.003 | -0.212 | -0.259 | -0.624 | -0.518 | -0.923 | -0.854 | -0.295 |

(a) PMI analysis between two features: hypothesis length and label for the SNLI

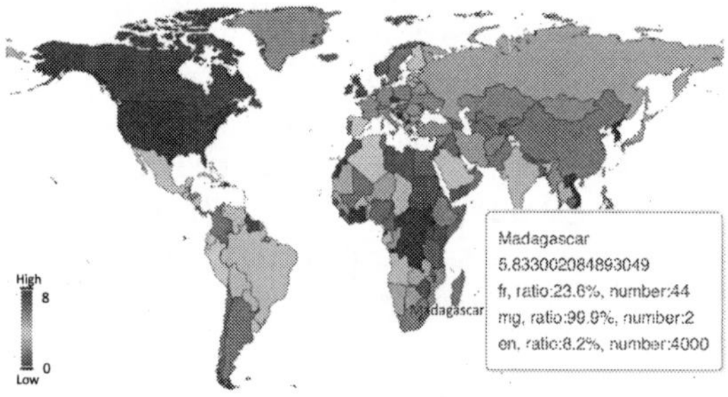


(b) Language map

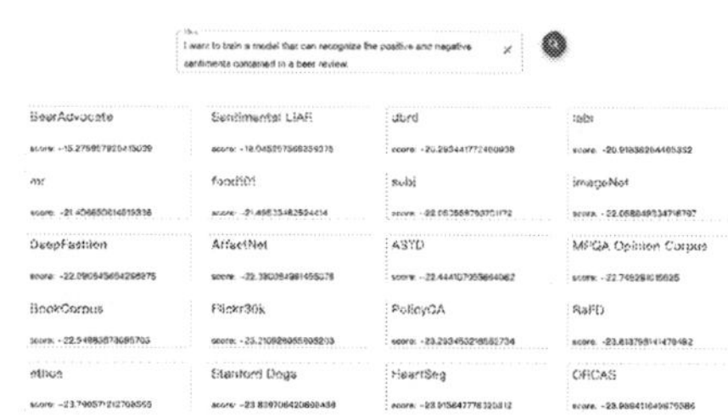

(c) Data recommendation

Figure 4: Case studies on artifact detection, systemic inequality, and dataset recommendation.

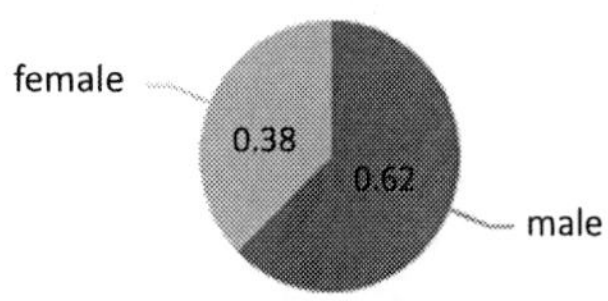


Figure 5: Gender bias analysis on SNLI.

## 5 Implications and Roadmap

DATALAB was born from our two visions (1) It is essential to standardize both the format of data and the interface of data-centric operations. (2) The standardization of data and operations allows more people in the community to contribute and share community wisdom. For example, in DATALAB, community researchers can easily contribute (1) new feature functions that enable us to conduct data analysis from more dimensions; (2) new datasets or the missing metadata. We hope that the unity of the platform can make it easier for *collective wisdom* to come into play.

In the future, we will extend DATALAB more broadly in terms of following perspectives: (1) index more data with different domains such as scientific and medical ones, and different modalities, such as image, video. (2) refine the current data typology over time, (3) add more built-in feature functions (e.g., labeling function (Ratner et al., 2020)). (4) introduce more effective data management methods into DATALAB, such as FAIR.[19]

## Acknowledgements

We thank all reviewers for their valuable comments and Antonis Anastasopoulos for sharing the mapping data between countries and languages, and thank Alissa Ostapenko, Yulia Tsvetkov, Jie Fu, Ziyun Xu, Chih-hao Wang, Lyuyang Hu, Yiran Chen, Zhengzheng Tang, Hiroaki Hayashi, Hector Liu, Xiachong Feng, Zhengfu He, Mingzhe Du, and Xiaodong Li for useful discussion and suggestions. This work was supported in part by Grant No. 2040926 of the US National Science Foundation, and the National Science Foundation of Singapore under its Industry Alignment Fund – Pre-positioning (IAF-PP) Funding Initiative. Any opinions, findings, conclusions, or recommendations expressed in this material are those of the authors and do not reflect the views of the National Research Foundation of Singapore and the US National Science Foundation.

## Ethics/Broader Impact Statement

If the platform works as expected, researchers, developers, and analysts can all benefit from it. Re-

[19] https://www.go-fair.org/fair-principles/

searchers can gain a deeper and broader understanding of the characteristics of the datasets, developers can more easily access the datasets and manipulate the data samples, and analysts can see some social insights from the datasets.

During the whole data analysis process, we tried to make it as transparent as possible, and the results of the analysis were well-grounded on sufficient evidence so that users could more reliably use it. Additionally, users are encouraged to report a case where the annotation results are not precise.

For those private datasets, we introduce three processing strategies for users: (1) users could flexibly use DATALAB SDK to deal with their data offline. (2) We introduce an account system[20] for users to set up a private space for their datasets. (3) We also open-source the code of DATALAB web platform[21] so that users can host this web service locally.

As no feature analysis method will ever be perfectly reliable,[22] to alleviate this issue, so far, DATALAB SDK provides several built-in feature functions for users to choose from and also make it customized by users. We are now working on benchmarking different feature functions in different domains of data so that users can have a better idea when choosing.

Currently, DATALAB only supports public datasets. In addition, knowing more about the characteristics of the test sets might make overfitting easier for model training. One possible approach is through multi-dataset evaluation, i.e., a good system should achieve good results across a series of different datasets.

DATALAB can privilege some datasets and data sources over others. To alleviate this problem, we introduce the dataset FINDER[23] functionality, where users can retrieve the dataset either from DATALAB and external resources like paperswithcode datasets[24] based on their requirement. Additionally, we will continue to keep the data corpus updated. For example, we recently added datasets from ACL2022.

Although DATALAB categorizes datasets into common tasks and paradigms, it still retains the original information provided by the creators of each dataset. For example, the text to be classified in `imdb` is named as "review" while in `ag_news` is named as "sentence". We introduce an intermediate variable[25] "text_column" to store the dataset-dependent naming information.

We appreciate any suggestions you have on how to make DATALAB better. Your issues are highly welcome,[26] and we will actively update.

[20] https://datalab.nlpedia.ai/user

[21] https://github.com/ExpressAI/DataLab_web

[22] Thank reviewers for raising the discussion of this issue.

[23] https://datalab.nlpedia.ai/dataset_recommendation

[24] https://paperswithcode.com/datasets

[25] https://github.com/ExpressAI/DataLab/tree/main/src/datalabs/tasks

[26] https://github.com/ExpressAI/DataLab/issues

## References


Pinkesh Badjatiya, Shashank Gupta, Manish Gupta, and Vasudeva Varma. 2017. Deep learning for hate speech detection in tweets. *CoRR*, abs/1706.00188.

Yonatan Belinkov and James Glass. 2019. Analysis methods in neural language processing: A survey. *Transactions of the Association for Computational Linguistics*, 7:49–72.

Damián Blasi, Antonios Anastasopoulos, and Graham Neubig. 2021. Systematic inequalities in language technology performance across the world's languages. *arXiv preprint arXiv:2110.06733*.

Su Lin Blodgett, Solon Barocas, Hal Daumé III, and Hanna Wallach. 2020. Language (technology) is power: A critical survey of "bias" in NLP. In *Proceedings of the 58th Annual Meeting of the Association for Computational Linguistics*, pages 5454–5476, Online. Association for Computational Linguistics.

Gerlof Bouma. 2009. Normalized (pointwise) mutual information in collocation extraction. *Proceedings of GSCL*, 30:31–40.

Samuel R. Bowman, Gabor Angeli, Christopher Potts, and Christopher D. Manning. 2015. A large annotated corpus for learning natural language inference. In *Proceedings of the 2015 Conference on Empirical Methods in Natural Language Processing*, pages 632–642, Lisbon, Portugal. Association for Computational Linguistics.

Isabel Cachola, Kyle Lo, Arman Cohan, and Daniel Weld. 2020. TLDR: Extreme summarization of scientific documents. In *Findings of the Association for Computational Linguistics: EMNLP 2020*, pages 4766–4777, Online. Association for Computational Linguistics.

Yiran Chen, Pengfei Liu, Ming Zhong, Zi-Yi Dou, Danqing Wang, Xipeng Qiu, and Xuanjing Huang. 2020. CDEvalSumm: An empirical study of cross-dataset evaluation for neural summarization systems. In

*Findings of the Association for Computational Linguistics: EMNLP 2020*, pages 3679–3691, Online. Association for Computational Linguistics.

James Clarke, Vivek Srikumar, Mark Sammons, and Dan Roth. 2012. An NLP curator (or: How I learned to stop worrying and love NLP pipelines). In *Proceedings of the Eighth International Conference on Language Resources and Evaluation (LREC'12)*, pages 3276–3283, Istanbul, Turkey. European Language Resources Association (ELRA).

Thomas Davidson, Dana Warmsley, Michael W. Macy, and Ingmar Weber. 2017. Automated hate speech detection and the problem of offensive language. In *Proceedings of the Eleventh International Conference on Web and Social Media, ICWSM 2017, Montréal, Québec, Canada, May 15-18, 2017*, pages 512–515. AAAI Press.

Jacob Devlin, Ming-Wei Chang, Kenton Lee, and Kristina Toutanova. 2019. BERT: pre-training of deep bidirectional transformers for language understanding. In *Proceedings of the 2019 Conference of the North American Chapter of the Association for Computational Linguistics: Human Language Technologies, NAACL-HLT 2019, Minneapolis, MN, USA, June 2-7, 2019, Volume 1 (Long and Short Papers)*, pages 4171–4186. Association for Computational Linguistics.

Kaustubh D Dhole, Varun Gangal, Sebastian Gehrmann, Aadesh Gupta, Zhenhao Li, Saad Mahamood, Abinaya Mahendiran, Simon Mille, Ashish Srivastava, Samson Tan, et al. 2021. Nl-augmenter: A framework for task-sensitive natural language augmentation. *arXiv preprint arXiv:2112.02721*.

Emily Dinan, Angela Fan, Ledell Wu, Jason Weston, Douwe Kiela, and Adina Williams. 2020. Multi-dimensional gender bias classification. *CoRR*, abs/2005.00614.

Marzieh Fadaee, Arianna Bisazza, and Christof Monz. 2017. Data augmentation for low-resource neural machine translation. In *Proceedings of the 55th Annual Meeting of the Association for Computational Linguistics (Volume 2: Short Papers)*, pages 567–573, Vancouver, Canada. Association for Computational Linguistics.

Fahim Faisal, Yinkai Wang, and Antonios Anastasopoulos. 2021. Dataset geography: Mapping language data to language users. *arXiv preprint arXiv:2112.03497*.

Steven Y. Feng, Varun Gangal, Jason Wei, Sarath Chandar, Soroush Vosoughi, Teruko Mitamura, and Eduard H. Hovy. 2021. A survey of data augmentation approaches for NLP. *CoRR*, abs/2105.03075.

Jinlan Fu, Pengfei Liu, and Graham Neubig. 2020a. Interpretable multi-dataset evaluation for named entity recognition. In *Proceedings of the 2020 Conference on Empirical Methods in Natural Language Processing, EMNLP 2020, Online, November 16-20, 2020*, pages 6058–6069. Association for Computational Linguistics.

Jinlan Fu, Pengfei Liu, Qi Zhang, and Xuanjing Huang. 2020b. RethinkCWS: Is Chinese word segmentation a solved task? In *Proceedings of the 2020 Conference on Empirical Methods in Natural Language Processing (EMNLP)*, pages 5676–5686, Online. Association for Computational Linguistics.

Matt Gardner, Joel Grus, Mark Neumann, Oyvind Tafjord, Pradeep Dasigi, Nelson F. Liu, Matthew Peters, Michael Schmitz, and Luke Zettlemoyer. 2018. AllenNLP: A deep semantic natural language processing platform. In *Proceedings of Workshop for NLP Open Source Software (NLP-OSS)*, pages 1–6, Melbourne, Australia. Association for Computational Linguistics.

Google. 2021. Explore datasets in know your data.

Jian Guo, He He, Tong He, Leonard Lausen, Mu Li, Haibin Lin, Xingjian Shi, Chenguang Wang, Junyuan Xie, Sheng Zha, et al. 2020. Gluoncv and gluonnlp: Deep learning in computer vision and natural language processing. *J. Mach. Learn. Res.*, 21(23):1–7.

Suchin Gururangan, Swabha Swayamdipta, Omer Levy, Roy Schwartz, Samuel R. Bowman, and Noah A. Smith. 2018. Annotation artifacts in natural language inference data. *CoRR*, abs/1803.02324.

Matthew Honnibal and Ines Montani. 2017. spaCy 2: Natural language understanding with Bloom embeddings, convolutional neural networks and incremental parsing. To appear.

Robin Jia and Percy Liang. 2017. Adversarial examples for evaluating reading comprehension systems. In *Proceedings of the 2017 Conference on Empirical Methods in Natural Language Processing*, pages 2021–2031, Copenhagen, Denmark. Association for Computational Linguistics.

Jeff Johnson, Matthijs Douze, and Hervé Jégou. 2017. Billion-scale similarity search with gpus. *arXiv preprint arXiv:1702.08734*.

Vladimir Karpukhin, Barlas Oguz, Sewon Min, Patrick Lewis, Ledell Wu, Sergey Edunov, Danqi Chen, and Wen-tau Yih. 2020. Dense passage retrieval for open-domain question answering. In *Proceedings of the 2020 Conference on Empirical Methods in Natural Language Processing (EMNLP)*, pages 6769–6781, Online. Association for Computational Linguistics.

Taku Kudo. 2020. Sentence piece. `https://github.com/google/sentencepiece`.

Quentin Lhoest, Albert Villanova del Moral, Yacine Jernite, Abhishek Thakur, Patrick von Platen, Suraj Patil, Julien Chaumond, Mariama Drame, Julien Plu, Lewis Tunstall, Joe Davison, Mario Sasko, Gunjan Chhablani, Bhavitvya Malik, Simon Brandeis, Teven Le Scao, Victor Sanh, Canwen Xu, Nicolas Patry, Angelina McMillan-Major, Philipp Schmid,

Sylvain Gugger, Clément Delangue, Théo Matussière, Lysandre Debut, Stas Bekman, Pierric Cistac, Thibault Goehringer, Victor Mustar, François Lagunas, Alexander M. Rush, and Thomas Wolf. 2021. Datasets: A community library for natural language processing. In *Proceedings of the 2021 Conference on Empirical Methods in Natural Language Processing: System Demonstrations, EMNLP 2021, Online and Punta Cana, Dominican Republic, 7-11 November, 2021*, pages 175–184. Association for Computational Linguistics.

Chin-Yew Lin. 2004. ROUGE: A package for automatic evaluation of summaries. In *Text Summarization Branches Out*, pages 74–81, Barcelona, Spain. Association for Computational Linguistics.

Zachary C Lipton. 2018. The mythos of model interpretability: In machine learning, the concept of interpretability is both important and slippery. *Queue*, 16(3):31–57.

Pengfei Liu, Jinlan Fu, Yang Xiao, Weizhe Yuan, Shuaichen Chang, Junqi Dai, Yixin Liu, Zihuiwen Ye, and Graham Neubig. 2021a. ExplainaBoard: An explainable leaderboard for NLP. In *Proceedings of the 59th Annual Meeting of the Association for Computational Linguistics and the 11th International Joint Conference on Natural Language Processing: System Demonstrations*, pages 280–289, Online. Association for Computational Linguistics.

Pengfei Liu, Weizhe Yuan, Jinlan Fu, Zhengbao Jiang, Hiroaki Hayashi, and Graham Neubig. 2021b. Pretrain, prompt, and predict: A systematic survey of prompting methods in natural language processing. *CoRR*, abs/2107.13586.

Zhengzhong Liu, Guanxiong Ding, Avinash Bukkittu, Mansi Gupta, Pengzhi Gao, Atif Ahmed, Shikun Zhang, Xin Gao, Swapnil Singhavi, Linwei Li, Wei Wei, Zecong Hu, Haoran Shi, Xiaodan Liang, Teruko Mitamura, Eric P. Xing, and Zhiting Hu. 2021c. A data-centric framework for composable NLP workflows. *CoRR*, abs/2103.01834.

Edward Loper and Steven Bird. 2002. Nltk: The natural language toolkit. *arXiv preprint cs/0205028*.

Christopher D Manning, Mihai Surdeanu, John Bauer, Jenny Rose Finkel, Steven Bethard, and David McClosky. 2014. The stanford corenlp natural language processing toolkit. In *Proceedings of 52nd annual meeting of the association for computational linguistics: system demonstrations*, pages 55–60.

Benjamin Marie, Atsushi Fujita, and Raphael Rubino. 2021. Scientific credibility of machine translation research: A meta-evaluation of 769 papers. In *Proceedings of the 59th Annual Meeting of the Association for Computational Linguistics and the 11th International Joint Conference on Natural Language Processing (Volume 1: Long Papers)*, pages 7297–7306, Online. Association for Computational Linguistics.

Julian John McAuley and Jure Leskovec. 2013. From amateurs to connoisseurs: modeling the evolution of user expertise through online reviews. In *Proceedings of the 22nd international conference on World Wide Web*, pages 897–908.

Tom McCoy, Ellie Pavlick, and Tal Linzen. 2019. Right for the wrong reasons: Diagnosing syntactic heuristics in natural language inference. In *Proceedings of the 57th Annual Meeting of the Association for Computational Linguistics*, pages 3428–3448, Florence, Italy. Association for Computational Linguistics.

Kishore Papineni, Salim Roukos, Todd Ward, and Wei-Jing Zhu. 2002. Bleu: a method for automatic evaluation of machine translation. In *Proceedings of the 40th Annual Meeting of the Association for Computational Linguistics, July 6-12, 2002, Philadelphia, PA, USA*, pages 311–318. ACL.

Amandalynne Paullada, Inioluwa Deborah Raji, Emily M Bender, Emily Denton, and Alex Hanna. 2021. Data and its (dis) contents: A survey of dataset development and use in machine learning research. *Patterns*, 2(11):100336.

Alexander Ratner, Stephen H. Bach, Henry R. Ehrenberg, Jason A. Fries, Sen Wu, and Christopher Ré. 2020. Snorkel: rapid training data creation with weak supervision. *VLDB J.*, 29(2-3):709–730.

Marco Túlio Ribeiro, Tongshuang Wu, Carlos Guestrin, and Sameer Singh. 2021. Beyond accuracy: Behavioral testing of NLP models with checklist (extended abstract). In *Proceedings of the Thirtieth International Joint Conference on Artificial Intelligence, IJCAI 2021, Virtual Event / Montreal, Canada, 19-27 August 2021*, pages 4824–4828. ijcai.org.

Brian Richards. 1987. Type/token ratios: what do they really tell us? *Journal of Child Language*, 14(2):201–209.

Gerard Salton and Christopher Buckley. 1988. Term-weighting approaches in automatic text retrieval. *Information processing & management*, 24(5):513–523.

Victor Sanh, Albert Webson, Colin Raffel, Stephen H. Bach, Lintang Sutawika, Zaid Alyafeai, Antoine Chaffin, Arnaud Stiegler, Teven Le Scao, Arun Raja, Manan Dey, M Saiful Bari, Canwen Xu, Urmish Thakker, Shanya Sharma Sharma, Eliza Szczechla, Taewoon Kim, Gunjan Chhablani, Nihal Nayak, Debajyoti Datta, Jonathan Chang, Mike Tian-Jian Jiang, Han Wang, Matteo Manica, Sheng Shen, Zheng Xin Yong, Harshit Pandey, Rachel Bawden, Thomas Wang, Trishala Neeraj, Jos Rozen, Abheesht Sharma, Andrea Santilli, Thibault Fevry, Jason Alan Fries, Ryan Teehan, Stella Biderman, Leo Gao, Tali Bers, Thomas Wolf, and Alexander M. Rush. 2021. Multitask prompted training enables zero-shot task generalization.

Maarten Sap, Dallas Card, Saadia Gabriel, Yejin Choi, and Noah A. Smith. 2019. The risk of racial bias in hate speech detection. In *Proceedings of the 57th Annual Meeting of the Association for Computational Linguistics*, pages 1668–1678, Florence, Italy. Association for Computational Linguistics.

Richard Socher, Alex Perelygin, Jean Wu, Jason Chuang, Christopher D. Manning, Andrew Ng, and Christopher Potts. 2013. Recursive deep models for semantic compositionality over a sentiment treebank. In *Proceedings of the 2013 Conference on Empirical Methods in Natural Language Processing*, pages 1631–1642, Seattle, Washington, USA. Association for Computational Linguistics.

Priyam Tejaswin, Dhruv Naik, and Pengfei Liu. 2021. How well do you know your summarization datasets? In *Findings of the Association for Computational Linguistics: ACL-IJCNLP 2021*, pages 3436–3449, Online. Association for Computational Linguistics.

TFData. 2021. Tensorflow datasets, a collection of ready-to-use datasets.

Alexander Tsesis. 2002. *Destructive messages: How hate speech paves the way for harmful social movements*, volume 27. NYU Press.

Xiao Wang, Qin Liu, Tao Gui, Qi Zhang, Yicheng Zou, Xin Zhou, Jiacheng Ye, Yongxin Zhang, Rui Zheng, Zexiong Pang, Qinzhuo Wu, Zhengyan Li, Chong Zhang, Ruotian Ma, Zichu Fei, Ruijian Cai, Jun Zhao, Xingwu Hu, Zhiheng Yan, Yiding Tan, Yuan Hu, Qiyuan Bian, Zhihua Liu, Shan Qin, Bolin Zhu, Xiaoyu Xing, Jinlan Fu, Yue Zhang, Minlong Peng, Xiaoqing Zheng, Yaqian Zhou, Zhongyu Wei, Xipeng Qiu, and Xuanjing Huang. 2021. TextFlint: Unified multilingual robustness evaluation toolkit for natural language processing. In *Proceedings of the 59th Annual Meeting of the Association for Computational Linguistics and the 11th International Joint Conference on Natural Language Processing: System Demonstrations*, pages 347–355, Online. Association for Computational Linguistics.

Jason W. Wei and Kai Zou. 2019. EDA: easy data augmentation techniques for boosting performance on text classification tasks. In *Proceedings of the 2019 Conference on Empirical Methods in Natural Language Processing and the 9th International Joint Conference on Natural Language Processing, EMNLP-IJCNLP 2019, Hong Kong, China, November 3-7, 2019*, pages 6381–6387. Association for Computational Linguistics.

Lee Xiong, Chuan Hu, Chenyan Xiong, Daniel Fernando Campos, and Arnold Overwijk. 2019. Open domain web keyphrase extraction beyond language modeling. In *EMNLP*.

Jieyu Zhao, Tianlu Wang, Mark Yatskar, Vicente Ordonez, and Kai-Wei Chang. 2018a. Gender bias in coreference resolution: Evaluation and debiasing methods. In *Proceedings of the 2018 Conference of the North American Chapter of the Association for Computational Linguistics: Human Language Technologies, NAACL-HLT, New Orleans, Louisiana, USA, June 1-6, 2018, Volume 2 (Short Papers)*, pages 15–20. Association for Computational Linguistics.

Jieyu Zhao, Tianlu Wang, Mark Yatskar, Vicente Ordonez, and Kai-Wei Chang. 2018b. Gender bias in coreference resolution: Evaluation and debiasing methods. In *Proceedings of the 2018 Conference of the North American Chapter of the Association for Computational Linguistics: Human Language Technologies, NAACL-HLT, New Orleans, Louisiana, USA, June 1-6, 2018, Volume 2 (Short Papers)*, pages 15–20. Association for Computational Linguistics.

Ming Zhong, Danqing Wang, Pengfei Liu, Xipeng Qiu, and Xuanjing Huang. 2019. A closer look at data bias in neural extractive summarization models. In *Proceedings of the 2nd Workshop on New Frontiers in Summarization*, pages 80–89, Hong Kong, China. Association for Computational Linguistics.

# A Appendix

## A.1 Detailed Statistics of DATALAB.

Here, we list more detailed statistics of DATALAB in Table 3.

| Aspect | | Number |
|---|---|---|
| Tasks | | 142 |
| Plain datasets | | 1,715 |
| Diagnostics datasets | | 3,583 |
| Language | | 331 |
| Organization | | 794 |
| Prompts | | 1,007 |
| Operation | Aggregate | 8 |
| | Preprocess | 4 |
| | Featurize | 16 |
| | Edit | 23 |
| | Prompt | 32 |
| Feature | Sample level | 138 |
| | Dataset level | 180 |
| Bias analysis | Hate speech datasets | 240 |
| | Gender bias datasets | 241 |
| | Gender bias samples | 18,520,130 |
| | Hate speech samples | 18,511,763 |
| Annotated Datasets | | 728 |
| Annotated samples | | 139,570,057 |
| Total samples | | 408,460,905 |

Table 3: More detailed statistics of the DATALAB. "Diagnostic Dataset" refers to a dataset obtained by applying transformations to the original version.[27] "Annotated" indicates datasets or samples where we compute features to obtain additional information that is not originally present in the dataset.

### A.2 Features

Features (e.g., `sentence length`) allow us to understand the characteristics of a dataset from different perspectives. Following Fu et al. (2020a), we define 318 features for 142 NLP tasks. Below, we list some core features at the sample- and dataset-level and suitable tasks.

#### A.2.1 Sample-level

**General Features** General features are task-agnostic and suitable for all NLP tasks.

- **Sentence length**: the number of tokens in a sentence.
- **Part-of-speech tags**: the part-of-speech tag for each token is automatically labeled by NLTK (Loper and Bird, 2002) Python tool.
- **Named entities**: entity names are automatically recognized by NLTK and SpaCy (Honnibal and Montani, 2017) Python tools.
- **Basic words ratio**: the proportion of words that appear in the basic English dictionary[28].
- **Lexical richness** (Richards, 1987): the proportion of unique words, obtained by dividing the number of unique words by the total number of words.
- **OOV density**: the proportion of words in a test sentence that do not appear in the training set.

**Specialized Features** In addition to general features, we also design task-specific features for some core NLP tasks. Below, we list some key task-specific features, as well as applicable tasks.

- **Span length**: the length of span. Span can be entity/answer/chunk/aspect. (*NER*, *QA*, *Chunking*, *ABSA*)
- **Label consistency of span** (Fu et al., 2020a): the visibility of a span and its label in the training set. (*NER*, *Chunking*)
- **Span frequency**: the frequency of entities in the training set. (*NER*, *Chunking*)
- **Span density**: the number of words belonging to entities in a sentence divided by the length of the sentence. (*NER*, *Chunking*)
- **Text similarity**: measures how similar two texts are. Here, we explore BLEU (Papineni et al., 2002) and ROUGE2 (Lin, 2004) for two texts. (*SUMM*, *Match*, *QA*)
- **Text length comparison**: measures the sentence-length relationship of sentence pairs, including addition, subtraction, and division operation of sentence lengths. (*Match*, *SUMM*,*QA*)
- **Answer/span position**: measures where the answer/span starts in the text. (*QA*, *ABSA*, *Chunking*)
- **Coverage ratio**: measures to what extent a summary covers the content in the source text. (*SUMM*)
- **Copy length**: the average length of segments in a summary copied from the source document. (*SUMM*)

The full names of the tasks mentioned above are as follows:

- NER: Named Entity Recognition
- Chunking: Chunkinig
- POS: Part-of-speech Tagging
- ABSA: Aspect-Based Sentiment Analysis
- QA: Question Answering
- Matching: Text Matching
- SUMM: Text Summarization

#### A.2.2 Dataset-level

- **Average on dataset-level**: a sample-level feature can be converted into a dataset-level feature by averaging that feature of each sample in the dataset (e.g. the average text length, the average span length).
- **Distribution of vocabulary**: measured by the word frequency of each word in the dataset.
- **Distribution of label**: characterize the number of samples contained in each category in the dataset.
- **Sample size of different splits**: characterize the number of samples contained in different splits.
- **Hate speech ratio**: characterize the degree of hate speech bias of the dataset.
- **Spelling errors ratio**: measures the extent of spelling errors contained in a dataset with the help of a detection tool[29].

### A.3 Bias

**PMI for Sentiment Classification** Taking the sentiment classification task as an example, we can use PMI to detect whether sentence length can indicate sentiment polarity. Given a sentence length sequence $L = \{l_1, l_2, \cdots, l_n\}$ with $n$ sentences, and a category sequence $C = \{c_1, c_2, \cdots, c_m\}$ with $m$ categories, the correlation measure PMI between sentence length and category can be defined

[28] wikipedia.basic_words

[29] spelling_error_detect_tool

| Observation | Conclustion |
|---|---|
| **SNLI** | |
| $\text{len}_{\text{hp}} > 8.4$, $\text{PMI}(\text{label}_{\text{neutral}}, \text{len}_{\text{hp}}) > 0.28$;<br>$\text{len}_{\text{hp}} \in [1, 4.7]$, $\text{PMI}(\text{label}_{\text{entailment}}, \text{len}_{\text{hp}}) = 0.359$; | Long hypotheses tend to be neutral.<br>Short hypotheses tend to be entailment. |
| $\text{flesch\_reading\_ease}_{\text{hp}} \in [-50, 1.352]$;<br>$\text{PMI}(\text{label}_{\text{entailment}}, \text{flesch\_reading\_ease}_{\text{hp}}) > 0.585$; | When the hypothesis is difficult enough to read,<br>the sample tends to be labeled as entailment. |
| $\text{male}_{\text{hp}} > 2$, $\text{PMI}(\text{label}_{\text{neutral}}, \text{male}_{\text{hp}}) > 0.317$;<br>$\text{female}_{\text{hp}} > 2$, $\text{PMI}(\text{label}_{\text{neutral}}, \text{male}_{\text{hp}}) > 0.377$; | Hypotheses with gender bias words<br>(male/female) tend to be neutral. |
| $X = \text{len}_{\text{pm}} - \text{len}_{\text{hp}}$, if $X \in [8, 30]$,<br>$\text{PMI}(\text{label}_{\text{entailment}}, \text{len}_{\text{pm}} - \text{len}_{\text{hp}}) > 0.084$;<br>while $X \in [0, 7]$; $\text{PMI}(\text{label}_{\text{neutral}}, \text{len}_{\text{pm}} - \text{len}_{\text{hp}}) = 0.045$ | When the length difference of hypothesis and premise is small<br>enough ([0,7]), the sample tends to be entailment, and when<br>it is large enough ([8,30]) the sample tends to be entailment. |
| $X = \text{len}_{\text{pm}} + \text{len}_{\text{hp}}$, if $X \in [4, 13]$,<br>$\text{PMI}(\text{label}_{\text{entailment}}, \text{len}_{\text{pm}} + \text{len}_{\text{hp}}) = 0.259$;<br>if $X > 22$, $\text{PMI}(\text{label}_{\text{neutral}}, \text{len}_{\text{pm}} + \text{len}_{\text{hp}}) > 0.105$; | When the sum of the lengths of hypothesis and premise<br>is small enough, the sample tends to be entailment, and when<br>it is large enough it tends to be neutral. |
| $X = \text{len}_{\text{pm}}/\text{len}_{\text{hp}}$, if $X < 2$,<br>$\text{PMI}(\text{label}_{\text{neutral}}, \text{len}_{\text{pm}}/\text{len}_{\text{hp}}) > 0.094$;<br>if $X > 2$, $\text{PMI}(\text{label}_{\text{entailment}}, \text{len}_{\text{pm}}/\text{len}_{\text{hp}}) > 0.141$; | When the lengths of hypothesis and premise are close enough,<br>the samples tend to be neutral, and when their lengths are<br>sufficiently different, samples tend to be entailment. |
| $\text{PMI}(\text{label}_*, \text{len}_{\text{pm}}) \approx 0$; | The length and gender features of the premise are<br>irrelevance with the label. |
| **SST2** | |
| $\text{len}_{\text{sent}} < 7$, $\text{PMI}(\text{label}_{\text{positive}}, \text{len}_{\text{sent}}) = 0.06$<br>$\text{len}_{\text{sent}} > 7$, $\text{PMI}(\text{label}_{\text{negative}}, \text{len}_{\text{sent}}) > 0$ | Sentences that are long enough tend to be negative,<br>while sentences that are short enough tend to be positive. |
| $\text{female}_{\text{sent}} \in [4.8, 5.4]$, $\text{PMI}(\text{label}_{\text{positive}}, \text{female}_{\text{sent}}) = 0.58$<br>$\text{female}_{\text{sent}} < 0.6$, $\text{PMI}(\text{label}_{\text{negative}}, \text{female}_{\text{sent}}) = 0.021$<br>$\text{male}_{\text{sent}} < 1.2$, $\text{PMI}(\text{label}_{\text{positive}}, \text{male}_{\text{sent}}) = 0.018$<br>$\text{male}_{\text{sent}} > 1.2$, $\text{PMI}(\text{label}_{\text{negative}}, \text{male}_{\text{sent}}) > 0.068$ | Sentences with low female bias tend to be negative,<br>with high female bias tend to be positive;<br>while sentences with high male bias tend to be negative. |

Table 4: Observations and conclusions of bias analysis with PMI on the SNLI and GLUE-SST2 dataset. "*hp*" and "*pm*" denote *hypothesis* and *premise*, respectively. "len" is a function that computes the length of a sentence. "*sent*" denotes "*sentence*".

as:

$$\phi_{\text{pmi}}(c_i, l_j) = \log(\frac{p(c_i, l_j)}{p(c_i)p(l_j)}), \tag{1}$$

where $c_i$ and $l_j$ denote the sentence length of the $i$-th sentence and the $j$-th category, respectively.

**Gender Bias** Given a male dictionary $K_{\text{male}} = [w_{m,1}, w_{m,2}, \ldots, w_{m,k_1}]$ with $k_1$ words, female dictionary $K_{\text{female}} = [w_{f,1}, w_{f,2}, \ldots, w_{f,k_2}]$ with $k_2$ words, and a dataset $D = [s_1, s_2, \ldots, s_N]$ with $N$ samples, the gender bias $gb$ of dataset $D$ can be defined as:

$$b_m = N_{\text{male}}/N, \tag{2}$$

$$b_f = N_{\text{female}}/N, \tag{3}$$

$$gb = b_m/b_f, \tag{4}$$

where $b_m$ and $b_f$ is the degree to which the dataset is biased towards men and towards women, respectively. $N_{\text{male}}$ and $N_{\text{female}}$ represent the number of words in the dataset D that appear in the dictionary $K_{\text{male}}$ and the number of words in the dictionary $K_{\text{female}}$, respectively. N is the sample size of dataset D.

## A.4 Calculation for Language Map

In language map, each country will be assigned a number that can be obtained by following steps: (1) for each country, collect the information that the languages spoken in this country and the proportion of people speaking each language. (2) for each data set, record the language of the data set (3) for each language, count the number of data set that belong to the language (4) for each language in the country, multiply the ration of the language and the number of data set belong to the language. Finally sum the score of all languages in the country.

### A.5 Customized Operation

```
from datalabs import load_dataset
from featurize import featurize

# Operation definition
@datalabs.feature
def get_length(text):
    return len(text.split(" "))


# Load dataset
dataset =
    load_dataset("ag_news")["train"]
# Apply operation
res = dataset.apply(get_length)
```

### A.6 Technical Implementation of Data Search

Our dataset search tool is designed to take as input a natural language description of a method and compare it against a search corpus of datasets.

We train our retrieval model with the Tevatron package.[30] The retrieval algorithm we use is effectively identical to Dense Passage Retrieval (DPR, Karpukhin et al. (2020)). Under this dual-encoder framework, the search corpus is indexed by encoding each document using the `CLS` embedding from BERT (Devlin et al., 2019). When our system receives a query, we first compute its embedding (again using the `CLS` embedding from BERT), then we rank the top documents using approximate nearest neighbor search (Johnson et al., 2017) on the shared inner product space of embeddings:

$$\text{score}(q, d) = \texttt{CLS}(\text{BERT}(q))^T \texttt{CLS}(\text{BERT}(d))$$

As a supervised learning-based retrieval method, this approach requires a large training set. To effectively generate a large training set, we adopt an automatic method for constructing annotations. We make the key observation that published AI/ML research papers reveal both a system description (contained in the abstract) as well as the datasets used to train or evaluate the system (usually found in the "Results" or "Experiments" section).

We use the abstracts of real papers as a proxy for natural language method descriptions, but we do not expect users to submit abstract-length queries into our system. Therefore, we pass these abstracts through the "TLDR" scientific abstract summarization system (Cachola et al., 2020) to generate brief method descriptions.

We next automatically extract the datasets used by a given paper, which are used as a proxy for the relevant (positive) documents for each query during training. We extract these using a heuristic: for a given paper, if it mentions a dataset by name twice in the "Results", "Experiments", or "Methods" section and also cites the paper that introduces the dataset, we register this dataset as being used by the given paper. By manually inspecting 200 automatic dataset tags, we found over 90% of the tags from this method were correct.

We also support traditional keyword queries in our system. To support these queries, we duplicate each example in our training set to replace the natural language description "query" with a keyword query. To generate keyword queries, we pass the abstract through a keyphrase extraction system trained on OpenKP (Xiong et al., 2019). We then train a single retriever using a training set containing these two heterogenous types of queries.

[30] `https://github.com/texttron/tevatron`

# Cue-bot: A Conversational Agent for Assistive Technology

Shachi H Kumar, Hsuan Su, Ramesh Manuvinakurike,
Maximilian C Pinaroc, Sai Prasad, Saurav Sahay and Lama Nachman
Intel Labs, Santa Clara, CA, USA
*{shachi.h.kumar, hsuan.su, ramesh.manuvinakurike,
maximilian.c.pinaroc, sai.prasad, saurav.sahay, lama.nachman }@intel.com*

## Abstract

Intelligent conversational assistants have become an integral part of our lives for performing simple tasks. However, such agents, for example, Google bots, Alexa and others are yet to have any social impact on minority population, for example, for people with neurological disorders and people with speech, language and social communication disorders, sometimes with locked-in states where speaking or typing is a challenge. Language model technologies can be very powerful tools in enabling these users to carry out daily communication and social interactions. In this work, we present a system that users with varied levels of disabilties can use to interact with the world, supported by eye-tracking, mouse controls and an intelligent agent Cue-bot, that can represent the user in a conversation. The agent provides relevant controllable 'cues' to generate desirable responses quickly for an ongoing dialog context. In the context of usage of such systems for people with degenerative disorders, we present automatic and human evaluation of our cue/keyword predictor and the controllable dialog system and show that our models perform significantly better than models without control and can also reduce user effort (fewer keystrokes) and speed up communication (typing time) significantly.

## 1 Introduction

Conversational agents, especially systems such as Alexa and Google Home, have become commodity items in people's homes. Such systems have enabled carrying out one-shot tasks such as setting reminders, playing music and accessing information simpler for the general population. We also have other PC and cloud based chatbots that are designed to perform certain goals or tasks, or to just engage in a casual conversation/chat with a user. The latter class of open-domain conversational agents have not yet seen widespread adoption besides mostly research exploration projects for developing conversational agents (Ram et al., 2018).

Large language models are being developed today with end-to-end pre-training. Large-scale pre-training has attained significant performance gains across many tasks within NLP (Devlin et al., 2019; Radford and Narasimhan, 2018), including intent prediction (Castellucci et al., 2019; Chen et al., 2019) and dialogue state tracking (Heck et al., 2020). Open-domain chatbots are also being trained using generative language modeling objective of minimizing perplexity on next word prediction task using large conversational corpora and transformer based models. These models have demonstrated surprising generality, with models like DialoGPT (Zhang et al., 2020b), Meena (Adiwardana et al., 2020) and Blender (Roller et al., 2020) achieving response generation performance competitive with humans in certain settings. These improving systems still suffer from issues such as repeated responses, hallucinated facts, and lack of controllability, grounding and embodiment (See et al., 2019).

With the availability of these pre-trained language enabling models, novel products and applications are emerging in several domains (Bommasani et al., 2021). One such accessesibility application we are exploring is aimed towards leveraging language modeling technology to support minority group of people with certain disabilities [1] to communicate with others effectively. One such example is Amyotrophic Lateral Sclerosis (ALS) or Motor Neuron Disease(MND), a progressive, degenerative, neurological disorder where people lose their muscle movement, voice and the ability to carry out a normal day-to-day communication. There have been technologies and platforms, one such example is Assistive Context-Aware Toolkit (ACAT)[2],

[1]According to WHO, there are more than 1 Billion people with disabilities

[2]https://01.org/ACAT



*Proceedings of the 60th Annual Meeting of the Association for Computational Linguistics*
*System Demonstrations*, pages 196 - 203

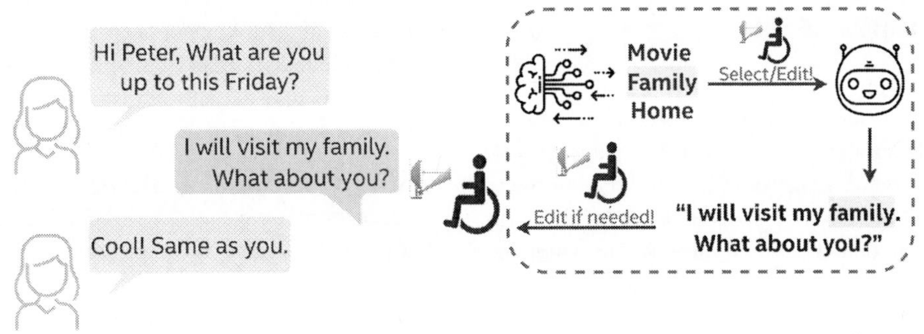


Figure 1: A dialog system for an assistive use-case can listen to a conversation and provide diverse cues to the user. These cues, provide human control to the dialog system that can generate relevant responses that can further be edited.

that enable these users to communicate, but it takes huge effort and time for these patients to communicate sentences character by character using various data input mechanisms that suit their situation such as gaze, fingers or muscle movements.

We want to enable full and faster communication and provide interaction support tools for people with such disabilities by having an intelligent agent be their voice and content assistent. The system should use very limited user input (e.g. gaze, single muscle movement, facial gesture, etc) and suggest cues and cue-based responses that can be interactively chosen and edited for near real time social interactions. The goal of such a system is to minimize the effort by minimizing the keystrokes input required for continued coherent interactions. Today's response generation systems suffer from several issues and are very hard to use as-is for our usage requirements. The system for our usage needs to be context-aware, personalized, should enable minimal user-intervention and most importantly, be assistive and controllable by the user. Fast response generation with response cues, editing and auto complete features can dramatically reduce the silence gap in the conversation resulting from users slower keystroke by keystroke input.

Our contributions in this work are, i) **Minority Group Application:** We bring forth a novel usage for open-domain chatbots/response generation systems, i.e., designing a reponse generation system that will represent users with communication disabilities and help them fulfill their day-to-day communication needs. ii) **Minimal user effort and intervention:** We show that the keyword predictor models can speed up communication time by suggesting cues to the user. We also present a technique for controllable response generation using these cues. We present human and automatic evaluation for this approach. iii) **Demo Interface:** We showcase a demo where a user can interact only using his/her eyes to control the interface, with minimum effort and time.

## 2 Motivation

To enable people with MND and other disabilities to communicate, Intel Labs developed ACAT, an open source platform that was originally developed for Professor Stephen Hawking. With ACAT, users have complete access to the capabitlies of their computers that they can control using various modalities and sensors such as proximity sensors, eye-gaze and further capabilities such as BCI-based controls are being developed. ACAT also includes word prediction, speech synthesis capabilities, this allows users to respond to ongoing conversations, and a range of tasks such as accessing emails, editing documents and browsing the web.

In ACAT, users can choose words that appear from the word predictors, or select letters to create words using the input modality that suits their condition. While this empowers users to communicate, this still involves a lot of effort in terms of the word/letter selections and involves a huge latency. With this work, we aim to reduce the user effort and intervention and also the time in generating a user response, by using the state of the art language modeling technology as will be described in the below sections. Our goal is to also integrate this work into the current ACAT system to enable the user to select entire responses based on input keywords, with minimum effort and intervention.

## 3 System Architecture

Figure 1 shows the interaction flow of the Cue-bot system. Consider an ongoing conversation between an interlocutor and the user. An Automatic Speech Recognition (ASR) system converts the interlocutor's current utterance to text. This, in addition to the dialog context, is input into the cue-generator model (described below), which outputs the possible cues or keywords for a potential response to the input that the user might want to respond with. In the figure, given the utterance "Hi Peter, what are you upto this Friday?", the cue-generator generates "movie", "family", "home" that the user can choose from. The interface also allows the user to enter his/her own cue or keyword, if the user needs, in case none of the suggested words are relevant. The user uses the Tobii eye-tracker and the OptiKey mouse controls to make a keyword selection or to type out a keyword of his/her choice.

Once the user chooses or enters a custom keyword, this information is sent to the Cue/Keyword-based Response Generation system (details below) that generates multiple responses relevant to the cue/keyword. The user can 1) choose one of these responses to use as his/her response to the interlocutor, 2) edit one of the responses or 3) type out the entire response if none of the suggested responses are relevant. These modules are described in detail below.

### 3.1 Models

The main software components of the system include the cue/keyword generator and the response generation models which are described in the sections below.

#### 3.1.1 Cue/Keyword Generator

In order to minimize the keystrokes in the interaction and hence user effort, we build a model that can generate keywords that could aid in generating the user's response in the conversation. We present two types of keyword generators in this section - extractive and generative. To train the model, we obtain the data by extracting 'key' terms from the dataset. This data is generated automatically, hence enabling end-to-end automatic pipeline, without the need for any other additional data collection or labeling efforts. Given a conversation context and a response output, keywords are extracted from the response utterance and incorporated into the model. We use keyBERT (Grootendorst, 2020) to extract meaningful keywords from the responses. This technique uses BERT-embeddings and cosine similarity to find the sub-phrases in a document that are most similar to the document itself.

**Extractive keyword predictor:** Given a conversation context, we use DialoGPT(Zhang et al., 2020b) with diverse beam search(Vijayakumar et al., 2018) to generate multiple responses (we use 10 beams, 2 groups and diversity_penalty of 5.5). We then use keyBERT(Grootendorst, 2020) to extract keywords from the beam outputs and present these as keyword suggestions.

**Generative keyword predictor:** We fine-tune a large pretrained language model, GPT2, to generate keywords for a given context, and present these as suggestions. We use the training and validation dataset from DailyDialog (Li et al., 2017a) to build the keyword predictor. For evaluation of these models, we use the top keyword prediction. We further use diverse beam search (same configuration as above) and generate multiple keyword suggestions.

**Cue/Keyword based Response Generation** Given the conversation context, we enable fine-grained control over the responses generated by training the model with important keywords automatically generated (as described above). For a given conversation context, we incorporate keywords into the model by adding new keyword-specific-tokens, in addition to dialog-state/speaker tokens that represent speaker turns in the dialog. We further extend the dialog-state embeddings to add 'keyword-state-embeddings' with special keyword separator token to indicate the positions of the keyword tokens.

In this work, we modify the HuggingFace TransferTransfo model (Wolf et al., 2019) architecture, a model is similar to the Transformer based architecture from (Radford and Narasimhan, 2018) that uses autoregressive and discriminative fine-tuning by optimizing a combination of two loss functions : 1) language modeling loss and 2) next-utterance classification loss. We incorporate fine-grained keyword-based control as model inputs and fine-tune this model on the DailyDialog dataset with multi-task objective.

### 3.2 Other Components

**Eye-Tracker** To support users with severe neurological disabilities who are unable to move, speak or type, we enable interaction with the system

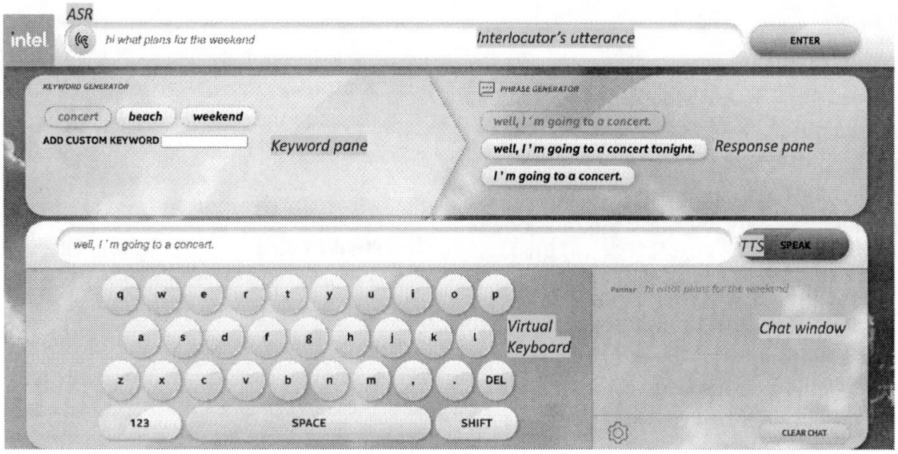


Figure 2: Cue-bot interface

through an additional input modality: eye-gaze tracking. We use the Tobii eye-tracker [3], (specifically the gaming version to lower the cost of the system), that works with Windows systems and can be mounted on the laptop or any other external monitor. This device needs to be calibrated to work for a user. This device has already been in use with the ACAT system supporting users with MND.

**Mouse Control** While the Tobii eye-tracker tracks the user's gaze, we need to translate the gaze to a mouse-click event. For this, we use OptiKey [4], which is an on-screen keyboard designed for users with MND, to interact with Windows systems. OptiKey can be integrated with the Tobii eye-tracker to allow users to control the system using eye-gaze only. We modify the OptiKey software to show the specific buttons needed to control the UI, such as left-click (single and double), right click, scroll up-down, finer mouse movement (in pixels).

**Automatic Speech Recognition** In a real system, where the user is communicating with an interlocutor, we need the cue-bot to be listening to the conversation in order to make relevant keyword and response suggestions to the user. To incorporate this in the web-interface as well, we integrate Google ASR that converts the interlocutor's speech to text that can be input into our models. This is enabled on a button-click on our user-interface as shown in Figure 2.

**User Interface Design** Figure 2 shows the user interface for this system. The top text area shows the placeholder for the interlocutor's utterance, that is obtained by converting speech-to-text using ASR. The interface is divided into two parts, the top area is further split into two panes 1) the left pane displays the generated keywords from the keyword predictor. The user can also add a custom keyword by clicking on the 'Add Custom Keyword' button. Once a keyword choice is made, 2) the right pane displays the generated responses from the keyword-based response generation model. The bottom area shows the virtual keyboard with buttons large enough to enable the gaze-tracker to detect gaze without ambiguities. Picking one of the generated responses from the right phrase pane, populates it into the textarea which can be edited by the user if needed. The 'Speak' button converts the user's response to speech. Finally, the chat window on the bottom-right keeps track of the ongoing conversation for the user's reference.

## 4 Experimental Setup

We initialize the TransferTransfo model with weights of DialoGPT 'medium' model with 345M parameters. We also use two candidates for the next utterance prediction task. We use a batch_size of 64 for training, nucleus sampling for generation with top_p set to 0.9. We fine-tune the model for 3 epochs. We compare the model trained without any information with a keyword-context model trained with keyword as auxillary input information.

[3]https://gaming.tobii.com/product/eye-tracker-5/
[4]https://github.com/OptiKey/OptiKey

### 4.1 Datasets

We use the Dailydialog dataset (Li et al., 2017b), which consists of 13,118 daily conversations involving various topics such as tourism, culture, and education among others. This dataset serves as a starting point for AAC applications as it contains suitable interactions for building applications to support social communication and daily life interactions. The training set has about 11,000 conversations, and the validation and test sets have 1000 conversations each. We use the test set, consisting of 6740 context-response pairs, to evaluate our models which will be discussed in the results section.

### 4.2 Automatic Evaluation

We use several automatic metrics to compute the performance of our models.

**Metrics for Evaluating Keyword Predictor Models** The keyword predictor model should be able to generate diverse keywords to present varied options for users to choose from. We evalute the extractive and generative models based on averaged cosine similarity between generated keywords as a measure of diversity; lower the similarity, higher the diversity. We hypothesize that meaningful keywords will result in generation of meaningful and context-relevant responses. Hence, we compute 'human-like' and coherence scores for the generated responses using DialogRPT (Gao et al., 2020), a model trained to predict human feedback dialogue responses.

**Metrics for Evaluating Controllable Response Generation Model** :

1) **Keyword Insertion Accuracy(KIA):** To evaluate the ability of the response generation model to induce a keyword into the response, thus enabling fine-grained control, we compute the keyword-insertion accuracies of the models.

2) **Similarity Based Metrics:** Because we intend to generate responses based on keywords, computing measures of similarity between the generated response and ground truth response (in the learnt embedding space) gives a good assesment for the model performance. We use BLEURT (Sellam et al., 2020), BERTScore (Zhang et al., 2020a) , Sentence-BERT (Reimers and Gurevych, 2019) to compute similarity between generated response and ground truth.

3) **Response Quality Metrics:** For response quality aspects of fluency and context-coherence, we perform language model based evaluation. We also perform n-gram based diversity evaluation. We also measure the perpelexity (PPL) by employing a pre-trained GPT-2 "medium" model.

### 4.3 Human Evaluation

**Keystrokes and Typing Time** One of the main focus of this work is minimizing user effort, time and intervention. With this in mind, we evaluate and compare the number of keystrokes and typing time taken by a user with and without our models (keyword prediction+response generation models). Please note that in absence of our models, the user will need to type out the entire response character by character. We consider two scenarios, 1) user picks a suggested keyword *(#keystrokes=1)*, 2) user enters his/her own keyword *(#keystrokes=#characters entered)*. We also consider edited responses *(#keystrokes=1)* and non-edited responses *(#keystrokes=#edits)*.

**Evaluation of the keyword-based response generation models** We randomly pick 100 dialog contexts and present the context along with the keyword and pairs of responses from the models and ask 3 annotators to rate the responses based on the following criteria: 1) Fluency: how natural and fluent the responses are, 2) Generic: are the responses too generic given the dialog context?, 3) Context relevance: how relevant and coherent is a response to a given dialog context, 4) Keyword relevance: how relevant is a response to the input keyword? We present pairs of responses from the no-keyword and the keyword-based model, and provide 4 options for for each of the above criteria: A better than B, B better than A, Both and, Neither.

## 5 Results

### 5.1 Automatic Evaluation Results

**Keyword Predictor Models:** From Table 2, we can observe that the generative keyword predictor tends to generate more diverse keywords (lower similarity score), which is very important in our use-case. The responses generated by choosing the keywords from the generative predictor are more coherent and human-like.

**Cue/Keyword controlled models:** Table 1 shows the performance of the response generation models. From the table, the KIA for the $no\_kw$ model is negligible, given the one to many nature

| | KIA | Similarity | BLEURT | BERT Score | Context | Diversity | Fluency | PPL↓ |
|---|---|---|---|---|---|---|---|---|
| no_kw | 0.083 | 0.271 | -1.035 | **0.868**/0.836/0.851 | 0.541 | 1.592 | **0.407** | **39.098** |
| kw_context | **0.672** | **0.539** | **-0.607** | 0.844/**0.853**/**0.868** | **0.568** | **1.789** | 0.403 | 41.752 |

Table 1: Performance of the keyword-based response generation model

| Kw Predictor | Coherence | Human-like | Diversity↓ |
|---|---|---|---|
| Generative | **0.903** | **0.641** | **0.227** |
| Extractive | 0.891 | 0.595 | 0.265 |

Table 2: Evaluation of keyword predictor models.

of open domain dialog. By guiding the model with cues or keywords, the KIA goes up to 67.2%. The cue/keyword based model outperforms the *no_kw* model in all of the similarity-based and response quality metrics, except perplexity where the *no_kw* model is lower.

### 5.2 Human Evaluation Results

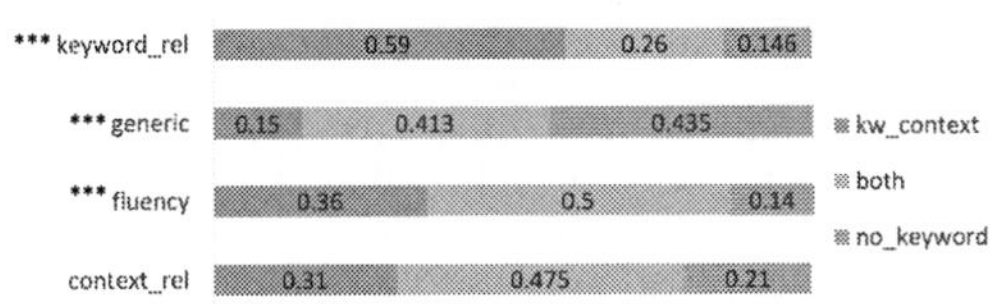


Figure 3: Results from human evaluation. (One-Sample Wilcoxon Signed Rank Test (mu=0) for the statistical tests.*** p<0.001, ** p<0.01, * p<0.05.)

**Keystrokes & Typing time** We compute both the interaction time and keystrokes to compare the keyword-based interaction models with typing out the entire sentences for 2 scenarios: 1) keyword picked from suggestion and 2) custom keyword entered. For 1) on average, using our models, it takes only 10% of the keystrokes taken to type out the entire sentence, and it takes 30% of the time to type the entire sentence, i.e., 70% of time is saved. For case 2) with our system, it takes about 35% of the keystrokes taken to type out the entire responses (with edits) and saves about 40% of the time to type the entire sentence.

**Keyword-based response generation evaluation** Figure 3 shows the scores for the response quality metrics for different model. From human ratings, we observe that the *kw_context* model outperforms the model without control, on all metrics significantly. The keyword-based model generates more fluent and relevant responses while at the same time, generating less generic responses compared to the *no_keyword* model.

## 6 Conclusion and Future Work

In this work, we present a system to support users with MND and other disabilities to carry out day to day social interactions with lesser effort, time and interventions. We use input modalities such as gaze tracking that allows users to control the entire interface only using their eyes. We build models that utilizes the ongoing conversations and suggests possible cues/keywords that the users can use, and generate relevant responses based on the selected keyword. We show through automatic and human evaluations that our models are better than the models without control and also save significant time and effort in interactions. For future work, we aim to integrate it with the ACAT toolkit that already supports MND users, to improve their quality of communication. We also aim to personalize the system by using user's data when available and also build a system that can continually learn through user interactions.

## 7 Ethics

CueBot aims to support users with disabilities and allow them to communicate while also enabling them to control the response generation. The system has been evaluated with automatic and human evaluation via AMT, where the AMT workers were fairly compensated (average >$15 per hour). Our tasks involved providing responses from humans and model which were rated by the AMT workers. We tried to mitigate any bias in the choices made by turkers by constantly shuffling the responses that we present. In our experiment we didn't collect any additional personal details (other than those collect by AMT by default) or identities from AMT workers', hence preserving their privacy. The next steps is to integrate this system with ACAT to enable user studies with ALS patients and further gain their feedback to improve the AI modules. Both the keyword suggestion and response generation modules use pre-trained language model DialoGPT (Zhang et al., 2020c) finetuned on DailyDialog dataset conversations. Given this, the responses generated could contain improper content or bias (from the large dataset these models are pre-trained on). This raises some important ethical questions that we intend to tackle as part of future work. In this current work we have not explored bias mitigation, which will also be a part of future work.

## 8 Acknowledgements

We thank the Torrey Frank (Intel Labs) and the team from French & Western for working with us in building the UI.

## References


D. Adiwardana, Minh-Thang Luong, D. So, J. Hall, Noah Fiedel, R. Thoppilan, Z. Yang, Apoorv Kulshreshtha, Gaurav Nemade, Yifeng Lu, and Quoc V. Le. 2020. Towards a human-like open-domain chatbot. *ArXiv*, abs/2001.09977.

Rishi Bommasani, Drew A. Hudson, Ehsan Adeli, Russ Altman, et al. 2021. On the opportunities and risks of foundation models.

Giuseppe Castellucci, Valentina Bellomaria, A. Favalli, and R. Romagnoli. 2019. Multi-lingual intent detection and slot filling in a joint bert-based model. *ArXiv*, abs/1907.02884.

Qian Chen, Zhu Zhuo, and W. Wang. 2019. Bert for joint intent classification and slot filling. *ArXiv*, abs/1902.10909.

Jacob Devlin, Ming-Wei Chang, Kenton Lee, and Kristina Toutanova. 2019. BERT: Pre-training of deep bidirectional transformers for language understanding. In *Proceedings of the 2019 Conference of the North American Chapter of the Association for Computational Linguistics: Human Language Technologies, Volume 1 (Long and Short Papers)*, pages 4171–4186, Minneapolis, Minnesota. Association for Computational Linguistics.

Xiang Gao, Yizhe Zhang, Michel Galley, Chris Brockett, and Bill Dolan. 2020. Dialogue response ranking-training with large-scale human feedback data. In *EMNLP*.

Maarten Grootendorst. 2020. Keybert: Minimal keyword extraction with bert.

Michael Heck, Carel van Niekerk, Nurul Lubis, Christian Geishauser, Hsien-Chin Lin, Marco Moresi, and Milica Gasic. 2020. TripPy: A triple copy strategy for value independent neural dialog state tracking. In *Proceedings of the 21th Annual Meeting of the Special Interest Group on Discourse and Dialogue*, pages 35–44, 1st virtual meeting. Association for Computational Linguistics.

Yanran Li, Hui Su, Xiaoyu Shen, Wenjie Li, Ziqiang Cao, and Shuzi Niu. 2017a. Dailydialog: A manually labelled multi-turn dialogue dataset.

Yanran Li, Hui Su, Xiaoyu Shen, Wenjie Li, Ziqiang Cao, and Shuzi Niu. 2017b. Dailydialog: A manually labelled multi-turn dialogue dataset. In *Proceedings of the Eighth International Joint Conference on Natural Language Processing, IJCNLP 2017, Taipei, Taiwan, November 27 - December 1, 2017 - Volume 1: Long Papers*, pages 986–995. Asian Federation of Natural Language Processing.

A. Radford and Karthik Narasimhan. 2018. Improving language understanding by generative pre-training.

Ashwin Ram, Rohit Prasad, Chandra Khatri, Anu Venkatesh, Raefer Gabriel, Qing Liu, Jeff Nunn, Behnam Hedayatnia, Ming Cheng, Ashish Nagar, Eric King, Kate Bland, Amanda Wartick, Yi Pan, Han Song, Sk Jayadevan, Gene Hwang, and Art Pettigrue. 2018. Conversational ai: The science behind the alexa prize.

Nils Reimers and Iryna Gurevych. 2019. Sentence-bert: Sentence embeddings using siamese bert-networks. In *Proceedings of the 2019 Conference on Empirical Methods in Natural Language Processing and the 9th International Joint Conference on Natural Language Processing, EMNLP-IJCNLP 2019, Hong Kong, China, November 3-7, 2019*, pages 3980–3990. Association for Computational Linguistics.

Stephen Roller, Emily Dinan, Naman Goyal, Da Ju, Mary Williamson, Yinhan Liu, Jing Xu, Myle Ott, Kurt Shuster, Eric Smith, Y-Lan Boureau, and Jason Weston. 2020. Recipes for building an open-domain chatbot.

Abigail See, Stephen Roller, Douwe Kiela, and Jason Weston. 2019. What makes a good conversation? how controllable attributes affect human judgments. In *Proceedings of the 2019 Conference of the North American Chapter of the Association for Computational Linguistics: Human Language Technologies, Volume 1 (Long and Short Papers)*, pages 1702–1723, Minneapolis, Minnesota. Association for Computational Linguistics.

Thibault Sellam, Dipanjan Das, and Ankur P. Parikh. 2020. BLEURT: learning robust metrics for text generation. In *Proceedings of the 58th Annual Meeting of the Association for Computational Linguistics, ACL 2020, Online, July 5-10, 2020*, pages 7881–7892. Association for Computational Linguistics.

Ashwin Vijayakumar, Michael Cogswell, Ramprasaath Selvaraju, Qing Sun, Stefan Lee, David Crandall, and Dhruv Batra. 2018. Diverse beam search for improved description of complex scenes. *Proceedings of the AAAI Conference on Artificial Intelligence*, 32(1).

Thomas Wolf, Victor Sanh, Julien Chaumond, and Clement Delangue. 2019. Transfertransfo: A transfer learning approach for neural network based conversational agents. *CoRR*, abs/1901.08149.

Tianyi Zhang, Varsha Kishore, Felix Wu, Kilian Q. Weinberger, and Yoav Artzi. 2020a. Bertscore: Evaluating text generation with BERT. In *8th International Conference on Learning Representations, ICLR 2020, Addis Ababa, Ethiopia, April 26-30, 2020*. OpenReview.net.

Yizhe Zhang, Siqi Sun, Michel Galley, Yen-Chun Chen, Chris Brockett, Xiang Gao, Jianfeng Gao, Jingjing Liu, and Bill Dolan. 2020b. DIALOGPT : Large-scale generative pre-training for conversational response generation. In *Proceedings of the 58th Annual Meeting of the Association for Computational Linguistics: System Demonstrations*, pages 270–278, Online. Association for Computational Linguistics.

Yizhe Zhang, Siqi Sun, Michel Galley, Yen-Chun Chen, Chris Brockett, Xiang Gao, Jianfeng Gao, Jingjing Liu, and Bill Dolan. 2020c. Dialogpt: Large-scale generative pre-training for conversational response generation. In *ACL, system demonstration*.

# M-SENA: An Integrated Platform for Multimodal Sentiment Analysis

**Huisheng Mao**[1,2]*, **Ziqi Yuan**[1,2]*, **Hua Xu**[1,2]†, **Wenmeng Yu**[1,2], **Yihe Liu**[1,3], **Kai Gao**[3]
[1]State Key Laboratory of Intelligent Technology and Systems,
Department of Computer Science and Technology, Tsinghua University
[2]Beijing National Research Center for Information Science and Technology(BNRist)
[3]School of Information Science and Engineering, Hebei University of Science and Technology
{mhs20,yzq21}@mails.tsinghua.edu.cn
xuhua@tsinghua.edu.cn

## Abstract

M-SENA is an open-sourced platform for Multimodal Sentiment Analysis. It aims to facilitate advanced research by providing flexible toolkits, reliable benchmarks, and intuitive demonstrations. The platform features a fully modular video sentiment analysis framework consisting of data management, feature extraction, model training, and result analysis modules. In this paper, we first illustrate the overall architecture of the M-SENA platform and then introduce features of the core modules. Reliable baseline results of different modality features and MSA benchmarks are also reported. Moreover, we use model evaluation and analysis tools provided by M-SENA to present intermediate representation visualization, on-the-fly instance test, and generalization ability test results. The source code of the platform is publicly available at `https://github.com/thuiar/M-SENA`.

## 1 Introduction

Multimodal Sentiment Analysis (MSA) aims to judge the speaker's sentiment from video segments (Mihalcea, 2012; Soleymani et al., 2017; Guo et al., 2019). It has attracted increasing attention due to the booming of user-generated online content. Although impressive improvements have been witnessed in recent MSA researches (Tsai et al., 2019; Rahman et al., 2020; Yu et al., 2021), building an end-to-end video sentiment analysis system for real-world scenarios is still full of challenges.

The first challenge lies in effective acoustic and visual feature extraction. Most previous approaches (Zadeh et al., 2017a; Hazarika et al., 2020; Han et al., 2021a) are developed on the provided modality sequences from CMU-MultimodalSDK[1]. However, reproducing exact identical acoustic and visual feature extraction is almost impossible due to the the vague description of feature selection and backbone selection (both COVAREP[2] and Facet[3] can not be directly used in Python). Moreover, recent literature (Tsai et al., 2019; Gkoumas et al., 2021; Han et al., 2021b) observe that the text modality stands in the predominant position while acoustic and visual modalities have few contributions to the final sentiment classification. Such results further arouse the attention on effective feature extraction of acoustic and visual modalities.

With the awareness of the importance of acoustic and visual feature extraction, researchers attempt to develop models based on customized modality sequences instead of provided features (Dai et al., 2021; Hazarika et al., 2020). However, performance comparison with different modality features is unfair. Therefore, the demand for reliable comparison of modality features and fusion methods is increasingly urgent.

Another factor that limits the application of existing MSA models in real scenarios is the lack of comprehensive model evaluation and analysis approaches. Models obtained outstanding performance on the given test set might degrade in real-world scenarios due to the distribution discrepancy or random modality perturbations (Liang et al., 2019; Zhao et al., 2021; Yuan et al., 2021). Besides, effective model analysis is also crucial for researchers to explain the improvements and perform model refinement.

The **M**ultimodal **SEN**timent **A**nalysis platform (M-SENA) is developed to address the above challenges. For acoustic and visual features, the platform integrates Librosa (McFee et al., 2015), OpenSmile (Eyben et al., 2010), OpenFace (Baltrusaitis et al., 2018), MediaPipe (Lugaresi et al., 2019) and provides a highly customized feature extraction API in Python. With the modular MSA pipeline, fair comparison between different features

* These authors contributed equally to this work.
† Hua Xu is the corresponding author.

[1]Features provided by CMU

[2]https://github.com/covarep/covarep

[3]https://imotions.com



*Proceedings of the 60th Annual Meeting of the Association for Computational Linguistics System Demonstrations*, pages 204 - 213
May 22-27, 2022 ©2022 Association for Computational Linguistics

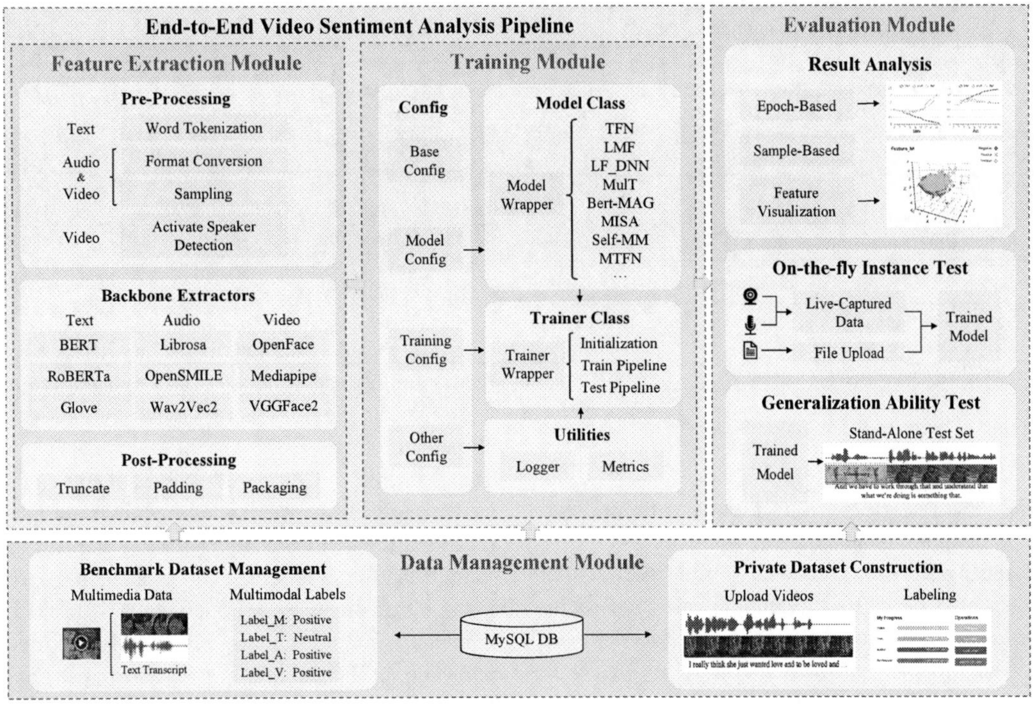


Figure 1: The overall framework of the M-SENA platform contains four main modules: data management module, feature extraction module, model training module and model evaluation module.

and MSA fusion models can be achieved. The results can be regarded as reliable baselines for future MSA research. Furthermore, the platform provides comprehensive model evaluation and analysis tools to reflect the model performance in real-world scenarios, including intermediate result visualization, on-the-fly instance demonstration, and generalization ability test. The contributions of this work are briefly summarized as follows:

1. By providing a highly customized feature extraction toolkit, the platform familiarizes researchers with the composition of modality features. Also, the platform bridges the gap between designing MSA models with provided, fixed modality features and building a real-world video sentiment analysis system.

2. The unified MSA pipeline guarantees fair comparison between different combinations of modality features and fusion models.

3. To help researchers evaluate and analyze MSA models, the platform provides tools such as intermediate result visualization, on-the-fly instance demonstration, and generalization ability test.

## 2 Platform Architecture

M-SENA platform features convenient data access, customized feature extraction, unified model training pipeline, and comprehensive model evaluation. It provides a graphical web interface as well as Python packages for researchers with all features above. The platform currently supports three popular MSA datasets across two languages, seven feature extraction backbones, and fourteen benchmark MSA models. Figure 1 illustrates the overall architecture of the M-SENA platform. In the remaining parts of this section, features of each module in Figure 1 will be described in detail.

### 2.1 Data Management Module

The data management module is designed to ease the access of multimedia data on servers. Besides providing existing benchmark datasets, the module also enables researchers to build and manage their own datasets.

**Benchmark Datasets.** M-SENA currently supports three benchmark MSA datasets, including CMU-MOSI (Zadeh et al., 2016), CMU-MOSEI (Zadeh et al., 2018b) in English, and CH-SIMS (Yu et al., 2020) in Chinese. Details of integrated datasets are shown in Appendix A. Users can filter

| Acoustic Feature Sets | |
|---|---|
| ComParE_2016 (Schuller et al., 2016) | Static (HSFs) |
| eGeMAPS (Eyben et al., 2015) | Static (LLDs) |
| wav2vec2.0 (Baevski et al., 2020) | Learnable |
| **Visual Feature Sets** | |
| Facial Landmarks (Zadeh et al., 2017b) | Static |
| Eyes Gaze (Wood et al., 2015) | Static |
| Action Unit (Baltrušaitis et al., 2015) | Static |
| **Textual Feature Sets** | |
| GloVe6B (Pennington et al., 2014) | Static |
| BERT (Devlin et al., 2018) | Learnable |
| RoBerta (Liu et al., 2019) | Learnable |

Table 1: Some of the supported features in M-SENA.

and view raw videos conveniently without downloading them to the local environment.

**Building Private Datasets.** The M-SENA platform also provides a graphical interface for researchers to construct their own datasets using uploaded videos. Following the literature (Yu et al., 2020), M-SENA supports unimodal sentiment labelling along with multimodal sentiment labelling. The constructed datasets can be directly used for model training and evaluation on the platform.

## 2.2 Feature Extraction Module

Emotion-bearing modality feature extraction is still an open challenge for MSA tasks. To facilitate effective modality feature extraction for MSA, M-SENA integrates seven most commonly used feature extraction tools and provides a unified Python API as well as a graphical interface. Part of the supported features for each modality are listed in Table 1 and described below:

**Acoustic Modality.** Various acoustic features have been proven effective for emotion recognition (El Ayadi et al., 2011; Akçay and Oğuz, 2020). Hand-crafted acoustic features can be divided into two classes, low level descriptors (LLDs), and high level statistics functions (HSFs). LLDs features, including prosodies, spectral domain features and others, are calculated on a frame-basis, while HSFs features are calculated on an entire utterance level. In addition to the hand-crafted features, M-SENA also provides pretrained acoustic model wav2vec2.0 (Baevski et al., 2020) as a learnable feature extractor. Researchers can also design and build their own customized acoustic features using the provided Librosa extractor.

**Visual Modality.** In existing MSA research, facial Landmarks, eyes gaze, and facial action units are

| Types | Scenarios | | |
|---|---|---|---|
| | Films(TV) | Variety Show | Life(Vlog) |
| Easy | 10 (en:4 ch:6) | 8 (en:4 ch:4) | 8 (en:4 ch:4) |
| Common | 9 (en:4 ch:5) | 11 (en:6 ch:5) | 8 (en:4 ch:4) |
| Difficult | 9 (en:4 ch:5) | 9 (en:5 ch:4) | 8 (en:4 ch:4) |
| Noise | 9 (en:4 ch:5) | 8 (en:4 ch:4) | 7 (en:2 ch:5) |
| Missing | 9 (en:4 ch:5) | 9 (en:5 ch:4) | 7 (en:3 ch:4) |

Table 2: Statistics of the generalization ability test dataset, where "en" represents "English", "ch" represents "Chinese".

commonly used visual features. The M-SENA platform enables researchers to extract visual feature combinations flexibly using OpenFace and MediaPipe extractors.

**Text Modality.** Compared with acoustic and visual features, semantic text embeddings are much more mature with the rapid development of pretrained language models (Qiu et al., 2020). Following previous works (Zadeh et al., 2017a; Rahman et al., 2020; Lian et al., 2022), M-SENA supports GloVe6B (Pennington et al., 2014), pretrained BERT (Devlin et al., 2018), and pretrained RoBerta (Liu et al., 2019) as textual feature extractors.

All feature extractors above are available through both Python API and Graphical User Interface(GUI). Listing 1 shows a simple example of default acoustic feature extraction using Python API. The process is similar for other modalities. Advanced usage and detailed documentation is available at Github Wiki[4].

```
from MSA_FET import
    FeatureExtractionTool

# Extract Audio Feature for MOSI.
fet = FeatureExtractionTool("librosa")

feature = fet.run_dataset(
    dataset_dir='~/MOSI',
    out_file='output/feature.pkl'
)
```

Listing 1: An example of acoustic feature extraction on the MOSI dataset using MMSA.

## 2.3 Model Training Module

M-SENA provides a unified training module which currently integrates 14 MSA benchmarks, including tensor fusion methods, TFN (Zadeh et al., 2017a), LMF (Liu et al., 2018), modality factorization methods, MFM (Tsai et al., 2018), MISA (Hazarika et al., 2020), SELF-MM (Yu et al., 2021), word-level fusion methods, MulT (Tsai et al., 2019), BERT-MAG (Rahman et al., 2020),

[4]https://github.com/thuiar/MMSA-FET/wiki

| Feature Combinations | TFN | | GMFN | | MISA | | Bert-MAG | |
|---|---|---|---|---|---|---|---|---|
| | Acc-2 (%) | F1 (%) | Acc-2 (%) | F1 (%) | Acc-2 (%) | F1 (%) | Acc-2 (%) | F1 (%) |
| CMU-SDK† | 78.02 | 78.09 | 76.98 | 77.06 | 82.96 | 82.98 | 83.41 | 83.47 |
| [T1]-[A1]-[V1] | 77.41 | 77.47 | 77.77 | 77.84 | 83.78 | 83.80 | 83.38 | 83.43 |
| [T2]-[A1]-[V1] | 70.40 | 70.51 | 71.40 | 71.54 | 75.22 | 75.68 | - | - |
| [T3]-[A1]-[V1] | 80.85 | 80.79 | 80.21 | 80.15 | 79.57 | 79.67 | - | - |
| [T1]-[A2]-[V1] | 76.80 | 76.82 | 78.02 | 78.03 | 83.72 | 83.72 | 82.96 | 83.04 |
| [T1]-[A3]-[V1] | 77.19 | 77.23 | 78.44 | 78.45 | 82.16 | 82.23 | 83.57 | 83.58 |
| [T1]-[A1]-[V2] | 77.38 | 77.48 | 78.81 | 78.71 | 83.2 | 83.14 | 82.13 | 82.20 |
| [T1]-[A1]-[V3] | 76.74 | 76.81 | 78.23 | 78.24 | 84.06 | 84.08 | 83.69 | 83.75 |

Table 3: Results for feature selection. For text, [T1] refers to BERT, [T2] refers to GloVe6B, [T3] refers to RoBerta. For acoustic, [A1] refers to eGeMAPS, [A2] refers to customized feature including 20-dim MFCC, 12-dim CQT, and f0, [A3] refers to wav2vec2.0. For visual, [V1] refers to action units, [V2] refers to landmarks, [V3] refers to both landmarks and action units. CMU-SDK† refers to modified CMU-SDK features with BERT for text.

multi-view learning methods: MFN (Zadeh et al., 2018a), GMFN (Zadeh et al., 2018b), and other MSA methods. Detailed introduction of the integrated baseline methods is provided in Appendix B. We will continue following advanced MSA benchmarks and put our best effort into providing reliable benchmark results for future MSA research.

### 2.4 Result Analysis Module

The proposed M-SENA platform provides comprehensive model evaluation tools including intermediate result visualization, on-the-fly instance test, and generalization ability test. A brief introduction of each component is given below, while a detailed demonstration is shown in Section 4.

**Intermediate Result Visualization.** The discrimination of multimodal representations is one of the crucial metrics for the evaluation of different fusion methods. The M-SENA platform records the final multimodal fusion results and illustrates them after decomposition with Principal Component Analysis (PCA). Training loss, binary accuracy, F1 score curves are also provided in M-SENA for detailed analysis.

**Live Demo Module.** In the hope of bridging the gap between MSA research and real-world video sentiment analysis scenarios, M-SENA provides a live demo module, which performs on-the-fly instance tests. Researchers can validate the effectiveness and robustness of the selected MSA model by uploading or live-feeding videos to the platform.

**Generalization Ability Test.** Compared to the provided test set of benchmark MSA datasets, real-world scenarios are often more complicated. Future MSA models need to be robust against modality noise as well as effective on the test set. Driven by the demand from real-world applications and observations, the M-SENA platform provides a generalization ability test dataset (consists of 68 Chinese and 61 English samples), simulating as many complicated and diverse real-world scenarios as possible. The statistics of the proposed dataset is shown in Table 2. In general, the dataset contains three scenarios and five instance types. Specifically, the three scenarios refers to films, variety shows, and user-uploaded vlogs, while the five instance types refer to easy samples, common samples, difficult samples, samples with modality noise, samples with modality missing. In addition, the dataset is balanced in terms of gender and scenario to avoid irrelevant factors. Examples of the generalization ability test dataset are shown in Appendix C.

## 3 Experiments on M-SENA

In this section, we report experiments conducted on the M-SENA platform. Comparison of different modality features are shown in Section 3.1, and comparison of different fusion models are shown in Section 3.2. All reported results are the mean performances of five different seeds.

### 3.1 Feature Selection Comparison

In the following experiments, we take BERT [T1], eGeMAPS (LLDs) [A1], and Action Unit [V1] as default modality features, and compare them with the other six feature sets. Specifically, we utilize GloVe6B [T2], RoBerta [T3] for text modality comparison; customized acoustic feature[A2](including 20 dimensional MFCC, 12 dimensional CQT, and 1 dimensional f0), wav2vec2.0 features [A3] for acoustic modality comparison; facial landmarks [V2], facial land-

| Model | MOSI | | | | MOSEI | | | | SIMS | | | |
|---|---|---|---|---|---|---|---|---|---|---|---|---|
| | Acc-2 | F1 | MAE | Corr | Acc-2 | F1 | MAE | Corr | Acc-2 | F1 | MAE | Corr |
| LF_DNN | 79.39 | 79.45 | 0.945 | 0.675 | 82.78 | 82.38 | 0.558 | 0.731 | 76.68 | 76.48 | 0.446 | 0.567 |
| EF_LSTM | 77.35 | 77.43 | 0.995 | 0.644 | 81.23 | 81.02 | 0.588 | 0.695 | 69.37 | 56.82 | 0.591 | 0.380 |
| TFN | 78.02 | 78.09 | 0.971 | 0.652 | 82.23 | 81.47 | 0.573 | 0.718 | 77.07 | 76.94 | 0.437 | 0.582 |
| LMF | 78.60 | 78.61 | 0.934 | 0.663 | 83.83 | 83.68 | 0.562 | 0.735 | 77.42 | 77.35 | 0.438 | 0.578 |
| MFN | 78.78 | 78.71 | 0.938 | 0.665 | 83.30 | 83.23 | 0.570 | 0.720 | 78.55 | 78.23 | 0.442 | 0.575 |
| GMFN | 76.98 | 77.06 | 0.986 | 0.642 | 83.48 | 83.23 | 0.575 | 0.713 | 78.77 | 78.21 | 0.445 | 0.578 |
| MFM | 78.63 | 78.63 | 0.958 | 0.649 | 83.49 | 83.29 | 0.581 | 0.721 | 75.06 | 75.58 | 0.477 | 0.525 |
| MulT | 80.21 | 80.22 | 0.912 | 0.695 | 84.63 | 84.52 | 0.559 | 0.733 | 78.56 | 79.66 | 0.453 | 0.564 |
| MISA | 82.96 | 82.98 | 0.761 | 0.772 | 84.79 | 84.73 | 0.548 | 0.759 | 76.54 | 76.59 | 0.447 | 0.563 |
| BERT_MAG | 83.41 | 83.47 | 0.761 | 0.776 | 84.87 | 84.85 | 0.539 | 0.764 | 74.44 | 71.75 | 0.492 | 0.399 |
| MLF_DNN | - | - | - | - | - | - | - | - | 80.44 | 80.28 | 0.396 | 0.665 |
| MTFN | - | - | - | - | - | - | - | - | 81.09 | 81.01 | 0.395 | 0.666 |
| MLMF | - | - | - | - | - | - | - | - | 79.34 | 79.07 | 0.409 | 0.639 |
| Self_MM | 84.30 | 84.31 | 0.720 | 0.793 | 84.06 | 84.12 | 0.531 | 0.766 | 80.04 | 80.44 | 0.425 | 0.595 |

Table 4: Experiment results for MSA benchmark comparison. All models utilize the Bert embedding and the provided acoustic and visual features in CMU-MultimodalSDK. Due to the requirement of unimodal labels, multi-task models, including MLF_DNN, MTFN, and MLMF, are tested on SIMS only.

marks and action units [V3] for visual modality comparison. Besides, we also report the model performances using the modality features provided in CMU-MultimodalSDK.

Table 3 shows the experiment results for feature selection. For Bert-MAG which is designed upon the Bert backbone, experiments are conducted only for Bert as text feature. It can be observed that, in most cases, using appropriate features instead of original features in CMU-MultimodalSDK helps to improve model performance. For textual modality, Roberta feature performs best for TFN and GMFN model, while Bert feature performs best for MISA model. For acoustic modality, wav2vec2.0 embeddings (without finetune) perform best for GMFN and Bert-MAG model. According to literature (Chen and Rudnicky, 2021; Pepino et al., 2021), finetuning wav2vec2.0 can further improve model performance which might provide more effective acoustic features for future MSA research. For Visual modality, the combination of facial landmarks and action units achieves the overall best result, revealing the effectiveness of both landmarks and action units for sentiment classification.

### 3.2 MSA Benchmark Comparison

Experiment results of benchmark MSA models are shown in Table 4. All models are improved using Bert as text embeddings while using original acoustic and visual features provided in CMU-MultimodalSDK. Besides recording reliable benchmark results, the M-SENA platform also provides researchers with a convenient approach to reproduce the benchmarks. Again, both GUI and Python API are available. We show an example of the proposed Python API in Listing 2. Detailed and Advanced usage is included in our documentation at Github[5]. We will continuously catch up on new MSA approaches and update their performances.

```
from MMSA import MMSA_run

# Load Default Training Config.
config = get_config_regression(
    model_name='tfn',
    dataset_name='mosi'
)

# Using User Designed Hyper-parameter.
config['post_fusion_dim'] = 32

# Modality Feature Selection.
config['featurePath'] = 'feature.pkl'

# Start Model Training.
MMSA_run(
    model_name='tfn',
    dataset_name='mosi',
    config=config,
    seeds=[1111]
)
```

Listing 2: An example to train model with M-SENA.

## 4 Model Analysis Demonstration

This section demonstrates model analysis results using the M-SENA platform. Intermediate result analysis is presented in Section 4.1, on-the-fly instance analysis is shown in Section 4.2, and generalization ability analysis is illustrated in Section 4.3.

[5]https://github.com/thuiar/MMSA/wiki

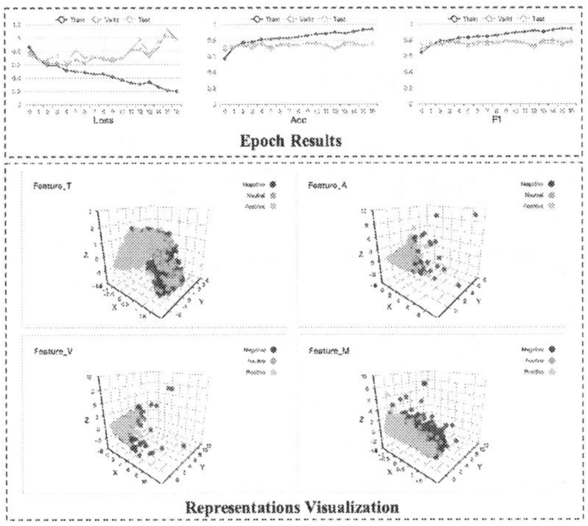


Figure 2: Intermediate Result Analysis for TFN model trained on MOSI dataset.

### 4.1 Intermediate Result Analysis

The intermediate result analysis submodule is designed to monitor and visualize the training process. Figure 2 shows an example of training TFN model on MOSI dataset. Epoch results of binary accuracy, f1-score and loss value are plotted. Moreover, the learned multimodal fusion representations are illustrated in an interactive 3D figure with the aim of helping users gain a better intuition about the multimodal feature representations and the fusion process. Unimodal representations of text, acoustic, and visual are also shown for models containing explicit unimodal representations.

### 4.2 On-the-fly Instance Analysis

M-SENA enables researchers to validate the proposed MSA approaches using uploaded or live-recorded instances. Figure 3 presents an example of the live demonstration. Besides model prediction results, the platform also provides feature visualization, including short-time Fourier transform (STFT) for acoustic modality and facial landmarks, eye gaze, head poses for visual modality. We will continuously update the demonstration to make it a even more intuitive and playable MSA model evaluation tool.

### 4.3 Generalization Ability Analysis

We utilized the model trained on MOSI dataset with [T1]-[A1]-[V3] modality features in Section 3.1 for generalization ability test. Experimental results are reported in Table 5. It can be concluded that all models present a performance gap between original test set and real-world scenarios, especially for the instances with noisy or missing modalities. Another observation is that the noisy instances are usually more challenging than modality missing for MSA models, revealing that noisy modality feature is worse than none at all. In the future, for the demand of real-world applications, MSA researchers may consider analyzing model robustness as well as performances on the test set, and design a more robust MSA model against random modality noise.

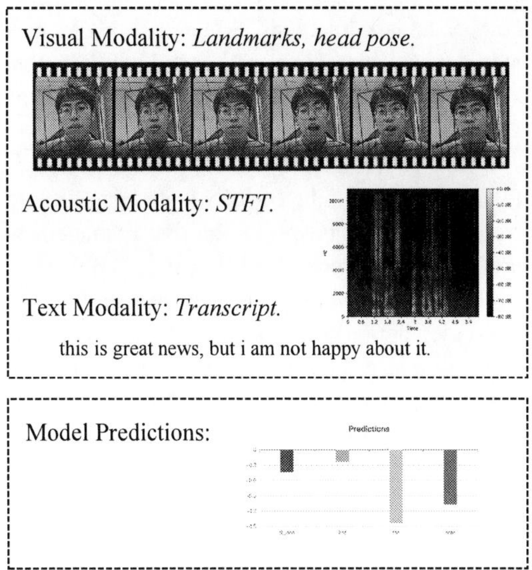


Figure 3: On-the-fly instance test example. The M-SENA platform also provides real-time modality feature visualization along with the model prediction results.

| Types | TFN Acc-2 / F1 | GMFN Acc-2 / F1 | MISA Acc-2 / F1 | Bert-MAG Acc-2 / F1 |
|---|---|---|---|---|
| Easy | 83.3 / 84.4 | 75.0 / 76.1 | 75.0 / 76.7 | 66.7 / 66.7 |
| Common | 71.4 / 74.5 | 85.7 / 82.3 | 71.4 / 75.8 | 78.6 / 78.6 |
| Difficult | 69.2 / 69.2 | 61.5 / 60.5 | 53.9 / 54.4 | 84.6 / 84.6 |
| Noise | 60.0 / 50.5 | 50.0 / 44.9 | 50.0 / 35.7 | 60.0 / 51.7 |
| Missing | 63.6 / 60.6 | 81.8 / 77.8 | 63.6 / 60.6 | 63.6 / 61.5 |
| Avg | 70.0 / 68.4 | 71.7 / 69.3 | 63.3 / 62.4 | 71.7 / 69.7 |

Table 5: Results for English generalization ability test. Binary accuracy and F1 scores are reported to show the effectiveness and robustness of the model.

## 5 Related Works

To the best of our knowledge, there are two widely used open-source repositories from CMU team[6] and SUTD team[7]. Both of them provide tools to load well-known MSA datasets and implement sev-

[6]https://github.com/A2Zadeh/CMU-MultimodalSDK

[7]https://github.com/declare-lab/multimodal-deep-learning

eral benchmarks methods. So far, their works have attracted considerable attention and facilitated the birth of new MSA models such as MulT (Tsai et al., 2019) and MMIM (Han et al., 2021b).

In this paper, we propose M-SENA, compared to previous works, the M-SENA platform is novel from the following aspects. For data management, previous work directly loads the extracted features, while the M-SENA platform focuses on intuitive raw video demonstration, and provides user with a convenient means for private dataset construction. For modality features, M-SENA platform first provides user-customized feature extraction toolkit and a transparent feature extraction process. Following the tutorial, Users can easily reproduce the feature extraction steps and develop their research on designed feature set. For model training, the M-SENA platform first utilizes a unified MSA framework and provide an easy-to-reproduce model training API integrating fourteen MSA benchmarks on three popular MSA dataset. For model evaluation, the M-SENA is the first MSA platform consisting of comprehensive evaluation means stressing model robustness for real-world scenarios, which aims to bridge the gap between MSA research and applications.

## Conclusion

In this work, we introduce M-SENA, an integrated platform that contains step-by-step recipes for data management, feature extraction, model training, and model analysis for MSA researchers. The platform evaluates MSA model in an end-to-end manner and reports reliable benchmark results for future research. Moreover, we further investigate comprehensive model evaluation and analysis methods and provide a series of user-friendly visualization and demonstration tools including intermediate representation visualization, on-the-fly instance test, and generalization ability test. In the future, we will continuously catch up on advanced MSA research progress and update new benchmarks on the M-SENA platform.

## Acknowledgement

This paper is funded by The National Natural Science Foundation of China (Grant No. 62173195) and Beijing Academy of Artificial Intelligence (BAAI). The authors thank the anonymous reviewers for their valuable suggestions.

## References

Mehmet Berkehan Akçay and Kaya Oğuz. 2020. Speech emotion recognition: Emotional models, databases, features, preprocessing methods, supporting modalities, and classifiers. *Speech Communication*, 116:56–76.

Alexei Baevski, Henry Zhou, Abdelrahman Mohamed, and Michael Auli. 2020. wav2vec 2.0: A framework for self-supervised learning of speech representations. *arXiv preprint arXiv:2006.11477*.

Tadas Baltrušaitis, Marwa Mahmoud, and Peter Robinson. 2015. Cross-dataset learning and person-specific normalisation for automatic action unit detection. In *2015 11th IEEE International Conference and Workshops on Automatic Face and Gesture Recognition (FG)*, volume 6, pages 1–6. IEEE.

Tadas Baltrusaitis, Amir Zadeh, Yao Chong Lim, and Louis-Philippe Morency. 2018. Openface 2.0: Facial behavior analysis toolkit. In *2018 13th IEEE International Conference on Automatic Face & Gesture Recognition (FG 2018)*, pages 59–66. IEEE.

Erik Cambria, Devamanyu Hazarika, Soujanya Poria, Amir Hussain, and RBV Subramanyam. 2017. Benchmarking multimodal sentiment analysis. In *International Conference on Computational Linguistics and Intelligent Text Processing*, pages 166–179. Springer.

Li-Wei Chen and Alexander Rudnicky. 2021. Exploring wav2vec 2.0 fine-tuning for improved speech emotion recognition. *arXiv preprint arXiv:2110.06309*.

Wenliang Dai, Samuel Cahyawijaya, Zihan Liu, and Pascale Fung. 2021. Multimodal end-to-end sparse model for emotion recognition. In *Proceedings of the 2021 Conference of the North American Chapter of the Association for Computational Linguistics: Human Language Technologies*, pages 5305–5316.

Jacob Devlin, Ming-Wei Chang, Kenton Lee, and Kristina Toutanova. 2018. Bert: Pre-training of deep bidirectional transformers for language understanding. *arXiv preprint arXiv:1810.04805*.

Moataz El Ayadi, Mohamed S Kamel, and Fakhri Karray. 2011. Survey on speech emotion recognition: Features, classification schemes, and databases. *Pattern recognition*, 44(3):572–587.

Florian Eyben, Klaus R Scherer, Björn W Schuller, Johan Sundberg, Elisabeth André, Carlos Busso, Laurence Y Devillers, Julien Epps, Petri Laukka, Shrikanth S Narayanan, et al. 2015. The geneva minimalistic acoustic parameter set (gemaps) for voice research and affective computing. *IEEE transactions on affective computing*, 7(2):190–202.

Florian Eyben, Martin Wöllmer, and Björn Schuller. 2010. Opensmile: the munich versatile and fast open-source audio feature extractor. In *Proceedings of the 18th ACM international conference on Multimedia*, pages 1459–1462.

Dimitris Gkoumas, Qiuchi Li, Christina Lioma, Yijun Yu, and Dawei Song. 2021. What makes the difference? an empirical comparison of fusion strategies for multimodal language analysis. *Information Fusion*, 66:184–197.

Wenzhong Guo, Jianwen Wang, and Shiping Wang. 2019. Deep multimodal representation learning: A survey. *IEEE Access*, 7:63373–63394.

Wei Han, Hui Chen, Alexander Gelbukh, Amir Zadeh, Louis-philippe Morency, and Soujanya Poria. 2021a. Bi-bimodal modality fusion for correlation-controlled multimodal sentiment analysis. In *Proceedings of the 2021 International Conference on Multimodal Interaction*, pages 6–15.

Wei Han, Hui Chen, and Soujanya Poria. 2021b. Improving multimodal fusion with hierarchical mutual information maximization for multimodal sentiment analysis. In *Proceedings of the 2021 Conference on Empirical Methods in Natural Language Processing*, pages 9180–9192.

Devamanyu Hazarika, Roger Zimmermann, and Soujanya Poria. 2020. Misa: Modality-invariant and-specific representations for multimodal sentiment analysis. In *Proceedings of the 28th ACM International Conference on Multimedia*, pages 1122–1131.

Zheng Lian, Bin Liu, and Jianhua Tao. 2022. Smin: Semi-supervised multi-modal interaction network for conversational emotion recognition. *IEEE Transactions on Affective Computing*.

Paul Pu Liang, Zhun Liu, Yao-Hung Hubert Tsai, Qibin Zhao, Ruslan Salakhutdinov, and Louis-Philippe Morency. 2019. Learning representations from imperfect time series data via tensor rank regularization. In *Proceedings of the 57th Annual Meeting of the Association for Computational Linguistics*, pages 1569–1576.

Yinhan Liu, Myle Ott, Naman Goyal, Jingfei Du, Mandar Joshi, Danqi Chen, Omer Levy, Mike Lewis, Luke Zettlemoyer, and Veselin Stoyanov. 2019. Roberta: A robustly optimized bert pretraining approach. *arXiv preprint arXiv:1907.11692*.

Zhun Liu, Ying Shen, Varun Bharadhwaj Lakshminarasimhan, Paul Pu Liang, AmirAli Bagher Zadeh, and Louis-Philippe Morency. 2018. Efficient low-rank multimodal fusion with modality-specific factors. In *Proceedings of the 56th Annual Meeting of the Association for Computational Linguistics (Volume 1: Long Papers)*, pages 2247–2256.

Camillo Lugaresi, Jiuqiang Tang, Hadon Nash, Chris McClanahan, Esha Uboweja, Michael Hays, Fan Zhang, Chuo-Ling Chang, Ming Guang Yong, Juhyun Lee, et al. 2019. Mediapipe: A framework for building perception pipelines. *arXiv preprint arXiv:1906.08172*.

Brian McFee, Colin Raffel, Dawen Liang, Daniel PW Ellis, Matt McVicar, Eric Battenberg, and Oriol Nieto. 2015. librosa: Audio and music signal analysis in python. In *Proceedings of the 14th python in science conference*, volume 8, pages 18–25.

Rada Mihalcea. 2012. Multimodal sentiment analysis. In *Proceedings of the 3rd Workshop in Computational Approaches to Subjectivity and Sentiment Analysis*, pages 1–1.

Jeffrey Pennington, Richard Socher, and Christopher D Manning. 2014. Glove: Global vectors for word representation. In *Proceedings of the 2014 conference on empirical methods in natural language processing (EMNLP)*, pages 1532–1543.

Leonardo Pepino, Pablo Riera, and Luciana Ferrer. 2021. Emotion recognition from speech using wav2vec 2.0 embeddings. *arXiv preprint arXiv:2104.03502*.

Xipeng Qiu, Tianxiang Sun, Yige Xu, Yunfan Shao, Ning Dai, and Xuanjing Huang. 2020. Pre-trained models for natural language processing: A survey. *Science China Technological Sciences*, pages 1–26.

Wasifur Rahman, Md Kamrul Hasan, Sangwu Lee, AmirAli Bagher Zadeh, Chengfeng Mao, Louis-Philippe Morency, and Ehsan Hoque. 2020. Integrating multimodal information in large pretrained transformers. In *Proceedings of the 58th Annual Meeting of the Association for Computational Linguistics*, pages 2359–2369.

Björn Schuller, Stefan Steidl, Anton Batliner, Julia Hirschberg, Judee K Burgoon, Alice Baird, Aaron Elkins, Yue Zhang, Eduardo Coutinho, Keelan Evanini, et al. 2016. The interspeech 2016 computational paralinguistics challenge: Deception, sincerity & native language. In *17TH Annual Conference of the International Speech Communication Association (Interspeech 2016), Vols 1-5*, pages 2001–2005.

Mohammad Soleymani, David Garcia, Brendan Jou, Björn Schuller, Shih-Fu Chang, and Maja Pantic. 2017. A survey of multimodal sentiment analysis. *Image and Vision Computing*, 65:3–14.

Yao-Hung Hubert Tsai, Shaojie Bai, Paul Pu Liang, J Zico Kolter, Louis-Philippe Morency, and Ruslan Salakhutdinov. 2019. Multimodal transformer for unaligned multimodal language sequences. In *Proceedings of the conference. Association for Computational Linguistics. Meeting*, volume 2019, page 6558. NIH Public Access.

Yao-Hung Hubert Tsai, Paul Pu Liang, Amir Zadeh, Louis-Philippe Morency, and Ruslan Salakhutdinov. 2018. Learning factorized multimodal representations. *arXiv preprint arXiv:1806.06176*.

Erroll Wood, Tadas Baltrusaitis, Xucong Zhang, Yusuke Sugano, Peter Robinson, and Andreas Bulling. 2015. Rendering of eyes for eye-shape registration and gaze estimation. In *Proceedings of the IEEE International Conference on Computer Vision*, pages 3756–3764.

Wenmeng Yu, Hua Xu, Fanyang Meng, Yilin Zhu, Yixiao Ma, Jiele Wu, Jiyun Zou, and Kaicheng Yang. 2020. CH-SIMS: A Chinese multimodal sentiment analysis dataset with fine-grained annotation of modality. In *Proceedings of the 58th Annual Meeting of the Association for Computational Linguistics*, pages 3718–3727, Online. Association for Computational Linguistics.

Wenmeng Yu, Hua Xu, Ziqi Yuan, and Jiele Wu. 2021. Learning modality-specific representations with self-supervised multi-task learning for multimodal sentiment analysis. In *Proceedings of the AAAI Conference on Artificial Intelligence*, volume 35, pages 10790–10797.

Ziqi Yuan, Wei Li, Hua Xu, and Wenmeng Yu. 2021. Transformer-based feature reconstruction network for robust multimodal sentiment analysis. In *Proceedings of the 29th ACM International Conference on Multimedia*, pages 4400–4407.

Amir Zadeh, Minghai Chen, Soujanya Poria, Erik Cambria, and Louis-Philippe Morency. 2017a. Tensor fusion network for multimodal sentiment analysis. In *Proceedings of the 2017 Conference on Empirical Methods in Natural Language Processing*, pages 1103–1114.

Amir Zadeh, Yao Chong Lim, Tadas Baltrusaitis, and Louis-Philippe Morency. 2017b. Convolutional experts constrained local model for 3d facial landmark detection. In *Proceedings of the IEEE International Conference on Computer Vision Workshops*, pages 2519–2528.

Amir Zadeh, Paul Pu Liang, Navonil Mazumder, Soujanya Poria, Erik Cambria, and Louis-Philippe Morency. 2018a. Memory fusion network for multi-view sequential learning. In *Proceedings of the AAAI Conference on Artificial Intelligence*, volume 32.

Amir Zadeh, Rowan Zellers, Eli Pincus, and Louis-Philippe Morency. 2016. Multimodal sentiment intensity analysis in videos: Facial gestures and verbal messages. *IEEE Intelligent Systems*, 31(6):82–88.

AmirAli Bagher Zadeh, Paul Pu Liang, Soujanya Poria, Erik Cambria, and Louis-Philippe Morency. 2018b. Multimodal language analysis in the wild: Cmu-mosei dataset and interpretable dynamic fusion graph. In *Proceedings of the 56th Annual Meeting of the Association for Computational Linguistics (Volume 1: Long Papers)*, pages 2236–2246.

Jinming Zhao, Ruichen Li, and Qin Jin. 2021. Missing modality imagination network for emotion recognition with uncertain missing modalities. In *Proceedings of the 59th Annual Meeting of the Association for Computational Linguistics and the 11th International Joint Conference on Natural Language Processing (Volume 1: Long Papers)*, pages 2608–2618.

# A Integrated Datasets

**CMU-MOSI.** The MOSI (Zadeh et al., 2016) dataset is a widely-used dataset that consists of a collection of 2,199 video segments from 93 YouTube movie review videos.

**CMU-MOSEI.** The MOSEI (Zadeh et al., 2018b) dataset expands the MOSI dataset by enlarging the number of utterances and enriching the variety of samples, speakers, and topics. For both MOSI and MOSEI datasets, instances are annotated with a sentiment intensity score ranging from -3 to 3 (strongly negative to strongly positive).

**CH-SIMS.** The SIMS dataset (Yu et al., 2020) is a Chinese unimodal and multimodal sentiment analysis dataset. It contains 2,281 refined video segments in the wild with both multimodal and independent unimodal annotations of a sentiment intensity score ranging from -1 to 1 (negative to positive, the score interval is 0.2).

# B Integrated Benchmarks

**LF-DNN.** The Late Fusion Deep Neural Network (Cambria et al., 2017) first extracts modality features separately and performs late fusion strategy for final predictions.

**EF-LSTM.** The Early Fusion Long-Short Term Memory (Cambria et al., 2017) is based on input-level feature fusion and conducts Long-Short Term Memory (LSTM) to learn multimodal representations.

**TFN.** The Tensor Fusion Network (TFN) (Zadeh et al., 2017a) calculates a multi-dimensional tensor (based on outer product) to capture uni-, bi-, and tri-modal interactions.

**LMF.** The Low-rank Multimodal Fusion (LMF) (Liu et al., 2018) is an improvement over TFN, where the low-rank multimodal tensors fusion technique is performed to improve efficiency.

**MFN.** The Memory Fusion Network (MFN) (Zadeh et al., 2018a) accounts for continuously modeling the view specific and cross-view interactions and summarizing them through time with a Multi-view Gated Memory.

**Graph-MFN.** The Graph Memory Fusion Network (Zadeh et al., 2018b) is an improvement of MFN, which can change the fusion structure dynamically to obtain the interaction between the modalities and improve the interpretability.

**MulT.** The Multimodal Transformer (MulT) (Tsai et al., 2019) extends multimodal transformer architecture with directional pairwise cross-modal attention which translates one modality to another using directional pairwise cross-attention.

**BERT-MAG.** The Multimodal Adaptation Gate for Bert (MAG-BERT) (Rahman et al., 2020) is an improvement over RAVEN on aligned data with applying multimodal adaptation gate at different layers of the BERT backbone.

**MISA.** The Modality-Invariant and -Specific Representations (Hazarika et al., 2020) is made up of a combination of losses including similarity loss, orthogonal loss, reconstruction loss and prediction loss to learn modality-invariant and modality-specific representation.

**MFM.** The Multimodal Factorization Model (Tsai et al., 2018) is a robust model, which can learn multimodal-discriminative and modality-specific generative factors, then reconstructs missing reconstruct missing modalities by adjusting for independent factors.

**MLF_DNN.** The Multi-Task Late Fusion Deep Neural Network (Yu et al., 2020) first extracts modality features separately and performs late fusion strategy for final predictions through unimodal labels training.

**MTFN.** The Multi-Task Tensor Fusion Network (Yu et al., 2020) calculates a multi-dimensional tensor (based on outer product) to capture uni-, bi-, and tri-modal interactions through unimodal labels training.

**MLMF.** The Multi-Task Low-rank Multimodal Fusion (Yu et al., 2020) is an improvement over MTFN, where low-rank multimodal tensors fusion technique is performed to improve efficiency through unimodal labels training.

**Self_MM.** The Self-Supervised Multi-Task Multimodal (Yu et al., 2021) design a label generation module based on the self-supervised learning strategy to acquire independent unimodal supervisions, which can balance the learning progress among different sub-tasks.

## C Generalization Ability Test Datasets

The examples of the proposed generalization ability test dataset are shown in Figure 4.

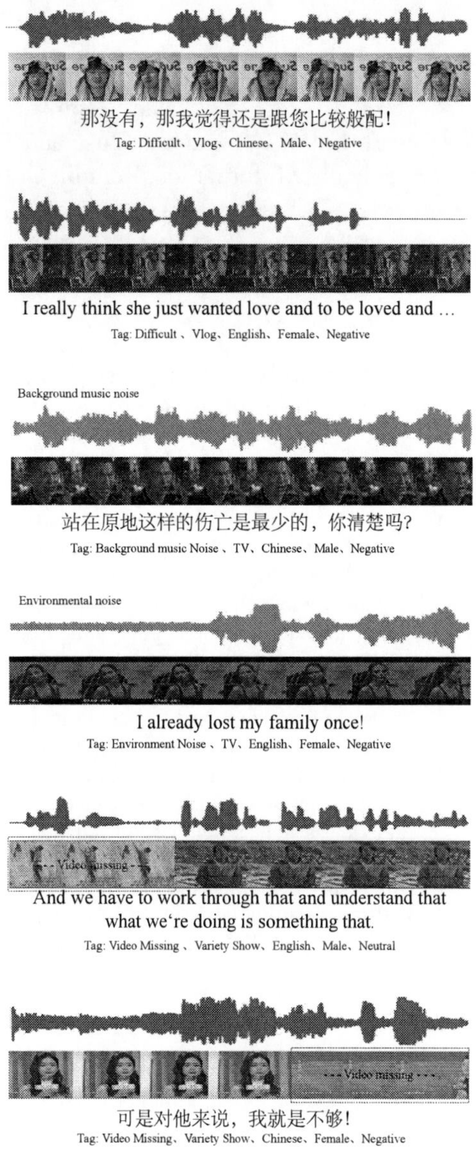


Figure 4: Examples of the constructed generalization ability test dataset.

# HOSMEL: A Hot-Swappable Modularized Entity Linking Toolkit for Chinese

**Daniel Zhang-Li[1], Jing Zhang[2]*, Jifan Yu[1], Xiaokang Zhang[2], Peng Zhang[1,3], Jie Tang[1], Juanzi Li[1]**

[1]Department of Computer Science and Technology, Tsinghua University, Beijing, China
[2]School of Information, Renmin University of China Beijing, China, [3]ZHIPU.AI
{zlnn21,yujf21}@mails.tsinghua.edu.cn,
{zhang-jing,zhang2718}@ruc.edu.cn,
peng.zhang@aminer.cn, {jietang,lijuanzi}@tsinghua.edu.cn

## Abstract

We investigate the usage of entity linking (EL) in downstream tasks and present the first modularized EL toolkit for easy task adaptation. Different from the existing EL methods that deal with all the features simultaneously, we modularize the whole model into separate parts with each feature. This decoupled design enables flexibly adding new features without retraining the whole model as well as flow visualization with better interpretability of the EL result. We release the corresponding toolkit, HOSMEL, for Chinese, with three flexible usage modes[1], a live demo[2], and a demonstration video[3]. Experiments on two benchmarks for the question answering task demonstrate that HOSMEL achieves much less time and space consumption as well as significantly better accuracy performance compared with existing SOTA EL methods. We hope the release of HOSMEL will call for more attention to study EL for downstream tasks in non-English languages.

## 1 Introduction

Entity linking (EL) is to extract the candidate mentions in the sentences and link them to their corresponding entities in the knowledge bases (KB) such as Freebase, Wikidata, and DBPedia. The linked entities encode rich knowledge from the KB, which can enhance many downstream tasks such as information retrieval (Raviv et al., 2016), recommendation (Guo et al., 2020), question answering (Feng et al., 2021; Zhang et al., 2021a), and language model pre-training (Zhang et al., 2019). As EL is usually deployed in the pre-processing stages of these tasks, an urgent demand for EL models is to guarantee a high accuracy to prevent potential error propagation.

Existing researches have fully explored the EL problem. From the matching-based methods (Chen et al., 2020, 2022; Logeswaran et al., 2019; Yamada et al., 2019; Wu et al., 2020; Zhang et al., 2021c) to the generation-based methods (Nicola De et al., 2020; De Cao et al., 2021), the SOTA models such as BLINK (Wu et al., 2020), GENRE (Nicola De et al., 2020), and EntQA (Zhang et al., 2021c), have considered different features such as mention, entity subtitle, and entity description, resulting in outstanding performances on various published EL benchmarks.

However, the existing advanced models usually aggregate all the features for training. Despite their excellent performance, they are difficult to be adapted to specific downstream tasks. Figure 2 illustrates an EL example for answering the question "*What religion does Luke's master believe in?*", by which multiple mentions are detected and linked to the entities in XLore[4] (Jin et al., 2019a) — one of the largest Chinese KBs. Depending only on the subtitle description of an entity, the mention, "*Luke*", can be highly probably linked to both the entity "*Luke Skywalker*" and "*Luke Cage*"[5]. Whereas in this scenario, we can accurately find that the former better matches because it has a relation "*master*" in XLore which is exactly the questioned aspect. This case presents a common phenomenon that downstream tasks usually require additional information invocation such as relation for better EL results.

Generally, developers need to annotate specific data and perform after treatments for EL model adaption. (For the above example, we need to annotate a new dataset such as the one including relation as the additional feature for question answering and retrain the EL model on the new dataset). However, in the era of advanced large EL models, such data

*Corresponding author.

[1]https://github.com/THUDM/HOSMEL

[2]https://www.aminer.cn/el/#/

[3]https://drive.google.com/drive/folders/1eh-dJnKWJulPuZGsORii4fPW-zCmWS5k?usp=sharing

[4]https://xlore.org/

[5]*Luke Skywalker* is a character in Star Wars and *Luke Cage* is a Marvel superhero.



*Proceedings of the 60th Annual Meeting of the Association for Computational Linguistics System Demonstrations*, pages 214 - 223

annotation and model retraining is quite costly and inefficient, which raises a natural question: *Can we develop an effective EL tool that can be easily adapted to downstream tasks?*

**Presented work.** We propose a **HO**t-**S**wappable **M**odularized **E**ntity **L**inking toolkit (HOSMEL) to solve the above problem. Compared with existing EL methods or toolkits, HOSMEL is more suitable for the downstream tasks because of its following characteristics:

- **Low coupled modules.** We modularize mention filtering, mention detection, and entity disambiguation by each entity attribute, ensuring each module can be trained separately and combined freely.
- **Incremental development.** The decoupled design turns the module of each step into a hot-swappable module, which enables flexibly adding the new features that were not previously considered without retraining the whole model.
- **Flexible to use (three usage modes).** We develop a corresponding toolkit for Chinese EL as Chinese has gained less attention than English. For flexible usage, we release three usage methods. The first one is a ready-to-use release for directly invoking the API or accessing the web application. The second one is a partial release for users who prefer to include parts of the release as a pre-step to improve the recall of their model. The third one is an easy-to-change release that enables adding additional features or training with self-defined data.
- **Flow visualization.** The decoupled design also enables a more explainable way for visualizing the results of each module, which provides user engineers a more effortless experience in deciding the useful features for optimizing the best outcome.

We select question answering as the downstream task to evaluate the proposed HOSMEL. We conduct extensive experiments on two question answering benchmarks. The results reveal three major advantages: (1) the training time of the lightweight HOSMEL is reduced by 4-5 times compared with two SOTA EL models, GENRE (Nicola De et al., 2020) and EntQA (Zhang et al., 2021c), in advance, the storage occupancy rate is also reduced by 78% compared with EntQA. (2) HOSMEL can achieve much better performance (+8.49-17.06% accuracy) than the best baseline EntQA on less training data. (3) We additionally evaluate the hot-swappable ability of HOSMEL and find that when adding a new feature relation, HOSMEL can be quickly updated and further improves 3.71-5.02% of accuracy.

**Contributions.** (1) We investigate the usage of EL in downstream tasks and raise the problem of adaptation for EL in downstream tasks. (2) We design a hot-swappable modularized EL system and release the corresponding toolkit in Chinese[1] and a live demo[2].

## 2 Problem Definition

A **knowledge base** (KB) $\mathcal{E}$ contains $n$ entities denoted by $\mathcal{E} = \{e_i\}_{i=1}^{n}$. Each entity $e_i$ is associated with a set of attributes denoted by $A_i = \{A_i^t\}_{t=1}^{T}$ where $A_i^t$ is the attributes of type $t$ and $T$ is the total number of attribute types. $A_i^t$ is further denoted by $\{a_{ij}^t\}_{j=1}^{n_i^t}$ with $a_{ij}^t$ as the $j$-th attribute of type $t$ and $n_i^t$ as the total number of attributes with type $t$. For example, an entity usually contains a title, a subtitle, a description, and multiple relations.

**Problem 1.** ***Entity Linking (EL):*** *Given an input text* $d = \{w_1, \cdots, w_n\}$ *and a KB* $\mathcal{E}$*, the output of EL is a list of mention-entity pairs* $\{(m_i, e_i)\}_{i=1}^{K}$*, where each mention* $m_i$ *is a text span extracted from d, and each entity* $e_i$ *is included in* $\mathcal{E}$*.*

We assume each mention has a valid gold entity in the KB and leave the out-of-KB prediction (i.e., nil prediction) to future works.

## 3 The Proposed HOSMEL

HOSMEL modularizes mention filtering, mention detection, and entity disambiguation by each entity attribute separately. Generally, given an input text, HOSMEL first selects all the possible mentions and then detects the useful ones, whose candidate entities are then measured by each attribute of them independently. Apart from mention filtering, each subsequent step aggregates the scores of all the previous steps and outputs a new top-K result to its next. Figure 1 illustrates the overall framework of the proposed HOSMEL, each step explained below.

### 3.1 Mention Filtering

Mention filtering is to filter out the possible mentions that can be linked to certain entities in KB. For example, in Figure 2, the input contains mentions "卢克*(Luke)*", "信仰*(religion)*", "师父*(master)*",

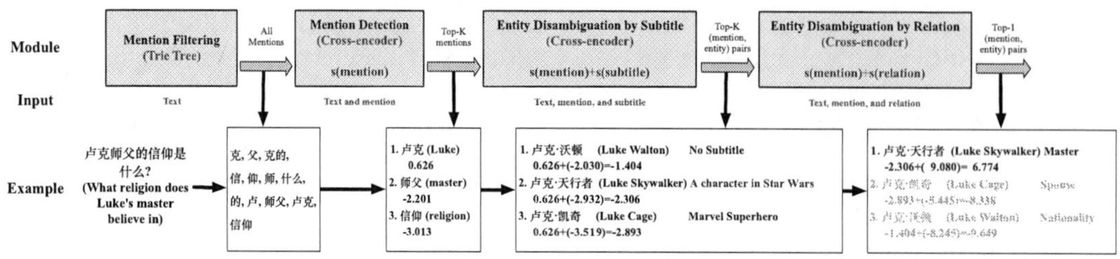

Figure 1: Illustration of the overall framework, where mention filtering, mention detection, entity disambiguation by subtitle, and disambiguation by relation are modularized. Each module aggregates the scores of all the previous modules and outputs a new top-K result to the next step.

etc. For this purpose, we build a Trie tree (Wilkes, 1974) with all the possible mentions, collected using titles and available alias names (Cf. Section A.2 for collecting details.) of all the entities in the KB. Previous works usually omit the steps of mention filtering and mention detection under the assumption that the mentions in an input text are known (Logeswaran et al., 2019; Yamada et al., 2019; Wu et al., 2020). Without this assumption, we can simply resort to the above Trie tree to find the mentions, because in our two EL benchmarks for question answering, by this kind of mention filtering, we can obtain an exceptionally high recall of the ground truth entities (Cf. Section A.2 in Appendix for details). For the datasets with mentions not exactly the same with the titles or alias names of the entities, users can change this Trie tree to other more suitable methods such as bi-encoder (Zhang et al., 2021c).

### 3.2 Mention Detection

Mention detection determines the top-K important mentions from all the possible mentions returned by the previous step. For example, in Figure 2, "卢克(*Luke*)" is more crucial to answer the question than the other mentions. For this purpose, we concatenate the input text $d$ and a mention $m_i$ into "$d$; $[SEP]; m_i$" as the input of a cross encoder, which is instantiated as MacBERT(Cui et al., 2020) in this and the subsequent steps. Then we apply a MLP layer on the CLS embedding of MacBERT to obtain the probability of $m_i$ given $d$. We take the logarithm of the probability as the mention's score $s(m_i) = \log(P(m_i|d))$ and output the top-K ranked mentions by $s(m_i)$ to the next step.

### 3.3 Entity Disambiguation

Entity disambiguation is to seek the correct entities from the KB for the detected mentions. Thanks to the Trie tree, we can quickly obtain the entity candidates stored as (title/alias, entity identifier) pairs with their title or aliases. For disambiguating an entity candidate, we match the input text and the mention with each type of attribute independently in the same way. Specifically, given an attribute type $t$, we concatenate the input text $d$, the mention $m_i$, and an attribute $a_{ij}^t$ of entity $e_i$ into "$d$; $[SEP]; m_i; a_{ij}^t$" as the input of MacBERT. We also apply a MLP layer on the CLS embedding to obtain the probability of attribute $a_{ij}^t$ given $d$ and $m_i$. We take the logarithm of the probability as $a_{ij}^t$'s score and get the maximal score from all the attributes $A_i^t$ as the pooling score of $A_i^t$, *i.e.*, $s(A_i^t) = \max_j \log(P(a_{ij}^t|d, m_i))$. When a type only has one attribute, such as a single subtitle, the maximal score is the score of the single attribute.

Then we rank the entities by the score of each $(m_i, e_i)$ pair, which is computed by the logarithm of the joint probability of $m_i$ and all the processed attributes of $e_i$ given the input text $d$, *i.e.*,

$$s(m_i, e_i) = \log P(A_i^1, A_i^2, \cdots, A_i^t, m_i|d), \\ = s(m_i) + \sum_{\tau=1}^{t} s(A_i^\tau), \quad (1)$$

where $s(m_i)$ and $s(A_i^\tau)$ are the scores of the mention $m_i$ and attributes $A_i^\tau$ respectively. The second equation is obtained according to the assumption of the independence of the mention and different attributes. The derivation details can be referred to Eq.(2) in Appendix. We return top-K ranked (mention,entity) pairs by $s(m_i, e_i)$ to the next step.

### 3.4 Training Strategy

The parameters of MacBERT are learned via optimizing the cross-entropy between the predicted scores and the ground truth mentions or the entity attributes. We train a separate MacBERT for computing each score, including the score of the mention and the score of each attribute type respectively. The training data is organized following the setting of multiple-choice question answering. For example, a data instance for training the mention detection model needs to include the input text and four candidate mentions, with one labeled as the ground truth. While for training the entity disambiguation model by an attribute such as the subtitle, it needs to include the input text, the mention to be linked, and four candidate subtitles with the ground truth label. Thanks to this separate training, we can adjust each module without influencing other modules. A new feature can be easily added as we only need to annotate a small amount of the training data about the new feature rather than re-annotate a new one with both the old and the new features.

## 4 The Usage of HOSMEL

We consider three different usage scenarios of the proposed HOSMEL and release the corresponding toolkit usage scripts with a live demo.

### 4.1 Ready-to-Use Release

The ready-to-use release is for users who need to link the input text to the general Chinese open domain KB. For this purpose, we train HOSMEL on XLore with the mention and entities' title, subtitle, and relations as features and release the model checkpoints. Users can download all the checkpoints and use them by the following scripts:

```
text = "卢克的师父信仰什么"
url = "http://localhost:9899/
    readyToUse/"
data = rq.urlopen(url+urllib.parse.
    quote(text)).read()
data = json.loads(data.decode("UTF-8"
    ))
# {"data": ["卢克", "bdi9202050",
# 6.774, "卢克的师父"]}
```

**Live Demo.** For this ready-to-use release, we also provide a live demonstration to observe each step's outputs in our pipeline, including mention filtering, mention detection, entity disambiguation by subtitle, and disambiguation by relation. In addition, it also comes with clickable links to XLore for closer observation of the entity. This could be useful for users who prefer a visualized front-end webpage for interpretability.

### 4.2 Partial Release

The partial release is for users interested in completing the EL process inside their downstream models or using parts of our release for entity candidate retrieval from XLore instead of the whole release. In this scenario, we expose each pipeline step for users to determine where to stop according to their needs. For example, if users only want to use mention filtering, mention detection, and disambiguation by subtitle, they can use the following scripts:

```
text = "卢克的师父信仰什么"
filtered_m = filter_mention(text)
# ["卢", "卢克", "什么", etc.]
detected_m = detect_mention(text,
    filtered_m,K=3)
# ["卢克", "师父", "信仰"]
entities = disambiguate_by_subtitle(
    text,detected_m,K=3)
# [["卢克", "bdi9203099", -1.404],
# ["卢克", "bdi9202050", -2.306],
# ["卢克", "bdi9201727", -2.893]]
```

Since loading the Trie tree into memory is time-consuming, which would bring a poor experience when debugging, we encapsulate the Trie tree into a web service using flask.

### 4.3 Easy-to-Change Release

As we illustrated in Figure 2, using specific features such as the relations of entities can potentially benefit the EL for downstream tasks. We provide a training script and a sample model usage implementation for users who have such a demand. In order to add a new feature, HOSMEL requires the users to: (1) format their training data into our format and (2) make a copy of the sample relation usage, and re-write the $generatePair$ method in it to retrieve the required feature. If the users prefer to change XLore into other KBs, they only need to rebuild the Trie tree. More usage details can be found in the released code and readme documents[6].

## 5 Experiment

In this section, we use two question answering benchmarks to evaluate the EL capacity of the proposed HOSMEL and also show its ability to easily add task-relevant features that can benefit the EL performance.

[6]https://github.com/THUDM/HOSMEL

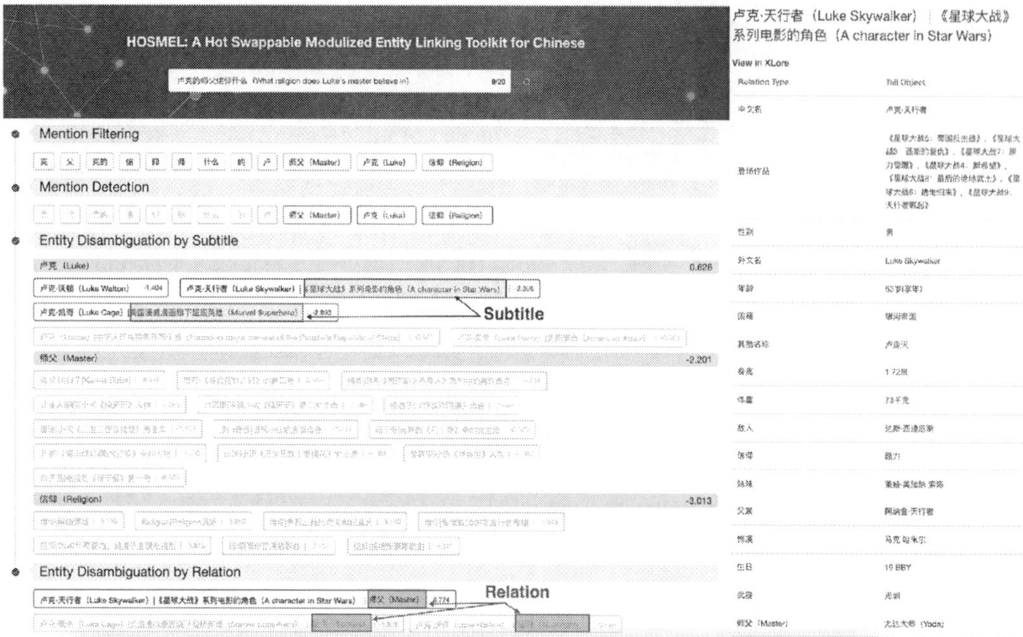


Figure 2: Illustration of the live demonstration. The input example "卢克的师父信仰什么? (*What religion does Luke's master believe in?*)" contains the mention "卢克(*Luke*)" that can be linked to the entity "卢克·天行者(*Luke Skywalker*)" with a relation "师父(*master*)".

### 5.1 Experimental Settings

**Datasets.**

*KB.* Since the 26,146,618 entities in XLore contain many uncommon entities, we create a subset of 16,095,248 entities from it for better usage and evaluation. To ensure precision, we consider various ways, such as ranking by edit times or removing certain entity types, during filtering.

*Test set.* We choose KgCLUE(Xu et al., 2020) and a hand-crafted dataset labeled by us as the test sets. Both of them are for one-hop question answering from the general Chinese open domain KB, each containing $1,673$ and $1,597$ questions labeled with the topic entities. We transfer KgCLUE's questions to our KB to increase ambiguity in order to challenge the EL model as our KB is much larger than KgCLUE's original KB (16M vs. 3M). Our dataset provides various formats of questions for the same answer, which also increases the EL difficulty.

*Basic Training data.* Unlike using hyperlinks and anchor texts in previous works (Logeswaran et al., 2019; Wu et al., 2020), we use the entity descriptions to construct a weak-supervised EL training dataset because hyperlinks are not always available in some KBs. Specifically, the description for each entity is parsed for its title or alias name to compose the training data, because the title or alias name occurred in its own description is highly possible to mention the entity, yielding a basic training data of 16 million (text, mention, entity subtitle) tuples.

*Additional Training data for Question Answering.* Since relation name is commonly used in question answering, we choose it as the additional feature. KgCLUE's training data, including 18,000 (question, mention, entity relation) tuples, allows us to train a model based on relation.

**Baselines.** We choose GENRE (Nicola De et al., 2020) and EntQA (Zhang et al., 2021c), the representations of the generative-based and matching-based methods, to be compared with our HOSMEL, as none of them need the pre-defined mentions, which is the same as the proposed HOSMEL.

**Evaluation Metrics.** We use the topic entities' top-1 accuracy as the evaluation metric for EntQA and HOSMEL. Since GENRE is different by returning zero or multiple entities without scores, we use recall for it instead of top-1 accuracy.

The details of the experimental settings can be found in Section A.2 in Appendix.

Table 1: Performance of all the models on the two benchmarks, where EntQA and HOSMEL report the top-1 accuracy and GENRE reports the recall rate.

| | KgCLUE | Hand-crafted |
|---|---|---|
| GENRE | 25.28 | 14.97 |
| EntQA | 80.99 | 60.34 |
| HOSMEL | 89.48 | 77.40 |
| HOSMEL + Relation | 94.50 | 81.15 |

Table 2: The recall rate of the mention detection result by HOSMEL and the bi-encoder result by EntQA.

| | KgCLUE | Hand-crafted |
|---|---|---|
| EntQA | 89.36 | 82.02 |
| HOSMEL | 99.46 | 95.12 |

### 5.2 Experimental Results

**Time and Space Efficiency.** Figure 3 shows the time and space cost of GENRE, EntQA, and HOSMEL. GENRE needs a full training of the entire 16 million training data to memorize the knowledge of all the entities in its parameters. EntQA also needs a full training of the dataset because of its bi-encoder. Besides, EntQA needs an additional 60GB storage space for the learned entity embeddings for quick retrieval while HOSMEL and GENRE only need 3.5GB for the Trie tree. The results demonstrate that HOSMEL is quite efficient in both time and space. In advance, we measured the average time used for inference. GENRE takes 21.39 seconds to process each test case, whereas EntQA and HOSMEL respectively only need 0.32 seconds and 0.26 seconds to output the results.

**Accuracy Performance.** Table 1 shows the performance of all the models on the two benchmarks, KgCLUE and hand-crafted. EntQA, GENRE, and HOSMEL are all trained on the basic training data with only the (text, mention, entity subtitle) tuples. GENRE presents a particularly poor performance, as the search space of the decoder in character-based languages like Chinese is much larger than the word-based languages like English. EntQA also performs worse than HOSMEL because the dense bi-encoder in EntQA is proved to remember the robust representations for common entities but struggles to differentiate rarer entities (Sciavolino et al., 2021). On the contrary, the proposed HOSMEL builds on a sparse Trie tree and a dense mention detection model for retrieving the entity candidates, which can attend to both the common and rare entities. The top-45 recall rates of HOSMEL and EntQA are also reported in Table 2.

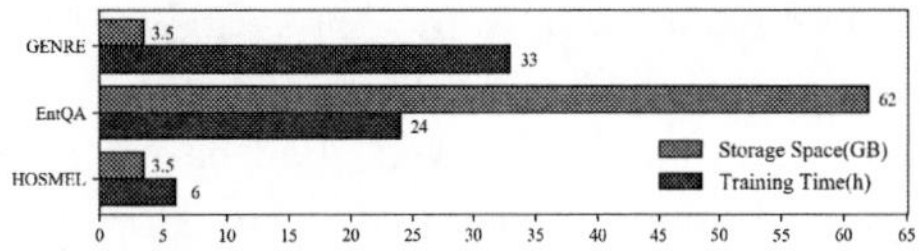


Figure 3: Time and space cost.

**Additional Feature's Performance.** We additionally evaluate the hot-swappable ability of HOSMEL. We find that when adding a new feature, we can easily train an additional MacBERT on relations and the resultant HOSMEL+Relation further improves $3.71 - 5.02\%$ accuracy. On the contrary, GENRE is unable to leverage the relation features. EntQA is also prevented as it needs to be retrained on the new training data where both the entity subtitle and relation are annotated.

## 6 Related Work

EL has attracted lots of attention, and many methods have been studied. Among them, matching-based methods (Logeswaran et al., 2019; Yamada et al., 2019; Wu et al., 2020; Jin et al., 2019b; Ferragina and Scaiella, 2012) and generation-based methods (Nicola De et al., 2020; De Cao et al., 2021) are two mainstreams. The former ones usually use a dense retriever based on the maximum inner-product search (MIPS) to retrieve entity candidates, followed by a cross-encoder to re-rank them. The later ones frame EL as a seq2seq model to autoregressively generate the text annotated with the entities' identifiers, such as their subtitles. However, both put all the features together for training, increasing the difficulty of adjusting for specific downstream tasks. Since the downstream tasks usually require specific filtering or additional information invocation for better EL results, these EL models need the newly annotated dataset for retraining, which is costly and inefficient. In addition, most of them are designed for English, and only a few (Jin et al., 2019b; Ferragina and Scaiella, 2012) have been released as a ready-to-use toolkit. HOSMEL is an EL toolkit for Chinese that can easily adjust to downstream tasks.

## 7 Conclusion and Future Work

We release a Chinese EL toolkit HOSMEL, which has shown to be an effective, efficient, and interpretable method due to the hot-swappable modulized structure. Moreover, for adapting to the downstream tasks, HOSMEL can be easily improved by training on additional features with limited training data. Experiments on two question answering benchmarks have demonstrated the time/space efficiency and the effectiveness compared with the SOTA EL models, as well as the easy task adaptation ability. An English version of the toolkit is planned to be released in the future.

## Acknowledgments

This work is supported by the National Natural Science Foundation of China 62076245, and the NSFC for Distinguished Young Scholar 61825602.

## References

Bo Chen, Jing Zhang, Jie Tang, Lingfan Cai, Zhaoyu Wang, Shu Zhao, Hong Chen, and Cuiping Li. 2020. Conna: Addressing name disambiguation on the fly. *IEEE Transactions on Knowledge and Data Engineering*, pages 1–1.

Bo Chen, Jing Zhang, Xiaokang Zhang, Xiaobin Tang, Lingfan Cai, Hong Chen, Cuiping Li, Peng Zhang, and Jie Tang. 2022. Coad: Contrastive pre-training with adversarial fine-tuning for zero-shot expert linking. In *AAAI 2022*.

Yiming Cui, Wanxiang Che, Ting Liu, Bing Qin, Shijin Wang, and Guoping Hu. 2020. Revisiting pre-trained models for Chinese natural language processing. In *Proceedings of the 2020 Conference on Empirical Methods in Natural Language Processing: Findings*, pages 657–668, Online. Association for Computational Linguistics.

Nicola De Cao, Ledell Wu, Kashyap Popat, Mikel Artetxe, Naman Goyal, Mikhail Plekhanov, Luke Zettlemoyer, Nicola Cancedda, Sebastian Riedel, and Fabio Petroni. 2021. Multilingual autoregressive entity linking. *arXiv preprint arXiv:2103.12528*.

Yu Feng, Jing Zhang, Gaole He, Wayne Xin Zhao, Lemao Liu, Quan Liu, Cuiping Li, and Hong Chen. 2021. A pretraining numerical reasoning model for ordinal constrained question answering on knowledge base. In *Findings of the Association for Computational Linguistics: EMNLP 2021*, pages 1852–1861.

Paolo Ferragina and Ugo Scaiella. 2012. Fast and accurate annotation of short texts with wikipedia pages. *IEEE Software*, 29(1):70–75.

Qingyu Guo, Fuzhen Zhuang, Chuan Qin, Hengshu Zhu, Xing Xie, Hui Xiong, and Qing He. 2020. A survey on knowledge graph-based recommender systems. *IEEE Transactions on Knowledge and Data Engineering*.

Hailong Jin, Chengjiang Li, Jing Zhang, Lei Hou, Juanzi Li, and Peng Zhang. 2019a. Xlore2: large-scale cross-lingual knowledge graph construction and application. *Data Intelligence*, 1(1):77–98.

Hailong Jin, Chengjiang Li, Jing Zhang, Lei Hou, Juanzi Li, and Peng Zhang. 2019b. Xlore2: large-scale cross-lingual knowledge graph construction and application. *Data Intelligence*, 1(1):77–98.

Lajanugen Logeswaran, Ming-Wei Chang, Kenton Lee, Kristina Toutanova, Jacob Devlin, and Honglak Lee. 2019. Zero-shot entity linking by reading entity descriptions. In *Proceedings of the 57th Annual Meeting of the Association for Computational Linguistics*, pages 3449–3460, Florence, Italy. Association for Computational Linguistics.

Mauricio Marrone. 2020. Application of entity linking to identify research fronts and trends. *Scientometrics*, 122(1):357–379.

Cao Nicola De, Izacard Gautier, Riedel Sebastian, and Petroni Fabio. 2020. Autoregressive entity retrieval. *arXiv: Computation and Language*. GENRE.

Hadas Raviv, Oren Kurland, and David Carmel. 2016. Document retrieval using entity-based language models. In *Proceedings of the 39th International ACM SIGIR conference on Research and Development in Information Retrieval*, pages 65–74.

Christopher Sciavolino, Zexuan Zhong, Jinhyuk Lee, and Danqi Chen. 2021. Simple entity-centric questions challenge dense retrievers. *arXiv preprint arXiv:2109.08535*.

Bhavani Thuraisingham. 2020. The role of artificial intelligence and cyber security for social media. In *2020 IEEE International Parallel and Distributed Processing Symposium Workshops (IPDPSW)*, pages 1-3. IEEE.

Catherine Tucker. 2019. 17. privacy, algorithms, and artificial intelligence. In *The Economics of Artificial Intelligence*, pages 423–438. University of Chicago Press.

MV Wilkes. 1974. The art of computer programming, volume 3, sorting and searching. *The Computer Journal*, 17(4):324–324.

Ledell Wu, Fabio Petroni, Martin Josifoski, Sebastian Riedel, and Luke Zettlemoyer. 2020. Scalable zero-shot entity linking with dense entity retrieval. In *Proceedings of the 2020 Conference on Empirical Methods in Natural Language Processing (EMNLP)*, pages 6397–6407.

Liang Xu, Hai Hu, Xuanwei Zhang, Lu Li, Chenjie Cao, Yudong Li, Yechen Xu, Kai Sun, Dian Yu, Cong Yu, Yin Tian, Qianqian Dong, Weitang Liu, Bo Shi, Yiming Cui, Junyi Li, Jun Zeng, Rongzhao Wang, Weijian Xie, Yanting Li, Yina Patterson, Zuoyu Tian, Yiwen Zhang, He Zhou, Shaoweihua Liu, Zhe Zhao, Qipeng Zhao, Cong Yue, Xinrui Zhang, Zhengliang

Yang, Kyle Richardson, and Zhenzhong Lan. 2020. CLUE: A Chinese language understanding evaluation benchmark. In *Proceedings of the 28th International Conference on Computational Linguistics*, pages 4762–4772, Barcelona, Spain (Online). International Committee on Computational Linguistics.

Ikuya Yamada, Koki Washio, Hiroyuki Shindo, and Yuji Matsumoto. 2019. Global entity disambiguation with pretrained contextualized embeddings of words and entities. *arXiv preprint arXiv:1909.00426*.

Jing Zhang, Bo Chen, Lingxi Zhang, Xirui Ke, and Haipeng Ding. 2021a. Neural, symbolic and neural-symbolic reasoning on knowledge graphs. *AI Open*, 2:14–35.

Shiyue Zhang, Benjamin Frey, and Mohit Bansal. 2021b. Chrentranslate: Cherokee-english machine translation demo with quality estimation and corrective feedback. In *Proceedings of the 59th Annual Meeting of the Association for Computational Linguistics and the 11th International Joint Conference on Natural Language Processing: System Demonstrations*, pages 272–279.

Wenzheng Zhang, Wenyue Hua, and Karl Stratos. 2021c. Entqa: Entity linking as question answering.

Zhengyan Zhang, Xu Han, Zhiyuan Liu, Xin Jiang, Maosong Sun, and Qun Liu. 2019. ERNIE: Enhanced language representation with informative entities. In *Proceedings of the 57th Annual Meeting of the Association for Computational Linguistics*, pages 1441–1451, Florence, Italy. Association for Computational Linguistics.

# A Appendix

## A.1 Proof of Eq.(1)

$$
\begin{aligned}
& s(m_i, e_i) \qquad (2)\\
= \;& \log P(A_i^1, A_i^2, \cdots, A_i^t, m_i|d),\\
= \;& \log(P(A_i^1|A_i^2, \cdots, A_i^t, d, m_i)P(A_i^2, \cdots, A_i^t, m_i|d)),\\
= \;& \log(P(A_i^1|d, m_i)P(A_i^2, \cdots, A_i^t, m_i|d)),\\
= \;& \log P(m_i|d)\prod_{\tau=1}^{t} P(A_i^\tau|d, m_i),\\
= \;& \log P(m_i|d) + \sum_{\tau=1}^{t} \log P(A_i^\tau|d, m_i),\\
= \;& s(m_i) + \sum_{\tau=1}^{t} s(A_i^\tau).
\end{aligned}
$$

As shown above, the second equation is obtained according to the Bayes Theorem. The third equation is derived based on the assumption that the probability of attribute $A_i^1$ is independent against the other attributes. Then we achieve the fourth equation according to the general assumption that the probabilities of attributes are independent against each other. Finally, by changing the log-product to sum-log, we show the score of a (mention, entity) pair is equal to the sum of the mention's score and all the attributes' scores.

## A.2 Experimental Settings

### Dataset

*KB.* For creating a concise KB from XLore, We filter out the entities that explain the Chinese characters and select the top 10% popular entities by the edit times. Since we filter the mentions based on the Trie tree created by the titles and alias names of all the entities in XLore, to ensure the recall of unseen mentions in the above popular entities, we keep the top 15 popular entities for each of these unseen mentions. The title, subtitle, and the relations except for the alias name of an entity are available in XLore. To improve the mention's coverage of the Trie tree, we collect the alias name of an entity from its relation named "alias" or the similar meaning.

*Test Set.* We choose KgCLUE(Xu et al., 2020) and a hand-crafted dataset, which contains real world questions with entities we collected from daily life conversations, as the test sets. Both of them are for one-hop question answering from the general Chinese open domain KB, which respectively contains 1,673 and 1,597 questions labeled with the topic entities. Note the fact that, instead of using classic entity linking data sets, question answering data sets are selected for evaluation because most previous entity linking data sets are closer to hyperlink labels, which makes it easier to achieve a better performance but lacks the connection to real-world applications, which is often less similar to the hyperlink labels. Although KgCLUE contains its own KB, a large number of useful entities are filtered out, and some important features such as the subtitle are unavailable. Thus we replace its KB with our created KB from XLore and align the topic entities in the questions to our KB. The hand-crafted test set contains the questions involving more common entities, which raises the difficulty of EL, as common entities are more likely to have ambiguity. We also provide several formats of the same question to increase the question answering difficulty as well as the topic entity linking difficulty.

*Basic Training Data.* Instead of collecting the hyperlinks and the corresponding anchor texts as the training data of EL (Logeswaran et al., 2019; Wu et al., 2020), we use the descriptions of the entities to construct a weak-supervised EL training dataset, as the hyperlinks are not always available in some KBs. Specifically, for each entity, we extract the first sentence from its description that explicitly mentions the entity's title or alias name to compose the training data because the title or alias name that occurred in the description is highly probably to mention the entity itself. As a result, we obtain about 16 million (text, mention, entity subtitle) tuples as the basic training data.

*Additional Training Data for Question Answering.* Since a commonly used feature for question answering is the relation name of an entity, we choose it as the additional feature. For training an additional model based on relations, we need to know the correct relation the input text mentions. KgCLUE's training data, including 18,000 (question, mention, entity relation) tuples, exactly satisfy this demand.

*Additional Training Data for Question Answering.* Since a commonly used feature for question answering is the relation name of an entity, we choose it as the additional feature. For training an additional model based on relations, we need to know the correct relation the input text mentions. KgCLUE's training data, including 18,000 (question, mention, entity relation) tuples, exactly satisfy this demand.

**Baselines.** GENRE trains a seq2seq model to translate the input text into the text annotated with the mentions and entity subtitles based on a pre-built Trie tree the same as HOSMEL. EntQA first trains a bi-encoder to retrieve the entity candidates and then trains a machine comprehensive model to extract the mention spans from the input text given the entity candidates. The scores of the two models are summed as the final score of a (mention, entity) pair.

For a fair comparison, all the models are trained on the basic training data. GENRE needs a full training of the entire 16 million training data to encode all the entity information into its parameters. EntQA also requires the use of the full data to improve the recall for the bi-encoder. HOSMEL doesn't suffer the need to train a bi-encoder, thus only needs a small amount of the training data. For training efficiency, we sample and create a multiple-choice-like training dataset from the basic training data with 406,420 (text, mention) pairs for training the mention detection model and 111,648 (text, mention, entity subtitle) tuples for training entity disambiguation by subtitle in our model. Only the proposed HOSMEL is trained on the additional training data because of its adaptation ability. Based on the KgCLUE's training data, we create an additional multiple-choice-like training data with 47,870 (text, mention, entity relation) tuples for training entity disambiguation by relation.

## B Ethical Considerations

For years the press has been arguing the use of AI and its pros and cons. One advance could be used in various ways and thus lead to different outcomes. To take a cultural look at how this work and other works in similar tracks will take effect, we would like first to take a brief on how might our work be used in both good and bad ways, then move on to applying our advance and ethical reasons for developing our toolkit, along with privacy issues.

For our demo, the outcome can shift in between justice and harmful outcomes. EL could be viewed as having an expert to extract key concepts from a given text, which means that it could be used in education to help the students find a related term in their reading before they fully understand the field. This could also be used in specialized domains such as biological and pharmaceutical for fast retrieval of useful concepts (Marrone, 2020). However, this could also be used in harmful ways. The chance of EL being used for detecting particular views in social media might be further applied to ban a specific group from expressing opinions, harming freedom of speech and equality. But if we look at it from a different perspective, if such use could be controlled by the users of the social media, potentially people who have difficulties can filter out the harmful languages to them (Thuraisingham, 2020) and find what they wanted faster.

To ensure our work could be used in the right way, we extracted our domain from XLore, where it's only a general KB without the worry of having harmful potential entities. We also separated the features. This raises the challenge to train the ranking model to favor a specific semantic pattern and thus makes it harder to be used against free speech. Our work purely ranks the similarity in context rather than learning the complete set of all entities, this could prevent the linking result from being biased to only popular entities (Sciavolino et al.,

2021), yet we still worry that specific context might lead to the linking of only popular entities. As a result, we strongly call for more work conducted to study the context and candidate similarity in retrievals instead of joining the popularity into final performance for better equality. We noticed that in recent years the protection for minor languages has finally drawn more attention (Zhang et al., 2021b), and one of the reasons for conducting our demonstration is the attempt in calling both English and Chinese, the two most popular languages, speakers to better consider the difference in languages and robustness while developing methods not only for the sake of equality between languages but also for better protection of the minor languages because not all languages are like English.

On the other hand, privacy has raised a significant portion of attention (Tucker, 2019). It is essential to discuss how our tool might relate to privacy. Our demo is based on XLore, which means it only uses data publicly available on the internet, but the risk of privacy leakage still remains while being applied to the downstream tasks. During usage, a level of caution to prevent privacy issues should still be kept for the sake of respect. In advance, we suggest usages of our method to be checked before actual deployment in a downstream system.

One overall solution to resolve the release of methods in data science is to discuss and consider the caution of ethics and respect during education. Some might argue the key is to take extra care during the development of such tools but to notice critical factors in a system that might lead to harmful usage requires strong integrity and respect to others. It is only with high ethical standards one could better consider the design and take better consideration of one's system during the design and before releasing.

# BMInf: An Efficient Toolkit for Big Model Inference and Tuning

**Xu Han**[1,2*], **Guoyang Zeng**[2,5*], **Weilin Zhao**[1,2*], **Zhiyuan Liu**[1,2,3,4,5†]
**Zhengyan Zhang**[1,2], **Jie Zhou**[2,5], **Jun Zhang**[1,2], **Chao Jia**[2,5], **Maosong Sun**[1,2,3,4,5†]
[1] Dept. of Comp. Sci. & Tech., Institute for AI, Tsinghua University
Beijing National Research Center for Information Science and Technology
[2] OpenBMB Group [3] Institute Guo Qiang, Tsinghua University
[4] International Innovation Center of Tsinghua University
[5] Beijing Academy of Artificial Intelligence, BAAI
zenggy@mail.tsinghua.edu.cn {hanxu17,zwl19}@mails.tsinghua.edu.cn
{liuzy,sms}@tsinghua.edu.cn

## Abstract

In recent years, large-scale pre-trained language models (PLMs) containing billions of parameters have achieved promising results on various NLP tasks. Although we can pre-train these big models by stacking computing clusters at any cost, it is impractical to use such huge computing resources to apply big models for each downstream task. To address the computation bottleneck encountered in deploying big models in real-world scenarios, we introduce an open-source toolkit for **B**ig **M**odel **Inf**erence and tuning (**BMInf**), which can support big model inference and tuning at extremely low computation cost. More specifically, at the algorithm level, we introduce model quantization and parameter-efficient tuning for efficient model inference and tuning. At the implementation level, we apply model offloading, model checkpointing, and CPU-GPU scheduling optimization to further reduce the computation and memory cost of big models. Based on above efforts, we can efficiently perform big model inference and tuning with a single GPU (even a consumer-level GPU like GTX 1060) instead of computing clusters, which is difficult for existing distributed learning toolkits for PLMs. BMInf is publicly released at `https://github.com/OpenBMB/BMInf`.

## 1 Introduction

Recent years have witnessed the great success of pre-trained language models (PLMs) (Han et al., 2021) in the NLP community. Various techniques of PLMs enable us to train big models containing billions of parameters from large-scale unlabeled corpora in a self-supervised fashion. Up to now, these big models (with billions of parameters like GPT-3 (Brown et al., 2020)) have achieved promising results on various NLP tasks and gained extensive attention from researchers. Despite the success

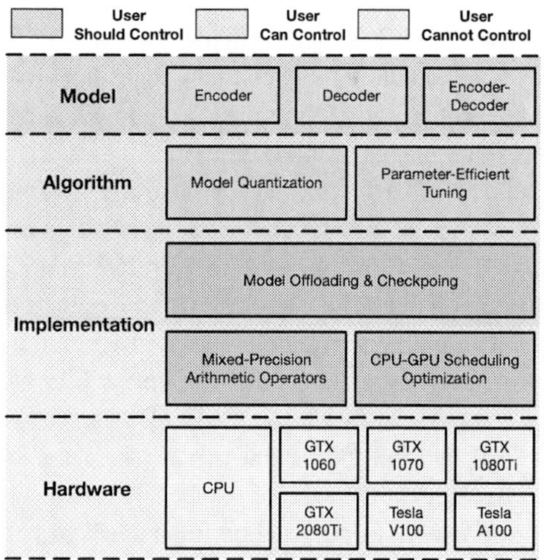


Figure 1: The overall framework of BMInf. To make BMInf convenient for users, the underlying implementation and the hardware adaptation will not be exposed to users, and these modules can be automatically executed.

of big models, the massive parameters of these big models also bring challenges to their inference and tuning. Since the pre-training process of big models usually requires to be completed once, the cost caused by massive parameters can be handled by stacking computing resources. However, the inference and tuning process of PLMs depends on specific application scenarios and will frequently use big models for computation. If we still stack devices to speed up the inference and tuning of big models, the cost of time, memory, and even money would become unbearable. In this paper, we introduce a toolkit BMInf, aiming at efficiently performing big model inference and tuning.

As shown in Figure 1, BMInf is built based on a four-level framework, the most important part of which lies in its algorithm level and implementation level. At the algorithm level, we introduce model quantization to compress big models from high-

* indicates equal contribution.
† indicates corresponding authors.



*Proceedings of the 60th Annual Meeting of the Association for Computational Linguistics System Demonstrations*, pages 224 - 230
May 22-27, 2022 ©2022 Association for Computational Linguistics

bit floating-point parameters to low-bit fixed-point ones, which can significantly reduce the memory cost of big models. The faster computation speed of low-bit numbers can also accelerate the computation of big models. Besides model quantization, we also introduce parameter-efficient tuning methods (Ding et al., 2022), which freeze the parameters of big models to reduce the computation and memory cost. By inserting additional learnable modules into big models, parameter-efficient tuning can tune these additional modules to help big models handle specific tasks. Some recent works (Lester et al., 2021; Gu et al., 2021; Hu et al., 2021) have shown that applying parameter-efficient tuning on big models can achieve results comparable to fine-tuning all model weights.

At the implementation level, we implement model offloading and model checkpointing, which can make full use of CPU memory to store massive parameters of big models. Moreover, model offloading and checkpointing can drop parameters and computation graphs during both the forward and backward propagation, which can further save GPU memory to operate more data. For the underlying arithmetic operators, we reimplement the mixed-precision CUDA arithmetic operators, which can better utilize the tensor cores of GPUs to further speed up the computation, especially accelerating the mixed-precision computation in model quantization. Considering model offloading and model checkpointing bring extra CPU-GPU communication to load offloaded model weights, we perform CPU-GPU scheduling optimization to synchronously execute weight loading and model computation. This CPU-GPU scheduling optimization can alleviate the time waiting for weight loading. All of model offloading, model checkpointing, and parameter-efficient tuning can benefit from the scheduling optimization.

Due to the algorithm-level and implementation-level efficiencies, BMInf can work on various GPUs at the hardware level, including both powerful GPUs (e.g. Tesla V100 and Tesla A100) and consumer GPUs (e.g. GTX 1060 and GTX 1080Ti). In Section 4, we will show that BMInf can run models with more than 10 billion parameters on a consumer GPU GTX 1060, which is quite difficult for existing PLM-related distributed toolkits such as Megatron (Shoeybi et al., 2019) and DeepSpeed (Rasley et al., 2020). At the model level, BMInf supports various possible architectures of

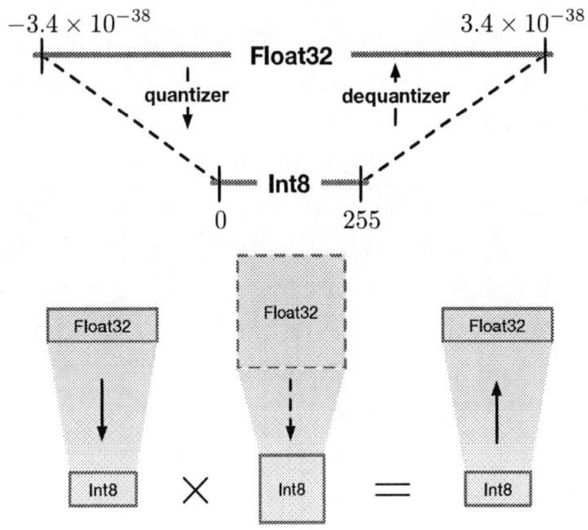


Figure 2: The illustration of model quantization. To balance both efficiency and effectiveness, we use 8-bit fixed-point numbers to represent the weights of all linear layers and higher-bit floating-point numbers (16-bit or 32-bit numbers) to represent hidden states. Here we use 32-bit floating-point numbers as an example. The dotted parts are only used for the low-bit adaptation training.

Transformer-based PLMs, and users can choose their own model architectures for inference and tuning. To make BMInf more convenient for users, the underlying implementation and the hardware adaptation are automatically executed and will not be exposed to users. In the following sections, we will show more details about BMInf, especially at the algorithm level and implementation level.

## 2 Algorithms to Support the Efficient Inference and Tuning of Big Models

In this section, we briefly introduce how BMInf supports big model inference and tuning in an efficient manner at the algorithm level, including model quantization and parameter-efficient tuning.

### 2.1 Model Quantization

The massive parameters of big models not only bring a huge amount of computation but also require a lot of memory to store parameters and computation graphs. Therefore, applying model compression is crucial to reduce the computation and memory cost of big models. Since we want big models to maintain generality after model compression, we choose model quantization rather than model pruning and model distillation for our toolkit. The latter two compression approaches are usually used to compress big models for specific tasks and will significantly change the model structure.

Model quantization aims to compress model

weights from high-bit floating-point numbers to low-bit fixed-point ones. Typically, PLMs are usually represented with 32-bit or 16-bit floating-point numbers, while their quantized models can be represented with 8-bit, 4-bit, or even 1-bit fixed-point numbers, saving much memory usage. In addition, GPUs have tensor cores specially designed for low-bit numbers, and thus model quantization can also speed up the computation. For Transformer-based PLMs, Zafrir et al. (2019) show that the 8-bit quantization has little impact on the model performance. To further alleviate the performance degradation, Shen et al. (2020) apply mixed-bit quantization where only those parameters with low Hessian spectrum are required to be quantized. Zhang et al. (2020) further utilize knowledge distillation to force low-bit models to imitate high-bit models.

Considering that training a 1-bit or 2-bit Transformer is still challenging due to the significant decrease in model capacity, our toolkit primarily quantizes high-bit (16-bit or 32-bit) models to 8-bit fixed-point ones. The performance of low-bit quantization is highly hardware-related, and those complex quantization mechanisms may only serve specific devices. Therefore, as shown in Figure 2, we apply a simple and effective mixed-bit quantization method, where hidden states are represented with high-bit numbers, while the weights of all linear layers are represented with 8-bit numbers. During the computation, we first quantize the input into 8-bit hidden states and perform computation operations, and then dequantize the output into high-bit states. To make the quantization less impactful on models, we use a small amount of pre-trained data for additional low-bit adaptation training. Specifically, in the low-bit adaptation stage, we still use high-bit numbers to represent model weights, but quantize these weights into low-bit forms for computation (the dotted parts in Figure 2). After the low-bit-adaptation stage, high-bit weights are discarded, and their corresponding low-bit weights are left for inference and tuning.

## 2.2 Parameter-Efficient Tuning

Vanilla fine-tuning (Radford and Narasimhan, 2018; Devlin et al., 2019) needs to tune all model weights, a mixed-precision PLM with $N$ parameters (Model weights are 16-bit numbers and optimizer states are 32-bit numbers) under this setting would require: (1) $N$ 16-bit weight states and $N$ 16-bit gradient states; (2) $N$ 32-bit master model weights; (3) $N$ 32-bit momentum states and $N$ 32-bit variance states for the optimizer. These add up to a total of $16N$ bytes memory consumption. Since a big model has massive parameters, this consumption is too large to compute.

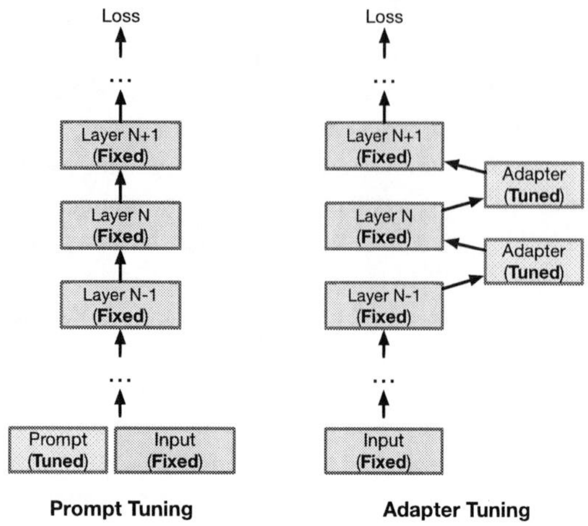


Figure 3: The illustration of parameter-efficient tuning. Here we take prompt tuning and adapter tuning as examples to show how to perform parameter-efficient tuning.

To efficiently tune big models for specific tasks, parameter-efficient tuning (Ding et al., 2022) has been proposed. As shown in Figure 3, the main idea of parameter-efficient tuning is to insert new modules into PLMs and only tune these additional modules, i.e. all PLM weights do not need to be tuned anymore. Under the setting of parameter-efficient tuning, we only need to store the forward and backward information of those tuned modules, which is significantly smaller than tuning all PLM weights. Prompt tuning (Lester et al., 2021; Gu et al., 2021) and adapter tuning (Stickland and Murray, 2019; Houlsby et al., 2019) are two typical parameter-efficient tuning approaches. Prompt tuning aims to better trigger the potential capabilities inside PLMs by only modifying the input. Since PLMs are mostly pre-trained on cloze-style tasks, prompt tuning first inserts several prompt embeddings into the input to adapt all downstream tasks to cloze-style tasks, which can bridge the pre-training and fine-tuning objectives, and then tunes the prompt embeddings to adapt PLMs to specific tasks. Adapter tuning mainly focuses on inserting extra adapter layers into PLMs to help adapt PLMs to handle downstream tasks.

Although freezing all PLM weights has been shown to perform moderately on downstream tasks (Lester et al., 2021), it is still one way to balance time efficiency, memory consumption, and model effectiveness. In fact, some recent parameter-efficient tuning methods (Hu et al., 2021) have achieved comparable results to fine-tuning all model weights. In our toolkit, we provide a unified interface to freeze all weights of big models and compute gradients for those additional modules, which can support various parameter-efficient tuning methods.

## 3 Implementations to Reduce the Computation and Memory Cost

In this section, we briefly introduce how BMInf reduces the computation and memory cost at the implementation level, including model offloading and model checkpointing, as well as CPU-GPU scheduling optimization. In fact, we also reimplement efficient mixed-precision arithmetic operators to better utilize GPU tensor cores. Since the reimplementation of CUDA operators is too detailed to be described in words, we will not show it here and recommend our readers refer to the source code.

### 3.1 Offloading and Checkpointing

Although we can exponentially compress big models through model quantization, it is still difficult for the GPU memory to support the storage of model weights and computation graphs. Therefore, we apply model offloading to utilize the CPU memory, which is often very large and cheap. As shown in Figure 4, the main idea of model offloading is to place model weights on the CPU. When the model is computed layer by layer, we load the offloaded weights from the CPU to the GPU for computation. After the computation is completed, we free the loaded weights and computation graphs to save the GPU memory. Since model weights can be divided into small pieces (such a piece is called a phase) to load, model offloading is quite important for running big models using low computing resources.

Although model offloading can well solve the forward propagation of big models, it cannot work for the back propagation, since much of the information used for the backward propagation needs to be computed and preserved in the forward propagation. The consumption of this memory is usually hidden behind the computation graph and often overlooked. In fact, the memory required for the back propagation is also quite huge. Take the matrix multiplication $\mathbf{y} = \mathbf{W}\mathbf{x}$ as an example, it is used almost everywhere in neural networks. Assuming that the gradient of $\mathbf{y}$ has been obtained and denoted as $\frac{\mathrm{d}\mathcal{L}}{\mathrm{d}\mathbf{y}} = \overline{\mathbf{y}}$, we have $\frac{\mathrm{d}\mathcal{L}}{\mathrm{d}\mathbf{x}} = \mathbf{W}^\top\overline{\mathbf{y}}$ and $\frac{\mathrm{d}\mathcal{L}}{\mathrm{d}\mathbf{W}} = \overline{\mathbf{y}}\mathbf{x}^\top$, where $\mathcal{L}$ is the final loss score. That is to say, the memory used for the matrix multiplication cannot be freed immediately after being used, leading to a conflict with model offloading.

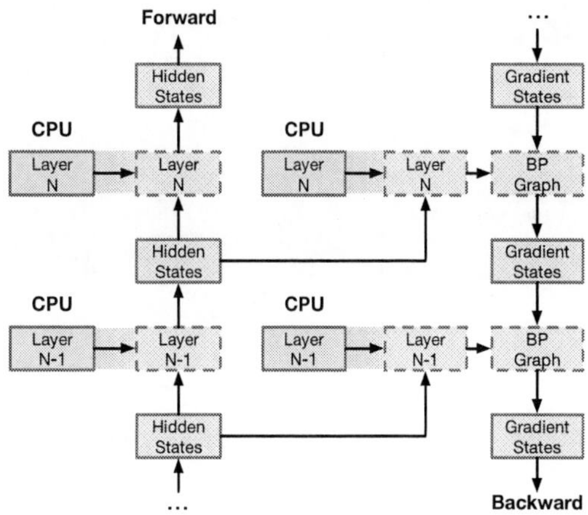


Figure 4: The illustration of model offloading and model checkpointing. All blue parts are stored in the CPU and all yellow ones are in the GPU. The dotted parts are temporary units, whose data and computation graphs will be freed from memory after computation.

To address the issue, we apply model checkpointing, which is also used by existing distributed frameworks such as Megatron and DeepSpeed to accelerate the pre-training of big models. The core of checkpointing is that it allows some of the information used in the back propagation not to be saved in the forward propagation, but to be recomputed in the back propagation. As shown in Figure 4, some hidden states are reserved for the back propagation and all other intermediate results are immediately freed. The reserved information is named "checkpoint". By dividing big models into several checkpoint-separated phases, freed intermediate results and computation graphs are recomputed as the back propagation passes through these phases, and then released immediately again after obtaining gradient states. Assuming the checkpointing is performed every $K$ operations, this approach reduces the memory footprint to at least $\frac{1}{K}$ of the original one, while only affecting the efficiency by one extra forward propagation time. Generally, offloading phases are consistent with checkpointing

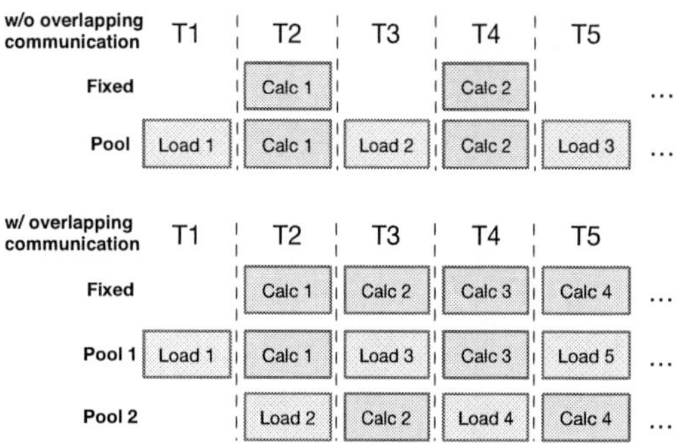


Figure 5: The illustration of overlapping weight loading and model computation. From the figure, we can find that through the CPU-GPU scheduling optimization, the time cost of weight loading can be negligible.

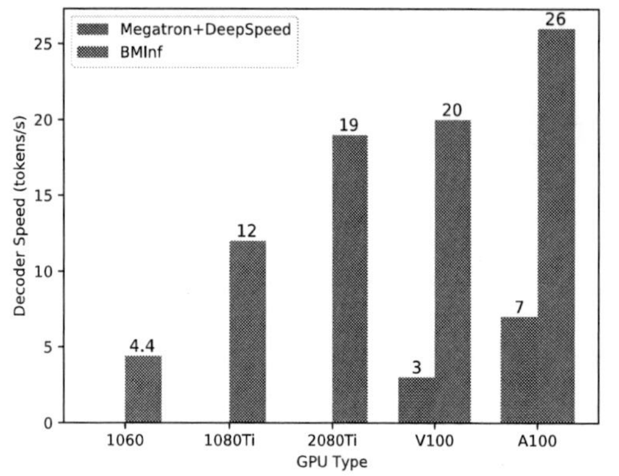


Figure 6: The decoding speed (tokens/s) when performing big model inference with different GPUs.

phases to avoid conflicts.

### 3.2 CPU-GPU Scheduling Optimization

One negative effect of offloading and checkpointing is that they lead to fragmented memory. In some widely-used deep learning frameworks such as PyTorch and TensorFlow, the GPU memory is allocated dynamically. However, checkpoints are long-lived while those freed and recomputed tensors are short-lived. Suppose the memory allocation is performed in an alternating pattern: long-lived, short-lived, long-lived, short-lived, $\cdots$, this may allow those long-lived tensors to be located in some fragmented regions of the GPU memory, which may affect the efficiency. In the worst case, when a block of $M$ bytes is required, the GPU memory indeed has more than $M$ bytes in total, but a contiguous block of $M$ bytes can never be found for allocation. Meanwhile, model offloading and model checkpointing require frequent communication between CPU and GPU to load model weights, which also brings lots of extra time overhead.

北京环球影城指定单日门票将采用价格滚动制度，即推出淡季日、平季日、旺季日和特定日门票。淡季日门票价格为418元，平季日门票价格为528元，旺季日门票价格为638元，特定日门票价格为688元。

Universal Studios Beijing will adopt a price rolling system, and the prices of low season tickets, mid-season tickets, high season tickets, and special season tickets will be different. The price of low season tickets is 418 RMB, the price of mid-season tickets is 528 RMB, the price of high season tickets is 638 RMB, and the price of special season tickets is 688 RMB.

Table 1: The Chinese text is an inference example of the CPM-2 implemented with BMInf. The underlined tokens are all generated by CPM-2. In this table, we also give the translated English text corresponding to the Chinese text.

To address these issues, we perform a CPU-GPU scheduling optimization. More specifically, we first pre-allocate those long-lived blocks into a contiguous section of the GPU memory ("Fixed" in Figure 5). Then, we pre-allocate two extra memory pools in the GPU to perform weight loading and model computation alternately ("Pool 1" and "Pool 2" in Figure 5). With these two pre-allocated pools, the CPU-GPU communication and the model computation can be synchronously executed, and the CPU-GPU communication time can be completely overlapped in the computation time. Owing to synchronously execution, the time cost of weight loading can be negligible.

## 4 Evaluation

In this section, we present some evaluation results of big model inference and tuning to show the efficiency of our toolkit BMInf. The following results are based on the model CPM-2 (Zhang et al., 2022). CPM-2 is a Chinese PLM with over 10 billion parameters. Since CPM-2 has an encoder-decoder architecture, it can be used for both text understanding and text generation. The original CPM-2 is implemented with the distributed toolkits DeepSpeed and Megatron, which are currently the most efficient open-source tools for running big models.

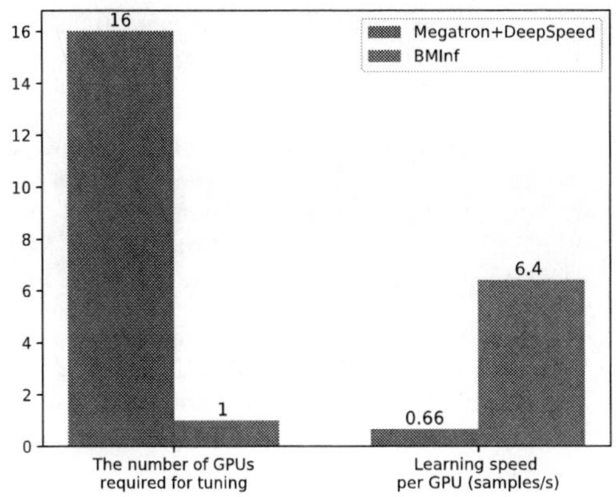


Figure 7: The minimum number of GPUs (Tesla V100) required for prompt tuning (batch size = 32) and the learning speed per GPU (samples/s) when taking minimum GPUs for tuning. Here, the model implemented using Megatron and DeepSpeed has 16-bit floating-point parameters, while the model based on BMInf has 8-bit fixed-point parameters.

### 4.1 The Results of Big Model Inference

As shown in Figure 6, we can find that models implemented with DeepSpeed and Megatron cannot perform model inference on some consumer GPUs with limited GPU memory, such as GTX 1060 and GTX 1080Ti. For BMInf, even on a GTX 1060 with only 6GB memory units can infer a big model with over 10 billion parameters.

On some powerful GPUs like Tesla V100 and Tesla A100, BMInf achieves $4 \sim 6$ times speedup. In addition to the decoding speed, we also give a case in Table 1, which can intuitively reflect the inference quality of the model implemented with BMInf.

### 4.2 The Results of Big Model Tuning

In order to evaluate the performance of BMInf on big model tuning, we follow the setting of CPM-2, use CCPM and LCQMC for experiments, and apply prompt tuning to adapt CPM-2 to these two datasets. CCPM is a text classification dataset related to Chinese poems, and LCQMC is a classification dataset of intent similarity.

From Figure 7, we can find that when performing prompt tuning (batch size = 32), the CPM-2 version implemented with DeepSpeed and Megatron requires 16 GPUs, while the version based on BMInf requires only one GPU. For the speed of processing samples, BMInf has achieved nearly 10 times speedup.

| Dataset | Model | ACC | GPU |
|---|---|---|---|
| CCPM | FT* | 91.6 | 32 |
| | PT(FP16)* | 90.9 | 16(↓ 50%) |
| | PT(INT8) | 87.4 | 1(↓ 97%) |
| LCQMC | FT* | 89.2 | 32 |
| | PT(FP16)* | 88.4 | 16(↓ 50%) |
| | PT(INT8) | 85.3 | 1(↓ 97%) |

Table 2: The comparison between fine-tuning (FT) and prompt tuning (PT). "PT(INT8)" is implemented based on the model quantization of BMInf. "*" means the result is from the CPM-2 paper (Zhang et al., 2022). "ACC" means the accuracy of models (%) and "GPU" means the minimum GPU number required for tuning. "↓" indicates a percentage decrease in the minimum number of GPUs required for tuning.

From Table 2 we can find that model quantization still affects the model performance to a certain extent. The reason is that the models with more parameters are more susceptible to the low-bit variance brought by the quantization methods. Although 8-bit quantization has been demonstrated the little impact on those models with millions of parameters, how to robustly quantify those big models with billions of parameters remains us an future work.

## 5 Conclusion and Future Work

In this paper, we introduce an efficient toolkit BMInf to provide a way to use large-scale PLMs. By applying model quantization, parameter-efficient tuning, model offloading, model checkpointing, CPU-GPU scheduling optimization, as well as the reimplementation of mixed-precision arithmetic operators, BMInf can perform big model inference and tuning with less than 1/30 of the GPU memory and 10 times speedup, as compared with existing open-source distributed toolkits for pre-training and fine-tuning PLMs.

In the future, our work to improve BMInf will focus on the following three directions:

(1) At the model level, we will gradually support more models;

(2) At the algorithm level, we will continue to improve our model quantization methods to achieve better performance, and work with other toolkits such as OpenPrompt (Ding et al., 2021) to explore more effective ways to tune big models;

(3) At the implementation level, we will provide long-term maintenance for this toolkit.

We hope this toolkit can help researchers utilize big models for their own works and advance the adaption of big models in the NLP community.

## Acknowledgements

This work is supported by the National Key R&D Program of China (No. 2020AAA0106502), Institute Guo Qiang of Tsinghua University, Beijing Academy of Artificial Intelligence (BAAI), and International Innovation Center of Tsinghua University.

## References

Tom Brown, Benjamin Mann, Nick Ryder, Melanie Subbiah, et al. 2020. Language models are few-shot learners. In *Proceedings of NeurIPS*.

Jacob Devlin, Ming-Wei Chang, Kenton Lee, and Kristina Toutanova. 2019. BERT: Pre-training of deep bidirectional transformers for language understanding. In *Proceedings of NAACL-HLT*, pages 4171–4186.

Ning Ding, Shengding Hu, Weilin Zhao, Yulin Chen, Zhiyuan Liu, Hai-Tao Zheng, and Maosong Sun. 2021. Openprompt: An open-source framework for prompt-learning. *arXiv preprint arXiv:2111.01998*.

Ning Ding, Yujia Qin, Guang Yang, Fuchao Wei, Zonghan Yang, Yusheng Su, Shengding Hu, Yulin Chen, Chi-Min Chan, Weize Chen, et al. 2022. Delta tuning: A comprehensive study of parameter efficient methods for pre-trained language models. *arXiv preprint arXiv:2203.06904*.

Yuxian Gu, Xu Han, Zhiyuan Liu, and Minlie Huang. 2021. Ppt: Pre-trained prompt tuning for few-shot learning. *arXiv preprint arXiv:2109.04332*.

Xu Han, Zhengyan Zhang, Ning Ding, Yuxian Gu, Xiao Liu, Yuqi Huo, Jiezhong Qiu, Liang Zhang, Wentao Han, Minlie Huang, et al. 2021. Pre-trained models: Past, present and future. *AI Open*.

Neil Houlsby, Andrei Giurgiu, Stanislaw Jastrzebski, Bruna Morrone, Quentin De Laroussilhe, Andrea Gesmundo, Mona Attariyan, and Sylvain Gelly. 2019. Parameter-efficient transfer learning for nlp. In *Proceedings of ICML*, pages 2790–2799.

Edward J Hu, Yelong Shen, Phillip Wallis, Zeyuan Allen-Zhu, Yuanzhi Li, Shean Wang, Lu Wang, and Weizhu Chen. 2021. Lora: Low-rank adaptation of large language models. *arXiv preprint arXiv:2106.09685*.

Brian Lester, Rami Al-Rfou, and Noah Constant. 2021. The power of scale for parameter-efficient prompt tuning. *arXiv preprint arXiv:2104.08691*.

Alec Radford and Karthik Narasimhan. 2018. Improving language understanding by generative pretraining. *OpenAI Blog*.

Jeff Rasley, Samyam Rajbhandari, Olatunji Ruwase, and Yuxiong He. 2020. DeepSpeed: System optimizations enable training deep learning models with over 100 billion parameters. In *Proceedings of KDD*, pages 3505–3506.

Sheng Shen, Zhen Dong, Jiayu Ye, Linjian Ma, Zhewei Yao, Amir Gholami, Michael W Mahoney, and Kurt Keutzer. 2020. Q-bert: Hessian based ultra low precision quantization of bert. In *Proceedings of AAAI*, pages 8815–8821.

Mohammad Shoeybi, Mostofa Patwary, Raul Puri, Patrick LeGresley, Jared Casper, and Bryan Catanzaro. 2019. Megatron-LM: Training multi-billion parameter language models using model parallelism. *arXiv preprint arXiv:1909.08053*.

Asa Cooper Stickland and Iain Murray. 2019. Bert and pals: Projected attention layers for efficient adaptation in multi-task learning. In *Proceedings of ICML*, pages 5986–5995.

Ofir Zafrir, Guy Boudoukh, Peter Izsak, and Moshe Wasserblat. 2019. Q8bert: Quantized 8bit bert. In *Proceedings of NeurIPS*.

Wei Zhang, Lu Hou, Yichun Yin, Lifeng Shang, Xiao Chen, Xin Jiang, and Qun Liu. 2020. Ternarybert: Distillation-aware ultra-low bit bert. In *Proceedings of EMNLP*, pages 509–521.

Zhengyan Zhang, Yuxian Gu, Xu Han, Shengqi Chen, Chaojun Xiao, Zhenbo Sun Yuan Yao, Fanchao Qi, Jian Guan, Pei Ke, Yanzheng Cai, et al. 2022. Cpm-2: Large-scale cost-effective pre-trained language models. *AI Open*.

# MMEKG: Multi-modal Event Knowledge Graph towards Universal Representation across Modalities

**Yubo Ma[1†*], Zehao Wang[2†*], Mukai Li[3†*], Yixin Cao[4*], Meiqi Chen[5†*], Xinze Li[1], Wenqi Sun[3], Kunquan Deng[3], Kun Wang[3], Aixin Sun[1], Jing Shao[3‡]**

[1] S-Lab, Nanyang Technological University [2] KU Leuven [3] SenseTime Research

[4] Singapore Management University [5] Peking University

yubo001@e.ntu.edu.sg

## Abstract

Events are fundamental building blocks of real-world happenings. In this paper, we present a large-scale, multi-modal event knowledge graph named MMEKG. MMEKG unifies different modalities of knowledge via events, which complement and disambiguate each other. Specifically, MMEKG incorporates (i) over 990 thousand concept events with 644 relation types to cover most types of happenings, and (ii) over 863 million instance events connected through 934 million relations, which provide rich contextual information in texts and/or images. To collect billion-scale instance events and relations among them, we additionally develop an efficient yet effective pipeline for textual/visual knowledge extraction system. We also develop an induction strategy to create million-scale concept events and a schema organizing all events and relations in MMEKG. To this end, we also provide a pipeline[1] enabling our system to seamlessly parse texts/images to event graphs and to retrieve multi-modal knowledge at both concept- and instance-levels.

## 1 Introduction

Recently, many Knowledge Graphs (KGs) have been curated (*e.g.*, Wikidata (Vrandečić and Krötzsch, 2014)) and successfully applied to various applications, ranging from information extraction (Lai et al., 2021) to information retrieval (Dong et al., 2014). KGs typically store billions of world facts in a directed graph, where nodes denote entities and edges denote their relations. Although simple yet effective, the expression ability of such entity-centric KGs is limited (Liu et al., 2020). How we can represent more complex knowledge, such as events, situations, or different modalities, becomes a key question for broader applications.

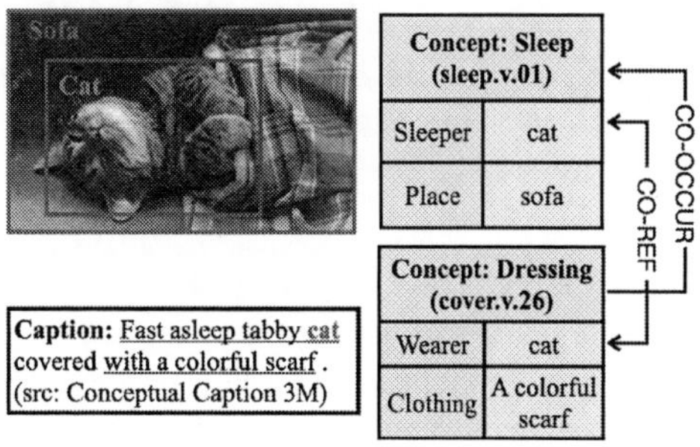


Figure 1: Examples of visual and textual events, and their relations. CO-REF denotes co-reference.

In this paper, we present a large-scale **M**ulti-**M**odal **E**vent **K**nowledge **G**raph (MMEKG) that bridges, complements, and disambiguates different modalities of knowledge, for better understanding or reasoning. Similar to real-world happenings, MMEKG takes events as its basic building blocks. Each event is defined by a concept, several arguments, and corresponding roles. Among events are various types of relations, such as causal, temporal, or sub-event relations. Thus eneities can be arguments in KGs. Figure 1 shows two example events: a visual *sleep* event with arguments *cat* (sleeper) and *sofa* (place), and a textual *dressing* event with arguments *cat* (wearer) and *scarf* (clothing), where argument roles are in brackets. The two events not only bridge the text and image with complementary arguments but also offer underlying commonsense knowledge — covering with a scarf usually happens when sleeping.

Compared with existing event KGs (Speer et al., 2016; Zhang et al., 2020; Hwang et al., 2021), MMEKG advances this field in the following three aspects: (1) A **large-scale ontology** contains 990 thousand concept events and 644 relation types, which covers most types of real-world happenings. (2) **Multi-modal knowledge** is naturally fused. To our best knowledge, it is the first event KG that bridges different modalities of data through fine-

*Equal Contribution.

†Work was done when Yubo, Zehao, Mukai and Meiqi were intern researchers at SenseTime Research.

‡Corresponding Author.

[1]System page: https:www.mmekg.com.



*Proceedings of the 60th Annual Meeting of the Association for Computational Linguistics System Demonstrations*, pages 231 - 239

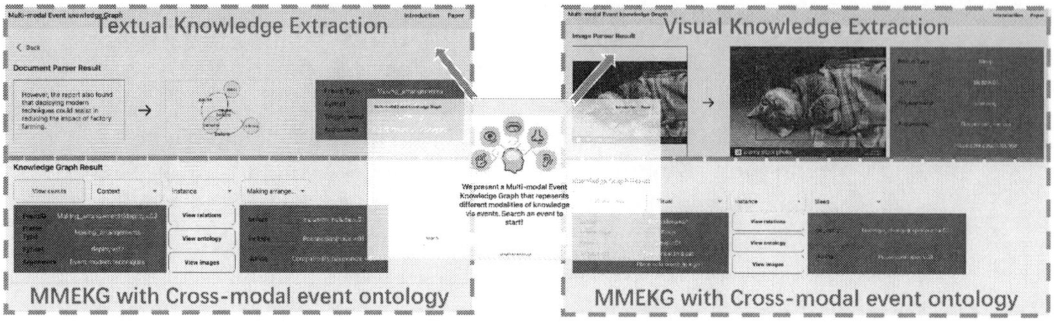


Figure 2: Illustration of Demo System. Any input texts/images can be parsed into event graphs, where nodes denote instance events and edges denote event-event relations. Each instance event also refers to detailed information: concept event, synset, arguments with corresponding roles, and the linked neighbors in MMEKG (blue tables). Note that a single image mainly contains one event.

grained alignments of events and arguments. (3) The **integration of concept and instance events** not only makes it possible to enlarge the ontology from instance events but also provides concept-level commonsense knowledge with contextual instances for comprehensive reasoning.

There are mainly two steps to build MMEKG. (1) To construct a schema and acquire concept events, we first manually combine FrameNet (Baker et al., 1998) and WordNet (Fellbaum, 1998) to initialize a high-quality event ontology; we then expand it automatically via ontology induction from instance events. For flexibility and exchangeability, we extend the Simple Event Model (SEM) (Van Hage et al., 2011) to define our ontology in Resource Description Framework (RDF). (2) To extract instance events from either texts or images, we developed a knowledge extraction system to support fast and massive extraction under the practical scenario. This system consists of event extraction and event relation extraction in both modalities, as well as the alignment between them. In addition, this system can parse any input texts/images to event graphs and seamlessly retrieve multi-modal knowledge from MMEKG.

To cover a variety of events, we apply our extraction system into multiple sources, including C4 News[2], Wikipedia[3], Bookcorpus[4], and CC3M&12M (Sharma et al., 2018; Changpinyo et al., 2021). These data sources result in 863 million instance events and 934 million relations. To ensure its quality, we evaluate both our extraction system and the constructed MMEKG. Compared with state-of-the-art models of each sub-tasks, our methods achieve comparable or better performance on standard benchmarks. The adaptation to practical corpus led to no significant degradation. We sample thousands of events and relations from MMEKG for manual evaluation. The precision is acceptable at both concept and instance levels.

## 2 Overview of MMEKG

### 2.1 Definitions

Our proposed MMEKG, as shown in Figure 3, is different from traditional event-centric KGs and has four types of nodes and four types of relations. Nodes include concept events, instance events, entities, and non-entity arguments *e.g.,* literals. Among them, concept events (color in purple in Figure 3) are modality agnostic and provide high-level summarization of instance events (color in yellow), and entities/literals (color in blue) could be event arguments. The four types of relations contain (1) relation between instance events. Such type of relation can be further categorized into more fine-grained sub-types, such as temporal, causal, co-occur, and other semantic relations, (2) relation between concept events, named as *subclassOf* which denotes a hierarchical relation, (3) relation between concept events and instance events, named as *instanceOf* relation that integrates concept and instance events, and (4) role relations that reflect the roles of arguments (entities or non-entities) to the linked events. Different concept events have different roles. Formally, we have:

**Definition 1** MMEKG $= \{(h,r,t)|h,t \in \mathcal{E}, r \in R\}$. $\mathcal{E} = \mathcal{E}_{cpt} \bigcup \mathcal{E}_{ins} \bigcup \mathcal{E}_{ent} \bigcup \mathcal{E}_{nent}$, where $\mathcal{E}_{cpt}$, $\mathcal{E}_{ins}$, $\mathcal{E}_{ent}$, and $\mathcal{E}_{nent}$ represent

[2]https://www.tensorflow.org/datasets/catalog/c4

[3]https://dumps.wikimedia.org/enwiki/

[4]https://www.gutenberg.org/

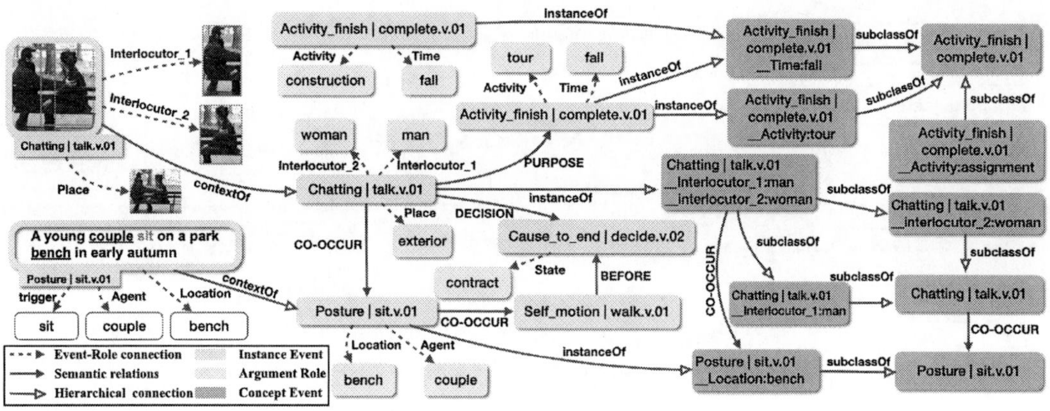


Figure 3: Three levels of MMEKG are illustrated from left to right. The left part is extracted multimodal context. The middle part shows the instance events aggregated from raw context. The right part are inducted concept events.

the set of concept event, instance event, entities, and non-entities, respectively. $\mathcal{R} = \mathcal{R}_{ins-ins} \bigcup \mathcal{R}_{cpt-cpt} \bigcup \mathcal{R}_{cpt-ins} \bigcup \mathcal{R}_{role}$, where $\mathcal{R}_{ins-ins}$ and $\mathcal{R}_{cpt-cpt}$ represent the set of relations between instance events or between concept events, $\mathcal{R}_{cpt-ins}$ represents the set of relations between instance events and concept events, and $\mathcal{R}_{role}$ denotes the set of argument roles. $w(h, r, t)$ denotes the relation weight of the triple $(h, r, t)$ in MMEKG, i.e., the confidence score of being true.

### 2.2 User Interface and System Architecture

As shown in Figure 2, based on MMEKG and the extraction system, we have developed a prototype system that can parse arbitrary texts or images to an event graph, where the nodes denote instance events and the edges denote their relations. For each instance event, we link it to a concept event in MMEKG by identifying the trigger word and its synset (Event Detection). According to the concept event and corresponding roles, we also extract arguments, either a span in texts or a region in images (Argument Extraction). These modules consist of two main components: **Textual Knowledge Extraction** and **Visual Knowledge Extraction** (no trigger word). Another main component is **Event Relation Extraction** which extracts various relations among events, including the fusion of textual and visual events. Note that concept events, synsets, and relation types, are defined by our **cross-modal event ontology**. The linked neighbors in MMEKG are also shown below for better understanding. The detailed architectures behind the demo system, MMEKG and the extraction system, are shown in Figure 3 and Figure 5 respectively.

## 3 Cross-modal Event Ontology

Ontology is critical because it not only confines what types of knowledge are concerned but also offers a reasoning ability — only the induction from instances to concepts brings new knowledge, *i.e.,* from the special to the general. The deduction from concepts to instances has no uncertainty but provides additional information. In this section, we introduce our RDF Schema to model ontology data (Section 3.1), an initial ontology by combining external resources (Section 3.2), and ontology induction for continuous expansion (Section 3.3).

### 3.1 Schema

Following prior work (Gottschalk and Demidova, 2019), we inherit and extend the basic Simple Event Model (SEM) (Van Hage et al., 2011; McBride, 2004) as a knowledge representation basis. An example schema is shown in Figure 4.

**Single event representation** is extended from SEM and FrameNet. (1) Each role has an associated *ekg:[role]* connecting instance event $e \in \mathcal{E}_{ins}$ and argument $a \in \mathcal{E}_{ent} \bigcup \mathcal{E}_{nent}$. (2) We additionally add virtual nodes connecting instance events with edge *ekg:contextOf* to represent a source of such event. Edges from the virtual node like *ekg:trigger*, *ekg:modality* and *ekg:content* indicate the trigger word, modality and sentence/image index of this source respectively.

**Event-event Relation** mainly includes (1) *rdf:instanceOf* to integrate instance and concept events, (2) *rdf:subclassOf* that indicates the hierarchy of concept events, and (3) other relations among instance events, such as temporal or causal relations. For such relations, we design a link-

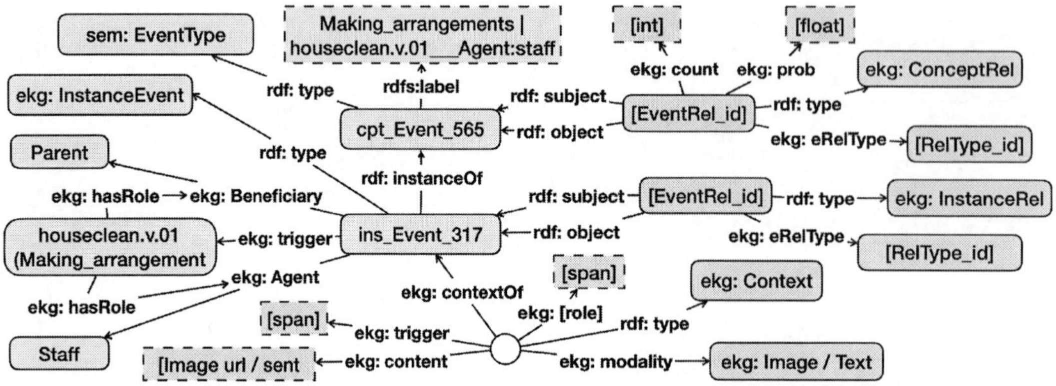


Figure 4: Illustration of Schema designed in MMEKG. Dashed boxes indicate literals and solid boxes indicate events, entities, and relations. We use different colors to represent different types of schema. **Blue**: Event-related. **Green**: Relation-related. **Yellow**: Information of related texts/images from which the system extracts instance events. The uncolored circle is a virtual node connecting an instance event and its source information.

ing node marked by [*EventRel_id*]. There are two advantages to this design: (a) Good extensibility. For possible N-to-1 event relations, multiple subjects and objects can be organized through the linking nodes. Conventional *subj-rel-obj* tuples cannot handle this case. (b) Integration of informative statistics and supplements. For example, we add the frequency and confidence score (obtained from ontology induction in Section 3.3) as prior to the events for reasoning with uncertainty.

### 3.2 Ontology Initialization

Based on schema, we initialize the ontology by merging WordNet (Fellbaum, 1998), FrameNet (Baker et al., 1998), and imSitu (Yatskar et al., 2016) Ontology. In specific, we map each verb and adjective synset in WordNet to a frame in FrameNet (for example, roast.v.01 $\longrightarrow$ Apply_heat). The frames are high-level concept events, and the aligned synsets become fine-grained concept events. Moreover, the WordNet taxonomy brings hierarchical information. For mapping, we first jointly consider the result from structural mapping (Leseva and Stoyanova, 2019) and cosine-similarity score between definitions about synsets and frames given by Sentence-BERT (Reimers and Gurevych, 2019). We randomly sample 100 synset-frame pairs to check whether the definitions of mapped synset and frame align well, and find 89% pairs are reasonable. Then we extend the ontology from imSitu dataset by manually aligning WordNet synset to annotated frame as our visual ontology.

### 3.3 Ontology Induction

This section details how to expand the initial ontology from the perspectives of hierarchical taxonomy and relation types.

**Taxonomy Induction** finds more fine-grained concept events hierarchically. For example, both complete, complete a tour and complete a tour in fall belong to the initialized concept event Activity_finish:complete.v.01, while they represent events with different granularity. Therefore we hope to discriminate them with a more hierarchical and fine-grained taxonomy structure.

Given an initialized concept event $o$ and one of its specific roles $r$, we first select all arguments connected by role $r$ with an instance event categorized to $o$. Then we cluster these arguments heuristically by lemmatizing the headword of each phrase. We further name each cluster by that lemmatized headword and calculate a salience score for each cluster by jointly considering (1) the confidence score $w$ of each event-role-argument triple clustered in and (2) how much information each cluster name provides. Finally, we select K clusters with the highest salience scores and create new concept events by combining role $r$ and these names with their trigger words. Corresponding instance events are also categorized into these newly derived concept events. As shown in Figure 3, we derive new concept events such as complete.v.01__Activity:tour and complete.v.01__Activity:tour__Time:fall. These fine-grained concept events summarize instance events via *instanceOf* relations and are summarized by complete.v.01 with *subclassOf* relations.

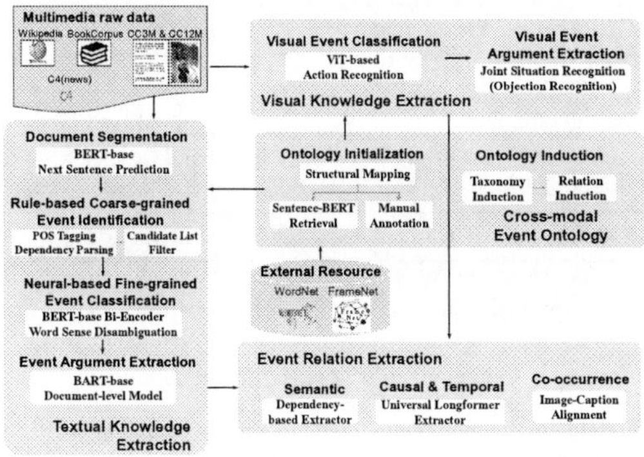


Figure 5: The architecture of Extraction System. There are four main components: Cross-modal Event Ontology, Textual Knowledge Extraction, Visual Knowledge Extraction, and Event Relation Extraction. We use the same ontology introduced in Section 3 for both MMEKG and this extraction system. Another three components are introduced in Section 4 respectively.

**Relation Induction** aims to discover commonsense relations between concept events, based on the relations between instance events. Similar to taxonomy induction, we calculate a salience score $s_r(o_h, o_t)$ for each pair of concept events $(o_h, o_t)$ on relation $r$. The score considers (1) the confidence score of relation $r$ between the children instance events. (2) the commonality of $o_t$ w.r.t. $r$. We add $(o_h, r, o_t)$ with a salience score exceeding a threshold to MMEKG. For example in Figure 3, since the salience score of the triple (talk.v.01, *co-occur*, sit.v.01) exceeds the threshold, we expand such relation from instance-level to concept-level.

## 4 Knowledge Extraction System

This section briefly introduces our knowledge extraction system collecting large-scale instance events and relations for MMEKG, which is shown in Figure 5. We follow the overall framework of previous knowledge extraction systems like GAIA (Li et al., 2020b) and RESIN (Wen et al., 2021), but extends and optimizes event-related components to enable it extracting billion-scale, high-quality events efficiently. With more advanced models, tuning strategy and component architectures, our system achieves comparable if not better performance on each component using a common benchmark. We also substitute all Cross-encoder in the system to Bi-encoder if possible and conduct a joint model of multi-task training during event relation extraction for efficiency.

### 4.1 Textual Knowledge Extraction

This component extracts nodes of the event graph from unstructured texts via event detection and argument extraction. (1) We **pre-process** the corpus as follows. First, we identify document boundaries using BERT-base Next Sentence Prediction (NSP) model and heuristic rules (5-10 sentences per document). Then, we obtain POS-tag and dependency tree via Stanza (Qi et al., 2020). Verbs and adjectives are regarded as candidate words triggering events. (2) Thanks to the synsets in our ontology, we convert **Event Detection** as an unsupervised word sense disambiguation (WSD) task to avoid costly training data. We apply a Bi-encoder model (Blevins and Zettlemoyer, 2020) to predict the most possible synset for candidate trigger words. Each synset refers to a concept event. We thus can link the texts with MMEKG. (3) We propose an efficient and effective method named PAIE (Ma et al., 2022) for **Event Argument Extraction**. The basic idea is to extend QA-based models (Du and Cardie, 2020) to predict all roles for a target event simultaneously. We propose to prompt PLMs for extraction tasks and design a role interaction prompt template for each concept event. All role embeddings serve as query vectors to identify argument spans as the answer. We train the model on annotations provided by FrameNet.

### 4.2 Visual Knowledge Extraction

For visual knowledge extraction, we design a two-stage extraction network. Both models are trained using the largest visual situation recognition dataset (Yatskar et al., 2016; Pratt et al., 2020). (1) For event detection, we leverage pre-trained ViT (Dosovitskiy et al., 2021) to obtain patched image features. Then, another layer of transformer is finetuned to classify images into our visual concept events. (2) Following Pratt et al. (2020), we use pre-trained ResNet-50 (He et al., 2016) as the backbone of Faster R-CNN (Ren et al., 2015), and conditional LSTM decoder to aggregate role information to extract arguments from images.

### 4.3 Event Relation Extraction

This component aims to extract temporal, causal, co-occur, and semantic relations between instance events. Co-occur includes text/image alignments.

**Temporal and Causal Relation**. For temporal and causal relations, we propose a novel method that builds a document-level graph to infer the relations

| Component | Sub-task | Benchmark | Metric | Our score | SOTA |
|---|---|---|---|---|---|
| Text Event Extraction | WSD | SemEval-2007 | Accuracy | 74.5 | 77.4 (Barba et al., 2021) |
| | EAE | ACE-05 | F1 | 67.0 | 65.4 (Du and Cardie, 2020) |
| Visual Event Extraction | VerbD | imSitu | Accuracy | 46.8 | 43.2 (Suhail and Sigal, 2019) |
| | EAE | imSitu | Accuracy | 23.8 | 19.5 (Suhail and Sigal, 2019) |
| Event Relation Extraction | ECI | Causal-TimeBank | F1 | 61.7 | 53.2 (Zuo et al., 2021) |

Table 1: Performance of each component. Abbreviation in column **Sub-task**: EAE: Event Argument Extraction. VerbD: Verb Detection. ECI: Event Causality Identification.

| | #Instance Event | #Concept Event | # Relation | # Relation Type |
|---|---|---|---|---|
| ConceptNet | _ | 74,989 | 116,097 | 4 |
| ATOMIC | _ | 309,515 | 877,108 | 8 |
| ASER (core) | 52,940,258 | _ | 52,296,498 | 14 |
| ASER (full) | 438,648,952 | _ | 648,514,465 | 14 |
| MMEKG-core | 12,310,716 | 990,123 | 48,599,695 | 644 |
| MMEKG-full | 863,428,946 | 990,123 | 934,413,371 | 644 |

Table 2: Statistics of MMEKG and existing event KG.

Table 3: Taxonomy induction.

| #Sample | Positive | Negative |
|---|---|---|
| 1000 | 80.1% | 19.9% |

| | Modality | Precision |
|---|---|---|
| Event | Textual | 84.0% |
| | Visual | 64.6% |
| Triple | Textual | 66.9% |
| | Cross-modal | 63.8% |

Table 4: Instance-level evaluation.

among events globally. Our method could conduct across-sentence reasoning without clear temporal/causal indicators and complicated heuristic rules. This enables us to identify all temporal and causal relations of a document simultaneously and efficiently. We jointly predict temporal and causal relations as multi-label multi-task classification and train the model based on Causal-TimeBank (Mirza, 2014). There are six relation types in total: *Before*, *After*, *During*, *Includes*, *Included*, and *Causal*.

**Co-occurrence Relation**. For textual co-occurrence, we identify it via dependency parsing if the trigger words have a *conj* relation. For cross-modal co-occurrence, we extract events from paired image-caption respectively and assume they co-occur. We also observe semantic shifts between different modalities. As shown in Figure 1, the textual *dressing* event may be a sub-event of the visual *sleeping* event. We will investigate it soon.

**Semantic Relation**. We claim that when an argument of event A is a gerund phrase B, B could also be viewed as a sub-event of A triggered by the gerund functioning as its semantic component. For example, we extract two events from sentence *Eating too much fried chicken cause overweight*: cause overweight (event A) and eat too much chicken (event B). Since A is also an argument of role *influencing_entity* for B, event eat too much chicken and cause overweight are connected with relation *influencing_entity*. Based on such assumption, we expand the relation types by exploiting the *frame elements* in FrameNet. We capture all event pairs in sentences satisfying (1) the trigger words are connected by *acl* or *acl:relcl* in dependency parsing, or (2) the trigger of one event is extracted as an argument of another event. Then we identify these two events having a relation labeled by the argument role.

## 5 Evaluation

### 5.1 MMEKG Statistics

Table 2 presents the statistics of MMEKG and other Event KGs. We build a full version, MMEKG-full, and MMEKG-core which filters out infrequent events ($< 3$ times), leading to a denser and more accurate version. MMEKG involves not only a much larger ontology but also more instance events.

### 5.2 Extraction System Performance

Table 1 shows the results of our components trained on publicly available datasets, since there is no unified benchmark to evaluate the entire extraction process. We can see that all of our knowledge extraction components, except WSD, achieve better performance. Our WSD model performs comparably and efficiently for massive event detection.

### 5.3 Instance-level Evaluation

Considering the different data distribution between training data and extracted corpus, we manually evaluate the instance-level quality of MMEKG. We randomly select 1,000 instance events in texts and

| Type | #Sample | Positive | Similar | Negative |
|---|---|---|---|---|
| Temporal | 134 | 65.7% | 15.7% | 18.6% |
| Co-occur | 139 | 57.6% | 20.1% | 22.3% |
| Semantic | 137 | 46.0% | 36.5% | 17.5% |
| All | 550 | 58.5% | 22.4% | 19.1% |

Table 5: Relation induction.

500 from images. Along with original contexts, we invite six colleagues to label whether the extracted event represents the semantic meaning of the original source or not. For instance event relations, we consider: (1) causal/temporal relations from texts and (2) cross-modal co-occurrence from image-caption pairs. We sample 200 textual relations and 300 cross-modality relations. Along with the contexts, we provide these extracted relations to the same six colleagues and ask them whether the relation extracted matches the original resource. Results in Table 4 demonstrate little performance degradation in precision[5] and an acceptable quality of our proposed MMEKG, considering the complexity of the entire pipeline.

### 5.4 Ontology-level Evaluation

Large-scale ontology is critical for knowledge reasoning. We further evaluate the quality of inferred taxonomy and relations. The difference from the instance-level evaluation is that no context is provided for reference in ontology evaluation. We construct pairs with one positive and one negative sample for comparison convenience, as illustrated in Figure 6, and ask the same six colleagues which sample agrees with our commonsense more. The results are shown in Tables 3 and 5. Both negatives are around 20%. In particular, for relation induction, some similar pairs are hard to tell which one is better. We attribute this to the low recall and random negative sampling, which may bring in false negatives. This also provides insights for future improvements.

## 6 Related Work

**Event Knowledge Graph** Existing event knowledge graphs (Speer et al., 2016; Sap et al., 2019; Zhang et al., 2020) usually face a dilemma about quality and quantity. ATOMIC (Sap et al., 2019) annotates manually and constructs high-quality

[5]We do not report recall here because (1) there is no annotated ground truth of instance events in extracted corpus. (2) precision is much more important since we extract events from large corpus to construct KG.

***Taxonomy Induction:***

```
positive: eat.v.01__Ingestibles:apple
negative: eat.v.01__Ingestibles:table
```

***Relation Induction:***

```
positive: (
  destroy.v.02__Patient:building, include,
    kill.v.01__Victim:people )
negative: (
  destroy.v.02__Patient:building, include,
    invalidate.v.01__Phenomenon:subpoena )
```

Figure 6: Examples of pair constructed for taxonomy (top) and relation induction (bottom). Each pair includes one positive and one negative sample. Positive ones are sampled from induced concept events or relations. Negative ones are generated by substituting the arguments (taxonomy) or tail events (relation) in positive samples.

knowledge bases, while ASER (Zhang et al., 2020) leverages defined patterns and automatic pipeline to build a large-scale graph. Compared with ASER, we not only develop a larger KG by larger corpus and advanced extraction system but also derive complicated ontology and incorporate information across modalities to control the quality of KG.

**Knowledge Extraction System** Previous multi-modal knowledge extraction systems, such as GAIA (Li et al., 2020b) and RESIN (Wen et al., 2021), jointly extract information of a small domain from relatively small-scale resource. Our system inherits their overall framework but is applied for extracting billion-scale and universal events. Therefore we optimize event-related modules targetedly for both efficiency and effectiveness.

**Cross-media Event Argument Alignment** Some previous works (Li et al., 2020a; Fung et al., 2021) also bridge texts and images through fine-grained alignments of event arguments for various tasks, such as multi-modal event extraction and fake news detection. Instead, we fuse knowledge from different modalities to construct such a large-scale KG.

## 7 Conclusion

We present the first Multi-modal Event KG (MMEKG) with a large-scale event ontology. It not only bridges and complements different modalities of knowledge via more expressive events but also benefits comprehensive reasoning with rich cross-modal contexts. Additionally, we provide a demo system that can seamlessly parse and link any texts/images via our knowledge extraction system.

## Acknowledgments

This study is supported under the RIE2020 Industry Alignment Fund – Industry Collaboration Projects (IAF-ICP) Funding Initiative, as well as cash and in-kind contribution from the industry partner(s). We also thank the KULeuven C1 project Macchina for support.

## References

Collin F. Baker, Charles J. Fillmore, and John B. Lowe. 1998. The Berkeley FrameNet project. In *36th Annual Meeting of the Association for Computational Linguistics and 17th International Conference on Computational Linguistics, Volume 1*, pages 86–90, Montreal, Quebec, Canada. Association for Computational Linguistics.

Edoardo Barba, Luigi Procopio, and Roberto Navigli. 2021. ConSeC: Word sense disambiguation as continuous sense comprehension. In *Proceedings of the 2021 Conference on Empirical Methods in Natural Language Processing*, pages 1492–1503, Online and Punta Cana, Dominican Republic. Association for Computational Linguistics.

Terra Blevins and Luke Zettlemoyer. 2020. Moving down the long tail of word sense disambiguation with gloss informed bi-encoders. In *Proceedings of the 58th Annual Meeting of the Association for Computational Linguistics*, pages 1006–1017, Online. Association for Computational Linguistics.

Soravit Changpinyo, Piyush Sharma, Nan Ding, and Radu Soricut. 2021. Conceptual 12M: Pushing web-scale image-text pre-training to recognize long-tail visual concepts. In *CVPR*.

Xin Dong, Evgeniy Gabrilovich, Geremy Heitz, Wilko Horn, Ni Lao, Kevin Murphy, Thomas Strohmann, Shaohua Sun, and Wei Zhang. 2014. Knowledge vault: A web-scale approach to probabilistic knowledge fusion. In *Proceedings of the 20th ACM SIGKDD international conference on Knowledge discovery and data mining*, pages 601–610.

Alexey Dosovitskiy, Lucas Beyer, Alexander Kolesnikov, Dirk Weissenborn, Xiaohua Zhai, Thomas Unterthiner, Mostafa Dehghani, Matthias Minderer, Georg Heigold, Sylvain Gelly, Jakob Uszkoreit, and Neil Houlsby. 2021. An image is worth 16x16 words: Transformers for image recognition at scale. *ICLR*.

Xinya Du and Claire Cardie. 2020. Event extraction by answering (almost) natural questions. In *Proceedings of the 2020 Conference on Empirical Methods in Natural Language Processing (EMNLP)*, pages 671–683, Online. Association for Computational Linguistics.

Christiane Fellbaum. 1998. *WordNet: An Electronic Lexical Database*. Bradford Books.

Yi Fung, Christopher Thomas, Revanth Gangi Reddy, Sandeep Polisetty, Heng Ji, Shih-Fu Chang, Kathleen McKeown, Mohit Bansal, and Avi Sil. 2021. InfoSurgeon: Cross-media fine-grained information consistency checking for fake news detection. In *Proceedings of the 59th Annual Meeting of the Association for Computational Linguistics and the 11th International Joint Conference on Natural Language Processing (Volume 1: Long Papers)*, pages 1683–1698, Online. Association for Computational Linguistics.

Simon Gottschalk and Elena Demidova. 2019. Eventkg–the hub of event knowledge on the web–and biographical timeline generation. *Semantic Web*, 10(6):1039–1070.

Kaiming He, Xiangyu Zhang, Shaoqing Ren, and Jian Sun. 2016. Deep residual learning for image recognition. In *Proceedings of the IEEE conference on computer vision and pattern recognition*, pages 770–778.

Jena D. Hwang, Chandra Bhagavatula, Ronan Le Bras, Jeff Da, Keisuke Sakaguchi, Antoine Bosselut, and Yejin Choi. 2021. Comet-atomic 2020: On symbolic and neural commonsense knowledge graphs. In *AAAI*.

Tuan Lai, Heng Ji, ChengXiang Zhai, and Quan Hung Tran. 2021. Joint biomedical entity and relation extraction with knowledge-enhanced collective inference. In *ACL*.

Svetlozara Leseva and Ivelina Stoyanova. 2019. Structural approach to enhancing WordNet with conceptual frame semantics. In *Proceedings of the International Conference on Recent Advances in Natural Language Processing (RANLP 2019)*, pages 629–637, Varna, Bulgaria. INCOMA Ltd.

Lily Li, Or Levi, Pedram Hosseini, and David Broniatowski. 2020a. A multi-modal method for satire detection using textual and visual cues. In *Proceedings of the 3rd NLP4IF Workshop on NLP for Internet Freedom: Censorship, Disinformation, and Propaganda*, pages 33–38, Barcelona, Spain (Online). International Committee on Computational Linguistics (ICCL).

Manling Li, Alireza Zareian, Ying Lin, Xiaoman Pan, Spencer Whitehead, Brian Chen, Bo Wu, Heng Ji, Shih-Fu Chang, Clare Voss, Daniel Napierski, and Marjorie Freedman. 2020b. GAIA: A fine-grained multimedia knowledge extraction system. In *Proceedings of the 58th Annual Meeting of the Association for Computational Linguistics: System Demonstrations*, pages 77–86, Online. Association for Computational Linguistics.

Kang Liu, Yubo Chen, Jian Liu, Xinyu Zuo, and Jun Zhao. 2020. Extracting event and their relations from texts: A survey on recent research progress and challenges. *AI Open*, 1:22–39.

Yubo Ma, Zehao Wang, Yixin Cao, Mukai Li, Meiqi Chen, Kun Wang, and Jing Shao. 2022. Prompt for extraction? paie: Prompting argument interaction for event argument extraction. *arXiv preprint arXiv:2202.12109*.

Brian McBride. 2004. The resource description framework (rdf) and its vocabulary description language rdfs. In *Handbook on ontologies*, pages 51–65. Springer.

Paramita Mirza. 2014. Extracting temporal and causal relations between events. In *Proceedings of the ACL 2014 Student Research Workshop*, pages 10–17, Baltimore, Maryland, USA. Association for Computational Linguistics.

Sarah Pratt, Mark Yatskar, Luca Weihs, Ali Farhadi, and Aniruddha Kembhavi. 2020. Grounded situation recognition. *ArXiv*, abs/2003.12058.

Peng Qi, Yuhao Zhang, Yuhui Zhang, Jason Bolton, and Christopher D. Manning. 2020. Stanza: A python natural language processing toolkit for many human languages. In *Proceedings of the 58th Annual Meeting of the Association for Computational Linguistics: System Demonstrations*, pages 101–108, Online. Association for Computational Linguistics.

Nils Reimers and Iryna Gurevych. 2019. Sentence-BERT: Sentence embeddings using Siamese BERT-networks. In *Proceedings of the 2019 Conference on Empirical Methods in Natural Language Processing and the 9th International Joint Conference on Natural Language Processing (EMNLP-IJCNLP)*, pages 3982–3992, Hong Kong, China. Association for Computational Linguistics.

Shaoqing Ren, Kaiming He, Ross Girshick, and Jian Sun. 2015. Faster r-cnn: Towards real-time object detection with region proposal networks. *Advances in neural information processing systems*, 28:91–99.

Maarten Sap, Ronan Le Bras, Emily Allaway, Chandra Bhagavatula, Nicholas Lourie, Hannah Rashkin, Brendan Roof, Noah A Smith, and Yejin Choi. 2019. Atomic: An atlas of machine commonsense for if-then reasoning. In *Proceedings of the AAAI Conference on Artificial Intelligence*, volume 33, pages 3027–3035.

Piyush Sharma, Nan Ding, Sebastian Goodman, and Radu Soricut. 2018. Conceptual captions: A cleaned, hypernymed, image alt-text dataset for automatic image captioning. In *Proceedings of the 56th Annual Meeting of the Association for Computational Linguistics (Volume 1: Long Papers)*, pages 2556–2565.

Robert Speer, Joshua Chin, and Catherine Havasi. 2016. Conceptnet 5.5: An open multilingual graph of general knowledge. In *AAAI Conference on Artificial Intelligence*.

Mohammed Suhail and Leonid Sigal. 2019. Mixture-kernel graph attention network for situation recognition. In *The IEEE International Conference on Computer Vision (ICCV)*, pages 10363–10372.

Willem Robert Van Hage, Véronique Malaisé, Roxane Segers, Laura Hollink, and Guus Schreiber. 2011. Design and use of the simple event model (sem). *Journal of Web Semantics*, 9(2):128–136.

Denny Vrandečić and Markus Krötzsch. 2014. Wikidata: a free collaborative knowledgebase. *Communications of the ACM*, 57(10):78–85.

Haoyang Wen, Ying Lin, Tuan Lai, Xiaoman Pan, Sha Li, Xudong Lin, Ben Zhou, Manling Li, Haoyu Wang, Hongming Zhang, Xiaodong Yu, Alexander Dong, Zhenhailong Wang, Yi Fung, Piyush Mishra, Qing Lyu, Dídac Surís, Brian Chen, Susan Windisch Brown, Martha Palmer, Chris Callison-Burch, Carl Vondrick, Jiawei Han, Dan Roth, Shih-Fu Chang, and Heng Ji. 2021. RESIN: A dockerized schema-guided cross-document cross-lingual cross-media information extraction and event tracking system. In *Proceedings of the 2021 Conference of the North American Chapter of the Association for Computational Linguistics: Human Language Technologies: Demonstrations*, pages 133–143, Online. Association for Computational Linguistics.

Mark Yatskar, Luke Zettlemoyer, and Ali Farhadi. 2016. Situation recognition: Visual semantic role labeling for image understanding. In *Conference on Computer Vision and Pattern Recognition*.

Hongming Zhang, Xin Liu, Haojie Pan, Yangqiu Song, and Cane Wing-Ki Leung. 2020. Aser: A large-scale eventuality knowledge graph. In *Proceedings of The Web Conference 2020*, pages 201–211.

Xinyu Zuo, Pengfei Cao, Yubo Chen, Kang Liu, Jun Zhao, Weihua Peng, and Yuguang Chen. 2021. Improving event causality identification via self-supervised representation learning on external causal statement. In *Findings of the Association for Computational Linguistics: ACL-IJCNLP 2021*, pages 2162–2172, Online. Association for Computational Linguistics.

# SOCIOFILLMORE: A Tool for Discovering Perspectives

**Gosse Minnema[1], Sara Gemelli[2], Chiara Zanchi[2], Tommaso Caselli[1], Malvina Nissim[1]**
1. University of Groningen, The Netherlands
2. University of Pavia, Italy
`g.f.minnema@rug.nl`

## Abstract

SOCIOFILLMORE is a multilingual tool which helps to bring to the fore the *focus* or the *perspective* that a text expresses in depicting an event. Our tool, whose rationale we also support through a large collection of human judgements, is theoretically grounded on frame semantics and cognitive linguistics, and implemented using the LOME frame semantic parser. We describe SOCIOFILLMORE's development and functionalities, show how non-NLP researchers can easily interact with the tool, and present some example case studies which are already incorporated in the system, together with the kind of analysis that can be visualised.

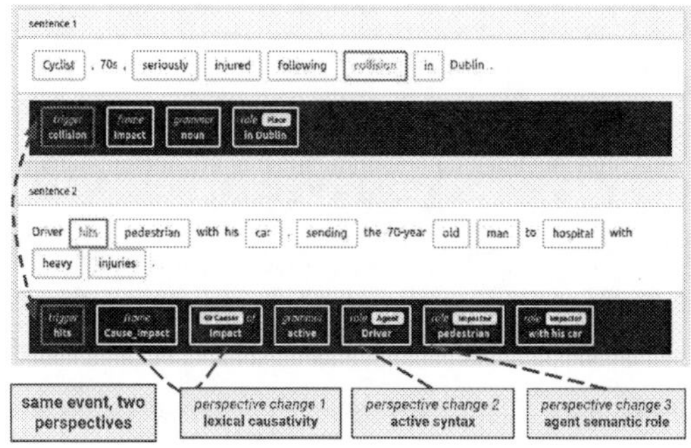


Figure 1: Analysis from SOCIOFILLMORE showing linguistic markers indicating the perspective changes in two descriptions of the same event. Words in boxes indicate triggers of semantic frames in the sentence.

## 1 Introduction

Descriptions of the very same event can vary widely. Sometimes completely different versions of a situation can be reported, while other times more subtle differences emerge by the way in which such situations or episodes are depicted by choosing specific natural language expressions. Figure 1 illustrates this: in the first sentence the car crash is lexicalized by the noun "`collision`" leaving the entire dynamic unknown and suggesting that the cyclist may have some responsibility. On the contrary, the second sentence uses the verb "`hit`" with a subject (the agent) and an object (the patient) making more transparent how the event happened and who is responsible for it.

This phenomenon is known as *framing* or *perspsectivization*, and can happen in any discourse either in full awareness or, more often, unconsciously (Horst, 2020). Politics, for instance, is the prime arena where intentional and biased framing takes place (Iyengar, 1994; Semetko and Valkenburg, 2000; Entman, 1993; Matthes, 2012), but this occurs also in other domains, such as sports. Indeed, representation alternatives, namely the different choices that language allows to describe the same event (not only at the lexical but also at the syntactic and pragmatic level), are key to expressing and understanding the ideological power of discourse (Haynes, 1989).

Different theoretical frameworks can guide the study of framing and perspectivization in discourse, such as Critical Discourse Analysis (CDA) (Fairclough, 2010; Van Dijk, 1995) and Frame Semantics (Fillmore, 1985; Baker et al., 2003). While NLP tools based on some of such frameworks do exist to potentially support large-scale text analysis of perspectivization, and more specifically of Fillmore's frame semantics (Xia et al., 2021), they are (i) recent, thus not yet established as analysis tools for specific perspectivization problems outside of the NLP community; (ii) technical, so that their adoption is basically impossible for the non-experts, who would though benefit from them. On the other hand, cognitive linguists have carried out cognitive linguistic analyses on the discourse regarding social issues and events (e.g. Pinelli and Zanchi (2021)), but these analyses usually imply manual scrutiny of data and, accordingly, deal with small datasets.

We fill this gap with the development of SOCIOFILLMORE, a user-friendly multilingual



*Proceedings of the 60th Annual Meeting of the Association for Computational Linguistics System Demonstrations*, pages 240 - 250
May 22-27, 2022 ©2022 Association for Computational Linguistics

tool based on frame semantics which allows users to conduct large-scale analyses of text by highlighting the perspectivization strategies they adopt.[1]

## 2 Context & Evidence

In this section, we highlight the theoretical frameworks that have guided the design of SOCIOFILLMORE and the empirical evidence we have collected to support its application to written corpora.

### 2.1 Frames, Constructions, & Perspectives

Being able to depict or report about events is part of the broader human ability of storytelling (Boyd, 2009; Gottschall, 2012). One of the key properties of telling a story is the presence of a *focus*, or a perspective (Bal, 1997), which is embedded and intrinsic into every communication act, as shown in Figure 1. Furthermore, the lexical units in a discourse are powerful access points to complex conceptual structures of encyclopedic knowledge and perspectives. This vision is at the core of Fillmore's frame semantics (Fillmore, 1971, 1985, 2006), and encoded into the FrameNet project (Baker et al., 2003). The availability of a computational resource and the strong linguistic orientation of Frame Semantics are the major driving reasons for preferring this framework over other existing ones.

Frames are powerful devices that express perspectives and they strongly interact with linguistic constructions (Langacker, 2006). In some cases, the construction used to present the events can even lead the evocation of different frames. This is clearly illustrated in Figure 1: the noun `collision` evokes the frame IMPACT, while the verb `hit` in an active voice evokes the frame CAUSE_IMPACT. The change of frames associated with different constructions triggers different perspectives and, in this case, also different responsibilities of the participants of the event.

In cognitive linguistic terms, these different constructional options are named *construals* (Langacker, 1991). Frames and construals are socially, culturally, and discursively constructed and constitutive (Dirven et al., 2007): they mirror our ideology, beliefs, and stereotypes and in turn contribute to building and enhancing them. Magnifying the connections between these two elements is a way to support users (e.g., social scientists, journalists, linguists, media studies scholars, among others) to identify and study the perpetration of biases and power structures in discourse.

### 2.2 Empirical Evidence

As a rationale for the validity of our tool two pieces of evidence are needed. The first concerns the feasibility and accuracy of (multilingual) frame semantic parsing, since any reasoning over the significance of finding one frame activated rather than an alternative one is meaningful only if frames can be accurately detected. For this, we ran an evaluation of LOME (Xia et al., 2021), a multilingual end-to-end frame parsing system which is the backbone of our tool, and found that it indeed produces reliable analyses. Details of the fine-tuning procedure and the evaluation are in Section 3.1.

The second piece of evidence concerns the relationship between frames and perspectives from a cognitive viewpoint, and more specifically on the human perception of semantic frames and/or of the interaction between syntactic and lexical semantic expressions of agentivity. Is it true that certain frames and/or constructions are associated with agentivity more than others? To test this, we ran a questionnaire where participants had to express judgements about their perception of the *focus* (i.e., *on which participant or entity is the main focus on the sentence?*) on a set of 400 sentences extracted from a large corpus on femicides in Italian (details in §4.1 and Appendix A). Judgements are expressed on a 5 point Likert-scale for four dimensions, namely focus on: 'the murderer', 'the victim', 'an object' (e.g., a weapon), or 'an abstract concept or emotion' (e.g., jealousy). The selected frames are reported in Table 1, together with the results, i.e., perception scores for each frame-construction pair (averaged over participants and sentences; every pair had approximately the same number of ratings). The highest level of focus on the murderer is found with the KILLING frame evoked by an active transitive construction; this makes sense, since this is the only situation in which the presence of a Killer role is required both syntactically and semantically.[2] On the other hand, constructions perceived as placing a high focus on the victim are found across all frames ex-

[1] An online demo and docker images of the app are available at `https://osf.io/8kh3d/`.

[2] Note that its syntactic realization appears to have a large influence on the perceived focus placed on the agent: on average, passive constructions evoking KILLING have a 'murderer' score of almost two points lower than their active counterparts.

| frame/construction | murderer** | victim** | object | concept / emotion* |
|---|---|---|---|---|
| CATASTROPHE | | | | |
| nonverbal | 1.319 | 2.713 | 0.760 | 2.190 |
| DEAD_OR_ALIVE | | | | |
| nonverbal | 1.195 | 3.387 | 1.386 | 1.993 |
| vrb:unaccusative | 1.983 | 3.529 | 1.566 | 1.539 |
| DEATH | | | | |
| nonverbal | 0.967 | 3.247 | 1.507 | 1.914 |
| vrb:unaccusative | 1.867 | 3.921 | 1.690 | 1.286 |
| EVENT | | | | |
| nonverbal | 1.431 | 1.503 | 1.186 | 2.339 |
| vrb:impersonal | 1.169 | 2.201 | 1.309 | 1.949 |
| KILLING | | | | |
| nonverbal | 2.007 | 2.387 | 1.032 | 1.673 |
| other | 2.410 | 2.345 | 1.198 | 1.663 |
| vrb:active | 3.897 | 2.659 | 1.570 | 1.651 |
| vrb:passive | 1.947 | 3.425 | 1.491 | 1.315 |

Table 1: Average scores for survey question "the main focus is on X". Legend: 'vrb' = verbal construction; '*' = differences between frame-construction pairs are significant at $\alpha = 0.05$, '**' = significant at $\alpha = 0.001$ (Kruskal-Wallis non-parametric H-test). Cells with a value $> 2.5$ are highlighted in green.

cept EVENT.[3] While the analysis presented here is limited to a specific domain, there is a clear pattern in the perception scores of frames and construals, granting sufficient ground for treating their automatically detected presence as a good proxy for how sentences perspectivize events in terms of foregrounding and backgrounding participants.

## 3 SocioFillmore

SOCIOFILLMORE consists of two parts: on the back-end side, there is a series of linguistic analysis components, and on the front-end side, there is a number of components for interacting with the user.

### 3.1 Linguistic Analysis Components

The linguistic analysis components are a combination of existing models and resources, linked by a set of rule-based bridging components.

**LOME** At the core of SOCIOFILLMORE is a frame semantic parser for annotating texts with FrameNet-based semantic frames and roles. While the rest of our architecture is agnostic as to what specific model is used, we decided to use LOME (Xia et al., 2021) as this is (i) one of very few available models capable of producing end-to-end frame analyses (i.e., taking raw text as input, without pre-specifying predicates to annotate), and (ii) based on XLM-R, it is the only model we are aware of that supports zero-shot multilingual FrameNet analysis. Zero-shot multilingual predictions (given English-only annotated) data are very useful given the complexities of Multilingual FrameNet and the limited availability of training data in languages other than English. In an effort to evaluate and improve LOME's multilingual capabilities, in Minnema et al. (2021), we tested LOME against an existing benchmark for Italian (the 2011 Frame Labeling over Italian Texts Task [FLAIT], Basili et al. 2013), and experimented with several methods for exploiting the limited available training data for Italian for improving on this. Interestingly, in a zero-shot setting, LOME underperformed versus the previous state-of-the-art SVM-based model, (Croce et al., 2013) by 24 percentage points (57% vs 81%) on the benchmark's frame detection task (i.e., predict semantic frames given gold predicates), but outperformed it on the frame boundary and argument classification tasks (i.e. predicting role spans and labels given predicates and frames). In our cross-lingual training experiments, we achieved best results training LOME on the concatenation of the available corpora for English and Italian, with a frame detection score much closer to the previous state of the art (77%). However, in a small-scale manual annotation experiment on texts from the RAI femicides corpus (see §4.1) focusing on a limited set of frames, we found that the zero-shot LOME model performed substantially better than the cross-lingually trained version, which seems to be largely due to a drop in predicate detection performance (i.e., given raw text, find all predicates that evoke frames); this can be explained by the nature of the available Italian annotations, which cover only one frame per sentence, making it hard for the model to learn which lexical units evoke frames. Thus, while being far from perfect, zero-shot LOME seems to be the best currently available option in practice for automatic frame annotation.

**Syntactic Analysis** The second main step of the SOCIOFILLMORE analysis pipeline is syntactic analysis. For each frame structure (i.e., a semantic frame together with its semantic roles) identified by LOME, we extract three types of syntactic information through a combination of a UD parse obtained with spaCy (Honnibal et al., 2020), the FrameNet database, and a set of hand-written rules: (i) syntactic construction, (ii) role-dependency links, and (iii) predicate-root status. We distinguish between

[3] This is consistent with the fact that, in FrameNet, the EVENT frame does not include any 'core' semantic roles apart from Place and Time, whereas all the other included frames include a Patient-like role that likely corresponds to the victim.

several types of syntactic constructions; Table 2 lists these constructions in increasing order of participant foregrounding (nonverbal and impersonal constructions do not require any event participant to be syntactically expressed, unaccusatives and passives require only a Patient-like argument, while actives also require an Agent-like role).

Constructions are classified based on three criteria. First, we look at the part-of-speech tags produced by the UD parser, in order to separate non-verbal from verbal constructions. Second, if the construction is verbal, we use FrameNet for determining which core semantic roles are required for the construction: if the triggered frame is EVENT, the construction is classified as impersonal; all other frames in FrameNet have been manually annotated as being either 'active' or 'non-active' based on the presence or absence of an Agent-like participant in the definition of the frame. This information is used to classify verbal constructions associated with non-active frames as unaccusative. Finally, semantically active frames are classified as instantiating either passive or active constructions based on the syntactic features taken from the dependency parse (e.g., finite or infinitive verb form, presence of passive auxiliary, etc.).

Two additional types of extracted syntactic information are role-dependency links and predicate-root status. The former are labels that indicate how a semantic role label is expressed syntactically relative to the frame trigger, and are extracted from the dependency tree by a rule-based algorithm that traverses the dependency tree, starting from the frame trigger, until it encounters a token that is included in the role argument span, or until a pre-set number of maximum traversal steps has been reached. Some possible role-dependency links are "`Event:nsubj↓`" (nominal subject, e.g. in *the [event]* ***happened***), "`Killer:*`" (self-referring link, e.g. in *the* ***[assassin]*** *of JFK*), and "`Suspect:↑-nsubj↓`" (subject of an intermediate node, e.g. in *the [prisoner] remains in* ***detention***). For the purposes of perspective analysis, role-dependency links can provide a useful extra layer on top of construction information: for example, it can help us distinguish between agent-centered and event-centered nonverbal constructions (e.g. ***assassin***, with a self-referential Killer role, vs. ***homicide***, without a Killer role) or detect active constructions in which the main focus is on an inanimate cause rather than on an animate agent (*the [accident]* ***killed*** *him* vs. *The [murderer]* ***killed*** *him*). On the other hand, predicate-root status refers to the position of the frame trigger in the syntactic tree, and serves as a proxy for how 'central' the construction is within the sentence. Verbal constructions are classified as 'roots' only if they are the root nodes of the dependency tree (i.e. are the main verb in the sentence), and nonverbal constructions are classified as 'roots' only if they are the the subject of the root node. The intuition behind this is that the main verbal construction in a sentence, or nonverbal constructions closely related to it, are more under focus than other constructions. For example, in *the* ***homicide*** *happened* (root) versus *he was arrested for* ***homicide*** *ten years later* (non-root), *homicide* is foregrounded in the former but backgrounded in the latter.

| Construction | Semantic Roles | Examples |
|---|---|---|
| non-verbal | none | *The *murder* of MLK*<br>*A *deadly* accident* |
| vrb:impersonal | none<br>[Event-like] | *It *rained**<br>*The event *occurred** |
| vrb:unaccusative | Patient-like | *The victim *died**<br>*He *fell* off the stairs* |
| vrb:passive | Patient-like | *She *was found* in her house*<br>*The cyclist *was hit* by a car* |
| vrb:active | Agent-like<br>[Patient-like] | *The girl *walked* to school*<br>*The police *arrested* the man* |

Table 2: Syntactic construction types used by SOCIOFILLMORE. Semantic roles between square braces are mandatory in a subset of constructions within the type. 'vrb'=verb-based constructions

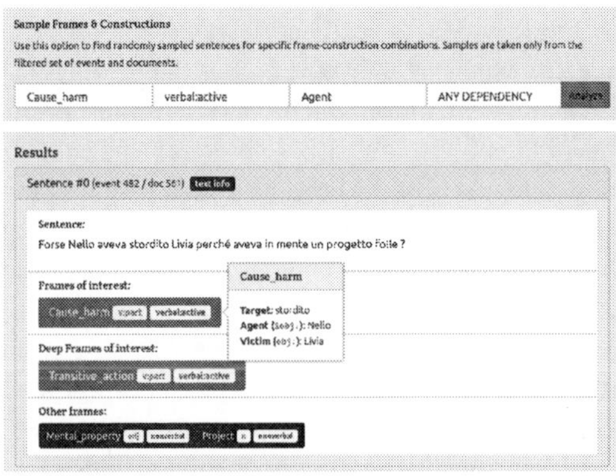


Figure 2: Explorer mode: visualize sentences matching specific linguistic features

### 3.2 User Interaction

SocioFillmore has two usage modes: one for exploring and analyzing existing, pre-processed corpora, and one for interactively exploring frame-based perspective analysis. The former mode is targeted towards domain experts interested in in-depth analysis of specific phenomena, while the latter is targeted to a broader community of (social) scientists who are unfamiliar with frame semantics but would like to learn about using linguistic frames and constructions for analyzing how events can be framed through language.

**Corpus Explorer** The corpus explorer is illustrated in Figure 2. It consists of three parts: first, the user can select relevant semantic frames from a pre-defined set (or add additional frames) that correspond to the perspective-taking phenomena that they want to investigate. Second, the user can specify which subset of the corpus they would like to analyze by adding document-based and event-based filters. Document-based filters (e.g. publication date, news outlet) can be added for any kind of corpus, while event-based filters (e.g. location of event, participants involved) can only be used for corpora that provide event-level metadata (i.e., each document is linked to some structured event representation). This second type of corpus is especially attractive for perspective analysis because it allows for investigating how similar real-world events are conceptualized in different documents that reference these events. Finally, having selected frames and filtered the corpus, the user can analyze the corpus in two ways: one can get global descriptive statistics over the selected part of the corpus, or visualize annotated sentences from the corpus. A wide range of descriptive statistics are available, for example, simple frequencies of semantic frames and constructions, frequencies of role dependencies per frame, and frame frequencies plotted as a function of time elapsed between the event occurrence and publication of the documents referencing it. On the other hand, when visualizing annotations from the corpus, there are two options: the user can either select specific documents from the corpus and analyze them sentence-by-sentence, or make a selection of linguistic features of interest (e.g. a combination of frames, constructions, and role dependencies) and request to see randomly sampled sentences matching these features.

As of now, we have implemented the corpus explorer for four different corpora on three domains

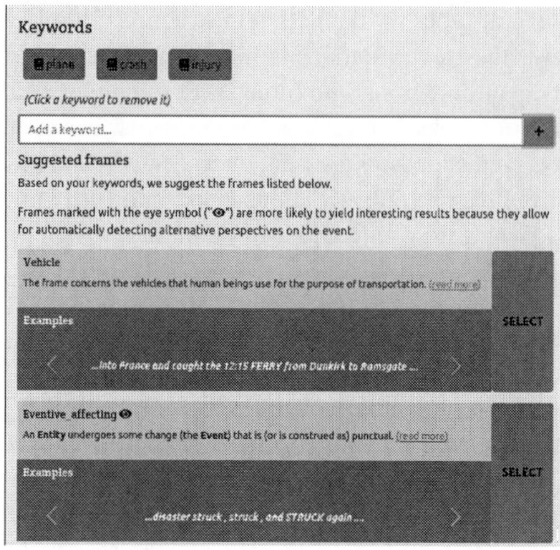


Figure 3: Interactive mode: keyword search interface

in two languages (femicides and migration in Italian, and traffic crashes in Dutch). We are planning to add additional corpora in the future, and also welcome contributed corpora from others. Adding an additional corpus requires some amount of expertise in NLP and FrameNet as well as in the domain of interest, and involves pre-processing the corpus and its metadata, running LOME and the SocioFillmore linguistic pipeline over the corpus, and adding corpus-specific logic (e.g. document/event filters) to the explorer interface. For future work, we are planning to develop a graphical UI to streamline this process and make it more accessible for users without a technical background.

**Interactive Mode** The interactive mode of SocioFillmore aims to make frame-based perspective analysis more accessible to people without a specific background in frame semantics. To this end, we provide three main features, as shown in Figure 3: a step-by-step interface with examples guiding the user through the stages of perspective analysis (event definition, frame selection, and document visualization), an interactive frame selection tool, and an on-demand version of LOME and the SocioFillmore linguistic pipeline with simplified annotation visualization. The most novel of these features is the interactive frame selection tool, which is meant to help users who are not familiar with the FrameNet database to find frames that are relevant for the event type that they would like to analyze. The frame selection tool consists of two components: an embedding-based keyword search function, and a rule-based algorithm for automatically finding frames that provide alternative perspectives on selected frames. The former of these makes use of 'bag-of-LU' frame embeddings that are computed using a similar method to that proposed in Alhoshan et al. (2019). Keyword searches are performed by retrieving GloVe vectors for the specified keywords, and then finding the frame embeddings with the top-N closest cosine distance to the centroid of the set of keyword embeddings. The suggested frames are then displayed to the user along with their definition and example sentences retrieved using the NLTK FrameNet API (Bird et al., 2009). Alternative representations for the creation of the frame and keyword embeddings (e.g., BERT embeddings) could be easily integrated in the tool. Complementary to the keyword search system, we use frame-to-frame relations to automatically add additional frames that provide alternative perspectives on the frames that the user specified.

## 4 Case studies

SOCIOFILLMORE has been applied (so far) to three case studies: Italian news reporting on femicides, Italian news reporting on migration, and Dutch news reporting on traffic crashes. In each of these cases, we target events where there is a potential imbalance of power between the actors involved and the attribution of responsibility for the happening to (at least) one of the participants of the event. This makes the study of the perspectives associated with the reporting of these events very suitable to investigate how responsibility is framed in news reports of such events, and where potential representation biases may emerge.

### 4.1 Femicides

For femicides, the domain of SOCIOFILLMORE developed most extensively to date, two corpora are currently available in the exploration tool. The first has been compiled by the CRITS research team at RAI (Radiotelevisione Italiana), composed by 2,734 news articles from 31 different Italian news sources, reporting on 937 femicides perpetrated between 2015 and 2017 (Belluati, 2021). The corpus is enriched with metadata (time, news source, etc.) and for each femicide event multiple news articles are available. For our analysis we selected 15 frames based on the examples in Pinelli and Zanchi (2021) - see Appendix B.

In Minnema et al. (2021), we applied

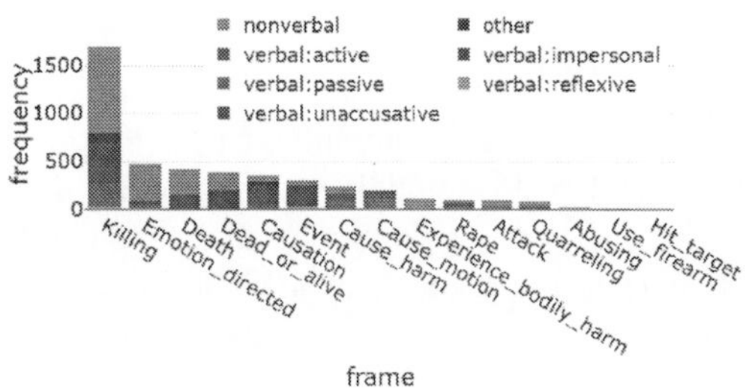


Figure 4: Femicides analysis: frequency of frames split by syntactic construction. Figure exported from SOCIOFILLMORE.

SOCIOFILLMORE on a randomly chosen 200K word subcorpus (10% of all events) of the RAI corpus. The main findings are shown in Figure 4. As expected, KILLING is by far the most frequent typical frame, followed by EMOTION_DIRECTED and DEATH. Concerning syntax, the *nonverbal* constructions (i.e., the predicate is either a noun or an adjective) are dominant across many frames, while *verbal:active* constructions are much rarer, as well as *verbal:passive* and *verbal:unaccusative*.

The combination of syntactic constructions and semantic frames is the key to magnifying perspectives. In particular, we observe that 60% of the instances of the frame KILLING are associated with constructions that foreground the victims and background the perpetrators. This reaches 79% of cases when the frame used to present the event is DEATH. In terms of perspective analysis, this indicates a bias in framing femicides as events where a killing takes place but no one is actually responsible for it.

### 4.2 Other domains

SOCIOFILLMORE has been productively used as well for studying the framing of traffic crashes and migrations in the Dutch and Italian media, respectively. Zanchi et al. (2021) used the tool for automatically identifying frames contributing to either dehumanizing or humanizing migrants in newspaper headlines (e.g. reporting on 'waves' of migrants, and thus collectively conceptualizing them as a non-human mass entity, vs. reporting on migrants as single and intentional individuals), and also compared the change in these frames over time relative to statistics about newly arrived migrants in Italy. We are also involved in ongoing work, in collaboration with the author of the original paper, aiming at reproducing the findings on traffic framing reported in Te Brömmelstroet (2020).

## 5 Conclusions

SocioFillmore is a multilingual tool that we have developed for studying perspectives in written text, grounded in Frame Semantics and Cognitive Linguistics. Through an interactive mode, the tool is easily accessible to non-experts, too. We support the rationale for the validity of our tool through a rigorous evaluation of the frame semantic parser at the core of our tool and a collection of human judgement on the connection between frames and perspectivization. The tool is available as a web interface (and as a docker release), it supports multiple languages, and already integrates a few large-scale case studies which can be browsed for research, but also for further understanding of the tool's functionalities.

## Ethical Statement

One of the key properties of SocioFillmore is its being agnostic on whether a perspective should be considered "good" or "bad". In this respect SocioFillmore is **not a prescriptive tool** on how news should be reported but rather a support tool that helps to magnify misuse of frames and biases that may mirror and strengthen asymmetric power dynamics existing in our societies.

SocioFillmore is based on state-of-the-art NLP technologies. While these tools achieve very good performances (also in zero-shot multilingual settings), none of them can be considered to reach nor mimic humans. The tools are based on powerful machine learning algorithms but they are far away from being artificial intelligent agents. We recommend **caution** when using SocioFillmore since margins of errors are present. At the same time, additional tests are needed before deploying SocioFillmore as an integrated tool or service that citizens or professionals may use for purposes other than research.

One of the services of SocioFillmore is corpus-assisted language analysis. The outcome of this service is highly sensitive to the data that are feeded to the tool. This requires users to pay particular attention to the curation of the data that will compose their corpus. Results on the presence of frames and bias are a direct consequence of what is input to the tool. The case studies we have illustrated are based on carefully curated corpus collections conducted by experts. We thus recommend that users of SocioFillmore should accompany the presentation of their results with a **documentation of their data collections** using tools such as data statements (Bender and Friedman, 2018) or data sheets (Gebru et al., 2021).

## References


Waad Alhoshan, Riza Batista-Navarro, and Liping Zhao. 2019. Semantic frame embeddings for detecting relations between software requirements. In *Proceedings of the 13th International Conference on Computational Semantics - Student Papers*, pages 44–51, Gothenburg, Sweden. Association for Computational Linguistics.

Collin F. Baker, Charles J. Fillmore, and Beau Cronin. 2003. The structure of the FrameNet database. *International Journal of Lexicography*, 16(3):281–296.

Mieke Bal. 1997. *Narratology: Introduction to the theory of narrative*. University of Toronto Press.

Roberto Basili, Diego De Cao, Alessandro Lenci, Alessandro Moschitti, and Giulia Venturi. 2013. Evalita 2011: The frame labelingover italian texts task. In *Evaluation of Natural Language and Speech Tools for Italian*, pages 195–204, Berlin, Heidelberg. Springer Berlin Heidelberg.

M. Belluati. 2021. *Femminicidio. Una lettura tra realtà e interpretazione*. Biblioteca di testi e studi. Carocci.

Emily M Bender and Batya Friedman. 2018. Data statements for natural language processing: Toward mitigating system bias and enabling better science. *Transactions of the Association for Computational Linguistics*, 6:587–604.

Steven Bird, Ewan Klein, and Edward Loper. 2009. *Natural language processing with Python: analyzing text with the natural language toolkit*. " O'Reilly Media, Inc.".

Brian Boyd. 2009. *On the origin of stories*. Harvard University Press.

Danilo Croce, Emanuele Bastianelli, and Giuseppe Castellucci. 2013. Structured kernel-based learning for the frame labeling over Italian texts. In *Evaluation of Natural Language and Speech Tools for Italian*, pages 195–204, Berlin, Heidelberg. Springer Berlin Heidelberg.

René Dirven, Frank Polzenhagen, and Hans-Georg Wolf. 2007. Cognitive linguistics, ideology, and critical discourse analysis. In *The Oxford handbook of cognitive linguistics*.

Robert M Entman. 1993. Framing: Towards clarification of a fractured paradigm. *Journal of Communication*, 43.

Norman Fairclough. 2010. *Critical Discourse Analysis: The Critical Study of Language (Second Edition).* Routledge.

Charles J. Fillmore. 1971. Subjects, speakers, and roles. *Synthese*, 21(3-4).

Charles J. Fillmore. 1985. Frames and the semantics of understanding. *Quaderni di semantica*, 6(2):222–254.

Charles J. Fillmore. 2006. Frame semantics. In D. Geeraerts, editor, *Cognitive Linguistics: Basic Readings*, pages 373–400. De Gruyter Mouton, Berlin, Boston. Originally published in 1982.

Timnit Gebru, Jamie Morgenstern, Briana Vecchione, Jennifer Wortman Vaughan, Hanna Wallach, Hal Daumé Iii, and Kate Crawford. 2021. Datasheets for datasets. *Communications of the ACM*, 64(12):86–92.

Jonathan Gottschall. 2012. *The storytelling animal: How stories make us human.* Houghton Mifflin Harcourt.

John Haynes. 1989. *Introducing stylistics.* Allen & Unwin Australia.

Matthew Honnibal, Ines Montani, Sofie Van Landeghem, and Adriane Boyd. 2020. spaCy: Industrial-strength Natural Language Processing in Python.

Dorothea Horst. 2020. Patterns 'we'think by? critical cognitive linguistics between language system and language use. *Yearbook of the German Cognitive Linguistics Association*, 8(1):67–82.

Shanto Iyengar. 1994. *Is anyone responsible?: How television frames political issues.* University of Chicago Press.

Robert W. Langacker. 1991. *Foundations of Cognitive Grammar, vol. II: Descriptive application.* Stanford University Press, Stanford.

Ronald W. Langacker. 2006. Dimensions of defocusing. In Tasaku Tsunoda and Taro Kageyama, editors, *Voice and grammatical relations: In honor of Masayoshi Shibatani*, page 115–138. John Benjamins Publishing.

Jörg Matthes. 2012. Framing politics: An integrative approach. *American behavioral scientist*, 56(3):247–259.

Gosse Minnema, Sara Gemelli, Chiara Zanchi, Viviana Patti, Tommaso Caselli, and Malvina Nissim. 2021. Frame semantics for social NLP in Italian: Analyzing responsibility framing in femicide news reports. In *Proceedings of the Eighth Italian Conference on Computational Linguistics.* Milan, January 26-28, 2022 (postponed).

Erica Pinelli and Chiara Zanchi. 2021. Gender-based violence in italian local newspapers: How argument structure constructions can diminish a perpetrator's responsibility. *Discourse Processes between Reason and Emotion: A Post-disciplinary Perspective*, page 117.

Holli A Semetko and Patti M Valkenburg. 2000. Framing European politics: A content analysis of press and television news. *Journal of communication*, 50(2):93–109.

Marco Te Brömmelstroet. 2020. Framing systemic traffic violence: Media coverage of dutch traffic crashes. *Transportation research interdisciplinary perspectives*, 5.

Teun A. Van Dijk. 1995. Discourse analysis as ideology analysis. In C. Schäffner and A.I. Wenden, editors, *Language and Peace.* Harwood Academic Publishers, Amsterdam.

Patrick Xia, Guanghui Qin, Siddharth Vashishtha, Yunmo Chen, Tongfei Chen, Chandler May, Craig Harman, Kyle Rawlins, Aaron Steven White, and Benjamin Van Durme. 2021. LOME: Large ontology multilingual extraction. In *Proceedings of the 16th Conference of the European Chapter of the Association for Computational Linguistics: System Demonstrations*, pages 149–159, Online. Association for Computational Linguistics.

Chiara Zanchi, Serena Coschignano, and Gosse Minnema. 2021. Numeri in arrivo anziché uomini e donne in partenza: Come i frame ci rendono inconsapevolmente ingiusti ['Numbers in arrival instead of men and women in departure: How frames render us unconsciously unjust']. In *Notize ai margini: IX rapporto Carta di Roma 2021 ['News at the margins: 9th report of the Rome Charter'].* `https://www.cartadiroma.org/`.

## A Questionnaire

The questionnaire has been conducted using the platform Qualtrics.

Participants have been recruited from several universities in Italy ($N$ = 239; Male = 86; Female = 153). Each participant was presented with 50 sentences and was asked to express a judgements on Likert-type scale from 0 to 5 for the perceived "amount" of focus placed on four dimensions, namely: 'the murderer', 'the victim', 'an object' (e.g., a weapon), or 'an abstract concept or emotion' (e.g., jealousy).

The sentences were selected by first automatically annotating the corpus with semantic frames and construals, determining a set of semantic frames that correspond to different ways of conceptualizing the femicides, selecting the set of most frequent construals for each frame, and then, for each frame-construal pair, randomly sampling sentences containing at least one instance of the pair from the corpus.

The frames that we selected were, in order of increasing level of detail and presence of event participants:

- EVENT, e.g., *the **incident** occurred*;
- CATASTROPHE, e.g., *the **tragedy** cost the life of ...*;
- DEAD_OR_ALIVE, e.g., *the victim was found **dead***;
- DEATH, e.g., *the victim **died** at the hands of...*; and
- KILLING, e.g., *the man **murdered** his wife.*

Each of these frames can occur in various syntactic configurations, but only KILLING can be evoked by a transitive verbal construction (actively or transitively used).

While it is possible that, in some cases, instances of these frames refer to another event referenced in the texts (e.g. KILLING could also refer to the perpetrator committing suicide, or to some other type of secondary murder; EVENT could also refer to other type of 'events' or 'incidents' mentioned in the text), but, from a manual inspection of the data, this seems to be fairly rare. We informed participants of the possibility of anomalous sentences occurring in the survey and instructed them to mark these as 'irrelevant' and to not assign any points to them.

The questionnaire has been approved by the Ethical Board of the University of Groningen. Participants were compensated with 5 euro. Each participant was asked to provide judgments on a set of 50 sentences. Participation is anonymized (there is no link between the questionnaire answers and the participants.) and we limit the collection of personal data to last name, initials, bank account and address only for payment purposes. After the payment, all personal data of the participant is deleted.

A screenshot of the original instructions provided to the participants is presented in Figure A.1. Translations in English of the instructions is given below:

```
INSTRUCTIONS:
Dear participant,
  the following questionnaire
is part of a project related to
```

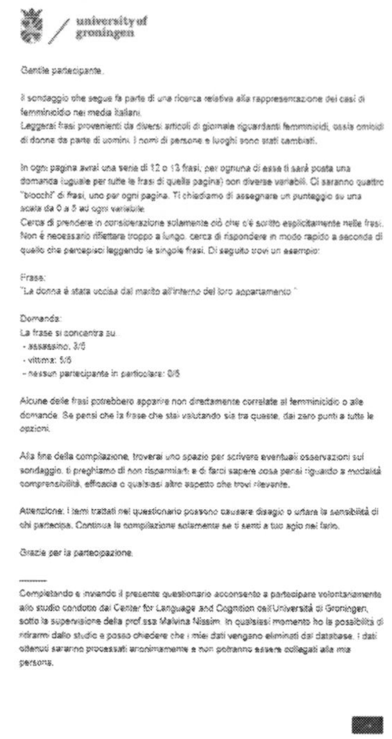
university of groningen

Gentile partecipante,

il sondaggio che segue fa parte di una ricerca relativa alla rappresentazione dei casi di femminicidio nei media italiani.
Leggerai frasi provenienti da diversi articoli di giornale riguardanti femminicidi, ossia omicidi di donne da parte di uomini. I nomi di persone e luoghi sono stati cambiati.

In ogni pagina avrai una serie di 12 o 13 frasi, per ognuna di esse ti sarà posta una domanda (uguale per tutte le frasi di quella pagina) con diverse variabili. Ci saranno quattro "blocchi" di frasi, uno per ogni pagina. Ti chiediamo di assegnare un punteggio su una scala da 0 a 5 ad ogni variabile.
Cerca di prendere in considerazione solamente ciò che c'è scritto esplicitamente nelle frasi. Non è necessario riflettere troppo a lungo, cerca di rispondere in modo rapido a seconda di quello che percepisci leggendo le singole frasi. Di seguito trovi un esempio:

Frase:
"La donna è stata uccisa dal marito all'interno del loro appartamento."

Domanda:
La frase si concentra su
- assassino: 3/5
- vittima: 5/5
- nessun partecipante in particolare: 0/5

Alcune delle frasi potrebbero apparire non direttamente correlate al femminicidio o alle domande. Se pensi che la frase che stai valutando sia tra queste, dai zero punti a tutte le opzioni.

Alla fine della compilazione, troverai uno spazio per scrivere eventuali osservazioni sul sondaggio, ti preghiamo di non risparmiarti e di farci sapere cosa pensi riguardo a modalità, comprensibilità, efficacia o qualsiasi altro aspetto che trovi rilevante.

Attenzione: I temi trattati nel questionario possono causare disagio o urtare la sensibilità di chi partecipa. Continua la compilazione solamente se ti senti a tuo agio nel farlo.

Grazie per la partecipazione.

---------
Completando e inviando il presente questionario acconsento a partecipare volontariamente allo studio condotto dal Center for Language and Cognition dell'Università di Groningen, sotto la supervisione della prof.ssa Malvina Nissim. In qualsiasi momento ho la possibilità di ritirarmi dallo studio e posso chiedere che i miei dati vengano eliminati dal database. I dati ottenuti saranno processati anonimamente e non potranno essere collegati alla mia persona.

Figure A.1: Original instruction given to the participant in the questionnaire for validating SOCIOFILLMORE.

```
the representation of femicides
in the italian media.  You
will read sentences extracted
from newspaper articles about
femicides, i.e.  murders in which
a man kills a woman.  The real
names un the sentences have been
changed.

  In each page you will be
presented with a series of 12
or 13 sentences; there are four
different "stacks" of sentences,
one for each page.  For each
sentence you will be asked a
question (the same of every
sentence in that page) followed
by different variables.  You will
be asked to rate every variable
on a scale from 0 to 5.

  While doing the task, try to
consider just what the sentence
explicitly expresses.  There is
no need to think for too long,
try to answer fast according to
what you perceive reading the
```

sentences. Example: *The woman was killed by her husband at home.* Question: The sentence focuses on...

- the murder: 3/5
- the victim: 5/5
- nobody in particular: 0/5

After the data analysis, the participants will receive an e-mail with a link to an online meeting in which we will briefly present the outcomes of the research.

Warning: the topics in the questionnaire could make you feel uncomfortable; please continue only if you feel at ease. Thank you for your time!

By filling in the following questionnaire I consent to participate voluntarily in the study conducted by the Center for Language and Cognition of the University of Groningen, supervised by prof. dr. Malvina Nissim. I can withdraw my participation at any time and have the data obtained through this study returned to me, removed from the database or deleted. The data obtained during this study will be processed anonymously and will therefore not be able to be traced back to me.

## B Frames and semantic roles

In Tables B.1, we provide the set of semantic frames and a mapping between their associated semantic roles and the main participants in the femicides.

| **frame** | **role:perpetrator_like** | **role:victim_like** | **role:cause_like** |
|---|---|---|---|
| Abusing | Abuser | Victim | - |
| Attack | Assailant | Victim | - |
| Causation | Causer | Affected | Cause |
| Cause_harm | Agent | Victim | Cause |
| Cause_motion | - | - | - |
| Dead_or_alive | - | Protagonist | Explanation |
| Death | - | Protagonist | Cause |
| Emotion_directed | - | - | - |
| Event | - | - | - |
| Experience_bodily_harm | Experiencer\|Body_part | - | - |
| Hit_target | Agent | Target | - |
| Killing | Killer | Victim | Cause |
| Quarreling | - | - | - |
| Rape | Perpetrator | Victim | - |
| Use_firearm | Agent | Goal | - |

Table B.1: Femicides: mapping frames, participants, and roles

# TimeLMs: Diachronic Language Models from Twitter

**Daniel Loureiro*♠, Francesco Barbieri*♣,**
**Leonardo Neves♣, Luis Espinosa Anke♢, Jose Camacho-Collados♢**
♠ LIAAD - INESC TEC, University of Porto, Portugal
♣ Snap Inc., Santa Monica, California, USA
♢ Cardiff NLP, School of Computer Science and Informatics, Cardiff University, UK
♠ daniel.b.loureiro@inesctec.pt , ♣ {fbarbieri,lneves}@snap.com,
♢ {espinosa-ankel,camachocolladosj}@cardiff.ac.uk

## Abstract

Despite its importance, the *time* variable has been largely neglected in the NLP and language model literature. In this paper, we present TimeLMs, a set of language models specialized on diachronic Twitter data. We show that a continual learning strategy contributes to enhancing Twitter-based language models' capacity to deal with future and out-of-distribution tweets, while making them competitive with standardized and more monolithic benchmarks. We also perform a number of qualitative analyses showing how they cope with trends and peaks in activity involving specific named entities or concept drift. TimeLMs is available at https://github.com/cardiffnlp/timelms.

## 1 Introduction

Neural language models (LMs) (Devlin et al., 2019; Radford et al., 2019; Liu et al., 2019) are today a key enabler in NLP. They have contributed to a general uplift in downstream performance across many applications, even sometimes rivaling human judgement (Wang et al., 2018, 2019), while also bringing about a new paradigm of knowledge acquisition through pre-training. However, currently, both from model development and evaluation standpoints, this paradigm is essentially static, which affects both the ability to generalize to future data and the reliability of experimental results, since it is not uncommon that evaluation benchmarks overlap with pre-training corpora (Lazaridou et al., 2021). As an example, neither the original versions of BERT and RoBERTa are up to date with the current coronavirus pandemic. This is clearly troublesome, as most of the communication in recent years has been affected by it, yet these models would barely know what we are referring to when we talk about *COVID-19* or *lockdown*, to name just a few examples. The lack of *diachronic specialization* is especially concerning in contexts such as social media, where topics of discussion change often and rapidly (Del Tredici et al., 2019).

In this paper, we address this issue by sharing with the community a series of *time-specific LMs specialized to Twitter data* (TimeLMs). Our initiative goes beyond the initial release, analysis and experimental results reported in this paper, as models will periodically continue to be trained, improved and released.

## 2 Related Work

There exists a significant body of work on dealing with the time variable in NLP. For instance, by specializing language representations derived from word embedding models or neural networks (Hamilton et al., 2016; Szymanski, 2017; Rosenfeld and Erk, 2018; Del Tredici et al., 2019; Hofmann et al., 2021). Concerning the particular case of LMs, exposing them to new data and updating their parameters accordingly, also known as continual learning, is a promising direction, with an established tradition in machine learning (Lopez-Paz and Ranzato, 2017; Lewis et al., 2020; Lazaridou et al., 2021; Jang et al., 2021). Other works, however, have proposed to enhance BERT-based topic models with the time variable (Grootendorst, 2020). With regards to in-domain specialization, there are numerous approaches that perform domain adaptation by pre-training a generic LM on specialized corpora. A well-known case is the biomedical domain, e.g., BioBERT (Lee et al., 2020), SciBERT (Beltagy et al., 2019) or PubMedBERT (Gu et al., 2021). In addition to these approaches to specialize language models, there have been similar temporal adaptation analyses to the one presented in our paper (Agarwal and Nenkova, 2021; Jin et al., 2021). In particular, these works showed that training language models in recent data can be beneficial, an improvement that was found to be marginal in Luu et al. (2021) in a different setting. In terms of continual lifelong learning, which is tangential to our

Authors marked with an asterisk (*) contributed equally.



*Proceedings of the 60th Annual Meeting of the Association for Computational Linguistics*
*System Demonstrations*, pages 251 - 260

main goal, Biesialska et al. (2020) provide a detailed survey on the main techniques proposed in the NLP literature.

More relevant to this paper, on the other hand, are LMs specialized to social media data, specifically Twitter, with BERTweet (Nguyen et al., 2020), TweetEval (Barbieri et al., 2020) and XLM-T (Barbieri et al., 2021) being, to the best of our knowledge, the most prominent examples. However, the above efforts barely address the diachronic nature of language. Crucially, they do not address the problem of specializing LMs to social media *and* putting the time variable at the core of the framework. Moreover, it is desirable that such time-aware models are released alongside usable software and a reliable infrastructure. Our TimeLMs initiative, detailed in Section 3, aims to address the above challenges.

## 3 TimeLMs: Diachronic Language Models from Twitter

In this section, we present our approach to train language models for different time periods.

### 3.1 Twitter corpus

For the training and evaluation of language models, we first collect a large corpus of tweets. In the following we explain both the data collection and cleaning processes.

**Data collection.** We use the Twitter Academic API to obtain a large sample of tweets evenly distributed across time. In order to obtain a sample which is representative of general conversation on that social platform, we query the API using the most frequent stopwords[1], for a set number of tweets at timestamps distanced by 5 minutes - for every hour of every day constituting a particular yearly quarter. We also use specific flags supported by the API to retrieve only tweets in English and ignore retweets, quotes, links, media posts and ads.

For our initial base model (2019-90M henceforth), we used an evenly time-distributed corpus from the API, for the period between 2018 and 2019, supplemented with additional tweets from Archive.org which cover the same period but are not evenly distributed.

**Data cleaning.** Before training any model, we filter each model's training set of tweets using the procedure detailed in this section. Starting with the assumption that bots are amongst the most active users, we remove tweets from the top one percent of users that have posted most frequently. Additionally, following the recommendation of Lee et al. (2021), we remove duplicates and near-duplicates. We find near-duplicates by hashing the texts of tweets after lowercasing and stripping punctuation. Hashing is performed using MinHash (Broder, 1997), with 16 permutations. Finally, user mentions are replaced with a generic placeholder (@user), except for verified users.

### 3.2 Language model training

Once the Twitter corpus has been collected and cleaned, we proceed to the language model pre-training. This consists of two phases: (1) training of a base model consisting of data until the end of 2019; and (2) continual training of language models every three months since the date of the base model.

**Base model training.** Our base model is trained with data until 2019 (included). Following Barbieri et al. (2020), we start from the original RoBERTa-base model (Liu et al., 2019) and continue training the masked language model on Twitter data. The model is trained using the same settings as Barbieri et al. (2020), namely early stopping on the validation split and a learning rate of $1.0e^{-5}$. This initial 2019-90M base model converged after around fifteen days on 8 NVIDIA V100 GPUs.

**Continuous training.** After training our base model, our goal is to continue training this language model with recent Twitter corpora. At the time of writing, for practical and logistical reasons, the decision is to train a new version of each language model every three months. The process to train this updated language model is simple, as it follows the same training procedure as the initial pre-training of the language model explained above. Our commitment is to keep updating and releasing a new model every three months, effectively enabling the community to make use of an up-to-date language model at any period in time.

### 3.3 TimeLMs release summary

In Table 1 we include a summary of the Twitter corpora collected and models trained until the date of writing. Models are split in four three-month quarters (Q1, Q2, Q3 and Q4). Our base 2019-90M model consists of 90 million tweets until the end of 2019. Then, every quarter (i.e., every three months) 4.2M additional tweets are added, and the model gets updated as described above. Our latest

[1] We use the top 10 entries from: google-10000-english.txt

released models, which are 2021-Q4 and 2021-124M (the latter was re-trained only once with all the data from 2020 and 2021), are trained on 124M tweets on top of the original RoBERTa-base model (Liu et al., 2019). All models are currently available through the Hugging Face hub at `https://huggingface.co/cardiffnlp`.

| Models | Additional | Total |
|---|---|---|
| 2019-90M | - | 90.26M |
| 2020-Q1 | 4.20M | 94.46M |
| 2020-Q2 | 4.20M | 98.66M |
| 2020-Q3 | 4.20M | 102.86M |
| 2020-Q4 | 4.20M | 107.06M |
| 2021-Q1 | 4.20M | 111.26M |
| 2021-Q2 | 4.20M | 115.46M |
| 2021-Q3 | 4.20M | 119.66M |
| 2021-Q4 | 4.20M | 123.86M |
| 2021-124M | 33.60M | 123.86M |

Table 1: Number of tweets used to train each model. Showing number of tweets used to update models, and total starting from RoBERTa-base by Liu et al. (2019).

In addition to these corpora for training language models, we set apart a number of tweets for each quarter (independent from the training set, with no overlap). These sets are used as test sets on our perplexity evaluation (see Section 4.2), and consist of 300K tweets per quarter, which were sampled and cleaned in the same way as the original corpus.

## 4 Evaluation

In this section, we aim at evaluating the effectiveness of time-specific language models (see Section 3) on time-specific tasks. In other words, our goal is to test the possible degradation of older models over time and, accordingly, test if this can be mitigated by continuous training.

**Evaluation tasks.** We evaluated the released language models in two tasks: (1) TweetEval (Barbieri et al., 2020), which consists of seven downstream tweet classification tasks; and (2) Pseudo-perplexity on corpora sampled from different time periods. While the first evaluation is merely aimed at validating the training procedure of the base language model, the second evaluation is the core contribution of this paper in terms of evaluation, where different models can be tested in different time periods.

### 4.1 TweetEval

TweetEval (Barbieri et al., 2020) is a unified Twitter benchmark composed of seven heterogeneous tweet classification tasks. It is commonly used to evaluate the performance of language models (or task-agnostic models more generally) on Twitter data. With this evaluation, our goal is simply to show the general competitiveness of the models released with our package, irrespective of their time periods.

**Evaluation tasks.** The seven tweet classification tasks in TweetEval are emoji prediction (Barbieri et al., 2018), emotion recognition (Mohammad et al., 2018), hate speech detection (Basile et al., 2019), irony detection (Van Hee et al., 2018), offensive language identification (Zampieri et al., 2019), sentiment analysis (Rosenthal et al., 2017) and stance detection (Mohammad et al., 2016).

**Experimental setting.** Similarly to the TweetEval original baselines, only a moderate parameter search was conducted. The only hyper-parameter fine-tuned was the learning rate ($1.0e^{-3}$, $1.0e^{-4}$, $1.0e^{-5}$). The number of epochs each model is trained is variable, as we used early stopping monitoring the validation loss. The validation loss is also used to select the best model in each task.

**Comparison systems.** The comparison systems (SVM, FastText, BLSTM, RoBERTa-base and TweetEval) are those taken from the original TweetEval paper, as well as the state-of-the-art BERTweet model (Nguyen et al., 2020), which is trained over 900M tweets (posted between 2013 and 2019). All the language models compared are based on the RoBERTa-base architecture.

**Results.** TweetEval results are summarized in Table 2. BERTweet, which was trained on substantially more data, attains the best averaged results. However, when looking at single tasks, BERTweet outperforms both our latest released models, i.e., TimeLM-19 and TimeLM-21, on the irony detection task[2] only. It is also important to highlight that TweetEval tasks include tweets dated until 2018 at the latest (with most tasks being considerably earlier). This suggests that our latest released model (i.e. TimeLM-21), even if trained up to 2021 tweets, is generally competitive even on past tweets. Indeed, TimeLM-21 outperforms the most similar TweetEval model, which was trained following a

[2]We note that the irony dataset was created via distant supervision using the #irony hashtag, and there could be a "labels" leak since BERTweet was the only model trained on tweets of the time period (2014/15) of the irony dataset.

| | Emoji | Emotion | Hate | Irony | Offensive | Sentiment | Stance | ALL |
|---|---|---|---|---|---|---|---|---|
| SVM | 29.3 | 64.7 | 36.7 | 61.7 | 52.3 | 62.9 | 67.3 | 53.5 |
| FastText | 25.8 | 65.2 | 50.6 | 63.1 | 73.4 | 62.9 | 65.4 | 58.1 |
| BLSTM | 24.7 | 66.0 | 52.6 | 62.8 | 71.7 | 58.3 | 59.4 | 56.5 |
| RoBERTa-Base | 30.8 | 76.6 | 44.9 | 55.2 | 78.7 | 72.0 | 70.9 | 61.3 |
| TweetEval | 31.6 | 79.8 | 55.5 | 62.5 | 81.6 | 72.9 | 72.6 | 65.2 |
| BERTweet | 33.4 | 79.3 | 56.4 | **82.1** | 79.5 | 73.4 | 71.2 | 67.9 |
| TimeLM-19 | 33.4 | **81.0** | **58.1** | 48.0 | **82.4** | 73.2 | 70.7 | 63.8 |
| TimeLM-21 | **34.0** | 80.2 | 55.1 | 64.5 | 82.2 | **73.7** | **72.9** | 66.2 |
| **Metric** | M-F1 | M-F1 | M-F1 | $F^{(i)}$ | M-F1 | M-Rec | AVG (F1) | TE |

Table 2: TweetEval test results of all comparison systems.

similar strategy (in this case trained on fewer tweets until 2019), in most tasks.

### 4.2 Time-aware language model evaluation

Once the effectiveness of the base and subsequent models have been tested in downstream tasks, our goal is to measure to what extent the various models released are sensitive to a more time-aware evaluation. To this end, we rely on the pseudo perplexity measure (Salazar et al., 2020).

**Evaluation metric: Pseudo-perplexity (PPPL).** The pseudo log-likelihood (PLL) score introduced by Salazar et al. (2020) is computed by iteratively replacing each token in a sequence with a mask, and summing the corresponding conditional log probabilities. This approach is specially suited to masked language models, rather than traditional left-to-right models. Pseudo-perplexity (PPPL) follows analogously from the standard perplexity formula, using PLL for conditional probability.

**Results.** Table 3 shows the pseudo-perplexity results in all test sets. As the main conclusion, the table shows how more recent models tend to outperform models trained when evaluated older data in most test sets (especially those contemporaneous). This can be appreciated by simply observing the decreasing values in the columns of the Table 3. There are a few interesting exceptions, however. For instance, the 2020-Q1 and 2020-Q2 test sets, which corresponding to the global start of the coronavirus pandemic, are generally better suited for models trained until that periods. Nonetheless, models trained on more contemporary data appear to converge to the optimal results.

**Degradation over time.** How long does it take for a model to be outdated? Overall, PPPL scores tend to increase almost 10% after one year. In general, PPPL appears to decrease consistently every quarterly update. This result reinforces the need for updated language models even for short time periods such as three-month quarters. In most cases, degradation on future data is usually larger than on older data. This result is not completely unexpected since newer models are also trained on more data for more time periods. In Section 6.1 we expand on this by including a table detailing the relative performance degradation over language models over time.

## 5 Python Interface

In this section we present an integrated Python interface that we release along with the data and language models presented in this paper. As mentioned in Section 3.3, all language models will be available from the Hugging Face hub and our code is designed to be used with this platform.

Our interface, based on the Transformers package (Wolf et al., 2020), is focused on providing easy single-line access to language models trained for specific periods and related use cases. The choice of language models to be used with our interface is determined using one of four modes of operation: (1) 'latest': using our most recently trained Twitter model; (2) 'corresponding': using the model that was trained only until each tweet's date (i.e., its specific quarter); (3) custom: providing the preferred date or quarter (e.g., '2021-Q3'); and (4) 'quarterly': using all available models trained over time in quarterly intervals. Having specified the preferred language models, there are three main functionalities within the code, namely: (1) computing pseudo-perplexity scores, (2) evaluating language models in our released or customized test sets, and (3) obtaining masked predictions.

Users can measure the extent to which the cho-

| Models | 2020-Q1 | 2020-Q2 | 2020-Q3 | 2020-Q4 | 2021-Q1 | 2021-Q2 | 2021-Q3 | 2021-Q4 | Change |
|---|---|---|---|---|---|---|---|---|---|
| **Barbieri et al., 2020** | 9.420 | 9.602 | 9.631 | 9.651 | 9.832 | 9.924 | 10.073 | 10.247 | N/A |
| **2019-90M** | 4.823 | 4.936 | 4.936 | 4.928 | 5.093 | 5.179 | 5.273 | 5.362 | N/A |
| **2020-Q1** | 4.521 | 4.625 | 4.699 | 4.692 | 4.862 | 4.952 | 5.043 | 5.140 | - |
| **2020-Q2** | 4.441 | 4.439 | 4.548 | 4.554 | 4.716 | 4.801 | 4.902 | 5.005 | -4.01% |
| **2020-Q3** | 4.534 | 4.525 | 4.450 | 4.487 | 4.652 | 4.738 | 4.831 | 4.945 | -2.15% |
| **2020-Q4** | 4.533 | 4.524 | 4.429 | 4.361 | 4.571 | 4.672 | 4.763 | 4.859 | -2.81% |
| **2021-Q1** | 4.509 | 4.499 | 4.399 | 4.334 | 4.439 | 4.574 | 4.668 | 4.767 | -2.89% |
| **2021-Q2** | 4.499 | 4.481 | 4.376 | 4.319 | 4.411 | 4.445 | 4.570 | 4.675 | -2.83% |
| **2021-Q3** | 4.471 | 4.455 | 4.335 | 4.280 | 4.366 | 4.394 | 4.422 | 4.565 | -3.26% |
| **2021-Q4** | 4.467 | 4.455 | 4.330 | 4.263 | 4.351 | 4.381 | **4.402** | **4.463** | -2.24% |
| **2021-124M** | **4.319** | **4.297** | **4.279** | **4.219** | **4.322** | **4.361** | 4.404 | 4.489 | N/A |

Table 3: Pseudo-perplexity results (lower is better) of all models in the Twitter test sets sampled from different quarters (each quarter correspond to three months. Q1: Jan-Mar; Q2: Apr-Jun; Q3: Jul-Sep; Q4: Oct-Dec). The last column reports difference in pseudo-perplexity, comparing the value obtained for each quarter's test set, between the model trained on the previous quarter and the model updated with data from that same quarter.

sen pretrained language models are aligned (i.e., familiar) with a given list of tweets (or any text) using pseudo-perplexity (see Section 4.2 for more details), computed as shown in Code 1.

```
from timelms import TimeLMs
tlms = TimeLMs(device='cuda')

tweets = [{'text': 'Looking forward to watching
    Squid Game tonight !'}]

pseudo_ppls = tlms.get_pseudo_ppl(tweets,
    mode='latest') # loads 2021-Q4 model
```

Code 1: Computing Pseudo-PPL on a given tweet using the most recently available model.

For a more extensive evaluation of language models using pseudo-perplexity, we provide a random subset of our test data across 2020 and 2021.[3] To evaluate other models from the Transformers package, we provide the 'eval_model' method (`tlms.eval_model()`) to compute pseudo-perplexity on any given set of tweets or texts (e.g., the subset we provide) using other language models supported by the Transformers package. Both scoring methods not only provide the pseudo-perplexity scores specific to each model (depending on specified model name, or TimeLMs specified mode), but also the PLL scores assigned to each tweet by the different models.

Finally, predictions for masked tokens of any given tweet or text may be easily obtained as demonstrated in Code 2.

```
tweets = [{"text": "So glad I'm <mask> vaccinated.",
    "created_at": "2021-02-01T23:14:26.000Z"}]

preds = tlms.get_masked_predictions(tweets, top_k=3,
    mode='corresponding') # loads 2021-Q1 model
```

Code 2: Obtaining masked predictions using model corresponding to the tweet's date. Requires tweets or texts with a <mask> token.

Note that while the examples included in this paper are associated with specific dates (i.e., the `created_at` field), these are only required for the 'corresponding' mode.

## 6 Analysis

To complement the evaluation in the previous section, we perform a more detailed analysis in three important aspects: (1) a quantitative analysis on the degradation suffered by language models over time; (2) the relation between time and size (Section 6.2); and (3) a qualitative analysis where we show the influence of time in language models for specific examples (Section 6.3).

### 6.1 Degradation analysis

Table 4 displays the relative performance degradation (or improvement) of TimeLMs language models with respect to the test sets whose time period is the latest where they have been trained on (diagonals in the table). The table shows how models tend to perform worse in newer data sets, with a degradation of performance up to 13.68% of the earlier 2020-Q1 model on the latest 2021-Q4 model (with data almost two years later than the latest data the language model was trained on).

In order to compare the effect of continuous training with respect to single training, Figure 1 shows the PPPL performances of 2021-124M (trained on all 2020-2021 data at once) and the

[3]Limited to 50K tweets, the maximum allowed by Twitter. IDs for all test tweets are available on the repository.

| Models | 2020-Q1 | 2020-Q2 | 2020-Q3 | 2020-Q4 | 2021-Q1 | 2021-Q2 | 2021-Q3 | 2021-Q4 |
|---|---|---|---|---|---|---|---|---|
| **2020-Q1** | 0.00% | 2.29% | 3.94% | 3.78% | 7.52% | 9.52% | 11.53% | 13.68% |
| **2020-Q2** | 0.04% | 0.00% | 2.46% | 2.59% | 6.24% | 8.16% | 10.42% | 12.75% |
| **2020-Q3** | 1.87% | 1.67% | 0.00% | 0.82% | 4.53% | 6.47% | 8.54% | 11.10% |
| **2020-Q4** | 3.95% | 3.74% | 1.57% | 0.00% | 4.82% | 7.14% | 9.22% | 11.43% |
| **2021-Q1** | 1.58% | 1.37% | -0.89% | -2.36% | 0.00% | 3.05% | 5.16% | 7.39% |
| **2021-Q2** | 1.21% | 0.82% | -1.55% | -2.83% | -0.77% | 0.00% | 2.83% | 5.19% |
| **2021-Q3** | 1.12% | 0.75% | -1.95% | -3.20% | -1.26% | -0.61% | 0.00% | 3.25% |
| **2021-Q4** | 0.10% | -0.17% | -2.97% | -4.47% | -2.51% | -1.83% | -1.37% | 0.00% |

Table 4: Difference across quarterly models and test sets comparing the pseudo-perplexity observed at the quarter corresponding to each model, against the pseudo-perplexity observed for that same model on both previous and future test sets. Highlights model degradation on future data, as well as how models fare on past data.

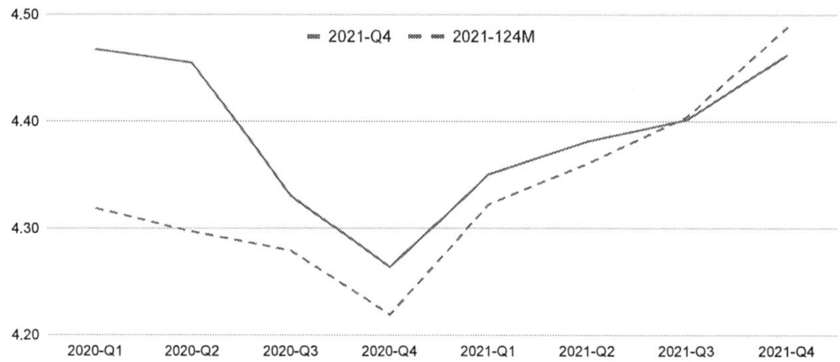


Figure 1: Performance (PPPL) of 2021-124M and 2021-Q4 models across the test sets.

2021-Q4 (updating 2021-Q3) models. Note how 2021-124M shows improved performance generally, with the largest differences being attained on the first two quarters of 2020, but not for the latest quarters where continuous training seems to work slightly better. While more analysis would be required, this result suggests that a single training is beneficial for earlier periods, while a quarterly training seems to be better adapted to the most recent data. However, there does not seem to be any meaningful catastrophic forgetting in the quarterly-updated model, as the differences are relative small.

### 6.2 Time and size control experiment

Given the results presented earlier, one may naturally wonder whether the improvement may be due to the increase in training size or the recency of additional data. While this question is not easy to answer (and probably the answer will be in-between these two reasons), we perform a simple control experiment as an initial attempt. To this end, we trained an additional language model with twice the training data of the third quarter of 2021 (2021-Q3). This way, the total number of training tweets is exactly the same as the model trained until the fourth quarter of 2021 (2021-Q4).

| Models | 2021-Q2 | 2021-Q3 | 2021-Q4 |
|---|---|---|---|
| **2021-Q2** | 4.445 | 4.570 | 4.675 |
| **2021-Q3** | 4.394 | 4.422 | 4.565 |
| **2021-Q3-2x** | **4.380** | **4.380** | 4.534 |
| **2021-Q4** | 4.381 | 4.402 | **4.463** |

Table 5: Results of the control experiment comparing quarterly models where the 2021-Q3 model is trained with twice the data from that quarter (2021-Q3-2x).

Considering the results on Table 5, we find that the model trained on twice the data for Q3 outperforms the model trained with the default Q3 data in all tested quarters. This confirms the assumption that increasing training data leads to improved language model performance. When comparing with the model trained until 2021-Q4, results show this 2021-Q3-2x model is only slightly better in the 2021-Q2 and 2021-Q3 test sets. However, as we could expect, the model trained in more recent data (i.e., until 2021-Q4) gets the best overall results on the more recent test set (i.e., 2021-Q4).

| Model | So glad I'm <mask> vaccinated. | I keep forgetting to bring a <mask>. | Looking forward to watching <mask> Game tonight! |
|---|---|---|---|
| **2020-Q1** | not<br>getting<br>self | bag<br>purse<br>charger | the<br>The<br>this |
| **2020-Q2** | not<br>getting<br>fully | mask<br>bag<br>purse | The<br>the<br>End |
| **2020-Q3** | not<br>getting<br>fully | mask<br>bag<br>purse | the<br>The<br>End |
| **2020-Q4** | not<br>getting<br>fully | bag<br>purse<br>charger | the<br>The<br>End |
| **2021-Q1** | getting<br>not<br>fully | purse<br>charger<br>bag | the<br>The<br>End |
| **2021-Q2** | fully<br>getting<br>not | bag<br>charger<br>lighter | the<br>The<br>this |
| **2021-Q3** | fully<br>getting<br>not | charger<br>bag<br>purse | the<br>The<br>This |
| **2021-Q4** | fully<br>getting<br>not | bag<br>lighter<br>charger | Squid<br>the<br>The |

Table 6: Masked token prediction over time using three example tweets as input (using mode='quarterly'). For each quarterly model, the table displays the top-3 predictions ranked by their prediction probability.

### 6.3 Qualitative analysis

In this section we illustrate, in practice, how models trained on different quarters perceive specific tweets. First, we use their masked language modeling head to predict a `<mask>` token in context. Table 6 shows three tweets and associated predictions from each of our quarterly models. The model belonging to the most pertinent quarter exhibits background knowledge more aligned to the trends of that period. In the two COVID-related examples, we observe increasing awareness of the general notion of being *fully vaccinated* (as opposed to *not vaccinated*, the top prediction from the 2020-Q1 model) in the former, and, in the latter, two instances where *forgetting a mask* is more likely than forgetting other apparel less related to a particular period, such as *a charger*, *a lighter* or *a purse*. Finally, note how, in the last example, "Looking forward to watching `<mask>` Game tonight!", it is only in 2021-Q4 that predictions change substantially, when the model has been exposed to reactions to the "Squid Game" show, overlapping in time with its global release.

Our second piece of analysis involves the visualization of pseudo log-likehood (PLL) scores for tweets requiring awareness of a trend or event tied to a specific period (Figure 2). Indeed, more recent models are better at predicting tweets involving popular events, such as NFTs or, again, the show "Squid Game". Conversely, we observe a stagnation (or even degradation) of the PLL scores for a tweet about a contestant of an older reality show.

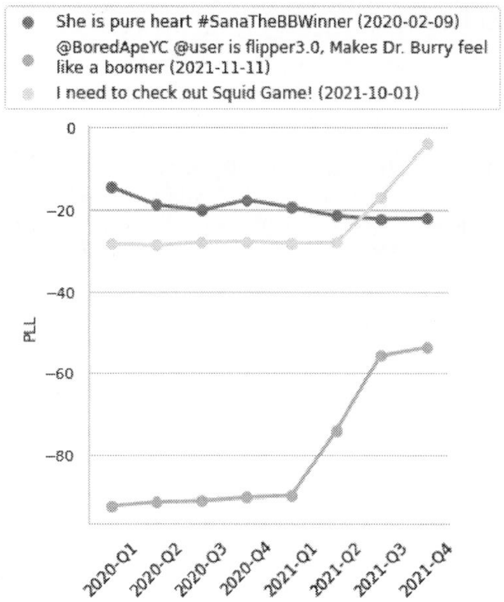


Figure 2: PLL scores of TimeLMs language models trained over different periods for three selected tweets.

## 7 Conclusion

In this paper we presented TimeLMs, language models trained on Twitter over different time periods. The initiative also includes the future training of language models every three months, thus providing free-to-use and up-to-date language models for NLP practitioners. These language models are released together with a simple Python interface which facilitates loading and working with these models, including time-aware evaluation. In our evaluation in this paper, we have shown how time-aware training is relevant, not only from the theoretical point of view, but also the practical one, as the results demonstrate a clear degradation in performance when models are used for future data, which is one of the most common settings in practice.

As future work, we are planning to explicitly integrate the time span variable in the language models, i.e., introducing string prefixes, along the lines of Dhingra et al. (2022) and Rosin et al. (2022).

## References


Oshin Agarwal and Ani Nenkova. 2021. Temporal effects on pre-trained models for language processing tasks. *arXiv preprint arXiv:2111.12790.*

Francesco Barbieri, Luis Espinosa Anke, and Jose Camacho-Collados. 2021. Xlm-t: A multilingual language model toolkit for twitter. *arXiv preprint arXiv:2104.12250.*

Francesco Barbieri, Jose Camacho-Collados, Luis Espinosa Anke, and Leonardo Neves. 2020. TweetEval: Unified benchmark and comparative evaluation for tweet classification. In *Findings of the Association for Computational Linguistics: EMNLP 2020*, pages 1644–1650, Online. Association for Computational Linguistics.

Francesco Barbieri, Jose Camacho-Collados, Francesco Ronzano, Luis Espinosa-Anke, Miguel Ballesteros, Valerio Basile, Viviana Patti, and Horacio Saggion. 2018. SemEval 2018 task 2: Multilingual emoji prediction. In *Proceedings of The 12th International Workshop on Semantic Evaluation*, pages 24–33, New Orleans, Louisiana. Association for Computational Linguistics.

Valerio Basile, Cristina Bosco, Elisabetta Fersini, Debora Nozza, Viviana Patti, Francisco Manuel Rangel Pardo, Paolo Rosso, and Manuela Sanguinetti. 2019. SemEval-2019 task 5: Multilingual detection of hate speech against immigrants and women in Twitter. In *Proceedings of the 13th International Workshop on Semantic Evaluation*, pages 54–63, Minneapolis, Minnesota, USA. Association for Computational Linguistics.

Iz Beltagy, Kyle Lo, and Arman Cohan. 2019. SciBERT: A pretrained language model for scientific text. In *Proceedings of the 2019 Conference on Empirical Methods in Natural Language Processing and the 9th International Joint Conference on Natural Language Processing (EMNLP-IJCNLP)*, pages 3615–3620, Hong Kong, China. Association for Computational Linguistics.

Magdalena Biesialska, Katarzyna Biesialska, and Marta R Costa-jussà. 2020. Continual lifelong learning in natural language processing: A survey. In *Proceedings of the 28th International Conference on Computational Linguistics*, pages 6523–6541.

A.Z. Broder. 1997. On the resemblance and containment of documents. In *Proceedings. Compression and Complexity of SEQUENCES 1997 (Cat. No.97TB100171)*, pages 21–29.

Marco Del Tredici, Raquel Fernández, and Gemma Boleda. 2019. Short-term meaning shift: A distributional exploration. In *Proceedings of the 2019 Conference of the North American Chapter of the Association for Computational Linguistics: Human Language Technologies, Volume 1 (Long and Short Papers)*, pages 2069–2075, Minneapolis, Minnesota. Association for Computational Linguistics.

Jacob Devlin, Ming-Wei Chang, Kenton Lee, and Kristina Toutanova. 2019. BERT: Pre-training of deep bidirectional transformers for language understanding. In *Proceedings of the 2019 Conference of the North American Chapter of the Association for Computational Linguistics: Human Language Technologies, Volume 1 (Long and Short Papers)*, pages 4171–4186, Minneapolis, Minnesota. Association for Computational Linguistics.

Bhuwan Dhingra, Jeremy R. Cole, Julian Martin Eisenschlos, Daniel Gillick, Jacob Eisenstein, and William W. Cohen. 2022. Time-Aware Language Models as Temporal Knowledge Bases. *Transactions of the Association for Computational Linguistics*, 10:257–273.

Maarten Grootendorst. 2020. BERTopic: Leveraging BERT and c-TF-IDF to create easily interpretable topics.

Yu Gu, Robert Tinn, Hao Cheng, Michael Lucas, Naoto Usuyama, Xiaodong Liu, Tristan Naumann, Jianfeng Gao, and Hoifung Poon. 2021. Domain-specific language model pretraining for biomedical natural language processing. *ACM Transactions on Computing for Healthcare (HEALTH)*, 3(1):1–23.

William L. Hamilton, Jure Leskovec, and Dan Jurafsky. 2016. Diachronic word embeddings reveal statistical laws of semantic change. In *Proceedings of the 54th Annual Meeting of the Association for Computational Linguistics (Volume 1: Long Papers)*, pages 1489–1501, Berlin, Germany. Association for Computational Linguistics.

Valentin Hofmann, Janet Pierrehumbert, and Hinrich Schütze. 2021. Dynamic contextualized word embeddings. In *Proceedings of the 59th Annual Meeting of the Association for Computational Linguistics and the 11th International Joint Conference on Natural Language Processing (Volume 1: Long Papers)*, pages 6970–6984, Online. Association for Computational Linguistics.

Joel Jang, Seonghyeon Ye, Sohee Yang, Joongbo Shin, Janghoon Han, Gyeonghun Kim, Stanley Jungkyu Choi, and Minjoon Seo. 2021. Towards continual knowledge learning of language models. *arXiv preprint arXiv:2110.03215.*

Xisen Jin, Dejiao Zhang, Henghui Zhu, Wei Xiao, Shang-Wen Li, Xiaokai Wei, Andrew Arnold, and Xiang Ren. 2021. Lifelong pretraining: Continually adapting language models to emerging corpora. *arXiv preprint arXiv:2110.08534.*

Angeliki Lazaridou, Adhiguna Kuncoro, Elena Gribovskaya, Devang Agrawal, Adam Liska, et al. 2021. Pitfalls of static language modelling. *arXiv preprint arXiv:2102.01951.*

Jinhyuk Lee, Wonjin Yoon, Sungdong Kim, Donghyeon Kim, Sunkyu Kim, Chan Ho So, and Jaewoo Kang. 2020. Biobert: a pre-trained biomedical language representation model for biomedical text mining. *Bioinformatics*, 36(4):1234–1240.

Katherine Lee, Daphne Ippolito, Andrew Nystrom, Chiyuan Zhang, Douglas Eck, Chris Callison-Burch, and Nicholas Carlini. 2021. Deduplicating training data makes language models better. *arXiv preprint arXiv:2107.06499*.

Patrick Lewis, Pontus Stenetorp, and Sebastian Riedel. 2020. Question and answer test-train overlap in open-domain question answering datasets. *arXiv preprint arXiv:2008.02637*.

Yinhan Liu, Myle Ott, Naman Goyal, Jingfei Du, Mandar Joshi, Danqi Chen, Omer Levy, Mike Lewis, Luke Zettlemoyer, and Veselin Stoyanov. 2019. Roberta: A robustly optimized bert pretraining approach. *arXiv preprint arXiv:1907.11692*.

David Lopez-Paz and Marc' Aurelio Ranzato. 2017. Gradient episodic memory for continual learning. In *Advances in Neural Information Processing Systems*, volume 30. Curran Associates, Inc.

Kelvin Luu, Daniel Khashabi, Suchin Gururangan, Karishma Mandyam, and Noah A Smith. 2021. Time waits for no one! analysis and challenges of temporal misalignment. *arXiv preprint arXiv:2111.07408*.

Saif Mohammad, Felipe Bravo-Marquez, Mohammad Salameh, and Svetlana Kiritchenko. 2018. SemEval-2018 task 1: Affect in tweets. In *Proceedings of The 12th International Workshop on Semantic Evaluation*, pages 1–17, New Orleans, Louisiana. Association for Computational Linguistics.

Saif Mohammad, Svetlana Kiritchenko, Parinaz Sobhani, Xiaodan Zhu, and Colin Cherry. 2016. SemEval-2016 task 6: Detecting stance in tweets. In *Proceedings of the 10th International Workshop on Semantic Evaluation (SemEval-2016)*, pages 31–41, San Diego, California. Association for Computational Linguistics.

Dat Quoc Nguyen, Thanh Vu, and Anh Tuan Nguyen. 2020. BERTweet: A pre-trained language model for English tweets. In *Proceedings of the 2020 Conference on Empirical Methods in Natural Language Processing: System Demonstrations*, pages 9–14, Online. Association for Computational Linguistics.

Alec Radford, Jeffrey Wu, Rewon Child, David Luan, Dario Amodei, Ilya Sutskever, et al. 2019. Language models are unsupervised multitask learners. *OpenAI blog*, 1(8):9.

Alex Rosenfeld and Katrin Erk. 2018. Deep neural models of semantic shift. In *Proceedings of the 2018 Conference of the North American Chapter of the Association for Computational Linguistics: Human Language Technologies, Volume 1 (Long Papers)*, pages 474–484, New Orleans, Louisiana. Association for Computational Linguistics.

Sara Rosenthal, Noura Farra, and Preslav Nakov. 2017. SemEval-2017 task 4: Sentiment analysis in Twitter. In *Proceedings of the 11th International Workshop on Semantic Evaluation (SemEval-2017)*, pages 502–518, Vancouver, Canada. Association for Computational Linguistics.

Guy D. Rosin, Ido Guy, and Kira Radinsky. 2022. Time masking for temporal language models. In *Proceedings of the Fifteenth ACM International Conference on Web Search and Data Mining*, WSDM '22, page 833–841, New York, NY, USA. Association for Computing Machinery.

Julian Salazar, Davis Liang, Toan Q. Nguyen, and Katrin Kirchhoff. 2020. Masked language model scoring. In *Proceedings of the 58th Annual Meeting of the Association for Computational Linguistics*, pages 2699–2712, Online. Association for Computational Linguistics.

Terrence Szymanski. 2017. Temporal word analogies: Identifying lexical replacement with diachronic word embeddings. In *Proceedings of the 55th Annual Meeting of the Association for Computational Linguistics (Volume 2: Short Papers)*, pages 448–453, Vancouver, Canada. Association for Computational Linguistics.

Cynthia Van Hee, Els Lefever, and Véronique Hoste. 2018. SemEval-2018 task 3: Irony detection in English tweets. In *Proceedings of The 12th International Workshop on Semantic Evaluation*, pages 39–50, New Orleans, Louisiana. Association for Computational Linguistics.

Alex Wang, Yada Pruksachatkun, Nikita Nangia, Amanpreet Singh, Julian Michael, Felix Hill, Omer Levy, and Samuel R Bowman. 2019. Superglue: A stickier benchmark for general-purpose language understanding systems. *arXiv preprint arXiv:1905.00537*.

Alex Wang, Amanpreet Singh, Julian Michael, Felix Hill, Omer Levy, and Samuel R Bowman. 2018. Glue: A multi-task benchmark and analysis platform for natural language understanding. *arXiv preprint arXiv:1804.07461*.

Thomas Wolf, Lysandre Debut, Victor Sanh, Julien Chaumond, Clement Delangue, Anthony Moi, Pierric Cistac, Tim Rault, Remi Louf, Morgan Funtowicz, Joe Davison, Sam Shleifer, Patrick von Platen, Clara Ma, Yacine Jernite, Julien Plu, Canwen Xu, Teven Le Scao, Sylvain Gugger, Mariama Drame, Quentin Lhoest, and Alexander Rush. 2020. Transformers: State-of-the-art natural language processing. In *Proceedings of the 2020 Conference on Empirical Methods in Natural Language Processing: System Demonstrations*, pages 38–45, Online. Association for Computational Linguistics.

Marcos Zampieri, Shervin Malmasi, Preslav Nakov, Sara Rosenthal, Noura Farra, and Ritesh Kumar. 2019. SemEval-2019 task 6: Identifying and categorizing offensive language in social media (OffensEval). In *Proceedings of the 13th International*

*Workshop on Semantic Evaluation*, pages 75–86, Minneapolis, Minnesota, USA. Association for Computational Linguistics.

# Adaptor: Objective-Centric Adaptation Framework for Language Models

**Michal Štefánik**[1,2] and **Vít Novotný**[1] and **Nikola Groverová**[2] and **Petr Sojka**[1]
[1]Faculty of Informatics, Masaryk University, Czech Republic
[2]Gauss Algorithmic

## Abstract

Progress in natural language processing research is catalyzed by the possibilities given by the widespread software frameworks. This paper introduces the Adaptor library[1] that transposes the traditional model-centric approach composed of pre-training + fine-tuning steps to objective-centric approach, composing the training process by *applications* of selected *objectives*. We survey research directions that can benefit from enhanced objective-centric experimentation in multi-task training, custom objectives development, dynamic training curricula, or domain adaptation. Adaptor aims to ease the reproducibility of these research directions in practice. Finally, we demonstrate the practical applicability of Adaptor in selected unsupervised domain adaptation scenarios.

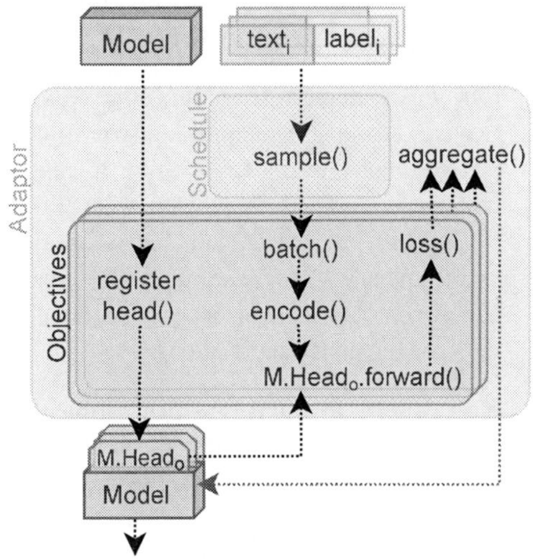


Figure 1: Overview of Adaptor's objective-centric training framework: Objective 1) registers its compatible head on top of the shared model, 2) performs specific input encoding, and 3) compute loss value based on its output. A Schedule implements a specific sampling curricula and Adaptor aggregates and propagates objectives' losses and performs optimization.

"The measure of intelligence is the ability to change."
— Albert Einstein

## 1 Introduction

Recent development in Natural Language Processing (NLP) heavily benefits from a high level of maturity of open-source frameworks, such as Fairseq (Ott et al., 2019) or HuggingFace Transformers (Wolf et al., 2020). Thanks to the standardized interfaces, these libraries allow for immediate experimentation with the most recent research results, practically fostering the speed of further progress in the area. While their use is seamless for countless conventional use-cases of transformer models and fine-tuning to a specific end-task (Devlin et al., 2019; Radford and Narasimhan, 2018), divergence from this framework requires feasible, but elaborate and complex customizations, increasing the risk of logical errors and complicating the reproducibility of experiments. A characteristic group of problems requiring significant changes to the standard pipeline are multi-step and multi-task adaptations.

This paper introduces the Adaptor library, which aims to simplify the more complex training processes that their training objectives can easier describe. Adaptor challenges the conventional *model-centric* framework, where data and task selection are constrained by the requirements of the selected language model architecture. Instead, it introduces an *objective-centric* training pipeline, with Objective as the central abstraction of the process.

The Adaptor framework aims to help NLP researchers and practicioners engage in projects that include any of the following:

- **Multi-objective training**: when training a language model on more than one task or data set, including languages, Adaptor can signif-

[1]`github.com/gaussalgo/adaptor`



*Proceedings of the 60th Annual Meeting of the Association for Computational Linguistics*
*System Demonstrations*, pages 261 - 269
May 22-27, 2022 ©2022 Association for Computational Linguistics

icantly simplify the custom code base that needs to be implemented. Even if the objective is custom, the user can avoid adjustments to other parts of the training pipeline.

- **Custom data schedule**: when users need to perform dynamic data sampling, Adaptor allows them to implement a custom Schedule (see Figure 2), leaving the data and model adjustment logic intact. This simplifies systematic experimentation and reproducibility, and minimizes the risk of errors.

- **Objectives design & evaluation**: Adaptor exposes top-level declaration of training objectives, which enables easy experimentation with custom objectives. Objective-level monitoring can provide custom behavioural insights and allows for pruning less promising experiments earlier in the lengthy training process, saving computational costs.

- **Robustness evaluation**: The objective-centric paradigm provides an easy robustness estimation by evaluating on out-of-distribution samples. In the standard *sequential* adaptation scenario, objective-centric evaluation exposes characteristic flaws of adaptation, like exposure bias or catastrophic forgetting.

This paper is structured as follows: Section 2 provides an overview of recent work demonstrating the potential of multi-objective training in domain and task adaptation. Section 2.4 also describes other software frameworks applicable for similar use cases. Section 3 describes the design of Adaptor, showing the users how to confidently integrate novel objectives and schedules. In Section 4, we describe and implement a set of non-trivial, yet promising domain adaptation experiments using Adaptor and collect their results. As Adaptor remains under active development, we close in Section 5 with an outline of the upcoming features. We welcome contributions of novel objectives and schedules.

## 2 Background

This section provides an overview of recent work that demonstrates the potential of multi-objective training and schedules that motivated the design of Adaptor. Our overview consists of a non-exhaustive list of applications that Adaptor aims to make more accessible for practical use and in future research.

### 2.1 Multi-Task Training

Multi-task training has a long history in both traditional machine learning (Caruana, 1997) and in deep learning (Crawshaw, 2020). This section describes examples of multi-task (i.e. multi-objective) training, outlining its benefits and potential.

Under some circumstances, multi-task training enhances distributional robustness of neural models. Tu et al. (2020) demonstrate this on adversarial data sets, exposing common heuristic biases of the language models (McCoy et al., 2019). Enhanced model generalization can also be achieved by introducing one or more latent tasks that do not directly correspond to the end task but reflect specific desired properties of the model. One of a few studies in this direction is Sharpness-Aware Minimisation of Foret et al. (2021), performing multi-objective training on image classification using cross-entropy and a novel, sharpness-aware objective, reflecting the model's monotonicity on the local neighborhood. In context of Neural Machine Translation (NMT), Wang and Sennrich (2020) incorporate Minimum Risk Training (MRT) objective (Ranzato et al., 2016), optimising an arbitrary sequence-level measure of outputs. In composition with the traditional token-level cross-entropy objective, MRT improves distributional robustness.

By aggregating multiple objectives, Xie et al. (2019) show that combining sentence classification objective with maximizing representation consistency to augmented samples fosters data efficiency.

The intuition on the benefits of multi-task training presumes that by optimizing the training by multiple cost functions, the final model is less prone to the weaknesses of a specific task (Collobert et al., 2011), possibly reflecting on higher-level, task-invariant properties of language (Bengio et al., 2013).

### 2.2 Data-Sampling Schedules

Exposing a model to training samples in a systematic schedule, also referred to as a *curriculum*, can lead to an improvement of the accuracy of the final model (Bengio et al., 2009). While the positive effects of more complex schedules based on sample "difficulty" with transformers remain to be explored, multiple studies show the potential of confidence-based sampling to improve accuracy and generalization. Biased samples can be identified, according to model's confidence (Pleiss et al., 2020; Swayamdipta et al., 2020) or using Bayesian methods such as the Product of Experts (Hinton, 2002). Then, they can be either eliminated (Bras et al., 2020) or downweighted (Utama et al., 2020).

More complex scheduling methods are applied in training NMT models. Bengio et al. (2015) use decay schedule to sample from both references and the previous outputs of a NMT model, minimizing the discrepancy between training and inference. Zhang et al. (2019) successfully use the same sampling strategy in a sequence-level objective. The results of Lu et al. (2020) underline the potential of sampling in NMT training, suggesting that the accuracy of transformers on reported MT benchmarks can be outperformed by simpler RNN models by combining objectives in decay schedule.

Despite the reported improvements, we find that custom scheduling strategies are rarely used. We attribute this to their complicated integration into the standard training process. To foster the research and applicability of scheduling methods, Adaptor makes the implementation of custom scheduling strategies easy, comprehensible, and reproducible.

### 2.3 Domain Adaptation

Objective-centric frameworks are well-suited for domain adaptation techniques, where Adaptor provides support for combining traditional end-task objectives with unsupervised adaptation or auxiliary-task objectives in a user-selected schedule. The goal of domain adaptation is to maximize performance on a specific data domain, often denoted as the *adapted* or *target domain* (Saunders, 2021).

Perhaps the most common adaptation approach using pre-trained language models is to continue pre-training on unsupervised samples of the adapted domain (Luong and Manning, 2015; Lee et al., 2019; Beltagy et al., 2019). This approach has been successfully extended in various directions. For instance, Gururangan et al. (2020) show that adapting to a shared task on different domain can enhance accuracy of the eventual application. If supervised data is sparse, other auxiliary tasks, described earlier in Section 2.1, can be used as concurrent objectives (Xie et al., 2019).

In cases where larger volumes of data of given task is available in a different language, adaptation using cross-lingual transfer can be considered. Pre-trained language models show that cross-lingual transfer works well with large-data unsupervised objectives (Conneau and Lample, 2019), but it can also be applied for low-resource supervised objective, such as very low-resource translation (Neubig and Hu, 2018).

If even unsupervised target-domain data is sparse, another option is to subset arbitrary unsupervised sources to automatically identify samples of adapted domain, by applying domain classifier (Jiang and Zhai, 2007; Elsahar and Gallé, 2019). If the boundary between the training and the adapted domain is known, an auxiliary objective can minimise a discrepancy of representations between the training and possibly low-resource target domain (Chadha and Andreopoulos, 2018).

Despite the possibilities, adaptation can also introduce undesired biases. In the scope of NMT, adaptation can cause problems of "catastrophic forgetting", when the model experiences performance degradation on the originally well-performing domains (Saunders, 2021), or "exposure bias", when the model overfits the non-representative specifics of the target domain, such as the artifacts of data collection (Ranzato et al., 2016). Additionally, by normalizing a single type of bias, such as lexical overlap (McCoy et al., 2019), the model might degrade its accuracy on other domains (Utama et al., 2020). Addressing multiple biases concurrently (Wu et al., 2020) can mitigate this problem.

Adaptor allows the knowledgeable user to construct a reproducible and robust adaptation pipeline using native multi-objective evaluation. Covering multiple domains in separate objectives, Adaptor can expose the above pitfalls, without the need to implement complex separate evaluation routines.

### 2.4 Related Software Frameworks

The *Adapters* architecture (Houlsby et al., 2019), having only a small set of parameters, might be a good fit when performing adaptation of transformer with modest hardware or data. Recently, the AdapterHub library (Pfeiffer et al., 2020) makes training and sharing of Adapters convenient. Compared to Adaptor, AdapterHub does not provide support for more complex adaptation cases, such as using multiple objectives, scheduling, or extended evaluation. However, since both libraries build upon the HuggingFace Transformers library (Wolf et al., 2020), their close integration is feasible.

If the robustness of models to heuristic shortcuts (McCoy et al., 2019) is the primary goal, the

```python
class ParallelSchedule(Schedule):
    def _sample_objectives(self, split: str) -> Iterator[Objective]:
        while True:
            for objective in self.objectives[split].values():
                yield objective
```

Figure 2: Adaptor provides a convenient base for implementing custom sampling schedules. ParallelSchedule in the figure demonstrates an implementation of the schedule sampling the update objectives in rotation. Further, the sampling can be easily conditioned on the state of Objectives such as the recent outputs, loss, or metrics evaluations.

Robustness Gym library (Goel et al., 2021) provides a comprehensive evaluation over an extendable set of different kinds of heuristic biases. Robustness Gym provides much deeper evaluation compared to Adaptor Evaluators, and could be integrated as an Adaptor Evaluator. Unlike Robustness Gym, Adaptor enables an evaluation of robustness also on generative tasks, with specified out-of-domain data sets.

## 3 Adaptor Design

This section describes the structure and functions of the Adaptor framework. We introduce its primary components bottom-up. Figure 3 depicts the relations of these components and compares user interaction with the traditional model-centric pipeline.

### 3.1 LangModule

A LangModule instance provides a management of inputs, outputs and objective-specific model components, referred to as *heads*. Once an objective with given LangModule is instantiated, an objective-compatible model is either initialised, or given by the user (see Section 3.2) and the parameters of this model are merged with the parameters of the previously-registered objectives.

The merge works as follows: If no previous objective was registered, then the model of the given objective is considered a base model. The models of the second- and later-registered objectives are then merged with the base model: first, pairs of PyTorch modules of the same name in the base and the new model are identified. If the dimensions and weights of these modules match, the respective module of the newly-adding model is replaced with a module of the base model.

In the case of pre-trained transformers, the weights of heads are initialized randomly by default, resulting in a registration of a distinct head for each objective and sharing the remaining parameters. Users can control which parameters (not) to merge by explicitly setting their respective weights as (non-)equal.

It is possible to use LangModule with any PyTorch module that uses a HuggingFace tokenizer, compatible with the given neural module. Therefore, LangModule is also suitable for other models such as recurrent networks.

### 3.2 Objective

Objectives are the primary component of Adaptor's training pipeline. Most importantly, an Objective serves two functions: sample encoding and loss computation. By implementing these and choosing the type of a model's head, Adaptor users can define and experiment with novel training objectives. If they additionally provide an explicit definition of the Objective's model (the `objective_module` attribute), the new objective does not even have to comply with common model heads; shared parameters of the given `objective_module` would still be merged with the given `lang_module`.

If no `objective_module` is given, the Objective will request that a LangModule assigns the Objective a module of the Objective's default `compatible_head` (see Section 3.1).

Additionally, every Objective instance performs its own logging, evaluation, and state updates, such as its convergence, based on a valuation of given `val_evaluators`, or draws a progress bar, based on the state of its sample iteration. However, the training flow is guided by a Schedule (see Section 3.3). Objectives can implement custom data sampling, but if possible, we recommended to do so in a custom Schedule instance.

Since data encoding is also objective-specific, Objectives expose a higher-level user interface of data inputs than other frameworks: instead of encodings, users provide an Objective with a `texts_or_path` and a `labels_or_path` containing raw texts and respective labels. Adaptor provides an implementation of standard Objectives for sequence and token classification and sequence-to-sequence tasks. When implementing a custom Objective, note that sampling and encoding are performance bottlenecks on current high-end GPUs.

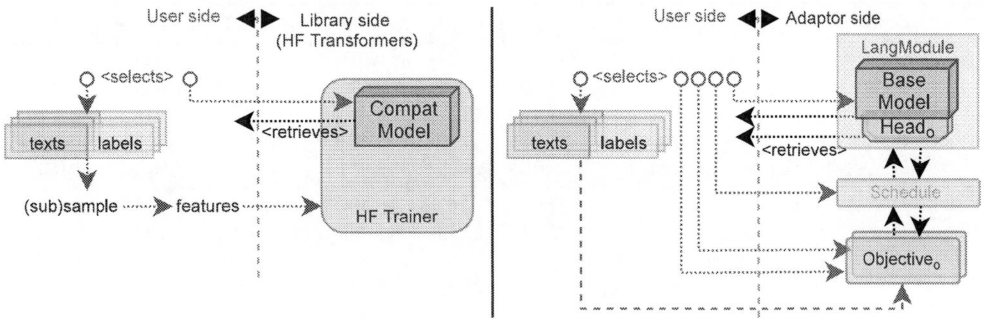


Figure 3: A comparison of interaction with a model-centric HuggingFace Trainer (left) and objective-centric Adaptor (right): While in model-centric approach, user resolves text processing, sampling and encoding compatible with selected model of specific objective, objective-centric approach delegates these functionalities to Objective instances. Explicit definition of Objectives and Schedule on Adaptor's user side makes otherwise complex multi-objective and custom-schedule experiments transparent and reproducible.

### 3.3 Schedule

Schedules control the training flow through the interfaces provided by HuggingFace Transformers library. Primarily, they deliver 1) a set of standard stopping strategies based on the state of the Objectives and 2) an IterableDataset instance, constructed by sampling Objectives according to a sampling strategy implemented in its `_sample_objectives`. A Schedule also ensures that outputs of distinct `lang_modules`' heads are delivered to the respective Objectives for loss computation.

This relatively complex sampling framework provides a very simple interface for custom Schedule implementations (see Section 2.2). For instance, a pre-defined `ParallelSchedule` is implemented with three lines of code (see Figure 2).

### 3.4 Adapter

An Adapter is customization of the HuggingFace Trainer with only minor adjustments. Specifically, Adapter redirects loss computation to a Schedule, which further distributes outputs to corresponding Objectives and extends native training logs with logs of Objectives' Evaluators. Furthermore, Adapter adjusts persistence of the models so that a model of every head can be reloaded without the use of Adaptor, by simply using HuggingFace Transformers' `AutoModelForXY.from_pretrained`.

Based on the actively-developed HuggingFace Transformers library, the Adaptor allows its users to benefit from all other native features of HuggingFace Transformers, such as the support for the most recent models, custom logging platforms, or distributed parallel training. Furthermore, it can simplify integration with other custom libraries (see Section 2.4).

## 4 Experiments

We use Adaptor in a set of domain adaptation experiments for a machine translation use-case, aiming to answer the following research question: **How well can unsupervised objective(s) substitute labeled parallel data**. In our methodology, we permute the easily-configurable parts of Adaptor's training configuration[2] and compare the results of the resulting model to a baseline adaptation scenario. We experiment with an architecture identical to the base model of Vaswani et al. (2017), with a configuration of Junczys-Dowmunt et al. (2018).

**Data.** We train the model on English-to-Czech translations on different domains of OPUS (Tiedemann, 2012) chosen for their significant distinctiveness: we use *Wikimedia* as a large-scale, supervised domain (denoted as *in-domain*, i.e. ID), *OpenSubtitles* as an Adapted Domain (AD) and *Bible* for the evaluation of a model's robustness on Out-Of-Domain (OOD) samples.

**Pre-training vs. fine-tuning.** We simulate two basic scenarios: training the model from a random initialization and fine-tuning the existing translation model with no control over its pre-training data. In the latter cases, we perform fine-tuning from the checkpoint of Tiedemann and Thottingal (2020).

**Schedules.** We implement and experiment with two objective schedules: i) **Sequential** schedule, sampling and differentiating the model sequentially

[2]Our code is available on `https://github.com/gaussalgo/adaptor/tree/reprod/demo.py`

| Schedule | | Objectives | $BLEU_{ID}$ | $BLEU_{AD}$ | $BLEU_{OOD}$ | $BERTS_{ID}$ | $BERTS_{AD}$ | $BERTS_{OOD}$ |
|---|---|---|---|---|---|---|---|---|
| Pre-training | | *1)* $Seq2Seq_{ID}$ | 28.18 | 5.34 | 0.91 | 0.833 | 0.738 | 0.671 |
| | Sequent. | *2)* $Seq2Seq_{ID}$+ $BackTr_{AD}$ | 5.10 | 15.01 | 2.57 | 0.740 | 0.805 | 0.733 |
| | | **3)* $Seq2Seq_{ID}$+ $Seq2Seq_{AD}$ | 4.96 | 17.37 | 2.64 | 0.756 | 0.816 | 0.726 |
| | Parallel | *4)* $Seq2Seq_{ID}$+ $BackTr_{AD}$ | 31.06 | 16.99 | 2.46 | 0.852 | 0.817 | 0.722 |
| | | **5)* $Seq2Seq_{ID}$+ $Seq2Seq_{AD}$ | 29.72 | 18.55 | 2.98 | 0.843 | 0.813 | 0.732 |
| Fine-tuning | | *6)* $Seq2Seq_{ID}$ | 37.97 | 17.62 | 6.50 | 0.875 | 0.808 | 0.758 |
| | | *7)* $BackTr_{AD}$ | 30.34 | 22.98 | 11.08 | 0.869 | 0.834 | 0.799 |
| | Parallel | *8)* $Seq2Seq_{ID}$+ $Denois_{AD}$ | 38.96 | 13.37 | 6.87 | 0.876 | 0.782 | 0.761 |
| | | *9)* $Seq2Seq_{ID}$+ $BackTr_{AD}$ | 38.25 | 21.47 | 9.03 | 0.873 | 0.831 | 0.791 |
| | | ***10)*** $Seq2Seq_{ID}$+ $Seq2Seq_{AD}$ | 40.72 | 23.35 | 6.97 | 0.880 | 0.836 | 0.772 |

Table 1: We evaluate the features of Adaptor on multi-objective domain adaptation in machine translation: our experiments compare the BLEU score and BERTScore of unsupervised adaptation (*Seq2seq + Denoising* or *Back-Translation*) applied in different schedules, to *no* adaptation ***(1, 6)*** and a hypothetical supervised adaptation ***(*3, *5, *10)***. Results show that the Parallel schedule eliminates *catastrophic forgetting* and that unsupervised Back-translation is able to reach performance that is close to the supervised adaptation.

by each objective until convergence by evaluation loss, or for a maximum of 100,000 updates. ii) **Parallel** schedule, concurrently sampling training batches uniformly from every given objective. Using gradient accumulation, we differentiate the model based on *all* given objectives. We perform updates until the convergence of *all* objectives, or for a maximum of 50,000 updates for each objective.

**Objectives selection.** We implement and experiment with the following Adaptor objectives:

- **Sequence-to-sequence** (seq2seq) objective, as introduced by Vaswani et al. (2017), maps a combination of encoder inputs in the source language and previously-generated outputs as decoder inputs to a distribution over the next-predicted tokens.

- **Denoising** objective introduced by Lewis et al. (2020) is an unsupervised instance of the seq2seq objective that performs random token permutation on the input and trains the model to map such 'noisy' text to the original version of the input. We use this objective on the target-data domain to enhance its comprehension by the model.

- **Back-translation** objective, as used e.g. by Sennrich et al. (2016) is also an unsupervised seq2seq objective, which uses an external translator in reverse direction to obtain pseudo-inputs. This objective is profitable when we have unlabeled data of the target domain.

Using these components, we construct the following experiments:

- **Baselines:** pre-training ***(1)*** and fine-tuning ***(6)*** on ID data from a domain different from the Application Domain (AD) using a single traditional *seq2seq* objective.

- **Sequential adaptation:** we pre-train using *seq2seq* on ID and afterwards adapt using either unsupervised *Back-translation* ***(2)***, or supervised *seq2seq* ***(3)*** on AD to quantify the unsupervised adaptation gap.

- **Parallel adaptation:** we concurrently train on both *seq2seq* and another unsupervised objective: *Back-translation* ***(4, 9)*** and *Denoising* ***(8)***. Again, we compare the gap to the supervised situation ***(5, 10)***.

### 4.1 Results

Table 1 evaluates the base transformer after the given number of updates on held-out deduplicated validation splits of In-Domain (ID), Adapted-Domain (AD), and the third Out-Of-Domain (OOD) data. Note that the results for the BLEU score are properly comparable only within the same domain.

We observe that the model trained on a single domain ***(1, 6)*** degrades on *all* other domains. In a pre-training scenario, domain robustness improves when incorporating data of adapted domain in *any* objective. However, in a sequential schedule, we observe catastrophic forgetting towards any most-recent domain of adaptation ***(2, 3)***. This is improved by using the Parallel schedule for a negligible price of in-domain accuracy ***(4, 5)***.

In the fine-tuning scenario, we show that incorporating unsupervised Back-translation to AD *(7, 9)* improves ID BLEU comparably to supervised adaptation *(10)*. Interestingly, Denoising on AD *(8)* improves in-domain performance but seems less efficient than Back-translation.

### 4.2 Adaptor Usage Complexity

To give an idea about the relative complexity of using Adaptor as compared to model-centric frameworks, we compare selected measurable code features of the complexity of our experimental implementation to an example implementation using the HuggingFace Trainer[3]. We pick the experiment of supervised pre-training + unsupervised fine-tuning, including evaluation, in the sequential schedule *(2)*, as this can still be addressed using HuggingFace Transformers relatively easily; Implementing the parallel multi-objective schedule in the Transformers framework would require major customisations of selected model and Trainer objects.

The training script using HuggingFace Trainer contains 654 lines of code, 135 variable assignments, 186 method calls and the initialisation of 9 custom objects. Additionally, in the pre-training + fine-tuning framework, this script has to be run twice, initialising the second training from the selected checkpoint of the first one, with updated configurations. Back-translated pseudo-labels are generated by a different script, not included in this assessment.

Using Adaptor, we construct an equivalent routine from the provided demo script. Our implementation contains 124 lines of code, 31 variable assignments, 37 method calls and the initialisation of 14 custom objects. Despite its brevity, our script wraps the whole training process, and hence, together with the associated version of Adaptor or its fork, it provides a reproducible fingerprint of the experiment.

## 5 Conclusion and Future Work

This paper introduces the Adaptor library, which provides objective-centric training framework well-suitable for multi-task and multi-domain training scenarios, and the development of novel objectives and sampling schedules. We find that even in the conventional single-objective training routines, Adaptor can reduce volumes of custom implementation and increases readability and reproducibility. Having used Adaptor already for several production use cases, we are happy to share it with the NLP community.

Our future work aims to further enhance Adaptor's user comfort with existing and novel unsupervised objectives, dynamic schedules, and demonstrations on novel use cases.

[3]For reference, we use *run_translation.py* example script on HuggingFace Transformers GitHub, version 4.17.0.

## 6 Broader Impact

Thanks to the ubiquity of objective-centric training, Adaptor can accelerate the applicability of the most recent research in multi-task and multilingual modeling and enrich the research with the practical experience of the industry.

We further identify the benefits of Adaptor's definite training pipelines in saving unnecessary financial and environmental expenses of reproducing the reported results of large language models, otherwise often including expensive hyperparameter optimization over unreported parameters. Due to these aspects, Adaptor could also ease the spread of state-of-the-art language technologies to under-resourced languages and more specialized domains with a sufficient amount of unsupervised sources.

Finally, objective-centric training might help expose the potential of unsupervised objectives to the generalization and interpretability of models. Adaptor can foster the research in unsupervised learning by lowering the relatively high entry level of technical proficiency needed for experimentation with novel language objectives.

## References

Iz Beltagy, Kyle Lo, and Arman Cohan. 2019. SciBERT: A Pretrained Language Model for Scientific Text. In *Proc. of the Conference on Empirical Methods in Natural Language Processing and the 9th Int. Joint Conference on Natural Language Processing (EMNLP-IJCNLP)*, pages 3615–3620, Hong Kong, China. ACL.

Samy Bengio, Oriol Vinyals, Navdeep Jaitly, and Noam Shazeer. 2015. Scheduled sampling for sequence prediction with recurrent neural networks. In *Advances in Neural Information Processing Systems*, volume 28. Curran Associates, Inc.

Yoshua Bengio, Aaron C. Courville, and Pascal Vincent. 2013. Representation Learning: A Review and New Perspectives. *IEEE Transactions on Pattern Analysis and Machine Intelligence*, 35:1798–1828.

Yoshua Bengio, Jérôme Louradour, Ronan Collobert, and Jason Weston. 2009. Curriculum Learning. In

*Proceedings of the 26th Annual International Conference on Machine Learning*, ICML '09, pages 41–48, New York, NY, USA. ACM.

Ronan Le Bras, Swabha Swayamdipta, Chandra Bhagavatula, Rowan Zellers, Matthew E. Peters, Ashish Sabharwal, and Yejin Choi. 2020. Adversarial filters of dataset biases. In *ICML*.

Rich Caruana. 1997. Multitask learning. *Machine Learning*, 28:41–75.

A. Chadha and Y. Andreopoulos. 2018. Improving Adversarial Discriminative Domain Adaptation. *CoRR*, abs/1809.03625v3.

Ronan Collobert, Jason Weston, Léon Bottou, Michael Karlen, Koray Kavukcuoglu, and Pavel Kuksa. 2011. Natural Language Processing (Almost) from Scratch. *J. Mach. Learn. Res.*, 999888:2493–2537.

Alexis Conneau and Guillaume Lample. 2019. Cross-lingual Language Model Pretraining. In *Proceedings of the 33rd International Conference on Neural Information Processing Systems (NIPS)*, Red Hook, NY, USA. Curran Associates Inc.

Michael Crawshaw. 2020. Multi-Task Learning with Deep Neural Networks: A Survey. *CoRR*, abs/2009.09796.

Jacob Devlin, Ming-Wei Chang, Kenton Lee, and Kristina Toutanova. 2019. BERT: Pre-training of Deep Bidirectional Transformers for Language Understanding. In *Proc. of the 2019 Conference of the North American Chapter of the ACL: Human Language Technologies*, pages 4171–4186, Minneapolis, USA. ACL.

Hady Elsahar and Matthias Gallé. 2019. To Annotate or Not? Predicting Performance Drop under Domain Shift. In *Proc. of the 2019 Conference on Empirical Methods in Natural Language Processing and the 9th International Joint Conference on Natural Language Processing (EMNLP-IJCNLP)*, pages 2163–2173, Hong Kong, China. ACL.

Pierre Foret, Ariel Kleiner, H. Mobahi, and Behnam Neyshabur. 2021. Sharpness-Aware Minimization for Efficiently Improving Generalization. *CoRR*, abs/2010.01412v1.

Karan Goel, Nazneen Fatema Rajani, Jesse Vig, Zachary Taschdjian, Mohit Bansal, and Christopher Ré. 2021. Robustness gym: Unifying the NLP evaluation landscape. In *Proceedings of the 2021 Conference of the North American Chapter of the ACL: Human Language Technologies: Demonstrations*, pages 42–55, Online. ACL.

Suchin Gururangan, Ana Marasović, Swabha Swayamdipta, Kyle Lo, Iz Beltagy, Doug Downey, and Noah A. Smith. 2020. Don't Stop Pretraining: Adapt Language Models to Domains and Tasks. In *Proc. of the 58th Annual Meeting of the ACL*, pages 8342–8360. ACL.

Geoffrey E. Hinton. 2002. Training Products of Experts by Minimizing Contrastive Divergence. *Neural Computation*, 14(8):1771–1800.

Neil Houlsby, Andrei Giurgiu, Stanislaw Jastrzebski, Bruna Morrone, Quentin De Laroussilhe, Andrea Gesmundo, Mona Attariyan, and Sylvain Gelly. 2019. Parameter-efficient transfer learning for NLP. In *Proceedings of the 36th International Conference on Machine Learning*, volume 97 of *Proceedings of Machine Learning Research*, pages 2790–2799. PMLR.

Jing Jiang and ChengXiang Zhai. 2007. Instance Weighting for Domain Adaptation in NLP. In *Proc. of the 45th Annual Meeting of the ACL*, pages 264–271, Prague, Czech Republic. ACL.

Marcin Junczys-Dowmunt, Roman Grundkiewicz, Tomasz Dwojak, Hieu Hoang, Kenneth Heafield, Tom Neckermann, Frank Seide, Ulrich Germann, Alham Fikri Aji, Nikolay Bogoychev, André F. T. Martins, and Alexandra Birch. 2018. Marian: Fast neural machine translation in C++. In *Proceedings of ACL 2018, System Demonstrations*, pages 116–121, Melbourne, Australia. ACL.

Jinhyuk Lee, Wonjin Yoon, Sungdong Kim, Donghyeon Kim, Sunkyu Kim, Chan Ho So, and Jaewoo Kang. 2019. BioBERT: a pre-trained biomedical language representation model for biomedical text mining. *Bioinformatics*.

Mike Lewis, Yinhan Liu, Naman Goyal, Marjan Ghazvininejad, Abdelrahman Mohamed, Omer Levy, Veselin Stoyanov, and Luke Zettlemoyer. 2020. BART: Denoising Sequence-to-Sequence Pre-training for Natural Language Generation, Translation, and Comprehension. In *Proc. of the 58th Annual Meeting of the ACL*, pages 7871–7880.

Wenjie Lu, Leiying Zhou, Gongshen Liu, and Quanhai Zhang. 2020. A mixed learning objective for neural machine translation. In *Proceedings of the 19th Chinese National Conference on Computational Linguistics*, pages 974–983, Haikou, China. Chinese Information Processing Society of China.

Minh-Thang Luong and Christopher Manning. 2015. Stanford neural machine translation systems for spoken language domains. In *Proceedings of the 12th International Workshop on Spoken Language Translation: Evaluation Campaign*, pages 76–79, Da Nang, Vietnam.

Tom McCoy, Ellie Pavlick, and Tal Linzen. 2019. Right for the Wrong Reasons: Diagnosing Syntactic Heuristics in Natural Language Inference. In *Proc. of the 57th Annual Meeting of the ACL*, pages 3428–3448, Florence, Italy. ACL.

Graham Neubig and Junjie Hu. 2018. Rapid adaptation of neural machine translation to new languages. In *Proceedings of the 2018 Conference on Empirical Methods in Natural Language Processing*, pages 875–880, Brussels, Belgium. ACL.

Myle Ott, Sergey Edunov, Alexei Baevski, Angela Fan, Sam Gross, Nathan Ng, David Grangier, and Michael Auli. 2019. fairseq: A fast, extensible toolkit for sequence modeling. In *Proceedings of NAACL-HLT 2019: Demonstrations*.

Jonas Pfeiffer, Andreas Rücklé, Clifton Poth, Aishwarya Kamath, Ivan Vulić, Sebastian Ruder, Kyunghyun Cho, and Iryna Gurevych. 2020. AdapterHub: A framework for adapting transformers. In *Proceedings of the 2020 Conference on Empirical Methods in Natural Language Processing: System Demonstrations*, pages 46–54. ACL.

Geoff Pleiss, Tianyi Zhang 0007, Ethan R. Elenberg, and Kilian Q. Weinberger. 2020. Identifying mislabeled data using the area under the margin ranking. In *Advances in Neural Information Processing Systems 33: Annual Conference on Neural Information Processing Systems 2020, NeurIPS 2020, December 6-12, 2020, virtual*.

Alec Radford and Karthik Narasimhan. 2018. Improving Language Understanding by Generative Pre-Training.

Marc'Aurelio Ranzato, Sumit Chopra, Michael Auli, and Wojciech Zaremba. 2016. Sequence Level Training with Recurrent Neural Networks. In *4th International Conference on Learning Representations, ICLR 2016, San Juan, Puerto Rico, May 2–4, 2016, Conference Track Proceedings*.

Danielle Saunders. 2021. Domain Adaptation and Multi-Domain Adaptation for Neural Machine Translation: A Survey. *CoRR*, abs/2104.06951.

Rico Sennrich, Barry Haddow, and Alexandra Birch. 2016. Improving neural machine translation models with monolingual data. In *Proceedings of the 54th Annual Meeting of the ACL (Volume 1: Long Papers)*, pages 86–96, Berlin, Germany. ACL.

Swabha Swayamdipta, Roy Schwartz, Nicholas Lourie, Yizhong Wang, Hannaneh Hajishirzi, Noah A. Smith, and Yejin Choi. 2020. Dataset cartography: Mapping and diagnosing datasets with training dynamics. In *Proceedings of the 2020 Conference on Empirical Methods in Natural Language Processing (EMNLP)*, pages 9275–9293, Online. ACL.

Jörg Tiedemann. 2012. Parallel Data, Tools and Interfaces in OPUS. In *Proc. of the Eighth International Conf. LREC*, pages 2214–2218, Istanbul, Turkey. ELRA.

Jörg Tiedemann and Santhosh Thottingal. 2020. OPUS-MT – building open translation services for the world. In *Proceedings of the 22nd Annual Conference of the European Association for Machine Translation*, pages 479–480, Lisboa, Portugal. European Association for Machine Translation.

Lifu Tu, Garima Lalwani, Spandana Gella, and He He. 2020. An Empirical Study on Robustness to Spurious Correlations using Pre-trained Language Models. *Transactions of the ACL*, 8:621–633.

Prasetya Ajie Utama, Nafise Sadat Moosavi, and Iryna Gurevych. 2020. Towards Debiasing NLU Models from Unknown Biases. In *Proc. of the 2020 Conference on Empirical Methods in Natural Language Processing (EMNLP)*, pages 7597–7610, Online. ACL.

Ashish Vaswani, Noam Shazeer, Niki Parmar, Jakob Uszkoreit, Llion Jones, Aidan N. Gomez, Łukasz Kaiser, and Illia Polosukhin. 2017. Attention is All You Need. In *Proc. of the 31st International Conference on Neural Information Processing Systems*, NIPS'17, pages 6000–6010, Red Hook, NY, USA. Curran Associates Inc.

Chaojun Wang and Rico Sennrich. 2020. On exposure bias, hallucination and domain shift in neural machine translation. In *Proceedings of the 58th Annual Meeting of the ACL*, pages 3544–3552, Online. ACL.

Thomas Wolf, Lysandre Debut, Victor Sanh, Julien Chaumond, Clement Delangue, Anthony Moi, Pierric Cistac, Tim Rault, Remi Louf, Morgan Funtowicz, Joe Davison, Sam Shleifer, Patrick von Platen, Clara Ma, Yacine Jernite, Julien Plu, Canwen Xu, Teven Le Scao, Sylvain Gugger, Mariama Drame, Quentin Lhoest, and Alexander Rush. 2020. Transformers: State-of-the-Art Natural Language Processing. In *Proc. of the 2020 Conf. EMNLP: System Demonstrations*, pages 38–45. ACL.

Mingzhu Wu, Nafise Sadat Moosavi, Andreas Rücklé, and Iryna Gurevych. 2020. Improving QA Generalization by Concurrent Modeling of Multiple Biases. *arXiv e-prints*, page arXiv:2010.03338.

Qizhe Xie, Zihang Dai, Eduard Hovy, Minh-Thang Luong, and Quoc V. Le. 2019. Unsupervised Data Augmentation. *CoRR*, abs/1904.12848v1.

Wen Zhang, Yang Feng, Fandong Meng, Di You, and Qun Liu. 2019. Bridging the gap between training and inference for neural machine translation. In *Proceedings of the 57th Annual Meeting of the ACL*, pages 4334–4343, Florence, Italy. ACL.

# QuickGraph: A Rapid Annotation Tool for Knowledge Graph Extraction from Technical Text

**Tyler Bikaun**(✉), **Michael Stewart** and **Wei Liu**
The University of Western Australia
35 Stirling Highway, Crawley, Western Australia
tyler.bikaun@research.uwa.edu.au
michael.stewart@uwa.edu.au
wei.liu@uwa.edu.au

## Abstract

Acquiring high-quality annotated corpora for complex multi-task information extraction (MT-IE) is an arduous and costly process for human-annotators. Adoption of unsupervised techniques for automated annotation have thus become popular. However, these techniques rely heavily on dictionaries, gazetteers, and knowledge bases. While such resources are abundant for general domains, they are scarce for specialised technical domains. To tackle this challenge, we present **QuickGraph**[1], the first collaborative MT-IE annotation tool built with indirect weak supervision and clustering to maximise annotator productivity.

QuickGraph's main contribution is a set of novel features that enable knowledge graph extraction through rapid and consistent complex multi-task entity and relation annotation. In this paper, we discuss these key features and qualitatively compare QuickGraph to existing annotation tools. A demonstration of our system is available at: https://youtu.be/ZlzH-AAoGXs.

## 1 Introduction

Hand-labelling is still the most reliable means to obtain quality training data to support deep learning applications; however, it is time-consuming and resource-intensive (Pustejovsky and Stubbs, 2012). Unsupervised approaches such as weak/distant supervision (Craven and Kumlien, 1999; Mintz et al., 2009) and data programming (Ratner et al., 2017) thus are usually attractive alternatives or starting points to human-annotation.

Leveraging unsupervised techniques, however, is predicated on the availability of relevant external resources such as semantically aligned knowledge bases, and a priori knowledge of phenomena/concepts in the corpus of interest. In general domains, these are widely available, e.g. YAGO (Suchanek et al., 2007), Freebase (Bollacker et al., 2008), Wikidata (Vrandečić and Krötzsch, 2014), DBPedia (Lehmann et al., 2015), whereas they remain scarce for emerging and specialised domains, such as engineering, industrial, medical, biological, law enforcement (Neves and Leser, 2012; Dima et al., 2021) which we refer to as technical domains. Due to their close real-world applications, technical domains are often more impactful and likely to have formal ontologies of engineered knowledge. Consequently, human-annotation remains critical and essential for obtaining quality training data for technical information extraction and instance population.

Numerous annotation tools exist, supporting many NLP tasks (Neves and Ševa, 2019). However, few tools support large-scale, hierarchical, multi-task, multi-label, entity and relation annotation that is required for translating NLP research to real-world industry applications in technical domains (Stenetorp et al., 2012; Yimam et al., 2013; Klie et al., 2018; Stewart et al., 2019; Abrami et al., 2019; Islamaj et al., 2020; Tang et al., 2020). Moreover, these tools lack features to optimise annotator productivity and return-on-time-invested. Such features are particularly essential for technical domains, as annotators are frequently subject matter experts, who are typically time-poor and costly.

Weak/distant supervision (Craven and Kumlien, 1999; Mintz et al., 2009) is a powerful paradigm for large-scale (potentially low-quality) automatic annotation. Surprisingly, the integration of this paradigm into annotation tools to accelerate labelled sample acquisition for deep learning applications remains unexplored.

To fill these gaps, we introduce **QuickGraph**, the first collaborative annotation tool for multi-task IE that is designed to be:

- *Fast*: Accelerates annotation via entity and relation propagation, and semantic clustering.

[1] *QuickGraph*. https://quickgraph.nlp-tlp.org



*Proceedings of the 60th Annual Meeting of the Association for Computational Linguistics*
*System Demonstrations*, pages 270 - 278

- *Powerful*: Supports complex multi-task entity and open/closed relation annotation and knowledge graph extraction.
- *Intuitive*: Simple to set-up and use.
- *Efficient*: Optimises annotation through easily-configurable relation constraints.
- *Insightful*: Builds real-time knowledge graphs from annotations[2], and provides three dimensions of inter-annotator agreement.

## 2 Related work

Many NLP annotation tools have been developed in recent years (Neves and Ševa, 2019), however few support entity and relation annotation as a single integrated task, nor do they contain purposely designed features to enhance annotator productivity. Here we discuss the most notable entity and relation annotation tools.

Historically, *brat* (Stenetorp et al., 2012) has been the most popular but routinely receives criticism for it's antiquated technology and set-up difficulty (Kummerfeld, 2019; Neves and Ševa, 2019). Similarly, *WebAnno* (Yimam et al., 2013), *INCEpTION* (Klie et al., 2018) and *TextAnnotator* (Abrami et al., 2019) are feature-rich and multi-purpose tools, but are challenging to use. *SLATE* (Kummerfeld, 2019) is a command-line-based tool, but lacks multi-task functionality and is restricted to technical end users because of its command-line design. *TeamTat* (Islamaj et al., 2020) is a powerful tool, but is oriented for small-batch complex annotation of large documents such as scholarly articles. Redcoat (Stewart et al., 2019) is an feature-rich entity typing tool and has been demonstrated to support MT-IE (Stewart and Liu, 2020), but is not purpose-built for relation annotation. SALKG (Tang et al., 2020) is a unique knowledge-graph annotation tool, yet lacks features for collaborative annotation and adjudication. Despite this, each of the aforementioned tools contain powerful elements, but universally lack features to support rapid large-scale, complex, annotation.

Recent tools enhance annotator productivity using active and proactive learning, including *APLenty* (Nghiem and Ananiadou, 2018), *Paladin* (Nghiem et al., 2021), *FitAnnotator* (Li et al., 2021) and *ActiveAnno* (Wiechmann et al., 2021). Inadequately, these tools cannot perform multi-task entity and relation annotation. Moreover, their performance using large ontologies remains unproven (Nghiem and Ananiadou, 2018; Li et al., 2021). Reliance on active learning may also result in unsatisfactory corpus quality due to sample acquisition and reliability concerns (Attenberg and Provost, 2011; Lowell et al., 2019).

[2]When both entity and relation annotation is performed.

## 3 System highlights

### 3.1 Key capabilities

QuickGraph is a multi-task document-level hierarchical entity and relation annotation tool. Our tool supports annotations that are: i) hierarchical, ii) multi-label, iii) multi-class, and iv) nested. These attributes enable annotation of tasks such as named entity recognition, coreference resolution, entity typing, part-of-speech tagging, relation extraction, semantic role labelling, and triple annotation. One of QuickGraph's novelties is its support for open[3] and closed[4] relation annotation, permitting open relation extraction tasks (Niklaus et al., 2018; Stanovsky et al., 2018).

Additional key contributions of QuickGraph are its novel features for indirect weak supervision through annotation propagation (Section 3.2.2), semantic clustering of documents to promote annotator consistency (Section 3.4.1), and real-time knowledge graph construction from text (Section 3.6.1). Each of these contributions enable rapid annotation of corpora to support deep learning applications without the need of external resources such as knowledge bases, dictionaries, or gazetteers.

### 3.2 Why is QuickGraph fast?

#### 3.2.1 Get started - quick

QuickGraph is available for free online and takes only minutes to create an account and set-up a project for rapid annotation. Our tool provides preset ontologies for popular entity and relation annotation tasks including ConceptNet-5.5 (Speer et al., 2017), CoNLL03 (Tjong Kim Sang and De Meulder, 2003), FIGER (Ling and Weld, 2021), SemEval-2007 Task 04 (Girju et al., 2007), and SemEval-2010 Task 8 (Hendrickx et al., 2010).

#### 3.2.2 Entity and relation propagation

QuickGraph's novel entity and relation propagation features enable annotators to make *a click worth a thousand annotations* (Figure 1B-D), analogous to the adage *a picture is*

[3]Relations are unbounded surface form linguistic expressions.

[4]Relations are bounded and predefined.

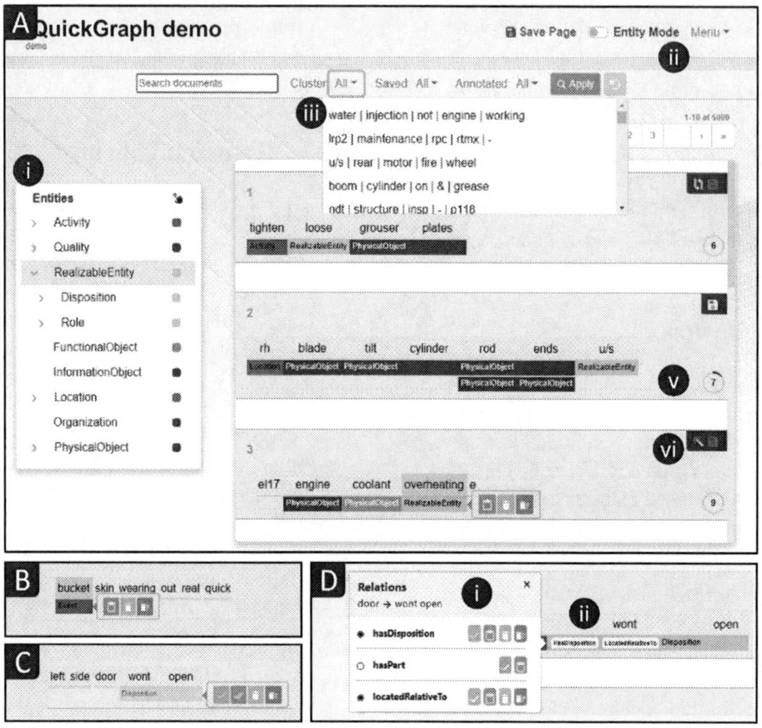


Figure 1: QuickGraph's annotation interface - A) main interface: i. hierarchical label palette, ii. annotation mode toggle, iii. cluster navigation, vi. document status tray, and v. cluster tray, B) *accepted* entity tooltip: buttons left-right: *apply all*, *delete one*, *delete all*, *quick search*, C) *suggested* entity tooltip: buttons left-right: *accept one*, *accept all*, *reject one*, *reject all*, *quick search*, and D) relation annotation: i. relation popover, and ii. applied relation.

*worth a thousand words*. Entity propagation is performed through case-insensitive sub-string matching, and relation propagation is implemented through a deterministic token/phrase offset matching algorithm. For unambiguous and consistently offset tokens and phrases, propagation can massively speed up annotation without compromising precision (Figure 1B-D). For example, users of QuickGraph can apply thousands of entities or hundreds or relations in a single click. As a result, these features enhance productivity and contribute to quickly capturing diverse contextual annotations to support deep learning applications.

The process of propagation involves cascading *suggested* (*weak*) annotations across the entire corpus, emulating weak supervision, but without the need for external resources. Throughout the annotation process, *suggested* annotations can be viewed and individually or bulk accepted, converting them into *accepted* (*silver*) annotations. At any point throughout the project, all created annotations can be downloaded. The presence of weakly labelled documents can be used in a similar fashion to their treatment in unsupervised learning methods (Ratner et al., 2017). Gold annotations are automatically generated by aggregating entity mentions and/or triples with respect to a desired inter-annotator agreement threshold.

### 3.2.3 Pre-annotation

Like other tools, our tool permits pre-annotation of corpora at project creation. Pre-annotation reduces annotation effort by pre-applying labels based on external resources such as gazetteers. A novel feature of QuickGraph is its ability to pre-annotate both entities and relations through sets of pre-labelled artefacts[5].

### 3.2.4 Built-in corpus pre-processing

QuickGraph supports corpus pre-processing as part of the project creation process rather than requiring external solutions. Consequently, corpora can be annotated end-to-end without external steps or dependencies, simplifying

[5]In the format of $\langle s_{span}, s_{type}, r_{type}, t_{span}, t_{type}, st_{offset} \rangle$ where s - source, r - relation, and t - target.

and speeding up the annotation process. Preprocessing stages currently consists of: i) character casing, ii) character removal, and iii) document deduplication.

## 3.3 Why is QuickGraph powerful?

### 3.3.1 Thousands of documents - at once

Unlike other tools, QuickGraph prospers with large-scale corpora. We have loaded and simultaneously annotated corpora consisting of 100,000 short user-generated texts with the tool whilst maintaining performance. While other tools limit annotators to a view small group of documents (Nghiem and Ananiadou, 2018; Kummerfeld, 2019; Islamaj et al., 2020; Li et al., 2021), QuickGraph users can view up to 100 documents simultaneously. Support for large document groups promotes quick identification of cross-document information, aiding annotators by viewing concepts in different contexts.

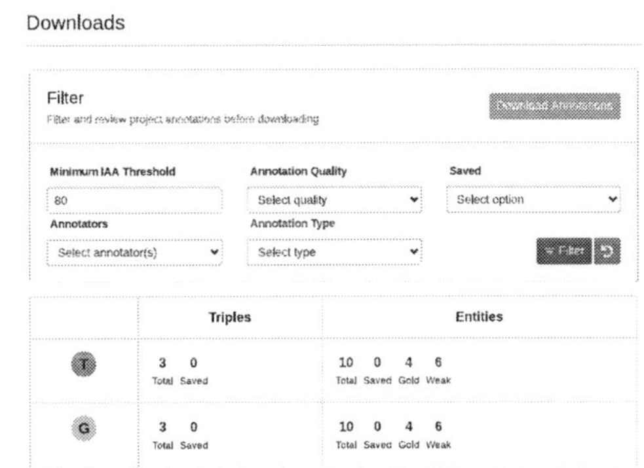


Figure 2: QuickGraph's flexible downloads component.

### 3.3.2 Annotation export flexibility

Exporting annotations to support deep learning applications is easy in QuickGraph (Figure 2). At any time, downloads can be filtered and exported. Our tool allows users to filter annotations based on their: i) inter-annotator agreement score, ii) quality (e.g. *gold*, *silver* or *weak*), iii) saved state, iv) annotator(s), and v) annotation type (e.g. entity mentions or triples).

## 3.4 How does QuickGraph help consistency?

### 3.4.1 Semantic clustering

An overlooked feature of current tools is document clustering to promote annotator productivity. Clustering is a core feature of QuickGraph, and has two primary benefits. First, annotators maintain a consistent mental model whilst annotating as clustered documents are likely to share semantic and express similar phenomena. Second, user actions are simplified as similar documents likely share similar concepts reducing the need to repetitively navigate through large hierarchical entity label spaces. Our tool implements agglomerative clustering of documents embedded with SBERT (Reimers and Gurevych, 2019) sentence embeddings.

### 3.4.2 Powerful ontology editor and relation constraints

Applying relation annotations consistently is difficult and time-consuming (Mintz et al., 2009). Besides preset ontologies available within QuickGraph, custom entity and relation ontologies can easily be created. Unlike other IE tools, our tool supports hierarchical entities and is the first to permit relation constraints through entity domain and ranges.

Relation constraints are made possible as QuickGraph applies relations between entities (*associated with token spans*) rather than on token spans directly (see Figure 1D). Consequently, this feature can enhance annotator productivity and consistency through restrained relation selection. For annotators using large formal ontologies, such as those found in technical domains, this can significantly reduce the search space of relations by using pre-defined domains and ranges.

## 3.5 Why is QuickGraph intuitive?

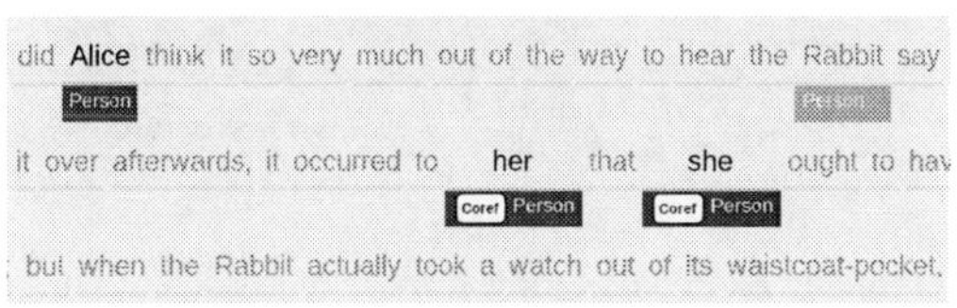


Figure 3: Example of relation annotation mode. *Alice* is the source entity.

### 3.5.1 Minimalistic interface

Instead of providing annotators with *everything but the kitchen sink*, akin to the current generation of annotation tools (Abrami et al., 2019, 2020), our tool has been designed with the tenet of minimalism. Significantly, this has been applied to the presentation of relations. Instead of rendering dependencies between entities and relations as free-flowing arrows, QuickGraph renders only what annotators choose to see, as means of promoting focused annotation (Figure 3). Additionally, toggling between entity and relation annotation is seamless, requiring only a single click or key press (Figure 1A.ii).

#### 3.5.2 Cluster annotation and navigation

At any time[6], QuickGraph users can drill in and out of document clusters with a single click (Figure 1A.v). Navigation between clusters is also trivial owing to interpretable cluster descriptions, each derived from their document sets top-n terms (Figure 1A.iii)

### 3.6 Why is QuickGraph insightful?

#### 3.6.1 Real-time knowledge graphs

Novel to QuickGraph is its real-time knowledge graph construction from annotations[7]. This feature enables annotators to gain insight into, and improve understanding of, their annotations. Two graph types are available for annotated documents: i) aggregated; documents are aggregated together, and ii) separated; documents are represented as sub-graphs.

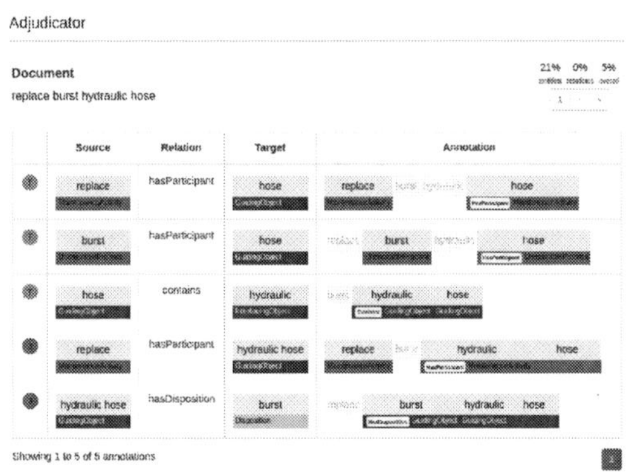


Figure 4: Example of three dimension adjudication for a terse document with two annotators.

#### 3.6.2 Multi-dimensional adjudication

Adjudication in our tool (Figure 4) is supported by three dimensions of inter-annotator agreement (IAA) : i) triples (referred to as *overall*), ii) entities, and iii) relations. Inspired by SemBLEU (Song and Gildea, 2019), pair-wise IAA is calculated through a modified-BLEU score (Papineni et al., 2002). Currently, IAA is strictly enforced on directionality and hierarchical entities and relation types. Adding relaxed IAA will be the focus of future development.

## 4 System architecture

QuickGraph is a multi-user tool built using the modern full-stack framework MERN[8], Python and Docker. Our tool consists of four containerised components (Figure 5): i) web client, ii) NoSQL database, iii) server, and iv) cluster server. Using Docker, our tool can be built and ready to annotate in minutes[9].

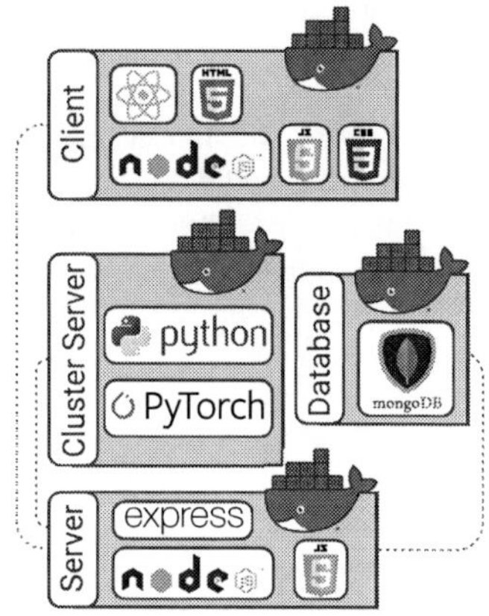


Figure 5: QuickGraph's system architecture and technology stack.

QuickGraph's NoSQL database consists of the three collections: `Projects`, `Texts` and `Users`. `Projects` contain information pertinent to the project's: manager, name, description, assigned annotators, settings, details of tasks, pre-processing operations, uploaded texts, clustering details, and entity and relation ontology information. `Texts` consist of all texts including details of their: original value, tokens, entity and relation markup, annotator saved states, weight, rank, and cluster designation. Lastly, the `Users` collection contains information such as the users: username, hashed and salted password, email, personalisation settings, and assigned and invited projects.

## 5 Comparison with existing tools

A qualitative comparison between QuickGraph and existing open-source annotation tools that support entity and relation annotation, or have

[6]If clustering was selected upon project creation.

[7]If entity and relation annotation was selected upon project creation.

[8]MongoDB-Express-React-Node. https://www.mongodb.com/mern-stack

[9]QuickGraph GitHub. https://github.com/nlp-tlp/quickgraph

| Tool | Annotation Type | Multi-label | Pre-annotation | Auto-annotation | Relation Constraints | Annotation Propagation | Document Clustering |
|---|---|---|---|---|---|---|---|
| **QuickGraph** | E/HE/R | ✓ | ✓ | - | ✓ | ✓ | ✓ |
| ActiveAnno | D | ✓ | ✓ | ✓ | - | - | - |
| APLenty | E | - | - | ✓ | - | - | - |
| brat | E/R | ✓ | - | - | - | - | - |
| FITAnnotator | E/R | - | - | ✓ | - | - | - |
| INCEpTION | E/R | ✓ | - | ✓ | ✓ | - | - |
| Paladin | D | ✓ | - | ✓ | - | - | - |
| RedCoat | E/HE | ✓ | ✓ | - | - | - | - |
| SALKG | T | - | ✓ | - | - | - | - |
| SLATE | E/R | ✓ | - | - | - | - | - |
| TeamTat | E/R | ✓ | ✓ | - | - | ✓ | - |
| TextAnnotator | E/R | ✓ | ✓ | ✓ | - | - | - |
| WebAnno | E/R | ✓ | ✓ | - | - | - | - |

Table 1: Comparison of QuickGraph's features to 12 popular, existing open-source annotation tools. Annotation type abbreviations: E - entity, HE - hierarchical entity, R - relation, T - triple, D - document.

design features to enhance annotator productivity, is provided in Table 1.

*Annotation type*: 75% of the reviewed tools support entity annotation, with most also allowing relation annotation. Only RedCoat (and QuickGraph) permit hierarchical entity annotation.

*Multi-label*: 75% of the reviewed tools support multi-label annotation. Of these, ActiveAnno and Paladin permit multi-labels, but are restricted to document classification tasks.

*Pre-annotation*: 50% of the reviewed tools allow pre-annotation of corpora prior to manual-labelling. These tools are limited to entities, while QuickGraph also supports relations through triples.

*Automatic annotation*: Less than 50% of the reviewed tools support automatic annotation. This feature is implemented through AI-assistance, typically using active learning, and is limited to entity annotation. QuickGraph purposely does not have this feature, as we believe uncontrolled automatic annotation for complex MT-IE can be unproductive.

*Relation constraints*: Of the reviewed tools, only INCEpTION allows for relation constraints. However, INCEpTION's constraints need to be expressed in a bespoke constraint language. In contrast, this feature of QuickGraph requires users to simply specify entity domain and ranges on relations.

*Annotation propagation*: Of the reviewed tools, only TextAnnotator provides annotation propagation via 'entity cascading'. However, this feature is restricted to entities, and the tool's interface is cumbersome and challenging to use. In contrast, QuickGraph allows easy and intuitive entity and relation propagation.

*Document clustering*: No reviewed tool offer document clustering. Only QuickGraph enables document clustering to improve annotator productivity and consistency.

## 6 Conclusion and future work

We introduced QuickGraph, a collaborative annotation tool for multi-task information extraction that accelerates annotator productivity. Distinguishing features of QuickGraph are its support for diverse information extraction tasks through hierarchical entity and open/closed relation annotation, annotation propagation, and semantic clustering.

Whilst QuickGraph is ready to use, there are features still under development, including: i) expanding available semantic embedding and clustering options, ii) improving annotation propagation processes, iii) relaxing inter-annotator agreement metrics, and iv) adding support for cross-document annotation.

## Acknowledgements

This research is supported by the Australian Research Council through the Centre for Transforming Maintenance through Data Science (grant number IC180100030), funded by the Australian Government. Additionally, Bikaun acknowledges funding from the Mineral Research Institute of Western Australia. Bikaun and Liu acknowledge the support from ARC Discovery Grant DP150102405.

The authors are grateful to Mrs. Shu Wong for her assistance and helpful feedback on the user-interaction and user-experience elements of QuickGraph.

## References


Giuseppe Abrami, Alexander Mehler, Andy Lücking, Elias Rieb, and Philipp Helfrich. 2019. Textannotator: A flexible framework for semantic annotations. In *Proceedings of the 15th Joint ACL-ISO Workshop on Interoperable Semantic Annotation (ISA-15). Association for Computational Linguistics, London, UK*, pages 1–12.

Giuseppe Abrami, Manuel Stoeckel, and Alexander Mehler. 2020. TextAnnotator: A UIMA based tool for the simultaneous and collaborative annotation of texts. In *Proceedings of the 12th Language Resources and Evaluation Conference*, pages 891–900, Marseille, France. European Language Resources Association.

Josh Attenberg and Foster Provost. 2011. Inactive learning? difficulties employing active learning in practice. *SIGKDD Explor. Newsl.*, 12(2):36–41.

Kurt Bollacker, Colin Evans, Praveen Paritosh, Tim Sturge, and Jamie Taylor. 2008. Freebase: A collaboratively created graph database for structuring human knowledge. In *Proceedings of the 2008 ACM SIGMOD International Conference on Management of Data*, SIGMOD '08, page 1247–1250, New York, NY, USA. Association for Computing Machinery.

M Craven and J Kumlien. 1999. Constructing biological knowledge bases by extracting information from text sources. In *Proceedings. International Conference on Intelligent Systems for Molecular Biology*, page 77—86.

Alden Dima, Sarah Lukens, Melinda Hodkiewicz, Thurston Sexton, and Michael P. Brundage. 2021. Adapting natural language processing for technical text. *Applied AI Letters*, 2(3):e33.

Roxana Girju, Preslav Nakov, Vivi Nastase, Stan Szpakowicz, Peter Turney, and Deniz Yuret. 2007. SemEval-2007 task 04: Classification of semantic relations between nominals. In *Proceedings of the Fourth International Workshop on Semantic Evaluations (SemEval-2007)*, pages 13–18, Prague, Czech Republic. Association for Computational Linguistics.

Iris Hendrickx, Su Nam Kim, Zornitsa Kozareva, Preslav Nakov, Diarmuid Ó Séaghdha, Sebastian Padó, Marco Pennacchiotti, Lorenza Romano, and Stan Szpakowicz. 2010. SemEval-2010 task 8: Multi-way classification of semantic relations between pairs of nominals. In *Proceedings of the 5th International Workshop on Semantic Evaluation*, pages 33–38, Uppsala, Sweden. Association for Computational Linguistics.

Rezarta Islamaj, Dongseop Kwon, Sun Kim, and Zhiyong Lu. 2020. Teamtat: a collaborative text annotation tool. *Nucleic acids research*, 48(W1):W5–W11.

Jan-Christoph Klie, Michael Bugert, Beto Boullosa, Richard Eckart de Castilho, and Iryna Gurevych. 2018. The inception platform: Machine-assisted and knowledge-oriented interactive annotation. In *Proceedings of the 27th International Conference on Computational Linguistics: System Demonstrations*, pages 5–9. Association for Computational Linguistics. Event Title: The 27th International Conference on Computational Linguistics (COLING 2018).

Jonathan K. Kummerfeld. 2019. SLATE: A super-lightweight annotation tool for experts. In *Proceedings of the 57th Annual Meeting of the Association for Computational Linguistics: System Demonstrations*, pages 7–12, Florence, Italy. Association for Computational Linguistics.

Jens Lehmann, Robert Isele, Max Jakob, Anja Jentzsch, Dimitris Kontokostas, Pablo N Mendes, Sebastian Hellmann, Mohamed Morsey, Patrick Van Kleef, Sören Auer, et al. 2015. Dbpedia–a large-scale, multilingual knowledge base extracted from wikipedia. *Semantic web*, 6(2):167–195.

Yanzeng Li, Bowen Yu, Li Quangang, and Tingwen Liu. 2021. FITAnnotator: A flexible and intelligent text annotation system. In *Proceedings of the 2021 Conference of the North American Chapter of the Association for Computational Linguistics: Human Language Technologies: Demonstrations*, pages 35–41, Online. Association for Computational Linguistics.

Xiao Ling and Daniel Weld. 2021. Fine-grained entity recognition. *Proceedings of the AAAI Conference on Artificial Intelligence*, 26(1):94–100.

David Lowell, Zachary C. Lipton, and Byron C. Wallace. 2019. Practical obstacles to deploying active learning. In *Proceedings of the 2019 Conference on Empirical Methods in Natural Language Processing and the 9th International Joint Conference on Natural Language Processing (EMNLP-IJCNLP)*, pages 21–30, Hong Kong, China. Association for Computational Linguistics.

Mike Mintz, Steven Bills, Rion Snow, and Daniel Jurafsky. 2009. Distant supervision for relation extraction without labeled data. In *Proceedings of the Joint Conference of the 47th Annual Meeting of the ACL and the 4th International Joint Conference on Natural Language Processing of the AFNLP*, pages 1003–1011, Suntec, Singapore. Association for Computational Linguistics.

Mariana Neves and Ulf Leser. 2012. A survey on annotation tools for the biomedical literature. *Briefings in Bioinformatics*, 15(2):327–340.

Mariana Neves and Jurica Ševa. 2019. An extensive review of tools for manual annotation of documents. *Briefings in Bioinformatics*, 22(1):146–163.

Minh-Quoc Nghiem and Sophia Ananiadou. 2018. APLenty: annotation tool for creating high-quality datasets using active and proactive learning. In *Proceedings of the 2018 Conference on Empirical Methods in Natural Language Processing: System Demonstrations*, pages 108–113, Brussels, Belgium. Association for Computational Linguistics.

Minh-Quoc Nghiem, Paul Baylis, and Sophia Ananiadou. 2021. Paladin: an annotation tool based on active and proactive learning. In *Proceedings of the 16th Conference of the European Chapter of the Association for Computational Linguistics: System Demonstrations*, pages 238–243, Online. Association for Computational Linguistics.

Christina Niklaus, Matthias Cetto, André Freitas, and Siegfried Handschuh. 2018. A survey on open information extraction. In *Proceedings of the 27th International Conference on Computational Linguistics*, pages 3866–3878, Santa Fe, New Mexico, USA. Association for Computational Linguistics.

Kishore Papineni, Salim Roukos, Todd Ward, and Wei-Jing Zhu. 2002. Bleu: A method for automatic evaluation of machine translation. In *Proceedings of the 40th Annual Meeting on Association for Computational Linguistics*, ACL '02, page 311–318, USA. Association for Computational Linguistics.

James Pustejovsky and Amber Stubbs. 2012. *Natural Language Annotation for Machine Learning: A guide to corpus-building for applications.* " O'Reilly Media, Inc.".

Alexander J. Ratner, Stephen H. Bach, Henry R. Ehrenberg, and Chris Ré. 2017. Snorkel: Fast training set generation for information extraction. In *Proceedings of the 2017 ACM International Conference on Management of Data*, SIGMOD '17, page 1683–1686, New York, NY, USA. Association for Computing Machinery.

Nils Reimers and Iryna Gurevych. 2019. Sentence-BERT: Sentence embeddings using Siamese BERT-networks. In *Proceedings of the 2019 Conference on Empirical Methods in Natural Language Processing and the 9th International Joint Conference on Natural Language Processing (EMNLP-IJCNLP)*, pages 3982–3992, Hong Kong, China. Association for Computational Linguistics.

Linfeng Song and Daniel Gildea. 2019. Sem-Bleu: A robust metric for AMR parsing evaluation. In *Proceedings of the 57th Annual Meeting of the Association for Computational Linguistics*, pages 4547–4552, Florence, Italy. Association for Computational Linguistics.

Robyn Speer, Joshua Chin, and Catherine Havasi. 2017. Conceptnet 5.5: An open multilingual graph of general knowledge. *Proceedings of the AAAI Conference on Artificial Intelligence*, 31(1).

Gabriel Stanovsky, Julian Michael, Luke Zettlemoyer, and Ido Dagan. 2018. Supervised open information extraction. In *Proceedings of the 2018 Conference of the North American Chapter of the Association for Computational Linguistics: Human Language Technologies, Volume 1 (Long Papers)*, pages 885–895.

Pontus Stenetorp, Sampo Pyysalo, Goran Topić, Tomoko Ohta, Sophia Ananiadou, and Jun'ichi Tsujii. 2012. brat: a web-based tool for NLP-assisted text annotation. In *Proceedings of the Demonstrations at the 13th Conference of the European Chapter of the Association for Computational Linguistics*, pages 102–107, Avignon, France. Association for Computational Linguistics.

Michael Stewart and Wei Liu. 2020. Seq2KG: An End-to-End Neural Model for Domain Agnostic Knowledge Graph (not Text Graph) Construction from Text. In *Proceedings of the 17th International Conference on Principles of Knowledge Representation and Reasoning*, pages 748–757.

Michael Stewart, Wei Liu, and Rachel Cardell-Oliver. 2019. Redcoat: A collaborative annotation tool for hierarchical entity typing. In *Proceedings of the 2019 Conference on Empirical Methods in Natural Language Processing and the 9th International Joint Conference on Natural Language Processing (EMNLP-IJCNLP): System Demonstrations*, pages 193–198, Hong Kong, China. Association for Computational Linguistics.

Fabian M. Suchanek, Gjergji Kasneci, and Gerhard Weikum. 2007. Yago: A core of semantic knowledge. In *Proceedings of the 16th International Conference on World Wide Web*, WWW '07, page 697–706, New York, NY, USA. Association for Computing Machinery.

Mingwei Tang, Cui Su, Haihua Chen, Jingye Qu, and Junhua Ding. 2020. Salkg: A semantic annotation system for building a high-quality legal knowledge graph. In *2020 IEEE International Conference on Big Data (Big Data)*, pages 2153–2159.

Erik F. Tjong Kim Sang and Fien De Meulder. 2003. Introduction to the CoNLL-2003 shared task: Language-independent named entity recognition. pages 142–147.

Denny Vrandečić and Markus Krötzsch. 2014. Wikidata: a free collaborative knowledgebase. *Communications of the ACM*, 57(10):78–85.

Max Wiechmann, Seid Muhie Yimam, and Chris Biemann. 2021. ActiveAnno: General-purpose document-level annotation tool with active learning integration. In *Proceedings of the 2021 Conference of the North American Chapter of the Association for Computational Linguistics: Human Language Technologies: Demonstrations*, pages 99–105, Online. Association for Computational Linguistics.

Seid Muhie Yimam, Iryna Gurevych, Richard Eckart de Castilho, and Chris Biemann. 2013. WebAnno: A flexible, web-based and visually supported system for distributed annotations. In *Proceedings of the 51st Annual Meeting of the Association for Computational Linguistics: System Demonstrations*, pages 1–6, Sofia, Bulgaria. Association for Computational Linguistics.

# Author Index

**Association for Computational Linguistics**
209 N. Eighth Street
Stroudsburg, Pennsylvania 18360

ISBN 978-1-7138-6724-1

CURRAN ASSOCIATES INC.
proceedings.com

# 19th Annual Meeting of the Young Researchers' Roundtable on Spoken Dialogue Systems (YRRSDS 2023)

Prague, Czech Republic
11-12 September 2023